Office 97:
The Complete Reference

Combine Information with Compound Documents

Use Binder to easily create compound documents (pages 121–126).

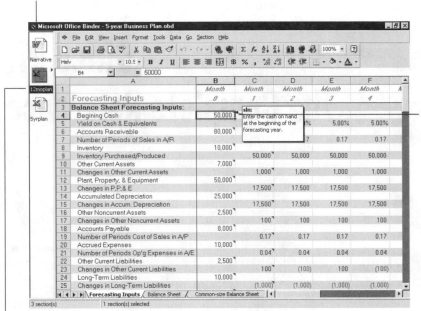

Work with binder sections in the same way you work with any Office document file. (See Chapter 6 for help with Word basics, Chapter 11 for help with Excel basics, and Chapter 20 for help with PowerPoint basics.)

Organize your compound document with sections (pages 121–126).

Use Binder to create compound documents: Microsoft Binder lets you easily create compound documents, which are documents that use chunks of information created by more than one Office program. A binder document might, for example, include a document created with Word, a workbook or chart created with Excel, and a presentation created with PowerPoint. (The chunks of information that make up a compound document are called OLE objects.)

Organize a compound document with sections: Binder lets you organize a compound document by placing different objects into different sections. You can create a new section either by inserting an existing Office document file or by creating a new, empty document file. You can name binder sections and arrange them within a binder document in any manner you wish.

Working with a section: To work with a particular section, you just select it from the section bar by clicking. When you're working with a particular section (for example, an Excel section), Binder supplies the correct set of Microsoft Office commands.

Create Your Own Toolbars, Menus, and Keyboard Shortcuts

Make buttons larger and easier to see and use (page 92).

Create menus for specific tasks—or for the commands you find most useful (pages 98–100).

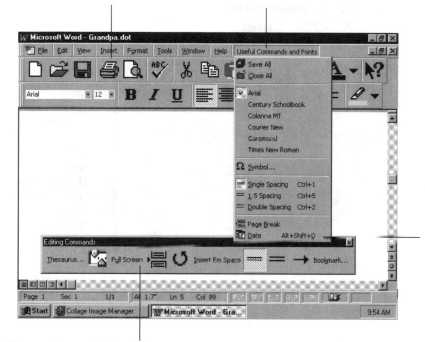

Assign your own keyboard shortcuts to commands (pages 105–106).

Build your own toolbar to help with the tasks you do in your work (pages 94–95).

Making buttons larger: On crowded toolbars, it's hard to tell what all the buttons are, so Office 97 offers a command for enlarging the buttons.

Create menus: Not only can you create a new menu from scratch—perhaps a menu with your favorite commands on it or one with commands that you find useful for a certain kind of work—you can also remove unwanted commands from menus, move commands from menu to menu, and even get rid of menus altogether.

Building a new toolbar: Office 97 offers many different toolbars for getting jobs done quickly, and you can create your own toolbars as well. What's more, you can remove buttons from and add buttons to toolbars; create buttons for macros, fonts, and styles; and even design your own buttons.

Assigning keyboard shortcuts to commands: Especially if you are a laptop user, your favorite commands should each have a keyboard shortcut. Office 97 lets you assign keyboard shortcuts you choose yourself to any command.

Take Advantage of Word 97's Numerous Desktop-Publishing Features

Lay out text in columns for a professional look (pages 269–270).

Decorate your files with clip art images (pages 83–84).

Dazzle your readers—turn text on its side (page 250).

Have text wrap—or snake its way—around graphics and text boxes (pages 256–260).

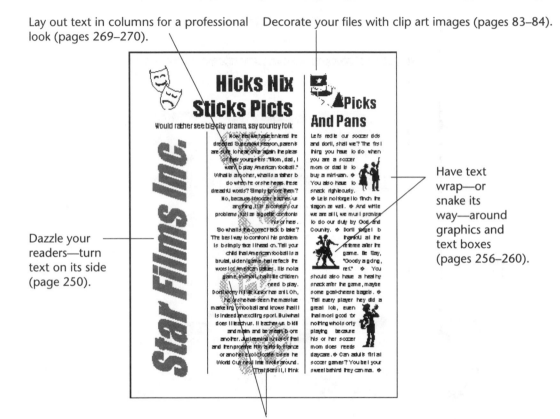

Make ghostly images called "watermarks" appear behind text (pages 260–264).

Import clip art images: What's a newsletter—or spreadsheet, or report, or notice, or announcement—without a graphic or two? The Office program comes with many clip art images. Use them to decorate and call attention to the files you create.

Lay out text in columns: Text looks great when it is laid out in newspaper-style columns. In columns, you can pack more text on the page. Word offers lots of options for laying out columns—you can create as many on a page as you want, draw lines between columns, and choose how wide you want them to be.

Rotate and flip text: Readers turn their heads when they see text that has been laid on its side. Thanks to Word's text boxes, you can do odd things to text. You can make a heading that straddles several columns in a newsletter, or create a boxed announcement that stands in the middle of the page for all to see.

Create a watermark: *Watermarks* are faint images that appear behind text. "Subliminal messages," you might call them. Word makes it pretty easy to include these sophisticated graphics in a word-processed document.

Wrap text around clip art images and text boxes: You can control how text behaves when it meets with or runs up against a graphic or text box on the page. Word offers many options for wrapping text.

Visualize Your Data in a Chart

Create numeric data with a worksheet (Chapter 11).

Choose from a wide variety of sophisticated chart types (pages 406–418).

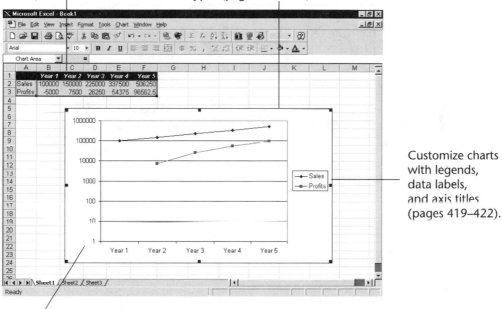

Customize charts with legends, data labels, and axis titles (pages 419–422).

Use special graph effects such as logarithmic axes, multiple value axes, and three-dimensionality (pages 410, 413–415, and 433).

Create numeric data: You can easily create or calculate the numeric data—called *data series*—that you want to plot in a chart, using an Excel worksheet. Simply enter the data series values into a row or column. You just want to be sure to include data series names (so that your chart will include a legend) and data category names (so that your chart's category axis will be labeled).

Choose from a chart type: Excel provides a variety of sophisticated chart types you can use, which means you can choose a chart that works well with your data and one that supports and emphasizes your chart's message. For example, you can use column and line charts of time-series analysis, and you can use XY (scatter) charts to explore relationships between data series.

Customize charts: You can customize your charts in a variety of ways, such as by choosing which colors various chart parts should use, specifying the size and placement of data markers, adding data labels that identify data point values or categories, and calibrating axes.

Use special graph effects: Excel allows you to use special effects such as logarithmic scaling when you want to plot the rate of change in a data series' values (rather than plotting just the data series values themselves). You can use more than one value axis if data point values can't all be reasonably calibrated using the same axis. And when necessary, you can add a third dimension of depth to your charts so that data series are segregated.

Perform Numerical Analysis with a Workbook

Create quantitative models that use formulas (Chapter 12).

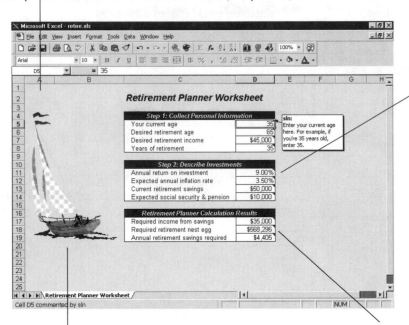

Retrieve raw data from other sources (pages 110–121 and 127–135).

Add nonnumerical data to your worksheets to make them more useful or interesting (pages 83–87).

Use powerful functions to make complex calculations (pages 384–391).

Create quantitative models: Within an Excel workbook, you can create quantitative models that use formulas to describe items such as a business's financial condition, an individual's retirement plans, or the results of a scientific study. You can even create formulas that manipulate text strings.

Use powerful functions: Some calculations are too complex or unwieldy to make with the standard arithmetic operation (addition, subtraction, multiplication, division, and exponentiation), but that's not a problem with Excel. It provides hundreds of easy-to-use, prefabricated formulas for making financial, trigonometric, and statistical calculations, as well as many other types of complex calculations.

Add nonnumerical data: While Excel's workbooks are specifically tailored for working with numeric data, you can also add other types of information to an Excel workbook. You can, for example, add Office Art drawing objects, pictures from the Microsoft Clip Gallery, and sound objects.

Retrieve raw data: Excel easily imports data created in other spreadsheet, accounting, and database programs. In addition, Excel, like the other Microsoft Office applications, lets you move information to and from Excel using OLE.

Track and Manage Data with Access 97

Use forms to enter and view data in a database table (pages 549–558).

Query to learn more about the people or items that your database tracks (pages 576–579).

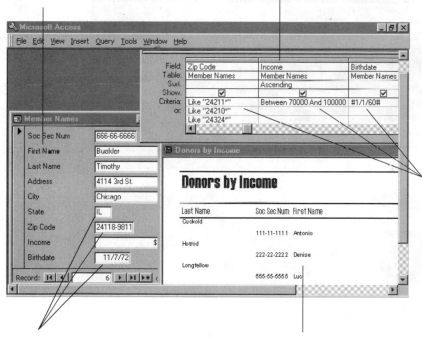

As part of a query, you can use expressions to pinpoint specific records (pages 588–592).

Assign field properties to promote accurate data entry (pages 520–526).

Generate a report that clearly shows what is in your database (pages 614–621).

Enter and view data on forms: Forms are one of the best ways to enter data in a database table. You can clearly see all the fields in a record on a form. And you can also see where data is supposed to be entered, because each place on the form is clearly labeled. Access even allows you to create very sophisticated forms that link data from different tables.

Field properties make entering data easier: Access offers field properties to make data entry go more smoothly. A field property is like a format. The Field Size property, for example, determines how many characters can be entered in a field. You can also create *input masks*—punctuation marks and preformatted spaces that make entering telephone numbers, social security numbers, and ZIP codes easier.

Construct queries to locate specific data: For example, you could construct a query that finds purchase orders submitted on a particular date. Or you could construct a query that finds purchase orders for an item that were made during a three-month period in states where sales tax is charged. With complex queries that include expressions, you can learn a lot about the items or people that your database tracks.

Generate and print reports about your data: When you want others to know about the information that a database tracks, you can print a report. Access offers many attractive ways to lay out the data in a report. And you can include as many or as few fields as you want.

Create Sizzling Presentations with PowerPoint 97

Put tables, graphs, charts, and
columns on slides (pages 666–669).

Draw on slides
to underscore
the high
points of a
presentation
(pages 683–684).

Looking to the Future...

	1998	1999	2000	
McCue	45	39	32	☒Growth
Cipherex	31	19	5	☒Creativity
O'Borne	24	33	42	☒Vision
				☒Teamwork
				☒Pep

The O'Borne Companies

Jump to any slide in a presentation—or
create a "kiosk" slide show that plays by
itself (pages 681–682 and 685).

Include a company logo or name on each
slide (page 657).

Put tables, graphs, columns, or charts on slides: Tables, graphs, and charts help make for a convincing
presentation. PowerPoint offers special slide layouts that are preformatted for tables, graphs, charts,
and columns.

Draw on slides during the presentation: Drawing on slides helps make a presentation livelier. Use
PowerPoint's pen to literally underscore the important points of your presentation.

Give a presentation tailored for your audience: You don't have to present slides from first to last. Also, if
the audience wants to go back and view a slide again, you can go directly to it. And you can also give
"kiosk"-style presentations that show themselves over and over again without your having to be there.

Include company logos and names on slides: By putting company logos, mottoes, and the like in the corner
of each slide in a presentation, you tell your audience exactly who is giving the presentation and help
hammer the message home.

Use Outlook to
Stay Organized and to Send and Receive E-mail Messages

Plan ahead and see exactly where you are supposed to be (pages 731–739).

Flag your e-mail messages and attach files to them (pages 703–707 and 708–709).

Store detailed information about friends, colleagues, and clients in one easy-to-reach place (pages 726–731).

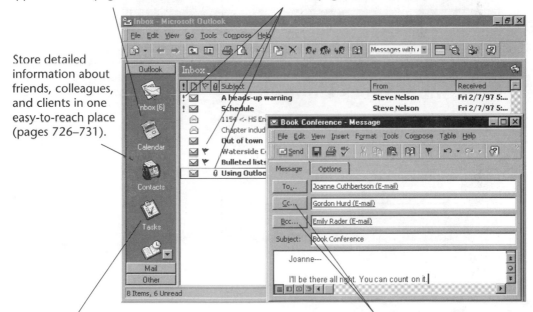

Juggle work tasks without dropping the ball (pages 739–745).

Send copies and blind copies of messages (pages 700–703).

Schedule appointments, meetings, and events: Outlook offers the Calendar screen for making sure you don't miss activities you have scheduled for yourself. After you schedule an activity, that activity appears on the Calendar screen, where you can see your daily, weekly, or monthly appointments.

Track the contact information of friends, colleagues, and clients: On the Contacts screen, you can keep street addresses, web page addresses, phone numbers of all types and varieties (such as pager numbers or FAX numbers), and even miscellaneous information such as anniversary dates and birthdays.

Prioritize tasks and manage your time better: Use the Tasks screen to find out which tasks need doing, how urgent each task is, when tasks need to be completed, and whether a task is overdue.

Mark messages as "urgent" or "confidential": Outlook offers many different ways to flag the messages you send. You can also be notified when a message has been received and send files with your e-mail messages.

Send copies and blind copies of messages: All you have to do to send a copy or blind copy of a message with Outlook is click a button and choose the recipient from a list of names. Outlook makes entering e-mail addresses very easy.

Publish Information to the World Wide Web

Create attractive and visually-exciting HTML documents (Chapter 26).

Add hyperlinks that point to other Internet resources using their URLs (pages 764–768).

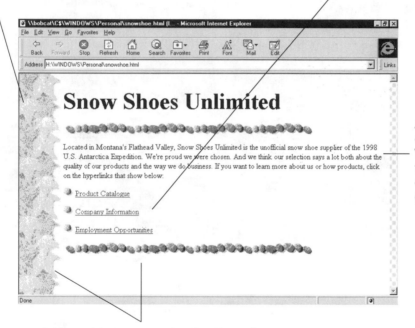

Add textual content using Word's familiar text-processing capabilities (Chapter 6).

Add graphic imagery using the Clip Gallery (pages 83 and 86–87).

Create HTML documents: Word comes with a wizard that gives you a head start building your own HTML documents. The Web Page Wizard, for example, lets you create ready-to-use web pages to which you simply add your content in the form of words and pictures.

Add hyperlinks: Word lets you easily add hyperlinks that point to any Internet resource (such as e-mail addresses, World Wide Web sites, FTP sites, and so forth) as well as local resources (such as Microsoft Office documents).

Add textual content: Using Word, you can add textual content to a web page document in the same way that you add textual content to regular Word documents. You can simply type the text onto the web page. You can copy or move text from another document, such as by using the Windows Clipboard. And you insert text files (including Word documents) directly onto the web page.

Add graphic imagery: You can insert graphic images onto the web pages you build with Word. Note, too, that the Microsoft Clip Gallery comes with a rich set of graphic images, which you can place onto web page documents as GIF or JPEG images, as well as photographic images, sounds, and even video clips.

Office 97:
The Complete Reference

Stephen L. Nelson
Peter Weverka

Osborne **McGraw-Hill**
Berkeley New York St. Louis San Francisco
Auckland Bogotá Hamburg London Madrid
Mexico City Milan Montreal New Delhi Panama City
Paris São Paulo Singapore Sydney
Tokyo Toronto

Osborne **McGraw-Hill**
2600 Tenth Street
Berkeley, California 94710
U.S.A.

For information on translations or book distributors outside the U.S.A., or to arrange bulk purchase discounts for sales promotions, premiums, or fundraisers, please contact Osborne McGraw-Hill at the above address.

Microsoft Office 97: The Complete Reference

234567890 DOC 9987

ISBN 0-07-882338-2

Publisher
Brandon A. Nordin

Editor-in-Chief
Scott Rogers

Acquisitions Editor
Joanne Cuthbertson

Project Editor
Emily Rader

Associate Project Editor
Cynthia Douglas

Editorial Assistant
Gordon Hurd

Technical Editors
Leigh Yafa
Eric J. Ray
Deborah S. Ray

Copy Editors
Kim Torgerson
Michelle Khazai
Dennis Weaver

Proofreaders
Linda Medoff
Karen Mead

Computer Designer
Peter Hancik

Illustrator
Lance Ravella

for Wiley Post,

The first man to circumnavigate the globe by air.

What a guy!

About the Authors

Stephen L. Nelson, a best-selling author and consultant, has written more than 50 books and more than 100 articles on using computers for personal and business financial management. His books have sold more than one million copies in English and have been translated into 11 different languages.

Peter Weverka is the author of *Dummies 101: Word for Windows 95*, *Word for Windows 95 for Dummies Quick Reference*, and *Quicken 6 for Windows for Busy People*. He has edited 80 computer books on topics ranging from word processors to databases to the Internet, and his humorous articles have appeared in Harper's.

Contents

Part III

Microsoft Excel

Part IV

Microsoft Access

Part V

Microsoft PowerPoint

Part VII

Web Publishing with Office

Part VIII

Appendixes

Acknowledgments

This book is a collective effort, and it owes a lot to many hard-working, talented people. First, we would like to thank acquisitions editor Joanne Cuthbertson, who cracked the whip of encouragement and whose many suggestions helped make this a better book.

Thank you to Gordon Hurd, who not only kept contracts and chapters flying up and down the West Coast but also helped tremendously to identify and collect the shareware and freeware programs included on the companion CD.

We would also like to thank our copy editors—Michelle Khazai, Kim Torgerson, and Dennis Weaver—who lent their editorial expertise to the book, and this book's technical editors, Leigh Yafa, Eric Ray, and Deborah Ray, who followed doggedly in our footsteps to make sure that all the instructions in this book are accurate.

Thanks also go to project editor Emily Rader, who cheerfully kept everything on track, and to Bob Richardson for his excellent index.

These Berkeleyites in the editorial offices of Osborne/McGraw-Hill gave their best to our book, and for that we are very grateful: associate project editor Cynthia Douglas; project editor Nancy McLaughlin; editing, design, and production director Steve Emry; production supervisor Marcela Hancik; designer Peter Hancik; illustrator Lance Ravella; and typesetters Jani Beckwith and Roberta Steele.

Thank you, too, to Kaarin Dolliver, our own editorial assistant extraordinaire, who word processed, reviewed manuscript, proofed pages, shot figures, collected all of the pieces and parts that make up the companion CD, and then (in her spare time) wrote the FrontPage appendix.

Hercules was a single man, but if he had been married and had had children, he would have completed his labors sooner. We would like to thank our families for encouraging us and, at times, for putting up with us during the long months it took to complete this book.

Introduction

This book is a comprehensive guide to using all the programs and all the different parts of Microsoft Office 97, the newest edition of the Office suite of programs. Put this book in a prominent place on your desk, and reach for it when you come to an impasse or you simply want to know a better way to complete a task.

The plain-language instructions in this book lay out exactly what you need to know to do a task well and then tell you, in step-by-step fashion, how to complete the task. This book does not pussyfoot around. We want you to do tasks well and do them quickly. And we want you to know enough to create Word documents, Excel worksheets, Access databases, PowerPoint presentations, Outlook messages, and Web pages that either stand out from the crowd or are so efficient they give you the opportunity to get your work done faster and better.

In this book are instructions, tips, tricks, advice, and shortcuts for getting the most out of Word, Excel, Access, PowerPoint, and Outlook, as well as the other parts of Office 97. What's more, this book comes with a CD on which you will find sample files for test-driving the features we explain on the pages of this book, templates for creating jazzy or useful files, and even ten shareware programs. In this book, you will also find instructions for creating Web pages with the Office 97 programs.

Whom This Book Is For

This book is for everybody who either uses one of the programs in the Office 97 suite or uses different programs in the suite to pass around and trade data. Office 97 makes it very easy to pass data back and forth between programs. Besides telling you how to use the features in each program, we tell you how the different programs work together. One of Microsoft's goals in designing the Office 97 suite was to keep users from having to enter information more than once. A table created in Access, for example, can also be used in a Word document. And an outline made in Word can be turned into the text for a PowerPoint presentation. In this book, you will learn how to save lots of time by passing data among the different Office 97 programs.

The Office 97 suite contains the following programs:

- *Word*   A word processing program
- *Excel*   A spreadsheet program
- *Access*   A database program
- *PowerPoint*   A presentation program
- *Outlook*   A combination e-mail and personal information manager program
- *Shared tools*   The clip art images, fonts, and many other features that you can take advantage of in all the programs in the Office 97 suite

No matter which version of Microsoft Office 97 you use, this book can help you. For the record, Microsoft offers two versions of Office 97:

- *Standard version*   The standard version of Office includes Word, Excel, PowerPoint, and Outlook.
- *Professional version*   The professional version includes all the programs in the standard version as well as Access.

 NOTE: Besides the versions of Office listed here, Microsoft offers the Small Office suite, which includes Word, Works, and Publisher; and the Home Office suite, which includes Word, Works, and Money. If you use either of these versions, you can still make use of this book. Part 1 covers the tools that all the Office programs share in common, which are also found in the Small Office and Home Office suites, and Part 2 covers Word.

Our "Best Possible Way" Philosophy

In Office 97 programs, there are almost always two ways to complete a task. Sometimes, in fact, a program offers three or four ways. Rather than waste your time explaining the two, three, or four ways, this book plunges in and explains what we believe is the best way. We chose our "best possible way" philosophy because we want to explain how to do tasks quickly and because, well, we have a lot of ground to cover. In the nearly 1,000 pages contained in this book, we have tried to cover all aspects of the Office 97 programs. To do that, we had to explain the "best possible way" and not waste pages explaining all of the ways to complete a task.

As part of our "best possible way" philosophy, we also explain which program to use to complete a task, and we ignore a part of a program if the task can be done better in another program. For example, Word includes a rather crude spreadsheet feature for making data calculations. Rather than use a Word table, this book steers you to an Excel worksheet, since calculations are much easier to make there than they are in Word. Meanwhile, Excel includes a simple lists feature for creating a name-and-address database. But, again, why use an Excel list when an Access table is easier to use and far more powerful?

What's in This Book, Anyway?

This book is organized to help you look up the information you need quickly. To get instructions, your best bet is to turn to the index or table of contents. To get the lay of the land, the following sections explain what you will find between the covers of this book.

"At a Glance" Pages

At the start of the book is a handful of "At a Glance" pages. These pages serve two purposes: They demonstrate some exciting features of the Office 97 programs and tell you which page to turn to in this book to learn about those exciting features. Be sure to look at the "At a Glance" pages. You might find one or two interesting things that you wouldn't discover on your own.

Part 1: Introducing Office

Part 1 starts by providing background information so you can be a proficient user of the Office 97 programs. It explains what the programs are and what they do, as well as how to manage Word documents, Excel workbooks, PowerPoint presentations, and so forth. You also learn how to customize the Office 97 programs to make them do your bidding and how to use tools such as the spell checker and clip art gallery, which are common to all the programs. Last but not least, you also learn how to share data amongst the different programs.

Part 2: Microsoft Word

Part 2 describes everything you need to know to use Microsoft Word. You learn how to work faster, how to create and use styles for consistent formatting, and how to desktop publish with Word. You also learn tried-and-true techniques for working on long reports and scholarly papers.

Part 3: Microsoft Excel

Part 3 describes and discusses the Excel spreadsheet program. You learn what workbooks are and how to enter labels and values into worksheet cells, as well as how formulas and functions work. Part 3 also describes how to use the ChartWizard to create charts, how to create sophisticated PivotTables, and how to use the advanced modeling tools.

Part 4: Microsoft Access

Part 4 covers the Access database program. In this part, you learn how to create an Access database, how to create and link database tables, and how to create forms, queries, and reports. Turn to Part 4 to get plain-language explanations of hideous database terms and to learn how to create useful databases that store information accurately and efficiently.

Part 5: Microsoft PowerPoint

Part 5 explains how to put together a PowerPoint presentation. You learn how to create the presentation, how to embellish it with artwork and animation, and how to create speaker's notes and other amenities to ensure that your presentation is a hit. Of course, you also learn how to give a presentation.

Part 6: Microsoft Outlook

Part 6 is divided into two chapters, one that covers how to send and receive e-mail and files, and another that explains how to use the personal information manager side of Outlook to keep track of appointments, contacts, and your to-do list.

Part 7: Web Publishing with Office

Part 7 goes into detail about how to use Office 97 to publish files on the World Wide Web. You get a primer on web publishing that explains what the World Wide Web is and what HTML does. Then you learn how to use hyperlinks to connect Office 97 files to the World Wide Web and how to publish web files with Word, PowerPoint, Excel, and Access. You also learn how to use Microsoft's Internet Explorer 4.0 with Office.

Part 8: Appendixes

Part 8 rounds out the book with three appendixes. Appendix A describes how to install and reinstall Office. Appendix B explains how to use FrontPage, Microsoft's program for creating web sites. (FrontPage isn't part of the Office 97 suite, but if you want to get serious about web publishing with Office, you need to know a bit about FrontPage.) Appendix C describes what is on the companion CD included with this book.

What's on the Companion CD?

Appendix C gives a thorough explanation of what is on the CD included with this book. The appendix also explains how to make use of the templates, sample files, and programs on the CD.

On the CD are

- *Templates* Over 50 "Headstart templates" that you can use to create Word documents, Excel worksheets, and PowerPoint presentations. Where Headstart templates are explained on the pages of this book, you see a Headstart icon.

- *Sample files* Close to 200 "Learn By Example" files. Use these sample files to test and get experience using the different features that are described on the pages of this book. Where you see a "Learn By Example" icon, read on to learn the name of a sample file that you can use to experiment with the feature that is being explained.

- *Shareware* Ten shareware programs that we thought are especially worthwhile. In fact, they are the ten best shareware programs that we could find.

Conventions Used in This Book

To make this book more useful and a pleasure to read, we joined heads with the publisher to create several conventions. Following are descriptions of the conventions in this book.

Icons

Occasionally, when we want to alert you to an important bit of advice, a shortcut, or a pitfall, you see a Note, Tip, or Warning icon and a few important words in the text.

NOTE: *This is a note. Notes define words, refer you to other parts of the book, or offer background information so you can make better use of an Office 97 program.*

TIP: *This is a tip. Tips give you shortcuts and handy pieces of advice to make you a better user of Office 97. Take a tip from us and read these tips attentively.*

WARNING: *This is a warning. When you see a warning, perk up your ears. Warnings appear when you have to make crucial choices or when you are about to undertake something that you might regret later.*

Besides Notes, Tips, and Warnings, you also see Headstart and Learn By Example icons.

HEADSTART
As we told you earlier in the introduction, the companion CD included with this book has over 50 Headstart templates. To alert you to the fact that you can use a Headstart template, the Headstart icon appears along with the name of the template you can use.

LEARN BY EXAMPLE
The Learn By Example icon tells you when a practice file is available that you can use to test an Office 97 feature. The text that accompanies these icons provides a description of the sample file and its name.

Sidebars

From time to time, we present information that is tangential to the main discussion. When that happens, the information is presented in a sidebar like this one.

Command Names

Rather than tell you to, for example, "choose Print from the File menu," this book presents commands in the order in which they are given: "Choose the File menu Print command." After all, to choose the Print command, you have to click File menu first, and then click Print. This convention was adopted to help you make better sense of commands and how to give them.

FYI

For the record, Stephen L. Nelson wrote all the chapters in Part 1 except Chapter 4. He also wrote Part 3, Part 7, and Appendix B. Peter Weverka wrote Chapter 4 in Part 1 as well as Parts 2, 4, 5, and 6. He also wrote Appendix A, Appendix C, and this introduction.

Bon Voyage!

We have thrown every tip, trick, and piece of useful advice that we know into this book. If you know a shortcut of your own that you would like to share with other readers, please send it to Peter_Weverka@msn.com so we can include it in the next edition of this book. For that matter, if you have a comment about the book or need advice for using a program, please e-mail a message to us. Meanwhile, best of luck using Office 97!

Part I

Introducing Office

The Complete
Reference

Office
97

Chapter 1

What Is Office?

L et's start by taking a look at Microsoft Office itself, how the parts of the Office suite of programs fit together, how this book is organized, and why you, the reader, are likely to benefit from this book. Even if you want to get on with your reading and learning, getting all this information up front helps you make better sense of Office and better use this book.

An Overview of Office

What is Microsoft Office? This question is actually one that's more difficult to answer than it should be. On the face of it, Office is simply four (or more) software programs sold in a bundle and installed together. If you purchase the standard version of Microsoft Office 97, you get Microsoft Word 97, Microsoft Excel 97, Microsoft PowerPoint 97, and Microsoft Outlook (new this year). If you purchase the professional version of Office, you get everything that comes in the standard version, as well as Microsoft Access 97.

What Is Word?

You use Word to create textual documents: letters, reports, books, and so on. Figure 1-1 shows a Word document. (The files that Word creates are called *documents*.) To create

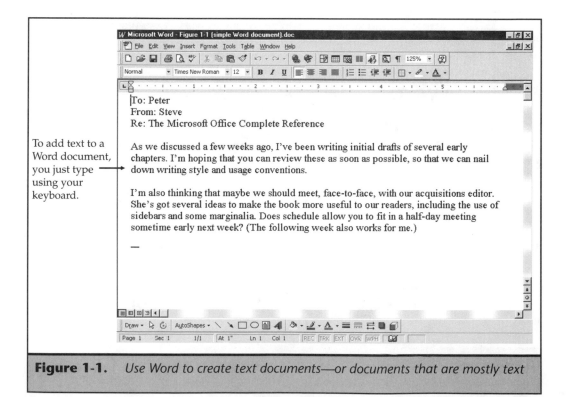

Figure 1-1.   *Use Word to create text documents—or documents that are mostly text*

a textual document, you simply start Word and then type in words and numbers. Chapters 6 through 10 talk in detail about working with and creating Word documents.

EXAMPLES

LEARN BY EXAMPLE
You can open the example Word document shown in Figure 1-1 from the companion CD. The sample document name, Figure 1-1 (simple Word document), *shows you what a Word document looks like. If you want to experiment with the sample document, just get to work—click someplace within the document to position the insertion point, and begin typing.*

NOTE: The easiest way to open a sample document is to use Windows Explorer to view the contents of the companion CD's Learn By Example folder. When you see the sample document you want to open, double-click it.

What Is Excel?

Excel lets you perform numerical analysis. That's just a fancy way of saying adding, subtracting, and other number-crunching calculations. Figure 1-2 shows a simple Excel workbook. (The files Excel creates are called *workbooks*.) In a nutshell, workbooks provide a grid of columns and rows that you use to describe and make calculations.

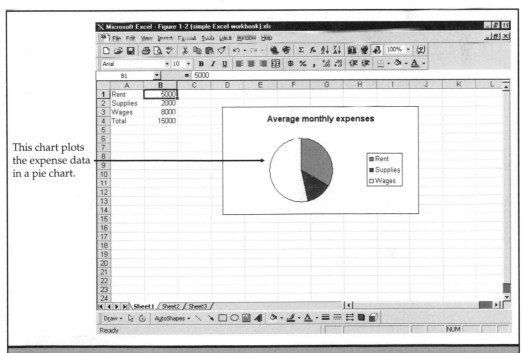

This chart plots the expense data in a pie chart.

Figure 1-2. *Use Excel to perform numerical analysis—such as when you want to create a budget or make a financial calculation—and to create charts*

Chapters 11 through 15 talk more about Excel workbooks, but for now note that what Figure 1-2 shows is just a simple budget. To create it, you would enter the budgeting categories Rent, Supplies, and Wages, and then the budgeted amounts for these categories. You'd also create a formula to total your individual budgeted amounts.

LEARN BY EXAMPLE

You can open the example Excel workbook shown in Figure 1-2 from the companion CD. The sample document name, Figure 1-2 (simple Excel workbook), *shows you what an Excel workbook looks like. If you want to experiment with the sample workbook, just click the cell containing the number 5000—the budgeted amount for rent, type the number* **2000***, and press* ENTER. *Notice that both the total shown and the pie chart change to reflect your alteration.*

What Is PowerPoint?

PowerPoint works much like Word does, except that rather than create pages of a textual document, you create colorful slides that you can use to produce 35mm slides, overhead transparencies, or, more likely, to display on your computer's screen in a slide show–like procession called a *presentation*. Figure 1-3 shows an example

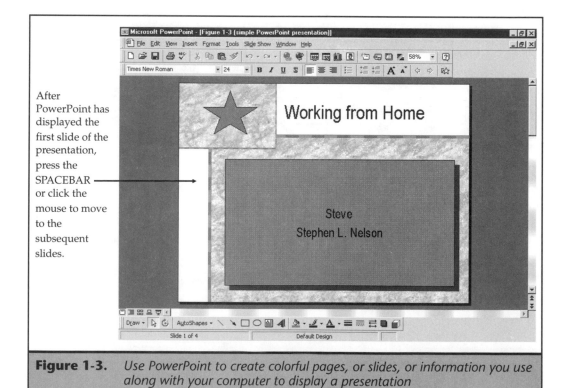

After PowerPoint has displayed the first slide of the presentation, press the SPACEBAR or click the mouse to move to the subsequent slides.

Figure 1-3. *Use PowerPoint to create colorful pages, or slides, or information you use along with your computer to display a presentation*

PowerPoint slide. You can't tell it from the figure, but this slide is actually in color. Typically, PowerPoint is used to create slide show presentations for sales calls, meetings, or speeches.

EXAMPLES

LEARN BY EXAMPLE

You can open the example PowerPoint presentation shown in Figure 1-3 from the companion CD. The sample document name, Figure 1-3 (simple PowerPoint presentation), *shows you what a PowerPoint presentation looks like. If you want to experiment with the sample document, choose the Slide Show menu's View Show command.*

What Is Outlook?

Outlook is a personal information manager. It lets you send and receive e-mail, keep a "To Do" list, maintain an appointment calendar, and keep a database of names, addresses, and telephone numbers. Figure 1-4 shows what the message window looks like (you would use this to e-mail someone a message). Figure 1-5 shows what the Outlook appointment calendar looks like.

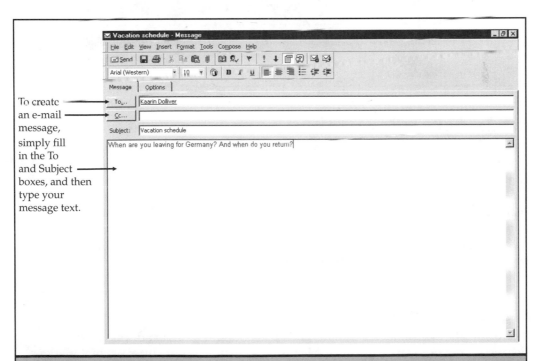

To create an e-mail message, simply fill in the To and Subject boxes, and then type your message text.

Figure 1-4.   *Outlook includes a handy e-mail program that you can use if your computer connects to a network or you use an online service like Microsoft Network*

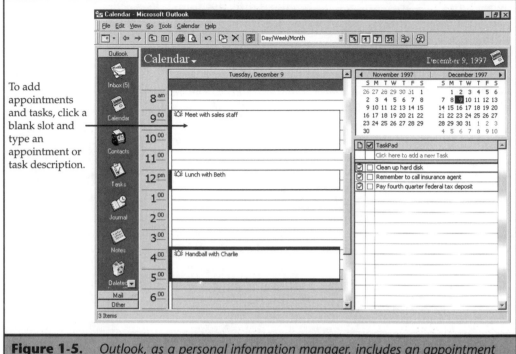

To add appointments and tasks, click a blank slot and type an appointment or task description.

Figure 1-5.   *Outlook, as a personal information manager, includes an appointment calendar and task list manager that you can use to better manage your workday*

What Is Access?

Access is a relational database management program. If you haven't used a database before, Access may sound like something that only computer experts and programmers can use. But that's not the case. Access simply helps you build and maintain lists of information, as shown in Figure 1-6. For example, if you work in a business, you maintain several lists of customer information. You keep a list of customer names, addresses, and telephone numbers, for example, as well as a list of the amounts that customers owe you. Access, as a database program, helps you keep, maintain, and better use exactly these sorts of lists. (Access calls its lists *tables,* by the way, and a collection of related tables a *database.*)

The Office Family

There are other versions of Office, but this book doesn't directly address those. Because of the popularity of Office, Microsoft is creating other suites of combinations. The Small Business Office suite, for example, includes Word, Excel, Outlook, Publisher,

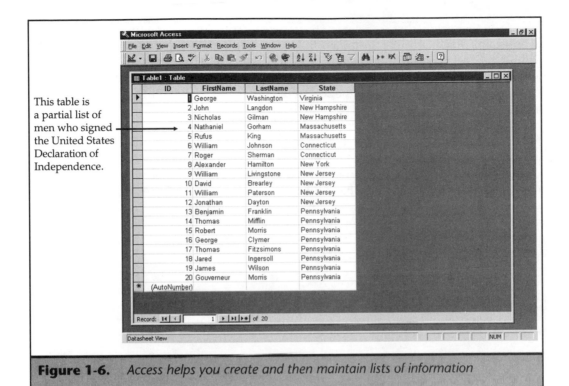

This table is a partial list of men who signed the United States Declaration of Independence.

Figure 1-6. *Access helps you create and then maintain lists of information*

AutoMap Streets Plus, and Small Business Financial Manager for Excel. There's even a Developer Office suite, which includes everything that the Professional Edition of Office does, as well as several additional developer tools. If you've purchased one of these other versions of Office, you can still get useful information from this book on those components that the standard and professional versions of Office have in common with your copy of Small Business or Developer Office.

How the Parts of Office Fit Together

Some people mistakenly think that Office is a single program. And the confusion is understandable because Microsoft markets Office in this manner. (You may have noticed that the Office logo shows four or five puzzle pieces tightly fitting together.) To be quite frank, however, Office isn't so much a technological innovation as a marketing gambit. In the opinion of the writers, Microsoft Corporation created Office as a way to win a bigger share of the word processor market and the spreadsheet market.

Marketing aside, there is a smart strategy to learning and using the Office suite of programs. Each Office program works with a different type of data: Word works with text, Excel works with numbers, PowerPoint works with pictures, Access works with lists of information, and so on. Given this, what you want to do is learn to use the Office programs that handle the sort of data that you work with. This makes sense, right?

In fact, this book assumes that you take this very approach: learning to use the *best* tool for working with a particular type of data. In this manner, you can save substantial reading and learning time by skipping coverage of features you don't need to use. And, more importantly, you'll get the biggest payback for your reading and learning investment since you'll be emphasizing the best tools. For example, Word includes a rather crude spreadsheet feature (called tables) that you can use to make calculations—such as for a budget. Excel's worksheets, however, are both easier to use and more powerful in what they can do. Similarly, Access's tables feature is both easier to use and more powerful than Excel's lists feature.

The
Complete
Reference

Office
97

Chapter 2

Managing Document Files

A lthough the different Office programs work with different types of data, their files are saved, opened, and printed in basically the same way. Because of these similarities, this chapter discusses document file management for all of the Office programs. It covers saving, opening, and printing document files, as well as creating new document files, working with file properties, and searching for lost document files. If you review this chapter—and then remember even a fraction of what you read—you'll be well equipped to work with Office document files.

Saving Document Files

Any time you create a document file you want to work with again, you'll want to save the document to your hard disk, a floppy disk, or even some other storage device. Fortunately, saving document files is easy. Extremely easy.

Saving a Document File for the First Time

To save a document for the first time, click the Save tool, which appears on the Standard toolbar. (You can also choose the File menu's Save As or Save command.) When the Office program displays the Save As dialog box, shown in Figure 2-1, follow these steps to save the document file.

1. Use the Save in drop-down list box to select the folder in which you want to save the document. (If you want to save a document file in your Favorites folder, click the Look in Favorites button. If you want to create a new folder to use for storing the document file, click the Create New Folder button and then, when prompted by Windows, provide a name for the new folder.)

2. Enter the filename you want to use for the new document file into the File name box.

 TIP: The Save As dialog box also provides several other buttons. For more information about any of these buttons, refer to the later chapter sections, "The Favorites Folder," "Changing the Open Dialog Box's File Listing Information," and "Using the Commands and Settings Menu."

Naming Your Document File

You can name your document files just about anything you want. For all practical purposes, there isn't a limit on the length of your document file. (You can use up to 255 characters, for example.) Don't, however, specify a three-character file extension yourself. Let the Office program add that bit of information for you. Office programs use the file extension (as well as other information stored in the file) to identify the format of the file.

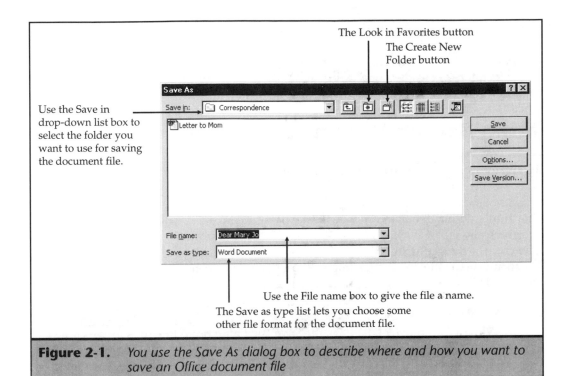

The Look in Favorites button

The Create New Folder button

Use the Save in drop-down list box to select the folder you want to use for saving the document file.

Use the File name box to give the file a name.

The Save as type list lets you choose some other file format for the document file.

Figure 2-1.   *You use the Save As dialog box to describe where and how you want to save an Office document file*

Resaving a Document File

Once you save a Document file, its new name appears on the document window's title bar. When you want to save it again, you simply click the Save tool or choose the File menu's Save command. The Office program saves the document file in the same location and with the same name, replacing your old version of the document file.

NOTE: If you've made changes to a document file since you last saved it, the Office program asks if you want to save your document file when you choose the File menu's Close or Exit commands to prevent you from accidentally losing your changes.

Saving a Document File with a New Name

You can save multiple copies of a document simply by giving the copies new names or by placing the copies in a different folder. (Typically, you'll want to give the document file a new name so that you don't get the document files mixed up.) To save a document file with a different name or in a different location, choose the File menu's Save As command. Then use the Save As dialog box to specify either a new filename or a new folder location. (This business of specifying either a new filename or a new folder location works the same way as it does when you originally specify a filename or folder location.)

Creating Backup Document Files

When you resave a document file, you actually replace the older version of the document file (the one you originally retrieved) with the new version that incorporates your most recent changes. Usually, this is exactly what you want—to replace the old version of some document file. But sometimes—particularly when someone else may later fiddle with a document file—you may want to have the Office program automatically create backup copies of your old document file whenever you save a new copy of the document file.

To automatically create a backup copy of the old versions of Word 97 documents and Excel 97 workbooks each time you resave a file, take the following steps:

1. Choose the File menu's Save As command.

2. When Word or Excel displays the Save As dialog box, click the Options button.

3. When the Office program displays the Save options dialog box, check the Always create backup copy box (if you're working with Word) or check the Always create backup box (if you're working with Excel).

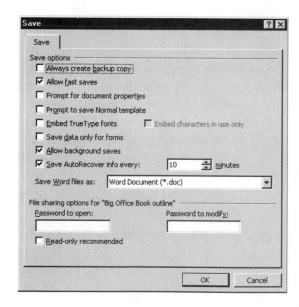

NOTE: *The preceding illustration shows Word's Save options dialog box. The Excel Save Options dialog box looks slightly different.*

Protecting Your Document Files and Using Passwords

If other people can grab your files—either because they can start and use your computer or because your computer connects to a network—you may want to consider using passwords for your most sensitive, confidential, or important document files. When you use passwords, people can't view document files you don't want them to see and, perhaps just as importantly, they can't change document files they shouldn't modify. Fortunately, this sort of control is easy to institute with both Word and Excel documents (although not with PowerPoint or Outlook) because both Word and Excel provide three levels of security in the Save options dialog box.

 NOTE: *You can control access to an Access database using passwords, too, but for Access the process works a little bit differently than it does for Word or Excel. In Access, you use the Tools menu's Security command to set passwords. Chapters 16 through 19 describe how Access works.*

Using the Read-Only Recommended Option

You can tell Word or Excel that it must require that people open a document file as "read-only." (Read-only means that someone opening the file can read the file, but not resave the file and thereby change it.) For example, if you collaborate with several other members of a project team to coauthor a monthly status report, you might want to make sure that someone doesn't inadvertently make changes to the report. In this situation, one easy way to minimize (although not eliminate) the chance of such a mistake would be to use the read-only recommended option. To do this, check the Read-Only Recommended box in the Save options dialog box.

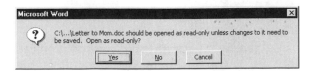

You've perhaps deduced as much, but it's important to make two quick observations about the read-only recommendation option. First of all, people aren't required to open a document file as read-only—they only receive a recommendation to do so. (In other words, the "read-only recommended" business is voluntary.) Another, somewhat less obvious characteristic of the read-only option is that someone can still save a new, modified copy of the document file as long as they use a new document filename.

Using the Password-to-Modify Option

If you want to control who can make changes to a document file but not who can read a document file, you use the password-to-modify option. With this option, anybody can open a file. But they must open the file as read-only unless they can supply the password-to-modify password. Actually, there are numerous uses for the password-to-modify option. Any time you have a document that can't be edited but can be freely circulated, you should probably use the password-to-modify option. By using the password-to-modify option, somebody *must* open your file as a read-only file unless he or she can supply the password.

To enable the password-to-modify option, enter a password in the Password to modify text box in the Save options dialog box. Your password can be up to 15 characters long, and it is case sensitive. (For instance, if you first enter the password as all lowercase letters, you must always use all lowercase letters when reentering the password.)

NOTE: When you click OK to close the Save options dialog box, the Office program asks you to confirm the password you entered—just to make sure that you really know your password—and it reminds you to remember your password.

After you assign a password-to-modify password, the Office program prompts anyone opening the file for the password:

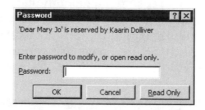

If you (or anyone else) can supply the correct password, you (or they) can open the document file, make changes, and then resave the document file. If someone doesn't know the password, he or she can open the file but won't be able to resave the document file. (Note, however, that someone can save a new copy of the file as long as the file gets a new name.)

Using the Password-to-Open Option

If you want to control access to the information in a document file, you use the password-to-open option. After you assign a password-to-open password, people who know (or can guess) the password can open the document. But nobody else can. To use the password-to-open option, just enter the password into the Password to open text box, which also appears in the Save options dialog box.

Opening Document Files

As you presumably know if you're reading this book, you can open document files using either the Document menu or the Windows Explorer. You can also open document files from within a program, however, by clicking the Open tool or by choosing the File menu's Open command.

Using the Office Shortcuts Toolbar

If you install Office in the usual way, the setup program adds the Office Shortcuts Toolbar program to your Startup group. (The Startup group is just a list of programs that Windows automatically starts whenever it starts.) The Office Shortcuts toolbar amounts to another way you can open document files and start programs. This book doesn't describe or discuss the Office Shortcuts toolbar, however, because standard Windows components that you can use for opening document files and starting programs—the Start menu, the Windows Explorer (in Windows 95) or the Windows NT Explorer (in Windows NT), the Documents menu, and shortcut icons—are superior to the Office Shortcuts toolbar and more general (because you can use them with any program and any document file).

The Basics of Opening Documents from Within an Office Program

To open an existing document, click the Open tool, which appears on the Standard toolbar, or choose the File menu's Open command. When the Office program displays the Open dialog box, shown in Figure 2-2, follow these steps to open the document file:

1. Use the Look in drop-down list box to select the folder that stores the document file you want to open. If the file you're looking for isn't in the default folder, activate the Look in drop-down list box to display a list of your drives. Click the drive that contains the document file you want, and then double-click folders until you locate your file. Alternatively, you can start looking through the folder hierarchy by clicking the Up One Level button next to the Look in drop-down list box.

2. To modify your search further, you can enter the filename into the File name drop-down list box. Refer to "Searching for Lost Document Files" later in this chapter for more information on this feature.

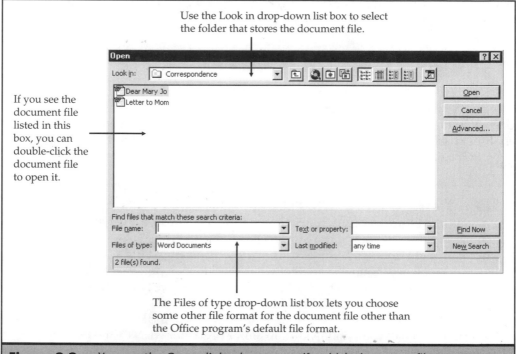

Use the Look in drop-down list box to select the folder that stores the document file.

If you see the document file listed in this box, you can double-click the document file to open it.

The Files of type drop-down list box lets you choose some other file format for the document file other than the Office program's default file format.

Figure 2-2.   *You use the Open dialog box to specify which document file you want to open and where the document file is located*

NOTE: You can also typically use the File menu to reopen the four document files you used most recently. They are listed at the bottom of the File menu. Just click a file to open it.

Searching the Web

If you click the Search the Web button, the Office program displays a Microsoft Network web page that you can use to conduct a search of the Internet using any of the popular Internet search services. For more information about how search services work, refer to Appendix B.

The Favorites Folder

When you install Office, the setup program creates a folder named Favorites in your Windows folder. You can use the two Favorites buttons (Add to Favorites and Look in Favorites) in the Open dialog box to access the Favorites folder. You can click the Add to Favorites button to add the selected folder or the selected document file to the

Favorites folder to create a shortcut icon to the folder or document file and then place the shortcut icon in the Favorites folder.

 NOTE: *When you click the Add to Favorites button, the Office program displays a menu with two commands: Add Selected Folder to Favorites, and Add Selected Item to Favorites.*

You can click the Look in Favorites button to display the contents of the Favorites folder in the box that appears beneath the Look in list box.

Once the Open dialog box displays the contents of the Favorites folder (this will be a list of shortcut icons), you can open a document file by double-clicking it.

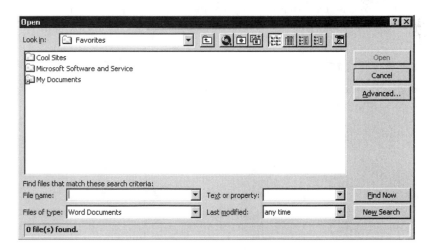

Changing the Open Dialog Box's File Listing Information

One of the major advantages of using the Open dialog box to open a document file (rather than, in comparison, the Documents menu or the Windows Explorer) is that you can easily specify how you want document files listed and described. More specifically, you can use the four display buttons to change the way document files get listed in the Open dialog box. The following table identifies and describes these buttons:

Button	Description
	The List button displays a simple list of document filenames and icons. If there are a large number of document files in the current folder, it makes more of them visible at once than any other display option.
	The Details button displays fewer document files, but gives you more details about each, such as file size and type. You can sort the listings differently by clicking on each heading.
	The Properties button displays a simple document file listing combined with a brief summary of the selected file's properties from the Properties dialog box.
	The Preview button also displays a simple document file listing, but combines it with a preview of the selected document file, if Save preview picture has been checked on the Summary tab of the Properties dialog box. (You use the File menu's Properties command to enable this feature.)

Using the Commands and Settings Menu

Clicking the Commands and Settings button displays a menu with an interesting assortment of commands:

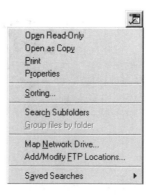

Because what a few of these commands do isn't all that apparent, you'll benefit from a quick review of what each does.

Open Read-Only

Use the Open Read-Only command when you want to open a document file, even
perhaps make changes to the document file, but don't want to replace the original
version of the document with some, new modified document file.

> *NOTE: Earlier in the chapter, in the section entitled, "Protecting Your Document Files
> and Using Passwords," this book describes how you can tell an Office program to
> recommend that people open a particular document file as read-only.*

Open as Copy

The Open as Copy command creates a copy of the selected document file and then
opens this copy rather than the original document file. When you use this command,
by the way, the Office program names the new, copied document file by adding the
words, "Copy of" to the original document filename. For example, if you use this
command to create a copy of a Word document named "Memo to Alfred," using this
command creates a new Word document named "Copy of Memo to Alfred." If you
use this command to create a copy of an Excel workbook named "Next year's
budget," using this command creates a new Excel document named "Copy of
Next year's budget."

Print

The Print command prints one copy of the selected document using the default
Windows printer. In effect, this Print command is equivalent to the Print toolbar
button, which appears on the Standard toolbars of all the Office program windows.

> *NOTE: Later in the chapter, in the section "Printing Document Files," this book
> describes in more detail how you print document files.*

Properties

The Properties command displays the properties dialog box for the selected document
file. This book talks more about document properties in the later chapter section,
"Working with Document File Properties."

Sorting

The Sorting command displays a dialog box you can use to specify which piece
of file information you want to use for sorting files listed in the Open dialog box and
whether files should be sorted in ascending or descending order. When you choose
this command, simply use the Sort files by drop-down list entries—Name, Size, Date

and Modified—to specify how document files should be sorted. Then use the Ascending and Descending option buttons to specify whether document files should be sorted in ascending or descending order.

Search Subfolders

The Search Subfolders command is, in effect, a toggle switch. If you choose this command to turn on the Search Subfolders switch, the Open dialog box not only displays a list of document files in the selected folder (which is the folder that shows in the Look in drop-down list box), the dialog box also displays a list of the document files in the selected folder's subfolders.

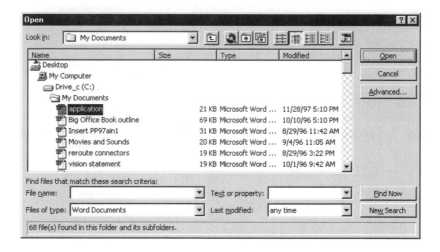

Group Files by Folder

If you turn on the Search Subfolders switch (see the preceding paragraph), you can use the Group files by folder command, which is actually another toggle switch, to specify that document files be grouped by folder—or not be grouped by folder. Typically, you do want to group files by folder when you've turned on the Search Subfolders switch.

NOTE: If the Search Subfolders switch or the Group files by folder switch is turned on, the Office program places a check mark in front of the command name.

Map Network Drive

The Map Network Drive command displays the Map Network Drive dialog box, shown in Figure 2-3, which allows you to map, or connect to, another computer's disk or storage device. (To connect to some other computer's disk or storage device, by the way, your computer needs to connect to a local area network.) After you choose the Map Network Drive, use the Path drop-down list box to provide the network drive path name in the form *computer name**disk name*. For example, if you want to use the hard disk drive named c$ on the computer named bobcat, you enter **bobcat****c$** into the Path drop-down list box.

Add/Modify FTP Locations

The Add/Modify FTP Locations command displays a dialog box you can use to build a list of useful FTP sites. (FTP is an Internet protocol that lets people move files between computer networks.)

Saved Searches

The Saved Searches command displays a list of document file search criteria you've previously saved. To search a disk again using a set of search criteria, you select the search criteria description from the Saved Searches list. (Later in the chapter in the section "Searching for Lost Document Files," this book describes how you create, use, and save search criteria.)

Using the Shortcut Menu

It turns out that it's really not an Office program like Word or Excel that displays the Open dialog box or the Save As dialog box. Windows displays both dialog boxes. The

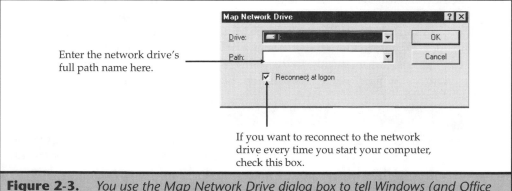

Figure 2-3. *You use the Map Network Drive dialog box to tell Windows (and Office programs) that you want to use another computer's disk drives or storage devices*

fact that it is Windows means that you actually can do far more with the document files you see listed than you might at first suspect.

If you right-click a document file listed in either the Open or Save As dialog box, Windows displays a shortcut menu of Windows file-management commands. On this menu you'll find some of the same commands that are on the Commands and Settings menu, including Print, Open Read-Only, and Properties. You may also find commands to let you create a shortcut to the selected file, delete or rename it, send the file to disk, and fax or e-mail it.

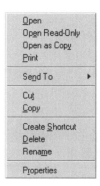

NOTE: *If you have questions about any of the shortcut menu commands, however, refer to the user documentation that came with your copy of Windows.*

Creating New Document Files

You create new document files in a variety of ways. Some programs, like Word and Excel, for example, create new document files when you start the program directly. And other programs, such as PowerPoint and Access, let you use wizards to create document files. Finally, in Outlook, you create new document files (or what Outlook calls "items") almost automatically. In the paragraphs that follow, this book briefly discusses how and when you create document files with each of the Office programs.

Creating a New Outlook Item

In Outlook (as described in more detail in Chapters 23 and 24), you create a new item simply by telling Outlook you want to write an e-mail message, add an appointment to your calendar, jot down a note or to-do list task, or record someone's name into your contacts folder. You don't, therefore, actually do anything special to create a new document file, or item. Item creation occurs automatically—and in the background. (To save the item, you typically do click a toolbar button named something like "Send" in the case of an e-mail item or "Save and Close" in the case of other Outlook items.)

Creating a New PowerPoint Presentation

In PowerPoint (as described in Chapter 20), you create a new presentation by indicating that you want to run the AutoContent Wizard. PowerPoint gives you the option of starting the AutoContent Wizard whenever you start the program.

Creating a New Access Database

In Access (as described in Chapters 16 through 19), you typically create a new database by indicating that you want to run the Database Wizard. Access gives you the option of starting the Database Wizard whenever you start the program.

NOTE: *You can also create new databases from scratch, although this book doesn't describe the mechanics of this more complicated approach.*

Creating New Word Documents and Excel Workbooks

In Word and Excel, you actually create blank document files simply by starting the program. What's more, in both of these programs, you can also create blank document files by clicking the New tool, which appears on the Standard toolbar.

Using the File New Command

While the New tool represents the fastest way to create new documents, you can also choose the File menu's New command. And you'll want to do this whenever you want to create a new document based on a template. (A template is just a document file that is partially complete—either because it already stores information or because it already contains formatting.)

To create a new document file using the File menu's New command, choose the command and follow these steps:

1. Click the New dialog box tab that most closely describes the type of document you want to create.

2. When you see the document template you want to use as the basis for creating your new document file (such as the Word template shown in Figure 2-4), double-click it.

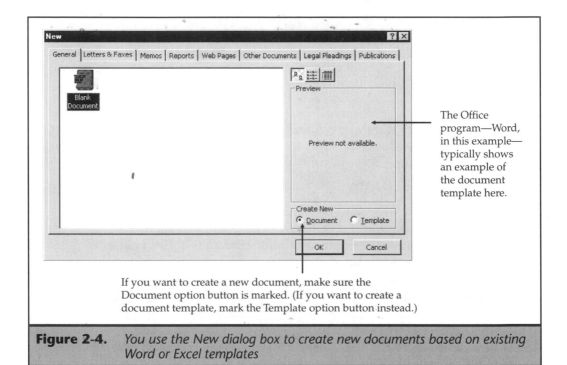

The Office program—Word, in this example—typically shows an example of the document template here.

If you want to create a new document, make sure the Document option button is marked. (If you want to create a document template, mark the Template option button instead.)

Figure 2-4. *You use the New dialog box to create new documents based on existing Word or Excel templates*

3. If a document template starts a wizard (some do), follow the wizard's instructions for completing the document.

 NOTE: *You can view the list of document templates in three different ways. Click the buttons above the Preview box to view the templates as large icons, in a list, or in a list with file details.*

Creating Your Own Document File Templates

If you use the same document file format over and over, you'll want to turn the document file into a template of your own. To do this, choose the File menu's Save As command and save the document file in almost the usual way. The only thing you need to do differently is select the Document Template option in the Save as type drop-down list box.

NOTE: *By default, the Office program saves document templates you create in its templates folder so they appear on the General tab of the New dialog box. If you instead want a document template to appear on some other tab, select the Templates folder subfolder that corresponds to the tab. (In other words, if you want a document template to appear on the Memos tab, you need to store it in the Memos subfolder of the Templates folder.)*

TIP: You can create new tabs for the New dialog box by creating new subfolders in the Templates folder. You can do this using the Windows Explorer or, as described in the earlier chapter section, "Saving Document Files," by using the Create New Folder button on the Save As dialog box.

Working with Document File Properties

While many of your document files will no doubt be similar in many respects, they will all have individual characteristics—properties, in other words—that distinguish them from one another. For example, they use different names, are of differing sizes, were probably created at different times, and so forth. These properties can be useful to you in a couple of important ways: they provide a valuable record associated with each document file, allowing you to describe document files, and they can make it easier for you to locate missing document files.

Describing Document File Properties

Document file properties can be divided into five general types, corresponding to the five tabs on the Properties dialog box, as shown in Figure 2-5.

The General tab, as you might expect, lists general information about a document file, including its name, type, location, and size. In addition, the General tab contains statistical information also found on the Statistics tab, and a record of certain file attributes.

The Summary tab (shown in Figure 2-5) lets you enter information about the document file, including its subject matter and notes or comments. In addition you can include keywords to make file searches easier.

The Statistics tab shows when the document file was created, and when it was last accessed, modified, and printed. Also included is the name of the person who last saved it (important for network users), the number of times it has been revised, the total time it has been open, and other bits of information as well.

The Contents tab describes the contents of a document file: the worksheets in an Excel workbook file, the headings in a Word document (if the Save Preview Picture check box has been enabled), the slides in a PowerPoint presentation, and so on.

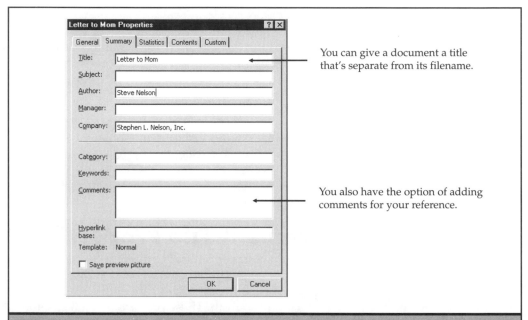

You can give a document a title that's separate from its filename.

You also have the option of adding comments for your reference.

Figure 2-5. *The Properties dialog box documents valuable information specific to each of your Document files*

Entering and Viewing Document File Properties

To describe your document files, choose the File menu's Properties command, and click on the Summary tab. (In Access, you actually choose the File menu's Database Properties command.) The Office program will have probably already entered your name and the company you work for, based on the information you provided at setup. Once the Office program displays the Properties dialog box, you can give your file a title, and enter the subject matter and any comments you may have, simply by filling in the text boxes. (For instance, you might make a note about assumptions used for sales projections, or name the client for whom you prepared the file.)

NOTE: To make your file easier to find later on, be as specific as you can here. If there's a keyword that you know you'll always associate with a file, include it in the summary properties. It could come in handy later. Also note that Outlook items possess a more limited set of properties than Word, Excel, and PowerPoint document files.

Searching for Lost Document Files

You've probably had the experience of knowing there's a document file somewhere on your hard disk that you need but that you also can't locate. Perhaps you can't remember in which folder you stored the document file. Or maybe you can't remember what the document file is called. You could try just browsing through your disk in Windows Explorer or Windows NT Explorer. And sometimes that will work. But there are much more powerful tools available to you.

Using the Find Feature

Your first line of attack is using the Find feature at the bottom of the Open dialog box, under the heading "Find files that match these search criteria." If you know the name of a file, but you just can't remember where it is, enter its name in the File name drop-down list box. (Pressing the downward pointing arrow next to this box will reveal a drop-down list of files you've previously searched for.) In the Files of type drop-down list box, you can specify the type of file (file extension type) you want to find. By default, an Office program assumes you want to find a "native" document file. For example, if you're working with Excel and choose the File menu's Open command, the default file style is "Microsoft Excel Files," meaning files with extension .xl*, as shown in Figure 2-6, but you can search all files if you prefer. Just click the downward pointing arrow to display the Files of type list and select All Files.

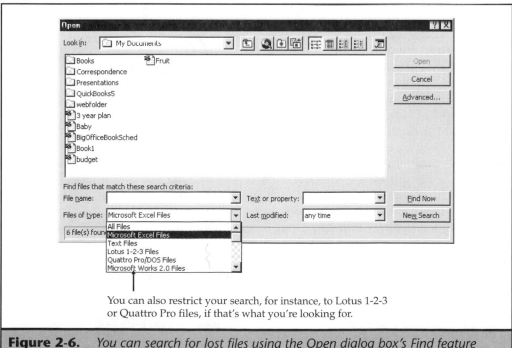

Figure 2-6. *You can search for lost files using the Open dialog box's Find feature*

If you know the directory (folder) where your file is located, enter it in the Look in drop-down list box. If not, click the downward pointing arrow to display the folder hierarchy, or use the Up One Level button, to tell the Office program where to search. You can search your entire disk drive by selecting it in the Look in box. Or, point to a floppy drive, if your file is on disk. Click Find Now to begin the search. In the Status bar, the Office program tells you how many files it has found that meet your criteria.

Searching for Specific Text or Properties

If you can't remember the name of the file, you may be able to remember some specific words or text in it, or perhaps some information that you entered on the Summary tab of the Properties dialog box. Enter whatever items of text you recall in the Text or property drop-down list box. (This box also "remembers" previously searched-for text.) Or, if you know when you last opened and modified the file, enter that in the Last modified drop-down list box. The default is "any time," but you can click the arrow and select from other time frames, like "today," or "last month." Click Find Now to start the search. Click New Search to erase criteria from a previous search and start over.

Using the Advanced Button

You can click the Advanced button to specify in even greater detail what the document file you want to find looks like. When you click the Advanced button, the Office program displays the Advanced Find dialog box, as shown in Figure 2-7.

You can add more criteria to your search using the Define more criteria section. The Property list box includes a drop-down list of the properties found in the Properties dialog box. (This illustrates the primary benefit, obviously, of filling out the Properties dialog box for all your files: The more specific and thorough you are in describing your document file properties, the easier time you have finding files later.)

The Condition list box allows you to specify an additional condition to zero in on the property you entered. The listings in the Condition box change depending upon the Property you select. For example, conditions that modify the Size property are limited to those expressing numerical relationships like "more than" or "equals."

In the Value list box, you can enter either text or numbers, to further define the criteria you chose in the Condition and/or Property boxes.

Let's say, for instance, that you are searching for an invoice, and you know the invoice number is above a certain value. Click the downward-pointing arrow next to the Property drop-down list box. Scroll through the list of properties and select Invoice Number. Then, in the Condition drop-down list box, select "more than." Finally, in the Value box, enter the appropriate value. Click Add to List, and your new criteria will appear in the large list box.

Use the And and Or buttons to tell the Office program whether each new criterion that you add is in addition to or instead of the previous criteria.

Any search criteria that you already specified in the Open dialog box will be carried over into an Advanced search.

As you add criteria in the Advanced Find dialog box, they will appear in the list box.

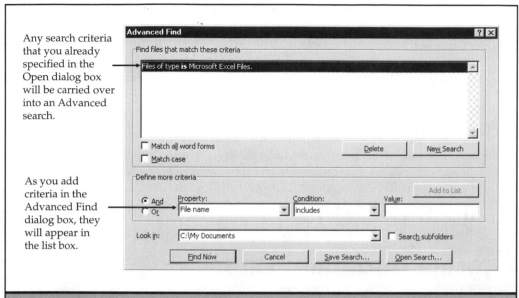

Figure 2-7. *You can use the Advanced Find dialog box to narrow down a file search*

 NOTE: *The Office program sometimes changes And to Or if it finds a contradiction in the criteria you select.*

If you want to delete a criterion, select it and click Delete. Clicking New Search clears the entire list box of all criteria, except for the File of type criterion, which is there by default. You can further define your search using the Match case option, which allows you to specify the case of the letters in the word you seek, and the Match all word forms option, which searches for words that use the same root as what you specify.

When you have entered all the criteria you want, click the Find Now button to begin your search.

Saving Advanced Search Criteria So You Can Use Them Again

Occasionally, you may need to repeat a search. Using the Save Search and Open Search buttons, you can save and revisit previous searches, saving yourself much time. When you click Save Search, Excel displays the Save Search dialog box.

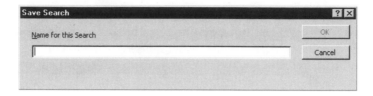

To use the Save Search dialog box, simply enter a name for the search, and click OK.

To later open a saved search, click the Open Search button in the Advanced Find dialog box to display the Open Search dialog box (see Figure 2-7). Select the search you want and click Open. You can delete and rename saved searches in this dialog box as well. You can also access saved searches on the Saved Searches submenu of the Commands and Settings menu, which appears when you click the Commands and Settings button in the Open dialog box.

Printing Document Files

The Office programs all make it very easy to print their document files. As a general rule, for example, you can click the Print toolbar button to print just about any Office document file—and usually in a way you'll find acceptable. Nevertheless, it's still extremely beneficial to go beyond this simple (although highly effective) technique because in doing so you'll learn how to print Office document files that look exactly the way you want.

Printing Basics

As mentioned in the preceding paragraph, you can print the open document file—Word document, Excel workbook, PowerPoint presentation, Access database file object, or Outlook item—by clicking the Print toolbar button. When you click the Print toolbar button, you in effect tell the Office program to print the open document file in the usual way. (The "usual" way just means with all of the default, or suggested, print settings.)

If you don't want to use the default, or suggested, print settings—or you want to verify the print settings—you can choose the File menu's Print command. When you do, the Office program displays a dialog box like that shown in Figure 2-8.

Changing the Printer

You use the Name drop-down list box to specify which printer (when you use more than one printer) you want to use to print the Office document file. To specify a different printer, simply select one from the Name list box.

If you want to change the way the printer works, you can click the Properties button, which appears just to the right of the Name drop-down list box, to display the printer's Properties dialog box. Different printers provide different properties, so it's impossible to describe here which printer options you can change with the printer's Properties dialog box. Typically, however, you use the printer's Properties dialog box to specify settings such as the page orientation (landscape versus portrait, for example), the paper size, and (when your printer includes multiple paper trays) the paper source.

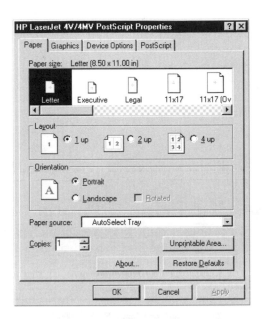

Setting the Number of Copies and Collating Them

You can tell an Office program how many copies of a document file you want to print, by entering a number in the Number of copies box in the Print dialog box. If you want them collated, check the Collate box. (Checking the Collate box tells the printer to print each copy complete, from the first page to the last, instead of printing all the first pages, followed by all the second pages, and so on.)

Printing to a File

Office programs let you print your document files to a file instead of to a printer. (Printing to a file means saving a copy of the document file in a form that can be read by a printer.) Printing to a file is not something you'll do with any frequency, but it can be useful when you want to print a document file later, on a different computer and printer, or if you want to use the file, say, in a desktop publishing program. Printer files use the file extension .prn.

To print to a file, check the Print to file box in the Print dialog box, and click OK. Give the file a name and select a destination folder in the Print to file dialog box, and then click OK again.

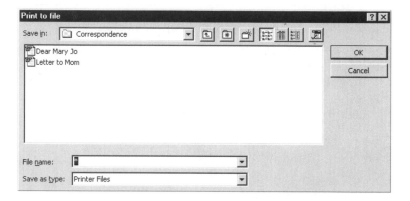

TIP: *You can also save a file as a printer file by choosing Save As on the File menu, and choosing Formatted Text in the Save as type drop-down list box in the Save As dialog box.*

Setting Word-Specific Print Options

Word provides several print options specific to its document files, as shown in Figure 2-9: Page range option buttons, the Print what drop-down list box, the Print drop-down list box, and the Options command button.

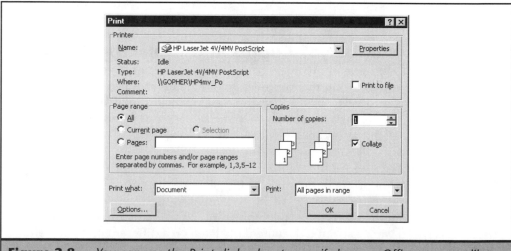

Figure 2-8.   *You can use the Print dialog box to specify how an Office program like Word should print a document file*

Use the Page range option buttons to indicate which pages of a document you want to print.

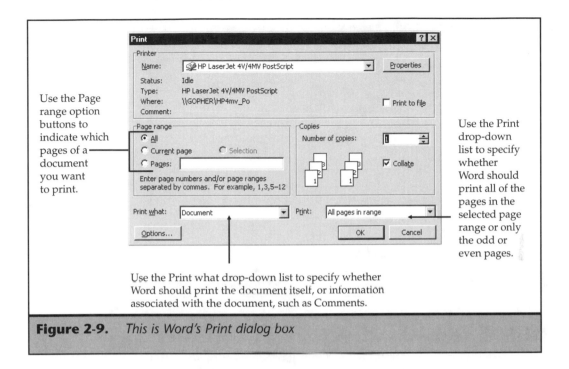

Use the Print drop-down list to specify whether Word should print all of the pages in the selected page range or only the odd or even pages.

Use the Print what drop-down list to specify whether Word should print the document itself, or information associated with the document, such as Comments.

Figure 2-9. *This is Word's Print dialog box*

As you might guess, you use the Page range option buttons to indicate which pages of a document file you want to print. If you want to print the entire Word document, select the All option button. If you want to print just the current page (the page that shows in the Word document window), select the Current page option button. If you want to print a particular page or range of pages, select the Pages option button; then enter page numbers and/or page ranges separated by commas.

You use the Print what drop-down list to specify which document file information you want to print: the document itself, a description of the document properties, a list of the comments you've used to annotate the document, and so forth.

The Print drop-down list box lets you specify which pages in the selected page range you want to print: all pages, just the even-numbered pages, or just the odd-numbered pages.

Finally, if you click the Options button, Word displays the Print Options dialog box. It essentially provides a large set of check boxes you use to further refine and more precisely control how Word prints the open document. If you have questions about one of the options in the Print options dialog box, click the What's This button and then click the check box you have a question about.

Setting Excel Workbook Print Options

Excel provides two print options specific to its document files, as shown in Figure 2-10: the Print Range option buttons and boxes and the Print What option buttons.

You use the Print range option buttons to indicate which pages of a workbook you want to print. If you want to print the entire Excel workbook, select the All option

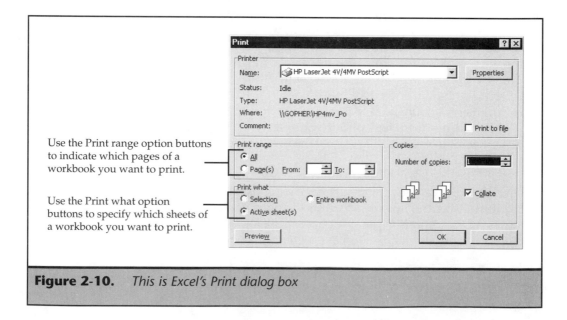

Figure 2-10. *This is Excel's Print dialog box*

button. If you want to print just specified pages, click the Pages option button and then use the From and To text boxes to enter page numbers or page ranges.

You can also use the Print what option buttons to specify what portion of a workbook you want to print: Selection (which means the selected range on a worksheet), Active sheet(s) (which means any selected worksheet), or Entire workbook.

Setting PowerPoint-Specific Print Options

PowerPoint provides three categories of print options specific to its presentations: the Print range option buttons and boxes, the Print what option buttons, and the check boxes that appear beneath the Print what option buttons. (See Figure 2-11.)

You use the Print range option buttons to indicate which slides of a presentation you want to print. If you want to print the entire PowerPoint presentation, select the All option button. If you want to print only the currently selected slide, select the Current slide option button. If you want to print just specified pages, click the Slides option button and then use the Slides text boxes to enter a slide number range. (The Custom Show button lets you print a subset of the presentation's slides that you've previously set up as a custom PowerPoint slide show.)

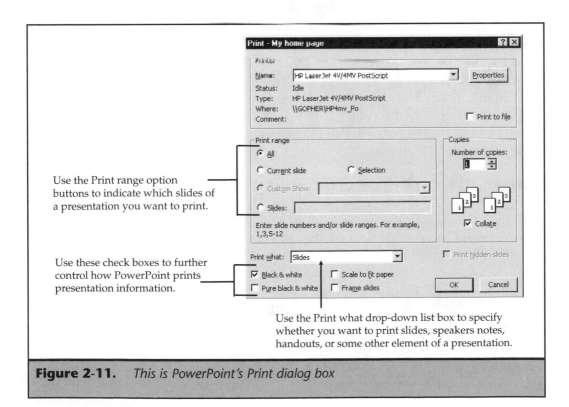

Figure 2-11. *This is PowerPoint's Print dialog box*

You use the Print what drop-down list box to specify what portion of a presentation you want to print: Slides (the actual slides or overhead transparencies), Handouts (pieces of paper with pictures of the slides but also plenty of extra room for taking notes), Notes Pages (speakers' note pages), and Outline View (an outline of the presentation).

 NOTE: If you have a question about speaker's notes or presentation outlines, refer to Chapter 20.

Finally, the check boxes that appear beneath the Print what drop-down list box let you exert even more control over the way that PowerPoint prints slides. You can check the Black & white box if you want PowerPoint to adjust the colors used in your presentation so that the printed copy of your presentation looks reasonable in black and white (and shades of gray). Or, you can check the Pure black & white box if you don't want PowerPoint to use shades of gray in its black and white printing. You can mark the Scale to fit paper box if you want PowerPoint to adjust the size of the printed slides so they fit nicely on whatever paper you use to print them. You can mark the Frame slides box if you want PowerPoint to draw a thin line around printed slides, handouts, and notes to frame the information.

Setting Access-Specific Print Options

Access provides several print options specific to its databases or database objects. (A database object is just a part of a database.) When printing Tables, Queries, and Forms, you can specify which records to print. When printing macros, the Print Macro Definition dialog box appears instead of the standard print dialog box. In essence, however, you basically have a subset of the same print options available to you in a program like Word or Excel.

Setting Outlook-Specific Print Options

Outlook provides numerous print options specific to its folders and items. But basically all of these program-specific print options simply boil down to different ways of organizing—what Outlook calls a print style—the Outlook folder or item information you want to print.

Controlling Page Setup in Office Programs

In all of the Office programs, you can also use the File menu's Page Setup command to control how the Office programs print. It's by using the Page Setup command, for example, that you change the print orientation from portrait to landscape or vice versa, that you easily adjust page margins, and that you specify paper sizes.

Page Setup Basics

In Word, Excel, Outlook, and Access, you make changes to the page setup by choosing the File menu's Page Setup command. (Some Office programs also include a Setup command button on their Print dialog boxes or on their Print Preview windows, but the File menu's Page Setup command is still usually the easiest way to make page setup changes—if only because the command is always available in Word, Excel, Outlook, and Access.) When you choose the Page Setup command, the Office program displays a dialog box—in some cases, a dialog box with multiple tabs—that lets you make your changes.

Making Word-Specific Page Setup Changes

When you choose the File menu's Page Setup command in Word, you see a Page Setup dialog box like the one shown next. The Margins tab lets you specify top, bottom, left, and right margins; gutters; and where headers and footers should appear. To specify a margin, for example, use the Top, Bottom, Left, or Right spin boxes. If you've added headers and footers to the Word document, use the Header and Footer spin boxes to indicate how far from the page's top or bottom edge the margin should be placed. You use the Apply to drop-down list box to indicate whether your margin settings apply to the entire document, the current section, or from the current page forward.

NOTE: A gutter is an extra amount of margin space added (usually) to the left margin for a document's binding.

Check the Mirror margins box if you want facing pages to use the same inside and same outside margins.

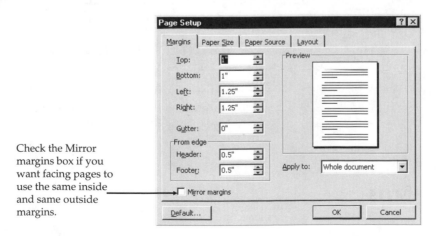

The Paper Size tab, shown here, lets you specify which size paper you're using and lets you choose a page orientation. As with the Margins tab, you can use the Apply to drop-down list box to indicate whether your paper size settings apply to the entire document or from the current page forward.

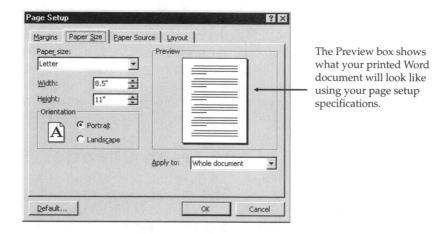

The Preview box shows what your printed Word document will look like using your page setup specifications.

The Paper Source tab, which isn't shown, lets you choose which printer tray you want to use for printing. For example, you may want the first page of a lengthy document to appear on letterhead paper, but the second and subsequent pages of the document to appear on plain, so-called "second-sheet" paper. Note that the paper source tab options that you see will depend on your printer.

The fourth and final Page Setup tab in Word, the Layout tab, lets you specify if a new section should start on a new page, a new column, or the next odd or even numbered page; how text should be vertically aligned on a page; and whether line numbers should be used to number each line of the document.

If you've added endnotes to your Word document, you can check this box if you don't want them to print.

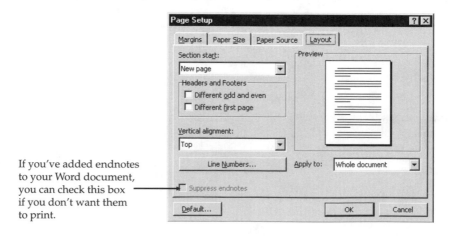

NOTE: *Chapter 6 describes how you create and use Word sections.*

Making Excel-Specific Page Setup Changes

When you choose the File menu's Page Setup command in Excel, you see a Page Setup dialog box like the one shown here. The Page tab lets you choose a page orientation, control the scaling of the printed worksheet, and specify which size paper you're using and what print quality you want. It also lets you specify the starting page number. How these options work will probably be obvious to you if you're familiar with Excel, but if you have questions, click the What's This button and then the box or button you have a question about.

 NOTE: *When you scale the size of a printout up or down, Excel adjusts both dimensions proportionally. For instance, choosing 200% normal size doubles both the width and the height of a printout.*

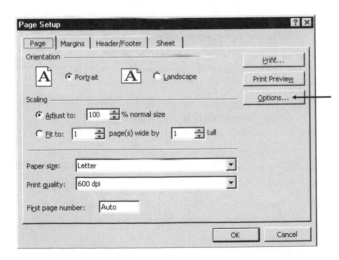

Click the Options command button to display the current printer's Properties dialog box if you want to make changes to the way this printer works.

The Margins tab, shown here, lets you specify top, bottom, left, and right margins; gutters; and where headers and footers should appear. To specify a margin, for example, use the Top, Bottom, Left or Right text boxes. If you've added headers and footers to the Excel workbook, use the Header and Footer spin boxes to indicate how far from the page's top or bottom edge the header or footer margin should be placed. You can also use the Center on page check boxes—Horizontally and Vertically—to indicate how you want a worksheet range aligned on a page.

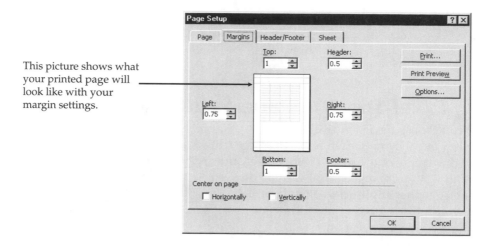

This picture shows what your printed page will look like with your margin settings.

The Header/Footer tab, shown here, lets you add headers and footers to your printed Excel workbook pages. To add a header or footer, select predefined headers or footers from the Header and Footer drop-down list boxes. When you do, Excel adds the header or footer to the page fragments shown above the Header drop-down list box and below the Footer drop-down list box.

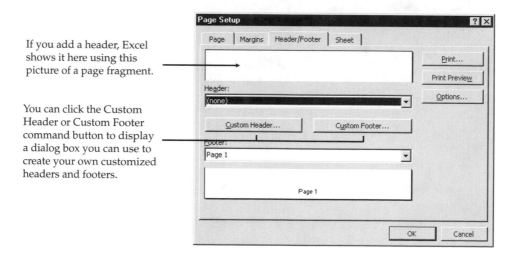

If you add a header, Excel shows it here using this picture of a page fragment.

You can click the Custom Header or Custom Footer command button to display a dialog box you can use to create your own customized headers and footers.

The fourth and final tab on the Excel's Page Setup dialog box, the Sheet tab, lets you make a rich variety of page setup specifications. If you want to print only a certain range of cells on a worksheet, you can enter that worksheet range (or multiple worksheet ranges) into the Print area text box. If you want to repeat a row or several rows at the top of each page, you can enter the worksheet range for the repeating row or rows into the Rows to repeat at top text box. (You use a repeating row to label your

INTRODUCING OFFICE

columns.) If you want to repeat a column or several columns on the left side of each page, you can enter the worksheet range for the repeating column or columns into the Columns to repeat at left text box.

You can click the two Page order option buttons to see a graphic display of the effect they produce.

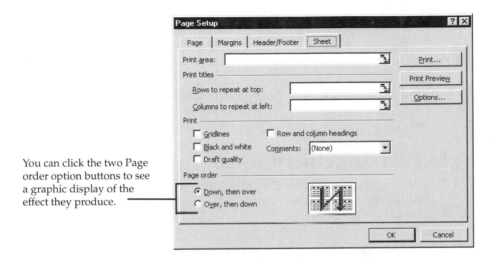

 TIP: *You can click the Collapse Dialog buttons, which appear at the right end of the Print area, Rows to repeat at top, and Columns to repeat at left text boxes to temporarily shrink the Page Setup dialog box so it's possible and easy to select a worksheet range with the mouse. When you're ready to expand the dialog box, click the button again.*

If you want the worksheet gridlines to appear in the printed worksheet, check the Gridlines box. You can check the Black and white box if you want your printer to ignore background color formatting (a good option to check if you have a black and white printer). If you want to speed up printing of the workbook, you can check Draft quality box. (In this case, Excel doesn't print gridlines and most graphic images.) You can check the Row and column headings box to tell your printer to print the standard row and column headings (such as A, B, 1, 2, and so on) that you see on the screen, but which normally don't show up on printouts. (This option might be of interest to you if, for instance, you wanted to refer back to particular worksheet cells, or formulas, in your printouts.) If you want to print the cell annotations that you can create using the Insert menu's Comments command, select one of the entries from the Comments drop-down list box. Finally, you can also use the Page order option buttons to specify how Excel should break a large worksheet range into page-sized chunks.

 NOTE: *Gridlines are the light solid lines displayed on your screen that separate rows and columns from each other. They won't show up on printouts unless you ask for them.*

Making Outlook-Specific Page Setup Changes

Outlook provides a set of page setup changes that are very similar to those already described for Word and Access. If you've read any of the preceding paragraphs or know Outlook reasonably well, you won't have any trouble working with Outlook's page setup options. For this reason and one other—the fact that describing Outlook's Page Setup options would require another ten or so pages of very repetitious information—this book doesn't go into any more detail about Outlook's page setup options.

TIP: *Remember that you can usually get helpful information about any dialog box button or box by first clicking the What's This button and then the button or box you have a question about.*

Making Access-Specific Page Setup Changes

When you choose the File menu's Page Setup command in Access, you see a Page Setup dialog box like the one shown in Figure 2-12. The Margins tab lets you specify top, bottom, left, and right margins, and where headers and footers should appear. To specify a margin, you simply use the Top, Bottom, Left, or Right text boxes.

NOTE: *Check the Print Headings box if you want a datasheet's column headings to print.*

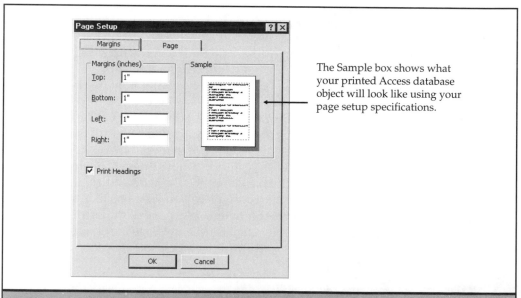

The Sample box shows what your printed Access database object will look like using your page setup specifications.

Figure 2-12. *The Margins tab of Access's Page Setup dialog box*

The Page tab, shown in Figure 2-13, lets you choose a page orientation, indicate which size paper you're using, and select a paper source. You can also specify that you want to use a particular printer by clicking the Use Specific Printer option button, clicking the Printer command button, and then selecting a printer from the dialog box that Access displays.

Using Print Preview

One of the most useful features in Word, Excel, Outlook, and Access is called Print Preview. (The Print Preview feature isn't available in PowerPoint.) It does just what its name suggests—it gives you the ability to preview what your printed page or pages will look like, before you print. Using Print Preview you can check, among other things, the way page breaks divide up your document file, how the margins are set, and how the header and footer appear.

To use the print preview feature, click the Print Preview button on the Standard toolbar or choose the File menu's Print Preview command. Using either approach, you'll see a window that will display an entire page of your document file as it will look when printed.

To page back and forth through the "printed document," use the PAGE UP and PAGE DOWN keys. To alternately zoom in and zoom out on the picture, click the picture.

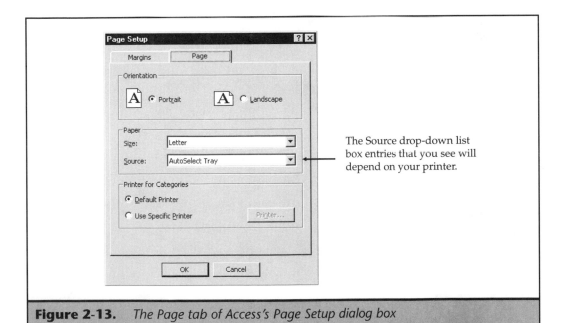

The Source drop-down list box entries that you see will depend on your printer.

Figure 2-13.   *The Page tab of Access's Page Setup dialog box*

> *NOTE:*   *The individual Office programs also provide command buttons for paging through a document file and for zooming, or magnifying, the document file. Unfortunately, however, there's no consistency among the programs in how you do this, so this section does not describe how you use these other methods.*

To print the document file when you've verified that it looks the way you want, click the Print button on the Print Preview toolbar. (In some Office programs, the Print command uses the label "Print," while in others the Office program just shows a picture of a printer.) Or, if you decide that you don't want to print the document showing in the print preview window, click the Close button on the Print Preview toolb. This closes the print preview, not the document.

Office
97

Chapter 3

Using the Common Office Tools

The individual Microsoft Office 97 programs share many of the same features, tools, and capabilities. They all use a sometimes annoying interface element called the Office Assistant to make your work easier. They check spelling in roughly the same way. They also provide common tools such as the Drawing tool.

This commonality produces a big benefit for you, the user, because it means that by learning to use a common feature, tool, or capability in one program—say Word—you've also indirectly learned how to use the equivalent feature, tool, or capability in another program like Excel or PowerPoint. To make sure that you understand and can use all of these features, tools, and capabilities, this chapter describes in greater and sometimes lesser detail all of these common elements.

Getting Help from the Office Assistant

You are probably already familiar with the Office Assistant. The Office Assistant is the usually helpful albeit sometimes annoying interface element that, in effect, acts as a knowledge cushion between you and the program you're working with.

The Office Assistant watches your work; makes occasional suggestions for working more efficiently; passes messages back and forth between you and the program; and, when asked, attempts to answer any questions you might have.

Turning on the Office Assistant

If you can see the Office Assistant's program window on your desktop (typically on top of an Office program window, as shown in Figure 3-1), you don't have to turn it on. It's already running. If you can't see the Office Assistant and you want to use it, click the Office Assistant button on the Standard toolbar.

Using the Office Assistant

To use the Office Assistant, enter a question into the Office Assistant balloon's only text box and then click the Search button. (If the balloon doesn't appear, simply click the Office Assistant.) Figure 3-1 shows the example question, "How do I print a document?"

TIP: *To get a tip about using the active program, click the Office Assistant's Tip button.*

Click this toolbar button to turn on the Office Assistant if it isn't already on.

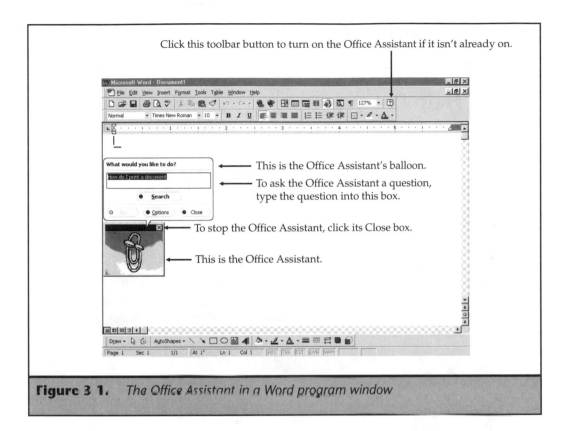

This is the Office Assistant's balloon.

To ask the Office Assistant a question, type the question into this box.

To stop the Office Assistant, click its Close box.

This is the Office Assistant.

Figure 3 1.   *The Office Assistant in a Word program window*

When the Office Assistant displays a list of Help topics (essentially just essays about how to accomplish certain tasks), click the button that corresponds to the Help topic you want to read:

For example, if you click the Print a document Help topic, as shown in the proceeding illustration, the Office Assistant starts the Help program and displays the help topic shown in Figure 3-2.

Using the Help Program

Once you select a particular Help topic from the Office Assistant balloon, the Office Assistant starts the Help program, directing it to open the Help information file for the active Office program. This book assumes that you're already familiar with how the Windows operating system works, including how its standard Help program works. Nevertheless, it's probably appropriate to make a few key points about the Help program.

In essence, the Help program lets you page through a heavily indexed text file with information about how to use a particular program. To display the Help information file's table of contents, choose Help, Contents and Index. If necessary, click the Contents tab. To open the Help information file to a particular chapter, double-click one of the book icons to the right of the chapters listed in the table of contents. To open a particular chapter section, double-click it. To view Help text, double-click the page icon to the left of the desired topic. In Figure 3-3 you can see what all of these little icons look like.

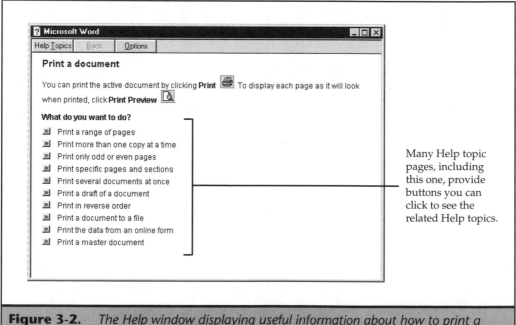

Figure 3-2.   *The Help window displaying useful information about how to print a Word document*

Double-click a chapter to display its list of sections and help topics.

Double-click a chapter section to display its help topics.

Double-click a Help topic to display its information.

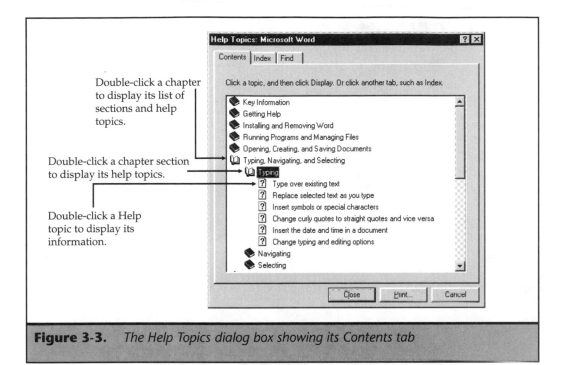

Figure 3-3. *The Help Topics dialog box showing its Contents tab*

If you can't find the Help topic you want by using the Contents tab, you can also use the Index or Find tabs. When you click the Index tab, Windows displays a two-level index of help topics. To find a Help topic, you can scroll through this list using the PGUP and PGDN keys or the scroll bar. You can also type a brief description of the Help topic you want to find into the text box, as I have done in Figure 3-4. When you see the help topic you want to read listed, just double-click it.

The Find tab, by the way, probably isn't one you'll use very often. It lets you search for specific words or phrases in the text of the Help information files. To use the Find tab, you first run a wizard (which Windows prompts you to do) to create a database of words and phrases. Once you do this, you enter the text or text fragment you're looking for into the text box provided, as shown in Figure 3-5. Next, select a word or phrase to narrow the search from the middle of the dialog box. Finally, double-click a Help topic from the list at the bottom of the dialog box.

NOTE: *For more information about the Help program, refer to the documentation that came with your copy of Windows, use the Help program itself to get help on Help, or acquire and read a good tutorial on your version of Windows.*

Customizing the Office Assistant

If you click the Options button on the Office Assistant's balloon (see Figure 3-1), Office Assistant displays the dialog box shown here. Its Options tab provides a series of check boxes that let you specify what the Office Assistant should and shouldn't do.

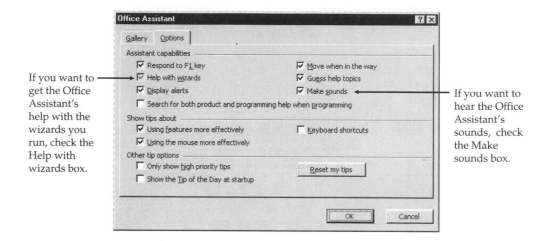

If you want to get the Office Assistant's help with the wizards you run, check the Help with wizards box.

If you want to hear the Office Assistant's sounds, check the Make sounds box.

TIP: *Remember that you can use the What's this button to get a more detailed description of what a check box does. To do this, click the What's this button and then the box or button you have a question about.*

The Gallery tab of the Office Assistant dialog box lets you choose a character for the Office Assistant. The default character, shown in the preceding figures and illustrations, is Clipit. You have several other choices, however, including a bouncing red dot, an Einstein-like professor, and a dog. To select a different character, use the Next and Back buttons until you see the character you want. Then click OK.

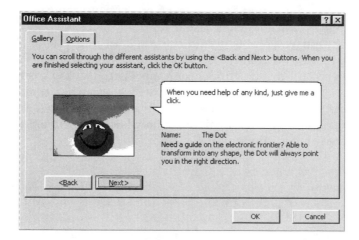

You can enter the first part
of the Help topic name into
this box to have Windows
search its index for what
you enter.

Double-click the help topic
you want to read.

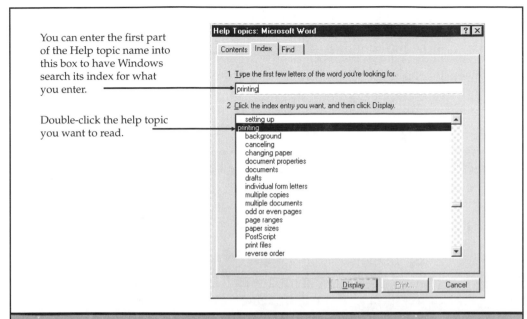

Figure 3-4.   *The Help Topics dialog box showing its Index tab*

You can type a word or phrase
into this box to have Help
search for matching words and
phrases in its text files.

Select a word or phrase here to
narrow the list of topics.

Double-click the help topic
you want to display.

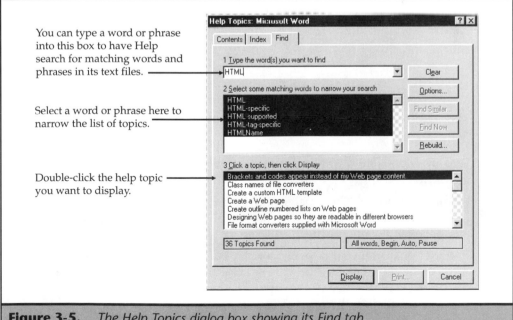

Figure 3-5.   *The Help Topics dialog box showing its Find tab*

Spell Checking Your Document Files

All of the Office programs let you easily spell check their document files. Curiously, however, the process doesn't work the same way in each Office program. Differences in spell checking mechanics exist. For this reason, the following paragraphs describe each Office program's spell checking in turn.

Spell Checking in Word

Word spell checks its documents automatically. If you type a word that's not in Word's spelling dictionary, Word underlines the possible misspelling with a red, wavy line:

If you know the correct spelling of the word, you can double-click the word and then type the correct spelling. If you don't know the correct spelling, you can right-click the word to display a shortcut menu:

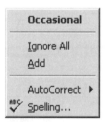

The shortcut menu provides several useful commands for dealing with the misspelled word:

■ Whenever possible, Word supplies a list of alternative spellings on the shortcut menu. You can correct the misspelling by choosing the correctly spelled word.

■ If Word thinks you've misspelled a word but you actually haven't, click the Ignore All command. Clicking Ignore All tells Word not to identify this word as misspelled in the document.

■ If Word thinks you've misspelled a word but you actually haven't, click the Add command. Clicking Add tells Word to place the selected word into your custom dictionary. Once you've placed a word into the custom dictionary, Word won't identify the word as misspelled in any document.

■ If you want Word to automatically fix this misspelling now and in the future, click AutoCorrect and then choose the correct spelling from the AutoCorrect submenu. (The later chapter section, "Using AutoCorrect," describes what AutoCorrect is and how it works.)

■ If you want to correct the misspelling in some way other than that already described here, click Spelling to display the Spelling dialog box. Then use its boxes and buttons to describe how you want the misspelling corrected. For example, using the Spelling dialog box, you can choose to ignore or change the selected occurrence of a misspelling or all occurrences of it.

NOTE: If Word isn't automatically spell checking your documents, choose the Tools menu Options command, click the Spelling & Grammar tab, and then check the Check spelling as you type box. Note, too, that the Spelling & Grammar tab provides more than a dozen other buttons and boxes that you can use to control the way Word checks spelling and grammar in your Word document.

Grammar Checking Your Word Documents

Word also checks the grammar of your documents as long as you haven't told it not to. If you turned off the grammar checker and you want to have Word check the grammar of your documents, choose the Tools menu Options command, click the Spelling & Grammar tab, and then check the Check grammar as you type box. When Word identifies a grammar error, it underlines the offending word, phrase, or sentence with a green wavy line. You can fix the grammar error manually by editing the text. Or, you can right-click the error to display a shortcut menu of commands similar to those you use to correct misspellings. If Word knows the correct word, phrase, or sentence, it displays it on the shortcut menu so you can select it. Word will also provide an Ignore Sentence command (which you can use to tell Word that it should ignore what it thinks is a grammar error) and a Grammar command (which you can use to display the Grammar dialog box and its additional grammar checking buttons and boxes).

Spell Checking in Excel

Excel's spell checking isn't automatic, but it's still very easy. To spell check a workbook or the selected range, choose the Tools menu Spelling command. If Excel identifies a misspelled word, it displays the Spelling dialog box (see Figure 3-6). Near the top of the dialog box, Excel writes the misspelled word and provides a list of suggested alternative spellings. If Excel is not able to supply alternative spellings, you can use the Change to text box to supply a new replacement word for the misspelled word. If the word isn't misspelled, you can click the Ignore button to ignore just this occurrence of the word or click the Ignore All button to ignore this and every other occurrence of the word.

If the Always suggest box is checked, Excel lists suggested replacements for the misspelled word here and even provides a best-guess replacement in the Change to text box. ——————

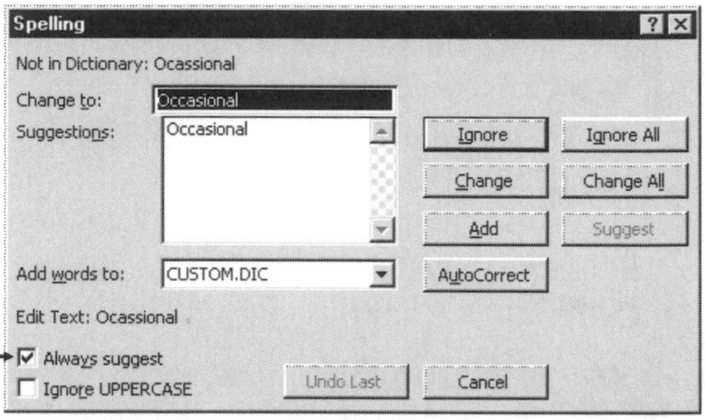

Figure 3-6.   *When Excel identifies a misspelled word, it displays the Spelling dialog box*

If you want to change the misspelling to what shows in the Change to text box, click the Change button to change only this occurrence of the word, or click the Change All button to change this and every other occurrence of the word.

If the word Excel thinks is misspelled isn't actually misspelled and you want Excel to stop identifying it as such, click the Add button. Clicking Add tells Excel to add the selected word to the custom spelling dictionary identified in the Add words to drop-down list box. Once a word has been added to the custom dictionary, it won't be identified as misspelled any more. You typically need to do this with words and terms you've created yourself (product names, trademarks, and so on), as well as with esoteric words and terms (shoptalk, industry-specific buzzwords, and so forth).

If you want to have Excel automatically correct a misspelling every time you enter it, click the AutoCorrect button. Clicking AutoCorrect tells Excel to add the selected word to its list of AutoCorrect entries.

Spell Checking in PowerPoint

PowerPoint's spell checking works almost identically to Word's spell checking. As does Word, PowerPoint automatically checks the spelling of words as you enter them. If PowerPoint identifies a misspelled word, it underlines the word with a red wavy line. To fix the misspelling manually, double-click the word and then type a replacement. Alternatively, right-click the word and then choose one of the alternative spellings or commands from the shortcut menu that PowerPoint displays. (If you have a question about what any of the commands on the shortcut menu does, refer to the earlier discussion of Word's spell checking.)

NOTE: *To control how PowerPoint's spell checking works, choose the Tools menu Options command, click the Spelling tab, and then use the boxes and buttons that PowerPoint displays to describe how and when you want spell checking to occur.*

Spell Checking in Access

Access's spell checking works almost identically to Excel's spell checking. To spell check the information shown in the open database object (an object is just a database building block, such as a table), choose the Tools menu Spelling command. If Access finds a word that isn't in its dictionary, it displays the Spelling dialog box shown in Figure 3-7. Near the top of the dialog box, Access writes the misspelled word and provides a list of suggested alternative spellings. If Excel is not able to supply alternative spellings, you can use the Change to text box to supply a new replacement word for the misspelled word. If the word isn't misspelled, click the Ignore Field, the Ignore, or the Ignore All buttons. If you want to change the misspelling to what shows in the Change to text box, click the Change button or the Change All button.

NOTE: *You can click the Ignore Field button to prevent Access from spell checking a field that contains textual phrases Access won't find in its spelling dictionary: alphanumeric strings (like product codes) and proper names (such as the names of companies and people).*

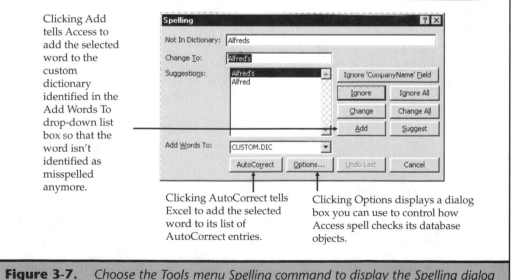

Clicking Add tells Access to add the selected word to the custom dictionary identified in the Add Words To drop-down list box so that the word isn't identified as misspelled anymore.

Clicking AutoCorrect tells Excel to add the selected word to its list of AutoCorrect entries.

Clicking Options displays a dialog box you can use to control how Access spell checks its database objects.

Figure 3-7.   *Choose the Tools menu Spelling command to display the Spelling dialog box in Access*

Spell Checking in Outlook

To spell check the information shown in an Outlook item, choose the Tools menu Spelling command. If Outlook finds a word that isn't in its dictionary, it displays the Spelling dialog box, which is for all practical purposes identical to the Spelling dialog box that Excel shows (see Figure 3-6). Near the top of the dialog box, Outlook writes the misspelled word and provides a list of suggested alternative spellings. If Outlook is not able to supply alternative spellings, you can use the Change to text box to supply a replacement word. If the word isn't misspelled, click the Ignore or the Ignore All button. If you want to change the misspelling to what shows in the Change To text box, click the Change button or the Change All button.

TIP: To tell Outlook that it should automatically check the spelling of any items you create before you send them, choose the Tools menu Options command, click the Spelling tab, and then check the Always check spelling before sending box. Note, too, that the Spelling tab also provides other boxes and buttons that you can use to customize the way Outlook spell checks items.

Using AutoCorrect

AutoCorrect, as mentioned briefly a handful of times already in this chapter, automatically fixes specified errors. For example, if you type the misspelling "recieve," an Office program like Word will automatically replace your misspelling with the correct spelling, "receive."

Perhaps the most useful aspect of AutoCorrect is that it occurs automatically—without intervention from you, the user. By default, if you make a mistake that AutoCorrect knows it should fix, it fixes the mistake.

To see which mistakes AutoCorrect fixes and to add new entries to its list, you choose the Tools menu AutoCorrect command. The Office program will display a dialog box like that shown in Figure 3-8.

NOTE: Figure 3-8 shows the Word program's AutoCorrect dialog box, but the AutoCorrect dialog boxes for the Excel, PowerPoint, and Access programs look and work in almost the same way. The only difference, in fact, is that the Word AutoCorrect dialog box includes three additional tabs not present on the AutoCorrect dialog boxes of other programs: the AutoFormat As You Type tab, the AutoText tab, and the AutoFormat tab. The AutoFormat As You Type and AutoFormat tabs provide boxes and buttons that you can use to control how Word's automatic formatting works. The AutoText tab lets you modify and add to the list of AutoText entries that Word will make. (An AutoText entry is a phrase or group of paragraphs assigned to a unique name. As soon as you type enough of the AutoText entry's name for Word to recognize it, Word displays the AutoText entry in a ScreenTip. If you want Word to replace the name you typed with the AutoText entry, simply press the ENTER key.)

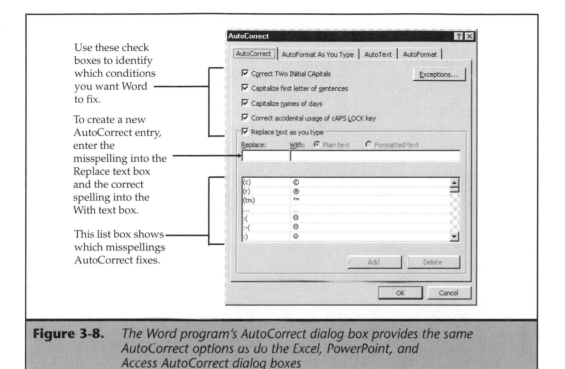

Use these check boxes to identify which conditions you want Word to fix.

To create a new AutoCorrect entry, enter the misspelling into the Replace text box and the correct spelling into the With text box.

This list box shows which misspellings AutoCorrect fixes.

Figure 3-8.   *The Word program's AutoCorrect dialog box provides the same AutoCorrect options as do the Excel, PowerPoint, and Access AutoCorrect dialog boxes*

Working with the Common Editing Tools

In general, you'll use the same tools for editing much of the data you enter into and store in your Office 97 document files. Each of the Office programs provides a Standard toolbar, which provides users with Cut, Copy, Paste, and Format Painter buttons—and you'll use these often. In addition, most of the Office programs' Standard toolbars also provide Undo and Redo buttons, which are equally handy. And then, of course, there are two or three Edit menu commands, which appear in most of the Office programs: Repeat, Find, and Replace. Because you'll want to use all of these tools in your work with Office and because they work in the same basic manner in each of the Office programs, this chapter also describes these tools.

The Cut, Copy, and Paste Toolbar Buttons

You use the Cut, Copy, and Paste tools to move and copy data within a document file and to move and copy data between document files. You can, for example, move or copy text you've selected in a Word document, a worksheet range you've selected in an Excel workbook, a piece of clip art you've placed in a PowerPoint presentation, an Access database object, and even entire Outlook items. In short, you can move or copy just about anything you can select.

NOTE: *To select text or objects in a document file, you typically drag the mouse across the text or click the object.*

Moving Data

To move data, for example, you use the Cut and Paste buttons in tandem, by following these steps:

1. Select the data you want to move.

2. Click the Cut button to move the selected data from the Office document file to the Windows Clipboard, a temporary storage area.

3. Position the insertion point at the exact location to which you want to move the data. (You can do this by clicking where the insertion point should be placed in the document.)

4. Click the Paste button to move the data you previously stored on the Windows Clipboard—you did this in step 2—to the insertion point location.

TIP: *You can use the Cut, Copy, and Paste tools and the Windows Clipboard not only to move and copy data within a document file but also between document files. Note, too, that almost all Windows programs provide Cut, Copy, and Paste buttons, which you can use in the manner described here.*

Copying Data

To copy data, you use the Copy and Paste buttons in tandem, by following these steps:

1. Select the data you want to copy.

2. Click the Copy button to store a copy of the selected data on the Windows Clipboard.

3. Position the insertion point at the exact location to which you want to copy the data. (You can do this by clicking where the insertion point should be placed in the document.)

4. Click the Paste button to copy the data you previously stored on the Windows Clipboard—you did this in step 2—to the insertion point location.

TIP: *All Office programs also let you move and copy data by dragging the selected text or object with the mouse. For example, you can move the selected data by dragging it. (This is called drag-and-drop.) And you can copy the selected data by holding down the CTRL key and then dragging the selection. As with the Cut, Copy, and Paste buttons, you can use the mouse to drag-and-drop data both within a document file and between document files. Note, however, that not every Windows program supports drag-and-drop editing.*

Using the Format Painter Button

The Format Painter button lets you copy formatting from one set of data to another set. For example, if you told Word to boldface and italicize some chunk of text, you could copy the formatting of that chunk—the boldfacing and the italicization—to some other chunk of text. Similarly, if you told Excel to format some set of numbers by adding dollar signs and decimal points, you could copy this number formatting to some other set of numbers.

NOTE: The later chapter section "Using the Formatting Toolbar" talks more about formatting data.

It's easy to use the Format Painter tool. You simply need to follow these steps:

1. Select the data containing the formatting you want to copy. (Typically you do this by clicking or dragging the mouse.)

2. Click the Format Painter button.

3. Drag the mouse across the data to which you want to copy the formatting.

Using Excel's Paste Special Command

When you copy an Excel cell or range, you actually copy more than just the cell's contents. If you've assigned any formatting to the cell's label or values, that formatting gets copied. If you've attached a cell comment, the comment gets copied, too. While normally it's okay that Excel copies all of this information, you can limit what Excel copies and at the same time exercise more control over how Excel completes the copy operation. To do this, however, you need to choose the Paste Special command instead of the Paste command. When you choose the Paste Special command, Excel displays the Paste Special dialog box, which asks what you want pasted into the destination range and how you want it pasted. You use the Paste option button set to indicate what parts of the copied selection you want pasted into the new range:

- Selecting All tells Excel to paste everything.

- Selecting Formulas tells Excel to paste only the cell's contents. (Selecting Formulas also results in labels and values being pasted.)

- Selecting Values tells Excel to paste only labels and values. (Excel converts any copied formulas to the values calculated by the formulas if you select this option.)

■ Selecting Formats tells Excel to paste only the formatting you assigned to the copied selection.

■ Selecting Comments tells Excel to paste only the cell notes attached to the copied selection.

■ Selecting Validation tells Excel to paste only the data validation logic you've created for the copied selection.

■ Selecting All except borders tells Excel to paste everything—cell contents, notes, and all the formatting—except for any cell borders.

The Paste Special dialog box also provides a set of Operation option buttons that let you arithmetically combine the values in the copied range with those in the range into which you'll paste the values: adding them, subtracting them, multiplying them, and so forth. Note that if you have questions about what one of the Paste Special option buttons does, you can click the What's This button and then the option button you have a question about.

The Undo and Redo Toolbar Buttons

What the Undo and Redo toolbar buttons do may be obvious. You click the Undo button to reverse the effect of your last editing operation. And you click the Redo button to, in effect, undo the effect of your last undo command. For example, if you've just copied data using the Copy and Paste buttons, you can click the Undo button to erase the effect of your copy-and-paste operation. If after clicking the Undo button, you realize that you've made a mistake because you *did* want the data copied, you can click the Redo button.

WARNING: You can't undo the effect of all editing operations. In general, for example, you can undo the effect of Edit menu commands and their equivalent toolbar buttons but not the effect of File menu commands and their equivalent toolbar buttons. Occasionally, you may not be able to reverse an action because of memory limitations. For example, if you select an entire worksheet in Excel and then apply a formatting command, Excel may warn you that there is insufficient memory available to reverse the action.

It's useful to note that the Undo toolbar buttons available in Word, Excel, and PowerPoint will undo more than one editing operation. Similarly, the Redo toolbar buttons available in Word, Excel, and PowerPoint will redo more than one undo operation. To undo multiple editing operations, click the arrowhead next to the Undo toolbar button. Then, when the Office program displays a list of previous editing operations, click the oldest editing operation you want to undo. (The Office program undoes the selected editing operation, as well as every more recent editing operation.)

NOTE: *The Outlook Standard toolbar doesn't provide an Undo or Redo toolbar button. Outlook's Edit menu does, however, provide an Undo command.*

To redo multiple undo operations, click the arrowhead next to the Redo toolbar button. Then, when the Office program displays a list of undo operations, click the oldest undo operation you want to reverse. (The Office program reverses the selected undo operation as well as every more recent undo operation.)

NOTE: *Access doesn't provide a Redo toolbar button—only an Undo toolbar button.*

Clear

Most of the Office programs supply a Clear command on their Edit menus. You can use this command or its keyboard equivalent, the DELETE key, to remove the selected data. For example, if you want to remove a word, you can select the word (such as by clicking it) and then you can choose the Edit menu Clear command. If you want to remove the labels and values you've entered into an Excel worksheet range, you can also choose the Edit menu Clear command or press the DELETE key. And, predictably, you can remove items on PowerPoint slides and Outlook items in the same way: select the thing you want to remove and then choose the Edit menu Clear command.

NOTE: Excel's Clear command works a bit differently. When you choose the Edit menu Clear command in Excel, Excel displays a submenu listing items you can delete from the selected worksheet range. This submenu lists four commands: All, Formats, Contents, and Comments. Choose All if you want to remove everything in the selected range. Choose Formats if you want to remove the formatting of the cells in the selected range. Choose Contents if you want to remove the labels, values, and formulas entered into the cells in the selected range. Finally, Choose Comments if you want to remove the comments you've used to annotate cells in the selected range.

Repeat

The Edit menus of Word, Excel, and PowerPoint supply a Repeat command that often lets you repeat the most recent editing command you've issued. For example, if you've just pasted the contents of the Clipboard into a document file, you can choose the Edit menu Repeat command to paste the contents of the Clipboard into a document file for a second time.

The Repeat command is a handy tool when you're making repetitive editing changes to a document file: formatting certain words to look the same way, repeatedly pasting the same Clipboard contents into a document file, inserting a series of clip art images into a document file, and so forth.

Using the Find and Replace Commands

If you've been working with a computer for very long, you've undoubtedly already come across the ubiquitous Find and Replace commands. As you may know, the Find command lets you search a document file for some bit of information, thereby eliminating the needle-in-a-haystack dilemma. The Replace command lets you easily make substitutions in a document—for example, swapping every occurrence of the word "Prince" with the phrase "The Artist Formerly Known As Prince." All of the Office programs supply their own variations of the Find and Replace commands. But they basically work in the same manner, so the Word program's Find and Replace commands are described here. (The Excel, PowerPoint, and Access programs supply both a Find command and a Replace command, but these commands' functionality amounts to a subset of the Word program command's functionality. Outlook supplies only a Find command but it, too, amounts to a "lite" version of Word's Find command.)

Using the Edit Menu Find Command

The Edit menu Find command lets you search through either an entire document file or the selected portion of the document file. (If you don't select some portion of the document file before choosing the command, the Office program assumes you want to search the entire Word document, active Excel worksheet, active PowerPoint slide, or active Access database object. To use the command, simply choose the Edit menu Find command. When the Office program displays the Find or Find and Replace dialog box, follow these steps to describe what you're looking for and how you want the Office program to perform its search:

1. Use the Find what box to enter the word or phrase you're looking for or to activate the drop-down list to select a word or phrase from a previous search. In Figure 3-9, you can see how I have entered the word "Thorgmorton."

2. Use the Search drop-down list box to indicate whether you want to search the entire document, from the insertion point forward, or from the insertion point backward.

3. Check the Match case box if case matters in your search. If you enter "Revenues" but don't want to find "revenues," for example, then case matters and you should mark the check box.

4. Check the Find whole words only box if, in order to be considered a match, what you enter in the Find text box can't be a fragment of a larger word.

5. Check the Use wildcards box if you want to use wildcard symbols in your search: an asterisk to represent any set of characters or a question mark to represent any single character. Note that if you don't check the Use wildcards box but you do use the asterisk or the question mark, Word assumes that these are actual characters you're looking for—not wildcard characters representing other characters or character strings.

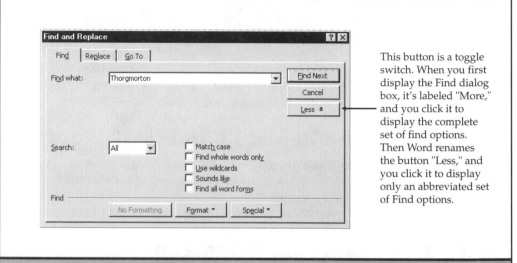

This button is a toggle switch. When you first display the Find dialog box, it's labeled "More," and you click it to display the complete set of find options. Then Word renames the button "Less," and you click it to display only an abbreviated set of Find options.

Figure 3-9. *The Find tab of Word's Find and Replace dialog box provides a superset of the options available in Excel, PowerPoint, Access, and Outlook*

TIP: *If you want to look for special characters, such as those that don't actually appear on your keyboard, check the Use wildcards box, click the Special button, and then choose the special character you want to find from the list that Word displays.*

6. Check the Sounds like box if you want to find words that are pronounced the same as what you enter in the Find what text box but are spelled differently: there and their, to and too, and so forth.

7. Check the Find all word forms box if you want to find words that use the same root but may be conjugated differently. For example, if you're looking for the word "want," it may also make sense for you to find "wants" and "wanted."

8. If you want to find words or phrases that are formatted a certain way, click the Format button, choose one of the formatting categories from the menu that Word displays, and then use the dialog box that Word displays to describe the formatting you're looking for.

NOTE: *If you later decide that you don't want to search for words or phrases that use formatting you've described in step 8, click the No Formatting button.*

9. After you describe the search you want to make, click the Find Next button. The Office program selects the first occurrence it can find that matches the search string you've entered into the Find what text box, and then selects the word or phrase. To continue searching, click the Find Next button again. (The Office progam leaves the Find dialog box open so you can do this.) If the Office program can't find a word or phrase like the one you're looking for, it displays a message box that alerts you to this fact.

Using the Edit Menu Replace Command

The Replace command does everything that the Find command does—and goes one step further. It lets you replace the occurrences you find of a particular word or phrase with some new word or phrase. To use the Edit menu Replace command, first open the document you want to search and, if necessary, select the portion of the document file that you want to search so as to limit your find and replace operation. Then, choose the Edit menu Replace command so that Word displays the Replace tab of the Find and Replace dialog box, as shown in Figure 3-10. Follow these steps to describe what you're looking for and want to replace:

1. Use the Find what text box to specify the word or phrase you're looking for, the so-called search string.

2. Use the Replace with text box to specify the word or phrase you want to substitute for occurrences of the search string.

3. After you describe the substitution you want to make, click the Find Next button. The Office program selects the next occurrence of the word or phrase that matches your search instructions. If you want to replace that occurrence, click Replace. Otherwise, you can click Find Next again to identify the next occurrence of the search string. To continue the substitutions, click the Replace button again. (The Office program leaves the Replace dialog box open so you can do this.) To make all the substitutions at once, click the Replace All button. When Word is finished replacing all of the words matching your search string, it reports how many substitutions were made. If Word can't find a word or phrase like the one you're looking for, it displays a message box that alerts you to this fact.

Working with the Formatting Toolbar

Word, Excel, PowerPoint, and even Outlook all provide a formatting toolbar that you can use to add formatting to the information you enter into a document file: Word documents, Excel workbooks, and PowerPoint presentations.

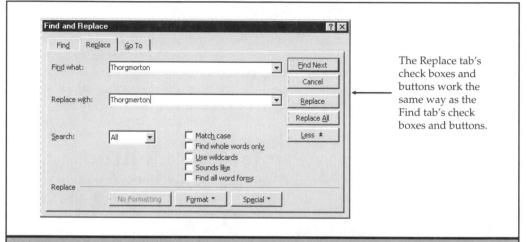

The Replace tab's check boxes and buttons work the same way as the Find tab's check boxes and buttons.

Figure 3-10. *The Replace tab of Word's Find and Replace dialog box provides a superset of the options available in Excel, PowerPoint, and Access*

NOTE: *Access also provides a formatting toolbar, but it isn't typically displayed and therefore isn't described here. Outlook provides a formatting toolbar, but you can use it only for message items so it isn't described here either. Note, however, that the Access and Outlook Formatting toolbars work in the same basic way as the Formatting toolbars available in the other Office programs.*

Because the Formatting toolbars work in basically the same way and supply almost the same set of tools for Word, Excel, and PowerPoint, this chapter describes all three formatting toolbars together.

Using the Formatting Toolbar

Using the Formatting toolbar's buttons is easy. You select the information you want to format. Then you click the button that represents the type of formatting you want. For example, if you want to boldface some chunk of text or a worksheet range, you select the text or range (such as by dragging the mouse across the text or cells), and then you click the Bold button. If you want to change the font, or typeface, used for a chunk of text or a worksheet range, you select the text or range and then you select a new font from the Font list box.

TIP: *Remember, if you point to any toolbar box or box, the Office program displays the tool name in a pop-up box called a ScreenTip.*

LEARN BY EXAMPLE
You can open the sample Word document Figure 3-A (example document for formatting) *if you want a simple document you can use for experimenting with the Word Formatting toolbar. You can open the sample Excel workbook* Figure 3-B (example workbook for formatting) *if you want a simple workbook that you can use for experimenting with the Excel Formatting toolbar. You can open the sample PowerPoint presentation* Figure 3-C (example presentation for formatting) *if you want a simple presentation that you can use for experimenting with the PowerPoint Formatting toolbar.*

Reviewing the Formatting Toolbar's Buttons

The Formatting toolbar provides drop-down list boxes and clickable buttons you can use to change the appearance of the information you've selected in a Word document, Excel workbook, or PowerPoint presentation. Table 3-1 describes each of these boxes and buttons, but your best route for learning what these tools do is simply to experiment with them.

NOTE: Perhaps not surprisingly, all of the Office programs provide many more tools you can use to customize the appearance of your document file contents. Both Word and Excel's Format menus, for example, provide an AutoFormat command, which you can use to richly format a Word document or Excel worksheet range. The Word and PowerPoint Format menus also all provide a Font command, which you can use to change the font typeface, style, point size, and color and to add special effects such as underlining, shadows, and so forth.

Using the Drawing Tools

All Office 97 programs supply the same new feature called Office Art. Office Art offers many drawing tools and capabilities that you can use to add drawn objects such as lines, arrows, boxes, and circles to your document files and then to format them.

Displaying the Drawing Toolbar

Before you can begin drawing, you need to add the Drawing toolbar to the Office program's window. In Word and Excel, you can do this by clicking the Standard toolbar's Drawing button. In PowerPoint, you choose the View menu Toolbars command and then you choose the Toolbars submenu Drawing command. Once you do this, the Office program adds the Drawing toolbar to the bottom of the program window, as shown in Figure 3-11.

NOTE: To subsequently remove the Drawing toolbar in Word or Excel, you click the Drawing toolbar button again. To subsequently remove the Drawing toolbar in PowerPoint, you choose the View menu Toolbars command and then the Toolbars submenu Drawing command again.

Button	Available In	What It Lets You Do
Normal ▾	Word	The Style button selects a style from a drop-down list box for the selection.
Times New Roman ▾	All	The Font button selects a font (typeface) from a drop-down list box for the selection.
14 ▾	All	The Font Size button specifies a point size for the selection. You can select a point size from the drop-down list or you can enter a point size into the box.
B	All	The Bold button boldfaces the selection.
I	All	The Italic button italicizes the selection.
U	All	The Underline button underlines the selection.
S	PowerPoint	The Shadow button adds a shadow to the selection.
≡	All	The Align Left button left-aligns the text in the selection.
≡	All	The Center button centers the text in the selection.
≡	All	The Align Right button right-aligns the text in the selection.
≡	Word	The Justify button justifies the text in the selection so the text is flush against both the left and right margin edges.

Table 3-1. *The Formatting Toolbar Buttons*

Button	Available In	What It Lets You Do
	Excel	The Merge & Center button concatenates the cell contents in each selected cell and then centers the new concatenated label across the selected columns.
	Word	The Numbering buttton turns the selected paragraphs into a numbered list.
	Excel	The Currency Style button formats the selected worksheet range to include a currency symbol, a comma as the thousands separator, and two decimal places.
	Excel	The Percent Style button formats the selected worksheet range to show values as percentages and adds the percent symbol (for example, the value 1 shows as 100%).
	Excel	The Comma Style button formats the selected worksheet range to include a comma as the thousands separator and two decimal places.
	Word and PowerPoint	The Bullets button turns the selected paragraphs into a bulleted list.
	Excel	The Increase Decimal button increases the number of decimal places shown for the selected worksheet range.
	Excel	The Decrease Decimal button decreases the number of decimal places shown for the selected worksheet range.
	Word and Excel	The Decrease Indent button reduces the indentation of the selection.

Table 3-1. *The Formatting Toolbar Button* (continued)

Button	Available In	What It Lets You Do
	Word and Excel	The Increase Indent button increases the indentation of the selection.
	PowerPoint	The Increase Paragraph Spacing button increases the space between paragraphs.
	PowerPoint	The Decrease Paragraph Spacing button decreases the space between paragraphs.
	PowerPoint	The Increase Font Size button increases the point size of the selection to the next larger size shown in the Font Size list box.
	PowerPoint	The Decrease Font Size button decreases the point size of the selection to the next smaller size shown in the Font Size list box.
	PowerPoint	The Promote button promotes the selected paragraph to the next higher level in the presentation's outline.
	PowerPoint	The Demote button demotes the selected paragraph to the next, lower level in the presentation's outline.
	PowerPoint	The Animation Effects button displays the Animation Effects toolbar.
	Word and Excel	The Outside Border button displays a list box you can use to add borders to the selection. (Note that in Word this tool includes the name of the current default border—Outside Border or Bottom Border, for example.)

Table 3-1.   *The Formatting Toolbar Button* (continued)

Button	Available In	What It Lets You Do
	Word	The Highlight button highlights the selected text using the color shown on the face of the toolbar button. (If you click the arrow next to the button, Word displays a drop-down list of colors you can use to choose your highlighting color.)
	Excel	The Fill Color button fills the selected worksheet range using the color shown on the face of the toolbar button. (If you click the arrow next to the button, Excel displays a drop-down list of colors you can use to choose your fill color.)
	Word and Excel	The Font Color button colors the text in your selection using the color shown on the face of the toolbar button. (If you click the arrow next to the button, Word and Excel display a drop-down list of colors you can use to choose your font color.)

Table 3-1. *The Formatting Toolbar Buttons (continued)*

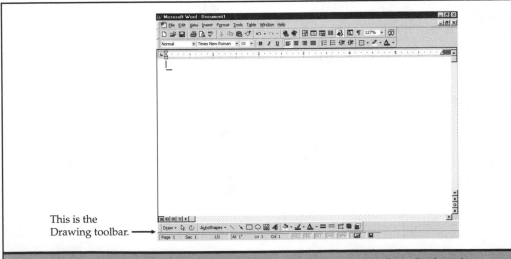

This is the Drawing toolbar. ⟶

Figure 3-11. *The Word program window with the Drawing toolbar displayed*

Reviewing the Drawing Toolbar's Tools

The Drawing toolbar provides the same set of tools no matter which program you use it with. Table 3-2 shows the toolbar buttons and provides brief descriptions of each tool.

Button	Description
Draw ▾	The Draw button displays the Draw menu of commands.
⬚	The Select Objects button tells the Drawing program that it should select the next object you click or the next group of objects that you drag across.
⬚	The Free Rotate button tells the Drawing program that you want to spin, or rotate, the selected object by dragging its rotation handles.
AutoShapes ▾	The AutoShapes button displays the AutoShapes menu of commands.
⬚	The Line button tells the Drawing program to draw a line from the starting point where you next click to the ending point where you release the mouse button.
⬚	The Arrow button tells the Drawing program to draw an arrow from the starting point where you next click to the ending point where you release the mouse button. (The Drawing program places the arrow head at the ending point.)
⬚	The Rectangle button tells the Drawing program to draw a rectangle. (You identify where you want the rectangle by dragging the mouse between the rectangle's opposite corners.)
⬚	The Oval button tells the Drawing program to draw an oval. (You identify where you want the oval by dragging the mouse between the two opposite points on the oval.)

Table 3-2. *The Drawing Toolbar Buttons*

INTRODUCING OFFICE

Button	Description
	The Text Box button tells the Drawing program to draw a text box, so you can later fill it with text. (You identify where you want the text box by dragging the mouse between the box's opposite corners.)
	The Word Art button starts the WordArt add-in, which lets you turn text into colorful graphic images.
	The Fill Color button colors the interior of the selected object with the color shown on the face of the button. (If you click the arrow next to the button, the Drawing program displays a drop-down list of colors you can use for your fill color.)
	The Line Color button colors the border of the selected object with the color shown on the face of the button. (If you click the arrow next to the button, the Drawing program displays a drop-down list of colors you can use for your border color.)
	The Font Color button colors the selected text with the color shown on the face of the button. (If you click the arrow next to the button, the Drawing program displays a drop-down list of colors you can use for your text.)
	The Lines button displays a drop-down list box of line styles so you can choose a line style (really a line thickness) for the border of the selected object.
	The Dash button displays a drop-down list box of dashed lines so you can choose a dashed-line style for the border of the selected object.
	The Arrow Styles button displays a drop-down list box of arrows so you can choose an arrow style for the selected line or arrow.
	The Shadow button adds a shadow to the selected object.
	The 3-D button adds a third dimension to the selected object.

Table 3-2. *The Drawing Toolbar Buttons* (continued)

Drawing Objects

As Table 3-2 implies, you use the same basic procedure for drawing any object—AutoShape, line, arrow, rectangle, oval, or text box—with the Drawing add-in tool. First, you click the drawing toolbar button or select the command that represents the object you want to draw. Second, you drag the mouse. For example, for a line or arrow, click either the Line or Arrow button and then you drag the mouse between the line's or arrow's endpoints:

For a rectangle or text box, you click either the Rectangle or Text Box button and then you drag the mouse between the shape's opposite corners:

For an oval, you click the Oval button and then you drag the mouse either from roughly the ten o'clock position to the four o'clock position or from roughly the two o'clock position to the seven o'clock position. (If this last sentence doesn't make sense, just try the Oval tool and you'll immediately see how it works.)

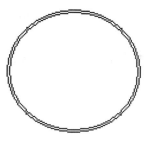

TIP: *To draw a square, you use the Rectangle tool but hold down the SHIFT key as you drag the mouse. To draw a circle, you use the Oval tool but hold down the SHIFT key as you drag the mouse.*

As mentioned in the preceding table, the AutoShapes tool displays a menu of commands, and each command corresponds to a particular category of shapes. When you choose an AutoShape menu command, the Drawing add-in displays a toolbar-like box with clickable buttons representing different shapes:

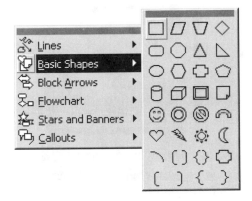

You click the button that shows the shape you want to draw and then you drag the mouse in the same way you do to draw lines, rectangles, and ovals.

 NOTE: *When you select an AutoShape, the Drawing add-in tool also adds a yellow adjustment handle to change the shape's most prominent feature. Use the other handles to change the size of the object.*

Editing, Moving, and Resizing Drawing Objects

You can most easily edit, move, and resize drawing objects by using the mouse. For example, to copy an object, click the object to select it, click the Copy button (on the standard toolbar), and then click the Paste button. To move an object, simply drag it. To resize an object, click the object to select it; then drag the object's selection handles. To remove an object, click it and then press the DELETE key.

 NOTE: *You can rotate, or spin, the selected object by clicking the Rotate button and then dragging the rotation handles on the object.*

TIP: You can select more than one object by clicking the Select Objects button and then dragging the mouse from the top-left corner to the bottom-right corner of a rectangle that includes the objects you want to select. This is the same technique, by the way, that you can use to select shortcut icons on the Windows desktop.

Working with Text Boxes

You create text boxes in the same way that you create rectangle objects except that after you've drawn the box, the Office program lets you enter text into the box:

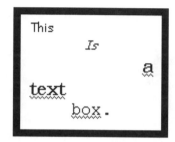

One interesting but very handy feature of text boxes is that you can format the text that appears in the box, as the preceding illustration shows. You'll usually want to do this with the Formatting toolbar's buttons.

TIP: To place existing text into a text box, first select the text and then click the Text Box button.

Formatting Drawing Objects

For the most part, you format drawing objects in the same manner that you format text in a Word document, PowerPoint presentation, or an Excel worksheet range. You select the item you want to format, such as by clicking it. Then you choose the Drawing toolbar button that supplies the formatting you want to apply. Some buttons—such as the Fill Color, Line Color, Line Style, Dash Style, and Arrow Style buttons—display or can display list boxes of formatting options. To choose an option you see listed, you simply click it.

Working with the Draw Menu's Commands

You won't need to use the Draw menu's commands if your use of the Drawing add-in tool is only casual or occasional. But if you become a frequent user of the Drawing toolbar—or you begin to use the Drawing toolbar for serious illustration work or drawing—you'll find the Draw menu's commands essential.

Grouping and Ungrouping Objects

You can group objects so that they are treated as a single object: edited together, moved or resized together, formatted together, and so on. To group a set of objects, follow these steps:

1. Click the Drawing toolbar's Select Objects button.

2. Drag the mouse from the top-left corner to the bottom-right corner of a rectangle that includes the objects you want to group. At this point, you've selected the objects.

3. Click the Draw button so that the Draw menu appears.

4. Choose the Draw menu Group command. Notice that the selection handles now surround the group instead of the individual objects in the group.

To ungroup a set of objects you've previously grouped, follow these steps:

1. Click the grouped objects set you want to ungroup.

2. Click the Draw button so that the Draw menu appears.

3. Choose the Draw menu Ungroup command.

 TIP: *You can undo the effect of your last Ungroup command by choosing the Draw menu Regroup command.*

Restacking Objects

If you choose the Order command from the Draw menu, the Drawing add-in tool displays a submenu of commands you can use for reordering, or restacking, the drawing objects you've created. The Order submenu includes commands for moving the selected object to the top or bottom of a stack of objects, or forward or backward in a stack of objects, and for moving the selected object behind or in front of text.

Working with a Grid

If you create complex drawings or illustrations that use a rich set of individual drawing objects—lines, rectangles, and ovals, for example—you can use the Draw menu Grid command in Word to add an invisible grid to the document file. You can then use this grid to more precisely locate your drawing objects. To add a grid, follow these steps:

1. Click the Draw button.

2. Choose the Grid command.

3. Check the Snap to grid box if you want the Drawing add-in tool to automatically move drawn objects so they are aligned against the vertical or horizontal lines in an invisible grid.

4. Use the Vertical spacing box to specify how far apart the vertical gridlines should be placed.

5. Use the Horizontal spacing box to specify how far apart the horizontal gridlines should be placed.

6. Use the Horizontal origin box to specify where, starting at the left edge of the page, the gridlines should begin.

7. Use the Vertical origin box to specify where, starting at the top of the page, the gridlines should begin.

8. Check the Snap to shapes box if you want drawn objects to align with additional gridlines that run along the vertical and horizontal edges of AutoShapes.

Nudging Objects

The Draw menu Nudge command displays a set of commands that nudge, or slightly move, the selected object. If you want to move an object left, for example, select it, click the Draw button, choose the Draw menu Nudge command, and then choose the Nudge submenu Left command. You can nudge objects in other directions by choosing one of the Nudge submenu other commands: Right, Up, or Down.

 TIP: *You can nudge the selected object in even smaller, one-pixel increments by selecting the object, holding down the CTRL key, and then pressing the arrow key that points in the direction that you want to nudge the selected object.*

Aligning and Distributing Objects

You can align or distribute the selected objects by using the Draw menu Align or Distribute command. When you choose this command—you need to click the Draw button and then choose the Draw menu Align or Distribute command—the Drawing add-in tool displays the menu shown next:

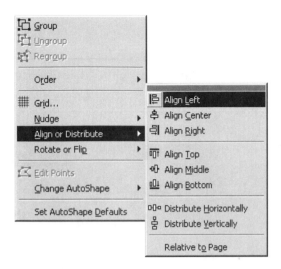

You choose the command that corresponds to the way that you want to align the selected objects. For example, if you've selected a set of ovals and you want to align them so they're all centered, you choose the Align or Distribute menu Align Center command. The other alignment commands work in the same basic way. If you want to align objects so their left edges all fall along the same line, you choose the Align or Distribute menu Align Left command. The Align or Distribute menu distribution commands—Distribute Horizontally and Distribute Vertically—don't align the objects. Rather, these two commands rearrange the selected objects within a vertical row or a horizontal row.

NOTE: By default, the Drawing add-in tool aligns or distributes the selected objects relative to each other. If you wish, you can align or distribute the selected objects relative to the page on which the drawn objects appear by selecting the Relative to Page command on the Align and Distribute submenu.

Rotating and Flipping Objects

You can use the Draw menu Rotate or Flip command to rotate, or spin, the selected object. To use this command, first select the object you want to rotate. Then click the Draw button, choose the Draw menu Rotate or Flip command, and choose the appropriate Rotate or Flip submenu command, shown next:

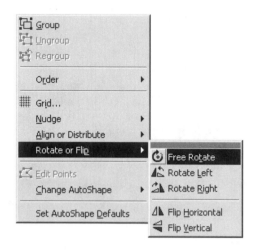

What most of the Rotate or Flip submenu commands do is obvious either from the command name or the tiny picture shown next to the command name. The only exception is the Free Rotate command, but it works exactly like the Free Rotate button, described earlier in this section.

Editing AutoShapes

The only three Draw menu commands not described in the preceding discussion—Edit Points, Change AutoShape, and Set AutoShape Defaults—let you edit AutoShapes you've added to a document file. For example, if you use the Lines AutoShape that's really a freeform shape, you can change the object's shape by selecting it, clicking the Draw button, choosing the Draw menu Edit Points command, and then dragging the selection handles. You can also create new editing point handles by clicking anywhere on the existing shape.

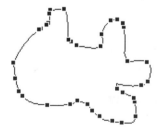

You can substitute a new AutoShape for the selected AutoShape by clicking the Draw button, choosing the Draw menu Change AutoShape command, choosing one of the Change AutoShape submenu commands (so the Drawing add-in tool displays a pop-up box of AutoShapes), and then choosing an AutoShape. This is easier than it sounds, so just experiment with the command if you have a question.

Finally, if you make changes to an object—perhaps you add a fill color and specify a line style—you can select the object and then tell the Drawing program that it should use the attributes you've assigned to the object as the default for other AutoShapes. To do this, select the object (as just mentioned), click the Draw button, and then choose the Draw menu Set AutoShape Defaults command.

 NOTE: *The default AutoShape attributes you specify apply only to the active document file.*

Working with the Clip Gallery

You can rather easily add clip art images, photographic pictures, sound, and even video to your Word documents, Excel workbooks, PowerPoint presentations, and Access database objects. In fact, Microsoft Office 97 comes with a rich set of clip art elements on its distribution CD. And you can use other clip art elements, too. (This book uses the term "clip art element" to refer not only to line art and bitmap images but also photographic images, sounds, and video clips.)

 NOTE: *You may need to first install the Microsoft Office 97 clip art if it wasn't installed at the same time that you installed the rest of the Office suite of programs. To do this, insert the Office CD into your CD drive, open the Clip Art folder, and then start the Clip Art Setup program. (Once you start the Setup program, you follow its onscreen instructions for installing the program.)*

Inserting Clip Art into a Document File

It isn't difficult to insert clip art elements into a Word document, an Excel workbook, or a PowerPoint presentation. To add clip art images, photographic pictures, sounds, and video clips to a document file, follow these steps:

1. Choose the Insert menu Picture command and then the Picture submenu Clip Art command. The Office program starts the Microsoft Clip Gallery add-in, as shown in Figure 3-12.

2. When the Microsoft Clip Gallery starts, click the tab that describes the type of clip art element you want to insert: Clip Art, Pictures, Sounds, or Videos.

3. Locate the clip art element you want to insert. You can do this by scrolling through the list box that shows clip art images, pictures, and video clips or, in the case of sounds, brief descriptions.

4. Double-click the clip art element you want to insert. The Clip Gallery inserts the clip art element into the document file at the insertion point location.

Editing Clip Art Elements

When you insert a clip art element into a document file, the Office program adds the Picture toolbar to the program window. You can use its buttons to edit the image. Table 3-3 identifies and describes the Picture toolbar's butons.

NOTE: If you perform a complete installation of Microsoft Office 97, the setup program installs the Microsoft Photo Editor program. You can also use it for editing photographic images.

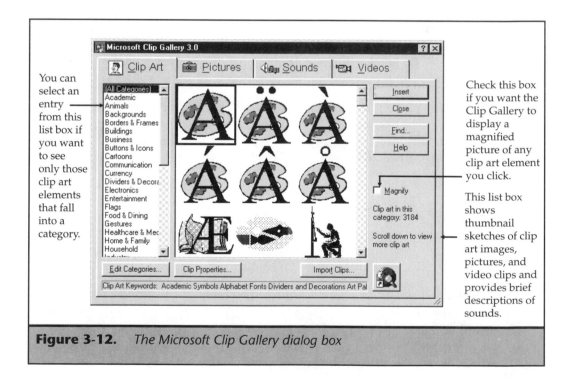

Figure 3-12. *The Microsoft Clip Gallery dialog box*

INTRODUCING OFFICE

Button	What It Does
	The Insert Picture button displays the Insert Picture dialog box, which works similarly to the Open dialog box. You can use this dialog box to insert another clip art element into the active document file.
	The Image Control button displays the Image Control menu, which provides settings for converting the selected clip art image to a grayscale image, a black-and-white image, or a transparent watermark image. (Note that the default image control setting, Automatic, tells the Clip Gallery to display the image using its original coloring.)
	The More Contrast button changes the colors of the selected image so that they show more contrast between the lightest and darkest colors.
	The Less Contrast button changes the colors of the selected image so that they show less contrast between the lightest and darkest colors used in the image.
	The More Brightness button increases the brightness of the selected image by adding white to the image's colors.
	The Brightness button increases the brightness of the selected image by removing white from the image's colors.
	The Crop button lets you crop the selected image by dragging its selection handles.
	The Line Style button displays a drop-down list box of line thicknesses you can use as a border for the selected image.
	The Text Wrapping button displays a drop-down list box of options for wrapping text around the selected image. (Note that the pictures shown next to the commands show what each text wrapping option does.)

Table 3-3.   *The Picture Toolbar Buttons*

Button	What It Does
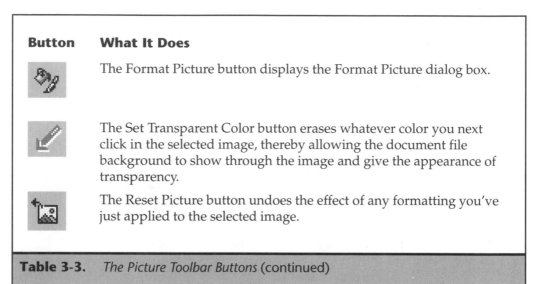	The Format Picture button displays the Format Picture dialog box.
	The Set Transparent Color button erases whatever color you next click in the selected image, thereby allowing the document file background to show through the image and give the appearance of transparency.
	The Reset Picture button undoes the effect of any formatting you've just applied to the selected image.

Table 3-3. *The Picture Toolbar Buttons* (continued)

Adding Clip Art Elements to the Gallery

While Office 97 provides a rich set of clip art elements, you aren't limited to using just these items. You can add other clip art images, photographic images, sounds, and video clips to the Clip Gallery. To do this, follow these steps:

1. Choose the Insert menu Picture command and then the Picture submenu Clip Art command. The Office program starts the Microsoft Clip Gallery add-in.

2. When the Microsoft Clip Gallery starts, click the Import Clips button. The Clip Gallery displays the Add clip art to Clip Gallery dialog box.

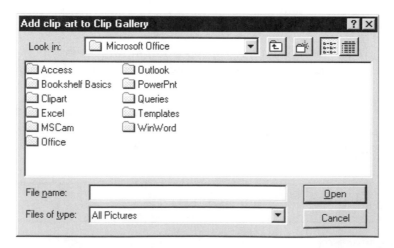

3. Use the Look in drop-down list box to identify the folder holding the clip art element you want to add to the Clip Gallery.

4. When the list box beneath the Look In drop-down list box shows the clip art element file that you want, double-click it.

Using Microsoft Camcorder

Microsoft Camcorder is an extra application that comes with all editions of Office 97. You can use Camcorder to make a movie of your computer screen, and you can narrate the movie if your computer has a microphone and a sound card.

Camcorder does not install automatically if you choose Typical when installing Office, so you have to install Camcorder separately. To do this, insert the Office 97 CD. When the contents of the CD appear on the screen, double-click the Valupack folder. Double-click the MSCam folder and then double-click Camcordr to begin the installation. To run Camcorder, click the Start button and choose Programs Microsoft Camcorder. To record a film, click the Record button. To record with sound, choose the Movie menu Preferences command and check the Capture Audio box.

At the time we were writing this book, Camcorder had several problems. First, in order to run Camcorder, your computer needs to have at least 16MB of memory. Second, Camcorder only works under Windows 95 and not under Windows NT. Finally, to get decent sound quality, you need an expensive microphone and an expensive sound card, as well.

Working with Macros and VBA Modules

You can create keystroke macros and Visual Basic for Applications (VBA) modules for Word document files, Excel workbooks, PowerPoint presentations, and Access databases. In essence, macros let you store and then later repeat, or replay, a sequence of keystrokes and mouse clicks. VBA modules amount to programming source code, which let you create customized applications on top of Word, Excel, PowerPoint, or Access.

How you use the Office programs as a development platform is beyond the scope of this book, but you should know that these tools exist. If you have more questions, refer to the Office program's online help, a book about using Office as a systems development platform, or confer with a systems consultant. Note that to use Office in these ways, it's generally extremely useful and perhaps essential that you have programming experience.

The Complete Reference

Office 97

Chapter 4

Customizing the
Office 97 Programs

After you become thoroughly familiar with an Office 97 program and learn which commands and buttons are your favorites, you might try tinkering with the program's toolbars, buttons, menus, and keyboard shortcuts to make them serve you better. In other words, you might try customizing the toolbars, menus, and keyboard shortcuts to your liking, which is the subject of this chapter.

Chapter 4 explains how to add buttons to and remove buttons from a toolbar, and how to create a toolbar of your own. It also describes how to create your own menus, remove commands from menus, and add commands to menus. Finally, this chapter tells you how to make keyboard shortcuts that are easy to remember.

NOTE: *You cannot change the menus, toolbars, or keyboard shortcuts in Outlook.*

Customizing a Toolbar

Most people don't use all the buttons on the Office 97 toolbars. If you never click a certain button, why keep it on the Standard or Formatting toolbar when you can replace it with a button you do use? For that matter, why not create a toolbar of your own with your favorite buttons or favorite commands on it? Some Office 97 toolbars are awfully crowded. You can do yourself a favor by making them less crowded or assembling the buttons you use frequently in a single toolbar.

This part of Chapter 4 explains how to remove buttons from and add buttons to toolbars; create buttons for commands, macros, and styles; and create your own toolbar. It also explains how to copy toolbars from template to template and how to remove a toolbar when you no longer need it. And, to start with, it explains how to put toolbars on the screen, remove them, and change their size and shape.

WARNING: *If others share the computer you work on, you might talk to them before you change the buttons on a toolbar. A coworker or family member who tries to click a button but discovers it isn't there any longer will receive an unpleasant surprise.*

Manipulating the Toolbars

Removing toolbars from the screen, placing toolbars onscreen, and changing the size and shape of toolbars is pretty simple. Figure 4-1 explains where to click and what to drag to manipulate toolbars. The following table gives all the details:

Displaying   Right-click on a toolbar or on the menu bar. When the shortcut menu appears, click the name of the toolbar you want to display.

Removing   Right-click on a toolbar or on the menu bar. On the shortcut menu, click the name of the toolbar you want to remove. You can also click a toolbar's Close button (the *X*) to remove it.

Repositioning   To drag a toolbar from the top or bottom of the screen to a side or the middle of the screen, click between the buttons and drag. After a toolbar has been dragged onscreen, its title bar appears. To make a toolbar that has been dragged onscreen go back to the top or bottom of the screen, double-click its title bar.

Reshaping   To change the shape of a toolbar that has been dragged onscreen, gently place the cursor on a side of the toolbar. When the cursor changes to a double-headed arrow, click and start dragging.

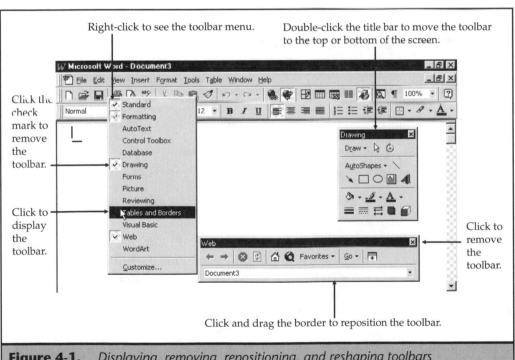

Figure 4-1.   *Displaying, removing, repositioning, and reshaping toolbars*

Larger Toolbar Buttons, Anyone?

Besides deciding for yourself which buttons should appear on toolbars, you can take advantage of three amenities that make toolbars and keyboard shortcuts easier to use and remember. Right-click on a toolbar, choose Customize, and click the Options tab of the Customize dialog box. The Options tab offers these check boxes:

■   *Large icons*   Makes buttons larger onscreen (not all the buttons can fit onscreen when the buttons are enlarged).

■   *Show ScreenTips on toolbars*   With this one checked, a caption appears below a button when you move the pointer over a button. The caption tells you the button's name.

■   *Show shortcut keys on ScreenTips*   With this one checked, a caption and the button's shortcut key equivalent, if there is one, appear below the button when you move the pointer over it.

Removing Buttons from and Adding Buttons to Toolbars

In the spirit of democracy, Office 97 lets you decide for yourself which buttons appear on toolbars. Adding and removing buttons is easy, and if you change your mind later and want the original toolbar back, you can get it with a few clicks of the mouse.

Removing Buttons from a Toolbar

To remove buttons from a toolbar, do the following:

1. Make sure that the toolbar whose buttons you want to remove is onscreen.

2. Right-click a toolbar or the menu bar and choose Customize from the shortcut menu. The Customize dialog box appears.

3. Move the pointer away from the dialog box and drag the button or buttons you want to remove from the toolbar. As long as the Customize dialog box is open, all you have to do to remove buttons is drag them from toolbars. As you drag, a black *X* appears below the pointer.

4. Click Close to close the Customize dialog box.

 NOTE: *In Word 97, changes to toolbars apply only to a specific template. To choose a template on which to make toolbar changes, click the Commands tab in the Customize dialog box. From the Save in drop-down list, choose the template to which the toolbar changes will apply.*

Adding Buttons to a Toolbar

Any command in Office 97, whether or not the program has assigned it a button, can be added to a toolbar. When you add a command such as What's This?, for which Office 97 has a button, the button is added to the toolbar. However, when you add a command for which no button exists, such as Next Window, the command name itself is placed on the toolbar. Figure 4-2 shows toolbars with both buttons and command names.

To put buttons on a toolbar, follow these steps:

1. Place the toolbar to which you want to add buttons on the screen.

2. Right-click a toolbar or the menu bar and choose Customize from the shortcut menu. You see the Customize dialog box.

3. Click the Commands tab, which is shown in Figure 4-2. By clicking category names on the left side of the Commands tab, you see different sets of commands in the Commands box. Some commands offer buttons that can be put on toolbars; some don't.

4. In the Categories box, click category names to search for the command you want to add to the toolbar. The commands are listed in the Commands box on the right side of the dialog box. (The All Commands category lists all commands in alphabetical order.) Some commands offer predefined buttons that you can put on toolbars; some don't.

5. When you've found the button or command name and it appears in the Commands box, click it.

TIP: *If you have trouble telling what a command does, click the Description button in the Customize dialog box. You see a brief explanation of the command.*

6. Gently drag the button or command name out of the Customize dialog box and place it on the toolbar. As you drag, a plus sign appears below the pointer to show that you are adding a button or command name.

7. If necessary, arrange the buttons on the toolbar by dragging them from place to place. If the buttons are too close together, gently drag them further apart. If you do this correctly, a faint line appears between the buttons so that you can arrange them into groups.

8. Click the Close button in the Customize dialog box when you have finished adding buttons to the toolbar.

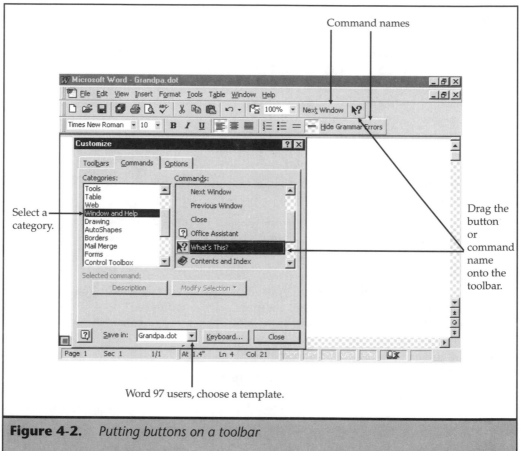

Figure 4-2. *Putting buttons on a toolbar*

HEADSTART

TEMPLATES

On the companion CD is a Word 97 template called Grandpa.dot. In this template, cumbersome toolbar buttons and esoteric commands have been removed. Meanwhile, buttons useful for writing simple documents have been added to the Standard and Formatting toolbars. Use Grandpa.dot to write letters, notes, and other simple documents.

Creating Toolbar Buttons for Macros, Styles, AutoText Entries, and More

In the previous section of this chapter, I described how to drag a button from the Customize dialog box to a toolbar. However, commands aren't the only things that can be put on toolbars. You can also place macro names, style names, AutoText entries, tables, queries, and other detritus. Because macros, styles, Access tables, and the like often have long names, Office 97 gives you the chance to shorten their names when you add them to a toolbar.

INTRODUCING OFFICE

To find out how to create toolbar buttons for the things in Office 97 that you name yourself, follow these steps:

1. Place the toolbar onscreen.

2. Right-click a toolbar or the menu bar and choose Customize to open the Customize dialog box.

3. Click the Commands tab (see Figure 4-2).

4. Scroll to the bottom of the Categories list. At the bottom of the list are entries called Styles, AutoText, Queries, and the like.

5. Click the type of item for which you want to create a toolbar button. When you click the item, a list of the styles, AutoText entries, queries, and whatnot that are available appears in the Commands box.

6. In the Commands box, click the thing for which you want to create a button and drag it onto the toolbar.

7. Right-click on the new button you just created. You see the following shortcut menu:

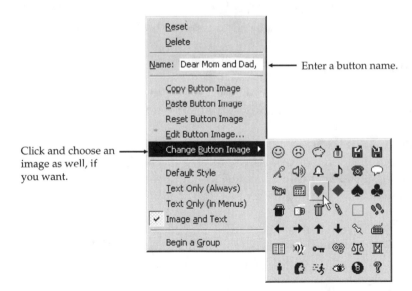

8. Type a button name in the Name box. If you are the decorative kind, you can also click Change Button Image and choose an image to go beside the button name.

TIP: *To see an image on a button, not a name, choose the Text Only (in Menus) option.*

9. Click the Close button in the Customize dialog box.

Restoring, Deleting, and Renaming Toolbars

It is fairly easy to go overboard when you add buttons to and remove buttons from toolbars. Therefore, this part of the chapter explains how to get an original toolbar back after you load it down with new buttons or strip it bare of its original set of buttons. It also tells how to delete a toolbar you created yourself (the subject of the next part of this chapter) and how to rename a toolbar you created.

 NOTE: *You can't delete the toolbars that Office 97 provides. Only toolbars you create yourself can be deleted. Likewise, you can't rename the toolbars that come with Office 97.*

Restoring a Toolbar

Suppose you make hash out of an important toolbar such as the Standard or Formatting toolbar and you want the original toolbar back. To get it back, do the following:

1. Right-click on a toolbar and choose Customize from the shortcut menu.
2. In the Customize dialog box, click the Toolbars tab, if necessary.
3. Click the name of the toolbar you want to restore.
4. Click the Reset button.
5. When you are asked if you really and truly want to restore the toolbar, click OK.
6. Close the Customize dialog box.

Deleting a Toolbar

Think twice about deleting toolbars. After a toolbar has been deleted, all the work that went into creating the toolbar is lost forever. You can't get a deleted toolbar back. To delete a toolbar, do the following:

1. Right-click on a toolbar and choose Customize from the shortcut menu.
2. If necessary, click the Toolbars tab in the Customize dialog box.
3. Click the name of the toolbar you want to delete.
4. Click the Delete button.
5. Click OK when the program asks if you are sure you want to delete the toolbar.
6. Close the Customize dialog box.

Renaming a Toolbar

To rename a toolbar you created yourself, do the following:

1. Right-click on a toolbar and choose Customize.

2. Click the Toolbars tab in the Customize dialog box, if necessary.

3. Click the name of the toolbar you want to rename.

4. Click the Rename button.

5. In the Rename Toolbar dialog box, type a new name for the toolbar and click OK.

6. Close the Customize dialog box.

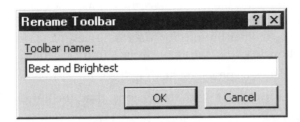

Creating Your Own Toolbar

To create a toolbar of your very own, you name the toolbar, spread it across the screen, and then call on the skills described in the previous handful of pages to add the buttons. Creating a toolbar doesn't take long and is well worth the effort. Instead of fishing in obscure program menus or aiming the pointer at hard-to-find buttons, all you have to do is line up your favorite commands and buttons on a toolbar and take it from there.

Follow these steps to create a toolbar you can call your own:

1. Right-click on a toolbar or on the menu bar and choose Customize at the bottom of the shortcut menu.

2. Click the Toolbars tab, if necessary.

3. Click the New button. You see the New Toolbar dialog box:

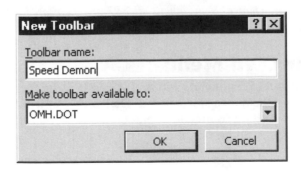

4. Type a name for the new toolbar in the Toolbar name box. The name you enter will appear on the shortcut menu beside the other toolbar names when you right-click on a toolbar. If you are creating a toolbar for Word 97, choose a template from the Make toolbar available to drop-down list.

5. Click OK. A very small toolbar with the name you typed appears onscreen.

6. Double-click the title bar of the new toolbar to make it appear along the top of the screen.

7. Click the Commands tab in the Customize dialog box and add the commands. See "Adding Buttons to a Toolbar" earlier in this chapter if you need help. See also "Creating Toolbar Buttons for Macros, Styles, AutoText Entries, and More" to find out how to add other things besides buttons and commands to a toolbar.

8. To rearrange buttons on a toolbar, drag the buttons to new places.

9. To make lines appear between the buttons, drag the buttons farther apart.

10. Click Close to close the Customize dialog box.

 TIP: Here is a fast way to assemble buttons from different toolbars on a single toolbar: Display the toolbars from which you want to take buttons, open the Customize dialog box, and drag the buttons to your new toolbar. Then restore the original toolbars with the Reset command in the Customize dialog box.

Changing What's on the Program Menus

In all the Office 97 programs except Outlook, you can create menus of your own, remove unwanted commands from menus, move commands from menu to menu, and even get rid of menus. This part of the chapter explains how. By the way, if you make mincemeat out of the menus, you can always get the originals back. The following pages explain how to do that, too.

 WARNING: If you share a computer with others, be sure to confer with them before you change the menus around. In Word 97, you can confine menu changes to a single template, but menu changes to the other Office 97 programs are for everyone to use or be confused by.

Creating Your Own Menu

Do you favor a handful of commands and find yourself using them most of the time? You might as well put them on a single menu. That way, you will know exactly where to find them. Besides putting command names on menus, you can put font names, AutoText entries, queries, and much else.

Follow these steps to create a menu of your own:

1. Right-click on a toolbar or on the menu bar and choose Customize from the shortcut menu. You see the Customize dialog box.

2. If necessary, click the Commands tab. It is shown in Figure 4-3.

3. Scroll to the bottom of the Categories list and choose New Menu. A single option, New Menu, appears in the Commands box.

 TIP: *Word 97 users may choose a template from the Save in drop-down list. By choosing a template, you tell Office 97 to make menu changes only to documents created with the template you chose.*

4. Click the New Menu option in the Commands box and drag it out of the Customize dialog box and onto the menu bar. If you do this correctly, a white box with a cross appears below the pointer as you drag.

 TIP: *You can also add menus to toolbars.*

5. Right-click on the menu you just created, and, in the Name box on the shortcut menu, type a name for the menu. To designate a hot key for the menu, enter an ampersand (&) before the letter that is to be the hot key. For example, entering **Spee&d** makes *d* the hot key, and the menu name looks like this on the menu bar: Spee<u>d</u>. Be sure to choose a hot key that doesn't appear in one of the other menu's names on the menu bar.

6. In the Categories box, click category names to search for the command you want to add to the new menu. (The All Commands category lists all commands in alphabetical order.) You likely have to scroll in the Commands list to find the command. Fonts, macros, queries, and other such things can be placed on menus. You will find them at the bottom of the Categories box.

7. In the Commands box, click the command, query, macro, or whatnot you want to add to the menu.

8. Drag the command out of the dialog box and onto the new menu. As you near the menu, a small gray box appears below the menu. Drop the new menu command inside that gray rectangle.

9. Repeats steps 8 and 9 to put more commands on the new menu. As shown in Figure 4-3, the new menu opens when you drag new commands onto it, and a vertical bar shows where the command will appear on the menu.

10. Click the Close button in the Customize dialog box when you have finished creating the new menu.

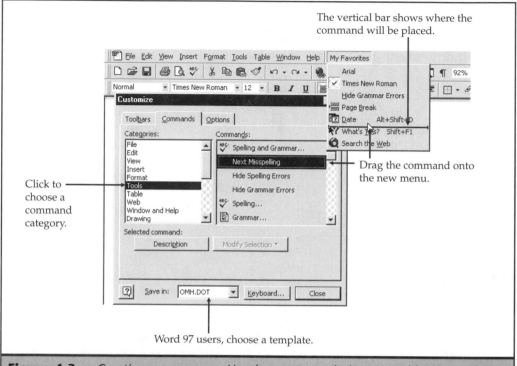

The vertical bar shows where the command will be placed.

Click to choose a command category.

Drag the command onto the new menu.

Word 97 users, choose a template.

Figure 4-3. *Creating a new menu. Use these same techniques to add commands to existing menus*

TIP: Sometimes horizontal lines appear on menus to separate commands. In Office 97 terminology, the horizontal lines separate "menu groups." To place a horizontal line on a menu, display the Customize dialog box and right-click the command that you want the line to appear directly above. Then, from the shortcut menu, choose Begin a Group and close the Customize dialog box.

A Quick Way to Open the Files You Recently Opened

As you know if you've used an Office 97 program for any length of time, the names of the files that were opened most recently appear at the bottom of the File menu. One of the fastest ways to open a file is to click its name at the bottom of the File menu. By default, four filenames appear, but you can add more files to the File menu by following these steps:

1. Choose the Tools menu Options command to open the Options dialog box.

2. Click the General tab.

3. In the entries box beside the Recently used file list check box, enter the number of files that you would like to see on the bottom of the File menu. At most, nine files can appear at the bottom of the File menu.

4. Click OK.

Adding, Removing, and Repositioning Commands

While the Customize dialog box is open, you can load an Office 97 menu with as many commands as you desire. For that matter, you can also prune menus to remove the commands that you think are extraneous and unnecessary. And you can reposition commands in menus and reposition menus themselves on the menu bar. Read on to learn the dirty details.

HEADSTART
The Grandpa.dot Word 97 template on the companion CD includes an extra menu with useful commands for writing simple documents. Create a Word 97 file with the Grandpa.dot template to see an example of a custom-made menu.

Adding Commands to Menus

To add commands to a menu, follow these steps:

1. Right-click on a toolbar and choose Customize from the bottom of the shortcut menu. The Customize dialog box appears.

2. Click the Commands tab (see Figure 4-3), if necessary.

3. Click the menu to which you want to add commands. The menu opens.

4. Click category names in the Categories box, and scroll to read command names in the Commands box, until you find the command you want to add to the menu. When you've found the command, click it.

5. Drag the command onto the menu. A horizontal bar shows where the command will appear on the menu. When the command is in the right place, release the mouse button.

6. Repeat steps 3 and 4 until you have added all the commands you want to add.

7. Click Close to close the Customize dialog box.

Removing Commands from Menus

Office 97 offers a quick but reckless technique for removing commands from menus, as well as a thoughtful, conscientious technique. Both are described here.

The reckless technique is to press CTRL+ALT+- (the hyphen key). The pointer changes into a black bar. With the black bar pointer, choose a menu command that you want to remove. That's right—choose the command as though you really wanted to select it. One by one, you can remove commands from menus this way.

The drawback of the CTRL+ALT+- technique is that it can't remove menu commands that offer submenus, nor can it remove commands that are grayed out. To remove those commands, you have to return to the Customize dialog box.

Follow these steps to remove commands from menus with the Customize dialog box:

1. Right-click on a toolbar or the main menu and choose Customize.

2. Gently click on the menu whose commands you want to remove. The menu opens.

3. One by one, click the names of the commands you want to remove and drag them off the menu.

WARNING: *Be sure to drag the commands away from the toolbars, menus, and Customize dialog box before you release the mouse button. If you fail to do so, you might move a command onto a toolbar or onto a different menu.*

4. Click Close in the Customize dialog box when you are done pruning menus.

Removing a Menu from the Menu Bar

To remove a menu, simply right-click on a toolbar to open the Customize dialog box, and then click on the menu you want to remove and drag it off the menu bar. Be sure not to drop it on a toolbar, however, because if you do, the menu will stick to the toolbar. Close the Customize dialog box when you are finished.

WARNING: *Menus you created yourself are gone forever after you remove them. You can, however, restore one of Office 97's built-in menus after you remove it. (See "Restoring and Renaming Menus," later in this chapter.)*

Repositioning Menus and Menu Commands

As long as the Customize dialog box is open, you can rearrange commands on menus until the cows come home. And you can also reposition menus on the menu bar. To change the position of menus and menu commands, follow these steps:

1. Right-click on a toolbar and choose Customize from the shortcut menu. The Customize dialog box appears (see Figure 4-3).

2. To change the position of a menu on the menu bar, drag the menu name sideways to a new position.

3. To change the location of a command on a menu, gently click the menu to open it, and then drag the command to a new place. A black horizontal bar shows you precisely where the command will land when you release the mouse button:

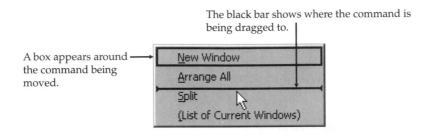

The black bar shows where the command is being dragged to.

A box appears around the command being moved.

4. Click Close in the Customize dialog box when you have finished rearranging menus and menu commands.

Restoring and Renaming Menus

If you make a mess of an Office 97 menu and want the original menu version back, all is not lost, because you can get it back very quickly. This part of the chapter explains how. It also explains how to recover a built-in Office 97 menu that you removed and how to rename a menu.

Restoring the Commands on a Built-In Menu

Follow these steps to restore a menu to its pristine state:

1. Right-click on a toolbar and choose Customize from the shortcut menu.

2. Right-click on the name of the menu whose commands you wish to restore.

3. Click Reset on the shortcut menu.

4. Click Close to close the Customize dialog box.

Restoring a Built-In Menu That You Removed

If you removed a built-in menu that came with an Office 97 program and you want to get the menu back, you have a bit of work to do:

1. Right-click on a toolbar or the menu bar and choose Customize.

2. Click the Commands tab in the Customize dialog box, if necessary.

3. Scroll to the next-to-last category in the Categories box, Built-in Menus, and click it. A list of standard, built-in menus appears in the Commands box:

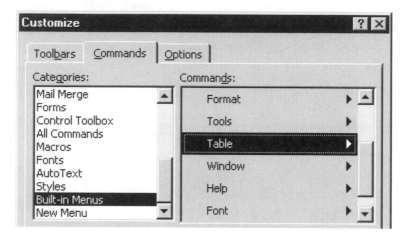

4. In the Commands box, click the name of the menu you want to restore (you might have to scroll to find the menu) and drag it back onto the menu bar.

5. Click Close to close the Customize dialog box.

Renaming a Menu

To rename a menu, right-click on a toolbar to open the Customize dialog box, and then right-click the menu to be renamed. A shortcut menu appears. On the shortcut menu, delete the name in the Name box and enter a new name. To establish a hot key for the menu, enter an ampersand (&) before the letter that is to be the hot key. Be sure to choose a hot key that doesn't appear in one of the other menus names on the menu bar.

Changing Keyboard Shortcuts

This part of the chapter explains how to fiddle with keyboard shortcuts. Are you particularly fond of a keyboard shortcut, perhaps a shortcut that figured prominently in WordStar or MultiMate or some other antique application that you knew and loved? If you are, you can make your favorite keyboard shortcut apply to a command in an Office 97 program.

Following are instructions for assigning keyboard shortcuts to commands and removing keyboard shortcuts. You will also find instructions here for restoring the original keyboard shortcuts, in case you make a hash of it and want to go back to the beginning.

WARNING: *If you share your computer with others, be sure to speak to them first before changing keyboard shortcuts.*

Assigning a New Keyboard Shortcut

Follow these steps to assign a keyboard shortcut to a command, font, AutoText entry, query, or other directive:

1. Right-click on a toolbar or on the menu bar and choose Customize from the shortcut menu.

2. Click the Keyboard button in the lower-right corner of the Customize dialog box. You see the Customize Keyboard dialog box shown in Figure 4-4.

NOTE: Word 97 users can make keyboard shortcuts apply only to documents created with a specific template. To do so, choose the template from the Save changes in drop-down list.

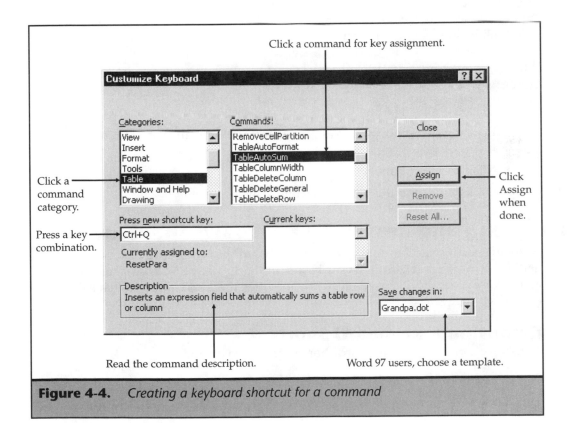

Figure 4-4. *Creating a keyboard shortcut for a command*

3. In the Categories list, click on the menu whose command you want to assign a keyboard shortcut to. At the bottom of the list are styles, AutoText entries, and other such items. You can assign shortcuts to those as well.

4. In the Commands list, find and click on the command, styles, or whatnot to which you want to assign a keyboard shortcut. Command names are hard to understand in this dialog box, so the Description box at the bottom of the Customize Keyboard dialog box tells you precisely what each command does.

5. Click on the Press new shortcut key box and press the shortcut key combination. In other words, if the shortcut key combination is CTRL+!, press the CTRL key and the exclamation point key simultaneously. Office 97 enters the names of the keys you pressed in the box and places a plus sign between the key names.

Shortcut key combinations can begin with the CTRL key, the ALT key, or any combination of the so-called modifier keys (CTRL, ALT, and SHIFT), as well as any letter, number, or symbol. For example, the following would all be valid shortcut keys: CTRL+!, ALT+P, ALT+9, CTRL+SHIFT+N, and ALT+SHIFT+5. It's very likely, however, that the key combination you want to assign is already claimed by another command. When that is the case, the words "Currently assigned to" and a command name appear below the Press new shortcut key box. Enter a new key combination, or else let yours stand if you want to override the preassigned key combination.

6. Click the Assign button.

7. Repeat steps 3 through 6 to assign other key combinations to commands, if you want.

8. Click the Close button.

9. Click the Close button in the Customize dialog box.

Removing and Restoring Keyboard Shortcuts

Following are instructions for removing a keyboard shortcut from a command and getting a program's original keyboard shortcuts back. Many an Office 97 user has assigned keyboard shortcuts, then swiftly forgotten them and longed to have the originals back.

Removing a Keyboard Shortcut

To remove a preassigned keyboard shortcut from a command:

1. Right-click on a toolbar and choose Customize from the shortcut menu.

2. Click the Keyboard button to open the Customize Keyboard dialog box (see Figure 4-4).

3. Find the command to which the keyboard shortcut has been assigned. To do that, click a category in the Categories box, and then click the command in the Commands box. If you have trouble finding the command, read descriptions in the Description box at the bottom of the Customize Keyboard dialog box.

When you find the command, its preassigned keyboard shortcut appears in the Current keys box.

4. In the Current keys box, click the keyboard shortcut you want to remove.

5. Click the Remove button.

6. Click Close to close the Customize Keyboard dialog box.

7. Click Close to close the Customize dialog box.

Restoring a Program's Original Keyboard Shortcuts

If you make a mess of assigning keyboard shortcuts to commands, you can always get the program's original keyboard shortcuts back by following these steps:

1. Right-click on a toolbar and choose Customize from the shortcut menu.

2. In the Customize dialog box, click the Keyboard button. The Customize Keyboard dialog box appears (see Figure 4-4).

3. Click the Reset All button. The program asks if you really want to unravel all your hard work

4. Click the Yes button.

5. Click Close twice to close all the dialog boxes.

 WARNING: Think twice before you reset the shortcut key assignments. After you click the Reset All button, all assignments you made are lost and you have to start all over.

Using the Tools Menu's Options Commands

At the bottom of the Tools menu on all five Office 97 programs is the Options command. When you click the Options command, you see the Options dialog box, an elaborate dialog box for customizing various parts of the program. Figure 4-5 shows the Options dialog box in the Outlook program.

Commands in the Options dialog boxes are mentioned throughout this book. For the time being, all you need to know is that the Options dialog boxes present many

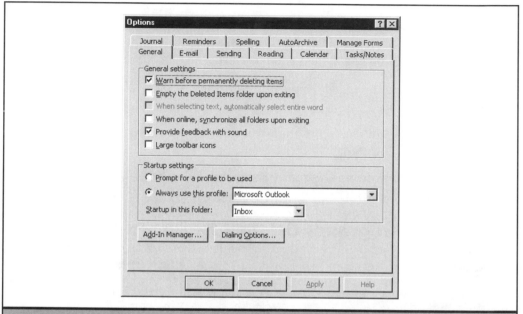

Figure 4-5.   *Each Office 97 program offers an Options dialog box for tweaking, customizing, and altering different features*

different ways to tell the programs how *you* want them to operate. Moreover, if you choose a command and find that it doesn't work the way you expected it to, it could be that someone fooled with an option in the Options dialog box. The moral: if you choose an option in an Options dialog box, make sure you know what you are doing.

The
Complete
Reference

Chapter 5

Sharing Information

One of the most useful aspects of the Microsoft Office 97 suite of programs—and, in fact, the reason it's even fair to call it a suite of programs—is that Office 97 makes it extremely easy to share information among its individual programs and among the people using Office. You can, for example, easily move an Excel worksheet range or chart to a Word document or a PowerPoint presentation. (In fact, this book assumes that this is the way you create tables and charts for Word and PowerPoint.) And you can move the text, clip art, and even drawing objects you create in one program—such as Word—to one of the other programs like PowerPoint or Excel.

Using OLE to Move and Share Information

OLE, an acronym for object linking and embedding, lets you share chunks of document files between programs—as long as the programs are OLE aware. What this means—and this is an important point—is that you can easily use information you create with one OLE-aware program with another OLE aware program.

 NOTE: *Many other popular programs are OLE aware too.*

Interestingly, OLE actually lets you share information in two distinct ways. You can simply make a copy of the information you want to share and then paste this copied information into the other document file. This is called *embedding*. Or, you can make a copy of the information you want to share, paste this information into the other document, *and* tell Windows that it should update the copy anytime the original information changes. This is called *linking*.

Understanding OLE Terminology

In both linking and embedding, two files are required: a source document file and a destination document file. The program in which you create the source document file is called the *server*, while the program in which you create the destination document file is called the *client*. If, for example, you embed a picture from a PowerPoint presentation into an Excel workbook, the PowerPoint presentation is the source document file, the PowerPoint program is the server, the Excel workbook is the destination document file, and the Excel program is the client.

The data that is embedded or linked is called an *object*, hence the term OLE. While an object is usually just a chunk of some document, an object can actually be just about anything: a file, text from a word processing program, a range of cells from a spreadsheet, a computer-drawn graphic image, a scanned photograph, a multimedia video clip—and the list goes on. The only real requirement is that the server program, as well as the client program, supports OLE.

When you embed, data created in the server program becomes a permanent part of the document file in the client program. As mentioned in the opening paragraphs of this section, even if the original data in the server document file should change, the data in the client document file would remain exactly the way it was when it was embedded.

When you link two files, however, the data itself never gets transferred to the destination document file—it remains in the source file in the server program. Instead of embedded data, the destination document file contains two other things: a marker indicating that the link to the source document file exists, and an address that tells the server where to find the linked data. As long as the link is maintained, any data changes in the server document file are reflected in the client document file.

Embedding and Linking Objects

The Office 97 programs provide two basic ways to embed and link objects: using the Copy and Paste Special commands and using the Insert menu's Object command. This section describes both methods, because they're useful in different situations.

Embedding Using Copy and Paste Special

To embed an object using the Copy and Paste Special commands, follow these steps:

1. Select data in the source file.

2. Copy the data to the Clipboard, using whatever commands the source file application provides for that purpose. (You can probably choose the Edit menu's Copy command or click the Copy tool on the Standard toolbar.)

3. Switch to the client program. Remember that this is the program that works with the destination document file. (You can do this by clicking on the program's Taskbar button, if the program is already running. Otherwise, use the Start menu to load the program.)

4. Choose the Edit menu's Paste Special command. The client program displays the Paste Special dialog box, as shown in Figure 5-1.

5. Make sure the Paste option button is enabled.

6. If necessary, select the first item in the As list.

7. Click OK.

To paste an object, select the first entry in this list box. The entry should describe what you're pasting as an object.

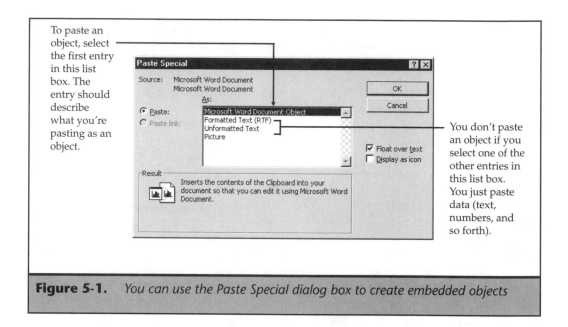

You don't paste an object if you select one of the other entries in this list box. You just paste data (text, numbers, and so forth).

Figure 5-1.   *You can use the Paste Special dialog box to create embedded objects*

Embedding Using the Insert Menu's Object Command

You can also use the Insert menu's Object command to embed an object. How you use this command, however, depends on whether the object you want to embed already exists. If the object doesn't already exist, you take the following steps:

1. With the client program active and the destination document file open, choose the Insert menu's Object command. Figure 5-2 shows Excel's Object dialog box.

2. If necessary, click the Create New tab to indicate that you want to create a new object.

3. Double-click the type of object you want to embed, and the appropriate program for creating the object opens.

4. Use the server program to create the new object.

5. After you create the new object using the server program, click away from the embedded document in the destination document to return to the client program.

Figure 5-3 shows a Word document with an Excel worksheet range embedded. Note that the Word document really uses the Excel worksheet range as a table.

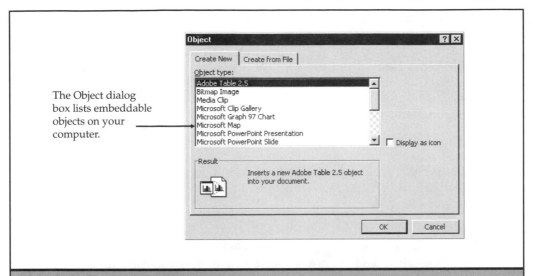

The Object dialog box lists embeddable objects on your computer.

Figure 5-2. *The Create New tab of Excel 97's Object dialog box, similar to the Object dialog boxes of Word 97, PowerPoint 97, and Access 97*

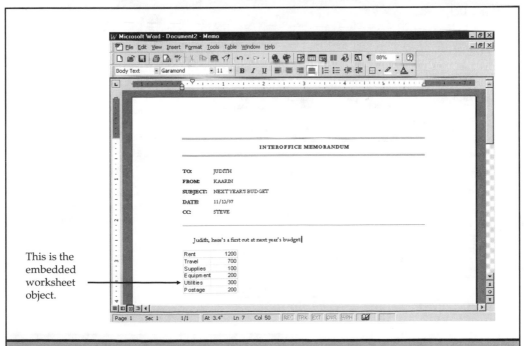

This is the embedded worksheet object.

Figure 5-3. *This Word document includes an embedded Excel worksheet range object*

EXAMPLES

LEARN BY EXAMPLE
You can open the example Word document shown in Figure 5-3, Figure 5-3 (a memo with next year's budget), *from the companion CD if you want to follow along with the discussion here. The example Excel workbook from which the worksheet range is copied is on the companion CD and is named* Figure 5-A (source file for budget memo). *The memo Word document without the embedded object is on the companion CD and is named* Figure 5-B (client file for budget memo).

If the object does exist, however, take the following steps to embed it:

1. With the client program active and the destination document file open, choose the Insert menu's Object command. Figure 5-4 shows Excel's Object dialog box again.

2. Click the Create from File tab.

3. Enter the complete path name for the file you want to link to in the File name text box. Or, if you don't know the complete path name, click the Browse command button and then use the Browse dialog box to locate and identify the file. The Browse dialog box works like the Open dialog box, which Office 97 programs display when you choose their File menu's Open command.

4. Click OK.

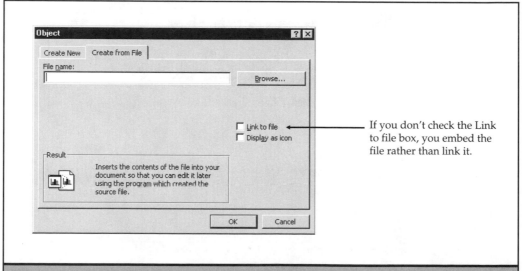

Figure 5-4. *The Create from File tab of Excel's Object dialog box, similar to the Object dialog boxes of Word, PowerPoint, and Access*

Editing Embedded Objects

If you ever need to edit an embedded object, just double-click it. When you do, the client program opens the server program, and then you use it to make your changes. The menus and toolbars for the server program replace those of the client program. This is called "editing in place." For example, if you wanted to edit the budget worksheet shown in Figure 5-3, you could double-click the object, make the necessary changes, and then click away from the embedded object in the destination document to simultaneously update the embedded object, close the server program, and return to the client program.

NOTE: In order to be able to edit the embedded object, of course, you must have the server program on your computer.

Linking Using Copy and Paste Special

To link an object using the Copy and Paste Special commands, follow these steps:

1. Select data in the source file.

2. Copy the data to the Clipboard, using whatever commands the source file application provides for that purpose. (You can probably choose the Edit menu's Copy command or click the Copy tool on the Standard toolbar.)

3. Switch to the client program. (You can probably do this by clicking on the program's Taskbar button.)

4. Choose the Edit menu's Paste Special command.

5. Enable the Paste link option button.

6. Select the list box entry that describes what you're pasting as an object. Figure 5-5 shows how I have selected to paste the link as a Microsoft Word Document Object, but the choices you will have in this box depend on what you have selected to paste.

7. Click OK.

Linking Using the Insert Menu's Object Command

You can also use the Insert menu's Object command to link an object. To use this approach, take the following steps:

1. With the client program active and the destination document file active, choose the Insert menu's Object command. Figure 5-6 shows PowerPoint's Object dialog box.

2. Click the Create from file option button.

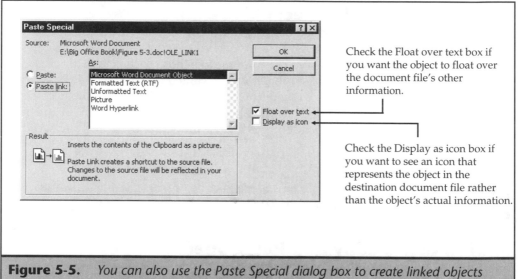

Check the Float over text box if you want the object to float over the document file's other information.

Check the Display as icon box if you want to see an icon that represents the object in the destination document file rather than the object's actual information.

Figure 5-5. *You can also use the Paste Special dialog box to create linked objects*

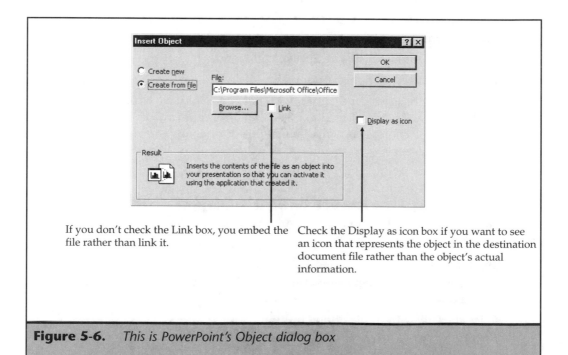

If you don't check the Link box, you embed the file rather than link it.

Check the Display as icon box if you want to see an icon that represents the object in the destination document file rather than the object's actual information.

Figure 5-6. *This is PowerPoint's Object dialog box*

3. Enter the complete path name for the file to which you want to link into the File name text box. Or, if you don't know the complete path name, click the Browse command button and then use the Browse dialog box to locate and identify the file. The Browse dialog box works like the Open dialog box, which Office programs display when you choose their File menu's Open command.

4. Click OK.

Figure 5-7 shows a PowerPoint presentation with a linked Excel chart.

NOTE: *To create a linked object, the file must already exist somewhere on your computer or, if you're connected to network, on the network.*

LEARN BY EXAMPLE

You can open the example PowerPoint presentation shown in Figure 5-7, Figure 5-7 (simple presentation), *from the companion CD if you want to follow along with the discussion here. The example Excel workbook from which the chart is copied is on the companion CD and is named* Figure 5-C (source file for budget chart). *The PowerPoint presentation without the embedded object is on the companion CD and is named* Figure 5-D (client file for budget presentation).

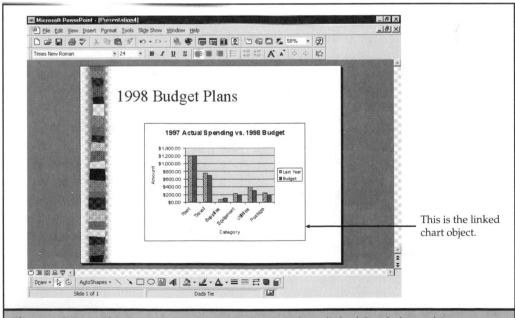

This is the linked chart object.

Figure 5-7.   *This PowerPoint presentation includes a linked Excel chart object*

Editing Linked Objects

If you ever need to edit a linked object, as is the case with embedded objects, you just double-click the object. When you do, the client program opens the server program, and then you use it to make your changes. For example, if you wanted to edit the chart object shown in Figure 5-7, you could double-click the object, make and save the necessary changes, close the server program, and then return to the client program. The linked object will be updated automatically.

 NOTE: *In order to be able to edit the linked object, of course, you must have the server program installed on your computer.*

Manual Links vs. Automatic Links

The links that connect linked objects to their source files can be either automatic or manual. An automatic link is updated automatically whenever the server document file changes. A manual link needs to be updated manually. While by default all links are automatic, if you have a good reason to change a link to manual status, you can do so.

To change the status of a link, or to update a manual link, choose the Edit menu's Links command. When you do this, the Office program displays the Links dialog box, which lists all the active links in the current document file and shows the status of each. To change a link to manual, select the Manual option. To update a manual link, click Update Now. By clicking the Open Source command button, you can open the source document file in the client program. When you are finished, click the Close button.

Importing and Exporting Document Files

In most cases, you'll have no problem importing and exporting document files among Word, Excel, PowerPoint, Access, and equivalent programs such as WordPerfect and Lotus 1-2-3. You simply use the File menu's Open and Save As commands. (You use the File menu's Open command to import document files and the File menu's Save As command to export document files.)

Using the Open Command

To import a document file created by another equivalent program, follow these steps:

1. Choose the File menu's Open command to display the Open dialog box, as shown in Figure 5-8.

INTRODUCING OFFICE

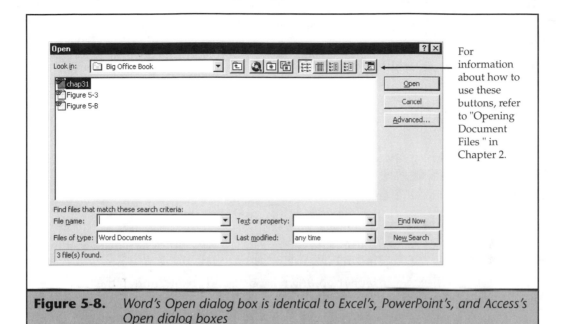

For information about how to use these buttons, refer to "Opening Document Files " in Chapter 2.

Figure 5-8.   *Word's Open dialog box is identical to Excel's, PowerPoint's, and Access's Open dialog boxes*

2. When the Office program displays the Open dialog box, select the appropriate file type or extension from the Files of type drop-down list box.

3. Use the Look in drop-down list box to identify the folder in which you've stored the document file.

4. When you see the document file that you want to import, double-click it.

NOTE: If you attempt to import a document file into Excel and Excel doesn't recognize or can't easily translate the file's information, Excel may start an Import Wizard, which will ask you questions about the file you want to import.

As a general rule, Excel has no trouble importing document files from common spreadsheet programs and Word has no trouble importing document files from common word processor programs. You can import Lotus 1-2-3 and Quattro Pro spreadsheets into Excel, for example. And you can import WordPerfect and Wordstar documents into Word. Import operations become trickier when you work with Access or PowerPoint, but it's still usually possible to import document files from other programs. If the Office program does not directly support the format of the file that you want to import, you may need to use the other (source) program to save the document file in a common file format such as the RTF format for a word processor file or the tab-delimited file for a spreadsheet.

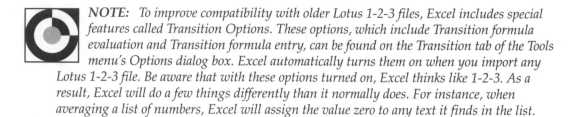

NOTE: *To improve compatibility with older Lotus 1-2-3 files, Excel includes special features called Transition Options. These options, which include Transition formula evaluation and Transition formula entry, can be found on the Transition tab of the Tools menu's Options dialog box. Excel automatically turns them on when you import any Lotus 1-2-3 file. Be aware that with these options turned on, Excel thinks like 1-2-3. As a result, Excel will do a few things differently than it normally does. For instance, when averaging a list of numbers, Excel will assign the value zero to any text it finds in the list. Needless to say, this can drastically change the result.*

Using the Save As Command

To export a document file created by an Office 97 program, follow these steps:

1. Open the document you want to export.

2. Choose the File menu's Save As command. The Office program displays the Save As dialog box shown in Figure 5-9.

3. Activate the Save as type drop-down list box, and scroll through the list of file types to find the one you want.

4. Use the Save in drop-down list box to specify in which folder you want to save the file.

5. In the File name text box, enter the name under which you want to save the file.

6. Click Save.

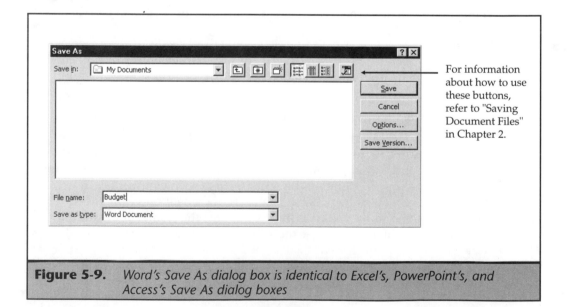

Figure 5-9.   *Word's Save As dialog box is identical to Excel's, PowerPoint's, and Access's Save As dialog boxes*

Sharing Document Files with the Apple Macintosh

The programs that make up Office 97 are highly compatible with their cousin programs that make up Office for the Macintosh suite of programs. As a result, you can easily transfer Office document files from PCs to Macintosh computers by saving a document file onto a floppy disk and then reading this floppy disk with the Macintosh. You just need to be sure to specify the file format as one that is acceptable to the Mac version of the Office program you're using. (You specify the file format using the Save as type drop-down list box, which appears on the Save As dialog box.)

> **NOTE:** *Newer Mac floppy disk drives generally read PC-formatted floppy drives, and the Macintosh operating system includes utilities for automatically converting PC-format files to Macintosh-format files.*

You should be able to move document files from a Macintosh to a PC by following the same steps in reverse order. In other words, you use the Mac to save a file to a floppy disk and then read this floppy disk using a PC. Be sure, however, to use a floppy disk that's been formatted by a PC, because the PC isn't smart enough to read disks that have been formatted by a Mac.

> **WARNING:** *The Mac version of Office doesn't have all of the features that the newest PC version of Office does. For this reason, you may lose document file information if you move a document file from the PC to the Macintosh.*

Working with Binder

Microsoft Office comes with a special program, called Binder, that lets you organize related Office document files so they appear to be one document. Once you've created a binder, you can open and print all of the documents as a group, and add page numbering and headers and footers that will apply to all of the documents in the binder. While Binder may sound complicated, it's really not—especially if you understand how OLE works.

Creating a Binder

To create a new binder, start the Microsoft Binder program. You start Binder in the same way that you start other programs. (It's probably listed on the Programs menu right after Microsoft Access and just before Microsoft Excel.) Binder, like Word and Excel, creates a blank, or empty, binder document when you start it, as shown in Figure 5-10.

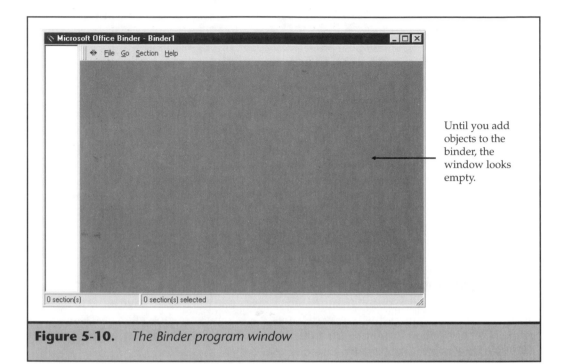

Until you add objects to the binder, the window looks empty.

Figure 5-10. *The Binder program window*

Adding Sections

You build a binder by adding sections. A section is just an Office document. (To be precise, Binder should actually call these documents *objects*, as described earlier in the chapter in the section, "Understanding OLE Terminology.")

To add a section by creating a new, blank Word document, Excel workbook, or PowerPoint presentation, follow these steps:

1. Choose the Section menu's Add command. Binder displays the Add Section dialog box, shown in Figure 5-11.

2. Click the dialog box tab that represents the category of Office template that you want to use as the basis for creating a new document file. If you don't know which category you want to use, click the General tab.

3. Double-click the template that you want to use as the model for creating a new document file. When you do, Binder adds a new section to the binder, as shown in Figure 5-12.

INTRODUCING OFFICE

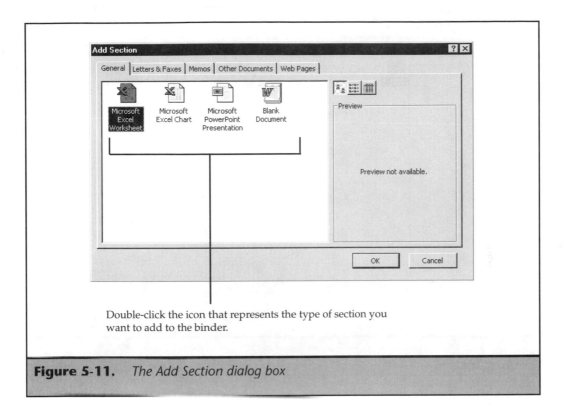

Double-click the icon that represents the type of section you
want to add to the binder.

Figure 5-11.   *The Add Section dialog box*

    TIP: *To delete a section, click its icon in the section pane and then press the* DELETE *key.*

To add a section using a document file that already exists, follow these steps:

1. Choose the Section menu's Add from File command to display the Add from File dialog box shown in Figure 5-13.

2. Use the Look in drop-down list box to select the folder in which you've stored the Office document file.

3. Double-click the document file you want to add to the binder.

Figure 5-14 shows an example binder document that includes four sections: a Word document section, an Excel worksheet section, an Excel chart section, and a PowerPoint presentation.

The section pane contains icons that represent the sections in a binder.

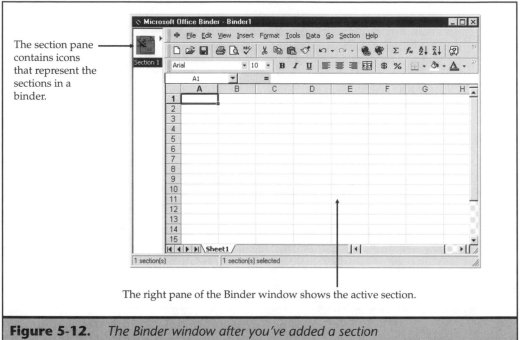

The right pane of the Binder window shows the active section.

Figure 5-12. *The Binder window after you've added a section*

This list box shows the Office document files in the active folder.

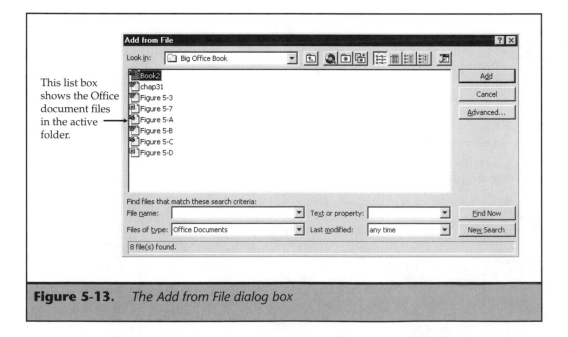

Figure 5-13. *The Add from File dialog box*

To move to a section, click its icon in the Section pane.

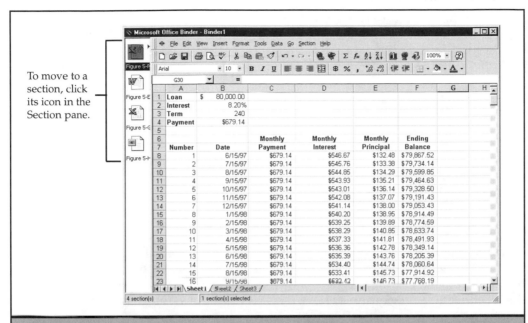

Figure 5-14. *The Binder window showing a binder with several sections*

LEARN BY EXAMPLE

EXAMPLES

You can open the example binder shown in Figure 5-14, Figure 5-14 (simple binder), from the companion CD if you want to follow along with the discussion here. The example Word document used for the binder's Word section is on the companion CD and is named Figure 5-E (Word section). *The example Excel workbook used for the binder's Excel workbook section is on the companion CD and is named* Figure 5-F (Excel workbook section). *The example Excel chart used for the binder's Excel chart section is on the companion CD and is named* Figure 5-G (Excel chart section). *Finally, the PowerPoint presentation used for the binder's PowerPoint presentation section is on the companion CD and is named* Figure 5-H (PowerPoint section).

Working with Sections

To work with a section, you simply click its icon in the Section pane. When you do this, Binder adds the server program's menus and toolbars to the Binder window. You can then work with the section the exact same way you work with a regular document file. For example, if you indicate you want to work with a Word section, you work with that section the same way you work with a regular Word document file. If you indicate you want to work with an Excel workbook section, you work with that section the same way you do with a regular Excel workbook.

TIP: Binder names your sections using labels such as "Section 1" and "Section 2" if you add them to the binder as blank documents. If you add a section using an existing file, the file name will be used as the section label. You can rename a section, however, by clicking its name in the Section pane and then typing the new name you want to use.

Printing Binders

You print binders by choosing the File menu's Print Binder command. When you choose this command, Binder displays the Print Binder dialog box, which looks and works very much like the Print dialog boxes used by other Office programs (see Figure 5-15). Unless you choose to print only the sections you've selected in the Section pane, Binder prints each section.

Saving and Opening Binders

You save and open binder documents in the same basic way that you save and open regular Office documents files. Use the File menu's Save Binder As command to save a binder document. Use the File menu's Open Binder command to open a binder document you've previously saved.

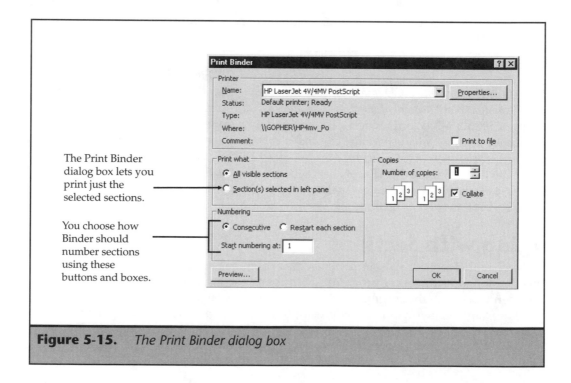

The Print Binder dialog box lets you print just the selected sections.

You choose how Binder should number sections using these buttons and boxes.

Figure 5-15. *The Print Binder dialog box*

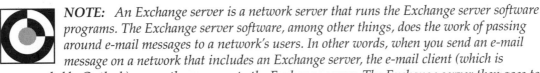

Sharing Document Files

These days it's quite likely that you will be using Word or Excel in a shared environment—on a network. Recognizing this feature of today's work environment, both Word and Excel provide special features that make it easy for you to share Word and Excel document files in work groups. What's more, Word, Excel, and PowerPoint all provide special commands you can use to easily e-mail documents to other network users (if the network includes an Exchange server) or to somebody with an Internet mail address if your computer connects to an Internet mail server.

NOTE: An Exchange server is a network server that runs the Exchange server software programs. The Exchange server software, among other things, does the work of passing around e-mail messages to a network's users. In other words, when you send an e-mail message on a network that includes an Exchange server, the e-mail client (which is probably Outlook) passes the message to the Exchange server. The Exchange server then goes to the work of delivering the message to the recipient's mailbox. An Internet mail server works the same basic way. Whenever someone sends a message, the message actually gets sent to the mail server. The mail server then goes to work—typically with the help of other Internet mail servers—delivering the message to the recipient's mailbox.

Sharing Document Files in a Workgroup

Both Word 97 and Excel 97 include features that make it possible to share a document file with other users. For example, Word (with the help of Windows) keeps track of the fact that more than one person has opened a Word document. And Word also provides tools for reviewing and merging the changes that multiple authors or editors make to the same document. Excel (also with the help of Windows) includes similar functionality.

WARNING: You need to be very careful when sharing documents. It's surprisingly easy to corrupt a document when you share it. If you want to try Word's and Excel's document sharing capability, consider first experimenting with the functionality using sample documents.

Sharing Word Documents

You save and open a shared Word document in the same manner that you save and open any Word document with one difference: you must save it to a shared drive, which is simply a drive accessible to other members of your workgroup. (Probably this means the drive is a network drive on a network file server, but the drive also could be a shared local drive on a workgroup member's desktop computer.)

NOTE: *The term "workgroup" simply refers to a group of people who work together. It isn't, in this context, a technical term.*

When you share a Word document, the first user to open the document opens the original document. Subsequent users open copies of the document and *not* the original document. To alert people that they're working with a copy of a document file, Word displays a message box before it creates and opens the copy:

To later successfully incorporate everyone's changes into the original document, you need to do three things. First, before making any changes to the document, everyone working with a copy of the document must turn on Word's Track Changes feature. People can do this by choosing the Tools menu's Track Changes command and then the Track Changes submenu's Highlight Changes command. When Word displays the Highlight Changes dialog box, check the Track changes while editing box shown here, and then click OK.

The second thing that people working with the original document and copies of the document must do is save multiple copies of the same document. Specifically, this means the person working with the original document can save the document using its original name, but everyone working with a copy of the document must save the document using a new document name. *This is critical.* If a user with a document copy saves the copy using the original document name, he or she may replace the original document with the copy of the document, which means that it's possible the most recent set of changes to the original document will be lost.

The final thing that somebody needs to do when multiple users share a Word document is merge the document changes. To do this, you (or someone else) needs to open the original document, choose the Tools menu's Merge Documents command, and then use the Select File to Merge Into Current Document dialog box to select the document copy with the changes you want to fold into the open document:

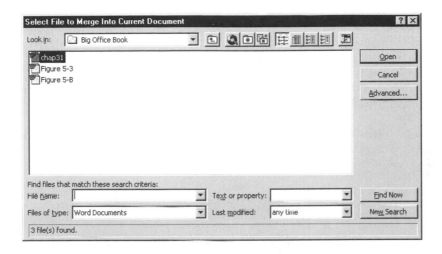

As Word adds changes from the document copy to the original document, it uses revision marks to show you where material is added or edited. You (or someone else) will later need to review these changes, resolve any conflicts, and then of course save the original document again.

NOTE: For more information about working with Word's revision marks feature and about merging documents, refer to Chapter 7.

Saving and Opening Shared Workbooks with Excel

You can also save and open an Excel workbook that you want to share just like any other workbook. As is the case with Word documents, predictably, you must store the workbook on a shared drive so other workgroup members have access to the workbook.

CREATING A SHARED WORKBOOK   As with a shared Word document, you can tell Excel that you want to share a workbook by choosing the Tools menu's Track Changes command, choosing the Track Changes submenu's Highlight Changes command, and then by checking the Track changes while editing box.

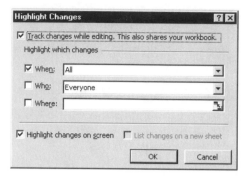

To make a file available for sharing you can also choose the Tool menu's Share Workbook command. Then, when Excel displays the Share Workbook dialog box check the Allow changes box:

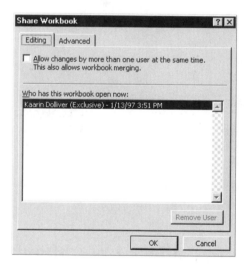

NOTE: *You can also use the Tools menu's Share Workbook command to find out who else is working with a shared workbook besides you. When you choose the command, Excel displays a list of all current users, giving the date and time that each opened the file.*

When you indicate you want to track changes or share a workbook, Excel asks your permission to save the file again to set it up as a shared workbook. After Excel does this, it indicates that your file is now shared by inserting the word "Shared" in brackets in the Title bar after the filename.

WORKING WITH A SHARED WORKBOOK   In many respects, working with a shared workbook is the same as working with an ordinary workbook. You can enter and edit numbers and text, and you can move data around within the workbook using the usual methods. You can also insert new rows and columns.

 NOTE: You can't perform all editing operations in a shared workbook, however. For a lengthy list of what you can't do in shared workbooks, choose the Help menu's Contents and Index command, click the Index tab, enter the phrase "shared workbooks, limitations" into the text box, and press ENTER.

To see the changes that other people are making to a shared workbook, save the workbook. When you do this, Excel describes the changes people have made and prompts you to choose which changes you want to make and to resolve conflicts.

You can also use the Tools menu's Merge Workbooks command to fold the changes of other users into the original copy of the Excel workbook. This command works in the same basic way as the Merge Documents command described earlier in "Sharing Word Documents."

Using the File Menu's Send To Commands

The File menu's Send To submenu provides commands you can use for sharing document files over a network, using e-mail to move document files, and even faxing Word documents. When you choose this command, the Office program displays a submenu of commands you can use for distributing a document file:

E-mailing a Document

If you choose the Send To submenu's Mail Recipient command, for example, the Office program starts your e-mail client (probably Outlook if you're using Office), creates a new e-mail message item, and attaches the document. to the message. To complete the e-mail message item, you identify the recipient and add any message text, and then click the Send button.

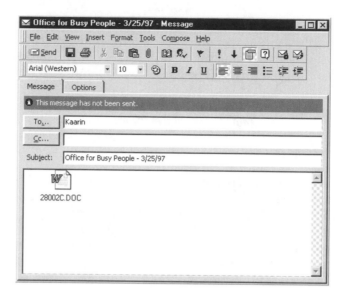

 NOTE: *For more information about creating e-mail messages with Outlook, refer to Chapter 23.*

Using the Send To Submenu's Routing Recipient Command

If your computer connects to a network that includes an Exchange server or any MAPI (Message Application Programming Interface)–compatible or VIM (Vendor Independent Messaging)–compatible mail system, you can use the Routing Recipient command on the Send To submenu. The Send To submenu's Routing Recipient command gives you more control over how your e-mail message is sent. It's especially useful for sending a message and document file to several members of a workgroup when you want to stay posted on who has received your message and who has replied. When you choose the Send To submenu's Routing Recipient command, the Office program displays the Routing Slip dialog box:

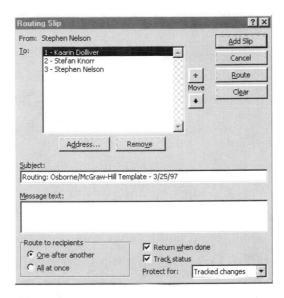

To use the Routing Slip dialog box, use the Address button to add the names of recipients to the To list box. Next, use the Subject and Message text boxes to provide the message subject and text you want to use for the routing slip. Once you click OK, the Office program sends the message—which includes both the document file and a routing slip—to the Exchange server. The Exchange server then sends the message to each of the recipients you identified.

 NOTE: *If you select the One after another option, the Office program waits for a reply from the first person on your address list (in the To box) before sending your message to the next recipient.*

To receive a notification each time the document file gets sent to a new recipient, select the Track status option. Select the Return when done option to route the document file back to you after all the recipients have replied.

Using the Send To Submenu's Exchange Folder Command

If you have Microsoft Exchange installed on your computer, you can use the Exchange Folder command on the Send To submenu. This command lets you post, or store, the open document in an Exchange folder. When you choose the command, the Office program displays the Send To Exchange Folder dialog box, which lets you choose the Exchange folder you want to store the document in:

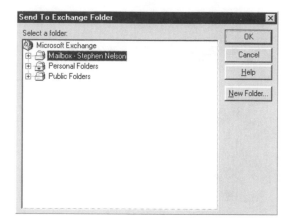

Using the Send To Submenu's Fax Recipient Command

If you're working with Word, the Send To submenu's Fax Recipient command lets you fax the open document to some recipient. When you choose this command, the Word starts the Fax Wizard. It asks you a series of questions about the fax you want to send, creates a fax cover letter (if you say you want this), and then sends the fax. To use the Fax Recipient command, you need to have a fax modem installed and working in your desktop computer.

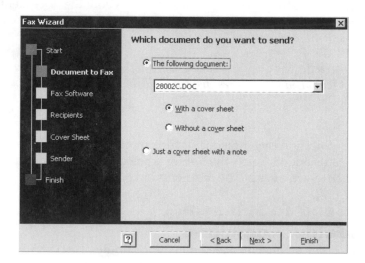

NOTE: *Some of the Office programs add other commands to the Send To submenu. For example, Word also adds a Microsoft PowerPoint command to the Send To submenu so you can export the open Word document to PowerPoint. Not to be outdone, PowerPoint adds a Microsoft Word command to the Send To submenu so you can export the open PowerPoint presentation to Word. PowerPoint also adds a Genigraphics command to the Send To submenu, which you can use to send a PowerPoint presentation to the Genigraphics service bureau so they'll create 35mm slides based on your presentation.*

Part II

Word

The Complete Reference

Office 97

Chapter 6

Laying Out a Document

139

Appearances count in word processing. To make a good impression on readers, a well-written, well-thought-out, and to-the-point Word 97 document should also look good on the page. This chapter, the first in Part II, explains how to lay out documents so that readers know that they are looking at a document that was created by someone who really knows word processing.

This chapter explains how to hyphenate text, how to control where one page ends and another begins, and how to handle tricky punctuation such as em and en dashes. It describes how to indent text and create hanging indents and hanging headings, as well as how to create section breaks for drastic layout changes. This chapter also explains how to determine how much empty space appears between lines and between paragraphs. It shows you how to number a document's pages and include headers and footers in documents.

Oscar Wilde said, "Appearances are everything." In word processing, how a page looks isn't necessarily everything, but it counts for a lot.

Laying Out the Text

In this part of the chapter, you learn how to tell Word 97 exactly where and how text should fall on the page. These pages explain how to hyphenate text, break sentences and pages in the middle, and keep paragraphs together on a single page. This part of the chapter also tells how to handle unusual punctuation, including dashes, ellipses, and quotation marks. It also tells how to align text by centering, justifying, right-aligning, or left-aligning it.

Hyphenating Text

One of the first things you should know about hyphenating text is that it may not be necessary. Text that hasn't been hyphenated is easier to read. Consider the pages of this book, for example. To make reading easier, words in this book aren't usually hyphenated on the right margin. In my opinion, it is only necessary to hyphenate text in formal documents, when you need to squeeze text into columns, and when text is justified.

Word 97 offers several different ways to hyphenate text. You can hyphenate a single word yourself by entering an optional hyphen, tell Word 97 to hyphenate the words automatically, review words one at a time and tell Word 97 where to hyphenate them, and even tell Word 97 not to hyphenate a word or a paragraph. Read on for the glorious details.

"Comparing the Hyphenation Techniques" explains all the different ways to hyphenate words, paragraphs, and documents. By the way, a hyphen is different from an em dash—a punctuation mark that is used to show an abrupt change of thought. It is also different from an en dash, a smaller dash that is used to show inclusive numbers or time periods. See "Handling Dashes and Quotation Marks" later in this chapter to learn how to use dashes correctly.

TIP: *You can tell Word 97 to hyphenate words as you enter them (by telling the program to hyphenate the document automatically), but doing so is a distraction. It hurts the eyes and makes the program run more slowly. I recommend typing the words first and then hyphenating them.*

Comparing the Hyphenation Techniques

Word 97 offers no less than four ways to hyphenate (or not hyphenate) a word, paragraph, or document. Which technique works best depends on what you are trying to accomplish in Word 97:

- *Automatic hyphenation* With this technique, Word 97 hyphenates the entire document very quickly. Unfortunately, you can't tell Word 97 *not* to hyphenate a single part of a document automatically. For example, you can't select a paragraph or two and hyphenate them automatically. Instead, Word 97 hyphenates the entire document. You can, however, remove hyphens that were made automatically very quickly.

- *Manual hyphenation* With this technique, you review each place where Word 97 suggests putting a hyphen, and you say *yes* or *no* to each suggestion. It takes longer to go this route than it does to hyphenate a document automatically, and if you change your mind about hyphens that were inserted manually, you have to delete them one at a time with the BACKSPACE or DELETE key. On the other hand, you get to choose where hyphens fall and you can also hyphenate part of a document. All you have to do is select the part of the document that you want to hyphenate first.

- *Optional hyphens* If a word is crying out to be hyphenated, you can insert a manual hyphen by pressing CTRL+- (hyphen) instead of going to the trouble of giving a hyphenation command.

- *Keeping paragraphs from being hyphenated* You can prevent a paragraph from being hyphenated by choosing the Format menu Paragraph command, clicking the Line and Page Breaks tab in the Paragraph dialog box, and clicking the Don't hyphenate check box.

- *Keeping hyphenated words from breaking across lines* Some words, such as *e-mail* and *X-Men*, should not be broken across two different lines. To keep these words from being broken, press CTRL+SHIFT+- (hyphen) instead of entering a plain hyphen.

Hyphenating Text in a Document

Word 97 offers two ways to hyphenate an entire document or many paragraphs at once—the automatic way and the manual way. In my experience, the best way to hyphenate an entire document is to hyphenate it automatically, review the paragraphs to see how Word 97 hyphenated them, and then manually hyphenate the paragraphs you think Word 97 didn't do a good job on. As the sidebar on the preceding page points out, you cannot automatically hyphenate a handful of paragraphs. When you opt for the automatic hyphenation technique, you have to go the whole hog and hyphenate the entire document.

Automatic Hyphenation

To hyphenate a document automatically:

1. Put the cursor anywhere in the document. All the text is hyphenated when you hyphenate automatically.

2. Choose Hyphenation from the Tools menu Language submenu. You see the Hyphenation dialog box shown in Figure 6-1.

3. Click the Automatically hyphenate document check box.

4. Click Hyphenate words in CAPS to remove the check mark if you want words in capital letters *not* to be hyphenated.

5. If you want, make an entry in the Hyphenation zone box to say how large the hyphenation zone should be. Word 97 tries to break words that cross

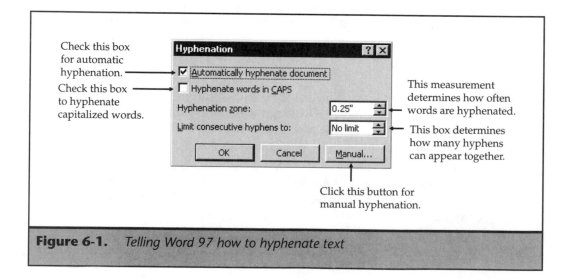

Figure 6-1. *Telling Word 97 how to hyphenate text*

into the hyphenation zone. With a large hyphenation zone, more words are hyphenated, but more white space appears between words. With a small hyphenation zone, fewer words are hyphenated but less white space appears between words. Figure 6-2 shows a paragraph that hasn't been hyphenated, the same paragraph with the hyphenation zone set to .2, and the paragraph yet again with the hyphenation zone set to .5.

TIP: *Small hyphenation zones work better with justified text. With text that hasn't been justified (when it is "ragged right"), use a large hyphenation zone.*

6. Make an entry in the Limit consecutive hyphens to box if you want no more than a certain number of hyphens to appear one after the other on the right side of a paragraph. In book publishing, the rule is to never allow more than two hyphens to appear together. In magazine publishing, the sky is the limit when it comes to how many hyphens can appear together.

7. Click OK in the Hyphenation dialog box.

EXAMPLES

LEARN BY EXAMPLE

If you care to experiment with hyphenating, open the Figure 6-2 (Hyphenation) *file on the companion CD.*

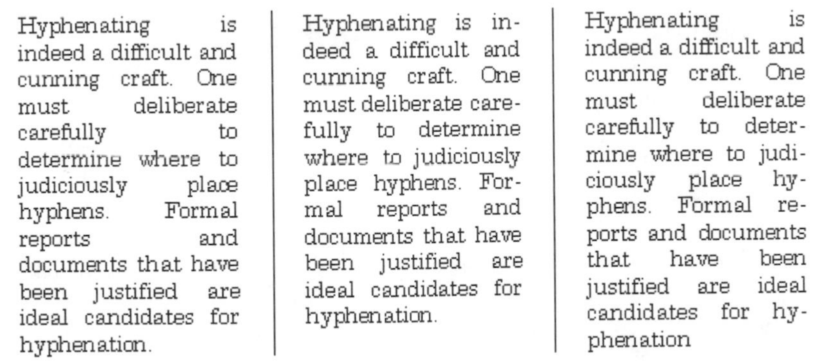

Hyphenating is indeed a difficult and cunning craft. One must deliberate carefully to determine where to judiciously place hyphens. Formal reports and documents that have been justified are ideal candidates for hyphenation.

Hyphenating is indeed a difficult and cunning craft. One must deliberate carefully to determine where to judiciously place hyphens. Formal reports and documents that have been justified are ideal candidates for hyphenation.

Hyphenating is indeed a difficult and cunning craft. One must deliberate carefully to determine where to judiciously place hyphens. Formal reports and documents that have been justified are ideal candidates for hyphenation

Figure 6-2. *Comparing hypenation settings: no hyphens (left); the hyphenation zone at .2 (middle); and the hyphenation zone at .5 (right)*

Hyphenating Text Manually

Follow these steps to review each hyphen that Word 97 proposes to enter as it hyphenates a document:

1. Place the cursor where you want to start hyphenating. To hyphenate part of a document, select it.

2. Choose Hyphenation from the Tools menu Language submenu. You see the Hyphenation dialog box (see Figure 6-1).

3. Follow steps 4 through 6 in the previous set of instructions to tell Word 97 how to hyphenate words that are in capital letters, how often words are to be hyphenated, and how many hyphens can appear consecutively.

4. Click the Manual button. You see the Manual Hyphenation dialog box. The cursor blinks at the place where Word 97 suggests putting a hyphen:

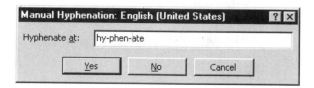

5. Click Yes or No to accept or reject the suggestion.

6. Keep clicking Yes or No until Word 97 tells you that it has finished hyphenating the document or the paragraphs you selected.

7. Click OK.

Optional Hyphens for Fixing Line Breaks

Rather than go to all the trouble of hyphenating an entire document or section of a document, you can simply insert an optional hyphen to keep lines from straying too far into the right margin or too far toward the right side of a column. An optional hyphen breaks the words. To insert an optional hyphen, press CTRL+- (hyphen).

The following illustration shows two identical sentences. In the sentence on the right, I pressed CTRL+- after *tintinnab* to insert an optional hyphen and make the line break. Now the three lines look better on the page. If I entered another word at the start of the sentence, *tintinnabulation* would move to the following line and the optional hyphen would disappear.

As he walked, he heard the tintinnabulation of the bells, which rang the hour, and he knew his time was up at last.	As he walked, he heard the tintinnab-ulation of the bells, which rang the hour, and he knew his time was up at last.

WARNING: *Whatever you do, don't enter a plain hyphen to solve a line-break problem. Your hyphen will remain in the text, even if half the words get pushed to the next line. Optional hyphens, on the other hand, disappear when they aren't breaking words in half on the right margin.*

Keeping Compound Words from Breaking

Contrary to breaking lines with hyphens, sometimes it is better for a line not to break over a hyphenated word. Consider the hyphens in the following sentence. When Word 97 encountered the hyphens in these compound words—*X-Men, G-Men,* and *e-mail*—it broke the lines where the hyphens appeared.

> If what you say about my heroes the X-
> men is true, and they were nixed by the G-
> Men, then you had better send me an e-
> mail message to say why.

But in cases like these, Word 97 should not have broken the lines at the hyphens. To keep words like these from breaking at the end of a line, press CTRL+SHIFT+- (hyphen) instead of entering a hyphen when you type the word.

Removing the Hyphens from Text

Unfortunately, the only way to remove hyphens from text that has been hyphenated manually is to remove the hyphens one by one by pressing the BACKSPACE or DELETE key. What a drag! On the other hand, removing hyphens that were put in automatically is quite simple:

1. Put the cursor anywhere in the document.
2. Choose Hyphenation from the Tools menu Hyphenation submenu. The Hyphenation dialog box appears (see Figure 6-1).
3. Click to remove the check mark from the Automatically hyphenate document check box.
4. Click OK.

Keeping Paragraphs from Being Hyphenated

Besides the myriad other ways to handle hyphens, Word 97 offers one more hyphenation tidbit—a way to keep paragraphs from being hyphenated. This option is chiefly for use with styles, but you can also use it to tag individual paragraphs to keep them from being hyphenated. After you've marked the paragraphs that you don't want to be hyphenated, you can run a quick and dirty automatic hyphenation over the entire document and be done with it.

To keep a paragraph from being hyphenated:

1. Either click in the paragraph or select the paragraphs that are not to be hyphenated.
2. Choose the Format menu Paragraph command.
3. Click the Line and Page Breaks tab. It is shown in Figure 6-3.
4. Click the Don't hyphenate check box.
5. Click OK.

 WARNING: If you can't hyphenate a paragraph, it is probably because someone unintentionally checked the Don't hyphenate check box.

Controlling Where Text Falls on the Page

This part of the chapter explains some tried-and-true techniques for making sure that text appears exactly where you want it to appear on the page. Following are instructions for breaking a sentence in the middle (without pressing the ENTER key),

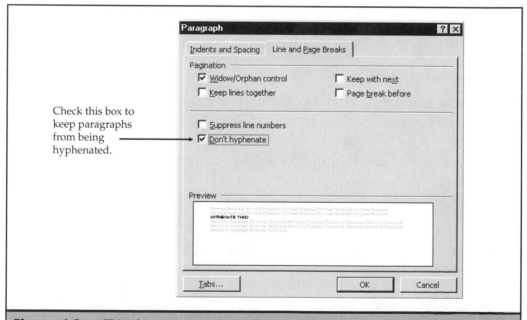

Figure 6-3. *This obscure option in the Paragraph dialog box keeps paragraphs from being hyphenated. Use it when you create styles*

ending a page before you've reached the bottom, making sure text appears at the top of a page, and keeping lines from being separated by a page break. You also learn to anchor a paragraph so it stays in one place and doesn't slide down the page if new text is placed above it.

Breaking a Sentence in the Middle

As you no doubt know, pressing the ENTER key starts a new paragraph and moves the cursor to the next line. But what if you want to move words to the following line without starting a new paragraph? In the following illustration, for example, the *We* at the end of the first line should probably move to the second line. That would plug the enormous hole that appears at the end of the second line. Typesetters and desktop publishers have to solve these kinds of problems all the time.

> "Let me be Frank," Frank said. "We are quite sad. We
> are thoroughly upset and unconditionally
> discombobulated. If the Los Angeles Dodgers dare to
> move back to Brooklyn, we will go berserk. Berserk I
> tell you!"

To move text to the following line without creating a new paragraph, press SHIFT+ENTER. For the following illustration, I placed the cursor before the *W* in *We* and pressed SHIFT+ENTER. Notice how the second line is filled up. Now the document is easier to read.

> "Let me be Frank," Frank said. "We are quite sad.
> We are thoroughly upset and unconditionally
> discombobulated. If the Los Angeles Dodgers dare to
> move back to Brooklyn, we will go berserk. Berserk I
> tell you!"

> *WARNING: Unless you click the Show/Hide button, it is impossible to tell where a line was broken by pressing SHIFT+ENTER. If you find yourself fiddling with text and can't understand why a line has moved down the page, click the Show/Hide button and look for the leftward-pointing arrow symbol. That symbol means that you or someone else pressed SHIFT+ENTER.*

Breaking a Page in the Middle

Word 97 gives you a new page to write on when you fill up one page. But what if you want to start a new page right away? In that case, press CTRL+ENTER. In Page Layout view, you see the top of the new page you created. In Normal view, the words "Page Break" and a dotted line appear across the screen:

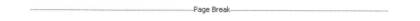

To remove a page break, switch to Normal view, click on the words *Page Break*, and press the DELETE key.

Incidentally, entering a page break is also the only way to make sure that text—a heading, for example—appears at the top of a page. Enter a page break before a heading if you want it always to be at the top of the page where everyone can see it.

Making Sure a Title or Heading Appears at the Top of a Page

To make sure that a chapter title or heading appears at the top of a page:

1. Click in the chapter title or heading that you want to appear at the top.

2. Choose the Format menu Paragraph command.

3. In the Paragraph dialog box, click the Line and Page Breaks tab (see Figure 6-3).

4. Click the Page break before check box.

5. Click OK.

Keeping Lines Together on the Page

When the last line on the page is a heading, you have a problem. Readers expect text to fall directly beneath a heading. However, when you are working on a long document, sometimes headings get pushed to the bottom of the page. To solve this problem, Word 97 offers two commands in the Paragraph dialog box for keeping lines of text together:

■ *Keep lines together* Keeps a paragraph from breaking across pages.

■ *Keep with next* Keeps a paragraph or several paragraphs and the paragraph that follows from breaking across pages.

 WARNING: The commands for keeping text on the same page are chiefly for use with styles. Sometimes Word 97 has to break a page early to make paragraphs and text stay together. As a result, empty, forlorn white space may appear at the bottom of pages.

To keep a heading and the paragraphs that follow it, two paragraphs, several lines, or a graphic and its caption from breaking across a page, do the following:

1. Select the stuff you want to keep on the same page. To keep paragraphs together, either place the cursor in the paragraph that you want to tie to the following paragraph, or select all the paragraphs to be kept together except the last one.

2. Choose the Format menu Paragraph command.

3. Click the Line and Page Breaks tab. It is shown in Figure 6-4.

4. Under Pagination, click a check box:

  ■ *Keep lines together*   Keeps the lines you selected from being broken across two pages.

  ■ *Keep with next*   Ties the paragraph or paragraphs to the paragraph that follows so that they all stay on the same page.

5. Click OK.

 NOTE: Word 97 offers a special command for keeping captions on the same page as the figures, charts, graphs, or whatnot that they describe. See "Captions for Figures, Graphs, Tables, and What All" in Chapter 10.

Preventing Widows and Orphans

On the Line and Page Breaks tab of the Paragraph dialog box (see Figure 6-4) is a check box called Widow/Orphan control. This check box is selected by default, and for no reason whatever should it be unselected.

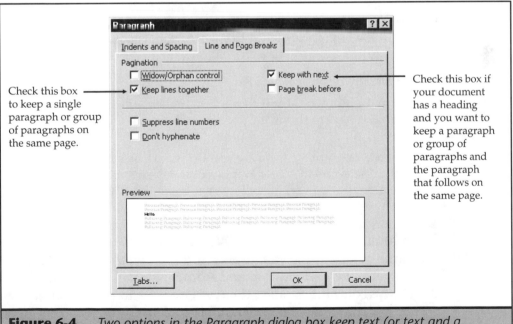

Figure 6-4.   *Two options in the Paragraph dialog box keep text (or text and a graphic) from breaking across two pages*

In typesetting terminology, a *widow* is the last line of a paragraph that appears at the top of a page. An *orphan* is the first line of a paragraph that appears at the bottom of a page. In the typesetting biz, widows and orphans are thought to be eyesores, but you can prevent orphans from appearing in your documents by never unchecking the Window/Orphan control check box.

Anchoring a Paragraph So It Stays in One Place

Suppose you are working on a company newsletter, and in the middle of the newsletter is an important announcement that has to stay smack-dab where it is. In other words, no matter how much company news gets inserted at the start of the newsletter, the announcement has to stay right in the middle of the page.

To keep a paragraph or graphic in one place, you can *anchor* it. After you drop anchor, text flows around the paragraph or graphic, and the paragraph or graphic never moves, no matter how many words or sentences you insert above it in the document.

 TIP: *To anchor text, put it in a text box first. See "Text Boxes for Announcements and Headings" at the start of Chapter 9 if you need instructions for doing so.*

To anchor text or a graphic, you start by telling Word 97 that you want to anchor it, and then you drag the text or graphic to the place where you want it to remain on the page. Follow these steps to anchor text or a graphic:

1. If you're not already there, switch to Page Layout view.

2. Click the Zoom drop-down list and choose 50%. When you are anchoring text or a graphic, it pays to shrink the document down so you can see most of the page.

3. Select the text box or graphic (if you are anchoring text, be sure to put it in a text box first). To select a text box or graphic, click inside it. Square selection handles appear on the corners and sides, as shown in this illustration:

> **The Annual Company Tug-of-War will take place on Friday afternoon at 4:30. This year, Sales and Marketing will do battle with Accounting and Administration.**
> **As always, only the winning team will be able to participate in the company's 401(k) plan.**

WORD

4. Choose the Format menu Picture command if you are anchoring a graphic or the Format menu Text Box command if you are anchoring a text box. Either the Format Text Box or the Format Picture dialog box appears.

5. Click the Position tab. Figure 6-5 shows the Position tab of the Format Text Box dialog box. The options in the Format Picture dialog box are the same.

6. Click the Lock anchor check box.

7. Click the Move object with text check box to remove the check mark. Notice that the Vertical From setting has changed to Page.

8. Choose Page from the Horizontal From drop-down menu.

 TIP: *Don't concern yourself with the Horizontal and Vertical settings on the Position tab. When you return to the document, you drag the text box or graphic to establish its horizontal and vertical position.*

9. Click OK to close the dialog box and return to the document.

 TIP: *After you anchor a text box or graphic, you likely have to click the Wrapping tab in the Format dialog box to tell Word 97 how text should behave when it encounters the text box or graphic. See "Wrapping Text Around Graphics and Text Boxes" in Chapter 9.*

10. Move the pointer to the border of the graphic frame or text box. The pointer changes into a four-headed arrow.

11. Drag the text box or graphic where you want it to remain on the page.

Figure 6-6 shows a company newsletter with an anchored announcement and an anchored graphic. No matter how much new text goes into this document, the announcement and graphic will stay in the same place—prominently on page 1.

LEARN BY EXAMPLE
To experiment with how text behaves beside an anchored text and graphic, open the Word 97 document Figure 6-5 (Anchoring) *on the companion CD.*

Aligning Text on the Page

When it comes to aligning text, Word 97 makes a distinction between aligning text in paragraphs with respect to the margins, and aligning all the text on the page with respect to the borders of the page. How to align text is the subject of this part of the chapter.

Click this tab to determine what text does
when it reaches the graphic or text box.

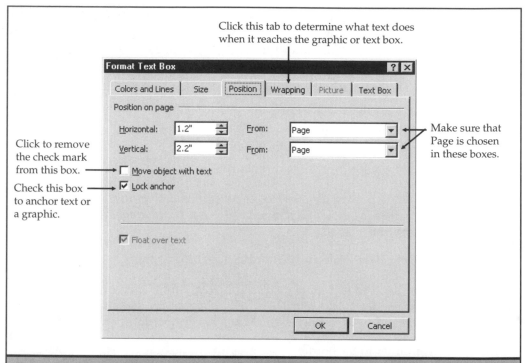

Click to remove
the check mark
from this box. →

Check this box →
to anchor text or
a graphic.

Make sure that
Page is chosen
in these boxes.

Figure 6-5. *Anchoring a text box or graphic to the page so it stays in one place*

A Word from Our President...

This year's profits showed a remarkable rise over last year's. Yes, the company is going great guns, and all of you are to thank for it. As your president, I would like to thank each and every one of you for coming to work

The Annual Company Tug-of-War will take place on Friday afternoon at 4:30. This year, Sales and Marketing will do battle with Accounting and Administration.
As always, only the winning team will be able to participate in the company's 401(k) plan.

on time, for your energy and spirit, and for doing exactly what I say at all times, no matter what.

You are part of a great tradition. For almost forty years now, employees have been doing exactly what I say. That is to be commended. The ability to follow orders is what made Sparta immortal in Grecian history. Indeed, "Spartan" has become an adjective oft employed by football coaches and the like. That's because being Spartan is good. And you're good, too. You are great employees.

Figure 6-6. *The announcement and graphic in this newsletter have been anchored to the page and will not move with the text*

Aligning Text with Respect to the Left and Right Margins

So important is aligning text with respect to the left and right margins, Word 97 offers buttons on the Formatting toolbar for doing it: the Align Left, Center, Align Right, and Justify buttons. Each aligns text in a different way, as shown in Figure 6-7. The figure itself explains the advantages of choosing one text-alignment technique over another.

To align paragraph text in a document, follow these steps:

1. Select the paragraphs you want to align. If you are aligning a single paragraph, all you have to do is click it.

2. Click an alignment button on the Formatting toolbar:

   ■ *Align Left*   Aligns text with the left margin or left side of the column.

   ■ *Center*   Centers the text between the margins or between the column boundaries.

   ■ *Align Right*   Aligns text with the right margin or right side of the column.

   ■ *Justify*   Aligns text with both the left and right margins and left and right sides of the column.

This text is right aligned. Right-aligned text sticks to the right margin or right side of the column. It can also be used for decorative purposes, as it is being used here.

This text is left aligned. Left-aligned text sticks to the left margin or left side of the column. It is supposed to be easiest to read; it creates a "ragged right" margin.

Headings, Like This One, Are Centered

This text has been justified. Justified text sticks to both the left and right margins or left and right sides of the column. Justified text looks good in formal documents and it is good for squeezing text into columns. I think that justified text should be hyphenated, too.

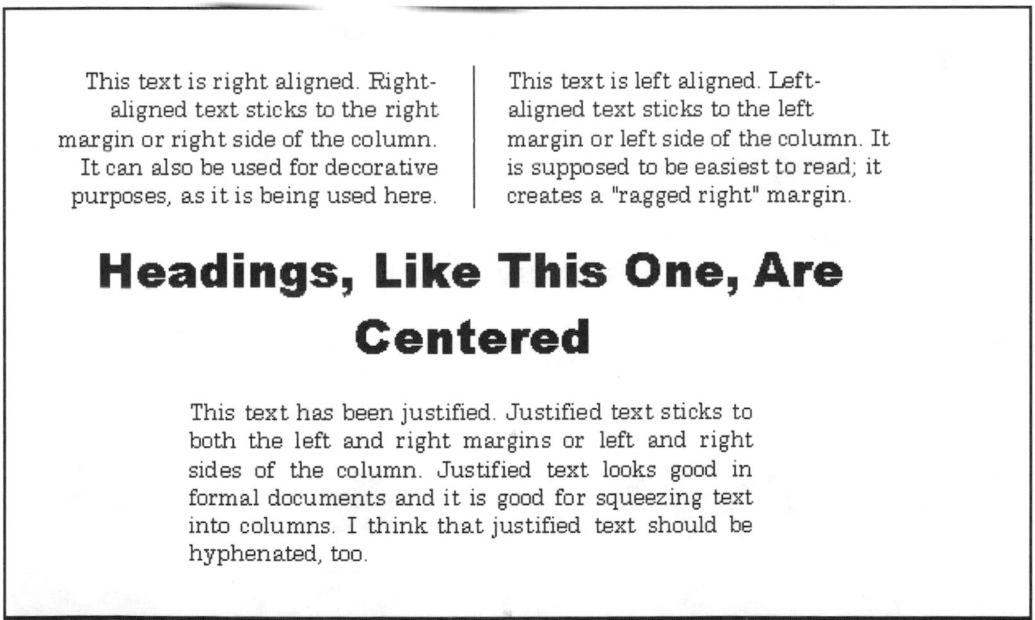

Figure 6-7.   *The four ways to align text: right-aligning, left-aligning, centering, and justifying*

TIP: *It isn't necessary to select an entire paragraph when you want to align text or give any command that pertains to paragraphs, for that matter. All you have to do is put the cursor in the paragraph or, to select more than one paragraph, select part of each one.*

You can also control text alignment by way of the Paragraph dialog box:

1. Choose the Format menu Paragraph command.
2. On the Indents and Spacing tab of the Paragraph dialog box, choose an alignment option: Left, Center, Right, or Justify.
3. Click OK.

Aligning Text with Respect to the Top and Bottom Margins

Word 97 also offers commands called Top, Center, and Justified in the Page Setup dialog box for aligning text with respect to the top and bottom margins of the page. The Justify setting only applies to pages that are filled up. When a page is only partly full, Word 97 aligns it with the top margin. Figure 6-8 shows the three ways to align text with respect to the top and bottom margins of the page.

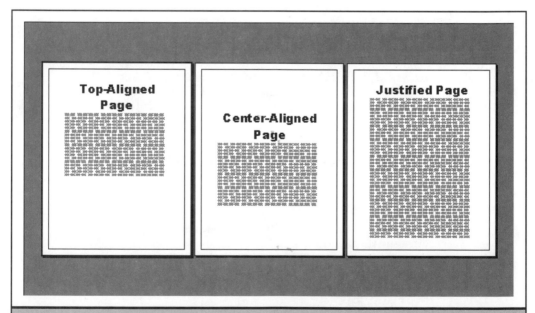

Figure 6-8. *From the Page Setup dialog box, you can tell Word 97 how to align all the text on a page with respect to the top and bottom margins*

To change the alignment of text vis-à-vis the top and bottom margins, follow these steps:

1. Click at the top of the page that is to be aligned in a new way. If you are aligning all the pages in a document, it doesn't matter where the cursor is before you give the command. If you are aligning all the pages in a section, make sure the cursor is in the section.

2. Choose the File menu Page Setup command.

3. Click the Layout tab in the Page Setup dialog box. The Layout tab is shown in Figure 6-9.

4. Under Vertical alignment, choose Top, Center, or Justified.

5. Under Apply to, tell Word 97 which pages in the document are to be aligned vertically: Whole document applies to the entire document; This point forward applies to all the pages from the cursor position to the end of the document; and This section applies to all the pages in the section that the cursor is in.

6. Click OK.

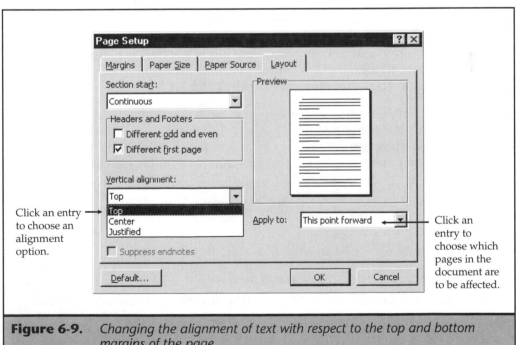

Click an entry to choose an alignment option.

Click an entry to choose which pages in the document are to be affected.

Figure 6-9. *Changing the alignment of text with respect to the top and bottom margins of the page*

Handling Dashes and Quotation Marks

This part of the chapter looks into a pesky aspect of Word 97: how to handle punctuation marks. As you must have noticed by now, the program occasionally reaches over your shoulder and enters punctuation marks for you. For example, Word 97 is geared for curly quotation marks and puts them in documents unless you tell it not to. And it enters ellipses (...) automatically as well. This part of the chapter explains how to usurp Word 97 and take command of punctuation marks.

Inserting Em and En Dashes

Dashes are punctuation marks and are different from hyphens. An *em dash* is used to show an abrupt change of direction in the middle of a sentence—know what I mean? It is called an em dash because it is the width of an *m* in whatever typeface it is set in. You can always spot an amateur desktop publisher because amateurs use dashes incorrectly. In the following illustration, the last sentence is the one with a proper em dash. The other em dashes were made by amateurs.

> An em dash looks like a hyphen-but it's wider.
> An em dash looks like a hyphen--but it's wider.
> An em dash looks like a hyphen - but it's wider.
> An em dash looks like a hyphen—but it's wider.

 NOTE: *Unless you've changed Word 97's default options, the program enters an em dash automatically when you type two hyphens in a row. If that isn't happening and you want it to happen, choose the Tools menu AutoCorrect command, click the AutoFormat as You Type tab, and click the Symbol characters (- -) with symbols (—) check box.*

Similar to an em dash, an *en dash* is used to show inclusive numbers or time periods. Amateurs let the hyphen do the work of the en dash. An en dash is the width of an *n* in whatever typeface it is set in. In the following illustration, en dashes appear in the first line, but hyphens appear in the second.

> pp. 9–17   Aug.–Sept. 1997   Exodus 16:11–1618
> pp. 9-17   Aug.-Sept. 1997   Exodus 16:11-1618

To include an em or en dash in a document, do the following:

1. Place the cursor where the dash is to appear.

2. Choose the Insert menu Symbol command. The Symbol dialog box appears.

3. Click the Special Characters tab. It is shown in Figure 6-10.

4. Either click Em Dash at the top of the list, or click En Dash, the second item on the list.

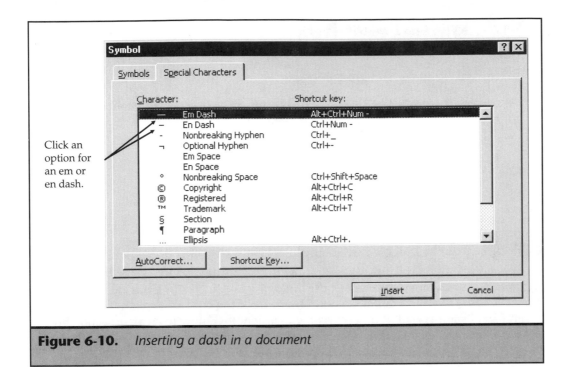

Click an
option for
an em or
en dash.

Figure 6-10.   *Inserting a dash in a document*

5. Click the Insert button.

6. Click the Close button.

TIP: *If you prefer pressing keys to clicking commands, you might prefer the keyboard shortcut for entering an em dash: simultaneously press the ALT key, the CTRL key, and the minus key on the numeric keypad (the key in the upper-right corner of the keyboard). To enter an en dash, simultaneously press the CTRL key and the minus key on the numeric keypad.*

Using Curly or Straight Quotation Marks

Until you fiddle with the default options, Word 97 puts curly quotes rather than straight quotes in documents. In the following illustration, curly quotes (also known as "smart quotes" because they know which way to turn on either side of text) appear in the first sentence and straight quotes appear in the second sentence:

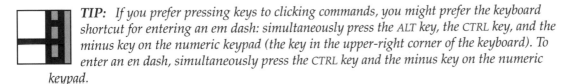

The problem with curly quotes is that they don't look good in some fonts, especially monospace fonts like Courier. And some people prefer straight quotation marks to curly ones.

To tell Word 97 to use straight quotes or curly ones, do the following:

1. Choose the Tools menu AutoCorrect command to open the AutoCorrect dialog box.

2. Click the AutoFormat As You Type tab. It is shown in Figure 6-11.

3. To use curly quotes, make sure a check mark appears in the "Straight quotes" with "smart quotes" check box.

4. Click OK.

Laying Out the Page

The second half of this chapter explores how to lay out the text in a Word 97 document. If you were to take your nose out of the text and hold the page at arm's length, would the page itself look good? This part of the chapter explains how to fashion an elegant layout. It describes how to indent text, how to create a section break when you want to change layouts in the middle of a document, how to adjust the

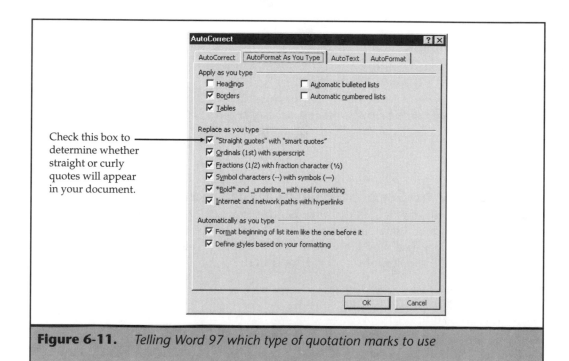

Figure 6-11. *Telling Word 97 which type of quotation marks to use*

spacing between lines and the spacing between paragraphs, how to number the pages in a document, and how to create a header or footer for document pages.

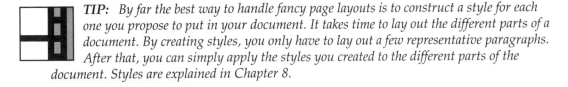

TIP: By far the best way to handle fancy page layouts is to construct a style for each one you propose to put in your document. It takes time to lay out the different parts of a document. By creating styles, you only have to lay out a few representative paragraphs. After that, you can simply apply the styles you created to the different parts of the document. Styles are explained in Chapter 8.

Indenting Text

The following pages explain how to indent text from the margin. The important thing to remember about indenting text is that text is indented with respect to the margins, not the edges of the page. In other words, if you indent a paragraph from the left margin by one inch and the left margin setting is one inch already, the text will fall two inches from the edge of the page. Margin settings are made from the edge of the page. Indentations are made from the margin.

Indents vs. Margins

"Margins" is kind of a dirty word in Word 97. To move text closer or farther away from the edge of the page, change the indentation of the text. The purpose of margin settings is to establish the overall look of the pages in a document. If you do change margin settings in the middle of a document, Word 97 inserts a page break and creates a new section where the new margins begin.

Word 97 offers no less than three ways to indent text. Moreover, when changing indentations, you can indent the first line of a paragraph, indent the entire paragraph, or create hanging headings. Better read on.

Indenting Text from the Margins

To indent text from the margins, you can drag markers on the ruler, click the Increase Indent and Decrease Indent buttons on the Formatting toolbar, or open the Paragraph dialog box and change indentation settings.

If you are doing a quick and dirty job on a document that needs to get out the door quickly, dragging the indent markers on the ruler is probably the way to go. However, to make sure that paragraphs are indented consistently from page to page, the best way to indent paragraphs is to use the Paragraph dialog box and enter exact measurements for indentations. In fact, the absolute best way is to create a style by way of the Paragraph dialog box. With the ruler, you have to "eyeball it" and hope for the best. With the buttons, you click away and watch the text get indented by one tab stop with each click of the mouse.

Indenting Text with the Paragraph Dialog Box

Follow these steps to indent text with the Paragraph dialog box:

1. Select all or part of the paragraphs you want to indent. If you are indenting a single paragraph, simply click in it.

2. Choose the Format menu Paragraph command. You see the Paragraph dialog box shown in Figure 6-12.

3. Under Indentation, make entries in the Left and Right boxes to say how far text is to be indented from the left and right margins. As you make choices, watch the Preview box. It gives you an idea of what your choices mean in real terms.

4. Click OK.

Indenting Text with the Indent Buttons

If you're in a hurry to change indentations, you might try clicking the Increase Indent or Decrease Indent buttons on the Formatting toolbar. These buttons move the text rightward to the next or previous tab stop (a half inch if you haven't changed the tab settings) and work only with respect to the left margin. In other words, if you click the Increase Indent button, the paragraph or paragraphs you selected move away from the left margin, but nothing happens on the right margin because the Indent buttons cannot move text with respect to the right margin.

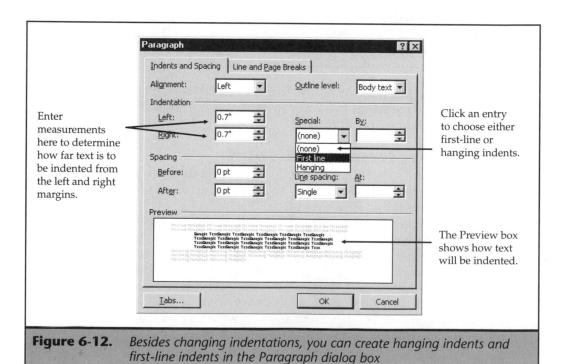

Enter measurements here to determine how far text is to be indented from the left and right margins.

Click an entry to choose either first-line or hanging indents.

The Preview box shows how text will be indented.

Figure 6-12.   *Besides changing indentations, you can create hanging indents and first-line indents in the Paragraph dialog box*

Click the Decrease Indent button if you clicked the Increase Indent button too many times and moved text too far from the left margin.

Indenting Text with the Ruler

By dragging markers on the ruler, you can change the indentation settings. Follow these steps to change indents with the ruler:

1. Choose the View menu Ruler command if the ruler isn't onscreen.

2. If you are indenting a single paragraph, simply click in it. Otherwise, select all or part of the paragraphs you want to indent.

3. Drag the left indent marker to change the left indentation setting; and drag the right indent marker to change the right indentation setting. As you move the pointer over a marker, a box appears to tell you its name. The left indent and right indent markers are shown in this illustration:

Left indent marker   Right indent marker

Indenting First Lines

In some kinds of documents, the first line is indented to mark the place where a new paragraph begins. To indent the first line of a paragraph most people press the TAB key once. In Word 97, pressing the TAB key indents the first line by a half inch or to the first tab setting, if you or someone else changed the tab settings. Word 97 offers two ways (three if you count pressing the TAB key) to establish the distance from the left margin that the first line is indented. You can do it by way of the Paragraph dialog box or with the ruler.

Indenting the First Line with the Paragraph Dialog Box

As you create a style, or if you merely intend to indent the first line of a paragraph or paragraphs, follow these steps to create a first-line indent:

1. Click in the paragraph or select all or part of the paragraphs whose first lines you want to indent.

2. Choose the Format menu Paragraph command. You see the Paragraph dialog box (see Figure 6-12).

3. Click the Special drop-down list to open it and then choose First line.

4. In the By box, enter the distance from the left margin that the first line is to be indented.

5. Click OK.

Indenting the First Line with the Ruler

To indent the first line with the ruler, follow these steps:

1. Choose the View menu Ruler command if the ruler isn't onscreen.

2. Click in a paragraph or select all or part of the paragraphs whose first lines you want to indent.

3. On the ruler, drag the first-line indent marker to the right. When you move the pointer over the marker, a box appears and tells you which marker it is.

First-line indent marker

Creating a Hanging Indent

A *hanging indent* is one in which the first line of the paragraph is closer to the left margin than the other lines in the paragraph are. Word 97 creates hanging indents automatically for numbered and bulleted lists. In those cases, the first line of the paragraph—the one with the number or bullet in it—is closer to the left margin than the other lines are. Notice where the first-line indent marker is in the following illustration. In this numbered list, the left-indent marker is directly on the left margin, but the second line in each paragraph is at the .25 inch mark:

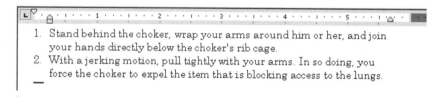

1. Stand behind the choker, wrap your arms around him or her, and join your hands directly below the choker's rib cage.
2. With a jerking motion, pull tightly with your arms. In so doing, you force the choker to expel the item that is blocking access to the lungs.

Hanging indents can be used for elegant effects in many different ways. Notice where the first-line indent marker is in the following list, which leaves the names of four famous moptops hanging:

John   The founder of the group, its rebel voice, rhythm guitarist, and madcap humor-maker
Paul   The melodious one, he of the soothing plaints and wooing love songs
George The handsome one with the eyes that sparkle, and trailblazer to the east
Ringo   The secret brains of the group whose winsome smile won so many hearts

To create a hanging indent, you can do so either by way of the Paragraph dialog box or the ruler.

LEARN BY EXAMPLE
To experiment with hanging indents, open the Word 97 document Figure 6A (Hanging Indents) *on the companion CD.*

Creating a Hanging Indent with the Paragraph Dialog Box

Do the following to create a hanging indent with the Paragraph dialog box:

1. Click in the paragraph or select all or part of the paragraphs for which you want to create hanging indents.

2. Choose the Format menu Paragraph command to open the Paragraph dialog box (see Figure 6-12).

3. Click the Special drop-down list and choose Hanging.

4. In the By box, enter the amount of space beyond the left indentation setting all lines in the paragraph after the first line are to be indented. In other words, if the left indentation setting is .5 inches and you enter 1 inch in the By box, the second and subsequent lines in the paragraph will be indented by 1.5 inches.

5. Click OK.

Creating a Hanging Indent with the Ruler

Follow these steps to create a hanging indent with the ruler:

1. Choose the View menu Ruler command if the ruler isn't onscreen.

2. Click in a paragraph or else select all or part of the paragraphs for which you want to create hanging indents.

3. On the ruler, drag the hanging indent marker to the right. As you drag, the left indent marker moves as well.

Hanging indent marker

You likely have to pull and tug, pull and tug on the hanging indent marker several times until you get it right.

Creating a Hanging Heading

A *hanging heading* is one that lies closer to the left margin than the text that falls below it. Hanging headings are quite elegant and they make it easier for readers to look up

WORD

information in a document. They make it easier because the headings stand out more and readers can find them more quickly. Figure 6-13 shows a document whose headings "hang."

As if you didn't expect it, Word 97 offers two ways to create a hanging heading:

■ *With the Paragraph dialog box* In the Special drop-down list, choose First line. Then enter a negative number in the Left box in the Indentation section of the dialog box.

■ *With the ruler* Click in the heading and drag the First-line indent marker on the ruler to the left instead of to the right, as shown in Figure 6-13.

LEARN BY EXAMPLE
To try your hand at hanging headings, open the Figure 6-13 (Hanging Headings) *file on the companion CD.*

Section Breaks for Drastic Layout Changes

Before you can change the headers and footers in the middle of a document, change the page-numbering scheme or sequence, put text in columns, or change the margins

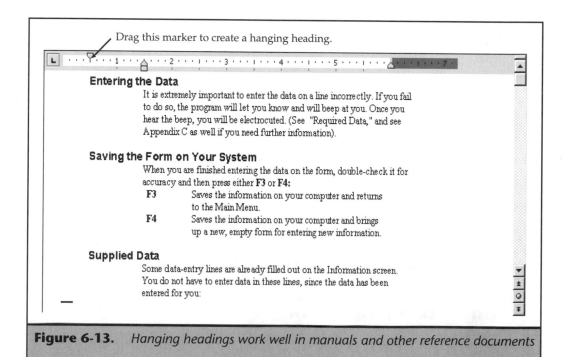

Drag this marker to create a hanging heading.

Entering the Data
It is extremely important to enter the data on a line incorrectly. If you fail to do so, the program will let you know and will beep at you. Once you hear the beep, you will be electrocuted. (See "Required Data," and see Appendix C as well if you need further information).

Saving the Form on Your System
When you are finished entering the data on the form, double-check it for accuracy and then press either **F3** or **F4**:
F3 Saves the information on your computer and returns to the Main Menu.
F4 Saves the information on your computer and brings up a new, empty form for entering new information.

Supplied Data
Some data-entry lines are already filled out on the Information screen. You do not have to enter data in these lines, since the data has been entered for you:

Figure 6-13. *Hanging headings work well in manuals and other reference documents*

for part of a document, you have to create a new *section*. As a matter of fact, Word 97 creates a new section for you when you change the margin settings or introduce columns. This part of the chapter explains how to insert a section break and how to remove one.

The sidebar below explains the four types of section breaks. In Normal view, you see the following when a section break is introduced: a double dotted line, the words "Section Break," and, parenthetically, the type of section break that has been introduced:

Section Break (Next Page)

Section Break (Continuous)

Section Break (Even Page)

Section Break (Odd Page)

The Four Kinds of Section Breaks

In the Break dialog box (choose the Insert menu Break command to get there), Word 97 offers four kinds of section breaks:

- *Next page* Creates a section break and a page break at the same time.

- *Continuous* Creates a section break in the middle of the page. This type of section break occurs, for example, between a heading and the two or three columns that appear below it in a newsletter. When margin settings are changed in the middle of a document, Word creates this kind of break.

- *Even page* Creates the section break on the next even-numbered page.

- *Odd page* Creates the section break on the next odd-numbered page. In conventional publishing, a new chapter always begins on an odd page. In a document with headers or footers that change from chapter to chapter, create an Odd page section break to start subsequent chapters on odd pages and you will be able to change headers or footers as well.

Inserting a Section Break

To insert a section break in a document and create a new section, do the following:

1. Place the cursor where the break is to occur.

2. Choose the Insert menu Break command. You see the Break dialog box:

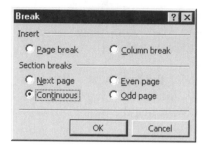

3. Under Section breaks, click the kind of break you want.

4. Click OK.

Deleting a Section Break

To delete a section break, do the following:

1. Switch to Normal view if you are in another type of view. It's hard to find section breaks in Page Layout view, for example.

2. Click on the words that tell where the section break is.

3. Press the DELETE key.

Adjusting Space Between Lines and Paragraphs

This part of Chapter 6 has to do with space, not outer space, but the kinds of decisions regarding space that sometimes have to be made when you are laying out a document. The following pages explain how to adjust the amount of space between lines, adjust for space between paragraphs, and fix spacing problems between characters in headings.

Adjusting the Space Between Lines

Double-spacing and single-spacing the lines in a document are two of the most common chores word processors do, so Word 97 offers special shortcuts for single- and double-spacing lines. The program offers many other line-spacing options as well. All line-spacing options are available in the Paragraph dialog box. Table 6-1 explains all of them.

NOTE: When Word 97 encounters a tall character or graphic that is too big to fit on a line, it automatically allows more space between lines to accommodate the tall character or graphic, except in the case of the Exactly option. When Exactly is chosen, the top of the tall character or graphic gets cut off by the line above.

To tell Word 97 how much space to put between lines in a document, do the following:

1. Select all or part of the paragraphs whose line spacing you wish to change. If you want to change line spacing in a single paragraph, click in it.

2. Choose the Format menu Paragraph command. You see the Paragraph dialog box shown in Figure 6-14.

3. Open the Line spacing drop-down list and choose an option (see Table 6-1).

4. If you chose At least, Exactly, or Multiple, enter a number in the At box:

■ *At least*   Enter, in points, the minimum distance that Word 97 can increase line spacing to accommodate tall characters.

■ *Exactly*   Enter, in points, the exact amount of space that is to appear between lines.

■ *Multiple*   Enter a number that expresses how much space goes between lines. For example, if you enter 3, the lines will be triple-spaced.

5. Click OK.

Option	Keyboard Shortcut	Description
Single-spacing	CTRL+1	Makes room for the tallest character in the line plus a small amount of extra space.
1.5 line spacing	CTRL+5	Puts one-and-a-half times the font size between lines. For example, if the characters are 12 points high, it puts 18 points between lines.
Double-spacing	CTRL+2	Puts two times the font size between lines. If the characters are 12 points high, it puts 24 points between lines.
At least		Normally, Word 97 adds extra space between lines to accommodate tall characters. This option tells Word 97 to adjust for tall characters, but only to a certain point—the point you specify with the At least option.
Exactly		Puts a specific amount of space between lines, no ifs, ands, or buts. With this option, Word 97 does not accommodate tall characters. Instead of increasing the amount of space, tall characters' heads are cut off.
Multiple		Works like double spacing, only the Multiple option allows for triple spacing, quadruple spacing, and so on.

Table 6-1.   *Line Spacing Options*

Adjusting the Space Between Paragraphs

The Paragraph dialog box offers commands for telling Word 97 how much space to put before each paragraph and after each paragraph. These commands are strictly for use with styles (Chapter 8 explains styles). Don't use them indiscriminately to put space before and after paragraphs because, used together, they can have unexpected consequences. For example, when a paragraph with such-and-such amount of space after it is followed by a paragraph with such-and-such amount of space before it, too much space may appear between the two paragraphs.

To tell Word 97 to put space before and after a paragraph, do the following:

1. Select all or part of the paragraphs whose before and after space settings you want to change. If you are working on a single paragraph, click it.

2. Choose the Format menu Paragraph command. The Paragraph dialog box appears (see Figure 6-14).

3. Under Spacing, enter an amount, in points, in the Before and After boxes.

4. Click OK.

Kerning to Fix Spacing Problems Between Characters

When letters are enlarged in headings, spacing problems sometimes appear between the letters. In the following illustration, for example, the *T* and the *w* in *Twins* appear

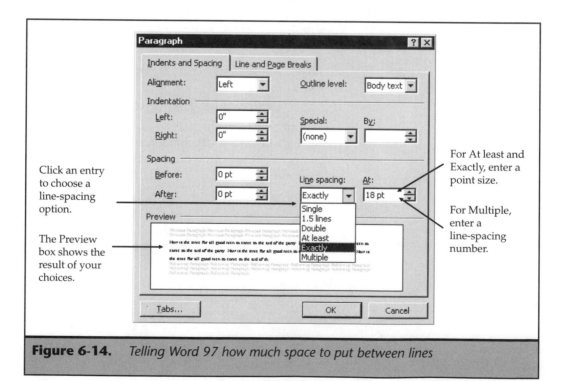

Figure 6-14.   *Telling Word 97 how much space to put between lines*

to be too far apart, and the *r* and the *n* in *Born* appear to be too close together and almost look like an *m*:

Twins Born in Twin Cities

NOTE: *Only proportional-spaced fonts can be kerned.*

Fixing spacing problems like the ones in the illustration is called *kerning*. Follow these steps to fix spacing problems between characters:

1. Select the two letters in question.
2. Choose the Format menu Font command.
3. Click the Character Spacing tab. It is shown in Figure 6-15.
4. In the Spacing menu, choose Expanded to put more space between the letters or Condensed to pack them closer together.

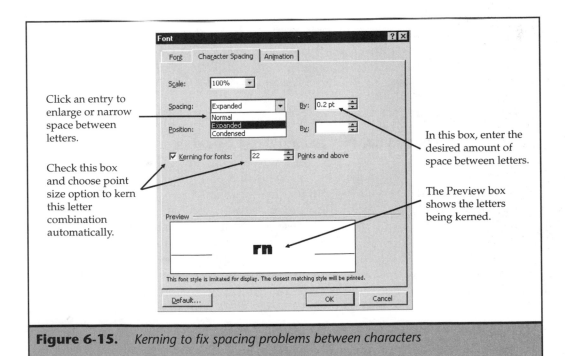

Figure 6-15. *Kerning to fix spacing problems between characters*

5. If you want, change the setting in the By box to make the letters closer together or farther apart. Word 97 makes a suggestion automatically, but if the letters in the Preview box don't look right, you can improve on Word 97's suggestion by making an entry of your own.

6. Click the Kerning for fonts check box if you want Word 97 to kern the letter combination you are working with automatically. In the Points and above box, make an entry to tell Word 97 at which point size to start kerning the letter combination.

7. Click OK.

Numbering a Document's Pages

It almost goes without saying, but long documents aren't worth much unless the pages are numbered. Readers want to know what page they are on and how many pages are in a document. And if the document is to have a table of contents or an index, pages absolutely must be numbered. This part of the chapter explains how to number the pages of a document, how to position page numbers on the pages, and how to choose a numbering scheme other than standard Arabic numbers. It also explains how to start from a number other than one and how to include chapter numbers in page numbers (1-1, 1-2, 1-3, and so on). Oh, I almost forgot. This part of the chapter also explains how to remove page numbers from a document.

TIP: If your document includes what publishers call "frontmatter"—a title page, table of contents, introduction, or other element that appears before the main text—create a new section for those elements and number them with Roman numerals. If you fail to take my advice and you number the entire document starting with page 1, your title page will start with page 1, and that will throw off the numbering scheme.

Page Numbers in Headers and Footers

Word 97 offers two ways to number the pages of a document—with standard page numbers or by including page numbers in headers and footers. If your document will include headers and footers, put the page numbers there (and see "Putting Headers and Footers on Pages" a few pages hence to find out how). When an automatic page number like the ones described in this part of the book is inserted in a document with headers and footers, the automatic page number overlaps the header and footer. That looks ugly. You can put page numbers in headers and footers or use Word 97's automatic page numbering feature, but you can't do both.

WORD

Positioning the Page Numbers

Follow these steps to tell Word 97 where page numbers should appear on the pages of a document:

1. Choose the Insert menu Page Numbers command. You see the Page Numbers dialog box shown in Figure 6-16.

2. In the Position drop-down list, tell Word 97 whether page numbers should be placed along the top or the bottom of the page.

3. In the Alignment drop-down list, tell Word 97 if the page number should go on the left side, center, or right side of the bottom or top of the page. The Alignment drop-down list also offers options called Inside and Outside. These options are for double-sided documents in which text appears on both sides of the page. Inside puts the page numbers near the binding; Outside puts them away from the binding (Outside is highly recommended). Watch the Preview box to see the effects your choices have on the sample page or pages.

4. Click OK.

Taking the Number off or Putting It on the First Page

In letters, informal documents, and notices, the standard practice is not to put page numbers on the first page. By default, Word 97 puts a page number on the first page of a document or section, but that doesn't mean you can't remove it.

To remove a page number from the first page of a document or section, choose the Insert menu Page Numbers command, and, in the Page Numbers dialog box (see Figure 6-16), make sure that no check mark appears in the Show number on first page check box.

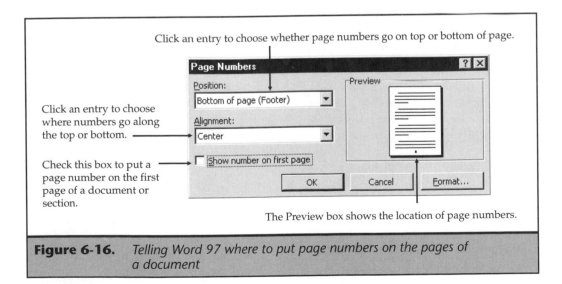

Click an entry to choose whether page numbers go on top or bottom of page.

Click an entry to choose where numbers go along the top or bottom.

Check this box to put a page number on the first page of a document or section.

The Preview box shows the location of page numbers.

Figure 6-16. *Telling Word 97 where to put page numbers on the pages of a document*

Numbering with Roman Numerals and Letters

Arabic numerals are not the only ones that can be used to number the pages of a document. In the spirit of multiculturalism and cultural diversity, Word 97 permits you to leave the Arabic world and return to Roman times, when computer documents were numbered with Roman numerals. The program offers other schemes for numbering pages as well.

To choose a numbering scheme for the pages of a document, follow these steps:

1. Choose the Insert menu Page Numbers command. You see the Page Numbers dialog box (see Figure 6-16).

2. Click the Format button. The Page Number Format dialog box appears, as shown in Figure 6-17.

3. Click the Number format drop-down list and choose a numbering scheme.

4. Click OK to close the Page Numbering dialog box.

5. Click OK in the Page Numbers dialog box.

Including Chapter Numbers in Page Numbers

To include chapter numbers in page numbers (1-1, 1-2, 2-1, 2-2, and so on), you must have assigned styles to the headings in your document (Chapter 8 explains styles). Truth be told, you must have diligently assigned the Heading 1 style to the first heading in each chapter. Not only that, but you must have chosen the Format menu Bullets and Numbering command, clicked the Outline Numbered tab, and chosen an

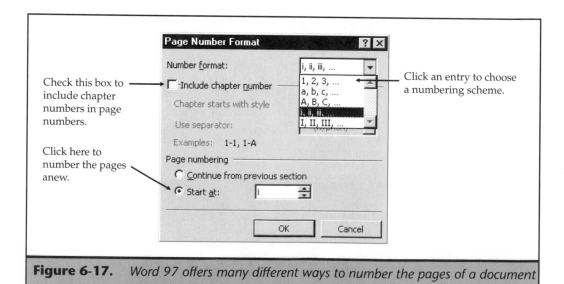

Figure 6-17. *Word 97 offers many different ways to number the pages of a document*

outline numbering scheme for the chapter titles. See "Numbering the Headings in a Document" in Chapter 10 for more instruction.

If you did all that, follow these steps to include chapter numbers in page numbers:

1. Choose the Insert menu Page Numbers command. The Page Numbers dialog box appears (see Figure 6-16).

2. Choose where the page number is to go on the pages (turn backward to "Positioning the Page Numbers" if you need help).

3. Click the Format button. The Page Number Format dialog box appears (see Figure 6-17).

4. Click the Include chapter number check box.

5. If necessary, click the Chapter starts with style drop-down list and choose Heading 1 from the list.

6. By default, Word 97 places a hyphen between the chapter number and the page number, but you can open the Use separator drop-down list and choose another symbol if you want.

7. Click OK in the Page Number Format dialog box.

8. Click OK in the Page Numbers dialog box.

LEARN BY EXAMPLE
To experiment with chapter numbers in page numbers, open the Word 97 document
Figure 6-18 (Page Numbers) *on the companion CD.*

Numbering the Pages Differently in the Middle of a Document

To start numbering the pages anew in a document, perhaps to choose a different numbering scheme or to start all over with page 1 in a new chapter, you must have divided the document into sections. Word 97 cannot change numbering schemes unless you create a section for the pages that are to be numbered a different way.

Follow these steps to number the pages in part of a document differently:

1. Choose the Insert menu Page Numbers command.

2. In the Page Numbers dialog box (see Figure 6-16), click the Format button. You see the Page Number Format dialog box (see Figure 6-17).

3. Click the Start at check box.

4. If the new set of pages is to start with a number other than 1, a, A, or I, enter the page number (or letter) in the box to the right of the Start at check box.

5. Click OK in the Page Number Format dialog box.

6. Click OK in the Page Numbers dialog box.

Removing Page Numbers

All right, you went to the trouble of numbering the pages in a document, and now you want to remove the page numbers. Follow these steps to remove them:

1. Choose the View menu Header and Footer command. As shown in Figure 6-18, the Header and Footer toolbar appears. If your page numbers are along the top of the pages, you see a page number. If your page numbers are along the bottom of the pages, click the Switch Between Header and Footer button on the toolbar to see the footer at the bottom of the page along with the page number.

2. Click on the page number. Hash marks appear around the page number.

3. Move the pointer over the hash marks, and when the pointer changes into a four-headed arrow, click. As shown in Figure 6-18, black squares appear around the page number.

4. Press the DELETE key.

5. Click the Close button on the Header and Footer toolbar.

Putting Headers and Footers on Pages

A *header* is a bit of text along the top of a page that tells readers what's what in a document. Usually, the header includes the title of the document, the author's name, and a page number. *Footers* do the same things as headers, only they do it along the bottom of the page, as befits their name.

This part of the chapter explains how to enter a header or footer; how to read and take advantage of the buttons on the Header and Footer toolbar; and how to include document information such as page numbers, dates, and times in headers. It describes how to create headers for odd and even pages and how to change the header in the

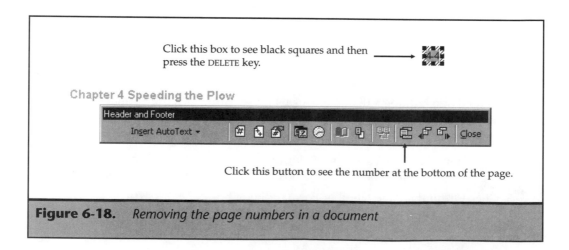

Click this box to see black squares and then press the DELETE key.

Chapter 4 Speeding the Plow

Header and Footer

Insert AutoText ▾

Click this button to see the number at the bottom of the page.

Figure 6-18.   *Removing the page numbers in a document*

middle of a document. It also explains how to remove a header or footer from the first page of a document.

Entering a Header and Footer

Follow these steps to enter a header and footer in a document:

1. Choose the View menu Header and Footer command. The Header and Footer toolbar appears along with a rectangle and the word "Header."

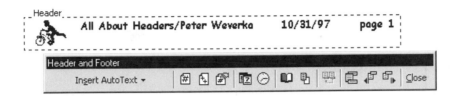

 TIP: In Page Layout view, you can simply double-click a header or footer to make the Header or Footer rectangle appear.

2. Type the header. As you do so, you can call on most of Word 97's formatting commands. For example, you can choose a new typeface, or boldface or italicize the letters. You can even put graphics in headers and footers, as the illustration demonstrates. The next section in the book explains how to include document information in headers and footers with buttons on the Header and Footer toolbar.

3. Click the Switch Between Header and Footer button on the toolbar. Now you see a rectangle and the word "Footer." The Switch Between Header and Footer button takes you back and forth between the header and footer.

4. Enter the text of the footer.

5. Click the Close button on the right side of the Header and Footer toolbar.

Including Document Information in Headers and Footers

The Header and Footer toolbar offers several buttons for entering information about the document you are working on in a header and footer. Table 6-2 explains why and when to click those buttons.

Button	Button Name	What It Does
Insert AutoText ▾	Insert AutoText	Opens a drop-down list with options for inserting document information. For example, you can list when the document was printed last, saved last, and the name of the person who created it.
[#]	Insert Page Number	Lists the page number.
[+]	Insert Number of Pages	Lists the total number of pages in the document. By typing **page**, clicking the Insert Page Number button, typing **of**, and clicking the Insert Number of Pages button, you can enter the following in a header or footer: page 1 of 20.
[7]	Insert Date	Lists the date the document was printed (not today's date or the date the header or footer was created).
[clock]	Insert Time	Lists the time the document was printed.

Table 6-2.   *Buttons on the Header and Footer Toolbar for Entering Document Information*

Creating Different Headers and Footers for the First Page

To create a different header or footer for the first page of a document, or to remove a header and footer from the first page of a document, follow these steps:

1. Click the Page Setup button on the Header and Footer toolbar or choose the File menu Page Setup command. The Page Setup dialog box appears.
2. Click the Layout tab. It is shown in Figure 6-19.

3. Click the Different first page check box.

4. Click OK.

5. Go to the first page of the document or section—the one whose header or footer is to be different.

6. Choose the View menu Header and Footer command. Now the header or footer box says "First Page Header" or "First Page Footer" to let you know that this header or footer can be different than the others in the section or the document:

7. Enter a header, a footer, or both. Or, leave the header and footer box blank if you don't want a header or footer on the first page.

8. Click the Close button on the Header and Footer toolbar.

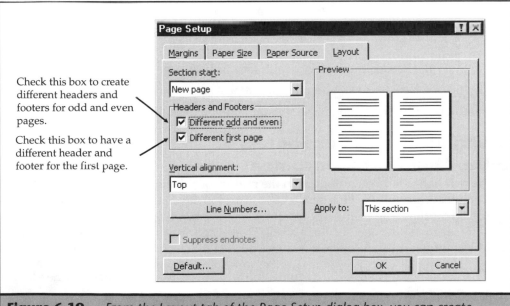

Check this box to create different headers and footers for odd and even pages.

Check this box to have a different header and footer for the first page.

Figure 6-19. *From the Layout tab of the Page Setup dialog box, you can create headers and footers for first pages and odd and even pages*

Headers and Footers for Odd and Even Pages

In two-sided documents in which text is printed on both sides of the paper, sometimes the header and footer on the even page and the header and footer on the odd page are different. In the book you are holding in your hands, as a matter of fact, the headers on even pages tell you the title of the book, and the headers on odd pages tell you which chapter you are in.

You, too, can create different headers and footers for odd and even pages by following these steps:

1. Either click the Page Setup button on the Header and Footer toolbar or choose the File menu Page Setup command. The Page Setup dialog box appears.

2. Click the Layout tab (see Figure 6-19).

3. Click the Different odd and even check box.

4. Click OK.

5. Move the cursor to an even page and choose the View menu Header and Footer command. Now the Header and Footer boxes tell you that you are entering a header or footer that will appear only on even pages:

Even Page Footer -Section 1-

6. Enter the header, the footer, or both for the even pages.

7. Move the cursor to an odd page and repeat steps 5 and 6.

8. Click the Close button on the Header and Footer toolbar.

Changing Headers or Footers in the Middle of a Document

In order to change headers or footers in the middle of a document, you must create a new section. When you create a new section, Word 97 assumes you want to keep the same headers and footers throughout, and it runs the headers and footers from the previous section in the new section as well. However, suppose you want to create new headers and footers for the section you created. To do that, follow these steps:

1. Click in the section of the document in which you want to create new headers and footers.

2. Choose the View menu Header and Footer command. The Header and Footer toolbar appears. This time, however, the Header (or Footer) box tells you which section you are in and that the header (or footer) is the same as that in the previous section:

Header -Section 2-_____Same as Previous_

Going the Whole Hog: A Proposal for Excellence   page 8

3. Click the Same as Previous button on the toolbar. Now the words "Same as Previous" disappear from the Header (or Footer) box and you can rest assured that the new header you type will be different from the old one.

4. Delete the header (or footer) contents and enter the new information.

5. Click the Close button on the Header and Footer toolbar.

TIP: *On the Header and Footer toolbar are buttons called Show Next and Show Previous. As you compose a new header (or footer), click these buttons to see what the header (or footer) in the next or previous section is.*

Removing a Header or Footer

Removing a header or footer is pretty simple. All you have to do is put the header and footer onscreen either by choosing the View menu Headers and Footer command or double-clicking the header or footer while the screen is in Page Layout view. Next, drag the pointer across the header or footer to select it. Then press DELETE.

WORD

The Complete Reference

Chapter 7

Working Faster and Better

In my humble opinion, computers were invented not so you can marvel at how wonderful technology is, but so you can get your work done faster and better. In this chapter, you will find shortcuts, tips, and techniques designed to get you out of the office quicker. Or, if you work at home, the advice in this chapter will enable you get away from your desk sooner so you can really start living.

This chapter provides instructions for moving around quickly in documents, viewing your work in different ways, and keeping errors to a minimum. You also learn how to select text, as well as two advanced techniques for copying text in Word 97. This chapter also explains how to find and replace text and organize your documents better.

Moving Quickly in Documents

The more you work on one, the longer a Word document gets. And when documents start to get very long, it is difficult to move around in them quickly. How do you get to the last page of a document if you are on the first page? And if you are on page 37, how do you get quickly to the heading that you know is somewhere between page 14 and 19? This part of the chapter explains techniques for getting there fast.

This part also explains keyboard and scrollbar techniques for moving around, how to use the Go To and Go Back command, and how to use the Select Browse Object button. You will also find instructions for moving around with the Document Map and for using bookmarks to mark the places you come back to often.

Keyboard and Scrollbar Techniques for Going Long Distances

When you have to get there in a hurry, the fastest way is to press either one of Word's keyboard shortcuts or use the scrollbars. The keyboard shortcuts are for people with nimble fingers; the scrollbars are for mouse mavens who prefer to click and drag. Both sets of techniques are described in the following pages.

Getting Around by Pressing Shortcut Keys

Word offers a host of keyboard shortcuts for moving from place to place. Table 7-1 explains the most useful ones.

TIP: *Pressing CTRL+PGUP or CTRL+PGDN doesn't move the cursor to the top of the previous or following page if you or someone else clicked the Select Browse Object button at the bottom of the vertical scrollbar to move the cursor to the previous or next comment, heading, bookmark, or whatever. "Using the Select Browse Object Button to Get Around," the next topic in this chapter, explains how the Select Browse Object button works. Suffice it to say, if the arrows are blue on either side of the button, pressing CTRL+PGUP or CTRL+PGDN does not take you to the previous or following page.*

Key(s)	Where the Cursor Moves
CTRL+HOME	To the top of the document
CTRL+END	To the bottom of the document
CTRL+PGUP	To the top of the previous page
PGUP	Up the length of one screen
PGDN	Down the length of one screen
CTRL+PGDN	To the top of the following page

Table 7-1. *Keyboard Shortcuts for Moving Around*

WORD

Getting Around with the Scrollbar

The other means of getting around quickly is to use the vertical scrollbar along the right side of the screen. Figure 7-1 labels the different parts of the vertical scrollbar. The following instructions explain how to use this valuable tool to get from place to place quickly:

To Move	Do This
Screen by screen	Click on the scrollbar but not on the scroll box or on the arrows.
Line by line	Click the single arrow at the top or bottom of the scrollbar.
Page by page	Click the double-arrows on either side of the Select Browse Object button. (Clicking the double-arrows when they are blue does not move the cursor page by page, but moves the cursor to the previous or next comment, heading, bookmark, or whatever.)
Very quickly up and down	Drag the *scroll box*, the square on the scrollbar. The scrollbar is shown in Figure 7-1. As you drag, a box appears and tells you which page will be displayed.

If you have assigned heading styles to the headings in your document, heading names appear as well when you drag the scroll box, as shown in the following illustration.

Page: 3

Getting Around with the Scroll...

TIP: *If the double-arrows on the bottom of the vertical scrollbar are blue but you want them to be black so you can move from page to page, click the Select Browse Object button and then click the Browse by Page button on the drop-down menu.*

By the way, a horizontal scroll bar lies along the bottom of the Word screen. Click its arrows or drag its scroll box to move a wide document from side to side onscreen so you can see either end of it.

LEARN BY EXAMPLE

The Figure 7-1 (Moving Around) *file on the companion CD provides a long sample document in case you want to practice the keyboard and scrollbar techniques described here for moving around.*

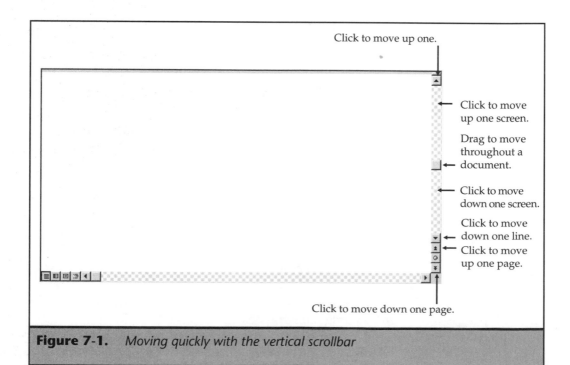

Figure 7-1. *Moving quickly with the vertical scrollbar*

Using the Select Browse Object Button to Get Around

Another way to get from place to place quickly is to click the Select Browse Object button. This button, a round one, is located in the lower-right corner of the screen. To begin with, the double-arrows on either side of it are black, and if you click the double-arrows, the cursor moves either to the previous page or the next page. However, you can tell Word to move the cursor to other places by making a choice from the Select Browse Object menu.

Click the Select Browse Object button and you see a drop-down menu with buttons. Each button represents either a command or a different element that you can move the cursor to. For example, in the following illustration, the cursor is on the Browse by Heading button. If you click this button, Word moves the cursor to the next heading in the document:

After you click a button on the Select Browse Object menu, the double-arrows on either side of the button turn blue. Now when you click the double-arrows, the cursor moves either to the previous or the next example of the element you chose from the Select Browse Object menu. For example, if you choose Browse by Heading and then click the blue double-arrows, the cursor moves either to the previous or the next heading in the document, depending on which double-arrows you click.

NOTE: *Choosing Browse by Page on the Select Browse Object menu tells Word to move the cursor from page to page. After this option is chosen, the double-arrows turn black.*

The Select Browse Object button is excellent for moving quickly from element to element in a document. Instead of giving commands over and over again, all you have to do is click the blue double-arrows.

NOTE: *The Find and Go To buttons on the Select Browse Object menu open, respectively, the Find tab and the Go To tab in the Find and Replace dialog box so you can give commands for finding text or moving the cursor to a specific part of a document. What's more, choosing the Edit menu Go To command or the Edit menu Find command from the menu bar and giving a command also turns the double-arrows beside the Select Browse Object button blue. After you give those commands, you can click the blue double-arrows to move around in a document.*

Using the Go To Command to Move to Numbered Pages and More

The Go To command can get you very quickly to numbered items in a document: page numbers, bookmark numbers, footnote numbers, and line numbers, for example. You can get there directly by telling Word the number of the item you want to get to, or you can click dialog box buttons to jump from item to item.

NOTE: *"Numbers, Numbers, and More Numbers" in Chapter 10 explains how to number the lines and headings in a document.*

Follow these steps to use the Go To command to get from place to place:

1. Choose the Edit menu Go To command, press F5, or click the Select Browse Object button and choose Go To on the drop-down list. As shown in Figure 7-2, you see the Go To tab of the Find and Replace dialog box.

2. In the Go to what scroll list, choose the item you want to move the cursor to.

3. Choose how you want to get there:

   ■ Click the Next or Previous button to go to the following or previous instance of the item you want to get to.

   ■ Enter a number in the Enter number box and click the Go To button to get there (the name of the box changes, depending on what you are trying to get to).

   ■ Enter a plus or minus sign and a number to skip ahead or skip behind several instances of the item you want to get to.

4. Word takes you to the item, but the dialog box stays open in case you want to keep searching. You can click buttons all over again, or make a new entry in the Enter number box if you want.

5. Click Close.

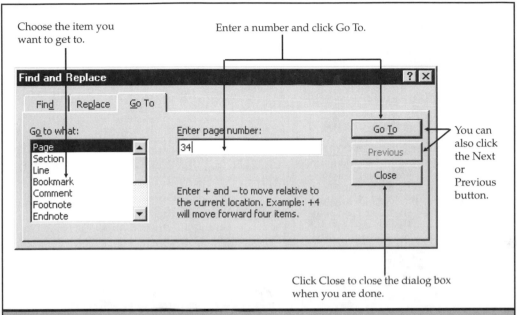

Choose the item you want to get to.

Enter a number and click Go To.

You can also click the Next or Previous button.

Click Close to close the dialog box when you are done.

Figure 7-2.   *With the Go To command, you can move the cursor to any element in a Word file that can conceivably be numbered*

Moving Around with the Document Map

As long as you applied heading styles to the headings in a document, you can get from place to place very quickly with the document map (Chapter 8 explains styles). As shown in Figure 7-3, the document map is a list of all the headings in a document. By scrolling down the list and clicking on the heading you want to move to, you can get there very quickly.

To see the document map, click the Document Map button on the Standard toolbar or choose the View menu Document Map command. To move the cursor to a heading, click on it. You may have to scroll to find the heading you want first. If you have trouble reading a heading, point to it with the cursor. As Figure 7-3 shows, all the words in headings appear when you point to them. You can also drag the border of the headings window to make more room onscreen for headings.

Click the Document Map button again or choose the View menu Document Map command to leave Document Map view.

LEARN BY EXAMPLE
The Figure 7-3 (Document Map) *file on the companion CD includes lots of headings in case you want to play around in Document Map view.*

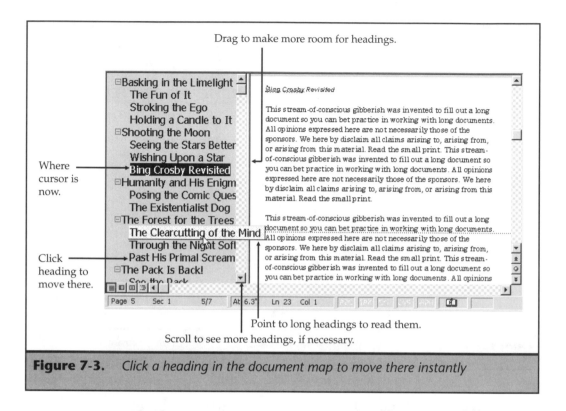

Figure 7-3. *Click a heading in the document map to move there instantly*

Using Bookmarks to Get from Place to Place

One way to get from place to place is to mark the places to which you will often return with bookmarks. Then, all you have to do to go to a place you've marked is give the Insert menu Bookmark command or use the Go To dialog box. As you will learn throughout this book, bookmarks have many uses. For example, in order to create a hyperlink or cross-reference to a sentence or paragraph in a document, you have to create a bookmark in the sentence or paragraph first.

To mark a place in a document with a bookmark, do the following:

1. Click where you want the bookmark to go.

2. Choose the Insert menu Bookmark command. The Bookmark dialog box appears, as shown in Figure 7-4.

3. Type a name in the Bookmark name box. Bookmark names can't include spaces, but you can get around that by typing underscores where spaces would go.

4. Click the Add button.

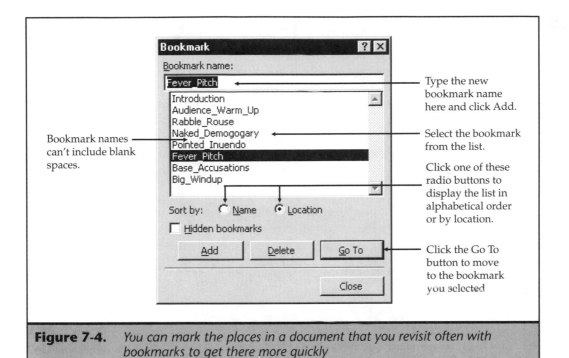

WORD

Figure 7-4. *You can mark the places in a document that you revisit often with bookmarks to get there more quickly*

Follow these steps to move to a spot in a document that you've marked with a bookmark:

1. Choose the Insert menu Bookmark command.

2. Either double-click the bookmark or click it and then click the Go To button. To help find the right bookmark, click the Name radio button to arrange the names on the list in alphabetical order, or click the Location radio button to arrange them by order in the document.

3. Click the Go To button.

To delete a bookmark, click its name in the Bookmark dialog box and then click the Delete button.

LEARN BY EXAMPLE

To try your hand at using bookmarks, open the Figure 7-4 (Bookmarks) *file on the companion CD that comes with this book.*

Different Ways to View Your Work

Depending on the kind of work you want to do, you might try viewing the screen in a different way. Normal view, for example, is good for writing first drafts, but when you want to focus on the layout, Page Layout view is best. Word offers six views in all. Each is explained in this part of the chapter. And, in case you want to be in two places at once, the following pages also discuss how to split the screen and view more than one document at a time.

Word's Six Document Views

Figure 7-5 demonstrates the six ways to view a document in Word. Table 7-2, meanwhile, describes each view. Each view has its advantages and disadvantages, but the important thing for you to remember is that changing views is easy. You can change views either by choosing commands on the View menu or by clicking the View buttons in the lower-left corner of the screen. (One view, Print Preview, was designed for reviewing documents before you print them, but I find this view so valuable that I count it among the views that Word offers.)

LEARN BY EXAMPLE
If you would like to test-drive Word's different views, open the Figure 7-5 (Views) *file on the companion CD.*

Working in More than One Place at a Time

Word offers commands for working on many different documents at the same time and for working on different parts of the same document. I can think of hundreds of reasons for using these valuable commands. For example, you might open a second document so you can review it and perhaps copy text from it to the document you are working on. And when you are working on a long report, you might split the screen or open a second window so you can see two parts of the document at the same time and make sure that the work is well-organized.

The following pages explain how to split the screen so you can see two different parts of the same document, put two different documents onscreen at the same time, and open a second (or third or fourth) window on the same document so you can work on several different parts at the same time.

Splitting the Screen

Splitting the screen means placing one part of a document on the top half of the screen and another part on the bottom half. Split the screen when you want to compare parts of the same document or move text from one part to another. Figure 7-6 shows an example of a split screen.

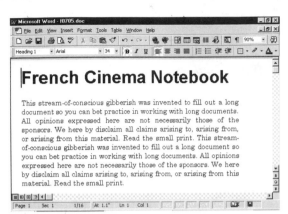

A   Normal View

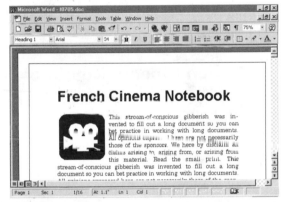

B   Page Layout View

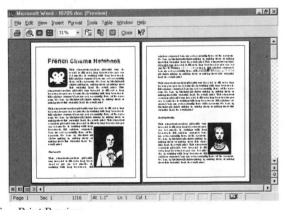

C   Print Preview

Figure 7-5. *The six ways to view a document in Word: A. Normal view, B. Page Layout view, C. Print Preview, D. Online Layout view, E. Outline view, F. Full Screen view*

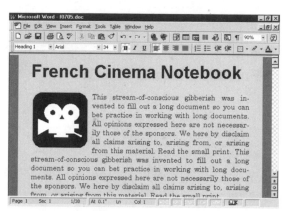

D   Online Layout View

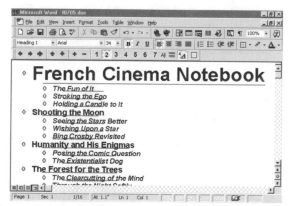

E   Outline View

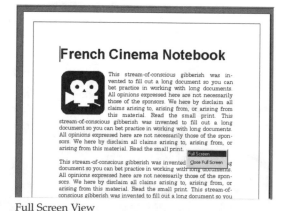

F   Full Screen View

Figure 7-5.   *The six ways to view a document in Word: A. Normal view, B. Page Layout view, C. Print Preview, D. Online Layout view, E. Outline view, F. Full Screen view (continued)*

View	Description
Normal	For writing first drafts and doing basic editing work. In Normal view, you can concentrate on the words. Sophisticated layouts, including graphics, either do not appear in Normal view or appear in the wrong places, as Figure 7-5 demonstrates. Click the Normal View button or choose the View menu Normal command to switch to Normal view.
Page Layout	As its name implies, for laying out documents. In Page Layout view, you can see precisely where columns begin and end, where the page's edges are, and where graphics and text boxes appear. In addition to graphics, page borders appear in Page Layout view, as Figure 7-5 shows. Click the Page Layout View button or choose the View menu Page Layout command.
Print Preview	For seeing more than one page at a time and getting a sense of how the entire document, not just a single page, looks. In Figure 7-5, two pages appear on the Print Preview screen, but you can display many more by clicking the Multiple Pages button and selecting several page icons from the drop-down menu. To get to the Print Preview screen, click the Print Preview button on the Standard toolbar or choose the View menu Print Preview command.
Online Layout	For laying out and dressing up documents that will be seen online. Use this view when you work on documents that won't be printed, but will be seen only on computer screens. In Figure 7-5, you can see the dark page background in Online Layout view, but not in any other view. Choose the View menu Online Layout command or click the Online Layout button.
Outline	For organizing material into headings. In Figure 7-5, I clicked the 2 button on the Outline toolbar to display first and second level headings only. Chapter 10 describes Outline view in detail. Choose the View menu Outline command or click the Outline View button.
Full Screen	For focusing on the task at hand. In Full Screen view, the menus, toolbars, status bar, and taskbar are stripped from the screen so you can see what the document will look like when it is printed. To give commands, either use keyboard shortcuts, right-click to see shortcut menus, or slide the pointer to the top of the screen, which makes the menu bar appear so you can choose commands. Choose the View menu Full screen command to switch to Full Screen view. To leave Full Screen view, click the Close Full Screen button or press the ESC key.

Table 7-2.   *Word's Six Views*

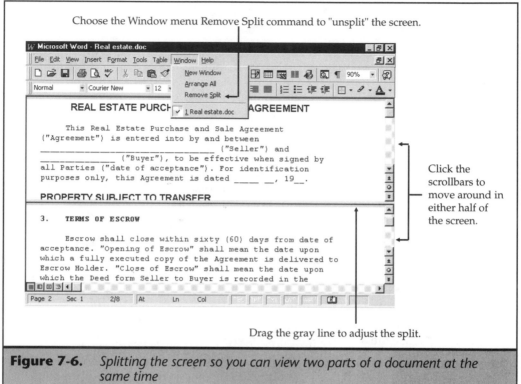

Figure 7-6. *Splitting the screen so you can view two parts of a document at the same time*

Follow these steps to split the screen:

1. Choose the Window menu Split command. A gray line appears across the middle of the screen. On the gray line is a cursor with two arrows that point north and south.

2. Drag the cursor up or down to the place where the screen is to be split.

3. Click the mouse button.

After the screen has been split, a solid gray line appears across the screen and scrollbars appear on either side of the split. Use the scrollbars or press shortcut keys to move to new places in the document. To move from one half of the split to the other, click in the other half or press F6. You can adjust the split by dragging the gray line to a new location.

Click on the side of the split you want to be in and then choose the Window menu Remove Split command to end the schizophrenic arrangement and get a single screen again.

TIP: *You can also split the screen by clicking on the tiny box above the up arrow on the vertical scrollbar and dragging the gray line to the middle of the screen.*

Opening Several Windows on a Document

Besides splitting the screen, another way to view more than one part of a document is to open more windows. With this technique, you open another window on the document. Then, in the window you just opened, you scroll to an important place that you intend to visit often. After that, when you want to revisit that place, you choose it on the Window menu.

On the Window menu shown here are five different windows of the same document. Each view is numbered. The check mark tells which window is onscreen. To switch to another window, simply choose it on the menu:

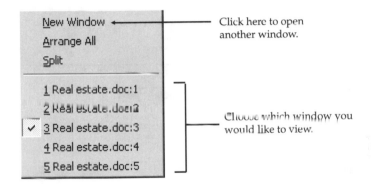

Click here to open another window.

Choose which window you would like to view.

Follow these instructions to open and close new windows on a document:

- ▪ *Opening* To open a new window on a document, choose the Window menu New Window command.

- ▪ *Closing* To close a window, click its Close button. The Close button is the *X* in the upper-right corner of the screen. Be sure to click the document window's Close button, not Word's Close button:

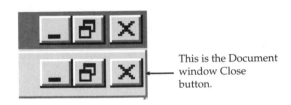

This is the Document window Close button.

WORD

NOTE: No matter how many windows of a single document are open, all work is saved to the same document file. You are working on a single document, not on several, when you choose the Window menu New Window command and work in a second window on a document.

Viewing More than One Document

Chapter 2 explained how to open several files at once and go from one file to the other by choosing its name on the Window menu. Another way to work on several files at once is to put them all onscreen. However, viewing several files at once is only good for comparing files and maybe copying or moving text from one file to another. When more than two files are onscreen, there isn't enough room to do any work.

To place several Word documents onscreen at the same time, follow these steps:

1. Open all the files that you want to see onscreen.

2. Choose the Window menu Arrange All command. Word endeavors to squeeze all the files on the screen, as shown in Figure 7-7.

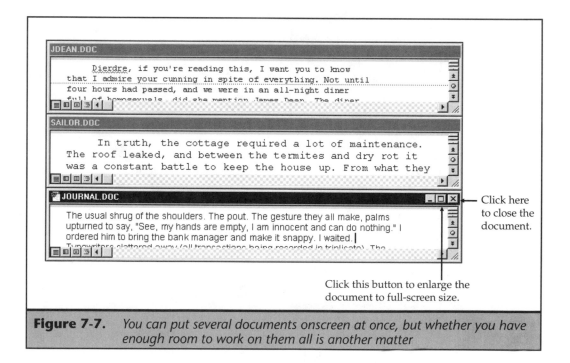

Figure 7-7.   *You can put several documents onscreen at once, but whether you have enough room to work on them all is another matter*

After the documents are onscreen, click in the one you want to work on. To close a document, click its Close button (the *X*). To enlarge a document so you can work on it, click its Maximize button. The document grows to full-screen size. You can shrink a document that is full-screen size by clicking its Restore button (the button shows two overlapping squares).

Techniques for Entering Text and Graphics Quickly

In your work, you no doubt enter certain things over and over again in Word documents. Your address, for example. Or the name of the company you work for. Perhaps a logo or other graphic. The following pages offer techniques for entering text and graphics quickly without having to retype or re-enter them.

AutoText for Entering Text and Graphics

Word has a special feature called AutoText for entering the blurbs, salutations, and what-all that people enter time and time again as they write letters, construct headers and footers, and do other things besides. By creating an AutoText entry or choosing one from Word's list, you spare yourself the trouble of typing them yourself. And you can also insert a graphic as an AutoText entry and spare yourself the considerable trouble of importing it, resizing it, and perhaps changing its color or hue. This part of the chapter explains how to make an AutoText entry as well as devise AutoText entries of your own.

Making an AutoText Entry in a Document

Figure 7-8 shows the AutoText entries on the Closing submenu. Click one of these entries to close a letter and save yourself the trouble of typing *Love, Respectfully yours, Yours truly*, or another letter closing. To insert one of Word's AutoText entries, follow these steps:

1. Place the cursor where the words in the AutoText entry should go.

2. Choose the Insert menu AutoText command.

3. On the submenu, click the name of the category in which the AutoText entry you want to make is found. In Figure 7-8, the category is "Closing." AutoText entries you create yourself appear on the Normal submenu.

4. On the submenu, click the word or words you want to insert.

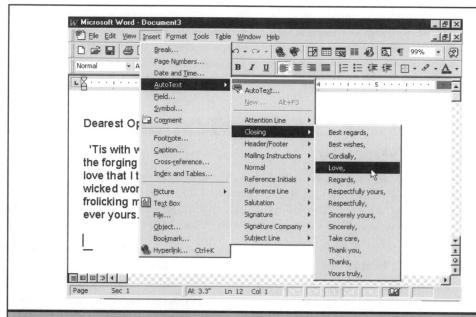

Figure 7-8. *AutoText entries save you the trouble of typing it or inserting it yourself*

"Automatic" AutoText Entries

AutoText entries on the Normal, Signature, and Signature Company submenus can be entered without choosing the Insert menu AutoText command. To enter one of those AutoText entries, type the first four letters. After the fourth letter, a small box appears and lists the rest of the AutoText entry. Press the ENTER key or F3 at that point to insert the entire AutoText entry:

The Flying Weverkas

"Yes ma'am, I'm a trapeze artist, a member of The F

Creating Your Own AutoText Entries

Besides making use of the generic AutoText entries in Word, you can create AutoText entries of your own. Homemade AutoText entries appear on the Normal submenu (choose the Insert menu AutoText command, and then click Normal). Follow these steps to create an AutoText entry of your own:

1. Enter or create the address, graphic, slogan, motto, logo, or whatnot that you want to be an AutoText entry.

2. Select the item you just created.

3. Choose the Insert menu AutoText command, and then click New. You see the Create AutoText dialog box:

4. Word 97 enters the first two words of the entry (if yours is a text entry), but you can enter a name of your own by typing it in the text box.

5. Click OK.

Deleting AutoText Entries

The AutoText submenus are crowded with AutoText entries, some of which you no doubt will never need or use. Therefore, you might consider pruning the list of AutoText entries to make the ones you do want easier to find. And if you change addresses or change names, you would have to delete a homemade AutoText entry, too.

Follow these steps to delete an AutoText entry:

1. Choose the Insert menu AutoText command, and then click AutoText. As shown in Figure 7-9, you see the AutoText tab of the AutoCorrect dialog box.

2. Find and click the AutoText entry you want to delete. The entries are in alphabetical order below the Enter AutoText entries here box.

3. Click the Delete button.

4. Click the Close button.

Using the AutoCorrect Feature to Enter Text Quickly

Chapter 3 explains Office 97's AutoCorrect mechanism. Even if you haven't read Chapter 3, you must have encountered AutoCorrect by now. When you start a sentence in Word with a lowercase letter, for example, Word automatically changes the lowercase letter to an uppercase letter. Try misspelling the word *weird*

WORD

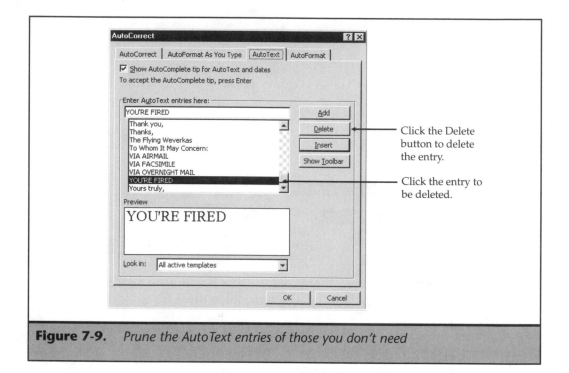

Figure 7-9.   *Prune the AutoText entries of those you don't need*

by typing it this way: *wierd*—Word immediately fixes the misspelling for you. With the AutoCorrect feature, you can tell Word 97 to correct—I mean autocorrect—the spelling errors that you make over and over again.

Although it wasn't necessarily designed that way, you can also use the AutoCorrect feature to quickly enter text. For example, suppose you are writing the definitive work about the Scotsman Thomas of Erceldoune, also know as Thomas the Rhymer, the thirteenth-century poet and seer. Rather than type *Thomas of Erceldoune* over and over again in the course of the work, you could arrange things such that every time you type **Erc/**, Word spells out *Thomas of Erceldoune*.

To use the AutoCorrect feature to enter text quickly, follow these steps:

1. Choose the Tools menu AutoCorrect command. The AutoCorrect dialog box appears, as shown in Figure 7-10.

2. In the Replace box, enter a code for the long word or phrase that you intend to enter over and over again. For Thomas of Erceldoune, for example, you could enter **Erc/**.

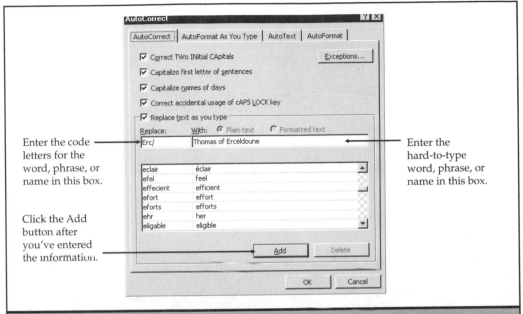

Enter the code letters for the word, phrase, or name in this box.

Enter the hard-to-type word, phrase, or name in this box.

Click the Add button after you've entered the information.

WORD

Figure 7-10. *With a little cunning, you can use the AutoCorrect feature to enter long or hard-to-type words, phrases, and place names*

*WARNING: Make sure that what you enter in the Replace box is not a real word. For example, if I enter **toe** for Thomas of Erceldoune and later try to write that word, the program will "autocorrect" the word toe." "I stubbed my toe" would become "I stubbed my Thomas of Erceldoune."*

3. In the With box, enter the word or phrase.

4. Click the Add button.

Each time you need to enter the long word or phrase, type the three or four characters you entered in the Replace box, then either press the SPACEBAR, press ENTER, press TAB, or type a punctuation mark. Word will automatically correct your entry.

Searching for the Right Word with the Thesaurus

Choosing the right word—*le mot juste*—is so important in writing, the French invented a special phrase for it and Microsoft included a thesaurus with its word processor. As you write, use the Thesaurus to find *synonyms*—words that have the same or a similar meaning. The Thesaurus is invaluable.

To find a synonym for a word, follow these steps:

1. Click the word for which you want a synonym.

2. Press SHIFT+F7 choose the Tools menu Language command, and then click Thesaurus. You see the Thesaurus dialog box shown in Figure 7-11.

3. Commence a search for the right word. Table 7-3 explains what the boxes and buttons in the Thesaurus dialog box do.

4. Click the Replace button when you've found a good synonym and it appears in the Replace with synonym box.

Word replaces the word you clicked in step 1 with the word in the Replace with Synonym box.

TIP: *If you can't quite think of the word you want but you know its antonym (its opposite), try opening the Thesaurus dialog box and seeing if the antonym has an antonym. The antonym of the antonym might be the synonym you are looking for. For example, if you need the word that means the opposite of* praise, *try looking up* praise *in the Thesaurus. If* Antonyms *appears in the Meanings box, click* Antonyms *and see if you can find the opposite of* praise *that way.*

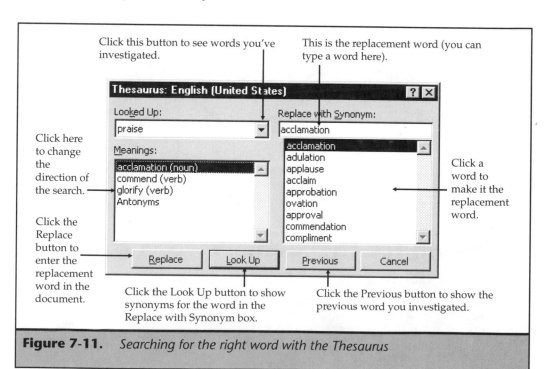

Figure 7-11.   *Searching for the right word with the Thesaurus*

Box/Button	What It Does
Looked Up	Lists the word for which you are seeking a synonym. Click the down arrow to see a drop-down list of all the words you have investigated in your search. To backtrack, click a word on the drop-down list.
Meanings	Lists word forms for the word you are looking up. In Figure 7-11, the program offers a noun form, verb form, and antonyms. Click an entry in the Meanings box to steer the search in a different direction.
Replace with Synonym	Lists what the program thinks is the best synonym for the word in the Looked Up box. When you click the Replace button, the word in this box replaces the one in the document for which you are seeking a synonym. Click a word in the box below this one to make it the replacement word, or else type your own replacement word in this box.
Replace	Enters the word in the Replace with Synonym box in the document. Click this button when your search is done.
Look Up	Tells the program to find synonyms for the word in the Replace with Synonym box, not the one in the Looked Up box. Click this button to look for a new set of synonyms.
Previous	Lists synonyms for the last word you investigated. Click this button when your search goes in the wrong direction and you want to backtrack.

Table 7-3. *Searching in the Thesaurus dialog box*

Fast Ways to Select Text

Numerous word processing tasks require you to select text first. Before you can change fonts or point sizes, you have to select text. Before you can delete text, you have to select it. Before you can move or copy text, you have to select it. Learn the many ways to select text in Word and you can become a much faster worker. The following pages explain speedy ways to select text.

Selecting Text with the Mouse

Table 7-4 describes techniques for selecting text with the mouse. To select some kinds of text, you must click in the selection bar. The *selection bar* is located on the left side of the document window. You can tell when the pointer is in the selection bar because it points to the upper-right corner of the screen, not to the upper-left corner, as is usually the case.

TIP: *You can also select an entire document by choosing the Edit menu Select All command or by pressing CTRL+A.*

Watch Out for the Paragraph Symbol When You Select Text

When you select text, whether you select the paragraph symbol at the end of paragraphs means a lot (click the Show/Hide button to see the paragraph symbols that Word puts at the end of paragraphs). In effect, the paragraph symbol holds all the formatting for the paragraph. For example, if you select text that is indented by an inch and you select it along with its paragraph symbol, it will be indented by an inch in the new location to which you move or copy it. On the other hand, if you select the text without selecting he paragraph symbol, the paragraph will be indented however far other text is indented in the location to which you move or copy it.

To select paragraph symbols when you select text, click in the selection bar when you make the selection. For example, double-clicking in the selection bar to select a paragraph selects the paragraph symbol as well as the text, but dragging the cursor over all the text in the paragraph selects all the text in the paragraph, but not the paragraph symbol.

"Extending" a Selection

Besides using the mouse, you can press F8 or double-click EXT (for "extend") on the status bar to select text. With this technique, you click where you want to start selecting text, press F8 or double-click EXT, and then click at the opposite side of the text you want to select. For example, to select the paragraph you are reading at this very moment, you would click at the start of the paragraph before the *B* in *Besides*, press F8 or double-click EXT, and then click after the period at the end of this sentence.

By the way, all the keyboard shortcuts for moving the cursor also work for selecting text after you press F8 or double-click EXT. For example, press F8 and then

To Select This	Do This
A word	Double-click the word.
A line	Click in the selection bar next to the line.
Several lines	Drag the mouse over the lines or drag the mouse down the selection bar. You can also click at the start of the text you want to select, hold down the SHIFT key, click at the end of the text, and let up on the SHIFT key.
A paragraph	Double-click in the selection bar next to the paragraph or triple-click in the paragraph.
A document	Triple-click in the selection bar or CTRL+click in the selection bar.

Table 7-4.   *Selecting Text with the Mouse*

press CTRL+END to select everything from the cursor to the end of the document. Or double-click EXT and press HOME to select to the start of the line.

TIP: *If a bunch of highlighted text is onscreen and you want it to go away but it won't (because you pressed F8 or double-clicked EXT to select it), double-click EXT again or press ESC.*

Advanced Techniques for Copying and Moving Text

It almost goes without saying, but copying and moving text are two of the most common word processing chores. Why enter text all over again when you can copy from a document or paragraph you've already written, or move it from another place in the document you are working on? The following pages explain advanced techniques for copying and moving text.

Copying Text Quickly

Word offers many different ways to copy text from one place to another. By one place to another, I mean from one part of a document to another, from one document to another document, and even from one program to another program. What's more, you can copy a single character to a new place, copy several paragraphs at once, or even insert an entire document into the document you are working on.

The following pages describe advanced techniques for copying text. Table 7-5 describes *all* the ways to copy text in Word.

Copy Technique	How It Works
Choose Edit | Copy	After you choose the Copy command, give a Paste command to copy the text.
Press CTRL+C	This is the keyboard shortcut for copying text.
Click the Copy button	The Copy button, located on the Standard toolbar, also copies text to the Clipboard.
Right-click and choose Copy from the shortcut menu	Shortcut menus also offer commands for copying and pasting text.
Press SHIFT+F2	After you press SHIFT+F2, move the insertion point where you want to copy the text, and then press ENTER.
Choose Insert | File	Copies an entire file into a document.
Drag the text to the Windows desktop	Creates a document scrap—an icon you can drag into a document for copying purposes.
Press CTRL+C, CTRL+F3, and then CTRL+V	Copies text to the Clipboard, copies it to the Spike, and then reinserts text from the Clipboard into your document. With this technique, you can use the Spike to copy text.
Select the text to be copied, then hold down the CTRL key as you drag the text to a new location	This is the drag-and-drop copying technique. Text is not copied to the Clipboard with this technique.

Table 7-5. *Techniques for Copying Text*

Comparing the Copy Techniques

Which copy technique is best for you? It depends on how adept you are with the mouse and keyboard, how many documents you are working on, and how far you want to copy text.

The quickest way to copy text is to use the drag-and-drop method, but to use it you have to be good with the mouse, and both the text you are copying and the place where you want to copy it have to be onscreen at the same time.

By choosing the Edit menu Copy command, pressing CTRL+C, or clicking the Copy button, you copy the text to the Clipboard. With that done, you can paste the text several pages back or forth in a document, in another document, in another window, or even in another Windows-based application. Copy text to the Clipboard when you want to copy it long distances or when you want to copy it several different times into a document.

To copy text from many different places, use document scraps or the Spike copying technique. Both are explained in this part of the chapter. With the Spike, copies are inserted in the order in which you copied them, but you can insert document scraps in any order you wish.

Word offers two other techniques for copying text. With Object Linking and Embedding (OLE), you can copy text so that changes made to the original are made instantaneously to the copy (OLE is explained in Chapter 5). With the AutoText feature, you can copy addresses, company names, quotations or anything else into a document by clicking a few buttons (AutoText is explained earlier in this chapter).

Copying Text with Drag and Drop

The fastest way to copy text is to "drag and drop" it. Use this technique to copy text to new locations on the screen. In theory, you can drag and drop text across a split window or from one open window to another, but that is more trouble than it's worth, because the screen has a habit of scrolling erratically when you drag text into a new window.

To copy text with the drag-and-drop method:

1. Select the text you want to copy.

2. Position the mouse over the text so the mouse pointer changes into an arrow.

3. Hold down the CTRL key, and then click and hold the mouse button down. A box with a cross in it appears below the pointer.

4. Drag the text to a new location.

5. Let up on the mouse button and release the CTRL key.

WARNING: *Don't forget to hold the* CTRL *key down when you drag and drop the text.* *If you don't hold it down, you will move the text instead of copying it.*

Besides being the fastest way to copy text, the drag-and-drop method has another advantage: it doesn't disturb what is on the Clipboard. If you've gone to the trouble of copying an ornate logo or long-winded passage to the Clipboard, you can keep it there and still copy text by using the drag-and-drop method.

Copying Text by Pressing SHIFT+F2

Word 97 offers another way to copy text without disturbing the Clipboard. What's more, you can use this technique to copy text to parts of a document that aren't onscreen or to other documents. To use this technique:

1. Select the text you want to copy.

2. Press SHIFT+F2. The status bar reads, "Copy to where?"

3. Move the cursor where you want to copy the text. To get there, you can click on the scroll bar, press keys to move the cursor, switch to another document, or open another document.

4. Press ENTER.

Copying Scraps for a Document

Suppose you want to copy text from many different places and assemble the text in a single document. That is hard to do with conventional copying techniques. You have to open one document, copy text, open another document, paste the text there, and start all over again. You could get a blister on your clicking finger that way.

Lucky for you, Word 97 offers *document scraps*, a handy technique for copying text from many different documents. With this technique, you drag the text you want to copy onto the Windows desktop. Then, with the text arranged neatly in "scraps" on the desktop, you drag the scraps into a document one at a time.

To copy text with the document scraps method:

1. Select the text you want to copy.

2. Click the Restore button in the upper, upper-right corner of the Word 97 window to make the window smaller onscreen. (Don't click the Restore button in the document window. If you do, you will shrink the document window, not the window that Word 97 is in.)

    At this point, you should see a patch of naked desktop to the right of the Word 97 window, as in Figure 7-12. Beginning with step 3, you will drag document scraps onto the desktop. If you intend to create several document scraps, you need room for all of them. Drag the Word window to the left side of the desktop by clicking and dragging its title bar. You might also shrink the window by dragging its borders.

3. Drag the text you selected onto the desktop to copy it there. You don't have to hold down the CTRL key to copy the text. Simply hold the mouse button on the text you selected in step 1, roll your mouse until the text is on the desktop, and then release the mouse.

As Figure 7-12 shows, Word creates a document scrap—an icon that appears to be torn at the bottom. The document scrap has a name to help you identify it. The name comes from the first few words of the text you copied, but you can change the name by right-clicking, choosing Rename from the shortcut menu, and typing a new name. A document scrap is a mini-file. By right-clicking on it, you can do a number of things from the shortcut menu, including deleting the document scrap. You can also drag document scraps to new places on the desktop.

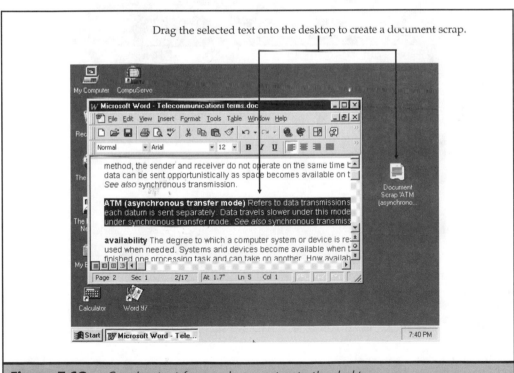

Figure 7-12. *Copying text from a document onto the desktop*

TIP: *If Windows is set up to "autoarrange" icons on the desktop, document scraps appear on the left side of the desktop when you copy them. To be able to drag document scraps on the desktop, you must tell Windows not to autoarrange the icons. To do that, right-click on the desktop, click Arrange Icons, and click Auto Arrange to remove the check mark from that opion.*

4. Select more text from the document that is open, or else open another document and select text from it.

5. Drag the next document scrap onto the desktop. You can put as many scraps on the desktop as you wish, provided you make room for them and you can remember what all of them are. Figure 7-13 shows several scraps on the Windows 95 desktop.

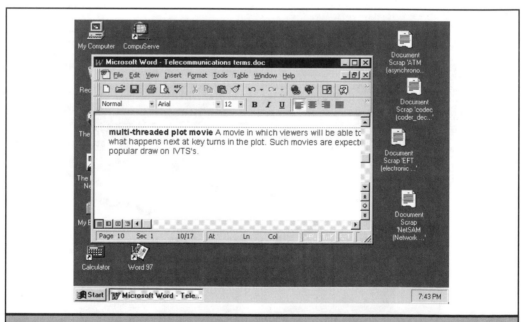

Figure 7-13. *Paste scraps in a document by dragging them from the desktop to a Word 97 document*

After you have copied all the scraps to the desktop, you are ready to paste them one at a time in a Word 97 document:

1. Open the document that is to receive all the scraps and scroll to the place where the first scrap is to be copied.

2. Drag a scrap from the desktop to the document. As you drag, a dotted line shows you where the text will go when you release the mouse button.

3. One by one, copy each scrap into your document.

When you are done, the document scraps remain on the Windows desktop. To remove them, right-click each scrap and choose Delete from the shortcut menu. When Word asks if you are sure you want to delete the scraps, click Yes.

 TIP: You can delete all the scraps at once by holding down the CTRL *key and clicking on each one. When all have been selected, either right-click on a scrap and choose* DELETE *from the shortcut menu or press the* DELETE *key. Word asks if you want to delete them all. Click Yes.*

Advanced Techniques for Moving Text

Chapter 3 explained how to move text by cutting and pasting it elsewhere. Cutting text to and pasting it from the Clipboard is fine if you're not in a hurry, but Word also offers a couple of advanced techniques for moving text. They are explained below.

Moving Text with Drag and Drop

Use the drag-and-drop technique to move text from one onscreen location to another. This technique doesn't work unless the place the text comes from and the place it will go to both appear on screen. To move text with the drag-and-drop method:

1. Select the text.

2. Slide the mouse over the text until the mouse pointer changes into an arrow.

3. Click and hold the mouse button down. A box appears below the pointer.

4. Drag the text to move it to a new location.

5. Release the mouse button.

Moving Text with the Spike

The *Spike* is a sort of supersonic Clipboard that you can use to cut text or graphics from many different places and then paste them in a document all at once. Instead of going to the trouble of cutting material from several different documents and pasting one thing at a time, you can cut and cut and cut and then paste all the material you cut in one fell swoop.

 NOTE: *Unfortunately, you can't use the Spike to copy text, although Table 7-5 describes a work-around technique for doing so.*

To use the Spike to move text from many different sources and assemble it in a single location, follow these steps:

1. Select the text or graphic.

2. Press CTRL+F3.

3. Repeat steps 1 and 2 as many times as necessary to cut other text or graphics.

4. Place the insertion point where all the text you cut is to go.

5. Press CTRL+SHIFT+F3 to simultaneously paste and clear the contents of the Spike. Alternatively, you can choose the Insert menu AutoText command, choose the AutoText command, select Spike, and then click the Insert button. This pastes the contents of the Spike and leaves the contents intact so you can paste them again.

Finding and Replacing Text and Other Things

This part of the chapter explains how to find text or formats in a document and how, if necessary, to replace them. Being able to find text or a format is important if you have to make a hasty, last-minute change. In any case, finding text or formats in a Word document takes but a few seconds and is far easier than reading a document to find whatever it is you are looking for. Finding and replacing text or formats is a great advantage, too. If you were writing the great American novel and you called the main character Jane but later decided to change her name to Jean, you could find Jane and replace her name with Jean throughout the hundreds of pages in your novel in about five seconds.

Finding Text and Text Formats in Documents

The following pages explain how to search for words, phrases, and formats in a document, as well as punctuation marks, section breaks, and other oddities.

Searching for Words and Phrases

To search for a word or phrase in a document, follow these steps:

1. Choose the Edit menu Find command or press CTRL+F. You see the Find and Replace dialog box.

2. If necessary, click the Find tab. The Find tab is shown in Figure 7-14. (Figure 7-14 shows the Find and Replace dialog box after clicking the More button.)

3. Type the word or phrase you are looking for in the Find what box.

TIP: *The Find what drop-down box lists the words and phrases you looked for recently. Click the down-arrow and choose a word or phrase if you already looked for it once since the last time you opened Word 97.*

4. To make the search go faster, you can click the More button and choose search options. When you click More, the dialog box grows larger and the following options appear:

   ■ *Search* Tells Word in which direction to search. Up searches from the cursor position to the start of the document; Down searches from the cursor position to the end of the document.

   ■ *Match case* Finds words with upper- and lowercase letters that exactly match those of the word or phrase you entered in the Find what box. For example, a search for *sit* finds that word but not *Sit* or *SIT*.

   ■ *Find whole words only* Be sure to click this box if you are looking for single words. Unless you click this box, a search for *sit* finds *sits, site, babysitter,* and all other words with the letters *sit* in them. Click this option and Word finds *sit,* not those other words.

   ■ *Use wildcards* Click here if you entered wildcards such as * and ? in the Find what box. (Use the asterisk to represent many characters and the question mark to represent a single character.)

   ■ *Sounds like* With this option, Word looks for words that sound like the one you are looking for. For example, a search for *sit* finds *set* as well.

   ■ *Find all word forms* Takes into account plurals, verb endings, and tenses in the search. For example, a search for *sit* finds *sits, sitting, and sat.*

5. Click the Find Next button. Word either finds and highlights the word or phrase you are looking for, or it tells you that it searched the document but couldn't find anything.

6. Click the Less button to shrink the Find and Replace dialog box and see the word or phrase onscreen.

7. Keep clicking the Find Next button to find other instances of the thing you are looking for, or else click Cancel to cease searching.

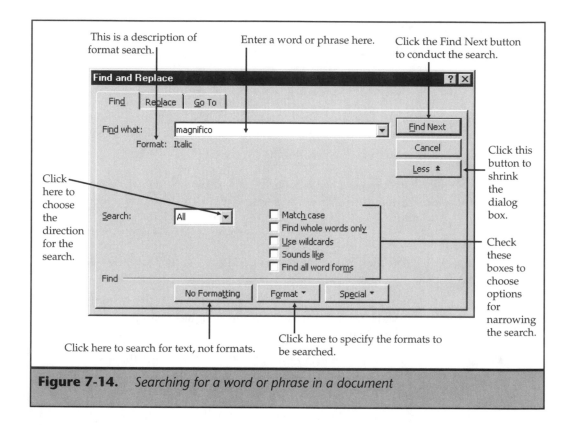

This is a description of format search.

Enter a word or phrase here.

Click the Find Next button to conduct the search.

Click here to choose the direction for the search.

Click this button to shrink the dialog box.

Check these boxes to choose options for narrowing the search.

Click here to search for text, not formats.

Click here to specify the formats to be searched.

Figure 7-14.   *Searching for a word or phrase in a document*

TIP: *After you tell Word to search for something, the arrows on either side of the Select Browse Object turn blue. You can click one of the blue arrows to search again without having to open the Find and Replace dialog box.*

Searching for Formats, Special Characters, and More

Besides searching for words and phrases, you can also search for formats and special characters in the Find and Replace dialog box. Figure 7-14, for example, shows a search for the word *magnifico* in italics, italics being the format.

SEARCHING FOR A FORMAT   To search for a format, follow these steps:

1. Choose the Edit menu Find command or press CTRL+F to open the Find and Replace dialog box (see Figure 7-14).

2. If you are looking for a word or phrase that has been formatted a certain way, enter the word or phrase in the Find what box.

3. Click the More button, if necessary.

4. Click the Format button. You see the following menu:

Font...
Paragraph...
Tabs...
Language...
Frame...
Style...
Highlight

5. Choose the type of format you are looking for. For example, to look for italicized text, click the Font option. When you click an option, the dialog box that was used to create the format opens.

6. In the dialog box, choose options to describe the format you are looking for. For example, to look for italicized text, choose Italic in the Font dialog box's Font style combo box.

7. Click OK to close the dialog box. In the Find and Replace dialog box, a description of the format you are looking for appears beneath the Find what box.

8. Click the Find Next button.

NOTE: *Click the No Formatting button in the Find and Replace dialog box when Word is set to search for formats but you no longer want to search for them.*

SEARCHING FOR SPECIAL CHARACTERS AND PUNCTUATION
To search for special characters and punctuation, follow the instructions for conducting a search, and click the Special button in the Find and Replace dialog box. You see a long list of things you can search for. Make a choice from the list and then click the Find Next button.

Replacing Text with Text and Formats with Formats

It almost goes without saying, but Word's Replace command is valuable indeed. Instead of painstakingly going through a document to find errors you made and fixing them one error at a time, you can use the Replace command to get the job done very quickly.

The Replace command works similarly to the Find command. First you tell Word what you want to replace by choosing the very same options that you choose when you tell Word what to look for with the Find command. Then you enter the replacement text or, if you are replacing a format, you tell Word what format will replace the one you told Word to find.

The following pages explain how to replace text with text, replace formats with formats, and use the Clipboard to get around the Find and Replace dialog box's 255-character limitation. It might seem impossible to replace the word *resume* with the frenchified *résumé* in a document because the Find and Replace dialog box doesn't permit you to enter accented characters. *Au contraire!* These pages explain how to replace *resume* with *résumé*.

> **WARNING:** *Always save a document before replacing text or formats. The Replace command is a powerful one indeed. It can wreak havoc on a document. By saving the document, you give yourself the opportunity to close it without saving your changes and thereby abandon all the mistakes that the Replace command introduced.*

Replacing Text with Text

Follow these steps to replace text with text:

1. Save the document.

2. Choose the Edit menu Replace command or press CTRL+H. You see the Find and Replace dialog box.

3. Click the Replace tab, if necessary. It is shown in Figure 7-15. (Figure 7-15 shows the dialog box after the More button has been clicked.)

4. Click the More button. The dialog box gets larger, as shown in Figure 7-15.

5. In the Find what box, enter the text that is to be replaced.

6. Click the Find whole words only check box.

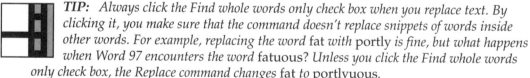

> **TIP:** *Always click the Find whole words only check box when you replace text. By clicking it, you make sure that the command doesn't replace snippets of words inside other words. For example, replacing the word* fat *with* portly *is fine, but what happens when Word 97 encounters the word* fatuous? *Unless you click the Find whole words only check box, the Replace command changes* fat *to* portlyuous.

Enter the word to be found in this box.

This is the format to be found.

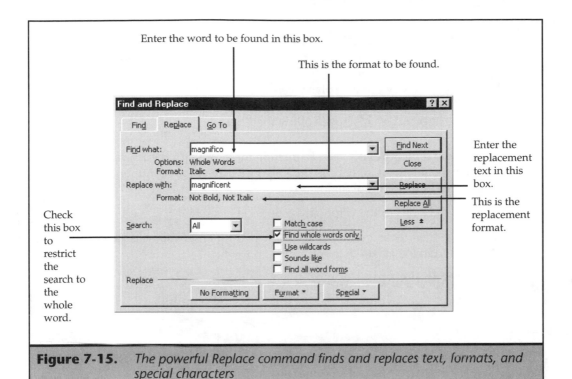

Check this box to restrict the search to the whole word.

Enter the replacement text in this box.

This is the replacement format.

Figure 7-15. *The powerful Replace command finds and replaces text, formats, and special characters*

7. Click the Find Next button. If Word finds the text you are seeking to replace, it highlights the text in the document.

8. Click the Find Next, Replace, or Replace All button:

■ *Find Next* Bypasses the text that Word found and does not replace it with the Replacement text.

■ *Replace* Replaces the text and highlights the next instance of the text in the document. Click this button to review each occasion in which Word wants to replace the text.

■ *Replace All* Replaces the text throughout the document immediately. Click this button if you are holding four aces and are absolutely certain that the text Word has found is the text you want to replace throughout the document.

Replacing Text with What Is on the Clipboard

Unfortunately, it is impossible to enter accent marks, umlauts, and other strange characters in the Find and Replace dialog box's Replace with box. That can be a problem. Suppose you want to replace *cooperate* with *coöperate*. Since you can't enter an umlaut in the Replace with text box, how do you make the replacement? By using the Clipboard, that's how. Follow these steps:

1. Type the replacement word. To include the accented characters or symbols, you probably have to choose the Insert menu Symbol command and make a choice in the Symbol dialog box.

2. Copy the word to the Clipboard.

3. Choose the Edit menu Replace command and enter the word to be replaced in the Find what box.

4. Click in the Replace with box.

5. Click the Special button. You see the following pop-up list:

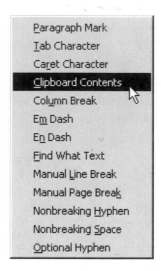

6. Choose Clipboard Contents. Word enters ^c in the Replace with box.

7. Click the Find Next button and start finding and replacing the text.

Reformatting Text with the Find and Replace Commands

Like the Find command, which offers a means of finding formats and finding words that were formatted a certain way, the Replace command can find formats and replace them with other formats. Turn back a few pages to "Searching for a Format" to find out how to tell Word which format to look for. The instructions for searching for a format also apply on the Replace tab of the Find and Replace dialog box.

After you have told Word which format to look for, use the same techniques to tell the program what the replacement format is. For example, click in the Replace with box, then click the Format button and choose Font to tell Word to replace plain text with italicized text. As shown in Figure 7-15, Word puts a description of the format you are seeking and the one that is to replace it underneath the Find what and Replace what text boxes.

 NOTE: You can also replace punctuation marks in the Find and Replace dialog box by clicking the Special button. If you entered em or en dashes incorrectly, for example, you can find and replace them by way of the Special button.

Chapter 8

Styles for Consistent and Easy Formatting

You needn't bother learning how styles work or how to apply styles if you never create documents longer than one or two pages. But if you create complex documents with headings and paragraphs that are formatted in different ways, creating and learning how to apply styles is well worth the effort. A *style* is a collection of fonts or paragraph formats to which a name has been given. Instead of going to the work of choosing fonts, line spacing options, indentation settings, and what-all for each paragraph in a document, you can bundle the different formatting commands in a style and simply apply the style to each paragraph that is to be formatted the same way. Applying a style takes but a second. Formatting paragraphs and headings one at a time is a tedious activity and is strictly for the birds.

This important chapter delves into the details of how styles work. It starts by explaining what a style is, the difference between paragraph and character styles, and what a template is. It shows how to create, apply, and redefine a style. This chapter tells how to copy styles between documents, delete and rename styles, and collect styles into a template so that you can use styles in more than one document.

How Styles Work

Styles are a bit confusing, even intimidating, at first. There are two kinds of styles: paragraph styles and character styles. And each Word document comes with a set of styles, but which styles it comes with depends on the template with which it was created. A *template* is a blueprint for a new document. Among other things, a template contains a collection of styles you can choose from for formatting documents. Word offers numerous templates, and you can create your own templates, too. The following pages explain everything you need to know to create and apply styles wisely.

Why Styles Are So Essential

By working with styles, you free yourself from having to visit and revisit numerous dialog boxes each time you want to format a paragraph or change the font and font size of text. After you create a style, you can simply choose it from the Style menu instead of giving formatting commands.

With styles, moreover, you can rest assured that headings and paragraphs throughout a document are consistent with one another. All headings given the Heading 1 style look the same. Paragraphs given the Intro Para style also look alike. And if you decide, for example, that the Intro Para style doesn't look quite right, you can change it and change as well every single paragraph to which the Intro Para has been assigned. You can do that instantaneously. Styles, besides making it easy to format paragraphs and headings, are a sort of insurance policy. If you change your mind about the look of a heading, all you have to do is redefine the style to which you've assigned it—and all headings that were given the same style are redefined as well.

In a business setting, styles are especially important. A company makes a good impression when the memos, faxes, and invoices that it sends to clients and customers have a similar look. You can give them a similar look by creating styles for faxes, memos, and invoices and saving them in a template. Creating styles for company correspondence also saves time. Instead of wrestling with Word's formatting commands, employees can simply choose styles from a menu as they create documents.

Some Word commands don't work unless the headings in the document have been assigned a style. For example, you can't create a table of contents unless each heading in the document was assigned a heading style. Nor can you take advantage of Outline view and the commands on the Outline toolbar. And you can't cross-reference headings or number the headings in a document. To create a table of figures or illustrations, you must have tagged their captions with the Caption style. The advantages of using styles are many. Do yourself a big favor by learning how styles work and how to apply styles.

What Is a Style, Anyway?

A style is a collection of commands that have been assembled under one name. To create a style, you tell Word that you are creating it, give several formatting commands, and then name the style. Later, when you apply the style by choosing it from the Style list, you really choose several commands at once. In effect, you choose all the commands that you chose when you or someone else created and named the style.

Figure 8-1 shows a style called Salutation being chosen from the Style list. After the user clicks Salutation, all the commands that are bundled into that style are applied to the text that is highlighted in the document—in Figure 8.1, a salutation. The Salutation style calls for 11 points of empty space to appear above and below the paragraph; and for the text to be set in 10-point Times New Roman.

Rather than apply the Salutation style, imagine how much trouble formatting a salutation would be if you had to format it anew each time you wrote a letter. You would have to do the following:

- ■ Choose the Format menu Paragraph command; under Spacing, enter **11** in the Before box and **11** in the After box; and click OK.

- ■ Select the text in the salutation, choose Times New Roman from the Font menu, and choose 10 from the Font Size menu.

LEARN BY EXAMPLE

EXAMPLES

The letter in Figure 8-1 was created with a Word template called Professional Letter. Open the Figure 8-1 (Styles) *file on the companion CD if you want to experiment with the styles in the Professional Letter template.*

Figure 8-1. *When you apply a style to text, you apply several commands at once and spare yourself the trouble of visiting lots of different menus and dialog boxes*

HEADSTART

To experiment with styles, open a file based on one of the templates in the New dialog box. Choose the File menu New command, click any tab besides General, click a template, and click OK. Then examine the styles on the Style list to get an idea of what styles are for.

Paragraph Styles and Character Styles

Word offers two kinds of styles, *paragraph styles* and *character styles*. By far the majority of styles are paragraph styles. Character styles merely apply to text, whereas paragraph styles apply to text as well as paragraphs:

■ *Paragraph style* Create a paragraph style for indentations, line spacing, tab settings, and all else that falls in the "formatting" category. A paragraph style, like a character style, can also include font and font size settings. When you assign a paragraph style, its format and font settings apply to *all* the text in the paragraph that the cursor is in (or to all the text in several paragraphs if you selected all or part of several paragraphs).

■ *Character style*   Create a character style for text that is hard to lay out (such as small capitals), for combinations of font and font size commands that are too troublesome to apply in conventional ways, for shaded text or text that is surrounded by borders, or for foreign words that the spell checker and grammar checker are to skip. Before you assign a character style, select text in the document. Character styles apply to selected text, not to all the text in a paragraph.

On the Style menu, paragraph styles are marked with the paragraph symbol (¶) and character styles are marked with the letter *a*:

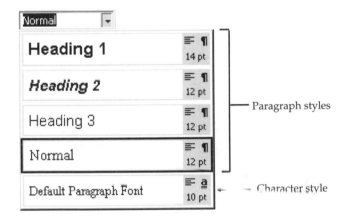

Commands That Can Be Bundled into a Style

In order to create a style, you visit the dialog boxes you would visit if you were applying formatting commands. A paragraph style can include formats made with all the commands in Table 8-1. A character style can include formats made with the commands that are marked with an asterisk in the table.

Styles and Templates

A *template* is a special type of file that can be used as the starting point for creating other files. In each Word template are many predefined styles for formatting documents. How many predefined styles are available depends on the template you choose when you create the document.

Whether you know it or not, all documents are created from templates. When you click the New button or press CTRL+N to create a new document, Word opens a generic document created from the Normal template. Choose the File menu New command and click a tab in the New dialog box, on the other hand, and Word presents many

Command	Formats for Styles
Format | Font*	Fonts, font styles, font sizes, font color, text effects (such as small capitals and embossed text), character spacing, animation
Format | Paragraph	Text alignment (Left, Center, and so on), indentation, before and after paragraph spacing, line spacing, outline level, widow and orphan control and other pagination instructions, hyphenation, suppressing line numbers
Format | Bullets and Numbering	Bulleted list formats, number schemes, heading numbering schemes
Format | Borders and Shading*	Borderlines for paragraphs, shading for paragraphs
Format | Tabs	Tab stop settings, leader settings
Tools | Language | Set Language*	Language for the spelling and grammar checkers

*For creating character styles only

Table 8-1.   *Commands for Building Styles*

templates for creating new documents. Figure 8-2 shows the templates on the Letters & Faxes tab. Choose one of these templates and you are presented with numerous predefined styles for laying out a fax or letter. (In Figure 8-1, you can see some of the styles that are available in the Professional Letter template.)

Besides creating files from the templates that Word provides, you can create your own templates and then create files from them. In fact, if you've gone to the trouble of creating elaborate styles for a document, you might as well save them in a template so you can make use of them again. The last third of this chapter explains how to create a template, copy styles to and from different templates, apply the styles in a template to a document you've already created, and turn a document into a template.

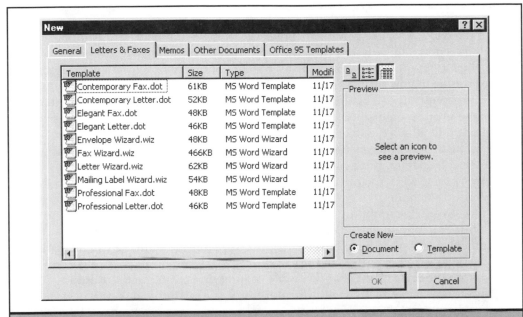

Figure 8-2. *Create a document from a template and you get many predefined styles to help with the layout*

Creating Styles

To create a paragraph style, either build it from the ground up by choosing the Format menu Style command and working inside the Style dialog box, or format a paragraph in a document and tell Word to make it a prototype for the style you want to create. To create a character style, you must choose the Format menu Style command and work inside the Style dialog box. Each method is explained in the following pages.

What Is the Best Way to Create a Style?

Word offers two ways to create a style: the prototype method and the ground-up method. Which is better?

The prototype method of creating a style has the advantage of letting you see exactly what the style looks like onscreen. With the prototype method, you format a paragraph, stare at it, change its formats if necessary, make sure it is just-so, type a style name in the Style list box on the Formatting toolbar, and press the ENTER key. When you assign the style you created to a paragraph, the paragraph looks exactly like the paragraph you used as a prototype.

Creating a style with the ground-up method takes longer, and you don't see what the style looks like onscreen, but you get to be more thorough. With the ground-up method, you start from the Style dialog box and visit the Font dialog box, the Paragraph dialog box, and any number of dialog boxes, where you tell Word precisely how the new style is going to format a paragraph.

The ground-up method offers several advantages over the prototype method. With the ground-up method, you can tell Word to redefine a style each time a paragraph to which the style has been assigned is changed. In other words, if you make a formatting change to a paragraph that has been assigned the Bold Text style, all paragraphs assigned the Bold Text style in the document are reformatted as well. You can also add the styles you create to a template with the ground-up method.

Moreover, the ground-up method gives you the opportunity to tell Word to always follow one style with another style. Suppose the Chapter Title style in a document is always to be followed by a paragraph tagged with the Chapter Intro style. For consistency's sake, and to save yourself the trouble of choosing a new style from the Style menu after you write chapter titles, you can tell Word to always follow Chapter Title with Chapter Intro.

Anyhow, most people aren't lucky enough or wise enough to create a perfect style the first time around. Maybe the best way to create a style is to go at it both ways, with the Style dialog box and the prototype method. Later in this chapter, "Redefining a Style" explains how to fine-tune a style. You can do that with the Style dialog box or the prototype method.

Creating a Style from a Prototype Paragraph

To create a style from a prototype paragraph, you start with a model paragraph whose formats are exactly the ones that the new style is supposed to embody. Follow these steps to create a style from a prototype paragraph:

1. Either find or create a model paragraph in your document.

2. Click in the paragraph.

NOTE: In Word, a paragraph is simply what you type onscreen before you press the ENTER key. Therefore, a heading is a paragraph. To create a heading style with the prototype method, click in a heading.

3. Click the Style menu box. If you do this correctly, the words in the Style box are highlighted:

Click in the Style list, type a style name, and press ENTER.

4. Type a name for the new style.

5. Press the ENTER key.

Choosing a Style Name

Choosing a meaningful style name that is nonetheless short enough to keep the Style menu from stretching out and covering half the document window is a real challenge. Style names can be 255 characters long, but only a prankster would choose a name longer than 20 or so characters. Consider the following Style list, whose names are too long. Working with this Style list would be well-nigh impossible.

Creating a Style from the Ground Up

To create a style from the ground up, follow these steps:

1. Click the paragraph or heading for which you want to create a new paragraph style, or select the text for which you want to create a character style.

2. Choose the Format menu Style command. You see the Style dialog box.

3. Click the New button. The New Style dialog box appears, as shown in Figure 8-3.

4. Enter a name for the style in the Name box. The name you enter will appear on the Style drop-down list.

5. In the Style type drop-down list, choose Character if you are creating a character style. Otherwise, let the Paragraph option stand.

6. Select the following options and check boxes as you deem fit:

   ■ *Based on*   Choose a style from the drop-down list to tie the style you are creating to another style. For example, by choosing the Default Paragraph Font style, you tell Word to always display text in the Default Paragraph Font, whatever that font happens to be. If you change the default font, styles based on that font will change as well. The style you are creating will inherit formats from the style that is chosen in the Based on drop-down list.

WORD

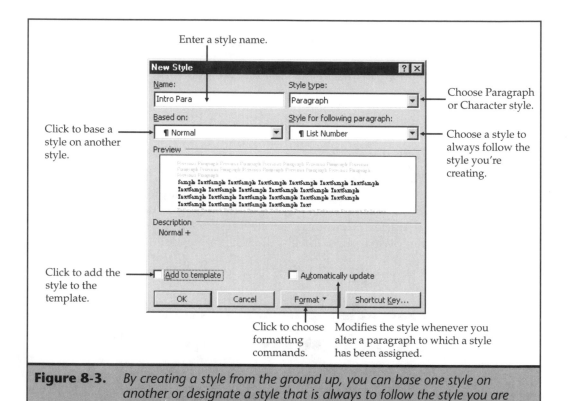

Enter a style name.

Click to base a style on another style.

Choose Paragraph or Character style.

Choose a style to always follow the style you're creating.

Click to add the style to the template.

Click to choose formatting commands.

Modifies the style whenever you alter a paragraph to which a style has been assigned.

Figure 8-3. *By creating a style from the ground up, you can base one style on another or designate a style that is always to follow the style you are creating*

WARNING: When you choose a style from the Based on drop-down list, either choose a bare-bones style like Normal or Default Paragraph Font, or choose (no style). If you choose an elaborate style from the drop-down list and you or someone else changes that style at a later day, changes to the elaborate style will be inherited by the new style. That can have bad consequences. But by sticking to a bare-bones style or no style at all, you can rest assured that changes to the based-on style won't have negative repercussions on the style you are creating.

■ *Style for following paragraph* If you want, choose a style from this drop-down list if the style you're creating is always to be followed by an existing style.

■ *Add to template* Click this check box if you want to add the style you are creating to the template with which you created the document. New styles are available only in the document for which they were created, unless this box is checked. Clicking this box saves the style you create in the document *and* in the template. A user who creates a file with the template can draw upon the style you create if this box is checked.

■ *Automatically update* Normally, when a formatting change is made to a paragraph, the style assigned to the paragraph does not change at all, but the style does change if you check this box. Checking this box tells Word to redefine the style each time a paragraph to which the style has been assigned is reformatted. With this box checked, all paragraphs in the document that were assigned the style are reformatted automatically each time you reformat a single paragraph that was assigned the style.

TIP: *If you are the type who likes to press keys to give commands, including style commands, click the Shortcut Key button. The Customize Keyboard dialog box appears. See "Assigning a New Keyboard Shortcut" in Chapter 4 to learn how to assign a keyboard shortcut to a style or command.*

7. Click the Format button. You see a menu of formatting choices (Table 8-1 lists the command equivalents of these options):

8. Choose an option to open a dialog box and give formatting commands. For example, choosing Paragraph opens the Paragraph dialog box.

9. In the dialog box, choose formatting options for the new style and then click OK.

10. Repeat steps 7 through 9 as many times as necessary to create the style.

11. Click OK to close the New Style dialog box.

12. Click Apply to format the paragraph or selected text with the new style.

Redefining a Style

It's not easy to create the perfect style the first time around. Very likely, you have to tinker with styles to make them come out right. Redefining a style, like creating a style, can be done two different ways: with the prototype method or the Modify Style dialog box.

NOTE: You can replace one style with another with the Edit menu Replace command. Choose the Edit menu Replace command, click the More button, click the Formats button, and choose Style. For the details, see "Finding and Replacing Text and Other Things" in Chapter 7.

Redefining Styles with the Prototype Method

To redefine a style with the prototype method, follow these steps:

1. Click in a paragraph to which you've applied the style that you want to redefine.

2. Reformat the paragraph. When you have finished redefining the style, paragraphs to which you've applied the style will look like the paragraph you reformatted.

3. Click in the Style menu. The letters of the style name are highlighted.

4. Press the ENTER key. You see the Modify Style dialog box:

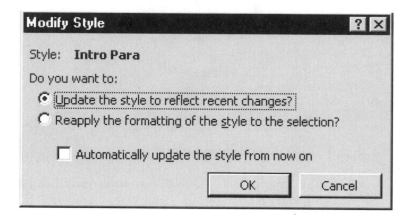

5. Make sure the Update the style to reflect recent changes? check box is checked.

6. Click OK.

NOTE: The Automatically update the style from now on? check box is the equivalent of the New Style dialog box's Automatically update check box (see Figure 8-3). Click this check box and all the paragraphs in the document that were assigned the style are reformatted each time you reformat a single paragraph that was assigned the style.

Redefining Styles with the Modify Style Dialog Box

The other way to modify a style is to use the Modify Style dialog box:

1. Click a paragraph whose style you want to redefine (or select the text if you are modifying a character style).

2. Choose the Format menu Style command to open the Style dialog box.

3. Click the Modify button. You see the Modify Style dialog box. If it looks frightfully familiar, that is because its options, check boxes, and buttons work exactly like those in the New Style dialog box (see Figure 8-3). See "Creating a Style from the Ground Up," earlier in this chapter, if you need instructions for filling in the Modify Style dialog box.

4. Modify the style in the Modify Style dialog box.

5. Click OK.

6. Click the Apply button to apply the new formats to all paragraphs or text in the document that were assigned the style you modified.

Applying a Style in a Document

After you have gone to the work of creating and redefining a style, applying it is easy. All you have to do is click in the paragraph to which you want to apply a style (or select the text if you are applying a character style) and then choose a style from the Style drop-down list. Or, to apply a style to several paragraphs, select all or part of all of them first. Figure 8-4 shows a style called Message Header First being chosen from the Style drop-down list. Sometimes you have to scroll to the bottom of the Style list to find the style you are after.

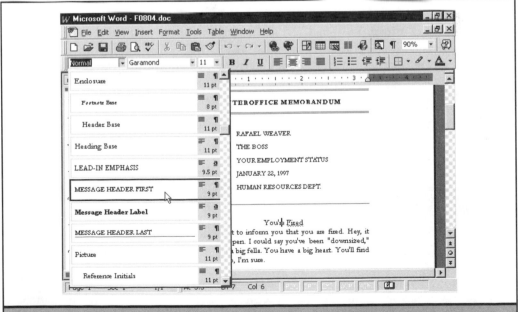

Figure 8-4. *Choosing a style from the Style drop-down list*

Notice that the Style list hints at what paragraphs will look like after a style has been chosen. Letters in the style names are shown in the same font as letters in the style itself. To the right of each style name is a box that tells how text is aligned, whether the style is a paragraph or a character style, and how many points high letters in the style are.

EXAMPLES

LEARN BY EXAMPLE
The memo in Figure 8-4 was created with a Word template called Professional Memo. Open the Figure 8-4 (Styles) *file on the companion CD if you want to experiment with the styles in the Professional Memo template.*

Working with Styles

This part of the chapter explains the in and outs of working with styles. It tells how to delete a style, rename a style, and copy styles to and from documents. The following pages offer a couple of tricks for finding out precisely which styles are which in a document and what to do if the modifications you make to a style keep fading out and disappearing. It happens.

Seeing Which Styles Are in Use

In complex documents with many styles, it is sometimes hard to tell which style is which. And it is also hard to remember what each style's formats are. Fortunately, you can rely on a special command in the Options dialog box to see exactly which styles are in use in a document. You can also use the Help menu What's This command to see how each style formats text and paragraphs.

The easiest way to tell which styles are in use is to make Word display style names along the left side of the document window, as shown in Figure 8-5. In the figure are styles named Caption, Body Text, and Special. With style names displayed this way, it is easy to see which style has been applied to which paragraph and what each style does in the way of formatting.

To display style names on the left side of the document window (Word calls it the *style area*), follow these steps:

1. Choose the Tools menu Options command to open the Options dialog box.

2. Click the View tab, if necessary.

3. Go to the Style area width scroll box in the lower-left corner of the View tab and click the up arrow button to enlarge the style area to .5 or .7 inches.

4. Click OK.

To remove the style names, repeat these steps, but shrink the style area to .0 inches.

To find out exactly what a style's formats do to a paragraph and text, choose the Help menu What's This command and click on a paragraph. As shown in Figure 8-5, a

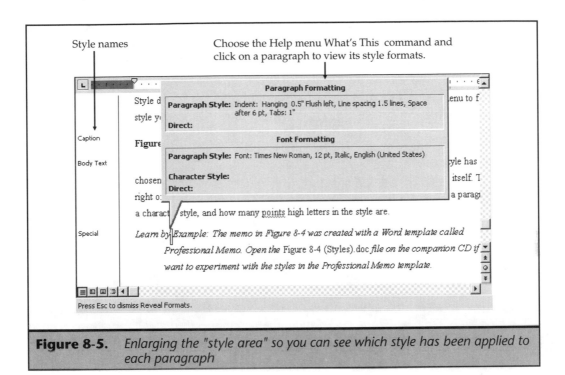

Figure 8-5.   *Enlarging the "style area" so you can see which style has been applied to each paragraph*

gray box appears and describes how the paragraph was laid out, which fonts were applied to its text, its character effects, and even its language setting. Press ESC when you have finished examining the gray box.

Help, Word Disregarded My Style Changes!

Many a Word user has gone to the trouble of redefining a style, only to discover later on that Word disregarded all changes made to the style. That happens because Word offers a feature by which styles in a document conform to the template's styles, not to the styles that individual users have modified or changed. For example, suppose you create a document based on the Contemporary Letter template, but you change one of the styles that is built into that template. When you close the file and open it again, Word may disregard the style change you made and reimpose the template's original style instead.

It can happen because Word has a special feature for updating all styles from the template and reimposing those styles each time a document is reopened. To turn that feature off and keep styles from being updated from the template, do the following:

1. Choose the Tools menu Templates and Add-Ins command. You see the Templates and Add-ins dialog box shown in Figure 8-6.

2. Uncheck the Automatically update document styles check box.

3. Click OK.

Uncheck this box to tell Word to let your style modifications stand.

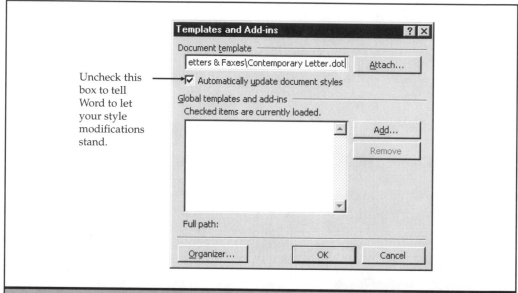

Figure 8-6. *Remove the check mark from the Automatically update document styles check box to keep styles from being updated from the template on which the document is based*

> **TIP:** *Sometimes users get the mistaken impression that Word is fooling with their styles because automatic updating is turned on and they don't know it. In the New Style and Modify Style dialog boxes is a check box called Automatically update. When that check box is selected, changes made to the formatting of individual paragraphs are made to the style itself, so all paragraphs in the document that have been assigned the same style are changed each time an individual paragraph's formats are changed. Redefine the style and uncheck the Automatically update check box to keep that from happening.*

Deleting and Renaming Styles

Long Style lists are a drag because they make it harder to find and apply styles. To keep Style lists from growing too long, Word gives you the opportunity to delete the styles you don't need to format documents. You can also rename styles. Rename a style to give it a more suitable name. And sometimes it is necessary to rename a style before copying it to another document. As the next part of this chapter explains, it is impossible to copy a style from one document to another if a style in the receiving document has the same name as the style being copied. Following are instructions for deleting and renaming styles.

Deleting a Style

When you delete a style, paragraphs to which the style was assigned are assigned the Normal style instead. Word doesn't let you delete the built-in styles that come with every Word document (Normal and the Heading styles, for example), but you can delete styles you fashioned yourself and the many extraneous styles that come with the templates. Follow these steps to delete a style:

1. Choose the Format menu Style command. The Style dialog box shown in Figure 8-7 appears.

2. Click the List drop-down menu and choose User-defined styles or Styles in use. By doing so, you trim the list of files in the Styles list and make it easier to find the style you want to delete.

3. In the Styles list, click the style you want to delete.

4. Click the Delete button.

5. Click Yes when Word asks if you really want to delete the style.

6. Click Close to close the Style dialog box.

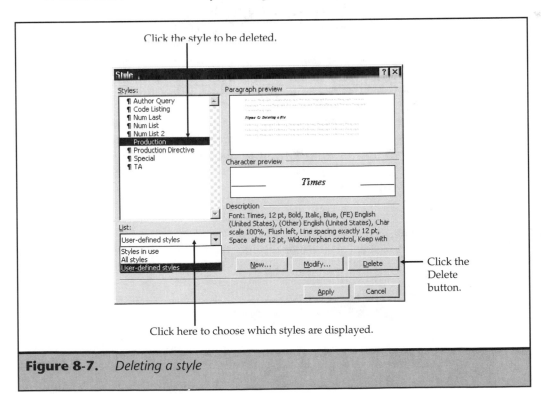

Figure 8-7. *Deleting a style*

Renaming a Style

It almost goes without saying, but you can't give a style a name that is claimed already by another style. Other than that caveat, renaming a style is similar to modifying a style. Choose Format | Style to open the Style dialog box. In the Styles list, click on the style you want to rename, and then click the Modify button. In the Modify Style dialog box, click in the Name text box and type a new name. Then click OK. If you want to apply the style to the current paragraph or selection, click Apply. Otherwise, click the Close button.

Copying Styles Between Documents

To copy a style from one document and make it available in another, all you have to do is copy a paragraph to which you've assigned the style from the first document to the second. As long as you copy an entire paragraph (including the paragraph symbol at the end of the paragraph), the style in the first document will land safely in the second and be available there as well. After you copy the paragraph, delete the text. Although the text has been deleted, the style it was assigned stays in the document and is available on the Style drop-down list.

WARNING: *You can't successfully copy a style from one document to another if the style you are copying has the same name as a style that is present in the document to which the copy is being made. To copy a style, its name must be different from all the style names in the document that is receiving the copy. Rename the style being copied, if necessary.*

By the way, the reason you have to copy an entire paragraph (by double-clicking in the left margin) is because Word formats—including styles—for each paragraph are stored in the paragraph symbol at the end of the paragraph. You can see this symbol by clicking the Show/Hide button. By copying the entire paragraph, you copy the paragraph symbol as well.

NOTE: *You can also use the Organizer to copy styles from one document to another. See "Assembling Styles for a Template" a bit later in this chapter. The same techniques for assembling styles for a template work for copying styles between documents.*

Constructing Word Templates

So far in this chapter you have learned to create styles and save them in a document. But suppose you go to all the trouble of creating intricate, elegant styles for a document and you want to use the styles over again for other documents. You could copy the styles one at a time, as the previous part of this chapter explained, but that would be a chore. It would be easier to create a new template for the new styles you created. That way, all you have to do to make use of the styles you so carefully crafted is choose the File menu New command and choose the template you created in the New dialog box.

The following pages explain how to assemble styles into a template, copy styles between templates, and choose a new template for a document.

Creating a Template for the Styles You Created

The fastest way to create a template for styles you created is to open the document for which you created the styles, save the document as a template, then open the template and delete the text. After you delete the text, the styles remain in the template and can be applied by anyone who uses the template to create a document.

To create a template for the styles you created in a document, follow these steps:

1. Open the document.

2. Choose the File menu Save As command. The Save As dialog box appears.

3. Click the Save as type drop-down list and choose Document Template. The Templates folder appears in the Save in list at the top of the dialog box. This is where Word stores templates that appear on the General tab of the Templates dialog box. If you want the template to reside in a different category, double-click the folder representing the template category you want.

4. Type a descriptive name in the File name box.

5. Click Save to complete the operation and close the Save As dialog box.

6. Delete all the text in the template.

7. Click the Save button to save your changes to the template.

8. Choose the File menu Close command to close the template.

As Figure 8-8 shows, templates you store in the Templates folder appear beside the Blank Document template on the General tab of the New dialog box. To create a document with the template you created, choose the File menu New command; click the General tab of the New dialog box, if necessary; click the template you created; and click OK.

Assembling Styles for a Template

Another way to create a template is to collect styles from different templates and documents and assemble them in a single template. Word offers a special tool called the Organizer for doing just that. Besides copying styles between documents and templates, you can copy macros, AutoText entries, and toolbars with the Organizer.

To create a template with the Organizer, you either create a brand-new template or open a template that you want to add styles to. Then you open the Organizer and start

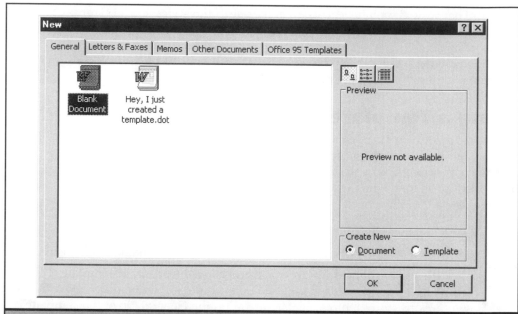

Figure 8-8. *To create a document from a template you created, choose File | New and click the category tab that corresponds to the name of the folder in which you stored the template*

copying styles (and macros, AutoText entries, and toolbars, too, if you want) from other templates and documents to the template you created or opened.

Follow these steps to copy styles from templates and documents to a template:

1. Either create a brand-new template or open the template that you want to copy styles to:

   ■ *Create a template* Choose the File menu New command. In the New dialog box, click the Template radio button in the lower-right corner. Then click OK. When the new template opens, click the Save button and save and name your new template.

   ■ *Open a template* Choose the File menu Open command. In the Open dialog box, click the Files of type drop-down list and choose Document Template. Find the folder with the template you want to copy styles to, click the template's name, and click the Open button. Click Enable Macros if Word asks how to open the template.

2. Choose the Format menu Style command. The Style dialog box opens.

3. Click the Organizer button. You see the Organizer dialog box shown in Figure 8-9 (if necessary, click the Styles tab). For now, don't worry that the arrows on the Copy button are pointing the wrong direction. In the next five steps, you will open a template or document on the right side of the dialog box, click the name of a style you want to copy, and thereby change the direction of the arrows on the Copy button.

4. Click the Close File button on the right side of the dialog box. The button changes its name to Open File.

5. Click the Open File button. You see the Open dialog box.

6. In the Open dialog box, find the template or document you want to copy files from, click the name of the template or document, and click Open. The styles in the template or document appear in the box on the right side of the screen.

7. If necessary, open the Styles available in drop-down list on the right side of the dialog box and choose either the current file or the Normal template to change which styles appear in the list of styles on the right side of the dialog box.

8. On the right side of the dialog box, click the name of a style you want to copy to your template or document on the left side of the dialog box. As soon as you click, the arrows on the Copy button point to the left. Notice the description of the style at the bottom of the Organizer dialog box.

9. Click the Copy button. The name of the style now appears in the box on the left as well as the right. The style has been copied.

10. Repeat steps 8 and 9 to copy more styles to the template or document on the left side of the screen.

11. Repeat steps 4 through 9 to open another document or template and copy styles from it as well.

12. Click the Close button in the Organizer.

13. Save your template or document now that you have copied the new styles.

EXAMPLES

LEARN BY EXAMPLE

On the CD is a sample template called Figure 8-9 (Organizer). *If you feel like experimenting, be my guest and use it to copy styles from other templates and documents.* Figure 8-9 (Organizer) *is on the CD that comes with this book.*

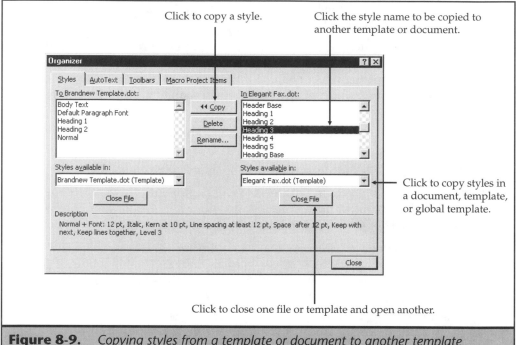

Figure 8-9. *Copying styles from a template or document to another template or document*

When Style Names Collide...

Do not copy styles with the same name from one template or document to the next. Word assumes that the style being copied takes precedence over the style that is already there, so you lose a style in the "copied to" document or template when you copy identically named styles.

To keep from losing a style, rename the style in the "copied to" template or document. To do that, click it and click the Organizer's Rename button. Type a new name in the Rename dialog box and click OK.

Choosing a Different Template for a Document

As you know, Word gives you the opportunity to create a style from a template. By choosing the File menu New command and selecting a template in the New dialog box, you can create a document with ready-made styles. But suppose you chose the wrong template. For example, suppose you chose the Contemporary Letter template for a letter, but after some thought, you realize that you should have chosen the Elegant Letter template. Oh my, feeling more elegant than contemporary these days, are we? Fortunately, you can always change horses in the middle of the stream and choose a new template for a document, even if you already created and formatted it.

Follow these steps to choose a different template for a document you have created:

1. Open the document.

2. Choose the Tools menu Template and Add-Ins command. You see the Templates and Add-ins dialog box shown in Figure 8-10. The template you used to create the document is listed in the Document template box.

3. Click the Attach button. The Attach Template dialog box appears.

4. Find and click the name of the template you want for the document, and then click the Open button. Back in the Templates and Add-ins dialog box, the name of the new template is listed in the Document template box.

5. Click the Automatically update document styles check box.

6. Click OK.

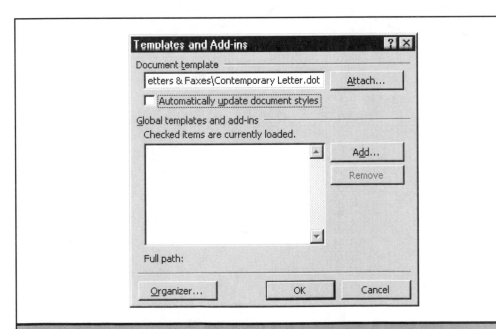

Figure 8-10. *Choosing a new template for a document*

The
Complete
Reference

Office
97

Chapter 9

Desktop Publishing with Word

bout ten years ago, I edited a book about PageMaker, the desktop publishing program. As I remember that book, the desktop-publishing features it described were no more sophisticated than the desktop-publishing features in Word 97. Word, in its own small way, has become a desktop publishing program in its own right. You can lay out and present text and graphics in many interesting ways with Word.

Chapter 9 describes Word's desktop-publishing features. It explains how to put text in a text box, shade a text box, and put borders around text boxes. It tells how to wrap text around graphics and text boxes in attractive, elegant ways. You also learn how to create a watermark and put art and text on the margin of a page. This chapter also explains how to arrange text in columns, create headers, and format and lay out a table.

Text Boxes for Announcements and Headings

To do anything fancy to text, you have to put it in a text box first. To put an announcement in the middle of a page, create a text box for the announcement. To put borders around text, shade it, or give it a color background, create a text box. If you are working on a newsletter and you want the story on page 1 to be continued on page 3, create two text boxes and link them together so that text from the text box on page 1 goes automatically to the second text box on page 3.

The following pages explain how to create a text box, change its size and shape, position it on the page, and remove the text box. They also explain how to flip and rotate text in a text box. See these parts of Chapter 9 to learn more about text boxes:

- "All About Borders, Shading, and Color" explains how to change the border and put a color or gray shade background in a text box.

- "Wrapping Text around Graphics and Text Boxes" explains how to tell Word how text should wind its way around a text box in a document.

- "Arranging Text in Newspaper-Style Columns" explains how to make text "float" from one text box to another.

Inserting a Text Box

The techniques for inserting and changing the size of text boxes are the same as those for inserting and changing the size of graphics. The only trick with text boxes is telling Word whether they should be attached to a paragraph and therefore move with that paragraph when it moves, or whether they should stay in one place.

TIP: *If you've already entered the text, you can select it and then give commands for putting a text box around it. You end up with a text box with your text inside of it. However, creating a text box by selecting text first wreaks havoc with the position settings of the new text box. It is much easier to create the text box first and then copy text into it.*

To begin with, don't worry about whether the text box is the right size or where it belongs on the page. You can handle that stuff after you have followed these steps to insert a text box in a document:

1. Scroll to the page where you want to insert the text box.

2. Choose the Insert menu Text Box command. The pointer changes into a cross and Word switches to Page Layout view, if you are not already there.

3. Click in what is to be the upper-left corner of the text box and drag the pointer across the page to what is to be the opposite corner. Lines appear to show where the borders of the text box are.

4. Release the mouse button. Square sizing handles and hash marks appear around the text box:

5. Click in the text box and start typing. You can format text in the text box by calling on most of Word's formatting commands, including the Align buttons and font settings.

Changing the Size and Shape of a Text Box

The easiest way to manipulate text boxes by far is to drag a *sizing handle*. Sizing handles are the hollow squares that appear on the corners and sides of text boxes. To change the size and shape of a text box, follow these steps:

1. Click in the text box to select it. Sizing handles and hash marks appear around the box.

2. Move the pointer over a sizing handle. When you do so, the pointer changes into a two-headed arrow. In the next step, you will drag a selection handle, but whether you drag a handle in a corner or on a side determines whether the text box keeps its proportions when you change its size:

■ *Changing size and proportions* Drag a sizing handle on a side of the text box. As the text box on the right side of Figure 9-1 shows, the text box changes shape.

TIP: *Hold down the* CTRL *key as you drag a handle on the side to drag both sides of the text box at the same time.*

■ *Changing size but keeping proportions* Drag a selection handle in the corner of the text box. As the text box in the middle of Figure 9-1 shows, the text box keeps its original shape but gets larger or smaller.

   a. Drag a sizing handle on a corner or a side of the text box. A dotted line shows how the text box is being changed.

   b. Release the mouse button.

LEARN BY EXAMPLE

Open the Figure 9-1 (Text Boxes) *file on the companion CD if you'd like to experiment with changing the size and shape of text boxes.*

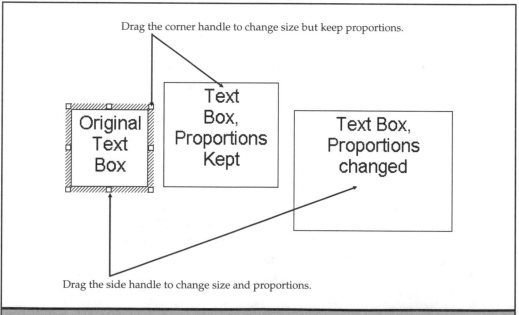

Figure 9-1. *To maintain the proportions of a text box when you change its size, drag a corner handle. To change its proportions, drag a side handle.*

Word offers a second way to change the shape and size of text boxes: choose the Format menu Text Box command, click the Size tab in the Format Text Box dialog box, and change the settings in the Height and Width boxes. Use this technique to create square text boxes and symmetrical text boxes.

TIP: *To create text boxes of the same size, copy the prototype text box, paste in the copy, remove the text, and enter new text. Before you can copy a text box, you have to select it. Do that by clicking on the perimeter of the box, not on the inside. If you click correctly, you see dots around the border of the text box instead of the usual hash marks.*

Positioning a Text Box on the Page

To position a text box on the page, drag it to a new location. Follow these steps:

1. Move the pointer over the perimeter of the text box, but not over a sizing handle. The pointer changes into a four-headed arrow.

2. Drag the text box to a new location. Dotted lines show where you are moving the text box.

3. Release the mouse button.

LEARN BY EXAMPLE
To try your hand at moving a text box, open the Figure 9-A (Text Boxes) *file on the CD that comes with this book.*

Positioning a Text Box Relative to the Column, Margin, or Page

Besides changing the position of a text box by dragging it, you can change positions in the Format Text Box dialog box shown in Figure 9-2. Choose the Format menu Text Box command, click the Position tab in the dialog box, and change the Horizontal From and Vertical From settings. Go this route if you are working with several text boxes and you want each to be in the same position relative to the column, paragraph, or page. Or, as "Anchoring a Paragraph So It Stays in One Place" in Chapter 6 explains, go this route if you want to lock the text box in one place and keep it from moving when text is inserted before it in a document.

On the Position tab are settings for telling Word where to position the left edge and top of a text box with respect to the margin, page, or paragraph in which the text box lies. Use the Horizontal From and Vertical From settings to enter the space settings:

- *Horizontal From* The space between the edge of the text box and the left edge of the column, margin, or page.

- *Vertical From* The amount of space between the top edge of the text box and the top of the margin, page, or paragraph.

Enter space between left edge of text box and
left edge of the column, margin, or page.

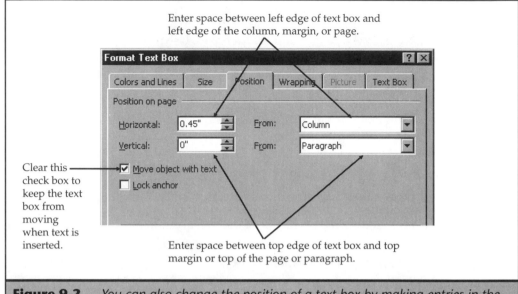

Clear this
check box to
keep the text
box from
moving
when text is
inserted.

Enter space between top edge of text box and top
margin or top of the page or paragraph.

Figure 9-2.   *You can also change the position of a text box by making entries in the Format Text Box dialog box*

Flipping and Rotating Text in a Text Box

On the Text Box toolbar is neat button for turning the text in a text box on its ear. After
you turn text on its side, you usually have to change the size of the text box to make all
the text appear onscreen. To flip or rotate text in a text box, follow these steps:

1. Click in the text box.

2. Right-click on a toolbar and choose Text Box to bring the Text Box toolbar
   onscreen, if necessary. It is shown in Figure 9-3.

3. Click the Change Text Direction button, the rightmost button on the Toolbar, as
   many times as necessary to flip the text.

LEARN BY EXAMPLE

Check out the Figure 9-3 (Text Boxes) *file on the companion CD. It offers text boxes
whose text you can flip and rotate to your heart's content.*

Removing a Text Box

All you have to do to remove a text box is select it by clicking on its perimeter,
and then press the DELETE key. To select a text box correctly, click when you see a
four-headed arrow. Text inside the text box is, alas, removed along with the text box,
so if you still need the text, copy the text elsewhere before you delete the text box.

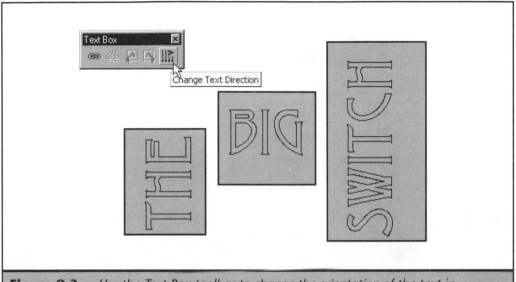

Figure 9-3. *Use the Text Box toolbar to change the orientation of the text in a text box*

WORD

All about Borders, Shading, and Color

One way to dress up graphics and text boxes is to put borders around them, fill them with color, or fill them with gray shades. You can create fanciful artwork this way. In Figure 9-4, different borders and gray shades appear around and in three text boxes and three graphics. The result is a little pastiche that describes what a wonderful country Mexico is.

The following pages explain how to put different kinds of borders on graphics, text boxes, and whole pages. They also describe how to "fill" a graphic or text box with color or a gray shade.

LEARN BY EXAMPLE
Open the Figure 9-4 (Borders) *file on the companion CD to experiment with borders, gray shades, and colors for text boxes and graphics.*

Drawing Borders Around Text Boxes and Graphics

Word puts a border around text boxes when you create them, but you can change the width and style of borders and even remove them. As for graphics, some have borders already. When you add a border to a graphic that already has a border, the graphic, in effect, gets two borders and grows thicker.

Figure 9-4. *By experimenting with borders, gray shades, and color, you can create fanciful artwork around text boxes and graphics*

WARNING: *Borders make graphics and text boxes wider and taller. That becomes a consideration when you line up text boxes or graphics in a row or line them up one below the other. Unless the borders on the text boxes and graphics are the same width, the text boxes and graphics do not line up with one another.*

DRAWING A BORDER   Follow these steps to draw a border around a text box or graphic:

1. Click the text box or graphic to select it.
2. Choose the Format menu Text Box or Picture command. The Format Text Box or Format Picture dialog box appears.
3. Click the Colors and Lines tab, which is shown in Figure 9-5. The options for creating borders around text boxes and pictures are the same.
4. Under Line, click the Color drop-down menu and choose a color for the border, if necessary.
5. If you want, click the down arrow on the Dashed drop-down list and choose a dashed line. Don't bother with this drop-down list if you want an unbroken line for the border.
6. Open the Style drop-down list and choose the type of line you want.
7. Enter how many points wide the line is to be in the Weight box.
8. Click OK.

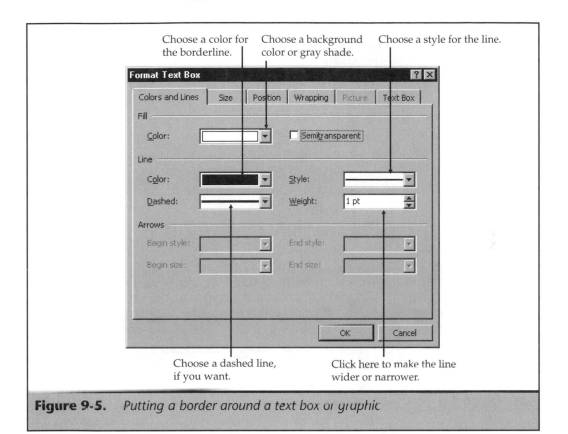

Figure 9-5. *Putting a border around a text box or graphic*

REMOVING A BORDER Follow these steps to remove the border around a text box or graphic.

1. Click the text box or graphic to select it.
2. Choose the Format menu Text Box or Picture command.
3. Click the Color and Lines tab, if necessary (see Figure 9-5).
4. Open the Color drop-down list and choose No Line.
5. Click OK.

Shading and "Colorizing" Text Boxes and Graphics

Another way to embellish a text box or graphic is to fill it with color or a gray shade. Announcements stand out when they are given a color or gray-shade background. By playing with the background of a clip art image, you can come up with interesting variations.

Follow these steps to give color or a gray shade to a text box or graphic:

1. Click the text box or graphic to select it.

2. Choose the Format menu Text Box or Picture command. You see the Format Text Box or Format Picture dialog box.

3. Click the Color and Lines tab, if necessary (see Figure 9-5).

4. Under Fill, open the Color drop-down list and choose a color or gray shade. The sidebar explains what the More Colors and Fill Effects options at the bottom of the drop-down list are for. Choose No Fill to remove a color or gray-shade background.

5. If you so desire, click the Semitransparent check box to render the fill color or gray shade a little bit dimmer.

6. Click OK.

By the way, you can get interesting effects by filling a text box with black and changing the text to white (with the Font Color button), as this illustration shows:

LEARN BY EXAMPLE
Open the Figure 9-6 (Fill Effects) *file on the companion disk that comes with this book to experiment with fill effects.*

More Colors, More Fill Effects

To get especially fancy, you can create a color of your own or create a "fill effect" for a graphic or text box. To do that, choose More Colors or Fill Effects from the Color drop-down list on the Color and Lines tab:

■ *More Colors*   To select a color apart from the 35 on the Color and Lines tab, click the More Colors option. You see the Color dialog box. On the Standard tab, click a color in the rainbow assortment of colors. On the Custom tab, either click a color in the rainbow assortment or enter hue, saturation, and brightness percentages, or red, green, and blue percentages to create a color. The New box in the lower-right corner of each tab shows precisely what color you are creating.

■ *Fill Effects*   When you choose Fill Effects at the bottom of the Color drop-down menu, you see the Fill Effects dialog box with its four tabs: Gradient, Texture, Pattern, and Picture. Figure 9-6 shows the kinds of fill effects you can get by clicking one of the tabs and playing with the options. To make a picture the background in a text box, you must either have installed the Microsoft Clip Art Gallery or have clip art of your own on-disk.

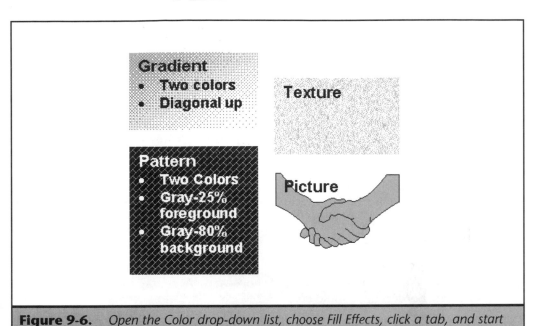

Figure 9-6. *Open the Color drop-down list, choose Fill Effects, click a tab, and start experimenting to create text boxes like these*

Drawing a Border around a Page

Besides drawing a border around text boxes and graphics, you can draw a border around one, two, three, or all four sides of a page. Borders can go around all the pages in a document or a select few. Some of the borders that Word offers are quite playful. This illustration shows Word's "pieces of cake" page border. It has been used to decorate a dessert menu:

The following steps explain how to put a border around all the pages in a document, some of the pages, or a single page. To put a border around a single page or a handful of pages in the middle of a document, create a section for those pages before following these steps:

1. Click on the page that you want to put a border around.

2. Choose the Format menu Borders and Shading command. You see the Borders and Shading dialog box.

3. Click on the Page Border tab. It is shown in Figure 9-7.

4. Under Setting, click the type of border you want. The None setting is for removing page borders. Click the Custom setting if you want to put borders on one, two, or three sides of the page or pages.

5. Under Style, click the type of line you want for the borders.

6. If you want, choose a color for the borderlines on the Color drop-down list.

7. Open the Width drop-down list and choose a point setting to tell Word how wide the borderlines should be.

8. If you want artwork instead of lines around the border, click the Art drop-down list and choose pieces of cake, umbrellas, or whatever tickles your fancy.

9. If you chose the Custom setting in step 4, either click one of the four buttons or click in the diagram in the Preview area to tell Word which side or sides to draw borders on.

10. If you want to draw borders around some, but not all, of the pages in the document, click the Apply to drop-down menu and make a choice to tell Word which pages in the document to put borders around.

11. Click OK.

If you want to get specific about how close the borderlines can come to the edge of the page or pages, click the Options button and make choices in the Border and Shading Options dialog box.

Wrapping Text Around Graphics and Text Boxes

In word processing terms, *wrapping* means to make text wind around the side or sides of a text box or graphic. Don't confuse "wrapping" with "rapping," which means to make words fly around the sides of a boom box or topic. Wrapping text is one of the easiest ways to create an elegant layout and impress your impressionable friends and employers.

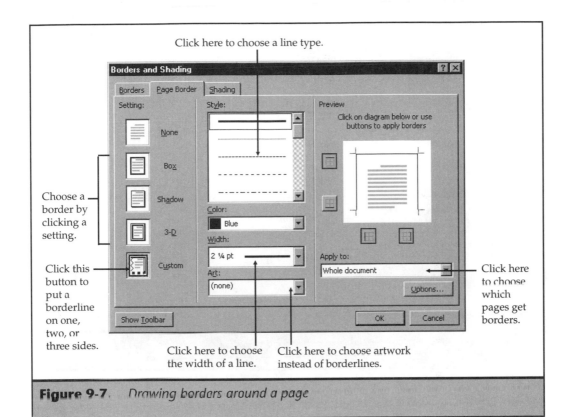

Click here to choose a line type.

Choose a border by clicking a setting.

Click this button to put a borderline on one, two, or three sides.

Click here to choose the width of a line.

Click here to choose artwork instead of borderlines.

Click here to choose which pages get borders.

Figure 9-7. *Drawing borders around a page*

TIP: To make the most of text wrapping, hyphenate and justify the text that is being wrapped. That way, the text can get closer to the graphic or text box.

Figure 9-8 illustrates several ways to wrap text. When you wrap text, you choose a wrapping style and you tell Word along which side or sides of the text box or graphic to wrap the text:

- *Wrapping style* The style choices are Square, Tight, Through, None, and Top and Bottom. When you choose Through, you can pull text as close to a text box or graphic as you want it to go. You can even make text overlap a text box or graphic. With the None style, text is not wrapped at all, and it appears on top of the text box or graphic.

- *Wrap to* The choices are Both sides, Left, Right, and Largest side. As Figure 9-8 shows, the Largest side choice wraps the text around the side of the graphic that allows the most room for wrapping, and it leaves empty space to the narrow side of the graphic.

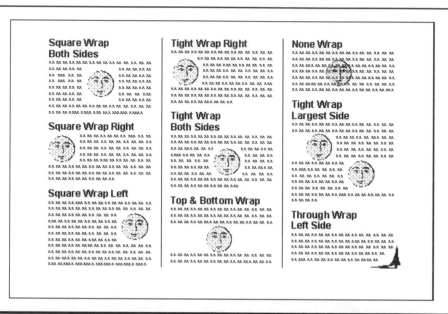

Figure 9-8. *Word offers many elegant ways to wrap text around a text box or graphic*

To wrap text around a text box or graphic, follow these steps:

1. Click the text box or graphic to select it.

2. Choose the Format menu Text Box or Picture command. The Format Text Box or Format Picture dialog box appears.

3. Click the Wrapping tab. It is shown in Figure 9-9.

4. Under Wrapping style, click a box to tell Word how to wrap text around the text box or graphic.

5. Under Wrap to, click a box to tell Word which side or sides of the text box or graphic to wrap the text around.

6. If you want to be specific about how close text can come to the graphic or text box, choose settings under Distance from text.

7. Click OK.

LEARN BY EXAMPLE

Open the Figure 9-B (Wrapping) *file on the companion CD if you want to try your hand at different wrapping styles and methods.*

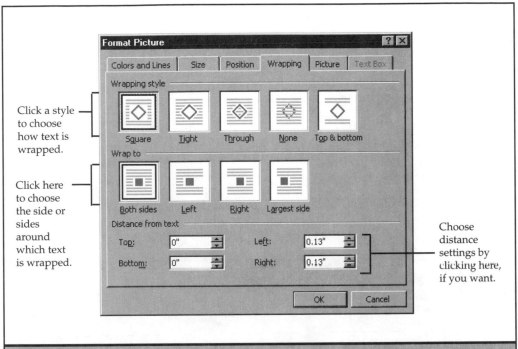

Click a style to choose how text is wrapped.

Click here to choose the side or sides around which text is wrapped.

Choose distance settings by clicking here, if you want.

Figure 9-9. *Telling Word how to wrap text and in which direction to wrap it*

Wrapping "Through" a Graphic

The Through wrapping style in the Format Picture dialog box is for making text wrap very, very close to a graphic or for making text overlap part of a graphic. After you choose the Through option and place the graphic in the text, you can make the text come closer by following these steps:

1. Click the graphic to select it.

2. Right-click on a toolbar and choose Picture to bring the Picture toolbar onscreen.

3. Click the Text Wrapping button and choose Edit Wrap Points from the shortcut menu, as shown in Figure 9-10. Black *wrap points*—small squares—appear on the graphic. You can see them in the figure.

4. Click and drag the wrap points inward to make text come closer to the graphic.

5. Click on the text when you are done.

The Wrapping Style option called Through in the Format Picture dialog box is for making text come very, very near to a graphic when it wraps around the graphic. To test this option, right-click on a toolbar and choose Picture to bring the Picture toolbar onscreen. Then click the Text Wrapping button and choose Edit Wrap Points from the shortcut menu to make wrap points appear around the graphic. Move the pointer over the wrap points and drag them inward, away from the text. By dragging them inward, you allow the text to get closer to the graphic.

- Square
- Tight
- Through
- None
- Top and Bottom
- Edit Wrap Points

Picture

Figure 9-10.   *Wrap points are the black squares that determine how close text can come to a graphic. Click and drag wrap points inward to make text come closer*

LEARN BY EXAMPLE
To doodle around with the Through option and see how wrap points work, open the Figure 9-10 (Through Wrap) *file on the companion CD.*

Creating a Watermark

The watermarks that you can create with Word are nothing like real watermarks and the Microsoft Corporation ought to be ashamed of itself for using the word *watermark* to describe putting text in front of a graphic or text box. Figure 9-11 shows examples of the so-called watermarks you can create in Word. A true watermark is made in the paper mold. It is impressed onto the paper and can be seen only when the piece of paper is held up to a light.

The techniques for creating a watermark with a graphic and text are slightly different. Both techniques are described in the following pages.

TIP: *To make a watermark appear on every page of a document, choose the View menu Header and Footer command before you create the text box or graphic for the watermark. By doing so, you tell Word to make the watermark part of the header, and it appears on every page of the document.*

LEARN BY EXAMPLE
Open the Figure 9-11 (Watermarks) *file on the companion CD if you want to noodle around with some watermarks I created.*

The following memo is top secret. It is not to be
discussed in the lunchroom on the penalty of death.

**Big Bear's Bed & Breakfast
2557 Roundabout Road
Big Bear, CA 92349**

Don't Have a Cow
About It!

Figure 9-11.   *You can create so-called watermarks like these with Word*

Creating a Watermark with a Graphic Image

To create a watermark like the one on the left side of Figure 9-11, you start by inserting
the graphic (see "Inserting Clip Art into a Document File" in Chapter 3). Then you tell
Word to make the graphic into a watermark, and to not wrap text around the graphic.
Next, you tell Word to put the graphic behind the text, and then you enter the text that
goes above the graphic.

TIP: *Solid black graphics work best for watermarks. Don't make a watermark from a
color graphic or one with lots of gray shades.*

TIP: *To make a watermark appear on each page of a document, choose the View
menu Header and Footer command and "attach" the watermark to the header box.
The watermark will not appear in the header, but it will appear on each page that the
header is on.*

Fasten your seat belts and follow these steps to create a watermark with a graphic:

1. Insert the graphic and make sure it is the right size.

2. Click the graphic to select it and choose the Format menu Picture command.
   You see the Format Picture dialog box.

3. Click the Picture tab. It is shown in Figure 9-12.

4. Under Image control, click the Color drop-down list and choose Watermark.

5. Click the Wrapping tab (see Figure 9-9) and choose None.

Use the Position tab to anchor the image to the page.   Click the Wrapping tab and choose None.

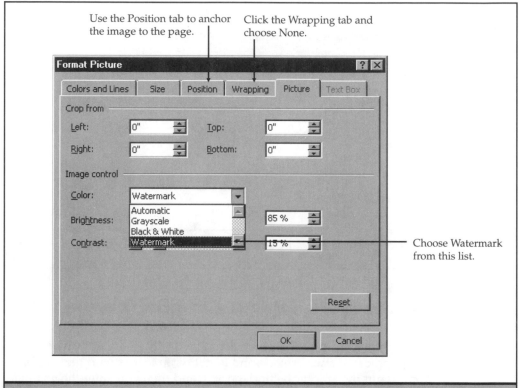

Choose Watermark from this list.

Figure 9-12.   *Choose Watermark from the Color drop-down menu to create a watermark with a clip art image*

TIP: *Before closing the Format Picture dialog box, you might click the Position tab and anchor the graphic to the page. Do that to make the watermark stay in a corner or in the middle of the page, for example. (See "Controlling Where Text Falls on the Page" in Chapter 6.)*

6. Click OK to close the Format Picture dialog box.

7. Right-click on the graphic and choose the Order menu Send Behind Text command from the shortcut menu:

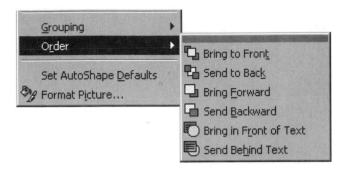

8. Type some text. It appears on top of the graphic image.

White Text over Dark Images

The right side of Figure 9-11 shows some white text over the black image of a cow. To create an image similar to that one, import a black image into a document, choose the Format menu Picture command, click the Wrapping tab in the Format Picture dialog box, and choose None. Click OK to close the dialog box, then right-click on the graphic and choose the Order menu Send Behind Text command. The text you type appears over the image. However, in order to read the text, it must be white. Click the Font Color drop-down list on the Formatting toolbar and choose White to get white text.

Creating a Watermark from Text

To create a watermark behind text like the "Top Secret" watermark in Figure 9-11, start by creating a text box and entering the "watermark words" inside it (see "Inserting a Text Box" at the start of this chapter). Choose gray for the text. Then follow these steps to make the text appear in the background:

1. Select the text in the text box, choose the Format menu Font command, click the Color drop-down menu in the Font dialog box, choose Gray-25% at the bottom of the menu, and click OK.

2. Choose the Format menu Text Box command. The Format Text Box dialog box appears.

3. Click the Colors and Lines tab, and, under Line, click the Color drop-down list and choose No Line to remove the border around the text box.

4. Click the Wrapping tab (see Figure 9-9) and choose None.

TIP: *If you want the "watermark words" to stay in one place on the page, click the Position tab in the Format Text dialog box and anchor the text box to the page. See "Controlling Where Text Falls on the Page" in Chapter 6.*

5. Click OK to close the Format Text Box dialog box.

6. Right-click on the text box and choose the Order menu Send Behind Text command from the shortcut menu.

When you type text, it appears over the words in the text box.

HEADSTART
On the companion CD that comes with this book is a template called Top Secret *that demonstrates how to use watermarks.*

Creating a Drop Cap

A *drop cap,* also known as a *drop capital,* is a letter that falls two, three, four, or more lines into the text. Figure 9-13 shows examples of drop caps. In Victorian times, it was considered very stylish to begin each chapter in a book with a drop cap, but drop caps can be used for other purposes, as the figure demonstrates.

Follow these steps to create a drop cap:

1. Click anywhere in the paragraph whose first letter is to be the drop cap.

2. Choose the Format menu Drop Cap command. The Drop Cap dialog box appears, as shown in Figure 9-14.

3. Choose Dropped or In Margin (the None setting is for removing drop caps):

   ■ *Dropped* Wraps text around the drop cap.

   ■ *In Margin* Places the drop cap in the margin beside the text. You cannot use this setting with text that has been laid out in columns.

4. Click the Font menu and choose a font for the drop capital letter. Choose a font that is different from the text in the paragraph that the letter is being "dropped in."

5. In the Lines to drop box, enter how many lines the letter is to drop. In Figure 9-13, for example, each drop cap drops four lines into the text.

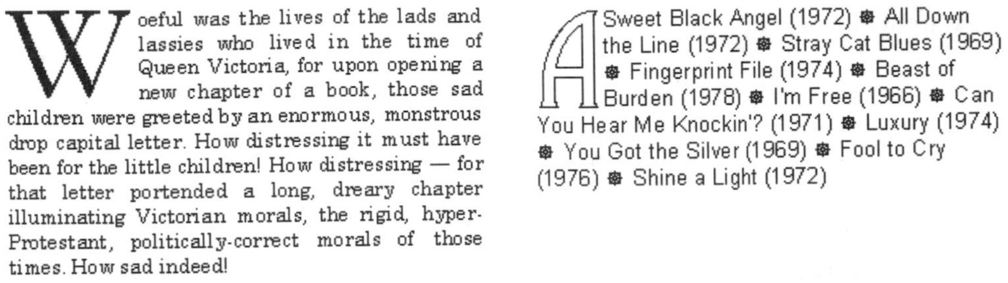

Woeful was the lives of the lads and lassies who lived in the time of Queen Victoria, for upon opening a new chapter of a book, those sad children were greeted by an enormous, monstrous drop capital letter. How distressing it must have been for the little children! How distressing — for that letter portended a long, dreary chapter illuminating Victorian morals, the rigid, hyper-Protestant, politically-correct morals of those times. How sad indeed!
A Sweet Black Angel (1972) ❁ All Down the Line (1972) ❁ Stray Cat Blues (1969) ❁ Fingerprint File (1974) ❁ Beast of Burden (1978) ❁ I'm Free (1966) ❁ Can You Hear Me Knockin'? (1971) ❁ Luxury (1974) ❁ You Got the Silver (1969) ❁ Fool to Cry (1976) ❁ Shine a Light (1972)

Figure 9-13. *Two uses of drop caps: at the start of an essay (left) and to mark the A side of a homemade cassette tape (right)*

6. In the Distance from text box, enter a number if necessary to put more space between the dropped letter and the text.
7. Click OK.

Click here to remove drop caps.
Click here to choose the type of drop cap
Drop Cap
Position
None
Dropped
In Margin
Options
Font:
Desdemona
Lines to drop:
4
Distance from text:
0.1"
OK
Cancel
Choose a font for drop caps here.
Enter the number of lines to drop here.

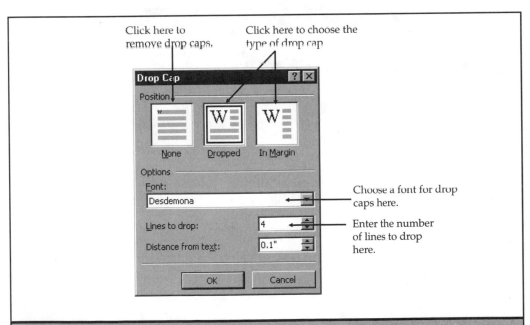

Figure 9-14. *Creating a drop capital letter*

To adjust the size of the drop cap or its distance from the text, choose the Format menu Drop Cap command again and choose different settings in the Drop Cap dialog box.

LEARN BY EXAMPLE
Open the Figure 9-13 (Drop Caps) *file on the companion CD if you want to play around with drop capital letters.*

Using One of Word's "Text Effects"

In the Font dialog box are a number of "text effects" that you can use to embellish text in various ways. Use the text effects along with boldface, italics, and underlining to draw readers' attention to headings and announcements in documents. The four most artful text effects—outlining, embossing, engraving, and shadowing—are shown in Figure 9-15. Some of the text effects look better on dark or black backgrounds.

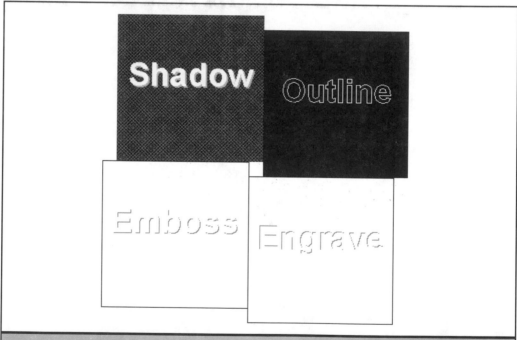

Figure 9-15.   *Use Word's text effects in text boxes to make headings and announcements stand out*

Follow these steps to apply one of Word's "text effects" to a document:

1. Select the text.
2. Choose the Format menu Font command. You see the Font dialog box.

TIP: *Most of the text effects work better when the text being "effected" has been boldfaced.*

3. Under Effects, click a check box. Don't be afraid to experiment and to choose combinations of text effects. You can see the results of your experiments in the Preview box at the bottom of the Font dialog box.
4. Click OK.

EXAMPLES

LEARN BY EXAMPLE
On the companion CD is a file called Figure 9-15 (Text Effects). *Open it if you care to experiment with Word's text effects.*

Arranging Text in Newspaper-Style Columns

Text looks great when it is laid out in newspaper-style columns. In columns, you can pack more text on the page. And you can put two or three stories on a page and give readers a choice as to which story they read first. This part of the chapter explains how to create newspaper-style columns in Word like the columns shown in Figure 9-16. It tells how to adjust the width of columns, break columns in the middle, create a heading that straddles columns, and make text in columns float to different pages.

However, before you take the plunge and create columns, I strongly recommend getting out a piece of scratch paper and designing your little newsletter. Decide how wide to make the columns, how much space to put between columns, how many columns you want, and how tall to make the headings. While you're at it, choose the File menu Page Setup command and tell Word how wide to make the margins. You usually don't need wide margins, headers, or footers in a newsletter. Word gives you lots of opportunities to tinker with columns and column sizes after you lay them out, but it takes a lot of time and shilly-shallying to do that. Better to get it right from the start and know precisely what you want to do.

WARNING: *You can only work with columns in Page Layout view.*

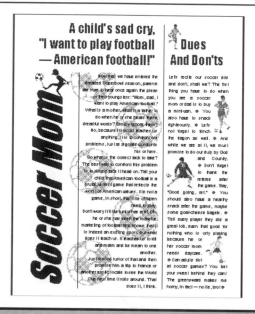

Figure 9-16. *You can create fancy column layouts with Word*

Should You Be Using a Table?

Some people create a two- or three-column document when they should be creating a table instead. Resumes, for example, are usually laid out in two columns (one for job titles, for example, and one for job descriptions), but you would be foolish to use Word's Column command to lay out a resume. Why? Because when you enter text at the top of the first column, text gets bumped downward to the bottom of the first column and into the second column. With Word's Column command, text "snakes" from one column to the next whenever you enter new text. If you were trying to create a resume or other document in which the text in one column has to refer to the text in the next column (Job Title to Job Description, for example), you would go through hell trying to line up text in the two columns. Each time you made an edit or entered a word or two, text would start snaking and everything would turn into chaos.

For resumes, schedules, and other two-column documents in which one column refers to the other, create a two-column table. Then remove the table borders. See "Working with Tables in Word" later in this chapter.

WORD

Creating and Adjusting Columns

The Columns button on the Standard toolbar offers a fast but dicey way to create columns, but I think you should be thorough about it. The Columns button simply throws out a number of columns and says, "Hello, I'm done." But columns are a tricky affair. It's hard to get them right the first time.

When you create columns, Word asks what part of the document to "columnize," so where the cursor is matters a lot when you give the command to create columns. You can columnize an entire document, everything past the position of the cursor, an entire section, or selected text. Word creates a new section when you create columns in the middle of a document.

Following are instructions for creating and adjusting columns after you have created them:

1. If you are creating columns, place the cursor in a section you want to columnize, select the text you want to columnize, or place the cursor at the position where columns are to begin appearing. If you are adjusting a column layout, click in a column.

2. Choose the Format menu Columns command. You see the Columns dialog box shown in Figure 9-17.

3. Either click a Presets box to choose a predesigned column layout of one, two, or three columns; or, if you want more than three columns, enter the number of columns you want in the Number of columns box.

4. Click the Line between check box if you want Word to draw lines between columns.

WARNING: *You can't have it both ways. If you click the Line between check box, lines appear between all the columns. You can't tell Word to place lines between one or two columns but not the others.*

5. If you want to, tell Word how wide each column should be and how much space to put between columns in the Width and spacing area. Watch the Preview box to see the effects of your choices. As you make entries in the Width and Spacing boxes, Word adjusts width and spacing settings so that all the columns can fit across the page. Be prepared to wrestle with these option boxes:

   ■ *Width* For each column, enter a number to tell Word how wide to make the column. Click the down arrow on the scroll bar, if necessary, to get to the fourth, fifth, or sixth column. (Make sure the Equal column width check box is cleared if you want columns of unequal size.)

■ *Spacing* For each column, enter a number to tell Word how much space to put between it and the column to its right.

6. In the Apply to drop-down list, tell Word to "columnize" the section that the cursor is in, the remainder of the document, the entire document, or text you selected.

7. Click OK.

Breaking a Column for Empty Space, a Text Box, or a Graphic

Suppose you want to break a column in the middle in order to insert a graphic, insert a text box, or merely to put some empty white space in the bottom of a column. Following are instructions for breaking a column.

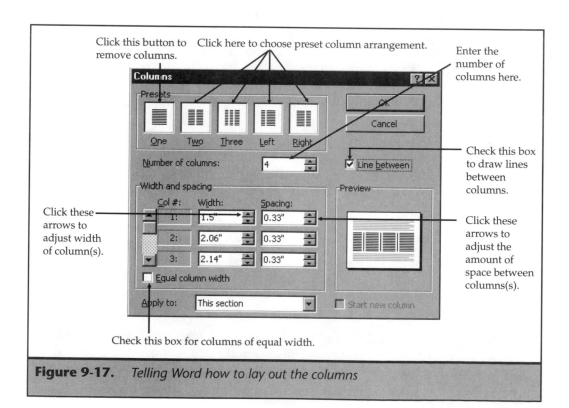

Figure 9-17. *Telling Word how to lay out the columns*

CREATING WHITE SPACE AT THE BOTTOM OF A COLUMN   To empty out the bottom of a column, click at the end of what is to be the last line in the column and either press CTRL+SHIFT+ENTER or choose the Insert menu Break command and click the Column break option button. Word breaks the column, and text that was at the bottom of the column is pushed into the next column, as shown in Figure 9-18.

BREAKING A COLUMN WITH A TEXT BOX OR GRAPHIC   To break a column with a text box or graphic, create a text box or import a graphic and tell Word to wrap the text around the graphic or text box. After you have imported the graphic or text box and positioned it roughly where it is to go, follow these steps:

1. Click the graphic or text box and choose the Format menu Picture or Text Box command.

2. In the Format dialog box, click the Wrapping tab and choose Top & bottom as the wrapping style.

NOTE: *You can also wrap text around the sides of a graphic. See "Wrapping Text around Graphics and Text Boxes" earlier in this chapter.*

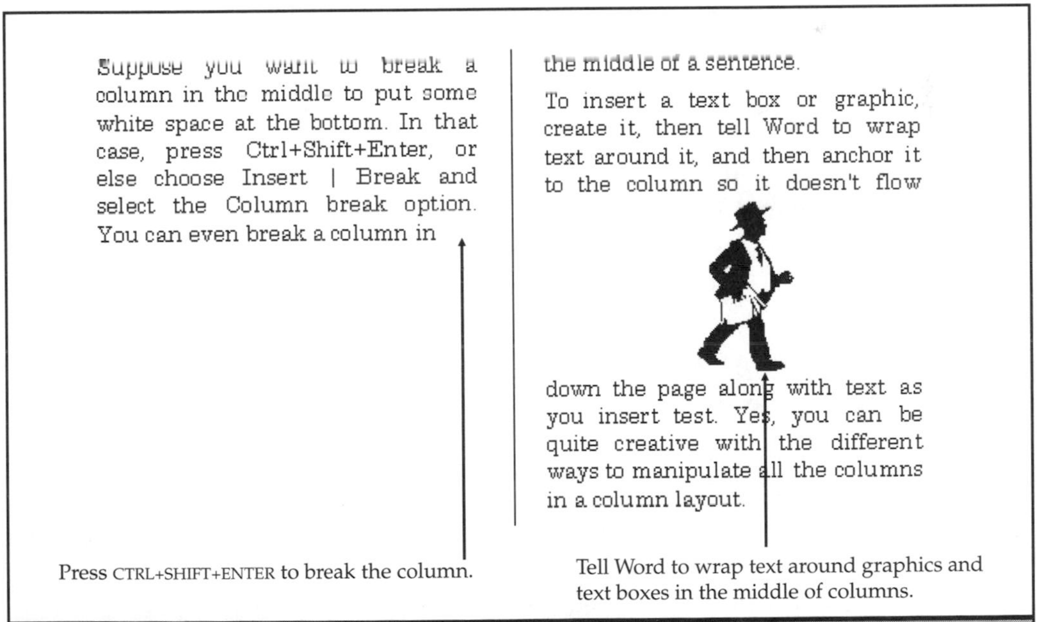

Suppose you want to break a column in the middle to put some white space at the bottom. In that case, press Ctrl+Shift+Enter, or else choose Insert | Break and select the Column break option. You can even break a column in

Press CTRL+SHIFT+ENTER to break the column.

the middle of a sentence.

To insert a text box or graphic, create it, then tell Word to wrap text around it, and then anchor it to the column so it doesn't flow

down the page along with text as you insert test. Yes, you can be quite creative with the different ways to manipulate all the columns in a column layout.

Tell Word to wrap text around graphics and text boxes in the middle of columns.

Figure 9-18.   *Ways of breaking a column*

3. Click the Position tab and uncheck the Move object with text check box.

4. Click OK to close the Format dialog box.

5. Drag the graphic or text box to locate it correctly in the column.

TIP: To find out where a column break was inserted and perhaps delete it, click the Show/Hide button on the Standard toolbar.

LEARN BY EXAMPLE

Open the Figure 9-18 (Column Break) *file on the companion CD if you want to experiment with column breaks.*

Creating a Heading that Straddles Columns

Creating a heading that straddles columns, like the heading in Figure 9-19, is similar to inserting a text box in the middle of a single column. All you have to do is create the text box and fill it with the heading. Then you anchor the heading to the page and tell Word to wrap text around the heading.

Follow these steps to create a heading that straddles columns:

1. Create the text box and type the heading inside it. Format the letters in the heading. Be sure to make the text box as small as is necessary to hold the heading.

2. Click the text box and choose the Format menu Text Box command. You see the Format Text Box dialog box.

3. Click the Colors and Lines tab and, under Line, choose No Line on the Color drop-down menu.

4. Click the Position tab and anchor the text box to the page. To do that, uncheck the Move object with text check box, click to put a check mark in the Lock anchor check box, and choose Page in the Horizontal From drop-down menu.

5. Click the Wrapping tab and choose Top & bottom as the wrapping style.

6. Click OK to close the Format Text Box dialog box.

LEARN BY EXAMPLE

On the companion CD is a sample file called Figure 9-19 (Heading Straddle) *that demonstrates a heading that straddles columns.*

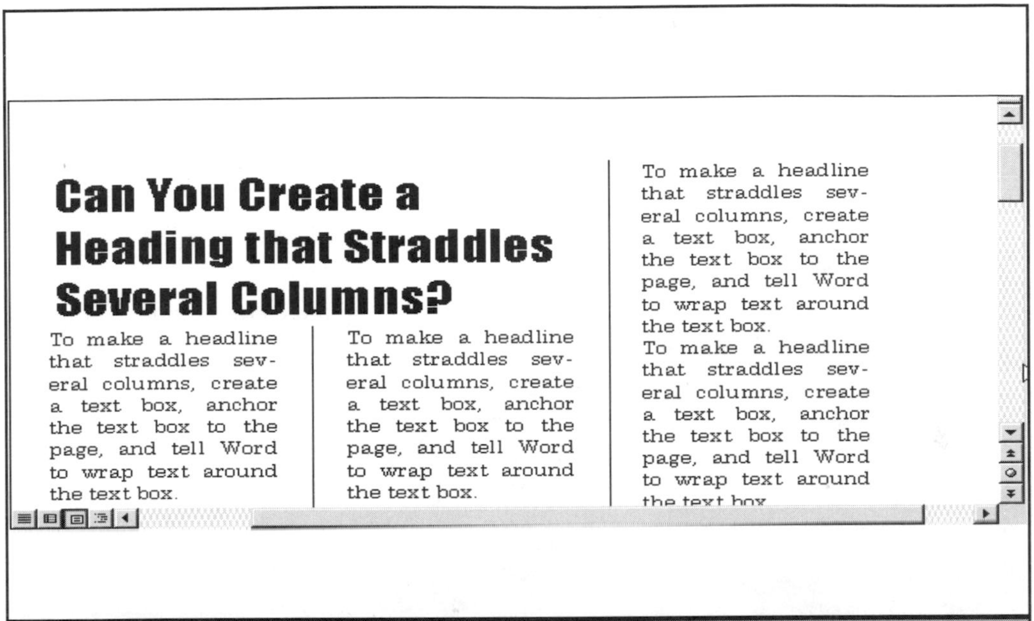

Can You Create a Heading that Straddles Several Columns?

To make a headline that straddles several columns, create a text box, anchor the text box to the page, and tell Word to wrap text around the text box.

To make a headline that straddles several columns, create a text box, anchor the text box to the page, and tell Word to wrap text around the text box.

To make a headline that straddles several columns, create a text box, anchor the text box to the page, and tell Word to wrap text around the text box.

To make a headline that straddles several columns, create a text box, anchor the text box to the page, and tell Word to wrap text around the text box.

Figure 9-19. *Create a text box to lay out a heading that straddles, or crosses, several columns*

Making Text in Columns "Float" to Different Pages

Word's Format menu Columns command is fine and good for laying out newsletters, but suppose a story begins on page 1 but resumes on page 3. What do you do then? In the Columns dialog box, Word offers no way to make text go from the front page to page 3 as the front page fills up. However, by tweaking Word, you can make linked text boxes so that text flows automatically from one page to the next when a story needs to be broken in the middle of the page. Doing so requires a little planning and forethought, but it can be done.

To make it work, you ignore the Format menu Columns command and create columns with text boxes. On the Text Box toolbar is a button for establishing a link between two text boxes such that text from the first goes automatically to the second when the first fills up. After you've linked all the text boxes, you paste text in the start of the first box and it flows into all the text boxes in the chain.

For this technique to work, you have to very carefully lay out the text boxes first. Word doesn't allow you to link text boxes in which text has already been put, so you have to plan carefully where the text boxes go. And you have to write all the text first and then be prepared to copy it in one shot into the text boxes. Follow these general steps to lay out and link the text boxes:

1. Create a text box for each column, as well as one for each heading and each "continued on" slug (the slug at the bottom of the column that says, "Cont'd on page 2," for example). All of the text boxes need not be columns. On page 2, for example, you could create large boxes, for the spillover text from page 1.

2. After you have created the text boxes, right-click on a toolbar and choose Text Box, if necessary, to see the Text Box dialog box.

3. Click the first check box in the chain of text boxes that text is supposed to pass to and from.

4. Click the Create Text Box Link button. The cursor changes into an odd-looking shape, something like a pitcher.

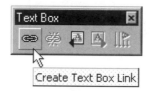

5. Move the pointer to the next text box in the chain and click it.

6. Copy the text you want to paste into the newsletter.

7. Click at the top of the first text box and give the Paste command. Text flows from the first text box into the next one.

8. Click in the second text box, if necessary, and repeat steps 4 and 5 to keep the text flowing to a third text box. You can link as many text boxes as is necessary this way.

TIP: *Also on the Text Box toolbar is the Break Forward Link button for breaking the relationship between text boxes that are linked together. Click the text box that is to be the last in the chain and then click the Break Forward Link button to break a link.*

TIP: *Click the Next Text Box or Previous Text Box button on the Text Box toolbar to go from text box to text box in a chain.*

EXAMPLES

LEARN BY EXAMPLE
Open the Figure 9-C (Text Float) *file on the CD that comes with this book if you would like to experiment with using text boxes in a newsletter to make text float from place to place. At the bottom of the document is some text. Copy it to the Clipboard, then follow the instructions above for linking text boxes in a chain.*

Removing the Columns

To remove columns, click anywhere in the columns and choose the Format menu Columns command. You see the Columns dialog box (see Figure 9-17). Under Presets, click One and then click OK.

Working with Tables in Word

Tables are an important part of any report or other kind of document that presents figures, so this part of the chapter explains how to create, enter numbers in, edit, change the layout of, and create header rows in a table.

TIP: Work on tables in Page Layout view. That way, you know precisely how close text comes to the margins. One of the biggest difficulties of working with tables is making all the data fit. One way to get around that problem is to print the page with the table on it in Landscape orientation.

Creating *a Table*

The best way to work on a table is to create a simple table, enter the data, and then worry about formats and layouts. Don't concern yourself with what the table looks like until you've entered all the text. That way, you can focus on the data itself and make sure it is accurate.

To create a table, click the Insert Table button on the Standard toolbar. When you click the button, a 4×5 grid appears. Move the pointer over the grid and click to tell Word how many columns and rows you want. To create a table bigger than four rows and five columns, hold the mouse button down, drag in a southeasterly direction , and then click. In this illustration, clicking would create a table that is six rows long and seven columns wide.

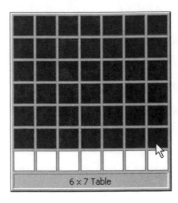

6 x 7 Table

Don't bother choosing the right number of rows and columns for now. As the following pages explain, it is easy to add and delete rows and columns.

TIP: *A fast way to create a table is to do it with the Draw Table tool. Right-click on a toolbar and choose Tables and Borders. Then click the Draw table tool and draw your table.*

Entering and Editing Table Data

After you have created the rows and columns, you can start entering the data. These instructions explain how to move from cell to cell to enter data, as well as how to move long distances in a table. You also find out how to delete and insert columns and rows, and how to select them. You can't insert or delete columns or rows without selecting them first.

Moving Around in a Table

As you enter data, you can press the arrow keys or click in cells to move from place to place. Use the following shortcut keys to go long distances:

Press	To Move Here
TAB	Next column in row
SHIFT+TAB	Previous column in a row
ALT+END	End of the row
ALT+HOME	Start of the row
ALT+PGDN	Bottom of the column
ALT+PGUP	Top of the column

NOTE: *A* cell *is the place where a row and column intersect. Each cell holds one data item.*

Selecting Rows and Columns

Before you can delete rows and columns, insert them, or change their formats, you have to select them:

- *Columns* To select a column, move the pointer to the top of the column. When the pointer changes into a black arrow that points down, click. To select several columns at once, continue to hold down the mouse button and drag the mouse to the right or left after you have selected the first column. Another way to select columns is to hold the ALT key and click anywhere in the column. To select adjacent columns with this technique, continue to hold the ALT key and drag across the desired columns.

- *Rows* To select a row, move the pointer to the left side of the row you want to select. When the pointer points to the upper-right corner of the screen, click. To select several rows, continue to hold down the mouse button and drag the mouse up or down.

- *Entire table* To select an entire table, either choose the Table menu Select Table command or hold down the ALT key and double-click in the table.

Deleting Rows and Columns

After you have selected rows and columns, deleting them is a lead-pipe cinch. First, right-click on the highlighted rows or columns that you selected. Then, choose Delete Columns or Delete Rows from the shortcut menu:

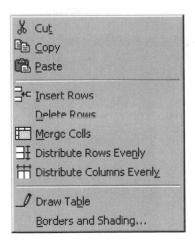

Inserting Rows and Columns

To insert a row or column, follow these steps:

1. Select the number of rows or columns you want to insert:

   - *Columns* Select a column or columns to the right of where the new columns are to go. In other words, if you want to create a new column 1, click the present column 1. After you create the new column, the one you select becomes column 2.

   - *Rows* Select a row or rows below where the new rows are to go. For example, to create a new fourth and fifth row, select the present fourth and fifth row. The two rows you insert will become the new fourth and fifth row, and the two rows you select will become the sixth and seventh row.

2. Right-click the columns or rows you selected and choose Insert Columns or Insert Rows from the shortcut menu.

TIP: *To insert a new last row in a table, click in the last column of the last row and press the TAB key.*

Formatting a Table

Word offers about a billion commands for formatting tables. However, unless you are the type who enjoys tinkering with table borders, shading, and other table formats, your best bet is to let Word do the work with the AutoFormat command. The following pages explain the AutoFormat command, how to align text in columns and rows, and how to change the width of columns and the height of rows.

Changing the Look of a Table

After the table has been "autoformatted," you can tweak it here and there to make it look better. First, however, let Word's AutoFormat command do the bulk of the work by following these steps:

1. Click in the table.

2. Choose the Table menu Table AutoFormat command. You see the Table AutoFormat dialog box shown in Figure 9-20.

3. In the Formats box, click the names of formats to find the one you like best. The Preview box shows what the formats look like.

4. Experiment with the Formats to apply and Apply special formats to check boxes to see how checking and unchecking the options affects the look of the table. Keep your eye on the Preview box as you do so.

5. Click OK when the table looks tip-top.

Aligning Text in Table Columns and Rows

Aligning text in columns is pretty simple. All you have to do is rely on the Align buttons on the Standard toolbar. Word offers a special menu for aligning the text across rows. Follow these steps to align the text in table columns and rows:

- *Columns* Select the column or columns and click the Align Left, Center, Align Right, or Justify button on the Standard toolbar.

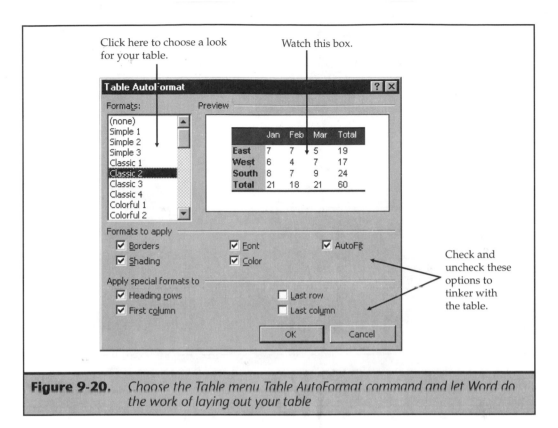

Figure 9-20. *Choose the Table menu Table AutoFormat command and let Word do the work of laying out your table*

- *Rows* Select the row or rows, right-click, and choose an option from the Alignment submenu. The following illustration demonstrates what the choices mean:

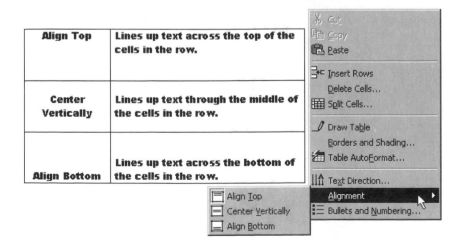

Changing the Width of Columns and the Height of Rows

In Page Layout view, drag column bars and row bars to change the width of columns and the height of rows. This illustration shows the row bars and column bars:

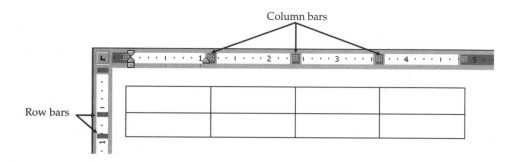

 TIP: *To make the rows in a table the same height or columns the same width, select the rows or columns, right-click, and choose the Table menu Distribute Rows Evenly or Distribute Columns Evenly command.*

The
Complete
Reference

Office
97

Chapter 10

Writing Reports
and Scholarly Papers

In this chapter, you will find advice and instructions for working on long documents such as reports, manuals, and scholarly papers. You will be glad to learn that Word has taken much of the drudgery out of writing long documents.

To help keep organized, you can work in Outline view or gather documents into a master document. That way, you always know where the various and sundry parts of your report or manual are and whether you need to rearrange things. Of course, no report or manual is complete without lots of lists and tables, so this chapter explains how to create numbered and bulleted lists, as well as how to create tables of contents and tables of figures, among other kinds of tables.

This chapter includes instructions for numbering the lines on a page and numbering the headings in a document. It tells how to create indexes and cross-references, as well as automatic captions for figures, graphs, and tables. Because footnotes and endnotes are such a chore, this chapter explains how to create footnotes and endnotes with Word's very excellent Insert menu Footnote command.

When I went to college during the Mesozoic era, students used typewriters to enter footnotes, figure tables, and the like. Perhaps this, and not disco culture, explains why I have never been nostalgic for those years.

Organizing Your Work

This part of the chapter delves into two techniques for making sure that a long report, manual, or whatnot is well-organized. It describes how to switch to Outline view to get a read on whether the work is organized well and how to rearrange documents in Outline view. The following pages also explain how to create a master document—a collection of subdocuments that, together, make up a single work. Create a master document for very, very big jobs.

LEARN BY EXAMPLE
Open the Figure 10-1 (Outline) *file on the companion CD if you want to test-drive Word's Outline view options.*

Organizing Your Work with Outlines

If your report or manual is a long one with many different headings in it, you can do yourself a big favor by assigning styles to the different headings and taking advantage of Outline view. In Outline view, you can glance at a single page and see how the different parts of a document fit together. And if they don't fit together correctly, you can rearrange headings and the text that comes below them. This part of the chapter explains how to do that, and it also explains how to edit headings, arrange headings in alphabetical order, and print an outline.

NOTE: *Styles are explained in Chapter 8. You can't see headings in Outline view unless styles have been assigned to the headings.*

Viewing the Outline of a Document

To see a document in Outline view, either click the Outline View button in the lower-left corner of the screen or choose the View menu Outline command. The Outline toolbar appears. To begin with, all headings and body text appear in the document window. However, by clicking buttons on the Outline toolbar, you can tell Word how much or how little of the document to show onscreen.

For Figure 10-1, I clicked the 4 button on the toolbar to tell Word to display headings to which I assigned the Heading 1, Heading 2, Heading 3, and Heading 4 styles. Now I can read the headings in the document and tell if I am presenting the material in the right way. You can tell which are the Heading 4 styles in the figure because they are indented farthest from the left side of the screen.

After a document is in Outline view, click buttons on the right side of the Outline toolbar to view the outline in different ways. Table 10-1 explains the buttons on the Outline toolbar.

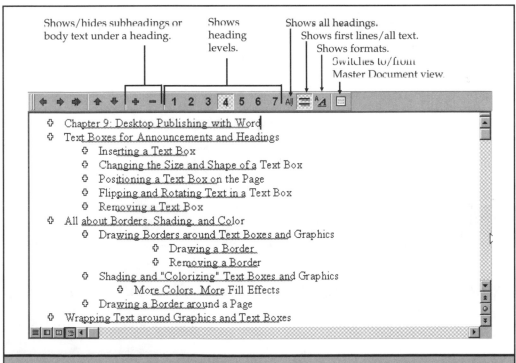

Figure 10-1.   *In Outline view, you can tell how good a job you did of organizing the material you want to present*

Button	What It Does
Expand	Shows the subheadings and subordinate text under a heading. Click on a heading and click this button to read its subheadings.
Collapse	Shows the heading only. Click this button after you click the Expand button.
1–7	Shows different heading levels in a document. Click the 1 button to see only the headings to which the Heading 1 style has been applied; click the 7 button to see headings to which the Heading 1, 2, 3, 4, 5, 6, and 7 styles have been applied.
All	Shows all the headings in the document.
Show First Line Only	Shows the headings and the first line in each paragraph of subordinate text. When this button is not clicked—when it is not "pressed down"—all the text is shown.
Show Formatting	Shows the font and type size of the text. The following illustration shows what an outline looks like after the Show Formatting button is pressed:

      ⊹ **Working with Tables in Word**
          ⊹ *Creating a Table*
          ⊹ *Entering and Editing Table Data*
              ⊹ Moving around in a Table
              ⊹ Selecting Rows and Columns
              ⊹ Deleting Rows and Columns
              ⊹ Inserting Rows and Columns

Table 10-1. *Outline Toolbar Buttons*

NOTE: *The Show First Line Only button only works when the All button has been clicked.*

Editing Text in Outline View

Yes indeed, you can edit text in Outline view as though you were editing it in Normal or Page Layout view. In fact, editing headings in Outline view is the best way to see many headings at once and make sure that they all have the same tone and are presented in an organized fashion in your scholarly report or chapter.

Rearranging a Document in Outline View

With a document in Outline view, you can do many things that would take far, far longer to do in Normal or Page Layout view. For example, you can promote or demote headings very easily. And if a heading and the text underneath it are in the wrong place, you can click toolbar buttons to move them—you don't have to visit the Cut and Paste commands.

The following pages explain how to promote and demote headings in Outline view and how to move headings forward or backward in a document. I've thrown in a neat trick for alphabetizing all the Heading 1s in a document, too.

PROMOTING AND DEMOTING HEADINGS   Suppose, after looking over a document in Outline view, you decide that a heading needs to be promoted or demoted or that a heading shouldn't be a heading at all, but should be turned into text. For example, if a Heading 3 should be a Heading 4 or should be turned into plain text, you can make it so by clicking one of the three buttons on the left side of the Outline toolbar. Notice that each button has an arrow on it. Click a button to promote or demote a heading and thereby move in the direction of or away from the left side of the screen.

Click the heading and then click one of the buttons on the Outline toolbar to promote and demote headings. Table 10-2 explains the buttons on the toolbar.

TIP: *To promote or demote several headings at once, select them first by dragging the pointer across the headings you want to select.*

MOVING HEADINGS (AND THE TEXT UNDERNEATH THEM) IN A DOCUMENT
Also on the left side of the Outline toolbar are two buttons, Move Up and Move Down, for moving headings and the text underneath them to new places in a document. Being able to move text in Outline view is convenient indeed. Instead of cutting the heading and text and pasting it elsewhere, you can simply move it in Outline view.

Button	What It Does
Promote	Click this button once, twice, or as many times as necessary to move a heading up the ladder. For example, pressing the Promote button while the cursor is in a Heading 3 heading turns the heading into a Heading 2 heading.
Demote	Click this button to bust a heading down a rank.
Demote to Body Text	Click this button to make a heading into text. Headings are assigned the Normal style when you click this button.

Table 10-2. *More Buttons on the Outline Toolbar*

When you move a heading in Outline view, the text underneath the heading moves along with the heading. Whether subheadings underneath the heading move as well depends on whether the subheadings are displayed on screen:

- If no subheadings are displayed beneath the heading when you move the heading, the subheadings move along with the heading.

- If subheadings are displayed beneath the heading, only the heading moves.

To see how this works, look at Figure 10-2. If I click the second heading, "Creating a Watermark," and click the Move Up button, it will become the first heading in the document, but "Creating a Watermark with a Graphic Image" will remain the third heading. It won't move along with its parent heading because I can see it onscreen. On the other hand, if I click "Creating a Watermark," then click the Collapse button to make the two subheadings below disappear, then click the Move Up button, "Creating a Watermark" and its two subheadings will become the first, second, and third headings in the document.

Follow these steps to move a heading forward or backward in a document:

1. Click the heading you want to move.

2. Tell Word whether you want to move subheadings (if there are any) below the heading:

   - To move the subheadings as well, click the Collapse button to fold the subheadings into the heading.

   - To move the heading independently of its subheadings, click the Expand button to display the subheadings in the window.

3. Click the Move Up or Move Down button as many times as necessary to land the heading in the right place.

Printing an Outline

When you print an outline, Word gives you whatever is onscreen in Outline view. In other words, to print the Heading 1s, Heading 2s, and Heading 3s, switch to Outline view and click the 3 button on the Outline toolbar. Expand or collapse subheadings by clicking the Expand or Collapse button.

When exactly what you want to print is on screen, click the Print button on the Standard toolbar. What you see is what you get.

Master Documents for Organizing Big Jobs

Word offers a special feature called a *master document* for working on book-length projects. If you were writing a 500-page Maileresque tome about the state of America and your ego, it would be a mistake to put all 500 pages in a single document. Imagine trying to find a paragraph or heading in such a long work. No, instead of hacking away at 500 pages at once, you could create a master document, a collection of subdocuments that are organized into one entity.

After the work has been organized into subdocuments, all you have to do is open a subdocument and start working on it. Changes made to the subdocument are all

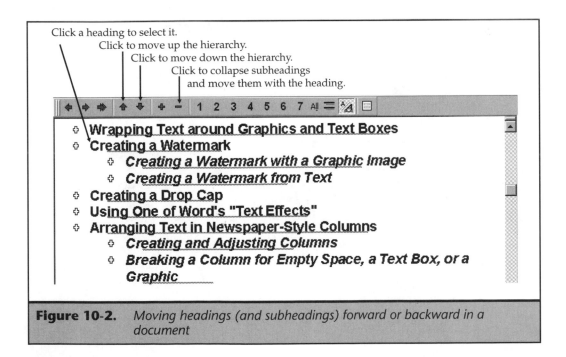

Figure 10-2.   *Moving headings (and subheadings) forward or backward in a document*

Arranging Headings in Alphabetical Order

To arrange the Heading 1 headings in a document in alphabetical order, follow these steps:

1. Switch to Outline view.

2. Click the 1 button on the Outline toolbar.

3. Choose the Table menu Sort command. The Sort Text dialog box appears. For this task, you needn't worry about the options in this dialog box.

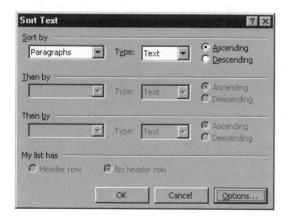

4. Click OK.

Text underneath the headings, and subheadings as well, are moved right along with the headings themselves.

recorded in the master document. And when you work in the master document, changes made there are recorded in the subdocument as well.

Everything that can be done in Outline view can be done to a master document, but you can do it all at once to two, three, five, seven, or seventeen subdocuments. In other words, you can see whether the work is organized well, and move headings and text from subdocument to subdocument, if necessary. So master documents, besides making it easier to work on long documents, offer all the advantages of Outline view.

WARNING: Knowing how to work in Outline view is important when you work with master documents. Don't create a master document unless you know how to use and operate all the buttons on the Outline toolbar.

To create a master document, you can assemble documents you've been working on for a while or start from scratch and devise a master document for a new project. Advice for doing both is offered on the pages that follow, where you will also find instructions for working on a master document and its subdocument and removing subdocuments from a master document. These pages also explain moving subdocuments, merging and splitting them, renaming them, and locking them so that no one can change them.

Creating a Master Document

Depending where you start from, the techniques for creating a master document are different. Following are instructions for creating a master document from scratch and assembling documents for a master document.

TIP: To keep things simple and moving smoothly, keep all subdocuments in the same folder. Moreover, Word gets very confused when subdocuments are created with different templates, so make sure that all the documents in the master document are founded on the same template.

LEARN BY EXAMPLE:
To try your hand at creating a master document, open the Figure 10-3 (Master Document) *file from the companion CD.*

CREATING A MASTER DOCUMENT FOR A NEW PROJECT   Follow these steps to create a master document from scratch:

1. Create a folder for the master document.

2. Create a new document.

3. Save the document in the folder you created in step 1. Congratulations. You just created the master document.

4. Choose the View menu Master Document command. As shown in Figure 10-3, the Master Document toolbar appears.

5. Enter the headings in the document. In other words, draw up an outline for your masterpiece. As you enter the headings, assign each one a heading style. In steps 6 and 7, you will divide the outline into sample documents, so be sure to assign the Heading 1 style to what will be the first heading in each subdocument.

6. Select the headings for the first subdocument. To do that, click the plus symbol beside a heading to which the Heading 1 style has been applied.

7. Click the Create Subdocument button on the Master Document toolbar. As shown in Figure 10-3, a gray box appears around the headings in the subdocument. Meanwhile, a subdocument icon appears in the upper-left corner of the box.

TIP: *You can click the cross next to a Heading 1 heading to select it and all its subheadings.*

8. Select the next batch of headings and click the Create Subdocument button again. Keep doing this until you have created all the subdocuments.

9. Save the master document.

When you save a master document, Word saves its subdocuments as well. Word gets subdocument names from each subdocument's first heading.

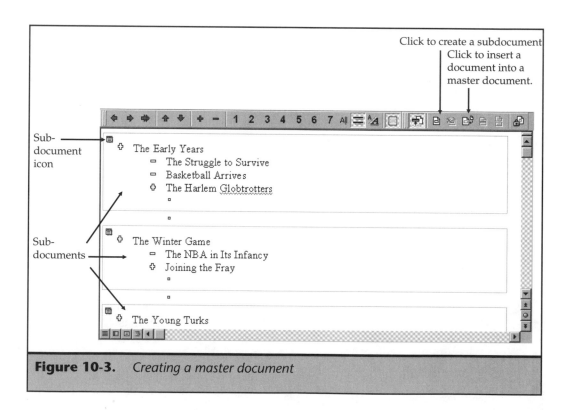

Figure 10-3. *Creating a master document*

ASSEMBLING DOCUMENTS FOR A MASTER DOCUMENT   If your masterpiece is half completed and comprises many documents in many different folders, you can still assemble the different documents into a master document by following these steps:

1. Create a folder for the master document.

2. Create a new document.

3. Save the document in the folder you just created. You just created a master document.

4. Choose the View menu Master Document command. The Master Document toolbar appears (see Figure 10-3).

5. Click the Insert Subdocument button. You see the Insert Subdocument dialog box.

6. Find and click the first file that you want to be part of the master document, then click Open.

7. Click the 1 or 2 button on the Master Document toolbar. It's easier to work in Master Document view with only one or two headings showing.

8. Go to the bottom of the master document and repeat steps 5 and 6 as many times as necessary to insert all the subdocuments.

Existing documents keep their original names when they are inserted into a master document.

Working on a Master Document and Its Subdocuments

To work on a master document or one of its subdocuments, you can either start from the master document or a subdocument. If you open a subdocument, all is well. You can open a subdocument, work on it, save it, and close it without ever knowing that it is part of a master document.

Open the master, however, and you see a document that looks something like Figure 10-4. Those underlined characters are hyperlinks. Notice that each lists the path to a subdocument. By clicking a hyperlink, you can open a subdocument and start working. (Chapter 25 explains hyperlinks in great detail.)

Or, if you are so inclined, you can work directly in the master document by clicking the Expand Subdocuments button. Do that and you see the master document in Outline view. Scroll to the part of the master document you want to work on and then click the Normal or Page Layout button to start working.

TIP: *You can open a subdocument in Master Document view. To do so, double-click a subdocument icon.*

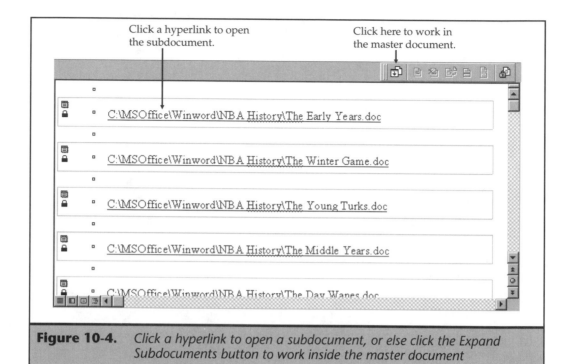

Figure 10-4. *Click a hyperlink to open a subdocument, or else click the Expand Subdocuments button to work inside the master document*

Reorganizing, Caring for, and Maintaining Master Documents

After you have created the master document, you can take advantage of all the buttons on the Outline toolbar to move headings and subheadings from place to place and to change the status of headings inside each subdocument. The previous section of this book explains how. For example, to move a heading to a new position inside a subdocument, click it, click the Collapse button if necessary, and then click the Move Up or Move Down button.

Suppose, however, that you want to rearrange the subdocuments inside a master document. Or you want to split a subdocument in two or merge two subdocuments. The following pages explain how to maintain, care for, and feed subdocuments in a master document.

TIP: *Except when splitting subdocuments, click the 1 button on the Master Document toolbar so you see only the first-level headings in the document. That makes it easier to move, merge, and remove subdocuments.*

REMOVING A SUBDOCUMENT To remove a subdocument, click its subdocument icon and then click the Remove Subdocument button, as shown in Figure 10-5. When

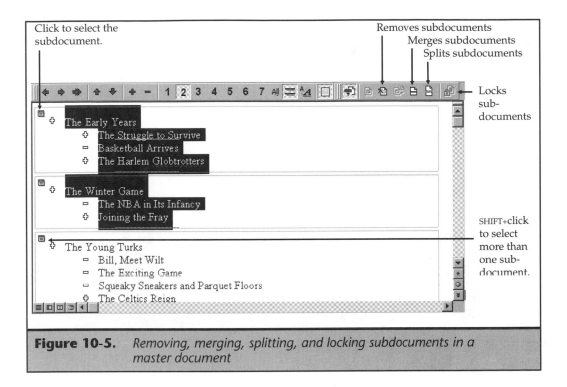

Click to select the subdocument.

Removes subdocuments
Merges subdocuments
Splits subdocuments

Locks sub-documents

SHIFT+click to select more than one sub-document.

The Early Years
    The Struggle to Survive
    Basketball Arrives
    The Harlem Globtrotters

The Winter Game
    The NBA in Its Infancy
    Joining the Fray

The Young Turks
    Bill, Meet Wilt
    The Exciting Game
    Squeaky Sneakers and Parquet Floors
    The Celtics Reign

Figure 10-5. *Removing, merging, splitting, and locking subdocuments in a master document*

you delete a subdocument this way, the document is not erased from the hard disk. It is simply removed from the master document.

DIVIDING A SUBDOCUMENT IN TWO   To divide a subdocument into two subdocuments, click the first heading in the subdocument and then click the Expand button. Next, click the heading that is to be the first heading in the new subdocument and click the Split Subdocument button.

MERGING SUBDOCUMENTS   To merge subdocuments, move the subdocuments so that they appear one below the other in the master document. Next, select the subdocuments. To do so, click the first subdocument's icon, then hold down the SHIFT key and click the subdocument icon of each subdocument you want to merge (see Figure 10-5). With that done, click the Merge Subdocument button.

MOVING SUBDOCUMENTS   I've found that the best way to move subdocuments is to remove them and then reinsert them. See "Removing a Subdocument" and "Assembling Documents for a Master Document" for more information.

LOCKING A SUBDOCUMENT SO OTHERS CAN'T EDIT IT   On the tail end of the Master Document toolbar is a button for locking subdocuments. *Locking* means to mark the subdocument so that others can read it but not alter it. To lock a subdocument, click anywhere inside it and then click the Lock Document button. To unlock it, click the Lock Document button again. Subdocuments that have been locked show a picture of a padlock next to their names:

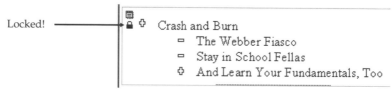

Locked! ─────── Crash and Burn
             The Webber Fiasco
             Stay in School Fellas
             And Learn Your Fundamentals, Too

Lists, Lists, and More Lists

This part of the chapter explains how to create bulleted lists, numbered lists, and numbering schemes for headings. Word offers some very convenient ways to handle lists. And if Word's numbers or bullets aren't good enough for you, you can invent numbering schemes or bullets of your own. The following pages explain how to create numbered lists, bulleted lists, and numbers for chapter headings.

Creating a Numbered List

Figure 10-6 shows a sample of the types of numbered lists you can create with Word. How fancy you want your lists to be is up to you. On the left is the list you get when you click the Numbering button on the Formatting toolbar. The two lists in the middle are preformatted lists that you can get simply by opening the Bullets and Numbering dialog box. The list on the right is a customized list. Although it takes a bit of work, you can create number formats on your own. This part of the chapter explains how. It also tells how to start, stop, and resume lists in documents.

EXAMPLES

LEARN BY EXAMPLE
To experiment with the many options for numbering lists, open the Figure 10-A (Numbered List) *file on the companion CD.*

1. Abbot and Costello	I. Abbot and Costello	a) Abbot and Costello	1 Abbot and Costello
2. Laurel and Hardy	II. Laurel and Hardy	b) Laurel and Hardy	2 Laurel and Hardy
3. The Marx Brothers	III. The Marx Brothers	c) The Marx Brothers	3 The Marx Brothers
4. The Three Stooges	IV. The Three Stooges	d) The Three Stooges	4 The Three Stooges

Figure 10-6. *A sampling of Word's numbered list formats*

Keeping Numbered Lists from Appearing Automatically

Word creates numbered lists automatically whether you like it or not when you type **1**, **A.**, or **i**; then enter a blank space or press TAB; type some text; and then press the ENTER key. Yours truly finds that extremely annoying. Perhaps you do, too. Follow these steps to tell Word *not* to create numbered lists automatically:

1. Choose the Insert menu AutoText submenu, then the AutoText command. You see the AutoCorrect dialog box.

2. Click the AutoFormat As You Type tab. It is shown in Figure 10-7.

3. Click the Automatic numbered lists check box to remove the check mark.

4. Click OK.

Creating a List

To create a simple list that isn't broken in the middle and doesn't require fancy formatting, type the items one at a time without any concern for numbers. Press ENTER after you have typed each item. When the list is done, select it and click the Numbering button on the Formatting toolbar.

The other way to create a simple list is to click the Numbering button and start typing. Each time you press ENTER, Word adds a new number to the list. When you are finished typing your list, press the ENTER key and then click the Numbering button to remove the last number.

Resuming and Restarting Numbered Lists

Suppose you write a list numbered 1 to 6, end the list, write a couple of explanatory paragraphs, and want to resume the list at 7. How do you tell Word to start numbering at 7? To resume a numbered list that you broke off earlier in a document, follow these steps:

1. Right-click where you want the list to resume.

2. Choose Bullets and Numbering from the shortcut menu. You see the Bullets and Numbering dialog box shown in Figure 10-8.

3. Click the Numbered tab, if necessary. It is shown in Figure 10-8.

4. Click the box that represents the type of numbered list you want to resume. For example, if you have been using ABC lists in the document, click the ABC list in the dialog box. A blue box appears around the list you chose.

5. Click the Continue previous list option button. The numbers in the blue box change.

6. Click OK.

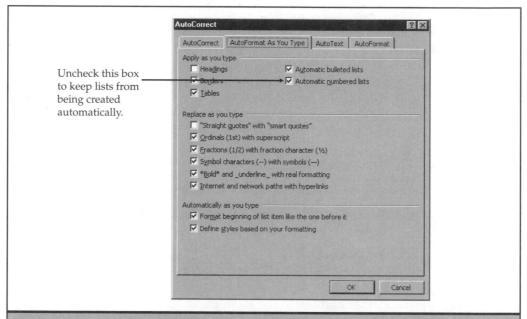

Uncheck this box to keep lists from being created automatically.

Figure 10-7.   *Telling Word not to create numbered lists automatically*

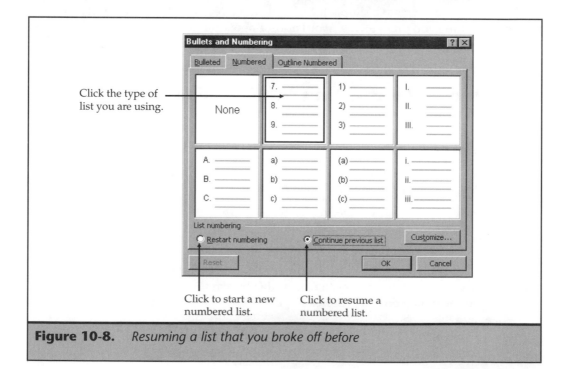

Click the type of list you are using.

Click to start a new numbered list.

Click to resume a numbered list.

Figure 10-8.   *Resuming a list that you broke off before*

Sometimes you click the Numbering button and Word resumes a list instead of starting one anew. To start a list under those circumstances, follow the instructions for resuming a list, but click the Restart numbering option button.

Changing the Numbering Scheme

Word offers seven numbering schemes in the Bullets and Numbering dialog box. Follow these steps to choose one of Word's numbering schemes:

1. Select the items to be included in the list; or, if you've already created the list and want to change its numbering scheme, select the list.

2. Right-click and choose Bullets and Numbering from the shortcut menu. You see the Numbered tab of the Bullets and Numbering dialog box (see Figure 10-8).

3. Click the type of list you want. A blue box appears around the list.

4. Click OK.

NOTE: *After you choose a new numbering scheme in the Bullets and Numbering dialog box, it becomes the default scheme for the document you are working on. After you chose Roman numerals or letters, for example, you get Roman numbers or letters when you click the Numbering button on the Formatting toolbar.*

Creating Your Own Format for Numbered Lists

If none of Word's formats do the trick, you can format the numbers on your own. You can choose a font for numbers and decide which punctuation mark follows the number. To be adventurous, you can tell Word how to align numbers and how far from the left margin to indent the text that follows the numbers.

Follow these steps to design a number format of your own:

1. Either select the items in the numbered list, or, if you haven't entered the items yet, place the insertion point where the list is to start.

2. Right-click and choose Bullets and Numbering. You see the Bullets and Numbering dialog box.

3. Click the Numbered tab (see Figure 10-8), if necessary.

4. Click the numbered list that most resembles the one you want to create on your own.

5. Click the Customize button. You see the Customize Numbered List dialog box shown in Figure 10-9.

6. If you want, change the punctuation mark that is to follow the numbers or letters in the list by clicking in the Number format box, erasing the period, and entering a new punctuation mark. For example, you could enter a colon (:) or hyphen (-).

7. Click the Font button to choose a new font and font size for the numbers or letters. The Font dialog box appears. Choose a new font and font size, and then click OK.

TIP: Besides choosing fonts, you can choose special effects and even animate the numbers or letters by choosing options in the Font dialog box.

8. In the Number position box, choose Left, Center, or Right to tell Word how the numbers or letters in the list are to be aligned with one another. The Preview box shows precisely what your choices amount to. In this illustration, numbers in a list are left-aligned, centered, and right-aligned:

Left	Centered	Right
8. Utah	8. Utah	8. Utah
9. Colorado	9. Colorado	9. Colorado
10. New Mexico	10. New Mexico	10. New Mexico
11. Arizona	11. Arizona	11. Arizona

9. In the Aligned at box, enter a number to tell Word at what point with respect to the left margin to align the numbers or letters. For example, if you enter .5" and the numbers or letters are left-aligned, all numbers or letters will appear directly to the right of the .5 inch mark. If you enter .5" and the numbers or letters are centered, all numbers or letters will be centered on the .5 inch mark on the horizontal ruler.

10. In the Indent at box, tell Word how far from the left margin to indent the text, not the numbers or letters, in the list. A large number puts a lot of space between the numbers or letters and the text; a small number puts little space.

11. Click OK to close the Custom Numbered List dialog box.

TIP: After you create your own format for numbered lists, Word applies it to the document you are working on when you click the Numbering button on the Formatting toolbar. Moreover, the format you created becomes an option in the Bullets and Numbering dialog box. It replaces the option you started with (in step 4 of the previous set of instructions) when you created your own number format. To get Word's old number format back, click the format you tampered with in the Bullets and Numbering dialog box, and then click the Reset button.

Working with Bulleted Lists

A *bullet* is a black, filled-in circle or other character that marks an item on a list. When you click the Bullets button, Word puts a bullet at the start of the paragraph. Besides

WORD

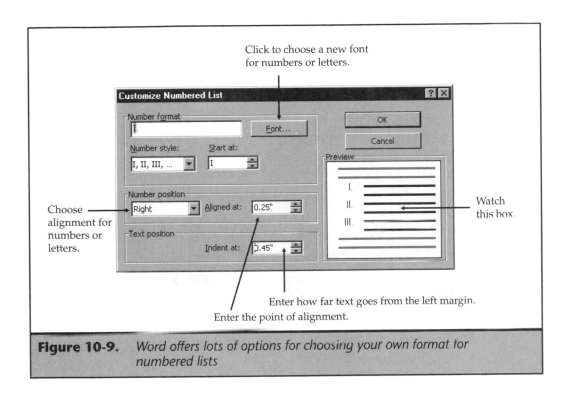

Click to choose a new font
for numbers or letters.

Choose
alignment for
numbers or
letters.

Watch
this box.

Enter how far text goes from the left margin.
Enter the point of alignment.

Figure 10-9. *Word offers lots of options for choosing your own format for numbered lists*

the standard bullet, you can use symbols as bullets. Figure 10-10 shows several different ways to present a bulleted list. The following pages explain how to create a bulleted list, use unusual characters as bullets, and format a bulleted list on your own.

LEARN BY EXAMPLE
To futz around with bulleted lists, open the Figure 10-10 (Bulleted List) *file on the CD that comes with this book.*

- Abbot and Costello
- Laurel and Hardy
- The Marx Brothers
- The Three Stooges

❑ Abbot and Costello
❑ Laurel and Hardy
❑ The Marx Brothers
❑ The Three Stooges

♦ Abbot and Costello
♦ Laurel and Hardy
♦ The Marx Brothers
♦ The Three Stooges

Abbot and Costello
Laurel and Hardy
The Marx Brothers
The Three Stooges

Figure 10-10. *In bulleted lists, you can use almost any symbol you care to use*

Creating a Bulleted List

To create a bulleted list, enter the items for the list, then select the list, and then click the Bullets button on the Formatting toolbar. Or, to create the list as you type it, click the Bullets button and start typing.

Removing bullets from a list is easy: select the list and click the Bullets button.

Choosing a Bullet Character

If the standard round bullet that Word provides doesn't do it for you, you can use another symbol for the bullets in your list. Word offers seven different kinds of bullets in the Bullets and Numbering dialog box, and if they don't do the job, you can use any symbol from the Symbol dialog box.

USING ONE OF WORD'S SYMBOLS FOR BULLETS   Follow these steps to use any one of Word seven bullet characters to mark items in a list:

1. Select the list if you've already entered it, or else place the cursor where the list is to begin.

2. Right-click and choose Bullets and Numbering.

3. If necessary, click the Bulleted tab. It is shown in Figure 10-11.

4. Click one of the eight boxes to choose a new symbol for the list.

5. Click OK.

NOTE: After you choose a new character for bulleted lists, it becomes the default bullet character. Click the Bullets button and you get the symbol you chose, not the standard round bullet. To get the standard bullet again, open the Bullets and Numbering dialog box and choose it on the Bulleted tab.

CHOOSING YOUR OWN SYMBOL FOR BULLETS   To use a character for lists apart from the seven on the Bulleted tab of the Bullets and Numbering dialog box, follow these steps:

1. Right-click and choose Bullets and Numbering.

2. If necessary, click the Bulleted tab (see Figure 10-11).

3. Click the box that holds the bullets you are least likely to need. Take this step because, when you are done choosing a new character for bulleted lists, it will appear on the Bulleted tab and take the place of the box you click in this step. Therefore, click a box whose bullets you don't care for.

4. Click the Customize button. You see the Customize Bulleted List dialog box shown in Figure 10-12.

5. Click the Bullet button. The Symbol dialog box appears.

6. Choose a symbol and click OK. The symbol you chose appears in the gallery of bullet characters and in the Preview box.

7. Click OK to close the Customize Bulleted List dialog box.

Creating a New Format for Bulleted Lists

Besides choosing bullet characters of your own, you can format a bulleted list to your own specifications. Word lets you decide how big the bullet character is and how far it goes from the left margin. You can also decide for yourself how far from the left margin to put the text that follows the bullet.

To format a bulleted list, select the list, right-click, and choose Bullets and Numbering to open the Bullets and Numbering dialog box. Then click the Bulleted tab (see Figure 10-11), if necessary, and click the Customize button to get to the Customize Bulleted List dialog box (see Figure 10-12). Do the following in the dialog box to format bullet lists:

- *Size of bullets*   Click the Font button, select a point size in the Size combo box, and then click OK.

- *Distance of bullet from left margin*   Under Bullet position, enter a setting in the Indent at box to tell Word how far from the left margin to place the bullets in the list. Keep your eyes on the Preview box to see what your choices mean in real terms.

- *Distance of list from left margin*   Under Text position, enter a setting in the Indent at box to tell Word how far from the left margin to place the text in the list.

Tables, Tables, and More Tables

This part of the chapter explains how to handle tables—tables of contents; tables of figures, tables, and graphs; and tables of authorities. Everybody knows what a table of contents is. In Word, you can create a table of the figures, graphics, equations, and other things in a document. You can also create a table of authorities. Lawyers and legal secretaries know what those are. If you don't know what a table of authorities is, count yourself among the blessed.

Generating a Table of Contents

Unless a long work has a table of contents, readers have a hard time using it as a reference. This part of the chapter explains how to generate a table of contents with Word. Doing so is pretty darn simple as long as you applied styles to the headings and other parts of the document that are to be included in the table of contents (TOC). Any part of a document that has been assigned a style can be included in the TOC (styles are explained in Chapter 8).

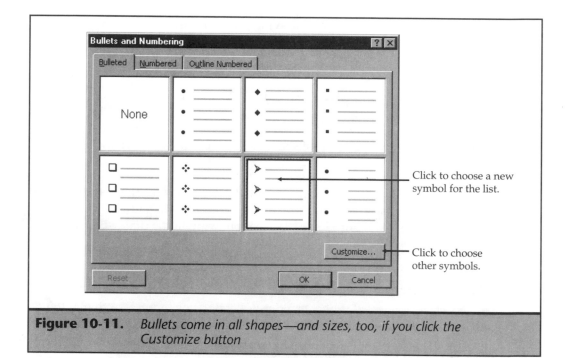

Figure 10-11. *Bullets come in all shapes—and sizes, too, if you click the Customize button*

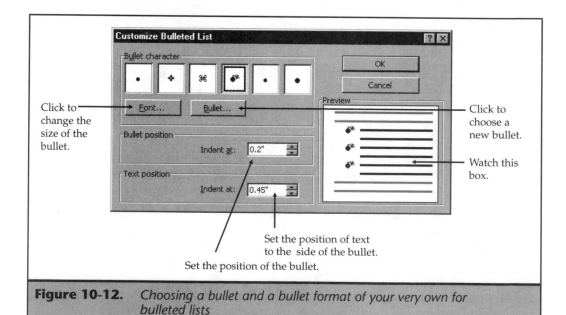

Figure 10-12. *Choosing a bullet and a bullet format of your very own for bulleted lists*

Some Advice About TOCs

Before you create a table of contents, create a new section in which to put it and number the TOC pages with Roman numerals. If you don't create a new section, the TOC will start on the first page and occupy the first handful of pages in the document. The first heading in the document, instead of appearing on page 1, will appear on page 2 or 3 or 4, because the TOC will push it there. It doesn't do to have a TOC whose first entry cites a heading on page 2 or 3 or 4.

TOCs should only include the first one, two, and at most three levels of headings. If your document goes seven headings deep, do not under any circumstances put all seven levels of headings in the TOC. That creates a long TOC that readers have to wade through to find what they are looking for. The object of a TOC is to help people find information. Having to read through many pages to find what you are looking for defeats the purpose of having a TOC.

Following are instructions for generating a TOC, telling Word what to put in the TOC and choosing a format for it.

LEARN BY EXAMPLE
On the companion CD is a file called Figure 10-13 (TOC). *Open that file if you would like to test out the TOC instructions in this book.*

Generating a Simple Table of Contents

To generate a simple table of contents with only the headings in a document, follow these steps:

1. At or near the start of the document, type **Table of Contents** and press ENTER once or twice.

2. Choose the Insert menu Index and Tables command.

3. Click the Table of Contents tab in the Index and Tables dialog box. It is shown in Figure 10-13.

4. In the Formats box, choose a format for the table of contents. As you click formats, watch the Preview box. It shows what the formats look like.

5. In the Show levels box, enter a number to say which headings should appear in the TOC. Entering 1, for example, puts only the Heading 1 headings in the TOC. Entering 3 puts Heading 1, Heading 2, and Heading 3 headings in the TOC.

6. Depending on the format you chose for your TOC, you might be able to tinker with it by choosing options at the bottom of the Table of Contents tab:

■ *Show page numbers* The TOC includes page numbers unless you click to remove the check mark from this check box.

■ *Right align page numbers* Page numbers are right-aligned so that the 1s and 10s line up underneath each other, but you can left-align them by clicking this check box and removing the check mark.

■ *Tab leader* A *leader* is a punctuation mark that steers the reader's eye in the TOC from the heading to the page number that the heading is on. Choose a leader from the drop-down list or choose (none) to keep a leader from appearing.

7. Click OK.

Including Tables, Captions, and More in the TOC

Besides heading styles, you can include any part of a document to which you have assigned a style in a TOC. Captions, paragraphs, and announcements for which you created a special style, for example, can be included in a TOC. As a matter of fact, you can exclude headings from a TOC as well.

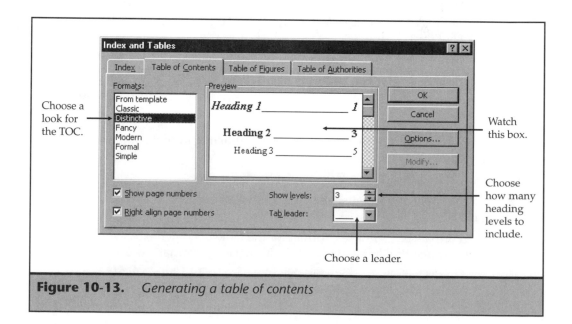

Figure 10-13.   *Generating a table of contents*

To choose exactly what goes into a TOC, choose the Insert menu Index and Tables command and click the Table of Contents tab in the Index and Tables dialog box (see Figure 10-13). Choose the kind of TOC you want, how many level of headings to include in the TOC, and so on, and then follow these steps:

1. Click the Options button. You see the Table of Contents Options dialog box shown in Figure 10-14.

2. In the TOC level box beside each style name, enter a level number to tell Word on which level the style is to appear on in the TOC. In Figure 10-14, for example, headings assigned the Digression style will be formatted like and indented as far as headings assigned the Heading 3 style, because a 3 is entered in the TOC level box beside both style names.

3. Click OK to close the Table of Contents Options dialog box.

4. Click OK in the Index and Tables dialog box.

Updating a TOC

Suppose you add one or two parts to your document, and each part has a heading. Meanwhile, you remove one or two other parts and their headings. Now the TOC you generated isn't accurate and up to date. To update the TOC, click it so it turns gray, and then press F9. That's all there is to it.

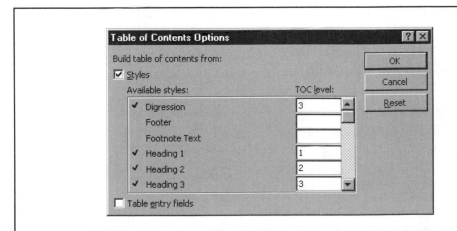

Figure 10-14. *In the box next to the style to be included in the TOC, enter a number*

Tables for Figures, Graphs, Tables, and What All

Sometimes reports and scholarly works, besides a table of contents, include other tables that list figures, graphs, and illustrations. Word can generate these kinds of tables as easily as it can generate a table of contents. For Word to generate the table, however, you must have used the Insert menu Caption command to put captions on figures, graphs, and so on, or you must have devised a style for the parts of a document that you want to compile into a table.

The following pages explain how to compile a table of figures, graphs, tables, equations, listings, or program lines that were given captions with the Insert menu Caption command. It also explains how to compile a table of all the parts of a document that were given the same style.

Generating a Table from Captions

Later in this chapter, "Captions for Figures, Graphs, Tables, and What All" explains how to use the Insert menu Caption command to put captions on figures, graphs, tables, equations, listings, and program lines. As long as you use the Insert menu Caption command to put captions on those things, you can generate a table with all the captions you wrote. For example, a report about agricultural production in Transylvania with graphs showing sorghum, soybean, and radish production could include a "Table of Graphs in this Report." The table would steer Transylvania scholars to the pages where the all-important agricultural data is given.

Follow these steps to generate a table of the figures, graphs, and what all that have been captioned with the Caption command:

1. Enter a title for the table near the start of the document and press ENTER once or twice.

2. Choose the Insert menu Index and Tables command.

3. Click the Table of Figures tab in the Index and Tables dialog box. It is shown in Figure 10-15.

4. In the Caption label box, choose which type of table to generate.

5. In the Formats box, choose a format for the table. As you click formats, watch the Preview box. It shows what the formats look like.

6. Depending on the format you chose for the table, you can fool with the options at the bottom to change the look of the table:

   ■ *Show page numbers* The table includes page numbers unless you click to remove the check mark from this check box.

   ■ *Right align page numbers* Page numbers are right-aligned so that the 1s and 10s line up underneath each other, but you can left-align them by clicking this check box and removing the check mark.

■ *Include label and number*   Click this box and remove the check mark to keep labels and numbers from appearing in the table. For example, entries in a table of figures would list the captions only. The word "Figure" and the figure number would not appear with each caption.

■ *Tab leader*   A leader is a punctuation mark that steers the reader's eye in the table to page numbers in the table. In Figure 10-15, a period is used as the leader. Choose a leader from the drop-down list, or choose (none) to keep a leader from appearing.

7. Click OK.

Generating a Table from Styles

As long as you thoughtfully applied a style to each sidebar heading, joke box, or whatever that you want to compile in a table, you can compile a "Table of Sidebars" or "Joke Boxes" at the start of a document. To do so, follow these steps:

1. Enter a title for the table near the start of the document, and press ENTER once or twice.

2. Choose the Insert menu Index and Tables command.

3. Click the Table of Figures tab in the Index and Tables dialog box (see Figure 10-15).

4. Choose a format for the table. ("Generating a Table from Captions" explains how to fill out the Table of Figures tab.)

5. Click the Options button. You see the Table of Figures Options dialog box:

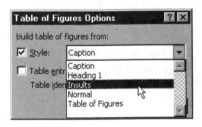

6. Make sure there is a check mark in the Style check box.

7. Click the Style drop-down menu and choose the style whose entries are to be compiled in a table.

8. Click OK to close the Table of Figures Options dialog box.

9. Click OK in the Index and Tables dialog box.

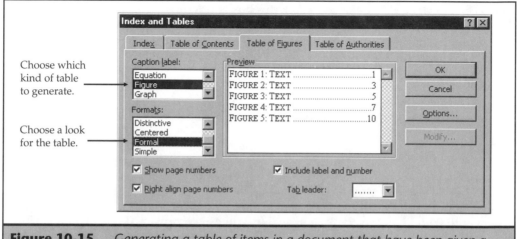

Choose which kind of table to generate.

Choose a look for the table.

Figure 10-15. *Generating a table of items in a document that have been given a caption with the Insert menu Caption command*

Updating the Table

To update a table of figures, graphs, or whatnot, all you have to do is click it, wait till it turns gray, and then press F9. If you add more figures, graphs, or whatnot, or remove some of them from a document, simply click the table and press F9 to get an entirely up-to-date table. Users who are averse to pressing F9 can right-click on the table and choose Update Field from the shortcut menu.

Creating a Table of Authorities

As every legal secretary and lawyer knows, a *table of authorities* is a list of the rules, cases, statues, regulations, and so on, cited in a legal document. Word makes it fairly easy to create these tables. The following pages explain how to enter citations for a table of authorities and how to generate the table itself.

Entering the Citations

Follow these steps to enter the citations in a table of authorities:

1. Go to the first citation and select it.

2. Press ALT+SHIFT+I. The Mark Citation dialog box appears, as shown in Figure 10-16. Your selection is listed in the Selected text and Short citation text boxes

3. In the Selected text box, edit the citation so that it looks like you want it to look in the table of authorities.

4. Choose a category from the Category drop-down list.

TIP: *If none of the categories in the Category list suits you, click the Category button to open the Edit Category dialog box. From there, either choose a category from the Category list or create a new category by entering it in the Replace with box and clicking the Replace button. Click OK when you are done.*

5. In the Short citation box, edit the citation for brevity. What you enter here determines what the citation looks like in the Mark Citation dialog box if you need to select it again.

6. Click the Mark button so that the citation appears in the table of authorities when you generate it. If other instances of this citation appear in your document, you can place them all in the table of authorities by clicking the Mark All button.

7. Click the Next Citation button. Word searches for other citations. To do so, it looks for cryptic examples of legalese such as *V* and *in re*. When Word finds another citation, the *V* or *in re* or whatever and the text that surrounds it appears in the Selected text box.

8. Click outside the dialog box and select the citation as you did in step 1. You may have to move the Mark Citation dialog box aside to do so. Click in the dialog box after you select the citation.

9. Repeat steps 2 through 7 to keep recording citations.

10. Click the Close button when you are done.

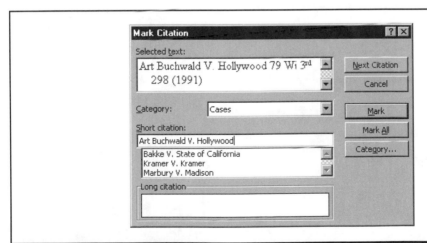

Figure 10-16. *Marking the citations for a table of authorities*

WORD

TIP: *If you have Show/Hide turned on, the field codes for the table of authorities now appear in your document and make it unreadable. Click the Show/Hide¶ button to wipe the codes off the screen.*

Generating the Table of Authorities

After you record all the citations for the table of authorities, you're ready to generate the table itself:

1. Place the cursor where you want the table to appear, type **Table of Authorities**, and press ENTER once or twice.

2. Choose the Insert menu Index and Tables command.

3. Click the Table of Authorities tab. It is shown in Figure 10-17.

4. Choose a format from the Formats list. The Preview box shows what the different formats look like. You can scroll down the Preview box.

5. In the Category drop-down list, choose which categories to include in the table.

6. If you leave the Use passim box checked, more than five references to the same citation are cited with the word *passim* instead of a page number. *Passim* means "scattered" in Latin. The word is used to refer to citations that appear throughout a legal document. Similarly, when possums are scattered throughout a meadow, they are said to be "passim possums."

7. The Keep original formatting text box retains the original formatting of long citations in the table. Uncheck this box if you want the table of authorities only to show short citations.

8. Choose a tab leader from the Tab leader drop-down list if you want something other than periods to appear between the citation and the page number in the table.

9. Click OK to generate the table of authorities.

Updating a Table of Authorities

To update a table of authorities after you have made changes to the citations in a legal document, either click the table and press F9 or right-click the table and choose Update Fields from the shortcut menu.

Numbers, Numbers, and More Numbers

The following pages explain how to number the lines in a document and how to number the headings. Lines in some kinds of legal documents have to be numbered. Passages in poems and religious texts are sometimes numbered as well to make it easier for scholars to cite specific lines. In scholarly papers and formal documents, headings are often numbered to make cross-referencing easier.

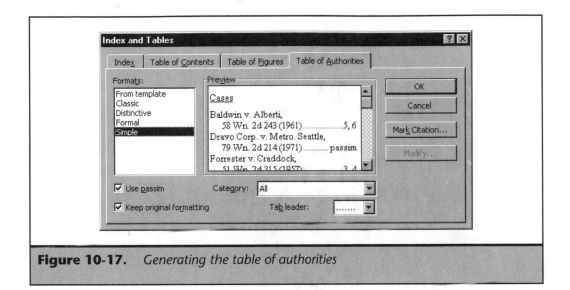

Figure 10-17. *Generating the table of authorities*

 NOTE: *If you came here to learn how to number the pages in a document, you came to the wrong place. Numbering pages is explained in Chapter 6.*

Numbering the Lines on Pages

Line numbers appear in the left margin. Follow these steps to number the lines in a document:

1. To number all the lines in a document, place the insertion point at the start of the document. Otherwise, place the insertion point at the start of a section to number all the lines in a section, or place the insertion point where you want to start numbering lines.

2. Choose the File menu Page Setup command. You see the Page Setup dialog box.

3. Click the Layout tab.

4. Click the Line Numbers button. The Line Numbers dialog box appears, as shown in Figure 10-18.

5. Click the Add line numbering check box.

6. Tell Word how the lines are to be numbered:

   ■ *Start at* To begin counting with a number other than 1, enter it.

   ■ *From text* The number in this box determines how far numbers are from the text. The larger the number, the further numbers are from the text and the closer the numbers are to the left side of the page.

- *Count by* Choose a number here to make numbers appear at intervals. For example, entering **10** makes intervals of ten (10, 20, and so on) appear.

- *Numbering* The numbers can begin anew on each page or at the start of each section. Choose Continuous to number all the lines consecutively.

7. Click OK to close the Line Numbers dialog box. You return to the Layout tab of the Page Setup dialog box.

8. Choose an Apply To option to tell Word which part of the document to number.

9. Click OK to close the Page Setup dialog box.

Line numbers can only be seen in Page Layout View. Since they appear in the margin, you likely have to scroll to the left side of the page to see them:

```
1          The death of Donald Turnupseed on July 14, 1995 freed me
2     from a moral burden I have borne for nearly ten years. May he rest
3     in peace. His Associated Press obituary says, "He was besieged
4     with interview requests ever since the crash on September 30,
5     1955. Mr. Turnupseed refused to talk publicly about the accident
6     except for an interview hours after the crash."
```

If you regret numbering the lines and want to remove the numbers, choose the File menu Page Setup command, click the Layout tab, and click the Line Numbers button. In the Line Numbers dialog box (see Figure 10-18), click the Add line numbering check box to remove the check mark, and then click OK twice.

LEARN BY EXAMPLE
To experiment with line numbers, open the Figure 10-18 (Line Numbers) *file on the companion CD and flail away.*

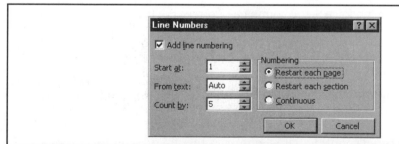

Figure 10-18. *Click the Add line numbering check box to number the lines in a document*

Numbering the Headings in a Document

As long as you applied Heading styles to the headings in a document, you can number the headings automatically with the Format menu Bullets and Numbering command. After the headings have been numbered, they are renumbered automatically when you remove or add a heading. So you can rest assured that all headings are numbered in sequence when you number the headings automatically.

Word offers a lot of different ways to number the headings. And you can also make words such as "Chapter," "Article," and "Section" appear in front of heading numbers automatically. Follow these steps to number the headings in a document:

1. Switch to Outline view. You get a better look at what you are doing from there.

2. Select the headings you want to number. To number all the headings, select the entire document.

3. Choose the Format menu Bullets and Numbering command. You see the Bullets and Numbering dialog box.

4. Click the Outline Numbered tab. It is shown in Figure 10-19.

5. Choose a numbering scheme by clicking on it. Notice the numbering schemes in the second row. The one on the left puts the word "Article" in front of Heading 1 headings and the word "Section" in front of Heading 2 headings. The one on the right puts the word "Chapter" in front of Heading 1 headings but does not number the headings below Heading 1.

6. Click OK.

To remove the numbers from headings, select the headings, open the Bullets and Numbering dialog box, click the None choice, and click OK.

EXAMPLES

LEARN BY EXAMPLE
Open the Figure 10-19 (Heading Numbers) file on the companion CD if you care to experiment with heading numbers.

Indexing a Document

A long document that readers will refer to often to get information is not complete without an index. Besides looking in the table of contents, looking in the index is the surest way to find out where information is. Unfortunately, writing an index is not easy, because Word cannot write the index entries for you, and writing a good index entry is certainly as hard as writing a good, descriptive heading.

Writing an index is not easy, but marking index entries and compiling an index is. The following pages explain how to do that.

Ways of Handling Index Entries

An index entry can be a cross-reference, a main entry, a subentry, or a sub-subentry. Moreover, index entries can refer to a single page or a page range. The following illustration shows the different types of index entries you can make with Word:

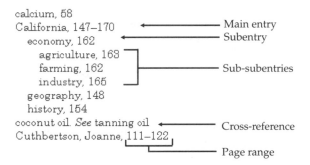

As you mark index entries, Word asks which type of entry you are marking. The Mark Index Entry dialog box offers option buttons and text boxes for entering the following types of entries in an index:

- *Cross-reference* A cross-reference refers the reader to another entry in the index. Make sure, when you enter a cross-reference, that the thing being referred to is really in the index.

- *Subentry* A subentry is subordinate to a main entry in the index. It offers specific information about a general topic listed in the index.

- *Sub-subentry* A sub-subentry is subordinate to a subentry (and the subentry's main entry, too). It offers very specific information about a sub-entry.

- *Page range* Besides referring to a single page, an index entry can refer to two or more pages. To make a page-range index entry, you must enter a bookmark that includes all the text in the page range. To create such a bookmark, select all text on the pages in question before you give the Insert menu Bookmark command.

As you mark index entries, ask yourself how you would search for information in an index and mark entries accordingly. Others will use your index to get information. Make sure your index entries don't lead them on a wild goose chase.

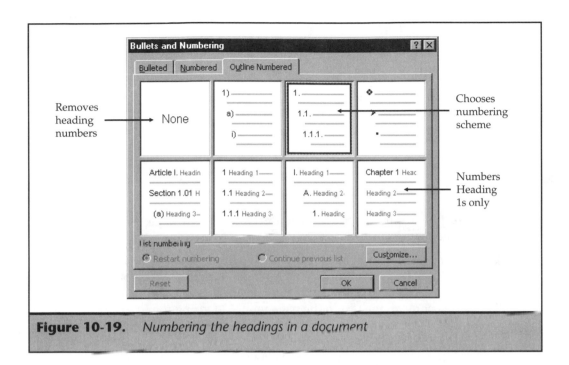

Figure 10-19.   *Numbering the headings in a document*

Marking the Index Entries

To mark index entries, you open the Mark Index Entry dialog box. After the box is open, you can tuck it in a corner, scroll through a document, and mark entries as you go along. Follow these steps to mark the index entries so you can compile them into an index later on:

1. Go to the first place where you want to make an index entry. If a word or phrase in the text can be included in the entry, select the word or phrase. You can save a little time that way.

2. Press ALT+SHIFT+X. You see the Mark Index Entry dialog box shown in Figure 10-20.

3. Tell Word how to handle the index entry:

   ■ *Main entry*   Enter the main entry here. If you selected a word or phrase in step 1, it appears in the Main entry box. Either edit the word or phrase or keep it. The word or phrase you enter in this box will appear in the index.

   ■ *Subentry*   Enter subentry or sub-subentry text in this box. Leave it blank if the index entry does not have a subentry. To enter a sub-subentry, type a colon (:) and then type the sub-subentry, as shown in Figure 10-20. What you type in this box will appear in the index.

4. Tell Word how to handle the page reference in the entry:

■ *Cross-reference*   To refer the reader to a main entry in the index, type the main entry's name in this box after the word *See*. What you type in this box appears in the index.

WARNING: *For cross-reference entries, be sure to refer the reader to a main entry that is really in the index. Word cannot double-check what you enter. You have to do that yourself and make sure that the cross-reference is accurate.*

■ *Current page*   Click to create an index reference to a single page in the document.

■ *Page range*   Click to create a reference to a range of pages. In order to create a page-range entry, you must create a bookmark that encompasses the page range. You can do that by clicking outside of the Mark Index Entry dialog box, selecting all the text in the page range, choosing the Insert menu Bookmark command, typing a name in the Bookmark name text box, and clicking Add. Then, in the Mark Entry dialog box, click the down arrow in the Page Range option button, and choose the bookmark from the drop-down list.

5. Click the Bold or Italic check box to tell Word if you want to boldface or italicize the page number or page range in the index entry. In some indexes, the page or page range where the topic is explained in the most depth is italicized or boldfaced so readers can go there first, if they want to.

6. Click the Mark or Mark All button:

■ *Mark button*   Enters the entry in the index.

■ *Mark All button*   As long as you selected a word in step 1, you may click Mark All to tell Word to mark all words in the document that are identical to the word in the Main Entry box.

7. Click outside the dialog box and find the next word or phrase for the index, and then repeat steps 2 through 6 to mark more index entries.

8. Click Close when you're done to close the Mark Index Entry dialog box.

When you're done, you see field codes in your document. That's distracting, but you can hide the field codes by clicking the Show/Hide button.

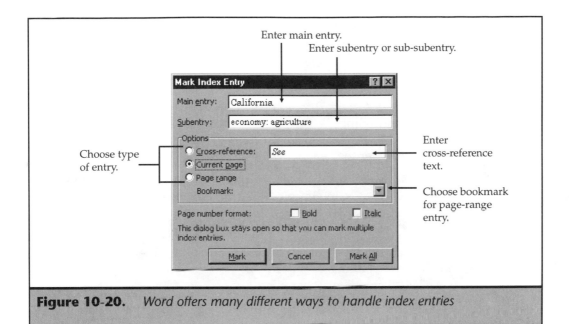

Figure 10-20.   *Word offers many different ways to handle index entries*

Generating the Index

After you have marked all the index entries, it is time to generate the index. Follow these steps to generate an index:

1. Go to the end of the document, insert a page break, type the word **Index**, and press ENTER a couple of times.

2. Choose the Insert menu Index and Tables command to open the Index and Tables dialog box.

3. Click the Index tab, if necessary. It is shown in Figure 10-21.

TIP: Watch the Preview box as you make choices. It shows very plainly what the options you choose in the Index and Tables dialog box amount to.

4. Under Type, choose Run-in instead of Indented if you want subentries and sub-subentries to fall directly below main entries. With the Indented option, subentries and sub-subentries are indented, as shown in the Preview box in Figure 10-21.

5. Click a format in the Formats box. Experiment at will, but keep your eyes on the Preview box.

6. Choose options in the bottom of the dialog box to get very specific about what the index should look like:

■ *Headings for accented letters*   Index entries that begin with accented letters are given their own headings if you click this box. In other words, an index entry called *übermensch* does not go with the *U*s, but goes instead between the *U*s and *V*s, under the heading *Ü*.

■ *Right align page numbers*   Page numbers appear right after entries, unless you click this check box, in which case page numbers appear right below one another.

■ *Columns*   If you can fit more than two columns on the page or want only one, make an entry in the Columns box. Indexes with sub-subentries cannot fit more than two columns on a page.

■ *Tab leader*   A leader is a series of punctuation marks. Choose a leader of your own to go between the index entry and the page number, if you want and if the index format you chose in step 5 calls for leaders.

7. Click OK to close the Index and Tables dialog box.

LEARN BY EXAMPLE
Open the Figure 10-21 (Index).doc *file on the companion CD to try your hand at forging an index.*

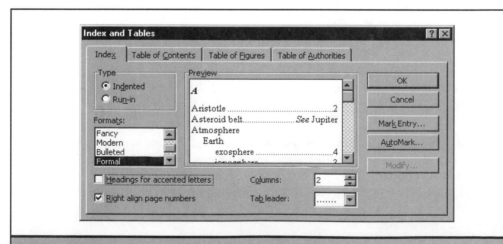

Figure 10-21.   *Generating the index*

Editing and Updating an Index

After you have generated the index, read it carefully. Make sure that all the entries are useful to readers. If you notice an unsuitable entry, find it in the document and either erase or edit the index field code. And be sure to update the index after you have finished editing it. The following pages explain how.

Editing Index Entries

Follow these steps to find and edit an index entry in a document:

1. If you cannot see the field codes and index entries in the text, click the Show/Hide button on the Standard toolbar.

2. Either scan the document for the entry or choose the Edit menu Find command, and in the Find and Replace dialog box, enter the entry you are looking for and then click the Find Next button. Enter the index entry verbatim. The Find command finds index entries as well as words—as long as you click the Show/Hide button.

3. If you decided to use the Find feature to locate the index entry, when Word finds the entry, click Cancel to close the Find and Replace dialog box. Index entries are enclosed in braces and quotation marks and are preceded by the letters _XE_, like so:

> { XE·"culture:defensive·posture·of" }¶

4. Either edit the index entry by clicking between the quotation marks and deleting and entering letters, or delete the entry by selecting it and pressing the DELETE key.

Updating an Index

To update an index after you have edited it or added entries to it, either right-click it and choose Update Fields from the shortcut menu, or click it and press F9.

Captions for Figures, Graphs, Tables, and What All

Word offers a special command for putting captions on figures, graphs, tables, equations, listings, and program lines. The command makes creating captions a little bit easier, but the chief advantage of the command is being able to number the captions automatically. When you add a caption or delete one, the other captions are automatically renumbered. What's more, the captions can be compiled in a table. "Tables for Figures, Graphs, Tables, and What All," earlier in this chapter, explains how to compile captions into a table so that readers can find out right away what page a certain graph or equation is on, for example.

To enter a caption, you start by selecting the thing that is to be captioned. In the case of figures, graphs, tables, and equations, all you have to do is click on them. By clicking, you select them. But to put a caption on a list or series of program lines, select all the lines first. Follow these steps to caption a figure, graph, or what all automatically:

1. Select the thing that is to be captioned.

2. Choose the Insert menu Caption command. You see the Caption dialog box shown in Figure 10-22.

3. In the Caption box, enter the caption. As Figure 10-22 shows, you have to enter the punctuation mark after the figure number yourself. Usually, a colon (:) or a period follows the figure number.

4. If necessary, click the Label drop-down list and tell Word what it is you are labeling in the caption.

TIP: You can create a label for an item that isn't on the Label drop-down list. To do so, click the New Label button, type a label in the Label box, and click OK.

5. Click the Position drop-down list and choose Above selected item or Below selected item to tell Word where the caption goes.

6. Click OK.

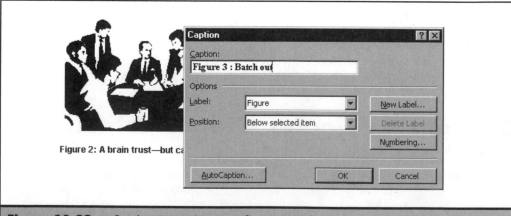

Figure 10-22.   *Putting a caption on a figure. Word numbers the captions automatically*

Managing Footnotes and Endnotes

Footnotes, the references, explanations, or comments that appear along the bottom of a page, are a chore, but at least Word relieves you of having to worry about numbering and formatting them. Yes, you still have to list authors, their works, and the dates their works were published correctly, but you don't have to worry whether a footnote is out of sequence or whether it fits on the page. Word takes care of all that. It also handles *endnotes*, which do exactly what footnotes do but do it at the end of the chapter or document.

Unless you fiddle with default options, footnotes go in the bottom margin of the page and endnotes go at the end of the document. Footnotes go directly above the footer, on the bottom of the page, unless you tell Word to put them directly below the text. A document can have both footnotes and endnotes. Word numbers footnotes with Arabic numerals and endnotes with Roman numerals.

This part of Chapter 10 explains how to enter a footnote or endnote, change the position of notes, change their numbering scheme, as well as move, delete, and edit notes.

Inserting a Footnote or Endnote

To insert a footnote or endnote, follow these steps:

1. Place the cursor where the note citation is to go. In other words, place the cursor where you want the number or symbol that marks the footnote or endnote reference to be.

2. Choose the Insert menu Footnote command. You see the Footnote and Endnote dialog box shown in Figure 10-23.

3. Under Insert, click Footnote to enter a footnote or Endnote to enter an endnote.

4. Under Numbering, tell Word whether the citation is to be a number or a symbol:

   ■ *AutoNumber* Click AutoNumber to make Word number the notes automatically.

■ *Custom mark*   Click Custom mark to mark the note with a symbol. To choose the symbol, either enter it yourself in the text box or click the Symbol button and choose a symbol from the Symbol dialog box.

5. Click OK. If you are in Page Layout view, Word takes you to the bottom of the page or the end of the document or section, where, beside the symbol or number, you can type the footnote or endnote. In Normal view, a notes box opens:

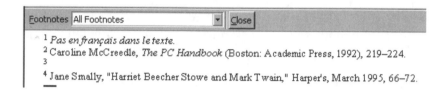

6. Type the footnote or endnote.

7. Click Close if you are in Normal view to leave the notes box. In Page Layout view, scroll up the page.

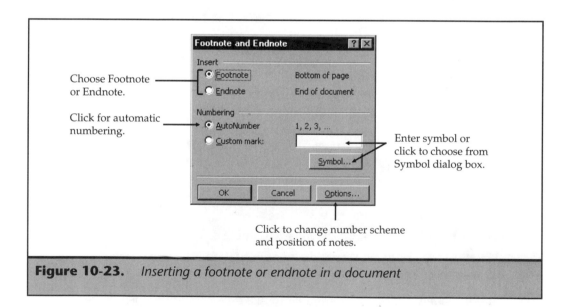

Figure 10-23.   *Inserting a footnote or endnote in a document*

Changing the Numbering Scheme and Position of Notes

By clicking the Options button in the Footnote and Endnote dialog box (see Figure 10-23), you can change the position or numbering scheme of footnotes and endnotes. Follow these steps to do so:

1. Choose the Insert menu Footnote command.

2. Click the Options button. You see the Note Options dialog box in Figure 10-24. The figure shows the options for footnotes on the All Footnotes tab. The options for endnotes on the All Endnotes tab are nearly the same.

3. Click the All Footnotes or All Endnotes tab and choose options:

   ■ *Place at* Word puts footnotes at the bottom of the page, but you can choose Beneath text to put footnotes below the last text line on the page, even if it appears in the middle of the page. For endnotes, either choose End of section (if the document is divided into sections) to make endnotes appear at the back of sections, or choose End of document to put the endnotes at the end of the document.

   ■ *Number format* Choose a numbering scheme. Choose Symbols if you want to use symbols.

   ■ *Start at* Enter a number or letter to start numbering the notes at a place other than 1, A, or i.

   ■ *Numbering* The Continuous option numbers the notes continuously from the start of the document to the end; the Restart each section option starts numbering anew at each section in the document. For footnotes, Restart each page begins numbering anew on each page.

   ■ *Convert* Choose this option to change all endnotes into footnotes, and all footnotes into endnotes.

4. Click OK to close the Notes Options dialog box.

5. Click OK in the Footnote and Endnote dialog box.

Editing, Moving, and Deleting Footnotes and Endnotes

Editing, moving, and deleting footnotes and endnotes is easy, I am happy to report. Following are instructions that explain how easy it is.

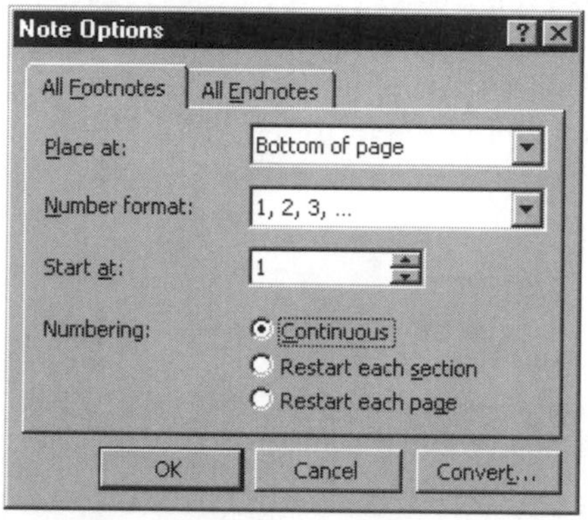

Note Options
All Footnotes
All Endnotes
Place at:
Bottom of page
Number format:
1, 2, 3, ...
Start at:
1
Numbering:
Continuous
Restart each section
Restart each page
OK
Cancel
Convert...

Figure 10-24. *Changing the position and numbering scheme of footnotes. The options on the All Endnotes tab are nearly the same as those on the All Footnotes tab*

Editing a Note

You can read footnotes and endnotes simply by placing the pointer on the note citation. When you do so, a box appears with the footnote or endnote text:

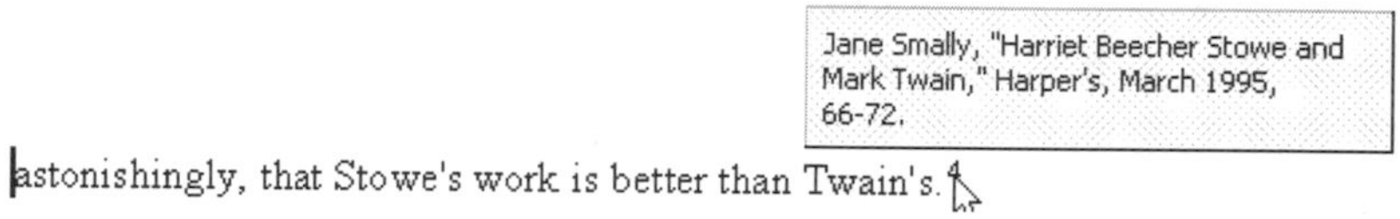

Jane Smally, "Harriet Beecher Stowe and Mark Twain," Harper's, March 1995, 66-72.
astonishingly, that Stowe's work is better than Twain's.

To edit a note, either scroll to the bottom of the page and find it in Page Layout view, or double-click its citation in the text in Normal view. With the note onscreen, change the text as you would normal text.

Moving a Note

To move a note, select its symbol or number and then either drag it where it is supposed to go or cut and paste it to a new location. When you move a note, all the other notes are renumbered, if that proves necessary.

Deleting a Note

To delete a note, select its symbol or number and press the DELETE key. Notes are renumbered when you delete one.

Including Cross-References in Documents

Word's cross-reference feature is mighty handy indeed. With it, you can refer readers to specific pages or to headings in a document (provided the headings have been assigned a style). Best of all, Word double-checks the references to make sure that all are accurate. If you refer to a page or a heading that isn't there, Word alerts you to the fact. And you can even include a hypertext link in a cross-reference (Chapter 25 explains hypertext links in detail).

The following pages explain how to insert cross-references, fix errant cross-references, and update the cross-references in a document.

Inserting a Cross-Reference

Follow these steps to insert a cross-reference:

1. Type the cross-reference text:

   - *To a page number* If your reference is to a page number, type something like this: **To learn more about the Canadian wilderness, turn to page**. Enter a blank space after the word *page*. A page number will appear after the blank space.

   - *To a heading* If your reference is to a heading, type something like this: **To learn more about our windswept northern neighbor, see "**. The heading will come directly after the quotation mark, so don't enter a blank space after the quotation mark.

2. Choose the Insert menu Cross-reference command. You see the Cross-reference dialog box shown in Figure 10-25.

3. In the Reference type drop-down list, choose what the cross-reference refers to. Except for bookmarks, you must have assigned a style or caption to all the options listed in the drop-down list if you want to refer to them. Bookmarks are for referring to page numbers in cross-references. To refer to the page a paragraph is on, click outside the dialog box, scroll to the paragraph, and put a bookmark there with the Insert menu Bookmark command.

4. In the Insert reference to drop-down list, what you chose in step 3 determines whether the reference is to a numbered item, text such as a heading, or a page number. Make the appropriate choice in the Insert reference to drop-down list. Do the following to make the cross-reference to text or a number, or a page number:

   - *Text* Choose this option (Heading text, Bookmark text, and so on) to include text in the cross-reference.

■ *Number* Choose this option to refer to a paragraph to which a bookmark has been applied.

5. Click to remove the check mark from the Insert as Hyperlink check box if you don't want to create a hyperlink as part of the cross-reference. Chapter 25 explains hyperlinks. By clicking a hyperlink, online users can go directly to the thing being cross-referenced.

6. You can add the word "above" or "below" to the cross-reference by clicking the Include above/below check box. (The check box is available with some Reference type options).

7. In the For which heading box, click on the thing that the cross-reference refers to, be it a heading, bookmark, footnote, or whatever.

8. Click the Insert button.

9. Click the Close button.

10. Finish writing the cross-reference text in the document.

Updating the Cross-References in a Document

To update all the cross-references in a document, select the entire document and either press F9 or right-click and choose Update Field from the shortcut menu.

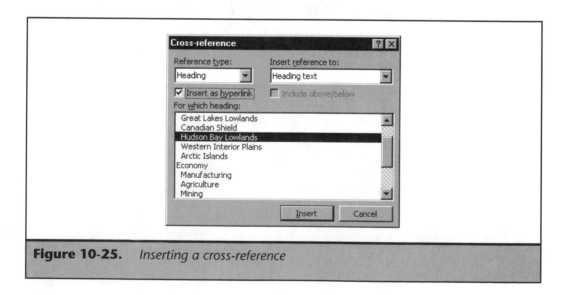

Figure 10-25. *Inserting a cross-reference*

Fixing Errant Cross-References

When a cross-reference refers to something that isn't there anymore because it has been deleted, you see an error message like this when you update the cross-references:

turn to the section called **"Error! Reference source not found.."**

To find and fix errors like those, use the Edit menu Find command to look for the word *Error!*. Then delete the cross-reference and either reinsert a new reference or abandon the cross-reference altogether.

Part III

Microsoft Excel

Chapter 11

Excel Basics

This chapter describes the basic construction techniques you'll use to build Excel workbooks. With the information that this chapter and the next chapter provide, in fact, you should be able to build almost any type of Excel workbook.

The first time you see Excel's program window and the workbook program window inside the program, they can inspire a certain amount of stress. Cryptic codes and pseudo-hieroglyphics appear scattered all over the program window. Clickable boxes and buttons abound, and a status bar along the bottom edge of the window displays all sorts of strange messages.

Touring the Excel Program Window

Despite all the seeming confusion, however, Excel's program window is actually pretty well-organized. And once you've had each of its component parts identified and described, you should find it easy to understand and use each of the parts of the window.

The top-most row of the program window is the program window title bar. It supplies a program control menu icon, which you'll probably never use (because it's largely redundant), names the program, and also supplies the program window

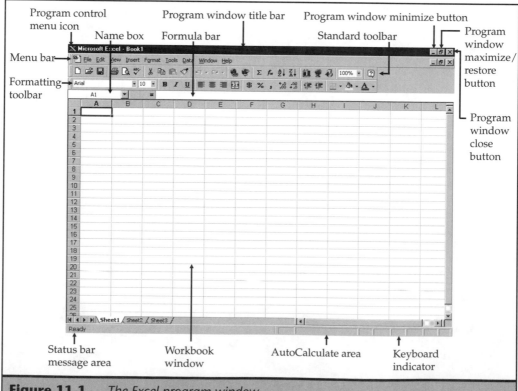

Figure 11-1. *The Excel program window*

buttons, which let you minimize, maximize/restore, and close the program window. The Minimize button shrinks the program window into a button that appears on the task bar. The Maximize/Restore button alternative increases the size of the program window so it fills the screen or restores it to its original, unenlarged size. The Close button closes, or stops, the Excel program.

Beneath the title bar are the menu bar and Excel's toolbars. The menu bar contains the menus of commands you'll sometimes use to perform tasks in the Excel program. The Standard and Formatting toolbars provide clickable buttons and boxes you can also use to issue commands to the Excel program. (Chapter 3 identifies and describes the Standard and Formatting toolbar tools.)

The area beneath the last toolbar provides a Name box and the Formula bar. The Name box provides the cell address or name of the active, or selected, cell. The Formula bar displays the contents of the active cell. You'll learn more about both of these items—the Name box and the Formula bar—in the paragraphs that follow.

The major portion of the Excel program window shows the workbook window described in detail in the next section.

At the bottom of the program window is the status bar. It provides a message area, the AutoCalculate area, and the keyboard indicator. Excel uses the message area to send you messages. For example, if Excel is ready to receive a command, the message area shows the one-word message, "Ready." If Excel is busy recalculating the formulas you've placed in a worksheet, it will display the message, "Calculating cells" followed by the percentage of cells it's calculated. The AutoCalculate area calculates the values in the selected cells using the function you specify—Sum, Average, Count, Count Nums, Min, or Max. Finally, the keyboard indicator just tells you whether you've turned on any of your keyboard's toggle switches: the CAPS LOCK key (identified with the abbreviation CAPS), the NUM LOCK key (identified with the abbreviation NUM), the Insert, or over-type, key (identified with the abbreviation OVR), and so forth.

Quick Math with AutoCalculate

The logic of AutoCalculate is that you can perform quick-and-dirty calculations on the selected area of the worksheet without actually having to create a formula. To sum, or add up, a range of cells, for example, you select all of the cells you want to sum. (The later chapter section, "Selecting Ranges," describes in detail how you select ranges of cells. Chapter 12 describes how you create formulas.)

AutoCalculate will also perform other calculations. To make a different calculation, right-click the AutoCalculate area. Excel displays a menu listing different AutoCalculate options: Average, which calculates the arithmetic mean of the values in the selected cells; Count, which counts the cells storing numbers, formulas, and anything else; Count Nums, which counts the cells storing numbers and formulas; Max, which finds the largest value in the selected cells; Min, which finds the smallest value in the selected cells; and Sum, which sums the values in the selected cells.

EXCEL

Touring the Workbook Window

As mentioned earlier, the workbook window occupies most of the program window. As shown in Figure 11-2, Excel uses the workbook window to display the workbooks— those stacks of worksheets—and to provide tools you'll use as you view explore, and modify a workbook.

The top-most row of the workbook window is the workbook window title bar. It supplies a workbook control menu icon, which you'll never need to use (because it's redundant), names the workbook, and also supplies the workbook window buttons. The workbook window buttons work like the program window buttons except that they affect the workbook window and not the program window. The Minimize button shrinks the workbook window into a button that appears along the button edge of the program window. The Maximize/Restore button alternative increases the workbook window so it fills the program window or restores it to its original, unenlarged size. The Close button closes the workbook. (If you've made changes to a workbook that

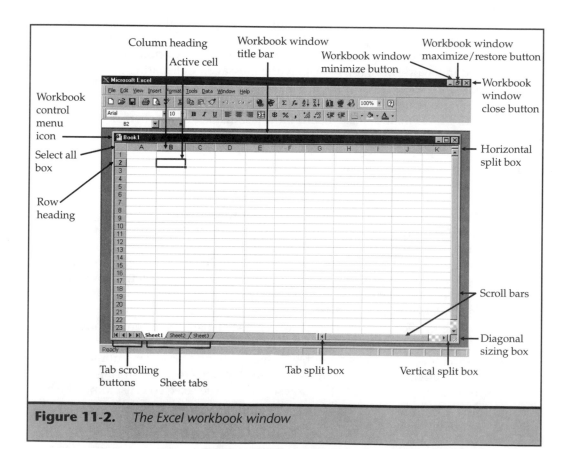

Figure 11-2.   *The Excel workbook window*

you haven't yet saved, Excel won't let you close the workbook without first confirming that you don't want to save your changes.)

The Select All box selects the entire worksheet. You might want to do this if you were making a change that affected the whole worksheet. But in practice, you'll rarely use this button.

The letters and numbers on the Column and Row heading buttons identify a worksheet's columns and rows and also identify the cells, or column-row intersections, that make up the worksheet. For example, the cell at the intersection of column B and row 2 is cell B2.

In Figure 11-2, by the way, cell B2 is the active cell. You can tell it's the active cell both because Excel places a dark border around the cell and because the Name box gives its cell address. Knowing which cell is the active one is important. Later in the chapter, the "Entering Data into Cells" section describes how you enter information into a worksheet—and usually the first step is clicking a cell to make it the active cell.

You actually see only a small portion of the worksheet in a workbook window. An Excel worksheet actually has 256 columns and 65,536 rows. To move the worksheet around so you can see different portions of it, you use the scroll bars. You use the vertical and horizontal scroll bars to move up and down and left and right in a worksheet. (Later in the chapter, the "Entering Data into Cells" section talks more about cells, columns and rows, so for now just note that these letters and numbers give you an easy way to specifically identify any cell in a worksheet.)

 NOTE: If you use the vertical or horizontal scroll bar to move your view of a worksheet page up and down or left and right, Excel displays a Row number or Column letter screen tip when you click the scroll bar. This screen tip, by providing you with a row number or column letter, lets you scroll more precisely.

As mentioned earlier, a workbook supplies a stack of worksheet pages. To flip through these pages, you use the worksheet tabs, which appear just left of the horizontal scroll bar. You just click a tab to move a particular worksheet to the top of the stack.

The preceding discussion describes the most usual and popular items in the workbook window, but there are a few more hidden features. The vertical split box and horizontal split box split the workbook window into two chunks, or panes, which you can scroll independently. By splitting a window into panes, you can view and compare nonadjacent portions of the workbook. To use either the vertical or horizontal split box, drag the split box up and down or left and right. (To remove a split, you drag the split box back to its original position.)

The Tab split box lets you change the number of sheet tabs that can be displayed and the size of the horizontal scroll bar. To make this change, you just drag the Tab split box left or right. This isn't difficult in practice. If you have questions, just try it. You'll immediately see how this works.

NOTE: The preceding paragraphs describe how you navigate, or move around, in a workbook using the mouse, but you can also navigate using the PGUP and PGDN keys as well as the CTRL+PGUP and CTRL+PGDN key combinations. The mouse method really is easiest, but if you're interested in learning how to use a keyboard—maybe you're a laptop user, for example—just open a workbook and experiment with the preceding keys and key combinations.

Entering Data into Cells

Excel's basic building blocks are its worksheet pages, which are simply tables, or grids, you use for storing information you want to manipulate—usually in calculations. For this reason, you'll want to learn as much as you can about entering data into a worksheet.

To enter some bit of information into a cell—which is really just a text box— you simply click the cell using the mouse and begin typing. When you press ENTER or click the Formula bar's Enter button, Excel places whatever you type into the cell. If you begin typing some entry and then realize that you don't want your entry placed into a cell, press ESC or click the Formula bar's Cancel button. Figure 11-3 shows an example Excel workbook with a bit of information.

WARNING: For purposes of the discussion that follows, this book assumes you are proficient both in entering data into a text box and in editing data already in a text box. If you don't already possess this knowledge, you'll benefit greatly by first acquiring it. You should be able to get this information from just about any good introductory Windows 95 or Windows NT tutorial.

EXAMPLES

LEARN BY EXAMPLE
You can open the example Excel workbook shown in Figure 11-3, Figure 11-3 (simple Excel workbook), *from the companion CD if you want to follow along with our discussion here.*

Editing and Erasing Data

When you want to change some cell's information, you have two choices. You can replace the cell's existing contents by typing over them. For example, you can click the cell, type your new entry, and press ENTER. Or you can edit the existing entry.

To edit some cell's contents, you double-click the cell. Excel turns the cell into an editable text box. You can then edit the cell's contents in the same manner that you edit the contents of any text box. To place the edited cell contents back into the cell, press ENTER or click the Formula bar's Enter button. To erase the contents of some cell, select the cell and press the DELETE key.

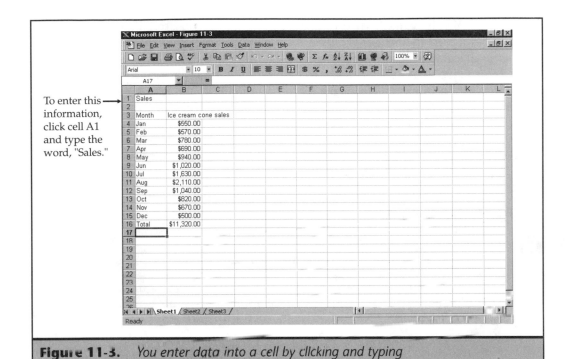

To enter this information, click cell A1 and type the word, "Sales."

Figure 11-3.   *You enter data into a cell by clicking and typing*

TIP: *You can't erase the cell data by clicking on a cell and pressing the* SPACEBAR. *While this technique appears to work, it really doesn't because all you're really doing is replacing the cell's current contents with a space character. This can cause problems later if the cell is included in calculations.*

Types of Cell Data

You can enter three types of data into the cells of a worksheet: labels, values, and formulas. Labels are text used to describe areas of the worksheet. Values are the data you want to use in a calculation. Formulas are the instructions that tell Excel what and how to calculate.

NOTE: *In Figure 11-3, cells A1 through A16 and cell B3 hold labels. Cells B4 through B15 hold values. Cell B16 holds a formula.*

Labels

As just mentioned, a label is a chunk of alphanumeric text. The main differentiating characteristic of a label is that the label isn't used in calculations. Typically, you use labels to describe the values you do want to use in calculations. In Figure 11-3, for example, all of the cell entries in column A are labels.

As a practical matter, you can enter labels as that are as long as you need. But if you type in a label that's wider than the column you're placing it in, you'll often need to adjust the column width. Here's the reason: While Excel will let a long label spill over into the adjacent cell or cells if they are empty, Excel displays only the portion of the label that fits in its own cell if the adjacent cell or cells store data. This sounds complicated, but really it's not. Take a look at the worksheet shown in Figure 11-4. Notice that the long labels in cells A1 through A5 spill over across cells B1 through B5. This is because cells B1 through B5 are empty.

NOTE: Technically, there is a limit to label length: you can't enter a label of more than 32,000 characters. Be careful though; only 1024 characters in a cell can be printed.

EXAMPLES

LEARN BY EXAMPLE
You can open the example Excel workbook shown in Figure 11-4, Figure 11-4 (incomplete income statement), *from the companion CD if you want to follow along with the discussion here.*

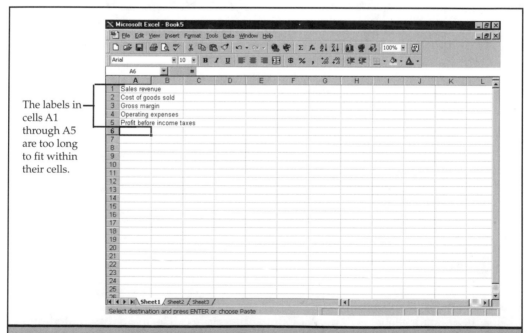

The labels in cells A1 through A5 are too long to fit within their cells.

Figure 11-4.   *Long labels spill over into adjacent cells—if there is room*

However, as soon as you enter another label or value into the adjacent cell, Excel truncates the long label. Figure 11-5 shows what happens when you do this.

LEARN BY EXAMPLE

You can open the example Excel workbook shown in Figure 11-5, Figure 11-5 (almost complete income statement), from the companion CD if you want to follow along with the discussion here.

When a label's display does get cut off because it can't spill over into adjacent cells or you don't want a label spilling over into adjacent cells, you just need to adjust the column width. There are a couple of quick ways to do this. If you want to make a column as wide as the widest piece of data it holds—a label or a value—you can double-click the right border of the column heading button. Alternatively, you can drag the right border of the column heading button using the mouse.

NOTE: *You can change the heights of rows using the same basic mechanics: You can double-click the bottom border of the row heading button or you can drag the bottom border of the row heading button.*

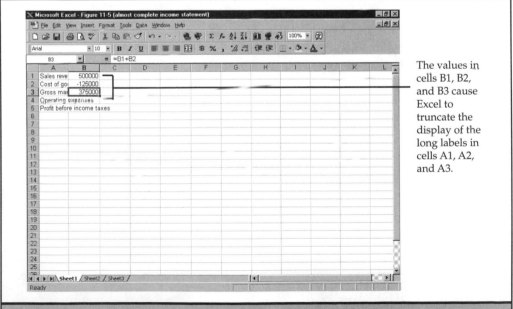

Figure 11-5. *The worksheet from Figure 11-4 after values have been entered into column B*

LEARN BY EXAMPLE
You can open the example Excel workbook shown in Figure 11-6, Figure 11-6 (complete income statement), *from the companion CD if you want to follow along with the discussion here.*

Label Entry Tools

Excel provides two handy tools that make data entry of labels easier: AutoComplete and Pick From List. AutoComplete works like this. When you begin entering a label in a column, Excel looks at each of the other entries in the column to see if it looks like your entry might just match one of those. If Excel finds that the first few characters of your entry match the first few characters of another entry, it automatically completes, or "AutoCompletes," your entry so it matches the earlier entry. This sounds kooky, perhaps, but let's take a quick look at a worksheet in which this AutoComplete tool

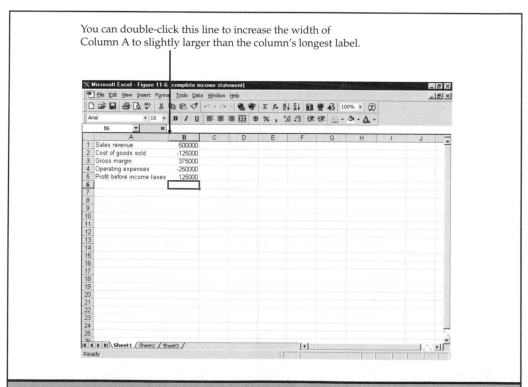

Figure 11-6.   *The worksheet from Figure 11-5 after Column A's width is increased*

would be really handy. Say you're building a list of customer names and addresses, and that you're using columns to store the individual fields of customer information. (See Figure 11-7.)

Take a close look at the entry started in row 6. When one begins typing the first part of the customer's city, *S*, there's a pretty good chance that one should finish the entry by typing *eattle*. In other words, it's very likely that some of the customers are located in the same town. So Excel finishes the city entry by typing out *eattle*. If you were doing this and you did want to enter that customer's city as Seattle, you press ENTER or click the formula bar's Enter button. If you want to enter something else, you just keep typing. Excel replaces *eattle* with whatever else you type. For example, if the customer described in row 6 really does business in San Francisco, when you type the next letters of the city name, Excel replaces the *eattle* with your entry—in this case *an Francisco*.

LEARN BY EXAMPLE

You can open the example Excel workbook shown in Figure 11-7, Figure 11-7 (customer list), if you want to follow along with the discussion here.

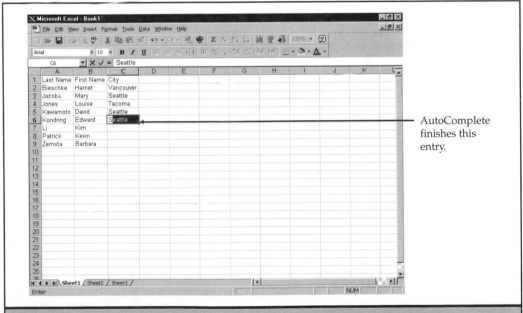

Figure 11-7. *A simple customer list illustrates the usefulness of AutoComplete*

NOTE: You don't have to do anything to turn the AutoComplete feature on. It's automatically turned on when you install Excel. If you find the AutoComplete feature irritating—and some users will—you can turn it off. To do so, choose the Tools menu Options command, click the Edit tab, and then uncheck the Enable AutoComplete for cell values box. (The check box is the last one shown on the Edit tab of options.)

The Pick From List feature also works to make data entry of labels easier. If you right-click a cell and choose the shortcut menu's Pick From List command, Excel displays a list of all the labels you've already entered in the column. (See Figure 11-8.) To enter one of the listed labels into the active cell, you just select it from the list.

LEARN BY EXAMPLE
EXAMPLES
You can open the example Excel workbook shown in Figure 11-8, Figure 11-8 (pick from list example) from the companion CD if you want to follow along with the discussion here.

Values

You use values in calculations. If you were building a worksheet that tallied the cost of an extended business trip to Europe, for example, you might build a worksheet like

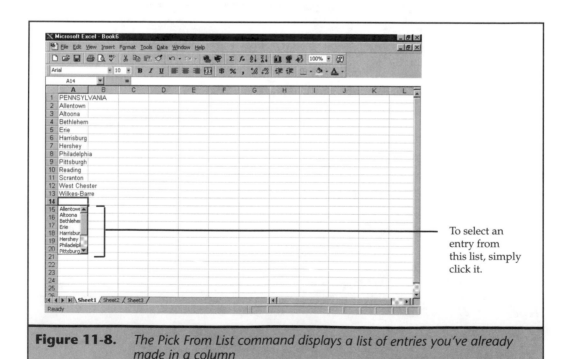

Figure 11-8. *The Pick From List command displays a list of entries you've already made in a column*

that shown in Figure 11-9. Notice that column A holds labels that describe the values and that column B holds the values—the estimated costs of the trip.

Basic Values

A few observations about cell values need to be made here. First, you typically don't type dollar signs, commas, and so forth. You usually add these symbols to the values by applying number formatting. You do need to include a decimal point if a value includes decimal values. In cell B4, for example, the cost of transportation is given as 839.86. To show the price in both dollars and cents, therefore, you use the decimal place between the dollars and the cents.

NOTE: Formatting is discussed further in Chapter 3.

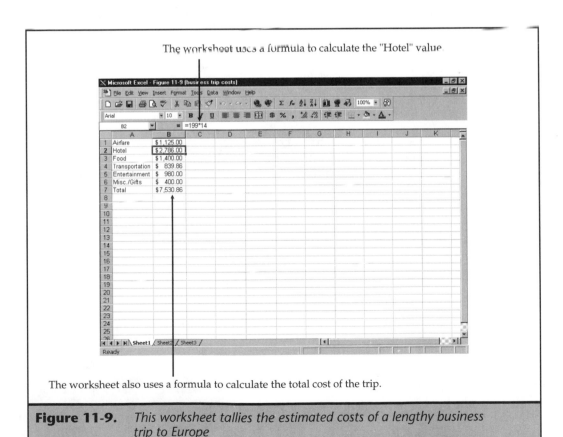

The worksheet uses a formula to calculate the "Hotel" value.

The worksheet also uses a formula to calculate the total cost of the trip.

Figure 11-9.   *This worksheet tallies the estimated costs of a lengthy business trip to Europe*

Figure 11-9 doesn't show any negative values, but worksheet cells accept negative values. To enter a negative value, just precede the number with the minus symbol. If you wanted to enter a "minus 200" into some cell, for example, you enter **-200**.

Special Values

Most of the time you will enter values like those shown in Figure 11-9. You should know, however, that Excel accepts values that look or work differently. (Remember that a value is just data you want to later use in a calculation.) For example, you can use scientific notation, date and time values, percentages, and fractions.

SCIENTIFIC NOTATION   Scientific notation amounts to a shorthand system for efficiently expressing very large or very small values. Using scientific notation, you express a value (sometimes only approximately) by multiplying a decimal value by ten raised or lowered to a specified power. For example, you might express the value 1,500,000 as the decimal value 1.5 multiplied by 106. (10^6 equals 1,000,000). Because 1.5 x 1,000,000 equals 1,500,000, the value 1,500,000 and the scientific notation value 1.5 x 10^6 are equivalent. In similar fashion, you might express the value .000000123 as the decimal value 1.23 multiplied by 10^{-7} (10^{-7} equals .0000001). Because 1.23 x .0000001 equals .000000123, the value .0000001232 and the scientific notation value .123 x 10^{-7} are equivalent.

NOTE: You may already know this, but 10^6 equals 10x10x10x10x10x10, or 1,000,000. 10^{-7} equals 1/10 x 1/10 x1/10 x 1/10 x 1/10 x 1/10 x 1/10, or .0000001.

You'll notice that as the power of ten increases, the number of zeros increases, and as the negative power of ten increases, the number of decimal places increases. And this is what makes scientific notation so useful. It's much easier, for example, to write 10^{100} than it is to write one with one hundred zeroes after it: values written using scientific notation take up less space because you use a special kind of shorthand to express them. In scientific notation, a decimal value, 1.23 x 10^{-7} is written as 1.23E-07. In other words, in place of the "x10" portion of the traditional notation, you just use an E.

	A	B
1	1E+20	
2	1.23E-07	
3		

Because scientific notation is so handy, you should know that if you do enter a really large or really small value in a worksheet cell—one that uses more than around twenty digits, Excel will convert your value to scientific notation. For example, if you enter the value:

100000000000000000000

Excel stores the following value in the cell:

10E+20

How Precise Is *Excel?*

Excel is more precise than most users will need. But you should know that Excel only uses the first 15 digits of a value. For example, if you enter the following 20-digit value:

12345678901234567890

Excel won't store this value in the cell. Rather, it will store the following 20-digit value:

12345678901234500000

Do you see what happens? Excel, in effect, loses the last five digits of this 20-digit number by converting them to zeroes. Note, too, that Excel hasn't done any rounding. So, what's really happened is that Excel has just dropped 67,890 from the value.

This same sort of lost-number problem occurs on the other side of the decimal place. If you entered the decimal value

.12345678901234567890

Excel would actually place the following value into the cell:

.123456789012345

While these dropped numbers sound terrible, it turns out that for most users, they don't really matter. If you were calibrating dollars, for example, how significant would roughly a $70,000 error be if you're talking about twelve million trillion? Not very.

EXCEL

DATE AND TIME VALUES   Excel considers dates and times to be values, too. This sounds weird when you first hear it, but treating dates and times as values means you can perform date and time arithmetic. You can easily calculate, for example, by which day you're supposed to pay an invoice due 45 days from today. And you can easily calculate how many hours you work if you start at 6:30 A.M., take a 45-minute lunch, and then continue working until 4:00 P.M.

To enter a date or time value, you just enter a value that looks like a date. Any of the following entries for February 8, 1998 looks like a date to Excel, for example:

February 8, 1998
Feb 8, 1998
8-Feb-98
2-8-98
02-08-98
2/8/98
02/08/98

 NOTE: Interestingly, as long as you haven't applied any specific cell formatting, if you enter a date value using either the first or second entry shown in the preceding list, Excel converts your entry to the third entry listed and also displays it this way. Similarly, if you enter a date value using the fourth entry shown in the preceding list, Excel converts your entry to the fifth entry listed and also displays it this way. While these conversions may seem strange, what's really happening is this: Excel recognizes that your entry is a date value, sees it has been entered incorrectly, and then converts it to an accepted date value syntax.

Time values work in a fashion that is similar to date values. If you enter into a cell something that looks like a time, for example:

1:00
2:30 AM
5:00:01 PM
16:45

Excel treats your entry as a time value. (Excel considers the entry 1:00 to be 1:00 A.M., by the way.) If you enter something that resembles a time value, but doesn't actually use the correct syntax—"1:00 p" for example, Excel edits your entry so it does use the correct syntax.

Here's another weird little twist on date and time values. While you can enter date and time values in the way just described—as little snippets of characters that look like a date or time—you can also enter them as regular values and then later format them to look like dates or times. According to Excel, for example, the integer 1, represents January 1, 1900. The integer 2 represents January 2, 1900. And the integer 3 represents January 3, 1900.

	A	B	C
1	225	August 12, 1900	
2	5490	January 11, 1915	
3	6704	May 9, 1918	
4	21070	September 7, 1957	
5	32111	November 30, 1987	
6			

TIP: *When you enter date or time values that look like date or time values, you're actually including formatting with the value. In other words, you're simultaneously entering a value into a cell and also telling Excel how to display, or format, the cell. Chapter 3 talks more about formatting values in Excel.*

Excel uses decimal values to represent time values. The decimal value .00, for example, represents 12:00:00 A.M. The decimal value .25 represents 6:00:00 A.M. The decimal value .5 represents 12:00:00 P.M., and so on. This business about time values being decimal values should make sense if you think about it for a minute. If Excel uses the whole number 1 to represent an entire day, then values less than one—in other words, decimal values—must be used to represent units of time less than a day: seconds, minutes, hours, and so forth.

	A	B	C
1	0.05	1:12 AM	
2	0.32	7:40 AM	
3	0.47	11:16 AM	
4	0.75	6:00 PM	
5	0.89	9:21 PM	
6			

Excel also lets you combine integers and decimal values to create date-and-time-value combinations. For example, the value 1.0 represents January 1, 1900 12:00:00 A.M. The value 2.25 represents January 2, 1900, 6:00:00 A.M. The value 3.5 represents January 3, 1900, 12:00:00 P.M.

Working with values that you enter as values is usually too confusing. You won't know the value 36,502.2 represents 4:48 A.M., December 8, 1999 until you format it. And, in fact, if you did enter the value 35,502.2 and then formatted it as a date, Excel would replace your entry (36,502.2) with the date value 12/8/1999 4:48 A.M.

NOTE: *For more information about formatting values, refer to Chapter 3.*

But you should still remember something about all this. And it's simply this: Each day's date value is one more that the previous day's date value. If you remember this, you'll be able to easily construct formulas that manipulate date values by adding values to date values. For example, if you want to know the precise date that falls 45 days after the date January 25, 1997, you can add the value 45 to the date value 1/25/1997. (The next chapter talks more about how you construct formulas.)

Splitting Hairs About Time Values

Some big office books also like to tell you that the value 0.041666667 represents one hour, that the value 0.000694444444444444 represents one minute and that the value 1.15741E-05 represents one second. The authors of this book don't think this information all that useful, however. If you remember that there are 24 hours in a day, 60 minutes in an hour, and 60 seconds in a minute, you can easily construct formulas that calculate the exact decimal values for any time value. The value 1 divided by 24 returns the decimal value for an hour. The decimal value for an hour divided by 60 returns the decimal value for a minute. And the decimal value for a minute divided by 60 returns the decimal value for a second.

PERCENTAGES AND FRACTIONS   You can enter percent values into worksheet cells by following the value with a percent symbol. Excel enters the decimal equivalent for the percent value into the cell, but displays the value as a percentage. Does that make sense? In other words, if you enter **75%** into a cell, Excel stores the decimal value .75 in the cell, but displays it as 75%.

You can also enter fractional values into worksheet cells as long as Excel understands that what you're entering is a fraction. If you enter **1 2/5** into a cell, for example, Excel figures that you're probably trying to enter a fraction. So it plops the value 1.4 into the cell, formatting it to look like a fraction. Note that the way you enter this is by typing the integer first (1), then a space, then the numerator (2), then a slash, and then the denominator (5).

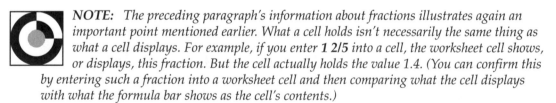 *NOTE: The preceding paragraph's information about fractions illustrates again an important point mentioned earlier. What a cell holds isn't necessarily the same thing as what a cell displays. For example, if you enter **1 2/5** into a cell, the worksheet cell shows, or displays, this fraction. But the cell actually holds the value 1.4. (You can confirm this by entering such a fraction into a worksheet cell and then comparing what the cell displays with what the formula bar shows as the cell's contents.)*

If you want to enter a fraction that doesn't contain a whole number and that could be misinterpreted by Excel as a date—for example, is the entry 2/5 a date value for February 5 or a fraction—just enter the fraction as **0 2/5**.

Wide Values

There's one final point you'll want to know concerning the values you enter into the cells of a worksheet: It's very likely that you'll want to enter values into cells that are wider than the column. But that's actually not a problem. If you enter a value with more digits than will fit into the width of a column, Excel does one of two things. If you haven't directly or indirectly told Excel to use special formatting for the cell, Excel displays the value using scientific notation, as cell B1 shows:

	A	B
1		3.578E+11
2		

If you have told Excel to use special formatting, Excel either attempts to widen the column when the number is entered or displays pound signs instead of the value as cell B2 shows:

	A	B
1		#########
2		

To make a column wide enough to display the value the way you want, double-click the right border of the column letter box. Alternatively, you can drag the right border of the column using the mouse. (These are the same techniques for changing column widths as mentioned earlier in the chapter in the discussion of wide labels.)

Formulas

The next chapter talks about formulas in detail. Before you finish reading this discussion of values, however, you should know that there's actually a final type of value called a *formula*. By entering a formula, you simply tell Excel to calculate a return using either values that the formula supplies or that the formula references. For example, if you enter the formula =2+2 into a cell, you tell Excel to add two and two together and display the result (which is four, of course). And if you enter the formula =A1+A2 into a cell, you tell Excel to add the value in cell A1 to the value in cell A2 and then display the result. This comment is relevant here because much of what you have read about values also applies to formulas. For example,

- Formula returns can be used in other formulas.
- Formulas can use and may display their results using scientific notation.
- Formulas are only precise to the 15 most significant digits.
- Formula results may be too wide to be displayed in a standard-width column.

Don't get hung up on this formula business. The next chapter explains everything. Do remember, however, that formulas are just another type of value.

Annotating Cells with Comments

Most people—at least when they're first working with Excel—enter data only into a worksheet's cells. But a worksheet's cells aren't the only place to enter and store information. You can also attach comments—electronic sticky notes, in effect—to cells. Why you do this is probably obvious: You can further document the contents of some cell without cluttering up the worksheet.

To attach a comment to a cell, follow these steps:

1. Click the cell to which you want to attach the note.

2. Choose the Insert menu Comment command. Excel displays a comment pop-up box.

	A	B	C	D	E
1	Airfare	$1,125.00			
2	Hotel	$2,786.00			
3	Food	$1,400.00			
4	Transportation	$ 839.86	Kaarin Dolliver:		
5	Entertainment	$ 980.00	Try to keep these costs		
6	Misc./Gifts	$ 400.00	down!		
7	Total	$7,530.86			
8					
9					

3. Enter the cell note into the pop-up box.

4. Click outside of the comment box when you're finished.

Once you've attached a comment to a cell, Excel places a small red triangle in the upper-right corner of the cell to show you that the cell has a comment. To later read the comment, place the mouse pointer over the center of the cell. Excel displays the comment in a small pop-up box, as shown in Figure 11-10. You can also later read all comments by all choosing the View menu Comment.

HEADSTART

TEMPLATES

The companion CD includes the retirement planner worksheet shown in Figure 11-10 (retire.xls) as a headstart template. The retirement planner worksheet uses cell comments to describe the inputs you supply to the headstart template and to explain the headstart template's outputs.

Working with Ranges

In the preceding pages of this chapter, the assumption is that you enter data into a worksheet one cell at a time. Your simplest approach to do this is just to click the cell

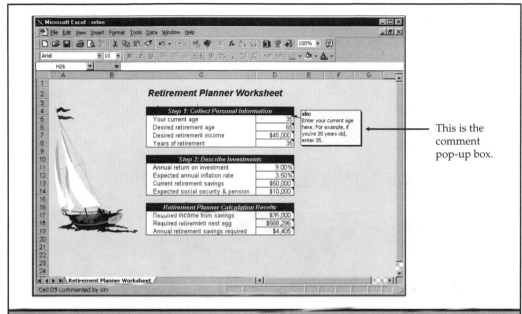

This is the comment pop-up box.

Figure 11-10. *When you place the mouse pointer over a cell to which you've attached a comment, Excel displays a small box with the cell comment*

and then type your entry. You can, however, select more than one cell at a time and enter data into more than one cell at a time. So, let's talk about this for a minute.

Selecting Ranges

To enter data into more than one cell at a time, you first need to know how to select a range of cells. Before you learn about range selection mechanics, however, let's quickly review how you select a single cell: You click the cell or move the cell selector to the cell using the arrow keys. When you do, Excel identifies your selection by placing a dark border around the cell. It also uses the Name box to give the selected cell's address.

When you select a group, or range, of adjacent cells, the process works very similar to this. Instead of simply clicking, however, you click on one corner of a rectangle of cells and then drag the mouse to the opposite corner, as shown in the next illustration . (If you're following along in front of your computer, make sure that you can duplicate this selection using the mouse.) When you select a range of cells, the Name box doesn't identify the entire selection—only the active cell in the selection. (The chapter talks about the significance of the active cell in a minute.)

You describe a contiguous range selection by giving the cell address of the top left corner of the range and the cell address of the bottom right corner of the range, separating the two addresses with a colon. For example, the range shown in the preceding illustration is B3:E8. You'll need to remember this bit of information because you'll often use range addresses in Excel dialog boxes and in constructing formulas.

 NOTE: You can also use the keyboard to select a range of cells. To do this, first select one corner of the range using the arrow keys. Then, while holding down the SHIFT key, use the arrow keys to increase the size of the selection. If this doesn't make sense to you—and it is hard to explain—just try it on your computer. You'll immediately see how it works.

A range can also be composed of nonadjacent cells. You can also select more than one range of cells using the mouse. To do so, select the group of cells, hold down the CTRL key, and then select the second and any subsequent groups of cells. The range address for the cells selected in the next illustration is B1:B2,B4:B6,B8,B12:B13,B15,B17.

	A	B	C
1	Algeria	213	
2	Belize	501	
3	Chile	56	
4	Croatia	385	
5	Equador	593	
6	Ethiopia	251	
7	France	33	
8	Guatemala	502	
9	Hungary	36	
10	Iran	98	
11	Japan	81	
12	Libya	218	
13	Morocco	212	
14	Netherlands	31	
15	Panama	507	
16	Sri Lanka	94	
17	Tunisia	216	
18	United Kingdom	44	
19	Vietnam	84	
20			

To select a three-dimensional range—in other words, to select the same group of cells on more than one sheet of a workbook—first group the worksheets. If all of the worksheet tabs are located next to each other, start by selecting the first worksheet tab and then holding SHIFT as you select the last worksheet tab. If the tabs for worksheets to be grouped are not next to each other, start by selecting the first worksheet tab, then hold CTRL as you click on each additional worksheet tab. Then, select the range on the active worksheet. You might want to select a three-dimensional range to quickly format more than one sheet at a time or if you are creating a formula that references the selected range on the selected sheets.

To select a column or row with the mouse, simply click the Column heading button that displays the column's letter or the Row heading button that displays the row's number. Excel selects the entire column or row.

TIP: To select a column or row with the keyboard, make sure the active cell is within the column or row you wish to select, then press CTRL+SPACEBAR to select the column or SHIFT+SPACEBAR to select the row.

Once you select a range of cells, you can begin to enter data into the range. You can do this either manually or using a command.

Entering Data into a Selected Range Manually

The white cell in a range selection is called the active cell, and it is into this cell that what you type gets placed. For example, if you select the range shown in the illustration below, type the word *Mississippi,* and then press ENTER, Excel places your entry into cell C19.

	A	B	C	D	E
1					
2					
3					
4					
5					
6					
7					
8					
9					
10					
11					
12			Delaware	321	
13			Hawaii	907	
14			Iowa	880	
15			Lousiana	450	
16			Maine	567	
17			Michigan	220	
18			Minnesota	567	
19					
20					

When you do select a range or multiple ranges, Excel lets you use the ENTER and TAB keys as well as the SHIFT+ENTER and SHIFT+TAB key combinations to easily place whatever you've typed into the active cell and to then change the active cell of the current range selection. Pressing ENTER and SHIFT+ENTER moves the active cell down and up the cells of the selected column. Pressing TAB and SHIFT+TAB moves the active cell right and left within the selected row.

At this point in a discussion of range selection mechanics, I could describe in a few paragraphs what happens when you get to the end of a column or row or rectangle and then again press ENTER, TAB, SHIFT+ENTER, or SHIFT+TAB. Instead, just try this out for yourself by selecting a few ranges on a worksheet, and then experiment with the keys and key combinations described here. You'll immediately see—and more importantly, remember—how these keys move the active cell around a worksheet's selected ranges.

One other thing you should know, however, concerns three-dimensional ranges. When you make one of these selections and then start entering data into the selection, what you enter on one worksheet of the selection gets automatically entered into the other worksheet's ranges. For example, if you select the range shown in the illustration that follows on the worksheets Sheet1, Sheet2, and Sheet3, and then enter the values shown, whatever you enter into the range B2:D4 of Sheet1 also gets placed into range B2:D4 of Sheet2 and range B2:D4 of Sheet3. If this doesn't quite make sense—or seems confusing—select the range B2:D4 in Sheet1, hold down the SHIFT key, and click the Sheet3 tab, and then enter the values shown in the illustration. When you're done, browse through Sheet1, Sheet2, and Sheet3, and you'll see exactly what happens.

	A	B	C	D	E
1		January	February	March	
2	Sales	15000	20000	10000	
3	Expense	12000	12000	12000	
4	Profit	3000	8000	-2000	
5					

TIP: *Manually entering data into a range selection may not seem like all that neat a data-entry technique. But it actually is. If you're entering a large quantity of data, you'll find it usually saves you time to select the worksheet range into which you want to enter the data first—and then later concentrate simply on entering the data, pressing ENTER, entering more data, pressing ENTER again, and so on. This will be especially true if you're a touch typist.*

Copying and Moving Worksheet Ranges

Once you know how to select a worksheet range, you can easily copy or move a worksheet range. To move the selected worksheet range, just drag the border of the selected range using the mouse. To copy the selected worksheet range, hold down the CTRL key, and then drag the border of the selected worksheet range using the mouse. As you drag the border of a selected range you're copying or moving, Excel displays an outline of the range to show you where the range is copied or moved.

WARNING: *When you copy or move a range, you replace the contents of the destination range.*

Using the Edit Fill Series Command

Range selection is a useful to know about if you want to enter, copy, or move data in a worksheet, but it's also useful if you're going to use Excel's Fill Series command, which is a terribly handy tool for quickly entering values that fit a easily identifiable pattern. For example, if you want to build a worksheet that describes how a loan balance is repaid over, say, 30 years with monthly payments, you might want to number and date the 360 monthly payment dates, as shown in the partially completed worksheet in Figure 11-11.

EXAMPLES

LEARN BY EXAMPLE
You can open the example Excel workbook shown in Figure 11-11, Figure 11-11 (loan amortization schedule), from the companion CD if you want to follow along with the discussion here.

Rather than manually entering this series of payment number and date values, you can use the Edit menu Fill Series command. You might also want to number the monthly payments made on such a loan: 1, 2, 3, and so on all the way to the 360th

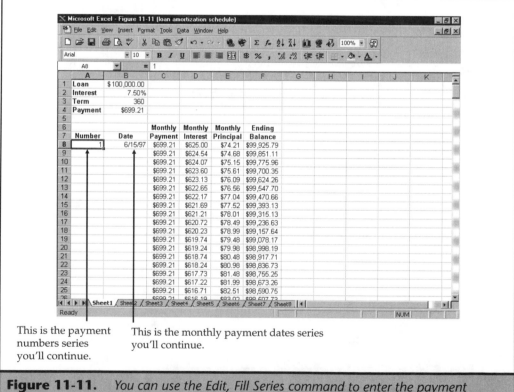

This is the payment numbers series you'll continue.

This is the monthly payment dates series you'll continue.

Figure 11-11. *You can use the Edit, Fill Series command to enter the payment numbers and monthly payment dates into this worksheet*

payment. Again, rather than manually entering this series of values, you can use the Edit menu Fill Series command. To use the Edit menu Fill Series command, follow these steps:

1. Enter the starting value for the pattern you're creating into the first cell of the range you'll select. In Figure 11-11, for example, you would enter the value 1 into cell A8 and the date value for the first monthly payment date, 6/15/97, in cell B8.

2. Select the range you want to fill. In Figure 11-11, for example, to fill the range A9:A367 with payment numbers, you select the range A8:A367. To fill the range B9:B367 with monthly payment dates, you select the range B8:B367.

3. Choose the Edit menu Fill command and then the Fill submenu Series command. Excel displays the Series dialog box.

4. Use the Step value text box to describe how the first cell's value changes as it's adjusted and placed into subsequent cells. (Optionally, you can enter the value that ends the pattern using the Stop value text box.)

5. Use the Series in buttons to indicate whether you want the range selection filled row by row or column by column. In the case where you're filling column A with payment numbers or column B with monthly payment dates, you mark the Series in Columns option button.

6. Use the Type buttons to indicate how the start value is adjusted using the Step value. The default pattern is for a Linear pattern, which simply means that the step value is added to the previous cell's value to get the current cell's value. (You would mark this option button to fill in the payment number series.) The Growth pattern means the step value is multiplied by the previous cell's value to get the current cell's value. The Date pattern tells Excel the series should follow the pattern you describe using the Date unit buttons. (You would mark this option button to fill in the monthly payment date series.) The AutoFill pattern tells Excel to look at the values you've already entered into the range (if you've done this) and then continue that pattern.

7. If you indicate you want to use a date series—you would do this by marking the Type date option button in step 6—you need to specify which date units you'll use to describe the series. You do this using the Date unit option buttons: Day, Weekday, Month, or Year. In the case of the monthly loan amortization schedule, for example, you would click the Month option button.

8. Enter the value which Excel should add to the first value in the series into the Step value text box. In the case of the payment number series, you would enter **1** since the next payment number should be created by adding one to the previous payment number. In the case of the monthly payment date series, you would also enter **1** since the next monthly payment date value should be created by adding one month to the previous monthly payment date.

9. Optionally, if you know the last value of the series, enter it into the Stop value text box. In the case of the payment number series, for example, you could enter **360** since there are only 360 payments in a 30-year mortgage with monthly payments. (You probably wouldn't know the last monthly payment date value.)

10. When the Series dialog box correctly describes the series, click OK. Excel fills the selected range with a data series like the one you describe.

TEMPLATES

HEADSTART

The companion CD includes several loan amortization headstart templates you can use: a 30-year fixed rate mortgage loan amortization schedule (30yrloan.xls), which actually shows how Figure 11-11 looks after the payment numbers and monthly payment dates have been entered; a 30-year adjustable rate mortgage loan amortization schedule (30yr-adj.xls); a 15-year fixed rate loan amortization schedule (15yrloan.xls); a 15-year adjustable rate loan amortization schedule (15yr-adj.xls); a 60-month fixed rate loan amortization schedule (60moloan.xls) such as might be used for a 60-month fixed-rate car loan; and a 60-month adjustable rate loan amortization schedule (60mo-adj.xls).

Using AutoFill with a Mouse

AutoFill, as mentioned earlier, refers to Excel's ability to identify a pattern from the values you've already entered and then continue the pattern. While you can choose the Edit menu Fill command and then the Fill submenu Series command to use AutoFill, you'll more often want to use the mouse. It's easier.

To AutoFill a range selection using the mouse, first enter the first few values of the pattern—just enough to clearly show the pattern. Then, select the range that holds those values. In Figure 11-12, for example, you would select the range A8:B9.

To continue the pattern, you drag the fill handle, which appears as a square with cross-hairs in the lower right corner of the range selection, into the range of cells that you want to fill. Actually using AutoFill is the best way to learn and appreciate its power. So do try it. Enter the date values shown in Figure 11-12, select the range holding the payment numbers and date values—A8:B9—and then drag the selected range's fill handle down several rows.

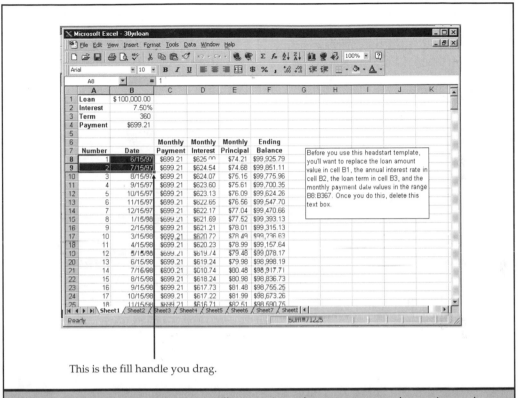

This is the fill handle you drag.

Figure 11-12. *You can use AutoFill to continue the payment number series and monthly payment date series already shown in A8:B9*

TIP: *You can also use AutoFill to copy the contents of single cell into a range. To do this, enter a label or value into a cell, select the cell, and then drag the cell's fill handle.*

Using a Custom List

AutoFill is a very powerful tool because Excel can identify almost any pattern you concoct: odd numbers, even numbers, a growth rate of 10%, days of the week, months of the year, and so on. There will, however, be patterns you'll enter that will be unique to your work. For example, you might have a list of employee names you enter frequently. Or a list of department names. Or product numbers. Anytime you start such a list, you actually know you are beginning a recognizable pattern. But the problem is that only you know the pattern. Excel doesn't. And this knowledge gap on the part of Excel is what Excel's custom lists address. In essence, by creating a custom list, you identify a special, unique pattern that Excel can use to AutoFill.

To create a custom list, first enter the labels or values that make up the list someplace in a worksheet. Then, select the range that holds the labels or values, choose the Tools, Options command, and click the Custom Lists tab. Excel displays the Custom Lists tab of the Options dialog box (see Figure 11-13). When you click the Import button, Excel creates a custom list based on the entries in the selected range. Click OK to close the Options dialog box.

NOTE: To edit the entries in a custom list, choose the Tools menu Options command and click the Custom Lists tab. Select the list you want to change from the Custom lists box. Then, make your changes using the List entries box. When you finish editing the list entries, click the OK button.

Once you define a custom list, AutoFill recognizes a custom list entry as the start of a pattern. To use a custom list therefore, all you have to do is enter the custom list's first entry in a cell. Then you drag that cell's fill handle.

NOTE: This chapter only briefly covered the topics of cell formulas—perhaps the most important type of entry you'll make in your worksheets. To learn more about formulas, you may want to turn to the next chapter. It describes in detail how formulas and a special formula tool, called functions, work.

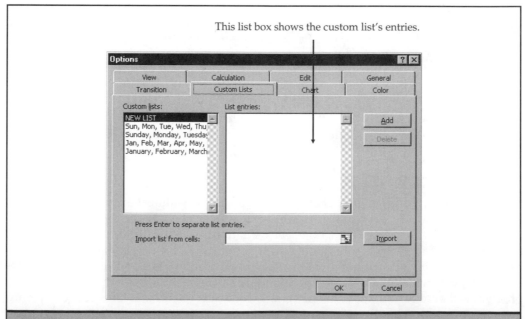

Figure 11-13. *You use the Options dialog box's Custom Lists tab to create and modify custom lists*

Office 97

Chapter 12

Excel Formulas and Functions

If you read the last chapter, you already know in general terms that Excel's cells also accept formulas. What you may not yet know is how powerful these formulas are. Excel lets you easily construct formulas that make complicated and cumbersome calculations. Excel even lets you create formulas that, instead of mathematically manipulating values, manipulate chunks of text. In this chapter, you'll learn how to use Excel's formulas to turn your Excel worksheets into powerful analytical tools.

Formula Basics

A formula simply takes input values, mathematically manipulates them, and then returns a result. All of the following are, for example, formulas:

```
2+2
99-1
5÷5000+2÷5000
```

Formulas may not seem like something you should get excited about, but they actually represent the foundation of Excel's power. Why? Because Excel lets you enter formulas into worksheet cells, and then it instantaneously calculates and displays the formula result.

Entering a Formula into a Worksheet Cell

Entering a formula into a worksheet cell is easy. You simply follow these steps:

1. Select the cell you want to place the formula into.

2. Type the equal sign to tell Excel that you're about to enter a formula.

3. Enter the formula using any input values and the appropriate mathematical operators that make up your formula.

The table that follows describes the five basic operators and provides examples of simple formulas that show how they're used.

Operator	Description	Example	Result
+	addition	=2+2	4
-	subtraction	=4-2	2
*	multiplication	=4*2	8
/	division	=12/4	3
^	exponentiation	=4^2	16

While the formulas in the preceding table can be useful ones to calculate, the neat part of Excel's formulas is that you don't have to include the actual values in the formula. In fact, you usually don't. You can typically reference the cells that hold the values. For example, let's say you want to calculate the monthly interest on a $100,000 loan that will charge 7 ½ percent interest annually. To make this calculation, you could construct a formula that looks like what follows:

=100000*7.5%/12

An easier method (because it lets you quickly change formula input values later) is to construct a simple worksheet that stores the loan values and then references these values in the actual formula. Figure 12-1 shows just such a worksheet. To construct it, enter the labels and values shown in the range A1:B2 as well as the label shown in cell A3. Then enter the formula **=B1*B2/12** into cell B3.

LEARN BY EXAMPLE

You can open the example Excel workbook shown in Figure 12-1, Figure 12-1 (loan interest calculation), from the companion CD if you want to follow along with the discussion here.

When you enter the formula into cell B3, you tell Excel to multiply the value in cell B1 by the value in cell B2 and to then divide that result by 12. (Notice that because cell B3 is the selected cell in Figure 12-1, its contents show on the formula bar: you now know why the formula bar is called the formula bar.)

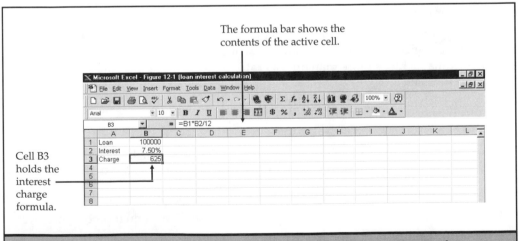

Figure 12-1.   *This simple worksheet calculates the monthly interest cost of an example loan*

The neat thing about the formula in Figure 12-1 is that, by using cell references in the formula rather than actual values, it's easy to recalculate the formula using different inputs. If interest rates pop up to, say, 9.75 percent, you can recalculate the monthly interest charge simply by replacing the existing value in cell B2, 7.5%, with the new value, 9.75%.

	A	B	C
1	Loan	100000	
2	Interest	9.75%	
3	Charge	812.5	
4			

NOTE: *The values 9.5 and 9.75 percent, by the way, are equivalent to the decimal values .095 and .0975.*

TIP: *While you can type out the cell addresses of all the cell references you want to use in a formula, it's often just as easy and usually more accurate to type the operators and then click the cells. For example, to create the formula =B1*B2/12, rather than typing =B1*B2/12, you could type =, click cell B1, type *, click cell B2, and then finally type /12. The reason this works is that if you've already told Excel that you're entering a formula—which you do when you type the first equal sign (=)—Excel assumes that any of the subsequent cells you click should be included in the formula.*

Operator Precedence

You need to keep in mind the issue of operator precedence as you write formulas. Operator precedence determines the order in which a formula's calculations are made when a formula includes more than one operator. Take, for example, the case of the following formula:

=1+2-3*4/5^6

Excel uses the rules of operator precedence to determine which calculations get performed first. The general rules that apply to the above formula are pretty easy:

- The exponential operation is performed first.
- The multiplication and division operations, which have equal precedence, are performed next and from left to right.
- The addition and subtraction operations, which also have equal precedence, are performed last and from left to right.

If two operators in a formula possess the same precedence—say a formula uses two multiplication operations or a multiplication and a division operation, for example—Excel calculates operators in left-to-right order. In the case of the formula given earlier, therefore, Excel first makes the exponential calculation, then does multiplication, then the division, then the addition, and finally the subtraction.

 TIP: *To verify that you understand how this works, try to calculate the above formula with a calculator and scratch pad and then test your result by entering the formula into an empty worksheet cell.*

To change the order in which Excel calculates a formula's operators, enclose the operator and its operands (the values it uses in its calculation) in parentheses. If you want to change the order of another additional formula operator, repeat the process: enclose the operator and its operands (which may actually include a calculation result) in parentheses.

For example, suppose that you want to use the formula =1+2-3*4/5^6 in some worksheet cell, but also want the operators used in exactly the opposite order that Excel would typically use them. In other words, rather than calculating the operators in the default order—exponentiation, multiplication, division, addition, and subtraction—you want them calculated in this order: subtraction, addition, division, multiplication, and finally, exponentiation. Here's how you would place your parenthesis marks:

=((1+(2-3))*(4/5))^6

You calculate the above formula by working from the innermost set of parentheses outward. After the first level of calculation is completed, the result is (0*0.262144)^6. The next level of calculation would be 0^6. The final result, then, is zero. If you had not changed the order of calculation by using parentheses, the result would have been 2.999232.

If you find this operator precedence business confusing—and it sometimes can be—your best bet is to keep your formulas simple. Don't construct lengthy formulas that use a bunch of different operators. If you can, substitute a function. (This chapter describes functions a bit later in the section, "Using Functions.") Or, alternatively, break a long formula into several shorter formulas, placing these shorter formulas into separate cells.

Boolean Algebra Operators

Excel supports another category of arithmetic operators called Boolean logic operators. These operators have lower precedence than any of the other five operators discussed up to this point. In other words, in any formula that includes them, the Boolean operations would be the last operations performed.

In effect, Boolean logic operators let you compare two values or labels by asking a question, such as "Is the value in cell A1 equal to the value in cell B1?" If the answer to the comparison question is yes, the operator returns a 1. If the answer to the comparison question is no, the operator returns a 0. The table that follows identifies, illustrates, and describes the Boolean operators that Excel provides.

Operator	Example	Comparison Made
=	A1=5	Is the value in cell A1 equal to 5?
>	A1>5	Is the value in cell A1 greater than 5?
<	A1<5	Is the value in cell A1 less than 5?
<>	A1<>5	Is the value in cell A1 not equal to 5?
=>	A1=>5	Is the value in cell A1 greater than or equal to 5?
=<	A1=<5	Is the value in cell A1 less than or equal to 5?

Boolean logic operators can seem sort of funny, but they actually become quite handy when you're using logical functions that return a value or label based on a result of the comparison test that a Boolean logic operator can make. For example, "If the student's test result is less than 60, return his letter grade as 'F'."

Interpreting Error Values

You can create formulas that don't make sense because they aren't possible. For example, no one knows how to divide a value by zero. That mathematical operation is undefined. So, if you enter a formula such as =1/0 into a cell, Excel can't calculate it. Instead, what Excel displays as the result of the formula calculation is an error, #DIV/0?. This error value tells you, first, that Excel can't calculate the formula, and, second, why Excel can't calculate it. In this case, it is because you're attempting to divide some value by zero, which is nonsensical. (In essence, you can think of division by zero as saying, "what formula result do I get if I *don't* divide some value?). The table on the next page provides a complete list of the error values that Excel can return when a formula calculation can't be made. Some of these won't make sense until you finish reading this chapter. But you'll want to have a complete list of error values someplace—and it makes more sense to do it here, rather than at the very end of the chapter or in some easy-to-miss appendix.

Error Value	Description
#DIV/0!	Formula attempts to divide some value by zero, which is an undefined mathematical operation.
#N/A	Formula references a cell that supplies the "Not Available" error value. A cell supplies this error value by using the =NA( ) function.
#NAME?	Formula uses a cell or range name that hasn't been defined, or the function name has been misspelled, or a text string is not enclosed in quotation marks.
#NULL!	Formula references a cell as the intersection of two ranges—except there is no intersection of the two ranges.
#NUM!	An invalid argument has been supplied for the function, where the function expects a numeric argument, or the result is either too large or too small to be represented in Excel.
#REF!	Formula references cells that no longer exist because you deleted them.
#VALUE!	Formula attempts to use the wrong argument or operand. For example, a chunk of text in a mathematical operation—which, of course, makes no sense.

If you do create a formula that returns an error value, use the error value to identify the type of error. (You can use the preceding table of error values to help you do this.) Then, if the error isn't temporary—perhaps a result of the fact that your worksheet still isn't complete—you'll need to correct the problem or problems that produce the error value.

How Excel Recalculates Formulas

Excel calculates the formulas you enter in the order they need to be calculated. For example, it first calculates any formulas that are independent of any other formulas. (These might be formulas that use only values and not cell references, or they might be formulas that reference only cells that hold values and not other formulas.) After Excel has calculated these independent formulas, it begins calculating the dependent formulas, working its way from your least dependent formulas to your most dependent formulas (A "dependent" formula needs other formulas' results in order to be calculated.)

NOTE: Excel calculates a worksheet's formula any time a formula's inputs change. On a fast computer or in a workbook that doesn't have a great number of complicated formulas, the recalculation usually happens so fast that you don't ever know it has occurred.

Most of the time this calculating happens automatically. You don't need to think about it. You don't need to worry about it. However, you can create something called a circular reference, and that typically creates problems.

A *circular reference* is a formula that either directly or indirectly depends on itself. With a circular reference formula, you can't calculate the formula because to calculate the formula you first need to calculate the formula. While that description sounds like gobbledy-gook, it's more common in real-life that you might think. (Pension fund calculations, for example, are often circular.) Say you were building a budgeting worksheet and that one of your formulas calculated an employee bonus that equaled, say, 10 percent of the profits after deducting the bonus. To calculate the bonus, you need to know the profits. But to calculate the profits, you need to know the bonus. You see the circular nature of this. Figure 12-2 shows an example workbook that makes just this calculation.

LEARN BY EXAMPLE

You can open the example Excel workbook shown in Figure 12-2, Figure 12-2 (circular reference example), *from the companion CD if you want to follow along with the discussion here.*

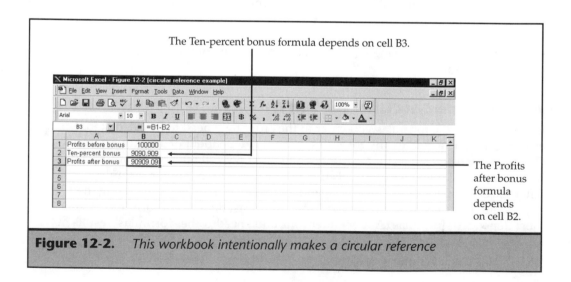

Figure 12-2. *This workbook intentionally makes a circular reference*

If you build a worksheet that makes a circular reference, Excel initially assumes you've made an error and displays the message shown here:

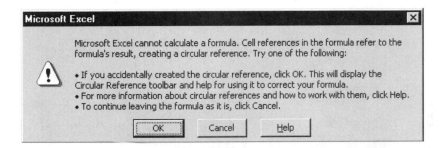

After you click the OK button in the alert box, Excel uses the status bar to identify the cell with the formula creating the circular reference. (The message says "Circular:" followed by the cell address with the circular reference formula.)

If you know you've made an error, click OK; Excel displays the Circular Reference toolbar. You can use its drop-down list box to display a list of the cell references that make up the circular reference and to move to any of these cell references. (The idea here, perhaps obviously, is that you move through each of the cells that make up the circular reference, looking for the formula that erroneously creates the circularity.)

TIP: You can also display the Circular Reference toolbar by choosing the View menu Toolbars command and then the Toolbars submenu Circular Reference command.

If you build a worksheet that intentionally uses a circular reference, Excel may be able to iteratively solve the circular reference. It turns out that some circular references—like the one about an employee bonus equaling ten percent of the profits after the bonus—converge to a single solution. All Excel has to do is repeatedly recalculate the worksheet. To tell Excel that you want it to repeatedly calculate a worksheet in an attempt to resolve a circular reference, choose the Tools menu Options command, select the Calculation tab, and then mark the Iteration check box.

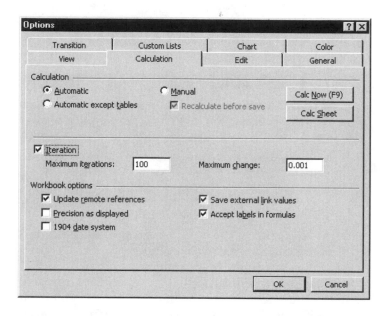

Note, however, that some circular references can't be solved. In this case, the formula that creates the circular reference doesn't converge to a single, correct solution. Sometimes, this lack of convergence results in formula results jumping around wildly. Other times, the lack of convergence causes the formula results either to continue to grow or decline—and usually at an accelerating rate. In practice, circular references that don't converge to a single solution are erroneous formulas. You've either made an error entering the formula—perhaps you referenced an incorrect cell or the cell itself with the formula. Or you've constructed a large, complex workbook—and your modeling logic has broken down someplace.

NOTE: Excel doesn't alert you to circular references if you've already told it you want it to make iterative, or repeated, workbook recalculations. Excel figures that if you've told it to do this, you know you've got circular references that you're trying to solve through convergence.

Creating Linking Formulas

Most of the formulas you create will reference other cells on the same worksheet. You aren't limited to doing this, however. You can pull values from cells located on other worksheets and even from cells in other workbooks.

The easiest way to do this, by the way, is to create the formula by typing the operators and then clicking the cells whose contents you want to use in the formula you're building. If you remember that you can display another worksheet page by clicking its sheet tab and you remember that you can display another workbook either by opening it or choosing it from the Window menu, you can display the cell you want to use and then click it.

You can also type out a formula that links to, or uses, cells on other worksheets or cells in a different workbook. To create a formula that uses a cell on another worksheet, just precede the cell address with the sheet name and an exclamation point. For example, to create a formula that multiplies the value in cell B2 on Sheet5 by 25, you use the following formula:

=Sheet5!B2*25

To create a formula that uses a cell in another workbook, precede the cell address with a single quote mark, the workbook name in brackets, the sheet name, a single quote mark, and an exclamation point. For example, to create a formula that multiplies the value in cell B2 on Sheet5 of the workbook named Budget by 25, you use the following formula:

='[Budget]Sheet5'!B2*25

By the way, if you change the name of a workbook—say from Budget to Budget 1996—Excel updates any linking formulas for you as long as the both the workbook you're renaming and the workbook that uses the linking formulas are open.

Using Arrays

An array is simply a string of values. For example, the following set of values is an array: 1, 2, 3, 4, and 5. The reason arrays are interesting—at least to Excel users—is that you can use arrays in formulas to create still other arrays. For example, you could add the following two arrays to create a third array:

	Array 1:	1	2	3	4	5
+	Array 2:	2	4	6	8	10
=	Result:	3	6	9	12	15

Do you see what's happened? When you add two, five-value arrays together, you create a third, five-value array. In the resulting array, the first value is calculated as the first value from array 1 (1) plus the first value from array 2 (2). The second value is calculated as the second value from array 1 (2) plus the second value from array 2 (4). The third value in the resulting array is calculated by adding the third values in array 1 and array 2, and so on.

Creating Array Formulas

While arrays may not seem all that useful, they can be very powerful in Excel worksheets—and once you see the actual mechanics, you'll understand why. Let's say you're creating a simple project time budget, in hours, that just coincidentally uses the same values as the array example. (See Figure 12-3.)

LEARN BY EXAMPLE

You can open the example Excel workbook shown in Figure 12-3, Figure 12-3 (project hours before array formula), from the companion CD if you want to follow along with the discussion here.

To create an array for the total values in row 4, first select the range B4:F4, type an equal sign (=), select the range B2:F2, type a plus sign (+), select the range B3:F3, and then press CTRL+SHIFT+ENTER. (You press these three keys simultaneously.) When you do this, Excel enters the array formula {=B2:F2+B3:F3} into each of the cells in the range B4:F4. (Note that you don't enter the curly brackets, Excel adds these when you press CTRL+SHIFT+ENTER.) Figure 12-4 shows the workbook from Figure 12-3 after adding an array formula.

Let's quickly review what's happening with this array formula to make sure that you understand how it works. In cell B4, the formula {=B2:F2+B3:F3} tells Excel to calculate its result by adding the values in B2 and B3. In cell C4, the formula tells Excel to add the values in C2 and C3. In cells D4, E4, and F4, the same basic mechanics

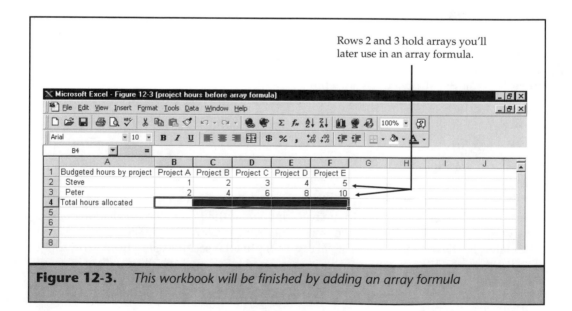

Figure 12-3. *This workbook will be finished by adding an array formula*

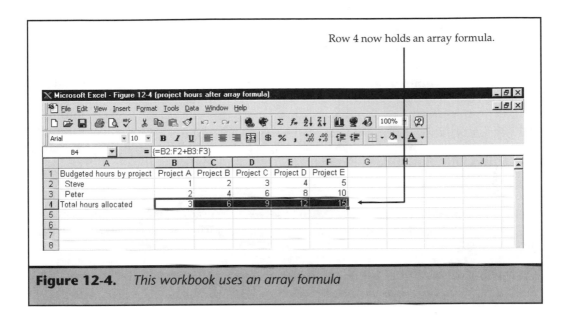

Row 4 now holds an array formula.

Figure 12-4. *This workbook uses an array formula*

apply: Excel calculates the correct column's total by adding the values in row 2 and row 3 of that column. You see how this works, right?

LEARN BY EXAMPLE
You can open the example Excel workbook shown in Figure 12-4, Figure 12-4 (project hours after array formula), from the companion CD if you want to follow along with the discussion here.

NOTE: *The array formula illustrated in Figure 12-4 provides a single-dimension array. You can create two-dimensional array formulas, however. To do this, you just need to select a two-dimensional range for the array formula and use a two-dimensional range in the formula itself.*

Now that you understand how array formulas work, you'll also understand why they are so powerful: You only have to enter a single formula to make several different calculations. Excel takes your single formula and stores it in the cells that hold the result array's values. But you've still only entered a single formula. That makes for less work, obviously. But there's a more important benefit when you're creating and working with large or complex workbooks: You'll have fewer formulas, which means you'll have fewer formulas to error-check and fewer formulas that may be incorrectly constructed and, therefore, returning erroneous results. Restated more simply: Array formulas simplify your workbooks by reducing the number of formulas. And that almost always reduces the number of errors, or bugs, in your workbooks.

Using Arrays as an Extension of Matrix Mathematics

In effect, what array formulas do is apply something you may remember as matrix mathematics from your school days. Using matrix mathematics, you simultaneously add, subtract, multiply, or divide matrices of values, thereby producing a new matrix of values. What's more, while you can always work with ranges that are of equal size, you can also work with ranges that are of unequal size—as long as Excel can figure out (applying the rules of matrix mathematics) what it's supposed to do. For example, Figure 12-5 shows a worksheet where the single cell range, B6, is multiplied by each of the values in the range B2:F4, returning the new values shown in the range B9:F11.

LEARN BY EXAMPLE
You can open the example Excel workbook shown in Figure 12-5, Figure 12-5 (project hours after contingency), *from the companion CD if you want to follow along with the discussion here.*

Using Array Constants

You should usually create array formulas that refer to ranges that contain your arrays. So that's the way this chapter initially describes arrays as working. You can, however, create array formulas in which the formulas themselves hold the array values. For example, to add the array 1, 2, 3, 4, and 5 to the array 2, 4, 6, 8 and 10, and place the

---

The values in the worksheet range B9:F11 are also produced by an array formula.

Microsoft Excel - Figure 12-5 (project hours with contingency)

File   Edit   View   Insert   Format   Tools   Data   Window   Help

Arial   10   **B** *I* U

B9   = {=B6*B2:F4}

	A	B	C	D	E	F	G	H	I	J
1	Budgeted hours by project	Project A	Project B	Project C	Project D	Project E				
2	Steve	1	2	3	4	5				
3	Peter	2	4	6	8	10				
4	Total hours allocated	3	6	9	12	15				
5										
6	Contingency factor	1.1								
7										
8	Scheduled hours by project									
9	Steve	1.1	2.2	3.3	4.4	5.5				
10	Peter	2.2	4.4	6.6	8.8	11				
11	Total hours allocated	3.3	6.6	9.9	13.2	16.5				
12										
13										

Figure 12-5.   *Array formulas also let you use matrix mathematics in your worksheets*

results in a worksheet range, you probably should follow the approach shown in Figure 12-4. You could also enter the following formula into the range B4:F4:

=\{1,2,3,4,5\}+\{2,4,6,8,10\}

When you press CTRL+SHIFT+ENTER, Excel places the following formula into the selected range:

\{=\{1,2,3,4,5\}+\{2,4,6,8,10\}\}

NOTE: *Notice that you would include the curly brackets when you type the array formula that includes the constants. Notice also that Excel adds its own set of curly brackets when you press CTRL+SHIFT+ENTER.*

Figure 12-6 shows an example Excel workbook that uses an array formula that uses constants.

LEARN BY EXAMPLE
You can open the example Excel workbook shown in Figure 12-6, Figure 12-6 (project hours using constant array formula), from the companion CD if you want to follow along with the discussion here.

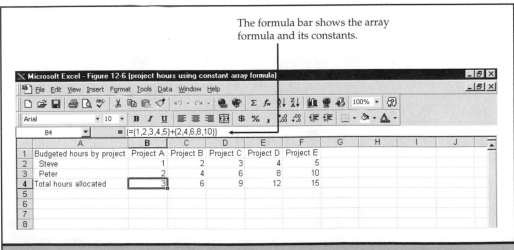

Figure 12-6. *The workbook shown here uses an array formula with constants*

Editing Array Formulas

You edit array formulas in almost the same way as you edit other formulas. Double-click the cell with the formula you want to edit. Then, when Excel displays the formula in an editable text box, make your changes. The one thing you need to remember is that when you finish making your changes, you must press CTRL+SHIFT+ENTER to update the array formula in all of the cells holding the formula.

NOTE: *Excel makes you press* CTRL+SHIFT+ENTER *to finish your editing. Excel won't let you break the array formula by mucking about with only one of the cells in which the array formula returns its results.*

Using Text Formulas

While most formulas only mathematically manipulate values, it turns out that you can also have text formulas. Obviously, you can't add two pieces of text together. But what you can do is concatenate, or moosh together, two or more pieces of text. To do this, you use the concatenation operator, &. This chapter won't spend much time on this concatenation business because it's pretty simple. Just take a look at the next table, which illustrates how the concatenation operator works:

Text Formula	What It Returns
="White"&"house"	Whitehouse
=A1&A2	Whitehouse (if cell A1 holds the label *White* and cell A2 holds the label *house*)
="Agatha"&" "&"Christie"	Agatha Christie

Notice, by the way, that the third text formula actually concatenates three chunks of text: the name "Agatha", a space enclosed in quotation marks, and the name "Christie".

Using Names in Formulas

When you have only a few formulas in a worksheet, it's usually pretty easy to keep track of what your formulas are doing. If you have to do a little research to figure out, for example, why some formula multiplies cell B81 by cell Z7, it's sort of a bother. But it's not an unbearable burden.

As soon as you begin creating some really substantial workbooks, however—workbooks with hundreds or thousands of formulas—you'll want to name many of the cells and ranges you use in your formulas. In this way, you'll be able to work with formulas that look like this:

=Interest_Rate*Loan_Balance

instead of formulas that look like this:

=B81*Z7

Naming Cells and Ranges

Excel provides probably a half-dozen different ways to name cells and ranges. But the easiest and usually the fastest way to name a cell or range is simply by using the Name box. The Name box is the box that shows the active cell's address; it appears at the left end of the Formula bar, just below the Formatting toolbar.

To name a cell or range, follow these steps:

1. Select the cell or range.

2. Click the Name box. Excel turns it into an editable text box and highlights the cell address (which is the cell address of the active cell).

3. Type the name you want to use for the selected cell or range. You can use numbers, letters, and the period (.), backslash (\), and underscore (_) symbols in your names, but you can't create cell or range names that resemble cell addresses.

Units		▼	=	20000	
	A	B	C	D
1	Units	20000		
2	Price	10		
3	Sales	200000		
4				

When you want to use the name in a formula, you can simply type it in place of the cell address. Or, if you're building formulas by clicking cell addresses, activate the Name box and choose the name from it.

To have Excel automatically update your worksheet formulas to use the new names you create in place of the equivalent cell or range references, you need to choose the Insert menu Name command and then the Name submenu Apply command. When Excel displays the Apply Names dialog box, select the name or names you want to substitute for cell or range addresses in your worksheet's formulas. Then click OK.

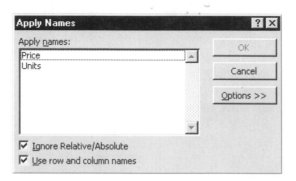

To later change the name of a cell or range or to change the cell or range a name refers to, choose the Insert menu Name command and then choose the Name submenu Define command. When Excel displays the Define Name dialog box, select the named cell or range from the Names in workbook list box. Then, make changes to the name using the Names in workbook text box and make any changes to the cell or range address using the Refers to text box. Then click OK.

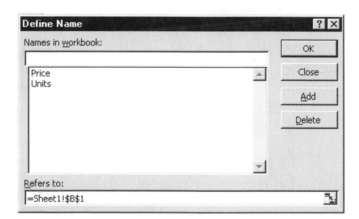

Natural-Language Formulas

The newest release of Excel supports natural-language formulas. Natural-language formulas let you write formulas that use label descriptions rather than cell references. As a result, you (and other people) can more easily read the formulas. For example, take a look at Figure 12-7. If you build this worksheet in the usual way, you might calculate the interest using the formula =B2*B3.

LEARN BY EXAMPLE:
You can open the example Excel workbook shown in Figure 12-7, Figure 12-7 (interest calculations), *if you want to follow along with the discussion here.*

This formula calculates the interest using the formula =B2*B3.

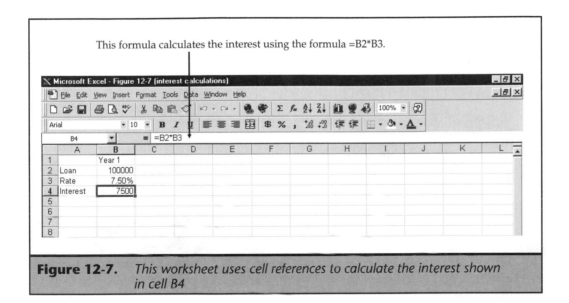

Figure 12-7.   *This worksheet uses cell references to calculate the interest shown in cell B4*

You can, however, rewrite the formula in cell B4 as =Loan*Rate, as shown in Figure 12-8.

EXAMPLES

LEARN BY EXAMPLE
You can open the example Excel workbook shown in Figure 12-8, Figure 12-8 (interest calculations using natural-language formulas), *if you want to follow along with the discussion here.*

This formula calculates the interest using the formula =Loan*Rate.

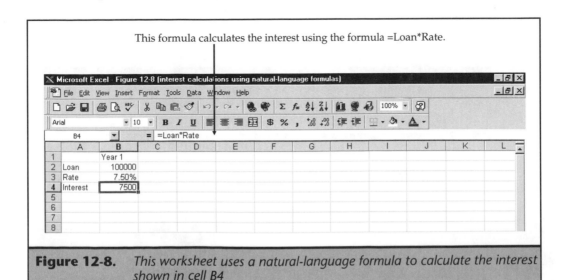

Figure 12-8.   *This worksheet uses a natural-language formula to calculate the interest shown in cell B4*

EXCEL

If you had a worksheet like the one shown in Figure 12-9, you could write the interest formula in cell B4 as =Year 1 Loan*Year 1 Rate. In this case, you could also write the interest formula in cell C4 as =Year 2 Loan*Year 2 Rate, and the interest formula in cell D4 as =Year 3 Loan*Year 3 Rate. (Notice that you put a space between the column heading and the row heading.)

LEARN BY EXAMPLE

You can open the example Excel workbook shown in Figure 12-9, Figure 12-9 (interest calculations using other natural-language formulas), if you want to follow along with the discussion here.

TIP: *You could also calculate the interest amounts in cells B4, C4, and D4 by using the same formula in all three cells, =Loan*Rate.*

The only trick to writing a natural-language formula is to have your formula use the same labels that your worksheet uses to identify some cell holding an input value.

Naming Constants

You can create named constant values and use these in worksheet formulas, too. If you were continually using, for example, a 4 percent inflation estimate in some large budgeting workbook, you could just name the constant, 0.04, as Inflation. This would

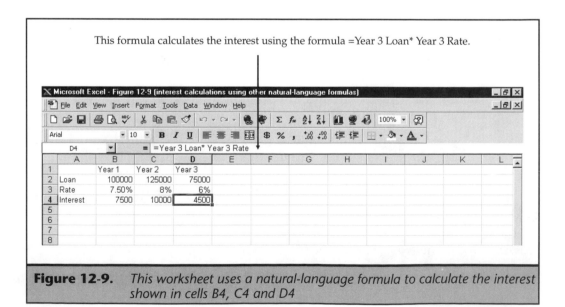

Figure 12-9. *This worksheet uses a natural-language formula to calculate the interest shown in cells B4, C4 and D4*

deliver a couple of benefits in your modeling: Your formulas would be more legible, and you would only have to change the constant in one place.

To name a constant, choose the Insert menu Name command and then choose the Name submenu Define command. When Excel displays the Define Name dialog box, enter the name you want to use to refer to the constant in the Names in workbook text box. Then, enter the constant in the Refers to text box. When you are finished, click OK.

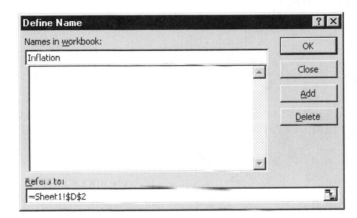

If you sometime later want to change the value of the named constant, once again choose the Insert menu Name command, and then the Name submenu Define command. Then, when Excel displays the Define Name dialog box, select the constant from the Names in workbook list box and edit the value shown in the Refers to text box. (A quick note, however: If you've got a constant you're occasionally changing, it isn't really a constant at all. So, it really belongs in a cell in your worksheet.)

Copying Formulas

Chapter 3 describes how you can use the Standard toolbar's Copy and Paste buttons to copy information in an Office document file. So you won't be surprised to learn that you can copy formulas, too. What may surprise you, however, is that Excel is smarter than you might at first think about the way it copies formulas. Specifically, Excel edits the formulas as it copies them so the formulas still make sense in their new location.

To demonstrate this, let's say, for example, that you are creating the worksheet shown in Figure 12-10 and that you enter the formula =B2+B3+B4 into cell B5 to total the Western Region's expenses. Notice that Figure 12-10 shows how the worksheet looks after you enter this formula. The formula bar shows the cell's formula.

Clearly, you would want to enter an equivalent formula into cells C4, D4, and E4. However, the formula in cell B6 wouldn't work for cell B13, right? The formula in cell B5 sums the values in the cells B2, B3, and B4. So, what do you do? Do you just enter

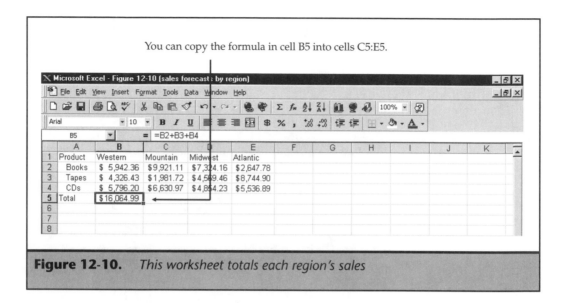

You can copy the formula in cell B5 into cells C5:E5.

Figure 12-10. *This worksheet totals each region's sales*

another formula into cell C5? No. It turns out that you can copy the formula in cell B5 to cell C5:E5 because Excel edits the formula so it works in its new location. For example, if you copy the formula in cell B5 into cell C5, Excel places the formula =C2+C3+C4 into cell C5. If you copy the formula in cell B5 into cell D5, Excel places the formula =D2+D3+D4 into cell D5. And if you copy the formula in cell B5 into cell E5, Excel places the formula =E2+E3+E4 into cell E5. In other words, Excel correctly adjusts the copied formula as it pastes the formula into its new locations.

NOTE: Copying a formula works in much the same way as copying a label or value. Just select the cell or range holding the formula or formulas that you want to copy. Then, while holding down the CTRL key, drag the border of the selection to the new location. Or, if you want to copy a formula across a continuous range, select the cell holding the formula and drag that cell's selection handle across the range.

The reason that Excel adjusts the cell references used in the formula is because Excel considers your cell references to be relative. In other words, while you might read the formula =B2+B3+B4 as saying "Sum the values in cells B2, B3, and B4," Excel reads it a bit differently. If, as in the worksheet shown in Figure 12-10, the formula appears in cell B5, Excel reads the formula =B2+B3+B4 as saying "Sum the values in the three cells directly above the cell with the formula." Do you see the difference? Excel figures, then, that when you copy the formula in cell B5 to its new location, it's still supposed to sum with the formula the three cells directly above the cell with the formula.

How Excel handles this formula-editing business is really pretty simple. If you copy a formula, say, seven rows down, Excel adjusts all the row numbers in your cell references by seven rows. If you copy a formula four columns left, Excel adjusts the column letters in your row numbers by four columns.

 NOTE: *The fact that Excel automatically edits formulas as you copy them is usually exactly what you want. You should know, however, that you can stop Excel from performing this formula editing by writing your cell references in a slightly different way. If you don't want Excel to adjust the column letter of a cell reference as the formula is copied into different columns, you precede the column letter with a dollar sign. For example, in the following formula, Excel would edit as necessary the row numbers but not the column reference: =$B2+$B3+$B4.*

If you don't want Excel to adjust the row number of a cell reference as the formula is copied into different rows, you precede the row number with a dollar sign. For example, in the following formula, Excel would edit as necessary the column letters but not the row numbers: =B$2+B$3+B$4.

Predictably, if you don't want Excel to adjust either the column letters or the row numbers, you precede both of these elements of the cell reference with dollar signs, like this: =$B$2+$B$3+$B$4. This type of cell reference is called an absolute reference.

TIP: *While you typically type the dollar signs used to convert a relative cell reference to an absolute cell reference, you can also use the F4 key. If you are entering or editing a cell reference, repeatedly pressing the F4 key cycles through the different ways you can write the cell reference. For example if you have just entered the cell reference B2 or you were editing a formula and the insertion point rested on the cell reference B2, pressing F4 repeatedly would rewrite the reference as $B$2, then B$2, then $B2, and finally B2.*

You can also rewrite range addresses so that they aren't edited in the usual way. For example, you could rewrite the formula =SUM(B2:B5) as =SUM($B$2:$B$5). And if you did, Excel won't adjust the range address as you copy the formula.

 NOTE: *The next section of this chapter, "Using Functions," describes what functions are and how you use them.*

A practical warning is in order here, however: If you start rewriting range addresses so some portions of the range address are adjusted while other portions aren't, you'll find it very difficult to monitor and error-check the formula editing that Excel is performing. Remember that a range address uses the cell addresses of the range's opposite corners. So, if you rewrite the formula =SUM(G20:G25) as =SUM($G$20:G25), you've fixed one corner of the range but not the other. In this case, Excel won't adjust the $G$20 corner of the range address as the formula is copied, but it will adjust the G25 corner of the range address. Unfortunately, this partial adjustment of the formula gets very confusing. If you copy your formula down rows or right across columns, for example, your range address actually grows larger and larger. But if you copy your formula up rows or left across columns, your range address first shrinks in size and then begins to grow. If you rewrite the formula =SUM($G20:G25), so Excel won't adjust the column of the first corner but will adjust the row, the formula adjustment gets even more confusing to monitor.

 NOTE: *It's important to note that Excel has no problem correctly adjusting the copied formulas. The problem is just that this sort of adjustment is difficult for you to monitor and error-check. For this reason, you may want to avoid constructing formulas that use partially fixed, or mixed range, references. You'll keep your worksheets much simpler and easier to error-check by doing so.*

Using Functions

Using the formula operators described thus far in the chapter, you can create formulas that make almost any calculation. But as a practical matter, some of your formulas—supposing you did do everything from scratch—would be very complicated. To make your formulas easier, Excel supplies predefined formulas called functions. One advantage of functions, then, is that they save you the time and trouble of building your own, more complicated formulas. But there's another advantage of functions, too. They are usually very clever and efficient about the way they accept and handle any inputs to the formula. If you're going to do any serious work with Excel, therefore, you'll want to know how to use Excel's functions.

Understanding How a Function Works

The best way to explain how a function works is to show you how they actually work in a workbook. Take a look at the worksheet shown in Figure 12-11. It supplies the sales orders booked by an imaginary team of sales people.

Let's suppose, for the sake of illustration, that you want to calculate the average sales orders of team members and place this value in cell B11. To do this, you could construct a formula like the one shown next and then enter it in your worksheet:

=(B2+B3+B4+B5+B6+B7+B8+B9+B10)/9

But an easier approach would be to use a prebuilt function that calculates the average of a set of values stored in the range B2:B10. To do this, you would enter the following formula into your worksheet:

=AVERAGE(B2:B10)

Clearly, using the AVERAGE function is easier even in this simple example. And you can imagine how much easier the function makes your calculations in the case

This formula calculates the average orders per salesperson.

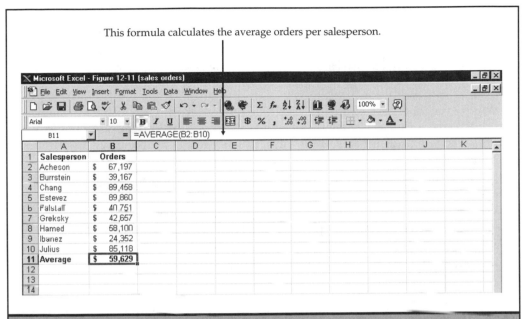

Figure 12-11. *This worksheet describes the sales orders booked by an imaginary team of salespeople*

where you might be calculating, say, the average orders of all the salespeople in a 100-person, or 1,000-person sales organization.

To create a function-based formula, you follow these steps:

1. Type the equal sign (=). (This is the way all formulas begin, of course.)

2. Type the function name followed by the begin parenthesis mark.

3. Enter the input values, or arguments, that the function needs or uses to make its calculation. The example AVERAGE calculation includes one argument, the range B2:B10. Many times, however, functions accept or expect more than one argument, and in that case, you separate the arguments with commas. For example, it wouldn't make much sense—because all you would be doing is increasing your work—but you could rewrite the AVERAGE function given earlier as:

    =AVERAGE(B2,B3,B4,B5,B6,B7,B8,B9,B10)

4. Type the end parenthesis mark and then press ENTER.

NOTE: *Not all functions require arguments. For example, Excel supplies a function that returns the mathematical constant for pi and it requires no arguments. In the case of functions that don't require arguments, you still follow the function name with the parenthesis marks, but you enclose nothing in between the parentheses. For example, the function-based formula to return the constant pi would look like this: =PI()*

While a function's arguments are often cell references, you can also use named constants, cells or ranges, actual values, and even other functions. For example, if you name the range B2:B10 as Salespeople's orders, you can calculate the average orders per salesperson using the following formula:

=AVERAGE(Salespeople's orders)

Or, you could use the actual Salespeople's orders values in the formula:

=AVERAGE(67197,39167,89458,89860,40751,42657,58100,24352,85118)

And you can use as arguments the results of still other functions. You get the basic idea: If a function wants a value as an argument, you can supply that value in a variety of different ways.

NOTE: *There are some functions that expect labels or text strings as arguments. To supply one of these text functions with an argument, you can also use cell and range addresses (as long as the cell or range holds the necessary label or labels), named cells or ranges, and even the actual text strings themselves. If you do include the actual text string as an argument, you need to enclose it in quotation marks.*

Using the Paste Function Command

As a practical matter, while functions are terribly useful, they present a couple of problems to users. The first problem is that it's usually tough to know whether Excel supplies a function that calculates a particular formula. You've already read earlier in this chapter that Excel provides a long list of functions. But you don't really know whether Excel supplies functions to calculate things like loan payments or logarithms or whatever else you want to calculate. And even if this chapter told you about each and every function, you wouldn't retain that knowledge for very long. (There are roughly 350 functions if you include those supplied by the Analysis ToolPak add-in.)

The second practical problem with functions is you'll find it nearly impossible to remember which arguments a function needs and in which order you're supposed to supply them. For example, the function for calculating a loan payment needs three arguments: the loan balance, the interest rate, and the number of payments. But you've got to enter these arguments in the right order, or the function can't make its calculations.

Fortunately, Excel provides something called the Paste Function command that cleverly addresses and almost entirely solves these two problems. The Paste Function command first helps you find the function (if any) that makes a particular calculation. Then, it explains which arguments you need to supply to the function and helps you to enter them in the right order.

To illustrate how all this works, suppose that you were considering the purchase of a new car and wanted to know what your monthly principal and interest payment would equal. As a practical matter, it would be impossible for you to construct a formula, from scratch, that made this calculation. So, you might decide to look for a function. And assuming you found such a function, of course, you would use it to make the calculation. Here's how you would use the Paste Function command to accomplish all of these things:

1. Click the Paste Function button on the Standard toolbar—or, choose the Insert menu Function command. When you do, Excel displays the Paste Function dialog box.

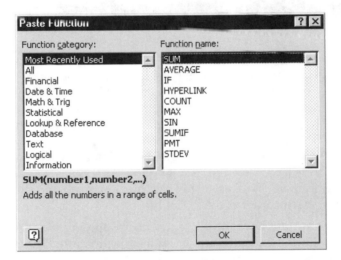

2. Use the Function category list box to select the category into which a function calculation falls. In the case of a loan payment calculation, for example, you would select Financial. When you do, Excel displays a list of the functions in the selected category using the Function name list box.

3. Select the appropriate function in the Function name list box. If you're not sure—and you won't be until you've used a function a few times—just click the function to select it and then read the description of the function that appears at the bottom of the dialog box. (If you still have questions about a function, you can click the Office Assistant button, click the Help with this feature button, and then click the Help on selected function button. Excel then

displays the Help window with a complete and detailed description of the function.) Once you've selected the function you want—the PMT function in the case of a loan payment calculation—click OK. Excel displays the Formula Palette—in the area just below the formula bar.

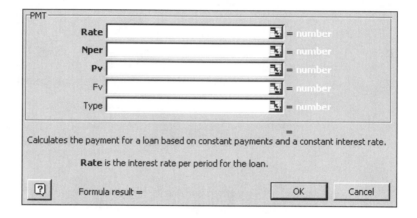

4. Supply the arguments by filling in the text boxes. You can enter values, cell addresses, or formulas into these text boxes. As you select an argument's text box, Excel describes what the argument should look like. Notice that to the right of each argument's text box, there's a Collapse dialog button. You can click this if you need to temporarily resize the dialog box so you can select cells on the worksheet. If you have additional questions about a particular argument, click the Office Assistant button. As soon as you've supplied the last needed argument, Excel calculates the function result and displays this value in the lower left corner of the dialog box.

5. Click the OK button when you've finished supplying the arguments. Excel closes the Formula Palette and places the function into the active cell. Figure 12-12 shows a car loan payment worksheet constructed in just this way.

LEARN BY EXAMPLE
You can open the example Excel workbook shown in Figure 12-12, Figure 12-12 (car loan payment), from the companion CD if you want to follow along with the discussion here.

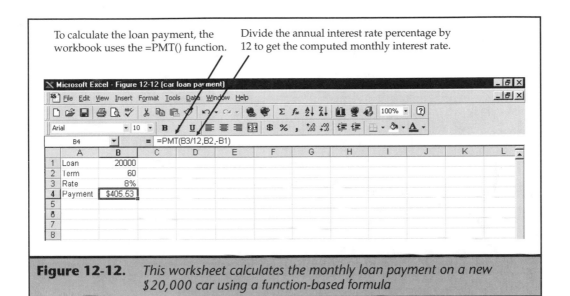

To calculate the loan payment, the workbook uses the =PMT() function.

Divide the annual interest rate percentage by 12 to get the computed monthly interest rate.

Figure 12-12. *This worksheet calculates the monthly loan payment on a new $20,000 car using a function-based formula*

HEADSTART

TEMPLATES

The companion CD includes a headstart template you can use for calculating loan payments in 60-month car loans: 60 mo-adj.xls, which calculates the payments and builds an amortization schedule for a 60-month, adjustable-interest-rate loan, and 60 moloan.xls, which calculates the payments and builds an amortization schedule for a 60-month, fixed-interest-rate loan.

Using the AutoSum Tool

Most of the time you'll either want to use the Paste Function button to enter function-based formulas into your worksheets or you'll just enter a function by typing it in. (Once you've used a function several dozen times, you may know its arguments well enough to enter them from memory.) But there is one function that is so commonly used, Excel's Standard toolbar provides a special tool, the AutoSum button, for it. That function is the SUM function.

To understand how the AutoSum button works, first know that the SUM function simply sums, or adds up, its arguments. That's all. While that doesn't sound very powerful, it turns out that this is something you'll be doing all the time. And, so, the SUM function is one you'll use over and over again. If you take a look at the worksheet shown in Figure 12-13, for example, both the total values shown in column F and the total values shown in row 6 get calculated by SUM functions.

Row 6 uses SUM-based functions to total costs by quarter.

Column F uses SUM-based functions to total costs by category.

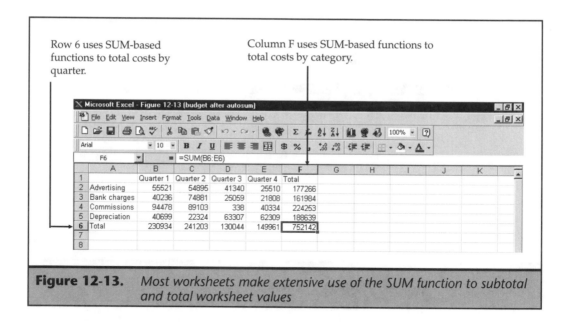

Figure 12-13. *Most worksheets make extensive use of the SUM function to subtotal and total worksheet values*

While you can enter these SUM functions individually into the cells or even using the Paste Function command, by far the easier method is simply to use the AutoSum button. To use the AutoSum button, you would first enter the labels and values shown in Figure 12-14. Next, you would select the range B2:F6 and then click the AutoSum button. Excel would add SUM functions to the range B6:E6 and F2:F6 to total the expenses by quarter and by expense category. Take a peek back at Figure 12-13 to see what your worksheet looks like after you click the AutoSum button.

LEARN BY EXAMPLE:
You can open the example Excel workbook shown in Figure 12-14, Figure 12-14
(budget before autosum), *from the companion CD if you want to follow along with the discussion here.*

Using the Analysis ToolPak Functions

As it's usually installed, Excel comes with roughly 200 functions. For most users, this function set is more than adequate. You'll rarely use more than a handful of functions. Some users, however, are going to need richer function sets. If you're a financial analyst, for example, Excel's basic financial functions may prove insufficient if you want to, say, calculate bond durations or yields to maturity. And statisticians, quantitative researchers, and engineers may find themselves in the same boat.

Fortunately, there's an easy way to expand the set of functions that Excel supplies. You can install the Analysis ToolPak, which supplies (roughly) another 150 functions

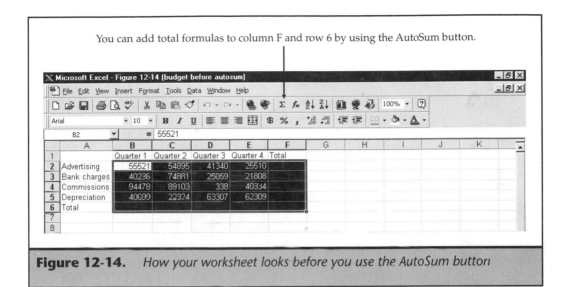

You can add total formulas to column F and row 6 by using the AutoSum button.

Figure 12-14. *How your worksheet looks before you use the AutoSum button*

to complement the (roughly) 200 functions that Excel initially supplies. To install the Analysis ToolPak, choose the Tools menu Add-Ins command. Then, when Excel displays the Add-Ins dialog box, mark the Analysis ToolPak entry in the Add-Ins available list box, and then click OK. (If the Analysis ToolPak entry is already marked, you or someone else has already installed this add-in.)

Auditing and Error-Checking Formulas

One final topic to discuss before this chapter concludes is Excel's formula auditing and error-checking tools. It's very likely that at some point in the not-too-distant future, you'll find yourself trying to solve some worksheet riddle by tracing how some formula result or value ripples through your worksheet, affecting dozens and perhaps hundreds of cells. Fortunately, Excel's auditing tools are both powerful and easy to use.

Tracing Precedents, Dependents, and Errors

If you want to see which cells supply inputs to the formula in the active cell, choose the Tools menu Auditing command, and then choose the Auditing submenu Trace Precedents command. If you used this tool with the simple worksheet shown in Figure 12-15 and your active cell, prior to choosing the command, is cell B5, Excel draws an arrow from cells holding the inputs to the cell with the formula.

LEARN BY EXAMPLE

You can open the example Excel Workbook shown in Figure 12-15, Figure 12-15 (mortgage payment calculator), *from the companion CD if you want to experiment with the auditing tools described here.*

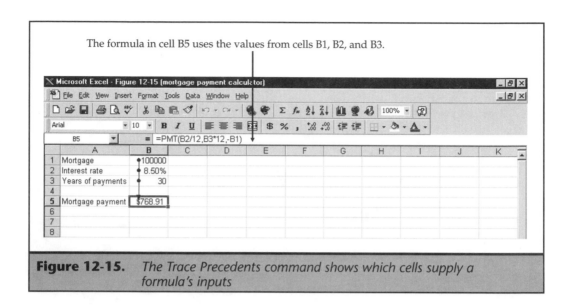

Figure 12-15.   *The Trace Precedents command shows which cells supply a formula's inputs*

NOTE: Excel provides another way to visually see which cells supply inputs to a formula. If you double-click a cell containing a formula, Excel colors the cell references supplying inputs and then draws a border around referenced cells using the same color. For example, in the example Excel workbook shown in Figure 12-15, the formula in cell B5 calculates the mortgage. This formula is =PMT(B2/12,B3*12,-B1). If you double-click cell B5—the cell with the formula—Excel colors the cell reference B2 in blue and draws a blue border around cell B2. Excel colors the cell reference B3 green and draws a green border around cell B3. Finally, Excel colors the cell reference B1 purple and then draws a purple border around cell B1. If the preceding description sounds confusing, just open the Learn By Example sample document for Figure 12-15 and then double-click cell B5.

If you want to see which cells rely on a particular cell's value or calculation result, select the cell, choose the Tools menu Auditing command, and choose the Auditing submenu Trace Dependents command. If you used this tool with the simple worksheet shown in Figure 12-15 and your active cell, prior to choosing the command, is cell B3, Excel draws an arrow that points from cell B3 to cell B5.

	A	B	C
1	Mortgage	100000	
2	Interest rate	8.50%	
3	Years of payments	30	
4			
5	Mortgage payment	$768.91	
6			

To see which cell returns the error value that results in the active cell's formula returning an error value, select the cell, choose the Tools menu Auditing command, and then choose the Auditing submenu Trace Error command. For example, in the illustration that follows, the simple mortgage payment worksheet used as the basis of our discussion has been modified by entering the formula =NA() in cell B3. (The NA() function returns the #N/A error value.) If after doing this, you select cell B5, choose the Tools menu Auditing command, and then choose the Auditing submenu Trace Error command, Excel draws a red arrow from cell B3 to cell B5 showing how this error value ripples through the worksheet.

	A	B	C
1	Mortgage	100000	
2	Interest rate	8.50%	
3	Years of payments	#N/A	
4			
5	Mortgage payment	#N/A	
6			

If you've been following along at your computer or you've at least looked at the Auditing submenu, you can guess how you get rid of the arrows that the Trace Precedents, Trace Dependents, and Trace Error commands draw. You choose the Remove All Arrows command.

NOTE: *The Auditing submenu also provides a Show Auditing Toolbar command. You can choose this command to display a toolbar with buttons you can click in place of choosing commands from the Auditing submenu. The toolbar includes buttons for tracing precedents, dependents, and errors, for removing tracing arrows, for attaching cell comments, and circling and uncircling invalid data. (You define valid and invalid data for a cell by choosing the Data menu Validation command.)*

Using the Go To and Info Boxes

If you choose the Edit menu Go To command, Excel displays the Go To dialog box. Almost ten years ago, now, this command was included in the original version of Excel as a quick and easy way to move around a worksheet. You can still use the Go To command and its dialog box this way. Simply choose the command and then, when Excel displays the Go To dialog box, enter the name or address of the cell or range to which you want to move. (If you select a range, the Go To command only searches that range. If you don't select a range, then the Go To command searches the entire worksheet.)

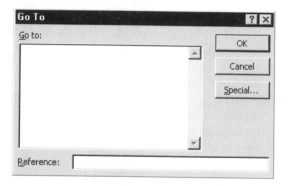

The Go To command has become more and more powerful over time, however. It now lets you move to or locate cells having specified attributes. To use the Go To command and dialog box in this manner, choose the command and then click its Special command button. Excel displays the Go To Special dialog box.

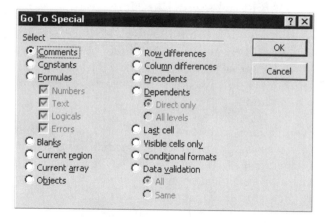

To use the Go To Special dialog box, use its buttons to describe the attributes of the cells you're looking for. Mark the Comments button, for example, to have the command select cells with comments. Mark the Constants button to have the command select cells with labels or number values (but not formulas or functions). Mark the Formulas button and use its check boxes to have the command select cells with formulas having specified characteristics, and so on. When you're ready to begin your search, click the OK button. Excel selects those cells that match the attributes you specified.

By the way, there are many other buttons on the Go To Special dialog box, as the preceding illustration shows. But you really don't have to worry about these. If you have a question about some button or box, click the What's This button (in the dialog box's upper right corner) and then click the button or box.

The
Complete
Reference

Office
97

Chapter 13

Using the Chart Wizard

W hile tabular presentations of data are very useful, it's also often very handy to both present and analyze your worksheet data visually—in other words, in a chart. This chapter prepares you to do this by first explaining how chart data is organized, and by then explaining how you create, use, and customize your Excel charts.

NOTE: You can easily use Excel charts in Word documents and PowerPoint presentations. In fact, this book assumes that you don't use the Microsoft Graph tool to create charts for Word or PowerPoint and do use Excel's Chart Wizard (because the Excel Chart Wizard is easier to use and more powerful).

Understanding Data Series and Data Categories

You need to understand what data series and data categories are—and how to arrange your worksheet data so that Excel easily identifies your data series and data categories—before you begin working with Excel's charting feature.

A data series is a set of values you'll plot in a chart. If you plot sales revenues over, say, the last ten years, the set of sales revenue values is a data series. If you plot expenses over, say, the same ten-year time frame, the set of expense values is another data series. The key thing to remember is that, fundamentally, data series are what you plot with charts.

Figure 13-1, for example, shows a chart with two data series: sales revenues and expenses.

EXAMPLES

LEARN BY EXAMPLE

You can open the example chart shown in Figure 13-1, Figure 13-1 (simple chart), from the companion CD if you want to follow along with the discussion here.

Note that on a chart that already exists, you can identify data series by looking at the data markers, which are the graphical objects that the chart uses to show the plotted values. The data markers for a data series are usually visually connected in some way. In Figure 13-1, for example, Excel plots each data series using a separate line. In a bar chart—and this chapter talks about bar charts a little later—the bars for a particular data series chart are all the same color. The same thing is true for a column chart. You get the idea.

Data categories, the other charting term you must understand, organize the data points—the individual values—within a data series. For example, in any chart that shows how some value changes over time—what's called a time-series chart—time is the data category. In a time-series chart, you use units of time—years, months, days, or whatever—to organize the individual data points within a data series. In Figure 13-1, for example, the data categories are years. You can, however, use data categories other than time to organize the data points in a data series. Take a look at Figure 13-2, for

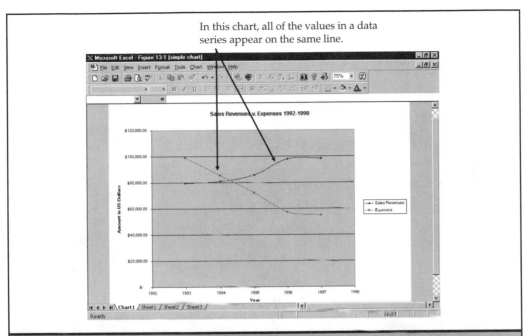

Figure 13-1. *You plot data series—such as the sales revenues and expenses shown here—with a chart*

example. Note how I've substituted the names of fictional corporations for the years. So these fictional companies have become the data categories that organize the data points in a data series. Note, too, that fundamentally the chart still plots sales revenue and expense information. The two data series are still sales revenues and expenses.

LEARN BY EXAMPLE
You can open the example Excel chart shown in Figure 13-2, Figure 13-2 (chart with company names as data categories), *from the companion CD if you want to follow along with the discussion here.*

Once you understand what data series and data categories are, you understand how Excel organizes your to-be-charted data. With this information, you'll find it easy to first collect chart data using a worksheet and then to later plot the data using Excel's Chart Wizard.

Collecting the Data You Want to Chart

Once you know which data series you want to plot and what your categories are, you're ready to enter your data into a worksheet. You can organize your data series

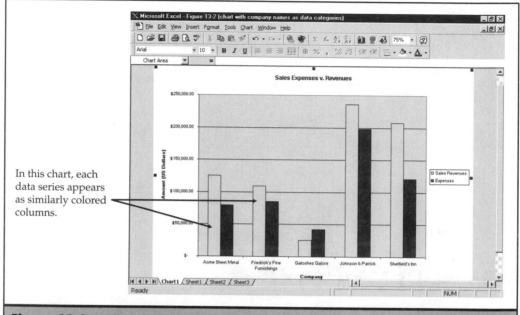

In this chart, each data series appears as similarly colored columns.

Figure 13-2. *This chart uses fictional corporations as the data categories*

into either rows or columns, as long as each data series has no more than 4,000 data points. (If data series do have more than 4,000 data points, you need to use separate columns for each data series—otherwise, you won't have room in a row for all of a data series' data points.)

NOTE: A chart can't show more than 255 data series. Each data series can't include more than 4,000 data points. A chart in total can't include more than 32,000 data points.

To collect the data you will plot in a chart, follow these steps:

1. Enter the data series names and values into the worksheet using a separate row or column for each data series. (The actual data points must be values, of course.) Figure 13-3 uses row 2 for the first data series, Sales, and row 3 for the second data series, Profits. It could just have well organized the data as shown in Figure 13-4, however, with the data categories organized by column.

LEARN BY EXAMPLE
You can open the example worksheet shown in Figure 13-3, Figure 13-3 (data series in rows), *from the companion CD if you want to follow along with the discussion here.*

LEARN BY EXAMPLE
You can open the example worksheet shown in Figure 13-4, Figure 13-4 (data series in columns), *from the companion CD if you want to follow along with the discussion here.*

NOTE: *Take a minute and look at both Figures 13-3 and 13-4 until you clearly see that they show the same information. The only difference is that Figure 13-3 organizes the data series by row, while Figure 13-4 organizes the data series by column.*

TIP: *You can provide the data points of a series by entering actual, numeric values into the cells or by supplying formulas that calculate the values.*

2. Enter values or labels that identify the data categories. In Figure 13-3, the data categories are described by the contents of the range B1:F1. In Figure 13-4, the data categories are described by the contents of the range A2:A6. Note the placement of the data category information: In Figure 13-3, which organizes the data series by row, the data category information appears in the row above the rows with the data series. In Figure 13-4, which organizes the data series by column, the data category information appears in the column to the left of the columns with the data series.

In this worksheet, each data series appears in its own worksheet row.

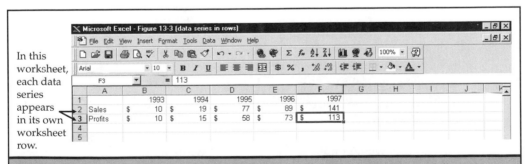

Figure 13-3. *This simple worksheet provides example data, which the following discussion uses to demonstrate the Chart Wizard*

In this worksheet, each data
series appears in its own
worksheet column.

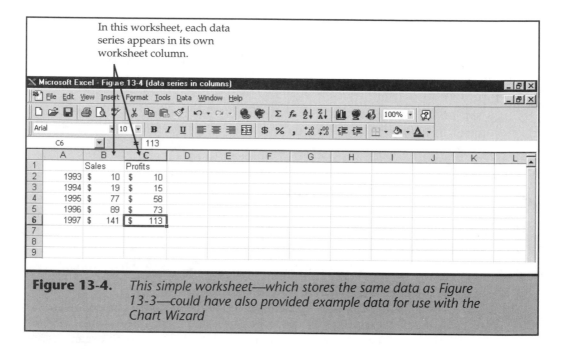

Figure 13-4. *This simple worksheet—which stores the same data as Figure 13-3—could have also provided example data for use with the Chart Wizard*

NOTE: *You don't have to enter or collect the data you'll plot into a contiguous worksheet range, as shown in Figure 13-3 or Figure 13-4. Doing so, however, makes it much easier to plot the data.*

Using the Chart Wizard

Once you've collected the data you want to plot, you're ready to use the Chart Wizard. To use the Chart Wizard, follow these steps:

1. Select the range that holds the data series and the data categories information. If you were plotting the sales and profit information shown in Figure 13-3, for example, you select A1:F3.

2. Choose either the Insert menu Chart command or click the Chart Wizard tool, which appears on the Standard toolbar. Once you do this, Excel starts the Chart Wizard. The Chart Wizard steps you through a series of four dialog boxes that ask, in essence, what you want your chart to look like.

3. When the first Chart Wizard dialog box asks which type of chart you want, select an entry from the Chart type list box. In Figure 13-5, the Column type is selected. Then select one of the chart's subtypes by clicking the button that shows a picture of the chart. In Figure 13-5, the Clustered Column subtype is selected. (A little later in the chapter, by the way, this book describes all 14 of

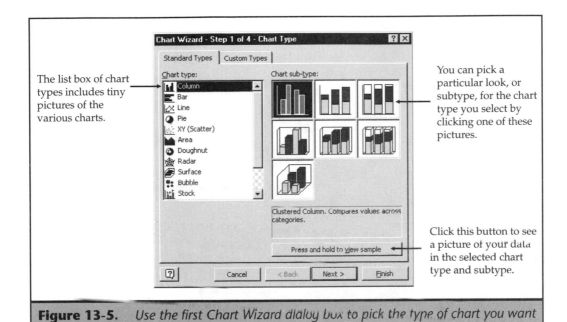

The list box of chart types includes tiny pictures of the various charts.

You can pick a particular look, or subtype, for the chart type you select by clicking one of these pictures.

Click this button to see a picture of your data in the selected chart type and subtype.

EXCEL

Figure 13-5. *Use the first Chart Wizard dialog box to pick the type of chart you want*

the Excel chart types and why you typically use each.) After you pick the chart type and subtype, click Next to continue.

4. When the second Chart Wizard dialog box asks you to confirm the worksheet range you selected before starting the Chart Wizard, as shown in Figure 13-6, verify that the range shown in the Data range text box is correct. (This range will be correct if you selected the worksheet range before clicking the Chart Wizard tool.) The second Chart Wizard dialog box also asks how you've organized your worksheet data. Use the Series in option buttons to tell Excel how you've organized your worksheet data. (Excel assumes that you'll have more data categories than you'll have data series, and marks either the Rows or Columns option button to show this assumption.) After you complete the second Chart Wizard dialog box, click Next.

5. When Excel displays the third Chart Wizard dialog box, shown in Figure 13-7, use its text boxes to add titles to the chart. To add a title to the chart, enter whatever you want to use for the title in the Chart title text box. Typically, people either use the name of the organization being described in the chart, or they summarize the chart's message. As shown in Figure 13-7, for example, you might give the name of the organization for which sales and profit data are plotted—Acme Trading Corporation, for example. Or, if you were trying

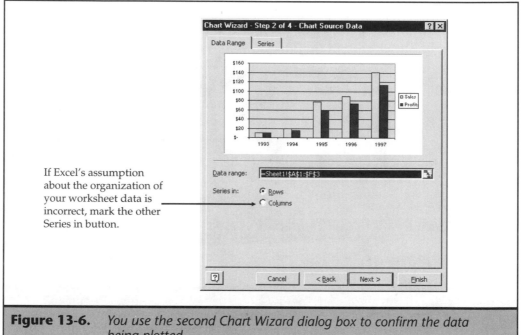

If Excel's assumption about the organization of your worksheet data is incorrect, mark the other Series in button.

Figure 13-6. *You use the second Chart Wizard dialog box to confirm the data being plotted*

to use the chart to make a point such as "Sales and profits continue to grow," you might use that message as the chart title.

The axis title text boxes let you add titles to the axis that shows the categories (in Figure 13-7, the horizontal axis) and to the axis that calibrates the data series' data points (in Figure 13-7, the vertical axis). If what the categories show and how the data series' points are calibrated are obvious, you don't need to include these extra chunks of text. However, if the categories aren't clear or the data series values aren't adequately calibrated, you can often use the axis titles to mitigate confusion. For example, if the values plotted as data points are actually thousands—in other words, you've omitted the zeros—you could and probably should use an axis title to make this clear. After you finish specifying whether you want a legend and adding any chart titles you want, click the Next button.

6. When the Chart Wizard displays the fourth and final Chart Wizard dialog box, use it to indicate where you want the new chart placed: on a new page, or sheet, of the workbook or as an embedded object floating over the top of an existing worksheet page. If you choose the As object in option button, as shown here, Excel embeds a chart object on the current worksheet. If you

You can use these other tabs to make additional changes to the chart, as described later in this chapter in the section, "Customizing Charts."

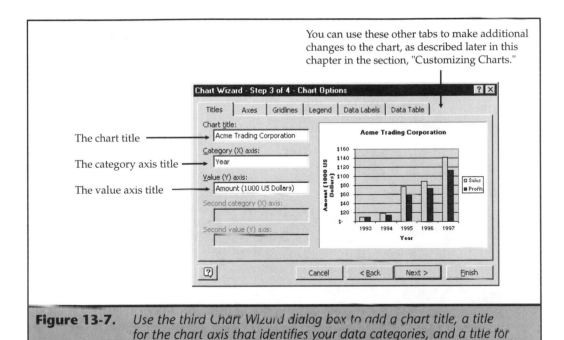

The chart title ⟶

The category axis title ⟶

The value axis title ⟶

Figure 13-7. *Use the third Chart Wizard dialog box to add a chart title, a title for the chart axis that identifies your data categories, and a title for the chart axis that calibrates your data series values*

choose the As new sheet option button, Excel adds a new chart sheet page to the worksheet and places your chart there.

Click this button to place the chart on a new chart sheet, or page.

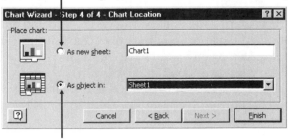

Click this button to place the chart onto an existing worksheet, or page, as an embedded object.

7. After you specify where you want the new chart created, click Finish. The Chart Wizard draws a chart like the one you've specified. Figure 13-8, for example, shows the same worksheet from Figure 13-3, but this time with the embedded chart.

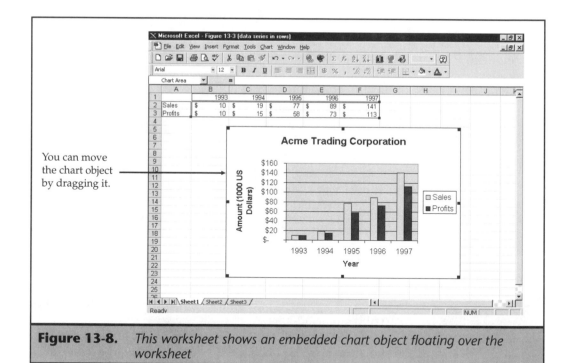

You can move
the chart object
by dragging it.

Figure 13-8. *This worksheet shows an embedded chart object floating over the worksheet*

LEARN BY EXAMPLE
You can open the example worksheet shown in Figure 13-8, Figure 13-8 (embedded chart), from the companion CD if you want to follow along with the discussion here.

As mentioned earlier, charts can either be embedded as objects that float on top of a regular worksheet or they can appear on their own chart sheets. (Figure 13-8 shows an embedded chart.) If in step 6 you would have chosen the As new sheet option button instead of the As object in option button, the Chart Wizard would have added a separate sheet to the workbook, named Chart1 if this were the first chart sheet you'd added, and placed the chart there. To expand the chart so it fills the screen, choose the View menu Sized with Window command.

Picking a Chart Type

You can pick a particular chart type either as part of using the Chart Wizard or, later on, after you've actually created the chart. If you pick the chart type as you're creating the chart with the Chart Wizard, you simply select your chart type using the first dialog box that the Chart Wizard displays, as shown in Figure 13-5.

If you change your mind about the chart type you want after creating the chart, Excel provides several ways to change your mind. The easiest method for changing the chart type is by using the Chart menu Chart Type command. And this raises an important distinction: Excel supplies a menu bar, but you use a different menu bar for working with charts. So, before you can use the Chart menu Chart Type command, you need to tell Excel that it should swap the chart menu bar for the standard, worksheet menu bar. How you do this depends on whether you want to work with an embedded chart (one that appears on a worksheet page) or with a chart that appears on its own chart sheet page. If the chart is embedded, you simply click it. Excel adds sizing handles to the chart to show it's selected, and replaces the standard worksheet menu bar with the chart menu bar. If the chart appears on its own chart sheet page, Excel actually swaps the menu bars when you display the page. In other words, if you display the chart sheet page, Excel knows that if you need any menu commands, they'll be the ones from the chart menu bar—and not the ones from the worksheet menu bar.

 TIP: *To unselect a chart object so that you work with the worksheet, click somewhere outside the chart.*

When you choose the Chart menu Chart Type command, Excel displays the Chart Type dialog box, shown in Figure 13-9, which lets you pick both a chart type and a subtype for the chart type. If you remember much about the Chart Wizard's operation,

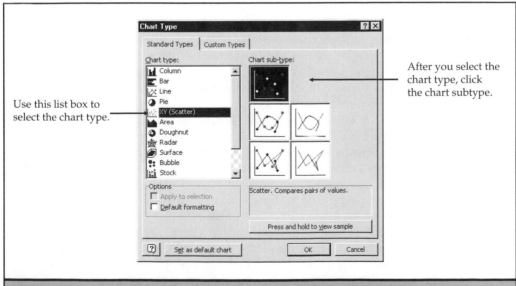

Figure 13-9. *The Chart Type dialog box lets you change both the chart type and the subtype*

EXCEL

you might recall that this is what you do in step 1 of the four-step chart-building process that the Chart Wizard steps you through.

Initially, the Chart Type dialog box shows the subtypes available for the existing chart type. These subtypes, as mentioned earlier, are simply different variations, or styles, of a particular chart type. To select another chart type, however, all you have to do is select the chart type from the Chart type list box. When you do, Excel displays pictures of the subtypes available for that chart type. You then select the subtype you want by clicking its picture. After you choose the chart type and subtype, click OK. Excel redraws your chart so it reflects your changes. It's that easy.

Reviewing the Different Chart Types

You can easily choose or change the chart type and subtype, but knowing why you change or choose a chart type and subtype is probably more important that knowing how you change or choose a chart type and subtype. For this reason, the next section of this chapter describes what each of the chart types does, points out some of the more unique subtypes, and gives you some hints as to when you might want to use particular chart types and subtypes.

Area Charts

The various area chart subtypes, as shown in Figure 13-10, plot your data series as colored areas. The unique thing about area charts is that Excel stacks these colored areas on top of each other. Excel creates the first data series' area by first drawing a line plotting the series' data point values and then coloring, or shading, this area. Excel creates the second data series' area, however, by drawing a line that plots the sum of the first and second data series' values and then coloring this new area. Subsequent data series are plotted in the same way: Excel creates the third data series' area by drawing a line that plots the sum of the first, second, and third data series' values and then coloring this new area.

Area charts, then, do two things really well. Best of all, they show how the data category totals of your plotted data change over time. For example, if you were plotting the sales revenues of all the major competitors in a particular industry, an area chart would emphasize how total industry revenues are changing over time. (The second and fourth subtypes let you make this visual analysis.) Another thing that area charts do, albeit not as well, is show you how the proportion of an individual data series changes over time relative to the total of all the data series' value. (The third and sixth subtypes let you make this visual analysis.) Take the example of an area chart that plots the sales revenues of all the major competitors in an industry,

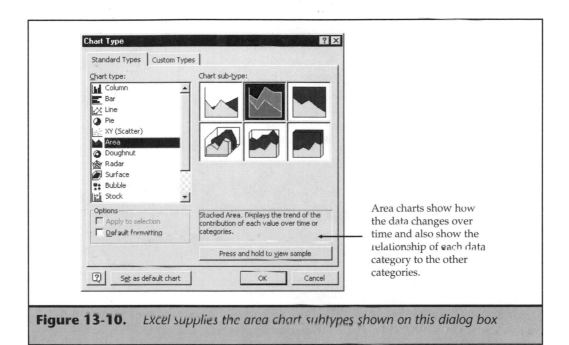

Figure 13-10. *Excel supplies the area chart subtypes shown on this dialog box*

for example. You might be able to use such an area chart to identify a trend, like "Competitor A is still growing, but they're becoming a less significant presence in the total market."

TIP: *A basic rule of charting is that your chart shouldn't have more dimensions than your data. As such, many of the chart subtypes that Excel provides don't use the third dimension of depth to organize your data.*

Bar Charts

Bar charts plot your data points as horizontal, individual bars, as shown in the following illustration. Because a bar chart uses individual data markers for each data point, they emphasize and let chart viewers compare the individual values. This is particularly true of the first and fourth subtypes (although this isn't as true of the other bar chart subtypes, which stack the bar data markers). In comparison, note that the area charts described in the previous section tend to emphasize changes in data point values rather than the actual data point values themselves.

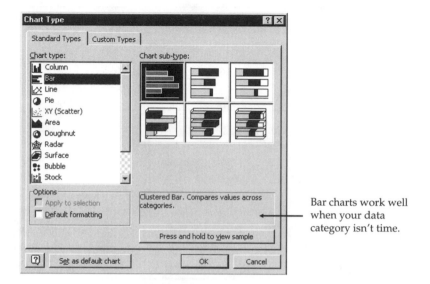

Bar charts work well when your data category isn't time.

One other important consideration with regard to the bar chart subtypes is that because the category axis is vertical rather than horizontal, the bar chart type often works well when your data category isn't time. The reason this is so is that people—or at least Europeans, as well as North and South Americans—are accustomed to using horizontal data category axes as chronological time lines. Therefore, if you use a vertical data category axis, the chart reader is less likely to mistakenly interpret your data category as a time unit.

Column Charts

Column charts work exactly like bar charts—and almost look like bar charts—except that they plot your data points using vertical rather than horizontal bars, as shown in the next illustration. Like the bar charts they resemble, column charts use individual data markers for each data point. In this manner, they emphasize and let chart viewers compare the individual values. Because the column chart uses a horizontal category axis, column charts work particularly well for comparing individual values over time.

NOTE: *The ability to compare individual values over time is particularly true of the first, fourth, and seventh column subtypes. The other column chart subtypes, in comparison, stack the data markers in a manner very similar to the way that the area chart types stack the areas they plot. So they work better for comparing the relationship among the data category totals over time.*

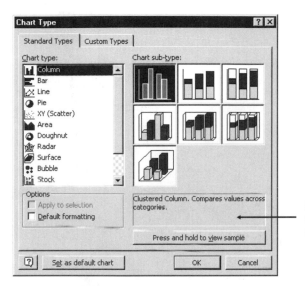

Column charts work
well when your data
category *is* time.

WARNING: *Despite the extra visual interest that the third dimension adds to a bar or column chart, it's rarely a good idea to use a third dimension when you choose either of these chart types. And here's why this is the case: The reason for choosing a bar data marker—and this could be in either a bar or column chart—is to compare the individual values within and between data series. However, that extra dimension of depth that Excel provides by showing you the "top" of the bar makes it more difficult to do this. By adding a "top" to a very short bar, for example, you can dramatically increase its visual presence—even though it may still be immaterial. If you use the extra dimension of depth to organize your data series by putting the first data series in front, the second data series in back behind the first one, and so on, things get even worse. In this case, because the data series appear at varying depths, you really shouldn't make comparisons between the different data series.*

Line Charts

Line charts, as the following illustration shows, plot the data points of a data series in a line. As such, they usually tend to de-emphasize the individual data point values (although some of the line chart subtypes include additional data markers on the actual line to show the individual values being plotted). What line charts typically do well, however, is show you how the plotted values change over equal increments of time.

EXCEL

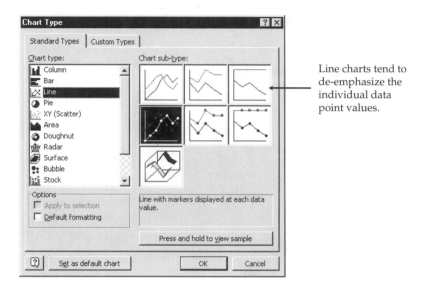

Line charts tend to de-emphasize the individual data point values.

WARNING: *There's also a subtle problem with the three-dimensional line chart subtype. To give the illusion of depth to a 3-D line chart, Excel elevates the far corner of the plot area. Unfortunately, this elevation reduces the apparent positive slope of line. And while that may not seem like such a big deal, it actually can be. The slope of the plotted line or lines indicates the change in the data series' values—which is what you're trying to show with the line chart anyway. Unfortunately, when Excel reduces the apparent positive slope of the line, it understates a positive change in the data series values or it overstates a negative change in the data series values.*

Working with Custom Subtypes

As you may have noticed, the Chart Type dialog box also includes a Custom Types tab. If you click this tab, Excel displays a lengthy list of more specialized and unusual-looking subtypes. The most interesting Custom Type subtype is the Logarithmic subtype, because it uses logarithmic scaling of the values axis. Logarithmic scaling lets you plot the range of change in a data series. This may seem too technical or esoteric to be of interest, but it's probably not. If you don't believe this statement and you have the time, create a line chart that plots the revenues of two companies: a $500,000,000 company growing at 5 percent annually over 10 years and a $1,000,000 company growing at 50 percent annually over 10 years. Then flip-flop back and forth between a regular line chart subtype (which doesn't use logarithmic scaling) and the Logarithmic Custom Type, which does. What you'll notice is that the significantly faster growth rate enjoyed by the smaller company doesn't even show up on a line chart. It does show up, however, on the Logarithmic chart that uses logarithmic scaling.

Pie Charts

Pie charts plot only a single data series, as the Chart Type dialog box shown in Figure 13-11 indicates. In a pie chart, each data point shows as a proportional slice of the pie (a segment of the circle). Pie charts typically aren't as useful as the other chart types. You typically can't plot more than a handful of data points in a pie chart because otherwise the slices of the pie get too small.

> *NOTE: The fact that 3-D pie charts exaggerate the size of slices shown in the foreground and minimize the size of slices shown in the background is often used to strengthen, dishonestly, a chart's message. Take a look, for example, at the next 3-D pie chart you see in a magazine or newspaper. You may see that if the newspaper or magazine wants to convince you that a certain pie slice is large, it will appear in the foreground. And you may see that if a newspaper or magazine wants to convince you that a certain pie slice is small, it will appear in the background.*

Doughnut Charts

Doughnut charts resemble pie charts, but they allow you to show more than a single data series by plotting the multiple data series as concentric circles. Each data point is

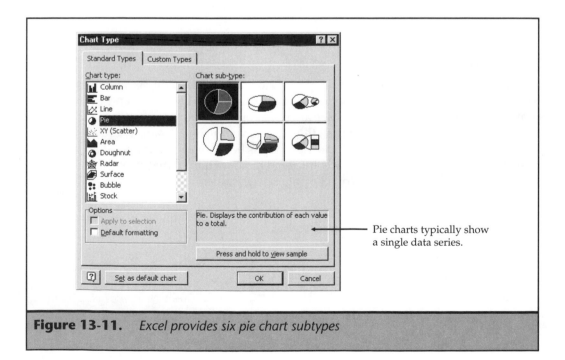

Figure 13-11. *Excel provides six pie chart subtypes*

Why You Probably Shouldn't Use Pie Charts

Because pie charts only show a single data series and because they limit you, practically speaking, to a handful of data points, you shouldn't use them very much— and maybe you shouldn't use them at all. As a practical matter, you'll usually present your information in a much cleaner and more meaningful way by just using a tabular format—in other words, a regular worksheet range.

Note, however, that there is one time when pie charts do seem to be very effective: They tend to be wonderful tools—because they are so simplistic—for explaining to children what charts do. Even very young children can see that larger pie slices indicate relatively larger values.

represented by a segment (or bite?) of the doughnut. While doughnut charts are popular in some cultures, you probably want to think carefully about their usefulness in your situation. A segment that represents the very same value will appear larger the farther away its concentric ring is from the center of the circle. What that means is that you can't compare values in different data series. And then that, of course, begs the question as to why you're plotting the multiple data series together in the first place. (If you did want to compare both the relative proportions of data series' values and values from different data series, a better option would be to use stacked bar or column chart subtypes.)

Radar Charts

Radar charts plot data points as radial points from a central origin, as shown in the following illustration. Each data series' points are connected in a line, and the radar chart uses as many radial axes as there are data points in your series. While radar charts can be a little confusing at first, they can be very useful. Radar charts allow you to more precisely calibrate each data series' points because each data point appears directly on an axis. The one other advantage of a radar chart is that it lets you compare the aggregate values—the totals of all a data series' values.

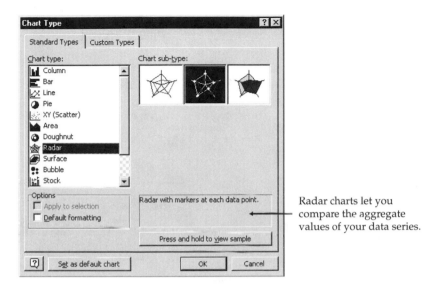

Radar charts let you compare the aggregate values of your data series.

XY (Scatter) Charts

The XY, or scatter, chart type is Excel's most useful chart type. It allows you visually to explore the relationship between two or more data series: an independent data series, which replaces the data categories that other charts use, and one or more dependent data series. Because this represents a change from the way that Excel's other chart types work—and because the XY chart is Excel's most useful chart—you'll probably benefit by being shown in detail how to actually use an XY chart.

Your first step is to create a worksheet range that shows at least two data series that you think may have a cause-and-effect relationship. Clearly, you expect some sort of cause-and-effect relationship here, but you probably wouldn't know the exact nature of the relationship: That would be what you wanted to explore by creating an XY chart.

TIP: *You can easily sort your data in ascending or descending order by selecting the range that holds both the independent data series and the dependent data series and then clicking the Standard toolbar's Sort Ascending or Sort Descending tools.*

If you select the range A1:B5 and then use the Chart Wizard to create an XY chart, you get a chart like the one shown in Figure 13-12. At first glance, this doesn't seem very interesting, perhaps. But it is. What the chart in Figure 13-12 shows you, among other things, is that while adding salespeople does increase your revenue, you get diminishing returns as a result. The chart shows this because the slope of the line in Figure 13-12 is flattening out.

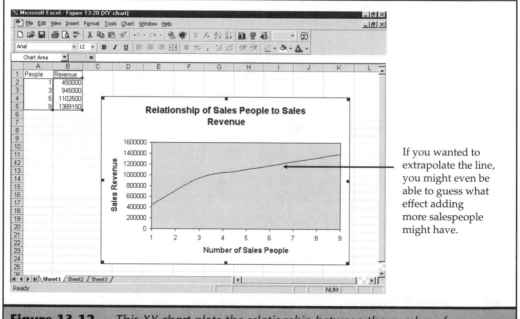

Figure 13-12. *This XY chart plots the relationship between the number of salespeople and a firm's sales revenue*

EXAMPLES

LEARN BY EXAMPLE
You can open the example chart shown in Figure 13-12, Figure 13-12 (XY chart), from the companion CD if you want to follow along with the discussion here.

If you're like most people, the significance of Figure 13-12 isn't all that apparent. So take a look at Figure 13-13. It shows the exact same information in a line chart. (You can tell this is so, because in Figure 13-13, Excel is using the contents of the range A2:A5 for data category names.) The thing to notice is that in Figure 13-13, the diminishing returns of the additional salespeople isn't at all obvious. In fact, it's basically hidden.

EXAMPLES

LEARN BY EXAMPLE
You can open the example chart shown in Figure 13-13, Figure 13-13 (line chart), from the companion CD if you want to follow along with the discussion here.

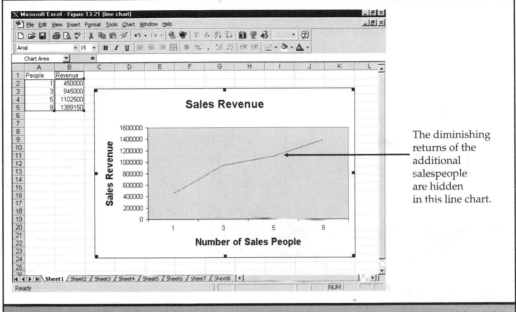

Figure 13-13.   *This line chart plots the same information as Figure 13-12, although in a much less meaningful way*

There are various chart subtypes available for the XY chart type. Most of the differences between the available subtypes relate to cosmetics: Some subtypes have gridlines, and some don't, for example. Some subtypes smooth the plotted lines (so they appear less jagged). And some use individual data markers for the dependent data series values and a line, while others don't.

Surface

Surface charts are probably Excel's most interesting and perhaps most useful three-dimensional chart type. What they let you do is plot a data set using a three-dimensional surface, as shown in the next illustration. By drawing a three-dimensional surface, a 3-D surface chart lets you explore relationships that exist both within a data series and with a data category. In fact, one indication of a data set that may be usefully plotted as a 3-D surface chart is when, even though you truly understand the difference between data categories and data series, you still have trouble defining which is which.

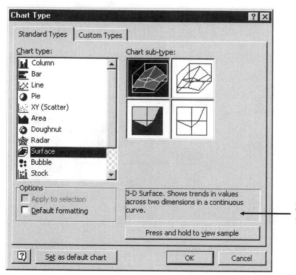

3-D surface charts plot a data set using a three-dimensional surface.

Bubble Charts

Bubble charts amount to a variant of Excel's XY scatter chart. Like an XY scatter chart, bubble charts plot an independent and dependent data series, thereby allowing you to visually explore correlation between the data series. A bubble chart adds a new wrinkle to the standard XY scatter chart, however, by allowing you to include a third data series. Excel uses the third data series' values to size bubble data markers. Excel has two bubble chart subtypes.

Stock Charts

Stock charts let you plot daily opening, high, low, and closing stock prices in a special variety of bar chart used by technical security analysts. (Two varieties of the stock chart also let you include a second values axis, which can be used to plot shares-traded volume.) The following illustration shows what the four stock chart subtypes look like. The lower two subtypes shown plot volume using columns.

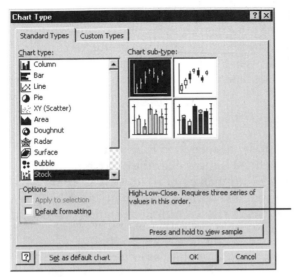

Excel tells you in which order your data series need to be arranged using the information in this box.

Cylinder, Cone, and Pyramid Charts

Cylinder, cone, and pyramid charts work like and resemble bar and column charts. The difference is that, rather than use a rectangular data marker, these chart types use three-dimensional cylinders, cones, or pyramids. For example, the next illustration shows how some of the cylinder chart subtypes resemble bar charts while others resemble column charts.

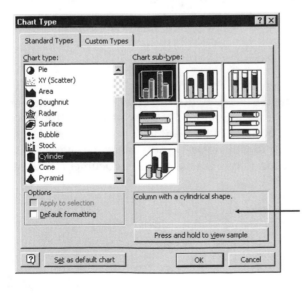

Excel displays a textual description of the selected subtype using this box.

Despite the fact that cylinder, cone, and pyramid charts look different, however, they should generally be used in the same manner as bar and column charts. For example, those chart subtypes that use a horizontal values axis are useful for comparing data point values when the data category isn't time. Those chart types that use a vertical values axis are useful for comparing data point values when the data category is time.

Printing Charts

Printing a chart isn't difficult. To print an embedded chart but not any of the worksheet page in which it's embedded, simply click the chart, and then click the Print tool on the Standard toolbar. To print an embedded chart as a part of an Excel worksheet page, Word document, or PowerPoint presentation in which it's embedded, print the worksheet, Word document, or PowerPoint presentation in the usual way.

NOTE: For more information about printing document files, refer to Chapter 2.

Saving Charts

Because charts are always part and parcel of an Excel workbook (the usual case), a Word document, or a PowerPoint presentation, you don't need to worry about separately saving a chart. When you save the document file with the embedded chart object or with the chart sheet, you also save the chart. As discussed in Chapter 2, you can save a document file in a variety of ways, but probably the easiest is just by clicking the Save tool on the Standard toolbar.

Sharing Charts

You can share a chart object between Excel and some other Office program by copying and pasting or cutting and pasting the chart. To do this, create and then select the chart you want to copy or move. Next, click the Standard toolbar's Copy button (if you want to copy the chart) or the Cut button (if you want to move the chart). Once you've done this, open the document file into which you want to place the chart, position the insertion point in the appropriate location in the destination document, and then click the Standard toolbar's Paste button.

NOTE: For more information on sharing objects between Office programs, refer to Chapter 5.

Customizing Charts

You can customize just about any aspect of a chart. You can add text that describes the chart or some element of the chart. You can add items such as gridlines or axes—or modify these items—to better calibrate the plotted data series for chart viewers. You can change the appearance of any of the parts of a chart. And you can even use special tools such as trend lines and error bars. The best part of all this is that none of this customization is difficult. As long as you understand how to create charts using Excel's Chart Wizard—which you already know how to do if you've read the previous portions of this chapter—you'll have no trouble customizing those charts.

Adding and Editing Titles, Legends and Data Labels

To annotate the data your charts plot or to emphasize their messages, Excel lets you add chart and axis titles, legends, and data labels to existing charts. Typically, you add titles and legends when you create the chart, of course; but you can add these later on, as well as data labels.

Adding Chart and Axis Titles

To add titles to an existing chart, you first need to display the chart's chart sheet if it's on its own chart sheet or to click the chart if it's embedded in a worksheet. When you do this, Excel replaces the worksheet menu bar with the chart menu bar.

To add a title to the chart or its axis, choose the Chart menu Chart Options command. When Excel displays the Chart Options dialog box, click the Titles tab; enter titles into the text boxes, as shown in the illustration that follows; and then click OK.

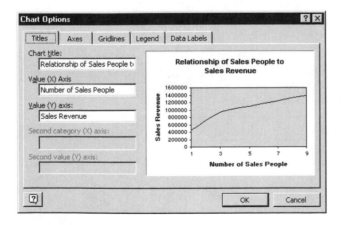

Editing Chart and Axis Titles

To edit a chart or axis title, click the title to select it. Then click the mouse to position the insertion point inside the title text box. Once you've done this, you can edit the chart title in the way you edit the contents of any text box. If you want to remove a title, click it and then press the DELETE key.

TIP: *To separate your title on different lines, click a chart title you've already added. (You can click on the chart sheet or the embedded chart.) Position the insertion point at the exact spot where you want to break the title into two lines of text, and then press CTRL-ENTER to end a line.*

Using Data Labels

Data labels annotate your data markers either by displaying the data point value (its relative percent of the data category total), or the data category name next to or above the marker. Many of the subtypes—particularly those supplied for the pie and doughnut chart types—initially supply data labels. You can add and remove data labels to or from any chart, however, by choosing the Chart menu Chart Options command and then clicking the Data Labels tab. When Excel displays the Data Labels tab of the Chart Options dialog box, you use its option buttons to indicate which type of data label you want. If you add data labels and then decide that you don't want them, you can easily remove them. Make the chart active either by displaying its chart sheet or clicking it (if it's embedded on a worksheet). Then click the data labels (to select them) and press the DELETE key.

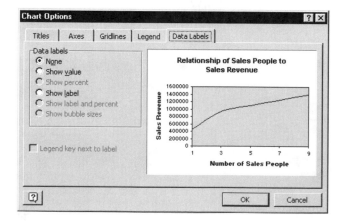

NOTE: *To format a data label in the active chart, first display its chart sheet page or click it (if it's an embedded chart) to make it active. Click the data label you want to format and then right-click the data label so Excel displays the shortcut menu. Choose the Format Data Labels command. When Excel displays the Format Data Labels dialog box, use the options that its four different tabs supply—Patterns, Font, Number, and Alignment—to specify exactly how you want the label displayed.*

Using Chart Legends

A chart legend simply names the data series. You have the choice of specifying that you want a legend when you create a chart with the Chart Wizard. Or, you can add one later by choosing the Chart menu Chart Options command, clicking the Legend tab, and then checking the Show Legend box. You can also control the placement of the legend in the same dialog box.

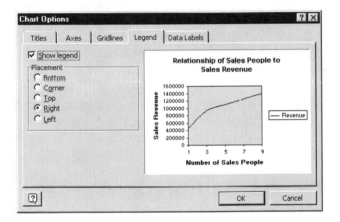

 TIP: *To add a meaningful legend, you must include the data series names in your initial worksheet range you select to plot. Otherwise, Excel uses the rather meaningless series names—Series 1, Series 2, Series 3, and so on.*

You can move a legend anywhere in the chart area by clicking the legend and then dragging it. You can also resize the legend (and thereby change the way it arranges the key information) by clicking the legend box and then dragging the sizing handles. (The sizing handles are those little black squares that appear on the corners and edges of a selected object—such as a selected legend.) You can remove a legend by clicking it and pressing the DELETE key. Finally, you can change the foreground and background pattern, the font, and the legend placement by right-clicking the legend to display the shortcut menu, and choosing the Format Legend command. When Excel displays the Format Legend dialog box, you can use its Patterns, Font, and Placement tabs to change the appearance and position of the legend box. The Patterns and Font tabs work in exactly the same way that these tabs work for formatting other objects. The Placement tab provides option buttons you can click to move the legend around the chart area.

Calibrating and Organizing the Data Markers

Excel provides two visual tools to make it easier for chart readers to better calibrate and organize a chart's data markers: axes and gridlines. While many of the subtypes use these tools, you can, of course, fine-tune the way Excel draws and uses chart axes and gridlines.

Adding and Removing Axes

To add axes to a chart, choose the Chart menu Chart Options command, and then click the Axes tab. (For the Chart menu commands to be available, as mentioned earlier, either the chart sheet must be active or the embedded chart on a worksheet must be selected.) When Excel displays the Axes tab, you can indicate which axes you want Excel to draw on the chart by marking check boxes. Or, if you want to remove an axis, of course, you can clear a check box. When you have finished, click the OK button and Excel will update the axes on your chart.

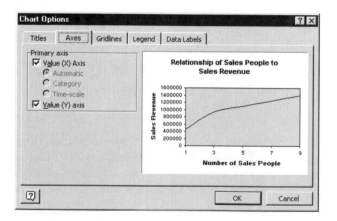

When Excel displays the Gridlines tab, you can indicate whether you want Excel to draw vertical and horizontal gridlines. Simply mark its check boxes to indicate whether you want major gridlines extending from an axis's major tick marks and minor gridlines extending from an axis's minor tick marks. (Gridlines aren't usually difficult to understand or use, so if you have questions, just experiment.)

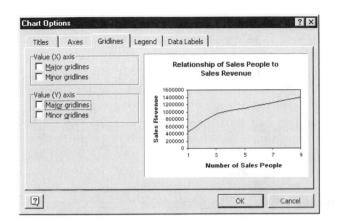

 TIP: *To better understand these options, your best bet is to just create an example chart or open a Learn By Example workbook and experiment with the Axes tab's and Gridlines tab's options.*

The only thing that's tricky about this axes business is that a chart can actually have as many as three primary axes and two secondary axes. For any chart type but the pie chart and doughnut chart—which don't use axes—you can supply a value axis to calibrate the data markers, and you can supply a category axis to identify the data categories. For some of the three-dimensional chart subtypes, you can also supply a series axis to identify the data series. These axes, when they exist, represent the chart's primary axes.

NOTE: *If you add a series axis to a three-dimensional chart, you don't need a legend. Series axes and legends do the same thing: they name and identify the plotted data series. Therefore, you only need one or the other. Because series axis are easier for the chart reader to use—they place the series names right alongside the series' data markers—you should usually employ them, when available, rather than legends. Note that series axes aren't available, however, for all of the three-dimensional chart types—only those that use the extra dimension of depth to organize, or segregate, the data series.*

Things get just a bit more complex in the case of a chart that uses a second value axis to calibrate and identify a chart's last set of data markers. In this special case, you also have a secondary set of axes: a secondary value axis to calibrate the second set of data markers, and a secondary category axis to identify the second set of data categories.

Formatting and Rescaling Chart Axes

You can change the way Excel draws your chart axes. To do this, right-click the axis to display the shortcut menu and then choose the Format Axis command. Excel displays the Format Axis dialog box, shown in the next illustration. Note that this chapter doesn't include the Font, Number, or Alignment tabs. They work the same way for a chart axis as they do for the cells of a worksheet (and this information is provided in Chapter 3). You will benefit, however, by taking a quick birds' eye tour of the Patterns and Scale tabs.

The Axis options on the Patterns tab lets you tell Excel whether it should even add an axis to the chart and, if so, what color, line style, and weight (or line thickness) it should use for the axis. The Tick mark labels options let you tell Excel whether it should label the tick marks and, if so, where it should place the tick marks. The Major and Minor tick mark type options let you tell Excel whether it should add tick marks, or little crosshatches, to the axis, and where they should be placed. You could spend several paragraphs reading in detail exactly how these options effect your charts. The best way for you to learn what they do, however, is to simply experiment with an existing chart.

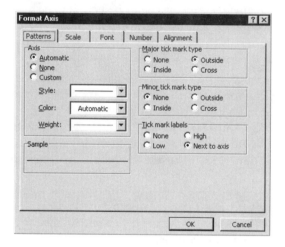

The Format Axis dialog box's Scale tab lets you control how Excel scales a value or category axis and how often it displays tick marks and tick-mark labels. The illustration that follows shows the Scale tab for a value axis. The Auto check boxes, if marked, tell Excel to scale the value axis by choosing where the value scale starts (its minimum value), where the value scale ends (its maximum value), which units of measurement should be used for the major and minor tick-marks, and where the category axis should intersect, or cross, the value axis. If you don't want Excel to automatically calculate these settings, you can unmark the check boxes and enter your own values into the text boxes. The Logarithmic scale check box tells Excel to use a logarithmically scaled value axis. (As noted in earlier in the chapter in the "Reviewing the Different Chart Types" section's discussion of the line chart subtypes, logarithmically scaled value axes can be a wonderful tool for showing the rate of change in the plotted data series' values.) The Values in reverse order check box tells Excel to flip-flop the standard order of the value axis, so everything looks upside down. Finally, the Category (X) axis crosses at maximum value check box tells Excel to draw the axis so, as the option label indicates, it intersects the value axis at the point of the largest plotted value.

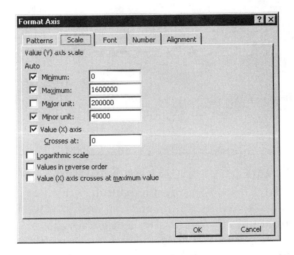

If you take a quick look at the illustration that follows, you see that the Scale tab for a Category axis looks quite a bit different from the Scale tab for a value axis. The dialog box provides three text boxes with self-explanatory labels: Value axis crosses at category number, Number of categories between tick-mark labels, and Number of categories between tick marks. In addition, the dialog box provides three check boxes. The Value (Y) axis crosses between categories check box tells Excel to draw the intersection of the value and category axes so that the lines cross someplace other than where a data marker is. The Categories in reverse order check box tells Excel to plot the categories in right-to-left order rather than in the usual left-to-right order. And the Value axis crosses at maximum category tells Excel to place the value axis after the last data category instead of before the first data category.

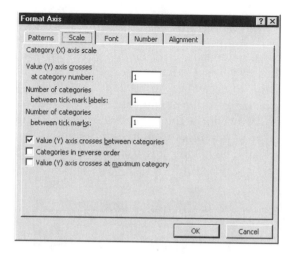

NOTE: *The Scale tab for a series axis provides a subset of the options available for a category axis.*

The Perils of Automatic Axes Scaling

Most of the time, you will want Excel to automatically scale your value axis by automatically selecting the axis minimum and maximum, as well as the units used to scale the axis. You should, however, verify that the way Excel has scaled an axis is reasonable and relevant. Excel tends to scale an axis in a way that emphasizes the differences in the plotted data points' values. Yet, if the differences in the plotted data points are insignificant, this probably doesn't make sense. (For a really good example of this sort of kooky value axis scaling, look at the way they plot the Dow Jones stock average the next time you watch the nightly news. What you'll see is that every single trading day of the year, the differences in the plotted data points' values show up as visually significant because the value axis maximum equals the daily high of the average and the value axis minimum equals the daily low of the average.)

One other time you'll want to consider overriding Excel's automatic scaling is when you're presenting several charts to viewers in one sitting. In this case, you should probably scale each of the charts using the same value axis so that viewers can make comparisons between the charts.

Adding a Data Table to a Chart

You can add a data table to a chart by selecting the chart, choosing the Chart menu Chart Options command, clicking the Data Table tab, and then checking the Show Data Table box. A data table simply shows the chart's data point values plotted in a table that appears beneath the chart. This is especially useful if you've created your chart on a separate chart sheet and then find that you need to include the source data in your printout.

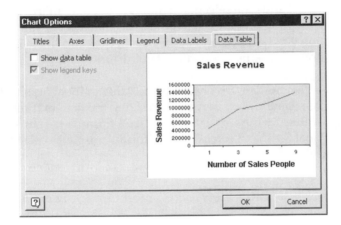

Working with the Data Markers

Excel also lets you customize the data markers. You won't be surprised to hear that you can change their color and shape, of course. But you may be surprised to learn about some of the other changes you can make. You can, for example, use clip art pictures in place of Excel's data markers. And you can add trend lines and error bars.

Changing the Plotted Data

Excel lets you make a couple of changes to the actual data plotted in a chart. You can add a new data series to chart, and you can adjust the actual data point value. Most people—and this probably includes you—aren't going to want to mess around with these sorts of changes. But just in case you want to do this, this book quickly describes how you make these changes.

To add another data series to a chart, display the chart sheet or, if the chart is embedded in a worksheet, click it. Then choose the Chart menu Add Data command. When Excel displays the Add Data dialog box, click the Range text box and then select the worksheet range that holds the data series you want to add to the chart.

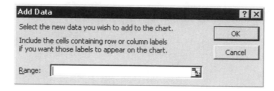

You can also change the actual data plotted in a bar, column, or line chart. To do this, hold down the CTRL key and click the data marker you want to show a different value. Then, when Excel adds the selection handles to the data marker, change the data marker's value by dragging the data marker. To change a bar or column chart, you drag the selection handle at the end of the bar. To change a line chart, drag the data marker that shows the actual plotted data point. (You can't drag just the line, in other words.)

As you drag the data marker, Excel adjusts the value in the worksheet cell that holds the plotted data value. So, by moving or resizing the data marker, you actually change the plotted value. By the way, if the cell uses a formula to return the plotted value, Excel starts Goal Seek so it can ask which formula input Excel should adjust so the formula returns the new value.

NOTE: *For more information about how Goal Seek works, refer to Chapter 15.*

Formatting the Data Markers

Mechanically, you can probably already guess how to format the data markers for a series. Click the marker to select the complete set of data markers for the data series. Then, right-click any of the selected data markers to display the shortcut menu and choose the Format Data Series command. Excel displays the Format Data Series dialog box, shown in the illustration that follows.

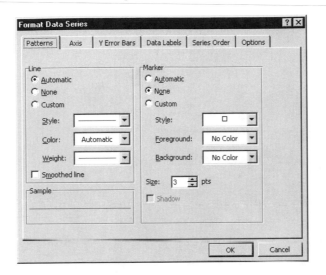

To reformat an individual data marker, click once on the marker to select the entire series, then click once again to select the individual data marker (the sizing handles will move to the data marker). Then, double-click the data marker to display the Format Data Point dialog box.

Using the Patterns Tab

The preceding illustration shows the Patterns tab for a line, but the Patterns tab looks different depending on the type of data marker you select. You actually make the same sorts of changes no matter which data marker type you're customizing, however. You can change the line that Excel uses to draw the data marker or its border. You can also change the color and pattern of the data marker or its interior. And, in some cases, you can make other changes to the data marker's pattern, too. For line and XY scatter charts, for example, Excel provides a Smoothed Line option. It tells Excel to smooth out, or soften, the plotted line's jaggedness.

USING THE AXIS TAB   The Axis tab lets you tell Excel which value axis a particular data series can be plotted against: the primary axis or the secondary axis. If a chart only has a primary axis, telling Excel to plot the data series on a second axis also results in the creation of a second axis.

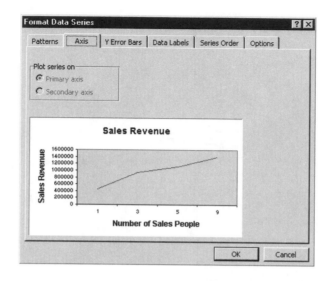

ADDING Y ERROR BARS TO A DATA SERIES' MARKERS To visually show that imprecision exists in your plotted data, you can add error bars. Error bars, in effect, show the chart reader that the plotted value isn't precise, but instead falls within an error range. To add error bars to the plotted data series, you use the Y Error Bars tab shown in the illustration that follows. Use the Display options to specify whether Excel should display plus or minus error bars, or both. Use the Error Amount options to specify how Excel calculates the error range: as a fixed amount added to and subtracted from the plotted value, as a percentage of the plotted value, as a specified number of standard deviation from the mean of the plotted value, as a standard error, or as some other amount you specify.

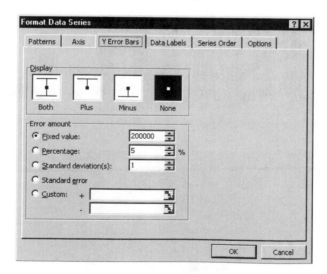

NOTE: *The Data Labels tab lets you add data labels to the selected data series. For information about how the Data Labels tab works, refer to the earlier chapter section, "Using Data Labels."*

Changing Series Order

The Series Order tab lets you choose the order in which Excel plots the different data series. It provides one list box and a couple of command buttons, Move Up and Move Down. To change the order of a particular series, select it from the list box and then, as you've guessed, click either the Move Up or Move Down button. To show you what effect your reordering has on the chart, Excel updates a preview of the chart within the dialog box.

Making Options Changes

The Options tab provides a bunch of rather miscellaneous settings for modifying the group of data markers. You can add drop lines to line charts and area charts. (Drop lines simply connect the plotted data markers to the horizontal axis.) You can control the width of the bars in bar and column charts and the gap, or spacing, between the bars. And you can make a bunch of other minor changes as well. The illustration that follows shows the Options tab for a line chart, but Options tabs for other charts look and work similarly.

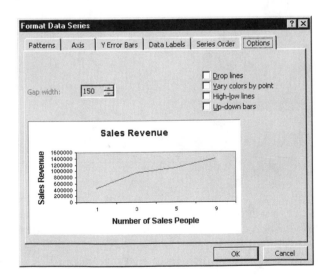

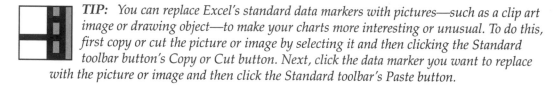

TIP: *You can replace Excel's standard data markers with pictures—such as a clip art image or drawing object—to make your charts more interesting or unusual. To do this, first copy or cut the picture or image by selecting it and then clicking the Standard toolbar button's Copy or Cut button. Next, click the data marker you want to replace with the picture or image and then click the Standard toolbar's Paste button.*

Working with Trend Lines

Trend lines represent the final customization opportunity you have with regards to data markers. Trend lines, however, don't actually change the way data markers look or how they're calibrated. What they instead do is show you the trend of a data series values by calculating and then drawing with a trend or regression line. To add a trend line, click the data series for which you want to add a trend line. Then choose the Add Trendline command from the Chart menu. When Excel displays the Trendline dialog box, use the Type tab to pick the type of trend line you want. Most people will probably want either the linear trend line (which simply plots the trend in a straight line) or a logarithmic trend line (which plots the trend as a rate of change). If you want to perform more sophisticated trend analysis, you can use the Polynomial, Power, Exponential, or Moving Average options.

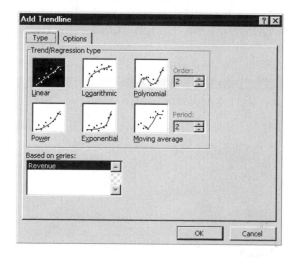

The Options tab of the Trendline dialog box lets you name the trend line. (In essence, the trend line is almost like another data series.) The Options tab lets you specify how far forward into the future or back into the past the trend line should continue. (You make these specifications using the Forecast options.) Use the check boxes at the bottom of the Options tab to tell Excel where the trend line should intercept the value axis, to provide the line's equation next to the line, and to display the R-squared value on the chart.

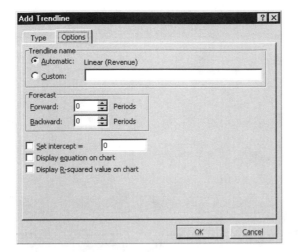

Adjusting the Elevation, Rotation, and Perspective of 3-D Charts

You can adjust the elevation, rotation, and perspective of any of Excel's three-dimensional charts. What this means is best illustrated by example. If you quickly create a three-dimensional chart and then choose the Chart menu 3-D View command, Excel displays the Format 3-D View dialog box. To change the elevation of the chart, click the buttons with the large arrows that point up and down. To change the rotation of the chart, click the buttons that show an arrow circling a line. If you want to change the perspective—basically, the perceived depth of the chart—clear the Right angle axes check box. Then, when Excel displays the two, new perspective buttons, click these to adjust the perspective. As you make changes to the elevation, rotation, or perspective, Excel updates the picture of the chart shown in the dialog box so you know the effect of your changes.

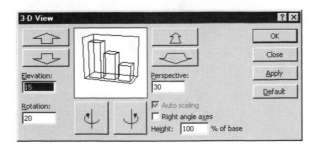

The
Complete
Reference

Office
97

Chapter 14

Working with PivotTables

PivotTables organize, analyze, and present information from worksheet lists. You can take a long, unwieldy list and reorganize it into a more compact and readable table. In the process, you transform some former list columns into PivotTable rows, and others into PivotTable columns. Then, if you want, you can "pivot" the table, exchanging, for instance, a row heading for a column heading, turning the table on its side, or inside out. That's what gives PivotTables their flexibility—they easily display the same information in a number of different ways, depending on what aspect you'd like to focus upon.

Excel provides a handy PivotTable Wizard to make it easy for you to create and modify PivotTables. In this chapter, you'll learn how to use the Wizard, and how to use PivotTables to analyze information, create charts, consolidate several tables into one, and more.

Working with Lists

PivotTables work with worksheet lists, which this book doesn't talk about—or at least talk about much. So a brief overview is in order. In essence, lists are databases that you create in an Excel worksheet. A database is simply a list of records, with each record containing a set of fields. The worksheet shown in Figure 14-1 is one example of a list: The worksheet lists records that describe a company's sales by region, quarter, product (flavor), units, and revenue. Another common example of a list might be a collection of records that describe each of your customers' names and addresses.

Although lists and list management are an important feature of Excel, this book will only talk about them in passing and in the context of PivotTables. The reason for this limited coverage is simple: Access database tables are a vastly superior replacement for Excel lists in almost all cases. Therefore, it doesn't really make sense to waste your reading time learning about an inferior information management tool.

Using the PivotTable Wizard

The list shown in Figure 14-1 contains two years' sales data for a company that makes ice cream and sells it nationwide. For each of the seven flavors it sells, the ice cream company has recorded sales by region for each quarter in the years 1996 and 1997. The sales report gives both unit sales and equivalent dollar amounts. The information shown in Figure 14-1 is exactly the sort of information that lends itself well to analysis with a PivotTable.

LEARN BY EXAMPLE
You can open the sample worksheet shown in Figure 14-1, Figure 14-1 (simple list for PivotTable), *from the companion CD if you want to follow along with the discussion here.*

Notice, by the way, that the data shown in Figure 14-1, while very detailed, doesn't provide much general information. You can't for example, easily discern trends in

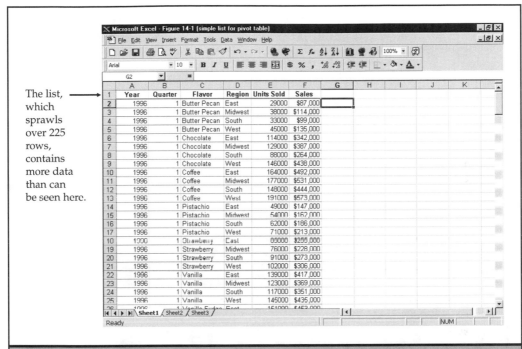

The list, which sprawls over 225 rows, contains more data than can be seen here.

Figure 14-1. *Here's the list of data we'll use to build a PivotTable. It contains ice cream sales figures over a two-year period*

sales from one year to the next or from one quarter to the next. You can't, without a great deal of effort, see in which sales region sales are strongest or which flavors sell best. You can get this information, however, by creating a PivotTable from the list shown in Figure 14-1.

Invoking the PivotTable Wizard

Once you've created a list with the information you want to analyze, click any cell in the list, and then choose the Data menu PivotTable Report command.

Excel displays the PivotTable Wizard Step 1 of 4 dialog box, as shown in Figure 14-2. The Wizard asks you the location from which to take data for the PivotTable. If a list is on an Excel worksheet, accept the default option, Microsoft Excel list or database. (Later in the chapter, the section entitled "Importing Data Into a PivotTable" examines some of the other options.)

Click on Next, and Excel will display the Step 2 of 4 dialog box, as shown in Figure 14-3. The list range will appear automatically in the Range text box. If the range selection is incorrect, you can reenter the correct range here. (You can simply type in the range reference, or select the list.)

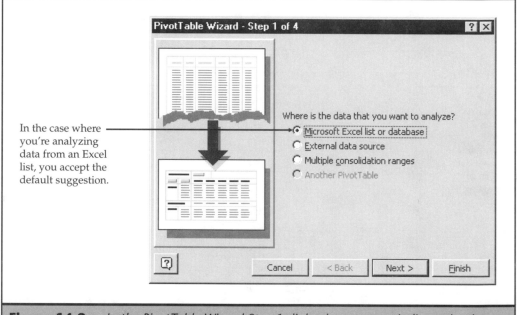

In the case where you're analyzing data from an Excel list, you accept the default suggestion.

Figure 14-2. *In the PivotTable Wizard Step 1 dialog box you can indicate the data source for your PivotTable*

Laying Out a PivotTable

When you've identified the range, click on Next again to move to the Step 3 of 4 dialog box, shown in Figure 14-4. It's in this dialog box that you specify the nuts and bolts of

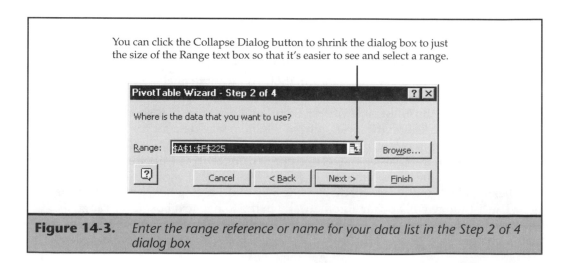

Figure 14-3. *Enter the range reference or name for your data list in the Step 2 of 4 dialog box*

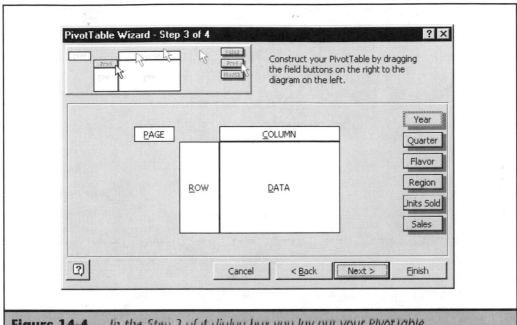

Figure 14-4.   *In the Step 3 of 4 dialog box you lay out your PivotTable*

your PivotTable. PivotTables make extensive use of Windows' drag-and-drop feature, which you can use to set up the row and column headings and data fields of your table now, and which you'll use to modify your table later.

The Step 3 dialog box has two main areas. On the right are a series of field heading buttons that the Wizard derived from your list. On the left is a plan of the PivotTable, showing how its parts are laid out with respect to one another. You get to choose which field headings go where by dragging them onto the PivotTable plan. You have many possible layout choices, but the discussion that follows illustrates one layout to keep the descriptions simple and focused. To begin creating an example PivotTable follow these steps:

1. Drag the Year and Quarter field buttons into the Column area. They will become column headings in the PivotTable.

2. Drag the Flavor and Region buttons into the Row area, to become row headings.

3. Drag the Sales heading into the Data area, because sales figures will be the data displayed in your table. (Don't worry about the Units Sold button for now—you can add that information to your table later.) The dialog box should appear as shown below:

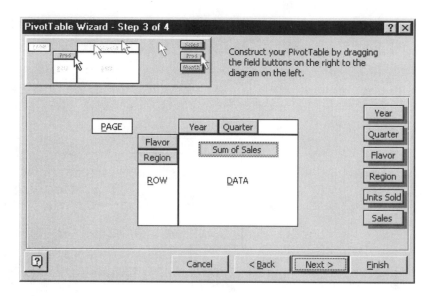

You'll notice that when you drag the sales heading into the Data area, the PivotTable Wizard renames it Sum of Sales. That's because the Wizard assumes you'll want to add up sales figures to arrive at subtotals and totals. By default, the Wizard will sum any numerical values and count any text entries you drag into the Data area.

TIP: You can override the defaults and apply different functions to field headings that you drag into the Data area. Double-click a heading in the data area to open the PivotTable Field dialog box, and you can see some of the other functions available. See "Using PivotTable Functions," later in the chapter, for more information.

4. Click on Next to move to the Step 4 of 4 dialog box, shown in Figure 14-5.

5. Click the New worksheet option button, if necessary, and then click Finish. The Wizard goes to work creating your table, and soon displays it in the location you selected. The Wizard is also displayed.

Taking a Closer Look at a PivotTable

Excel creates a table based on your specifications, as shown in Figure 14-6. If you put the Quarter and Year field headings in the Column area as shown above, Excel creates a column heading for each quarter and one for each year's total. In addition, there is a column heading for the grand total of two years' sales. These headings are said to be along the column axis of the table.

LEARN BY EXAMPLE

You can open the PivotTable shown in Figure 14-6, Figure 14-6 (simple PivotTable), from the companion CD if you want to follow along with the discussion here.

You can tell the PivotTable Wizard where to display your PivotTable and select from among various display options.
PivotTable Wizard - Step 4 of 4
Where do you want to put the PivotTable?
New worksheet
Existing worksheet
Click Finish to create your PivotTable.
Cancel
Options...
< Back
Next >
Finish

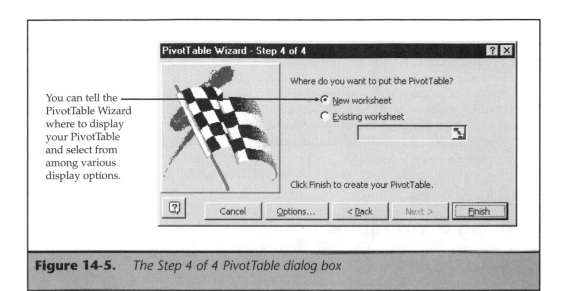

Figure 14-5. *The Step 4 of 4 PivotTable dialog box*

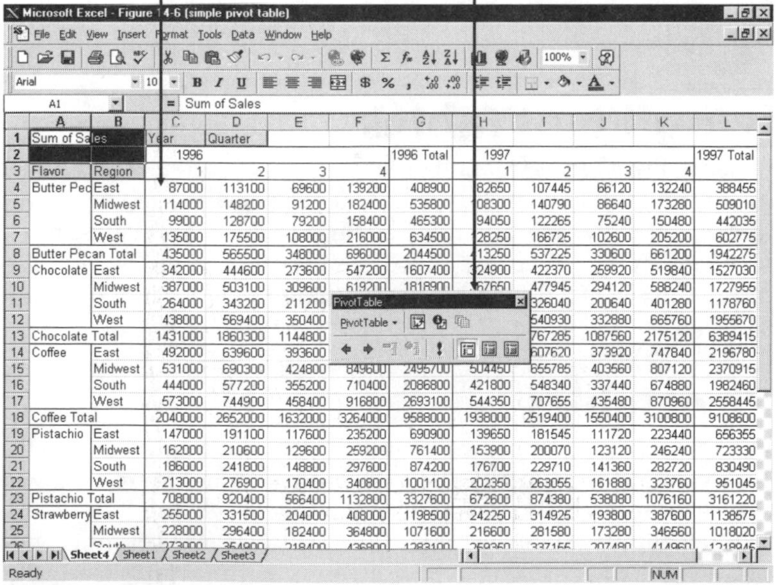

At each row and column intersection you can find the sales of a particular flavor, in a particular region for a particular quarter, in a particular year.
The PivotTable toolbar.
Microsoft Excel - Figure 14-6 (simple pivot table)
Sum of Sales
Year
Quarter
Flavor
Region
PivotTable

Figure 14-6. *Using the example data and the preceding step-by-step instructions, the PivotTable Wizard would create this PivotTable*

Along the row axis of the table are headings corresponding to the field headings you dragged to the row area in Figure 14-4: Region and Flavor. Within each of the four regions, each flavor has its own row. Because you dragged the Sales button into the Data area, sales figures appear in the body of the table.

Excel also adds rows showing regional subtotals and national grand totals for each quarter and year. Because these totals represent the sum of the Sales figures, Excel places the title Sum of Sales at the top of the table.

When you create a PivotTable, Excel displays the PivotTable toolbar, which contains several buttons useful for working with PivotTables. Later in the chapter, the book talks more about the individual buttons as I discuss various aspects of working with PivotTables.

Refreshing PivotTables

As the data changes in the list upon which the PivotTable is based, you need to refresh the PivotTable, because although a PivotTable is linked to its source data, that link is not automatically updated. You can refresh a PivotTable in either of two ways: by choosing the Data menu Refresh Data command, or by clicking on the Refresh Data button on the PivotTable toolbar.

TIP: *The Refresh Data toolbar button is the one that shows an exclamation point. Remember, too, that you can point to any toolbar button and an office program will display the button's name in a ScreenTip.*

Modifying PivotTables

What distinguishes PivotTables from other kinds of tables is the ease with which you can rearrange, or "pivot" them. For example, you can reshape a table by moving column headings to the row axis and row headings to the column axis. You can simplify a table by moving either row or column headings to the page axis. And you can change the emphasis of a PivotTable by changing the order in which headings and totals are displayed.

Pivoting PivotTables

Pivoting refers specifically to switching headings from the column axis to the row axis and vice versa. A couple of examples easily illustrate this. In Figure 14-7, you can see that the Flavor heading has been moved from the row axis to the column axis. Doing so produces quite a different looking table. The new table is 53 columns wide, but only 9 rows high. Now each flavor seems to have its own "mini-table," showing quarterly and yearly totals by region. Regional grand totals are displayed at the extreme right edge of the table. It's important to emphasize that pivoting the table hasn't changed the information displayed—just how it's displayed.

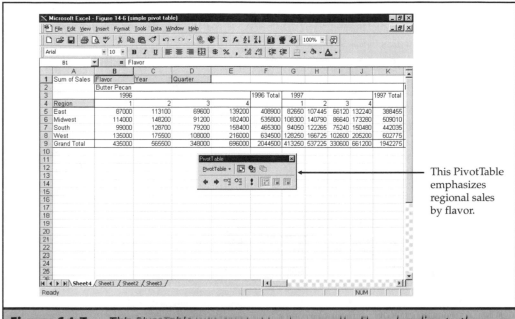

This PivotTable emphasizes regional sales by flavor.

Figure 14-7. *This PivotTable was created by dragging the Flavor heading to the column axis*

LEARN BY EXAMPLE
You can open the PivotTable shown in Figure 14-7, Figure 14-7 (pivoted PivotTable), from the companion CD if you want to follow along with the discussion here.

In Figure 14-8, the Flavor heading has been dragged back to the row axis, and the Year heading has been dragged to the row axis as well. Now each year appears to have its own table, one on top of the other, and quarterly grand totals are displayed at the bottom of the table.

LEARN BY EXAMPLE
You can open the sample PivotTable shown in Figure 14-8, Figure 14-8 (PivotTable emphasizing yearly sales), from the companion CD if you want to follow along with the discussion here.

Reordering Fields

PivotTables have a hierarchy of fields, depending on how you place their headings in the table. On the row axis, for example, the field you place to the outside (to the left) is the outer field, while the one to the inside (to the right) is the inner field. The outer field is higher in the hierarchy: all inner field items are repeated for each outer field item. For example, if Flavor is an inner field and Region is an outer field, each region

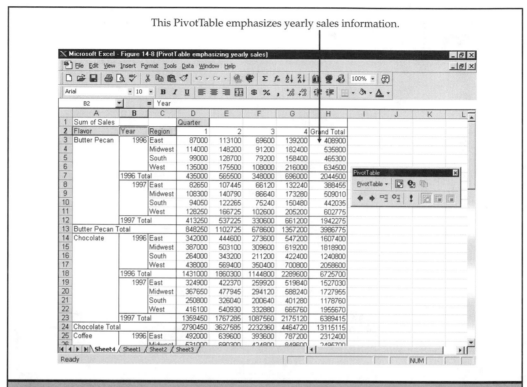

Figure 14-8. *This PivotTable was created by dragging the Year heading to the row axis, displaying the same data in a very different fashion*

is broken down by flavor. You can easily reverse their positions, so that each flavor would be broken down by region. To do this, you would just drag the Flavor heading to the left of the Region heading.

Creating Page Fields

In the table shown in Figure 14-8, data for one year seems to be stacked upon data for the other. It's useful to view the data by year, but the resulting table is cumbersome. Luckily, there's a better way to view sales figures for each year—using the page axis. When you move a field to the page axis, you divide that field into a series of separate pages, each of which can be viewed individually. In Figure 14-9, the Year field has been dragged to the page axis, in the upper left-hand corner of the table. (When the mouse pointer changes to three cascaded pages, you know you've found the page axis.)

You can focus on each year's figures separately by moving the Year field to the page axis.

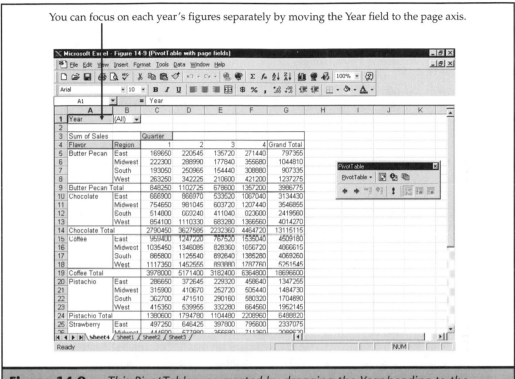

Figure 14-9. *This PivotTable was created by dragging the Year heading to the page axis*

LEARN BY EXAMPLE
You can open the sample PivotTable shown in Figure 14-9, Figure 14-9 (PivotTable with page fields), *from the companion CD if you want to follow along with the discussion here.*

By clicking the downward-pointing arrow next to the Year heading you can display a drop-down menu, where you can choose to view figures for 1996, 1997, or both years combined (All). In a like manner, you can drag any of the other headings to the page axis to divide them into a series of pages. To narrow your focus even more, you can drag more than one heading to the page axis.

Displaying Pages on Separate Worksheets

By clicking the Show Pages button on the PivotTable toolbar when you use page fields, you can create a separate worksheet for each page in the field. When you click the Show Pages button, Excel displays the Show Pages dialog box:

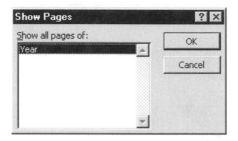

Select a page field, click OK, and Excel creates a page worksheet for each item in that field. For example, if you select the Year field, Excel creates separate worksheets for 1996 and 1997. Excel places each of the worksheets adjacent to the PivotTable worksheet, and names each of the new sheets appropriately for the page item it displays, as shown in Figure 14-10.

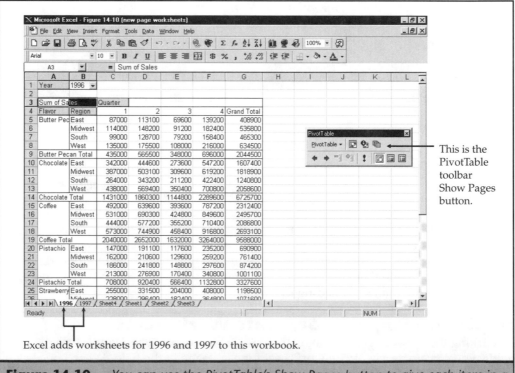

Figure 14-10. *You can use the PivotTable's Show Pages button to give each item in a page field its own worksheet*

LEARN BY EXAMPLE
You can open the sample worksheet shown in Figure 14-10, Figure 14-10 (new page worksheets), *from the companion CD if you want to follow along with the discussion here.*

Adding New Fields and Deleting Existing Fields

To add a new field or delete an existing field, select any cell in the table. Click the PivotTable Wizard button on the PivotTable toolbar.

When Excel displays the PivotTable Wizard Step 3 dialog box, which looks the way you last left it, make changes to the table layout by dragging fields in and out of the table. Note that you can display more than one set of data in the Data area of the table. To add the Units Sold field to the table, for example, drag it into the Data area, click Next, and then click Finish. Figure 14-11 shows the PivotTable after the Units Sold field has been added.

In order to display the additional data effectively, Excel adds another heading named Data to the table. Each data category, Sales and Units Sold, is displayed on separate rows, and subtotals are given for both categories.

This row shows sales revenue in dollars data.

This row shows unit sales data.

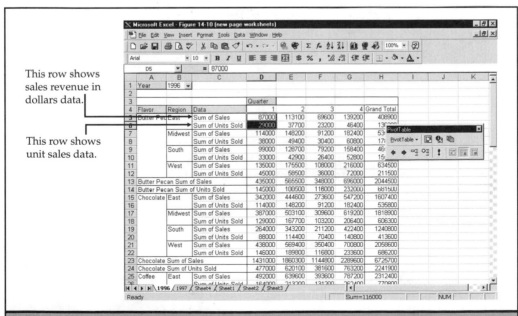

Figure 14-11. *This Pivot Table shows two fields in its data area: sales revenue in dollars and units sold*

TIP: *To rename a field heading, simply select the heading and edit it in the formula bar. If you change a heading name the change affects all instances of the name in the table, including in subtotals and totals.*

Showing and Hiding Fields

You can hide any of the items in a field to narrow the focus of a PivotTable. Suppose, for example, you'd like to concentrate on only four of the seven flavors in the Flavor field. To filter your data in this manner, double-click on the Flavor field heading, and Excel displays the PivotTable Field dialog box, as shown below.

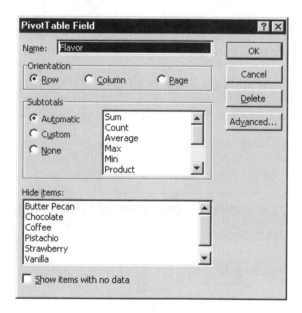

To use the PivotTable Field dialog box, select the item you want to hide in the Hide items list box and then click OK. Excel displays the PivotTable and hides the items you selected. (When you hide items, those items are excluded from subtotals and grand totals as well.) Repeat this procedure to redisplay the data.

Working with Data in PivotTables

You can manipulate PivotTable data in various ways. You can sort data in ascending or descending order, group and ungroup data items, and perform calculations upon data. In addition, you can change how totals and subtotals are displayed.

Sorting Data in PivotTables

You can sort data field items in ascending or descending order. You can either sort labels alphabetically, or numbers by value. When Excel first creates your PivotTable, it sorts field items in ascending order. In Figure 14-6, for example, Excel lists the regions in alphabetical order: starting with East; it lists flavors, starting with Butter Pecan; and it lists quarters, starting with 1.

To change the sort order, select an item in the field you want to sort and choose the Data menu Sort command. When Excel displays the Sort dialog box, as shown below, select either the Descending or Ascending option and click OK. Excel resorts the list information in the specified order.

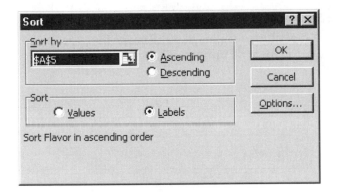

 NOTE: *You can sort labels in alphabetic order and you can sort values in numeric order.*

Grouping Data in PivotTables

To make your PivotTables easier to read and understand, or to provide different perspectives on the same data, you can create custom groupings of field items. Suppose that you really were working with a list like the one shown in Figure 14-1 and that you wanted to see how well flavors containing either vanilla or chocolate fared compared with the other flavors. You can create a special Vanilla-Chocolate group, and group the rest of the flavors together as Other.

To create a group, select all the flavors you want to place in the group. (If you press the CTRL key, you can select items that aren't adjacent to one another.) When you've selected all the items in the first group, click the Group button on the PivotTable toolbar.

Excel names the groups using the generic description Group1, and creates a new column with the heading Flavor2. (To rename a group or a heading, select it and type in a new name.)

You can further improve the table's appearance and readability by hiding the individual flavor names. You can accomplish that simply by double-clicking the names of the new groups you've created. Your PivotTable will look like the one in Figure 14-12. (In Figure 14-12, I've also dragged the Flavor heading off the table using the PivotTable Wizard Step 3 dialog box, and renamed the new heading "Flavor Groups.")

LEARN BY EXAMPLE
You can open the sample worksheet shown in Figure 14-12, Figure 14-12 (PivotTable with grouped data), from the companion CD if you want to follow along with the discussion here.

Grouping Numeric Items

If you have a long list of numeric items like ZIP codes that you want to group, you often don't have to select them all individually. You may be able to specify a range of

The Group 1 field item includes the Chocolate, Vanilla, and Vanilla-Fudge flavors.

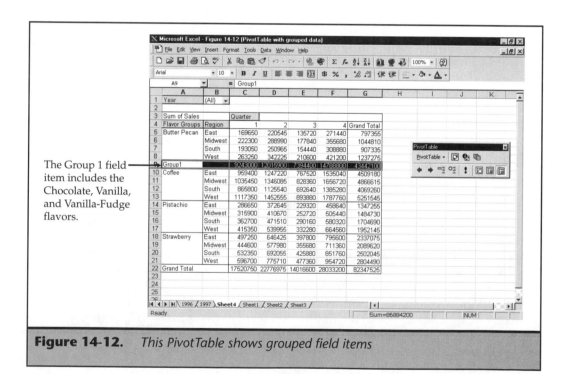

Figure 14-12. *This PivotTable shows grouped field items*

items to group. To group numeric items instead of labels, try the following method: Instead of selecting all the items you want to group, just select one. Next, click the Group button, so that Excel displays the Grouping dialog box, as shown below.

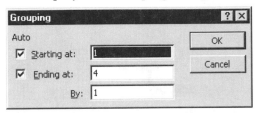

In the Grouping dialog box, enter the number of the first and last items you want to group together, and an interval between items. Click OK. If you select the Auto option, Excel will fill in the values for you.

> **TIP:** *To ungroup items and return the table to its former appearance, select the item you want to ungroup and click the Ungroup button on the PivotTable toolbar.*

Using PivotTable Functions

As mentioned earlier in the chapter, the PivotTable Wizard provides other functions besides summing that you can use to operate upon data field items. Those other functions include counting; averaging; and finding minimum and maximum values, standard deviations, variances, and products.

To specify which function you want the PivotTable to use, click the PivotTable Wizard button to display the PivotTable Wizard if it isn't already displayed, and then double-click the data heading button once you've moved it to the data area:

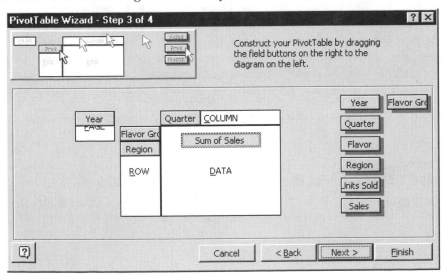

Once you do this, the PivotTable Wizard displays the PivotTable Field dialog box. To specify which calculation you want, select an entry from the Summarize by list box.

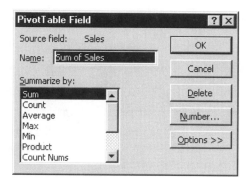

TIP: When you drag the heading of a text field into the data area, the Wizard automatically applies the COUNT function to that field.

Using PivotTables to Create Charts

Creating a chart from a PivotTable is easy. The first step is to select the worksheet ranges that hold the data series you want to plot. Because PivotTables often contain a great deal of information, you need to be careful as you select data, and try to limit the information you include on a single chart. Figure 14-13 shows how I selected rows 4 through 7 from the PivotTable in Figure 14-6 to plot the sales of butter pecan ice cream by region over each quarter. Because I did not want to include the subtotals for each year and the total for 1996 and 1997 in my chart, I had to hide columns G, L, and M.

Once you have selected the data you want to chart, just click the Chart Wizard button on the Standard toolbar, and follow the prompts. Charts created from PivotTables will reflect any changes subsequently made to the table. Figure 14-14 shows the chart I created based upon the data from Figure 14-13.

TIP: For more information about creating charts, refer to Chapter 13.

Importing Data into a PivotTable

If you want to create a PivotTable based on data in a database or other external application, you can select the External data source option in the first PivotTable Wizard dialog box.

Columns G, L, and M have been hidden by dragging the column sizing lines so that the width of the column equals zero.

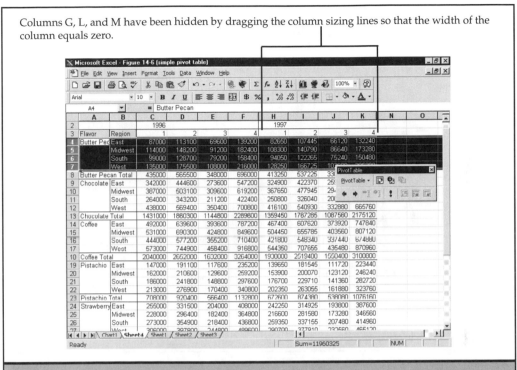

Figure 14-13. *Here's the data I selected to chart*

When you take on this task, use the Query Wizard to get the data you want. In step 2 of the PivotTable Wizard, click the Get Data button. This starts the Query Wizard. To use the Query Wizard to import a database, follow these steps:

1. In the first Query Wizard dialog box, make sure that the Use the Query Wizard to create/edit queries box is checked, as shown in Figure 14-15. Choose from the list of databases and queries on the Databases and Queries tabs. If the data source you want is not listed, or if no databases are defined, click New Data Source in the list box on the Databases tab and click OK.

1. If you create a new data source, the Query Wizard asks you to name the source and select the driver as shown in Figure 14-16. You might also need to install the driver if it hasn't already been installed. Click Connect when you are done.

2. Click Select and select the database or query you want to import.

3. Choose the columns or fields you want to include and click Next.

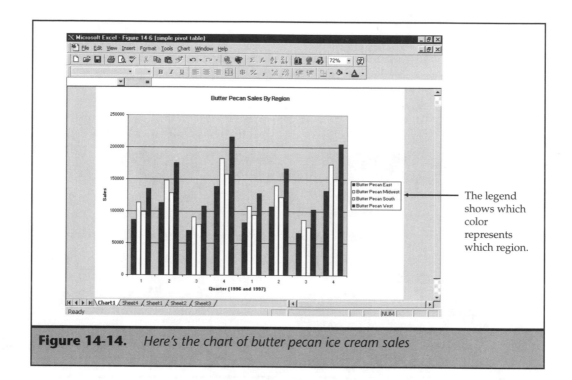

The legend shows which color represents which region.

Figure 14-14. *Here's the chart of butter pecan ice cream sales*

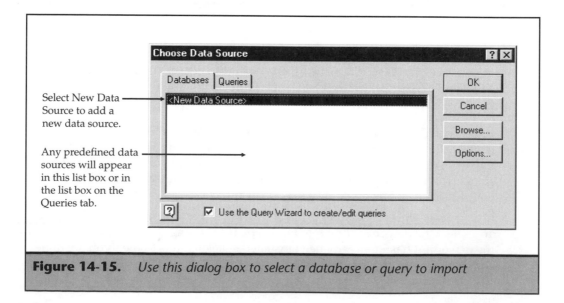

Select New Data Source to add a new data source.

Any predefined data sources will appear in this list box or in the list box on the Queries tab.

Figure 14-15. *Use this dialog box to select a database or query to import*

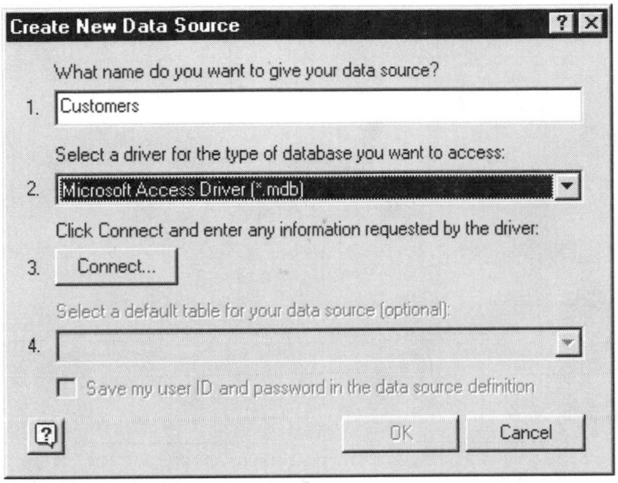

Figure 14-16. *Use the Create New Data Source dialog box to name your data source and select a driver for the database*

4. (Optional) In the last two dialog boxes of the Query Wizard, you can filter or sort the order of your fields. When you are done, click Finish to return to the PivotTable Wizard.

5. You complete the third and fourth PivotTable Wizard dialog boxes in the same way you create the PivotTable.

Should you ever wish to modify the query the table is based upon, you need to click the PivotTable Wizard button to restart the PivotTable Wizard and then use the second PivotTable Wizard dialog box to reopen the query and make any changes to the query.

Combining Worksheets in PivotTables

You can consolidate, or combine, data from separate Excel worksheets into a single PivotTable. Then, using the drop-down list of the page axis, you can still display separately data that originated in each worksheet. You can also use the same procedure to combine data from several ranges in the same worksheet.

To generate the consolidated table, select the Multiple consolidation ranges option in the first PivotTable Wizard dialog box, and click on Next. In the Step 2a dialog box, select the Create a Single Page Field For Me option (which is the default).

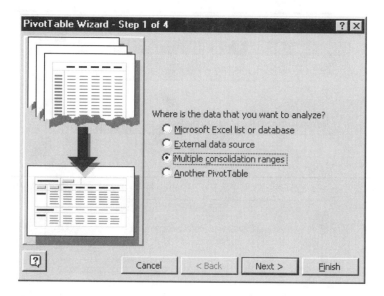

Then, click on Next. When Excel displays the Step 2b dialog box, select each of the ranges you want to consolidate and click Add. The ranges will appear in the All Ranges list box.

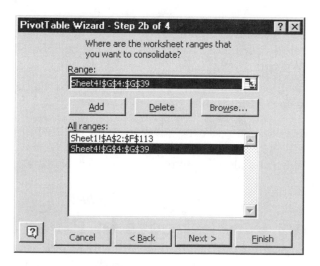

Click Next, and Excel displays the Step 3 dialog box, which will be familiar to you. Complete the rest of the PivotTable creation process as before.

The Complete Reference

Office
97

Chapter 15

Advanced Modeling Techniques

457

E xcel provides a rich set of advanced modeling tools that you can use to examine, manipulate, and even create data. These analytical tools, which are described in this chapter, aren't going to be tools you employ all the time. But they do dramatically enhance your ability to perform real-life, complicated modeling. With the Data menu's Table command and the Scenario Manager, for example, you quickly simulate the effect of changing input variables. With the Goal Seek command, you can work backward from the formula results you want to the input values you need. With the Data menu's Consolidate command, you get an easy yet powerful way to combine and mathematically manipulate data from multiple worksheet ranges. Finally, by using the Solver add-in, you can perform sophisticated optimization modeling.

 NOTE: Excel's PivotTable feature is described in Chapter 14.

Using Data Tables

Data tables let you show how a formula result changes as you supply different input values. While this may sound very simple, data tables are extremely useful for performing what-if analyses. For example, if you want to estimate the future value of a retirement savings account based on $2,000-a-year contributions and a 10 percent annual rate of return after 10, 20, and 30 years, data tables provide the easiest means for performing this analysis. (In this example, the input values that you supply are the different forecasting horizons of 10, 20, and 30 years, and the formula result is the future value of the retirement savings account.) If you want to experiment with the gross income delivered by selling a consulting service at $80 an hour, $100 an hour, and $120 an hour, data tables again provide the easiest means for performing this analysis. (In this example, the input values are the different hourly billing rates and the formula result is the gross income.)

Two varieties of data tables exist: one-variable data tables (which accept only one input variable but allow you to calculate more than one formula result) and two-variable data tables (which predictably accept two input variables but only allow you to calculate a single formula result). But that's enough background information about data tables. The best way to understand what they do and when you'll want to use them is to see exactly how they work and exactly how you build them.

Creating a One-Variable Data Table

To make this example more concrete, let's suppose that you really did want to estimate the future value of a $2,000-a-year retirement savings program based on a 10 percent and a 12 percent annual return. In this case, as shown in Figure 15-1, you might enter the input values into the range B4:B7. In constructing a one-variable data table, then, you first enter the input values you want to supply to a formula into a range of cells in a single column.

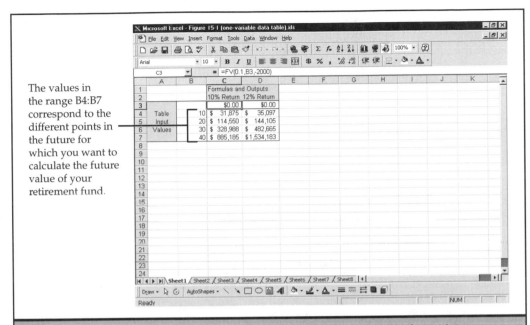

The values in the range B4:B7 correspond to the different points in the future for which you want to calculate the future value of your retirement fund.

Figure 15-1.   *This worksheet shows you how to organize a vertical, one-input-variable data table*

> **NOTE:**   *It turns out that you can organize one-variable data tables in two ways—either vertically, with the input values and formula results stored in columns, or horizontally, with the input values and formula results stored in rows. This chapter only shows you how to organize a vertical one-variable table here, however. Both tables do the same work for you. And it gets unnecessarily confusing to flip-flop table orientation.*

The only trick in building this one-variable worksheet is to make sure that there's an extra, empty row above the row in which you begin storing your input values. In other words, in Figure 15-1, row 3 of column B needs to be empty when you start building your data table.

LEARN BY EXAMPLE
You can open the example Excel workbook shown in Figure 15-1, Figure 15-1 (one-variable data table), *from the companion CD if you want to follow along with the discussion here.*

Your next step is to enter the formulas you want to calculate into the subsequent columns—except that you need to enter the formula or formulas into the empty row that's above the row in which the first input value appears. In Figure 15-1, for example, there are two formulas: one for cell C3 and one for cell D3. These are the formulas that Excel will repeatedly recalculate using each of the input values supplied by the range B4:B7. The formula in cell C3, =FV(0.1,B3,–2000), estimates the future value of the $2,000-a-year retirement savings using a 10 percent rate of return. The formula in cell D3, =FV(0.12,B3,–2000), estimates the future value of the $2,000-a-year retirement savings using a 12 percent rate of return.

Notice that both formulas refer to the empty cell B3. In effect, what a data table does is use this cell, called the *column input cell*, to temporarily store the input values from the range B4:B7. Excel will calculate the formula using each of the inputs. Excel then stores the formula results in the same rows as the input values producing the results.

Once you've got your input values and your formulas entered, follow these steps to create your data table:

1. Select the range that includes both the input values and the formulas. In Figure 15-1, for example, this range would be B3:D7.

2. Choose the Data menu's Table command.

3. When Excel displays the Table dialog box (see Figure 15-2), click the Column input cell text box and then click cell B3. This tells Excel that for your vertically organized one-variable table, your formulas use cell B3 as the input cell.

4. Click OK.

After you click OK, Excel places a special function-based formula based on the =TABLE() function into the ranges C4:C7 and D4:D7. This formula calculates the estimated future value of your retirement savings at various points in the future. For example, in cell C5, the formula returns $114,550, suggesting that you'll accumulate

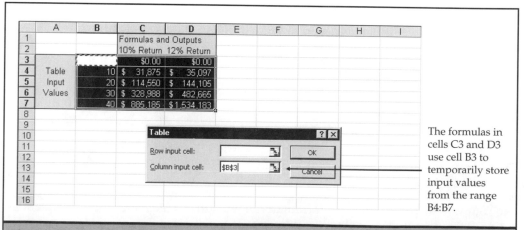

Figure 15-2.   *The Table dialog box asks for the cell your formulas reference and into which Excel should temporarily store information*

this amount if you save $2,000 a year for 20 years and earn 10 percent annually. And in cell D7, the formula returns $1,534,183, suggesting that you'll accumulate this amount if you save $2,000 a year for 40 years and earn 12 percent annually.

NOTE: *In a horizontally organized one-variable table, you don't use the Column input cell text box. You use the Row input cell text box.*

One-variable data tables are neat for a couple of reasons. One is that it turns out that the table only uses one =TABLE() formula for calculating its outputs. Each of the cells in the range C4:D7, for example, holds the same formula, ={TABLE(,B3)}. The benefit of this single-formula approach is probably obvious: the fewer formulas you use, the fewer formula errors your worksheets will contain.

The other neat thing about these data tables is that you can easily change the table's results simply by supplying new inputs. You can do this either by entering new values into the input value range (B4:B7 in the example) or by editing the formulas used to return the future value amounts. Figure 15-3 shows another version of the same data table shown in Figure 15-1 with only a few minor differences. Figure 15-3

The formulas in cells C3 and D3 use different interest rates.

The range B4:B7 holds different input values.

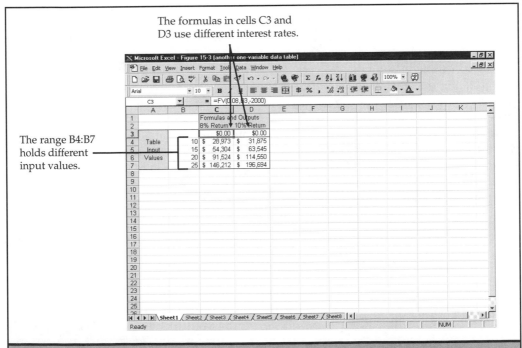

Figure 15-3.   *You can create this data table simply by updating the values in B4:B7 and the formulas in cells C3 and D3*

uses a different set of forecasting periods: 10 years, 15 years, 20 years, and 25 years. And Figure 15-3 uses different annual return percentages—8 percent and 10 percent—in the two future-value formulas in cells C3 and D3. (Figure 15-3 also, of course, shows different labels in cells C2 and D2 so the data table correctly describes the annual returns used in those two columns' calculations.)

LEARN BY EXAMPLE
You can open the example Excel workbook shown in Figure 15-3, Figure 15-3 (another one-variable data table), *from the companion CD if you want to see a completed version of the one-variable data table worksheet after changing the input values and editing the formulas.*

Creating a Two-Variable Data Table

Two-variable data tables allow you to experiment with how changing two values affects a single formula's result. In constructing a two-variable table, you enter one set of input values into a range of cells in a single column and another set of input values into a range of cells in a single row. To make this discussion more concrete, however, let's suppose that you want to further analyze the future value of retirement savings, but this time you want to experiment with the effect of varying both the annual contribution amount and the annual return, while keeping the number of years until retirement constant. In this case, as shown in Figure 15-4, you might enter the varying contribution amount input values into the range B3:B6. And you might enter the fluctuating annual return percentages into the range C2:E2.

You enter the formula that you want the data table to repeatedly recalculate into the cell that represents the intersection of the input value's row and column. In Figure 15-4, for example, that means the formula goes into cell B2. The tricky part of entering this formula, however, isn't simply clicking the right cell. Rather, it's the fact that the formula needs to reference two empty cells, which the Data menu's Table command will use as temporary storage locations for each of the input values you supply. In Figure 15-4, the formula =FV(A1,25,–B1) calculates the formula result shown in cell B2. Notice that cells A1 and B1 are both empty. These then are the temporary storage locations just mentioned.

LEARN BY EXAMPLE
You can open the example Excel workbook shown in Figure 15-4, Figure 15-4 (two-variable data table), *from the companion CD if you want to see a completed version of the two-variable data table worksheet discussed here.*

HEADSTART
The companion CD includes a headstart template (retire.xls) that you can use for retirement savings calculations. The companion CD also includes a headstart template (savings.xls) that you can use for making general savings calculations.

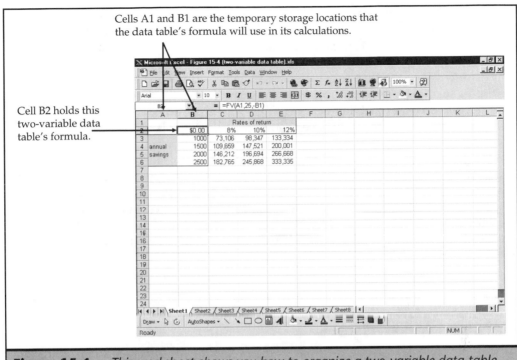

Cells A1 and B1 are the temporary storage locations that the data table's formula will use in its calculations.

Cell B2 holds this two-variable data table's formula.

Figure 15-4. *This worksheet shows you how to organize a two-variable data table*

Once you enter the input values and the formula, you're ready to build the data table. To do this, follow these steps:

1. Select the range that includes both sets of the input values and the formula. In Figure 15-4, for example, you would select the range B2:E6.

2. Choose the Data menu's Table command.

3. When Excel displays the Table dialog box, click the Row input cell text box and then click the cell that you want Excel to use for temporarily storing the input values from the range C2:E2. (In Figure 15-4, you would click cell A1.)

4. Click the Column input cell text box and then click the cell that you want Excel to use for temporarily storing the input values from the range B3:B6. (In Figure 15-4, you would click cell B1.)

5. Click OK.

After you click OK, Excel places the special function-based formula based on the =TABLE() function into the range C3:E6. This formula calculates the estimated future value of your retirement savings after 25 years based on varying contribution amounts and different annual returns. For example, in cell C4, the formula returns 109,659, suggesting that you'll accumulate this amount if you save $1,500 a year and earn 8 percent annually. In cell D6, the formula returns 245,868, suggesting that you'll accumulate this amount if you save $2,500 a year and earn 10 percent annually.

The only trick to using a two-variable data table is that you need to be sure, in the process of supplying the input values to the formula that the =TABLE() function uses in its calculations, that you don't get the input values mixed up. For example, in Figure 15-4, the real formula that keeps getting recalculated is =FV(A1,25,–B1). According to the =FV() function, this means cell A1 is supposed to supply the annual return percentage and that cell B1 is supposed to supply the annual savings amount. (This annual savings amount gets included as a negative amount because it represents a cash outflow.) When you choose the Data menu's Table command to display the Table dialog box, therefore, you need to enter **$A$1** into the Row input cell text box and **$B$1** into the Column input cell text box. If you get your Row input cell text box and Column input cell text box entries mixed up and criss-crossed, your formula won't return the correct results.

Using Goal Seek for Simple What-If Analysis

While typically you calculate formulas by supplying the input values and then asking Excel to calculate the formula's result, or output, you can work the other way. In other words, you can supply a formula, the result you want it to return, and then all of the input values except for the one Excel calculates for you. In effect then, Excel works backward from the calculation result to get one of your inputs.

To illustrate how Excel does this, suppose that you had calculated the monthly payment required for a home you want to purchase, as shown in Figure 15-5. As this simple worksheet shows, with a $100,000 loan balance, an 8 percent annual interest rate, and 360 months (30 years) of payments, your monthly principal and interest payment equals–$733.76. (The loan payment amount is a negative value because you'll pay out the money.)

TIP: Note that the formula in cell B5 divides the annual interest rate in cell B2 by 12 to convert it to a monthly interest rate so you can calculate your monthly payment.

LEARN BY EXAMPLE

EXAMPLES

You can open the example Excel workbook shown in Figure 15-5, Figure 15-5 (mortgage payment analysis), from the companion CD if you want to see a completed version of the worksheet described here.

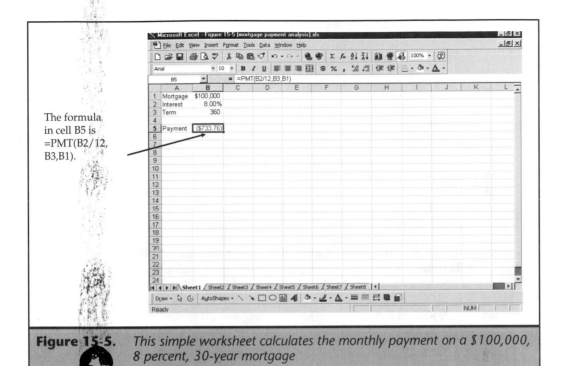

The formula in cell B5 is =PMT(B2/12, B3,B1).

Figure 15-5. *This simple worksheet calculates the monthly payment on a $100,000, 8 percent, 30-year mortgage*

Now, for the sake of our illustration, assume that the largest monthly principal and interest payment you can possibly afford is $700. Rather than build new formulas that, for example, calculate the interest rate needed for a $700 payment, you can tell Excel to work backward by using the Tools menu's Goal Seek command.

HEADSTART

The companion CD includes a headstart template (homebuy.xls) that you can use for making mortgage qualification and home affordability calculations.

TEMPLATES

Here's how this would work in the case of the $700 mortgage payment example we're talking about here:

1. Click the cell with the formula that you want to return a specified result. (In Figure 15-5, for example, you would click B5.)

2. Choose the Tools menu's Goal Seek command. Excel displays the Goal Seek dialog box. Note that Excel enters an absolute address for the cell with the formula into the Set cell text box.

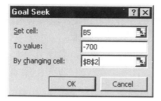

3. Specify the value you want the formula to return using the To value text box. For this example, the value in the To value text box is –700 because you want your monthly principal and interest payment to equal $700. (Notice that the payment amount, because it's a cash outflow—an amount you pay out—needs to be specified as a negative value.)

4. Click the By changing cell text box.

5. Click the cell that holds the input value you want Excel to adjust so the formula returns the result you want. If you want to calculate which interest rate is necessary in order for you to enjoy a $700 mortgage payment on a 30-year, $100,000 mortgage, simply click cell B2. Excel enters the absolute address for the cell, $B$2, into the By changing cell text box.

6. Click OK. Excel begins its calculations. If, by working backward, it can find an input value that causes the formula to return the specified result, it replaces the input value and it displays a dialog box that tells you it has done so.

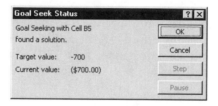

If you click OK, Excel updates the worksheet so the formula returns the result you want. (If you don't see any changes, make sure that you have specified two decimal places when applying the number formatting.)

	A	B	C	D
1	Mortgage	$100,000		
2	Interest	7.51%		
3	Term	360		
4				
5	Payment	($700.00)		
6				
7				
8				

Using the Scenario Manager

As mentioned in the first part of this chapter, Excel's data tables let you experiment with the effect of changing one or two variables at a time. That's handy, to be sure. But, in reality, you're much more likely to consider changes that involve many more variables at a time. And this modeling reality is what the Scenario Manager addresses. Using the Scenario Manager, you can change up to 32 variables at a time. You can also store (and easily retrieve) sets of input values.

While the Scenario Manager isn't difficult to use, you'll find it much easier to follow the discussion here with a concrete example. Let's suppose, for the sake of illustration, that you're working with a worksheet like the one shown in Figure 15-6.

TIP: To name the cells in the range B1:B3, select the range A1:B3, choose the Insert menu's Name, Create command, and then click OK. To name cell B5, select the range A5:B5, choose the Insert menu's Name, Create command, and then click OK again.

EXCEL

Cell B5 uses the formula =PMT(B2/12,B3,B1) to calculate the mortgage payment.

Each of the cells holding values is named.

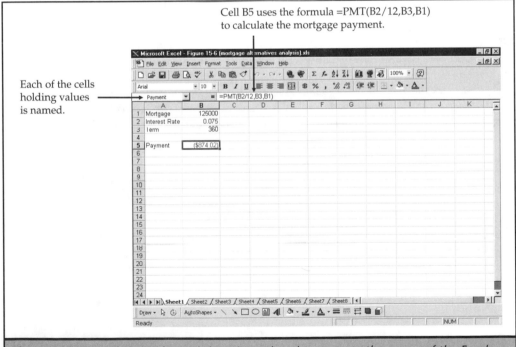

Figure 15-6.   *This simple worksheet is used to demonstrate the power of the Excel Scenario Manager*

LEARN BY EXAMPLE
You can open the example Excel workbook shown in Figure 15-6, Figure 15-6
(mortgage alternatives analysis), *from the companion CD if you want to see a
completed version of the worksheet described here.*

Creating a Scenario

Once you have a worksheet that you want to use in your what-if analysis, you're
ready to begin creating your scenarios. To do this, follow these steps:

1. Choose the Tools menu's Scenarios command.

2. When Excel displays the Scenarios dialog box, click the Add command button.

3. When Excel displays the Add Scenario dialog box, shown in Figure 15-7, name
   or describe the scenario using the Scenario name text box.

4. Click the Changing cells text box and then, using the mouse, select each of
   the cells or ranges into which you want the Scenario Manager to place values.
   In Figure 15-7, for example, you would select the range B1:B3. Remember that
   you
   can select multiple ranges or cells by holding down the CTRL key as you
   click and drag.

*NOTE: You can protect scenarios (in a manner very much like you protect cells and
sheets) so other users can't change or modify the scenario. To protect or hide a scenario,
first mark the Prevent changes and Hide check boxes that appear at the bottom of the Add
Scenario and Edit Scenario dialog boxes. Then to turn on sheet protection, you choose the
Tools menu's Protection command and the Protection submenu's Protect Sheet command.*

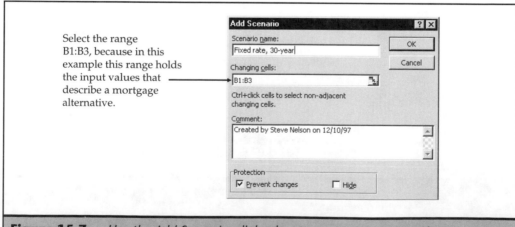

Figure 15-7. *Use the Add Scenarios dialog box to create a new scenario*

5. After you identify the cells the Scenario Manager can change, click OK.

6. When the Scenario Manager next displays the Scenario Values dialog box (see Figure 15-8), use this dialog box to provide the values you want Scenario Manager to place into the cells. To enter a value, click the text box and enter the value. Notice in Figure 15-8 that the Scenario Manager uses the cell names to identify the cells. If you don't name the cells before you add the scenario, Scenario Manager just uses the cell addresses—which makes it a lot harder to keep your input values straight.

7. Click OK. Excel adds your scenario to its list of scenarios and returns you to the Scenario Manager dialog box (see Figure 15-9). It now lists your new scenario.

If you want to add additional scenarios, you repeat the process described in the preceding step-by-step instructions: you can click the Scenario Manager's Add button and complete the dialog boxes that Excel displays. Figure 15-9, by the way, shows several scenarios added in just this way.

Working with Scenarios

To use a scenario, display the Scenario Manager dialog box and then double-click the scenario you want. (See Figure 15-9.) That's it. Excel then enters the scenario's values into the input cells you specified. To use another scenario, repeat the process. Note that you can undo the changes that the Scenario Manager makes: simply click the Standard toolbar's Undo button.

WARNING: *When the Scenario Manager enters input values into the specified cells, it replaces those cell's current contents. This means that it's possible to inadvertently lose data if you're not careful. For example, the Scenario Manager can replace a formula with a constant value.*

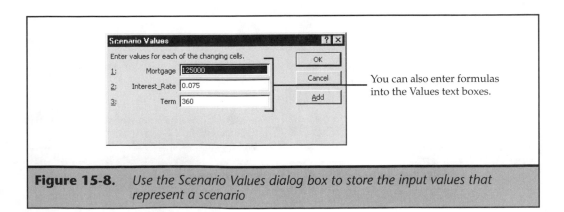

Figure 15-8. *Use the Scenario Values dialog box to store the input values that represent a scenario*

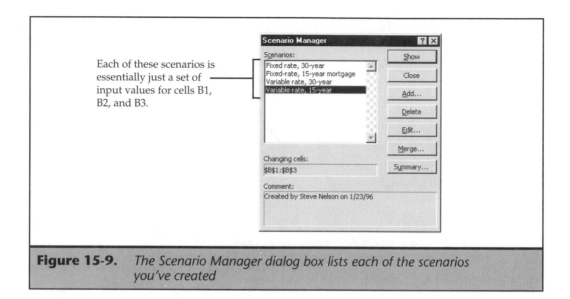

Each of these scenarios is essentially just a set of input values for cells B1, B2, and B3.

Figure 15-9. *The Scenario Manager dialog box lists each of the scenarios you've created*

To prepare a report that summarizes all of your scenarios, display the Scenario Manager dialog box and then click the Summary button. Excel displays the Scenario Summary dialog box that asks whether you want to prepare a Scenario Summary or a Scenario PivotTable. (See Figure 15-10.) Click the button that corresponds to your choice. Next, click the Result cells text box and then select, by clicking and dragging, the cells you want to view on the summary report. When you finish with this, click OK and Excel adds a new sheet to the worksheet with the report you chose. Figure 15-11, for example, shows a summary report. It describes each of the scenarios from Figure 15-9 and can be expanded or collapsed to either show or hide detail.

NOTE: For more information about Excel's PivotTables, refer to Chapter 14.

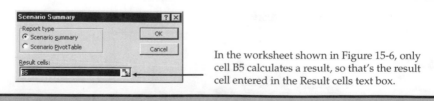

In the worksheet shown in Figure 15-6, only cell B5 calculates a result, so that's the result cell entered in the Result cells text box.

Figure 15-10. *The Scenario Summary dialog box asks how you want Excel to prepare a report that describes the scenarios you've created*

Each column summarizes a scenario.

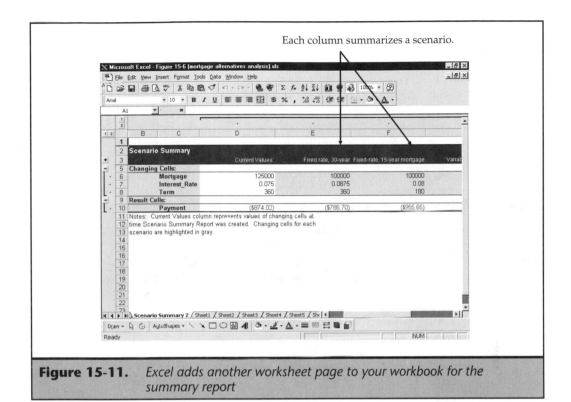

Figure 15-11. *Excel adds another worksheet page to your workbook for the summary report*

Merging Scenarios from Other Sheets and Workbooks

Scenarios are stored with specific worksheets and, therefore, get stored with Excel workbooks. You can retrieve scenarios you or someone else has created in another worksheet or workbook, however, by opening the workbook and then using the Scenario Manager's Merge button. When you click this button, Excel displays a dialog box that asks for the name of the workbook and the name of the worksheet from which you want to view and possibly retrieve scenarios, as shown in the following illustration:

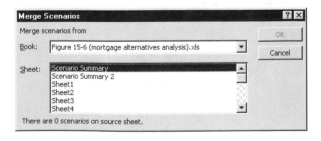

As you can probably guess, you use the Book list box to select the workbook with the scenarios you want and you use the Sheet list box to select the actual scenario. After you provide this information, click OK.

This is probably obvious, but to actually use a scenario you retrieve from some other sheet or worksheet, plopping the scenario's input values into the specified cells must make sense. What this usually means, then, is that each of the sheets and each of the workbooks should look and work the same way. If you've used cell names to refer to cells, for example, the scenarios should all use the same names and reference the same cell addresses.

Using the Data Consolidate Command

The Data menu's Consolidate command lets you aggregate data so you can analyze the consolidated data. For example, if you built individual budgets by company department, you might choose to use the Data menu's Consolidate command to calculate the total amounts budgeted for all departments (wages, travel and entertainment, office supplies, and so on) or to calculate the average amount budgeted for, say, department office supplies.

Not surprisingly, your first step in consolidating data is to create the workbook or workbooks with the data you will later consolidate. Figure 15-12 shows the first worksheet, Administration, of such an example workbook. You can't tell it from Figure 15-12, but for this workbook, both the second and third worksheet pages, Research and Marketing, mirror the first. They use a range of the exact same dimensions to store the budget numbers, and they use the same labels to describe the contents of rows and columns. The only real difference is that the sheet names and data are different.

Once you set up a workbook with the ranges you want to consolidate and then collect the data in those ranges, you're ready to use the Data menu's Consolidate command. To do this, follow these steps:

1. Select the top left corner of the worksheet range into which you want to place the consolidated data. (You'll often want to set up this consolidation range on a separate worksheet.)

2. Choose the Data Consolidate command. Excel displays the Consolidate dialog box, as shown in Figure 15-13.

EXAMPLES

LEARN BY EXAMPLE
You can open the example Excel workbook shown in Figure 15-12, Figure 15-12 (pre-consolidation), from the companion CD if you want to experiment with the Data menu's Consolidate command but don't want to build the workbook described here.

The second and third worksheet pages, Research and Marketing, mirror the first worksheet page, Administration.

Figure 15-12.   *This chapter uses this workbook to illustrate how data consolidation works*

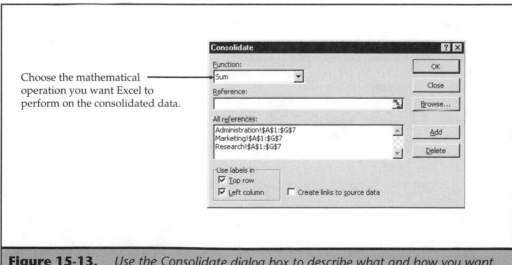

Choose the mathematical operation you want Excel to perform on the consolidated data.

Figure 15-13.   *Use the Consolidate dialog box to describe what and how you want Excel to consolidate*

3. When Excel displays the Consolidate dialog box, activate the Function drop-down list box and choose the mathematical operation you want Excel to perform on the consolidated data. The table that follows describes these operations.

Function	What It Does
Sum	Sums the values in the consolidation ranges
Count	Counts the number of cells that aren't empty
Average	Calculates the average of the values
Max	Finds the largest value in each cell of the consolidation ranges
Min	Finds the smallest value in each cell of the consolidation ranges
Product	Multiplies the values in the consolidation ranges
CountNums	Counts the number of cells that hold values
StdDev	Calculates the sample standard deviation of the values
StdDevP	Calculates the population standard deviation of the values
Var	Calculates the sample variance of the values
VarP	Calculates the population variance of the values

4. To identify the worksheet ranges that you want to consolidate, click the Reference text box. Then select the first worksheet range you want to consolidate (by clicking and dragging) and click the Add button. Select the second and any subsequent worksheet ranges you want to consolidate in the same manner and continue this process until you identify each of the worksheet ranges you want to consolidate. As you do this, Excel creates a range of addresses for each of the worksheet ranges you select and add and lists them in the All references box at the bottom of the Consolidate dialog box. (See Figure 15-13.)

NOTE: *You can consolidate data from workbooks that aren't open, too. To do this, click the Browse button to display a Browse dialog box, which works like the regular Open dialog box that Excel displays when you choose the File Open command. When you find the workbook file that you want to reference using the Browse dialog box, click OK. Excel writes the first part of the linking formula needed to reference the workbook. Note, however, that you will need to supply the worksheet name and range.*

5. After you identify the ranges, mark the Use labels in Top row and the Use labels in Left column check boxes, which the Consolidate dialog box also

provides, to tell Excel to retrieve the labels that describe the values (if you want to do this).

6. If you want Excel to update the information shown in the consolidation range any time data in the source worksheet ranges change, mark the Create links to source data check box. This tells Excel to create linking formulas that calculate the values for the consolidation range rather than simply plopping constant values into this range. It also tells Excel to create the consolidation as an outline so you can show or hide item detail.

7. When you finish describing how and what you want Excel to consolidate, click OK. Excel consolidates the data in the ranges you specified. Figure 15-14, for example, shows the simple budgeting worksheet from Figure 15-12. It shows the company-wide budget amounts by summarizing the individual budgets for the three departments, Administrative, Marketing, and Research.

LEARN BY EXAMPLE

You can open the example Excel workbook shown in Figure 15-14, Figure 15-14 (post-consolidation), *from the companion CD if you want to see a consolidated workbook.*

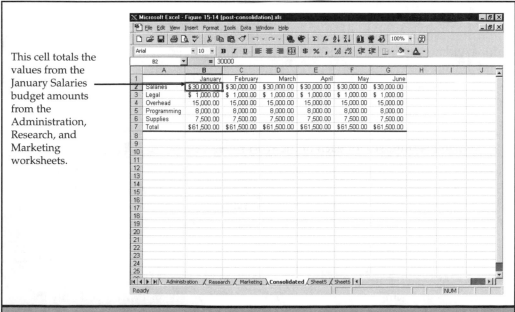

This cell totals the values from the January Salaries budget amounts from the Administration, Research, and Marketing worksheets.

Figure 15-14. *This worksheet shows the result of the consolidation*

Consolidating by Position vs. Consolidating by Category

It turns out that you can actually have Excel consolidate data in two ways: by position or by category. By position just means that you work with ranges that are all exactly the same size. By category means that you use the same labels to identify the rows and columns. The workbook that you see in Figure 15-12 (and again in 15-14) can be consolidated either by position or by category because the source ranges are all the same size and because the labels that identify the contents of the worksheets' rows and columns are identical. But you should know that consolidating by category is usually preferable.

Category-based consolidation is more powerful because it lets you consolidate sets of data that aren't identical. In the case of the workbook shown in Figure 15-12, for example, if you budgeted a particular expense—say, legal fees—only for the Administration department and then budgeted another expense—say, programming—only for the Research department, you could still consolidate the department budgets. The consolidated data would show company-wide budgeted expenses for all of the departments: both those expenses that are common across all your departments and those expenses that are unique to departments.

The trick in category-based consolidation is to use the exact same labels. If you use "Salaries" to describe the salaries expense in one department, for example, and then use "Salaries & Wages" to describe the salaries expense in another department, you'll see both expenses in the consolidated data range: "Salaries" and "Salaries & Wages."

Optimization Modeling with Solver

Optimization modeling is a sophisticated tool. What it does, in brief, is optimize a certain function subject to specified constraints. Unfortunately, the mechanics of optimization modeling are daunting to solve manually. And that's where Excel comes in: using Excel, you can rather easily and very quickly solve optimization modeling problems.

Understanding Optimization Modeling

Optimization modeling can seem a little confusing if you hear it discussed only in abstract terms. So, let's suppose you own and operate a 5,000-acre farm in eastern Oregon. On your farm, let's pretend, you do just two things: you raise cattle and you grow wheat. One of your basic business dilemmas, then, would be how to divide your resources between cattle and wheat in a way that maximizes your farming profits. Optimization modeling helps you make just such decisions.

Optimization modeling works like this. Your first step is to create what's called an objective function. This is simply the formula that calculates some value you want to optimize either by maximizing or minimizing the formula's calculation result. But let's put this in context of the imaginary farm you now own and operate. If you make $400 for each head of cattle you raise and $2.20 for each bushel of wheat you grow, your profits can be described with the following formula:

=400*Cattle+2.2*Wheat

So this formula is the objective function. And what you want to do, of course, is maximize your profits by raising as many head of cattle and by growing as many bushels of wheat as you can.

But, of course, there are limits to the number of cattle you can raise and the bushels of wheat you can grow. Optimization modeling incorporates these limits by way of constraints, which are simply formulas that describe the limits. For example, in the case of your farm, you would be limited by your farm's acreage. If each head of cattle requires ten acres of land and each bushel of wheat requires at least 1/50 of an acre, ten times the number of cattle and 1/50 times the number of bushels of wheat must be less than or equal to the number of acres you farm. You can describe this constraint using the following formula:

10*Cattle+1/50*Wheat<=5000

Similarly, if you're limited to 5,000,000 gallons of water a year and each cow requires 1,500 gallons of water of year while each bushel of wheat requires 25 gallons of water, the water limit is another constraint. It can be quantified this way:

+1500*Cattle+25*Wheat<=5000000

And just for fun, let's say you have a couple of other constraints, too. For example, it may be that you must grow at least 50 head of cattle for your own needs—perhaps you have a big barbecue every Labor Day. And maybe you need to grow at least 1,000 bushels of wheat because you've contracted to supply that much to a local bakery. These limits would set other constraints on the objective function, as quantified this way:

+Cattle>=50

+Wheat>=1000

To summarize, what you really want to do is make as much money farming as you possibly can, except you can't farm more than 5,000 acres, you can't use more than 5,000,000 gallons of water, and you have to raise at least 50 head of cattle and grow at least 1,000 bushels of wheat.

You probably see the problem. Short of trial-and-error experimentation, there's no easy way to figure out the number of cattle you should raise and the bushels of wheat you should grow to make the maximum amount of profit. And that's where Solver comes in. By creating a formula that describes the objective function and formulas that quantify the constraints, Solver will tell you how to optimize the objective function. Or, restated in terms of your farm, it will tell you exactly how many cattle to raise and how much wheat to grow.

Using Solver

Once you understand the sorts of optimization modeling problems that Solver addresses, you'll often find it surprisingly easy to use Solver in modeling. You set up a worksheet that describes the particular optimization modeling problem you want to solve. Next, you describe to Solver how it finds the information it needs to begin its calculations. Finally, you review Solver's calculation results and, optionally, Solver's special reports.

Creating the Solver Worksheet

To use the Solver tool, your first step is to create a worksheet that names the variables of your objective function, describes the objective function, and then describes the constraints. Figure 15-15 shows a worksheet that does these three things for the example farming problem described in the preceding section. To review, that problem's objective function, which simply says your profits equal $400 times the head of cattle you raise and $2.20 times the bushels of wheat you grow, is

Profits=$400*Cattle+$2.2*Wheat

The following constraints, however, limit this objective function:

10 acres * Cattle + 1/50 acre * Wheat <= 5000 acres

1500 gallons * Cattle + 25 gallons * Wheat <= 5000000 gallons

Cattle >= 50

Wheat >= 1000

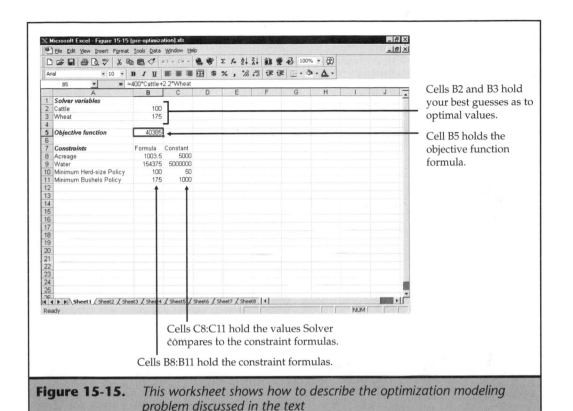

Cells B2 and B3 hold your best guesses as to optimal values.

Cell B5 holds the objective function formula.

Cells C8:C11 hold the values Solver compares to the constraint formulas.

Cells B8:B11 hold the constraint formulas.

Figure 15-15.   *This worksheet shows how to describe the optimization modeling problem discussed in the text*

NOTE: *Constraint formulas can be a little difficult to interpret the first time you encounter them, so a quick description is probably in order. The first constraint says that you can't farm more than 5,000 acres since that's the size of your farm. The second constraint says you can't use more than 5,000,000 gallons of water. The third constraint says you need to raise at least 50 head of cattle. And the fourth constraint says you need to grow at least 1,000 bushels of wheat.*

You'll need a worksheet like the one shown in Figure 15-15 to provide the information that the Solver needs. If you want to build the worksheet yourself, enter the labels shown in the range A1:A11. Next, enter the values shown in cells B2 and B3. (To start, it really doesn't matter which values you enter here. Typically, however, these represent your best guesses as to which modeling variable values are optimal.) Next, name cell B2 *Cattle* and cell B3 *Wheat*.

TIP: The easiest way to name the cells is to select the range A2:B3, choose the Insert, Name, Create command and then click OK.

To describe the objective function, enter the formula **=400*Cattle+2.2*Wheat** into cell B5. Excel's Solver will look for the modeling variable values that optimize—in this case, maximize—the calculation result this formula returns.

LEARN BY EXAMPLE
You can open the example Excel workbook shown in Figure 15-15, Figure 15-15 (pre-optimization), from the companion CD if you want to perform optimization modeling without actually constructing the workbook shown in Figure 15-15 yourself.

Your next step is to describe the constraints that limit the number of cattle you raise and the amount of wheat you grow. To describe the acreage constraint, for example, enter the following formula into cell B8:

=10*Cattle+1/50*Wheat

Then enter the number of acres, 5000, into cell C8.

To describe the formula part of the water constraint, enter the following formula into cell B9:

=1500*Cattle+25*Wheat

Then enter the gallons of water, 5000000, into cell C9.

To describe the formula part of the minimum-herd-size constraint, enter the following formula in cell B10:

=Cattle

Then enter the minimum head of cattle you've decided you must raise, 50, in cell C10.

Finally, to describe the formula part of the minimum number of bushels of wheat you need to raise, enter the following formula into cell B11:

=Wheat

Then enter the minimum number of bushels of wheat you've promised the local brewery, 1000, in cell C11.

Optimizing the Objective Function

After you create a worksheet that describes the linear programming problem you want to solve, you're ready to use Solver to optimize the objective function. To do this, follow these steps:

1. Choose the Tools menu's Solver command so that Excel displays the Solver Parameters dialog box (shown in Figure 15-16).

NOTE: *Solver is an add-in, which means to use it, it needs to be installed. If your Tools menu doesn't show the Solver command, choose the Tools Add-Ins command. When Excel displays the Add-Ins dialog box, mark the Solver Add-In entry, which appears in the Available Add-Ins box. Then click OK.*

2. To identify which cell holds the objective function, click the Set Target Cell box and then click the worksheet cell holding your objective function. In the case of the worksheet shown in Figure 15-15, for example, you would click cell B5 because it holds the objective function formula that calculates your farming profits.

3. Describe how Solver optimizes the objective function using the Equal To option buttons. In the case of a profit function, for example, you would click the Max button since you want to maximize your profits. If the objective function instead described costs you wanted to minimize, you would mark the Min button. And if your objective function needs to return a specific value, mark the Value of button and then enter the value using the Value of box.

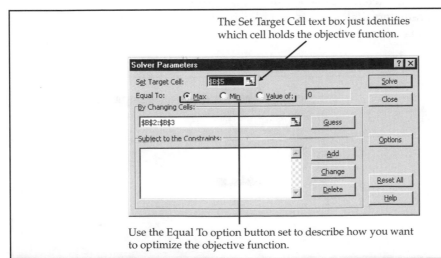

The Set Target Cell text box just identifies which cell holds the objective function.

Use the Equal To option button set to describe how you want to optimize the objective function.

Figure 15-16. *Use the Solver Parameters dialog box to tell Solver how you arranged your worksheet information and to provide the additional information needed to fully describe the constraints*

4. Identify the cells Solver should adjust to optimize the objective function. (In the discussion that follows, these are called the *adjustable cells*.) In the case of the Cattle-versus-wheat problem described in this chapter, that means you need to identify which adjustable cell holds the number of cattle you're supposed to be raising and which adjustable cell holds the bushels of wheat you're supposed to be growing. To do this, click the By Changing Cells text box and click each of the adjustable cells. (In Figure 15-15, for example, you would click cells B2 and B3.)

5. Click the Add button to begin identifying the constraints.

6. When Excel displays the Add Constraint dialog box (shown here), first click the Cell Reference box and then click the cell holding the formula part of a constraint. Next, use the Constraint drop-down list box to select the comparison operator that compares the formula to the constant value. Finally, click the Constraint box and then the cell that provides the constant value. To add the other three constraints, repeat steps 5 and 6.

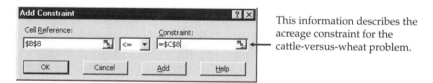

This information describes the acreage constraint for the cattle-versus-wheat problem.

7. When you finish describing the constraints, click OK. Excel returns you to the Solver Parameters dialog box shown in Figure 15-17. (In Figure 15-17, the Solver Parameters dialog box is completely filled out to solve the cattle-versus-wheat problem.)

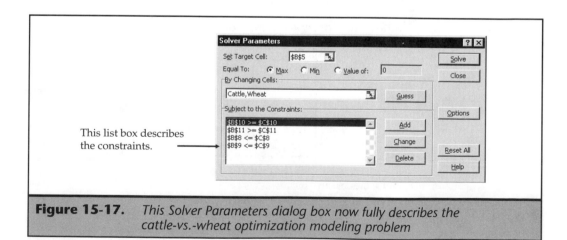

This list box describes the constraints.

Figure 15-17.   *This Solver Parameters dialog box now fully describes the cattle-vs.-wheat optimization modeling problem*

NOTE: If you make a mistake describing a constraint, you can remove the constraint by selecting it in the Solver Parameters dialog box and then clicking the Delete button. You can also edit the constraint by selecting it in the Solver Parameters dialog box and then clicking the Change button. When Excel displays the Change Constraint dialog box, you use it to modify the constraint. The Change Constraint dialog box, by the way, works like the Add Constraint dialog box. Finally, if you want to start over from scratch and erase all of your inputs—the Target Cell and By Changing Cells settings, and the constraints—click the Reset All button.

EXCEL

Using Integer Constraints

It may be that as another constraint you want the objective function to return integers (whole numbers) to the adjustable cells. In the case of the cattle-versus-wheat problem, for example, you might want to verify that Solver returns the optimal number of cattle and the optimal bushels of wheat as integer values. To make this specification, you create an integer constraint using "int" as the constraint operator and "integer" as the constraint formula result.

While integer constraints make theoretical sense in many cases, they also make it much more difficult for Solver to finish its calculations. For this reason, you may choose to accept noninteger values in the adjustable cells—even though they don't make practical sense. In the case of the cattle-versus-wheat problem, for example, you might happily accept a noninteger number of cattle as part of your optimal solution, and then round up or down to the next, nearest integer.

8. After you specify your constraints, click Solve. Excel attempts to optimize the objective function. If it can, it displays the Solver Results dialog box shown here. It gives you the option of replacing the original values in the adjustable cells with the optimal values that Excel calculates. Or you can restore the original values you entered into the adjustable cells.

Click this button to have Solver replace the current contents of the adjustable cells.

Click this button to create a scenario for the optimal values.

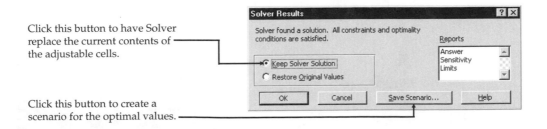

9. When you click OK, Solver replaces the values you originally used as the starting variable values.

Figure 15-18 shows the solution to the cattle-versus-wheat problem. Cell B2 holds the value 113.6364, indicating the optimal number of cattle to raise is either 113 or 114. Cell B3 holds the value 193181.9, indicating that the optimal bushels of wheat to raise is roughly 193,182. If you really were a farmer, you would presumably convert this bushels-of-wheat figure into an acres-planted-in-wheat figure. This means that you would plant 3,864 acres of wheat since, according to our worksheet model, you get 50 bushels of wheat an acre.

EXAMPLES

LEARN BY EXAMPLE
You can open the example Excel workbook shown in Figure 15-18, Figure 15-18 (post-optimization), *from the companion CD if you want to see an optimized workbook.*

Using Solver's Reports

Knowing which combination of adjustable cell values causes your objective function to return its optimal value is interesting. But if you begin to use the Solver tool, you'll quickly find yourself interested in digging deeper into the details of the optimal solution. You may want to know by how much Solver changed the adjustable cell

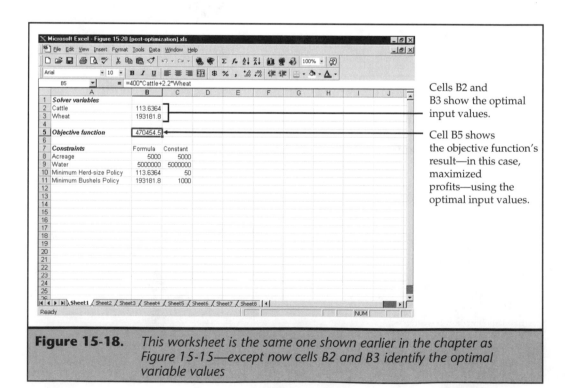

Figure 15-18. *This worksheet is the same one shown earlier in the chapter as Figure 15-15—except now cells B2 and B3 identify the optimal variable values*

values you started with, for example. You may want to know the extent to which Solver improved the result that your objective function originally returned. And you'll certainly want to know which constraints limit, or bind, your objective function.

To gain these insights, you can tell Solver to prepare special reports that provide this information. To do this, use the Solver Results dialog box shown previously. Simply click the reports you want in the Reports box. When you click OK to close the Solver Results dialog box, Excel not only updates the values in the adjustable cells, it also adds new worksheet pages to your workbook. Figure 15-19 shows the Answer Report, which is probably the most useful report that Solver prepares.

At the top of the Answer Report, for example, Solver shows the values the target cell returned before and after Solver optimized the objective function. If the initial values in the adjustable cells reflect your plans before running Solver, this change-in-the-target-value information lets you see what improvement, if any, Solver has been able to suggest. Solver also reports on how the values in the adjustable cells changed after you used Solver to optimize the function.

You can tell by how much Solver improved your objective function by comparing cells D8 and E8.

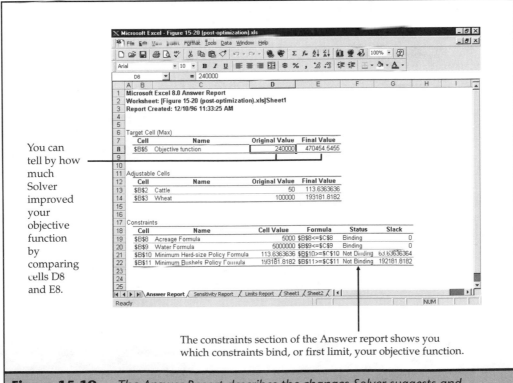

The constraints section of the Answer report shows you which constraints bind, or first limit, your objective function.

Figure 15-19. *The Answer Report describes the changes Solver suggests and identifies which constraints limit further improvement in the objective function*

At the bottom of the Answer Report, Solver identifies those that have no effect on the objective function as "nonbinding" and those that have an effect as "binding." In Figure 15-19, for example, both the acreage and the water constraints limit the objective function. (What this means, practically speaking, is that if you wanted in this example to increase your profits, you would need both more water and more land first.)

Figure 15-20 shows another of Solver's reports, the Sensitivity Report. For the adjustable cells, it shows the final, optimal values and something called the *reduced gradient*. The reduced gradient shows you how much the objective function's result would change if the adjustable cell's value increased by one. (In the cattle-versus-wheat problem, for example, it shows how much your farming profit increase if you raise one more cow or grow one more bushel of wheat.) For the constraints, the Sensitivity Report shows the final values of the constraint formulas and something

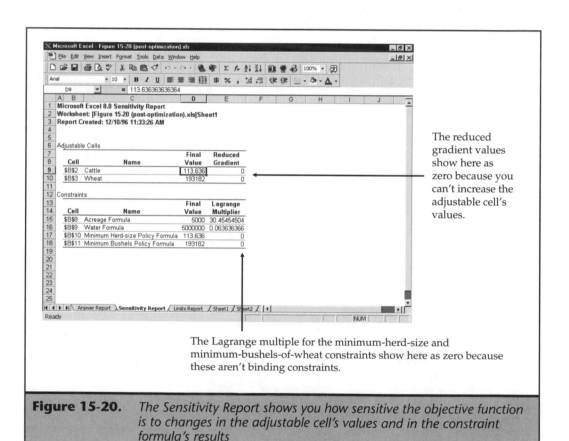

The reduced gradient values show here as zero because you can't increase the adjustable cell's values.

The Lagrange multiple for the minimum-herd-size and minimum-bushels-of-wheat constraints show here as zero because these aren't binding constraints.

Figure 15-20.   *The Sensitivity Report shows you how sensitive the objective function is to changes in the adjustable cell's values and in the constraint formula's results*

called the *Lagrange multiple*. The Lagrange multiple shows you how much the objective function's result would change if the constraint formula's result increased by one. (In the cattle-versus-wheat problem, for example, it shows how much your farming profit change if you have one more acre of land, one more gallon or water, and so forth.)

The Limits Report, shown in Figure 15-21, is the final report. It shows you how much the values in your adjustable cells can change without bumping up against your constraints.

Fine-Tuning Solver's Operation

If you take a peek back at Figure 15-17, you'll notice that the Solver Parameters dialog box provides an Options button. You can click this button to display the Solver Options dialog box, shown here. It lets you fine-tune the way Solver works. For example, the Max Time setting lets you place a limit on the time Solver takes to solve some problem.

The initial Max Time setting is 100 seconds, but you can set a Max Time value up to 32,767 seconds (which is slightly more than 9 hours).

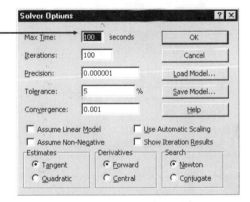

The Iterations setting lets you limit the number of calculations Solver makes in its attempt to solve the model. Again, you can enter a value as high as 32,767. The suggested setting of 100 seconds, however, is more than adequate for small linear programming problems such as the one discussed in the cattle-versus-wheat scenario.

The Precision setting, of course, tells Solver how precise it should be in calculating the adjustable cell values. You can specify a precision setting anywhere from 0 to 1, with smaller values representing increased precision. With the precision setting of .00001, for example, you get a more precise result than with the precision setting of .01. As you might expect, the more precision you require, the longer it takes Solver to finish its calculations.

The Tolerance setting lets you specify an acceptable error percentage in the objective function's result when you're working with integer constraints. As you would expect, the larger the acceptable error percentage, the more quickly Solver finishes its calculations.

The Lower Limit cells show the lowest possible values
for your adjustable cells, given the model constraints.

The Upper Limit cells show the highest
possible values for your adjustable cells,
given the model constraints.

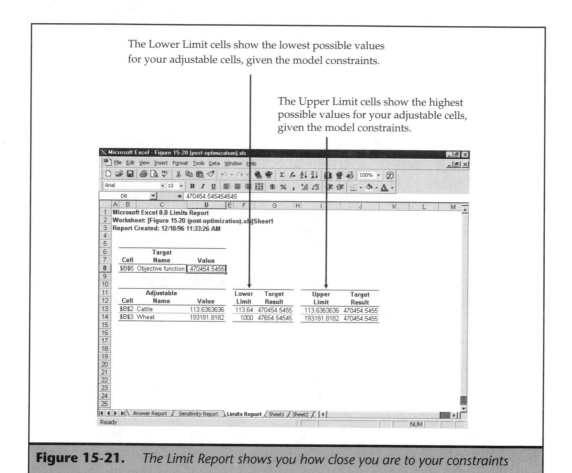

Figure 15-21. *The Limit Report shows you how close you are to your constraints*

In addition to those settings already discussed, Solver provides several other options you can use to exert even more control over the way Solver works and to solve more complex and much larger optimization modeling problems: Assume Linear Model, Show Iteration Results, Use Automatic Scaling, Estimates, Derivatives, and Search. Discussion of these options reaches far beyond the scope of this book. (If you want to learn more about linear programming, consult an upper-division or graduate-level operations research text such as *Operations Research, Applications and Algorithms*, by Wayne L. Winston (Boston: PWS-Kent Publishing Co., 1991).

Part IV

Microsoft Access

The Complete Reference

Office 97

Chapter 16

Creating a Database

This chapter, the first in Part IV, explains how to create a database with Microsoft Access 97. Before you can create a database that will serve you well, however, you need to know a little database theory, which this chapter explains. It also explains how the different tables in a database fit together and what a relational database is. This chapter will also define strange database terms such as *records*, *fields*, *forms*, and *queries*.

In this chapter you will find advice for structuring a database. You learn how to get around on the Access screen and how to create a database table as well. Because creating databases can be an onerous task and requires more know-how than the other Office 97 programs require, you can call on the wizards to do much of your database work. This chapter explains how to use the Database Wizard and the Table Wizard to create databases and database tables.

How a Database Works

Unfortunately, it is impossible to jump in and get to work in a database program like Access without knowing a bit about database theory. In a database, information is stored in very specific ways. What's more, the data in a database can be stored in more than one database table. In fact, as the following pages explain, it is to your advantage to store data in more than one table if you intend to track large numbers of people, sales items, inventory items, or whatever it is you want to track with your database. And, apart from putting data in database tables, there is more than one way to get data out of a database, too. You can query the database, filter it, or create a report, for example.

The following pages explain what you need to know about databases before you create a database of your own. They also explain what extremely dreary database terms like *filter, relational database,* and *form* mean. Of all the computer terminology, database terminology is the most dreary—and that's saying a lot, because computer terminology as a rule is the dreariest jargon on the planet. I wish one or two literate people had been in the room to object when the propeller-heads who invented database terms coined words like *relational query, dynaset,* and *primary key.*

Storing the Data in Tables, Records, and Fields

The data in a database is stored in different tables. Like the tables you create in Excel or Word, database tables are divided into columns and rows. In a database table, however, rows are called *records* and columns are called *fields*. Actually, to be precise, each row in a database table is a record, and each record is divided into several fields. For example, seven records have been entered in the Phone Numbers database table shown in Figure 16-1. Each record is divided into four fields—Social Security Number, Last Name, First Name, and Telephone Number.

A record comprises all the data about one person or thing. A field is one category of information. As "Designing Your Database" a little later in this chapter explains, one of the most important choices you make when you design a database is which fields to

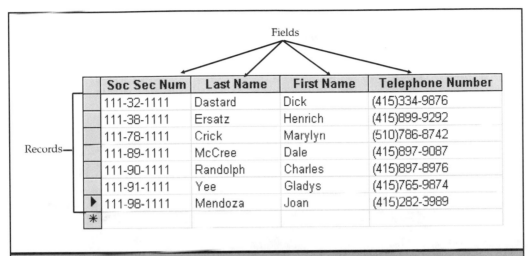

Fields

Soc Sec Num	Last Name	First Name	Telephone Number
111-32-1111	Dastard	Dick	(415)334-9876
111-38-1111	Ersatz	Henrich	(415)899-9292
111-78-1111	Crick	Marylyn	(510)786-8742
111-89-1111	McCree	Dale	(415)897-9087
111-90-1111	Randolph	Charles	(415)897-8976
111-91-1111	Yee	Gladys	(415)765-9874
111-98-1111	Mendoza	Joan	(415)282-3989

Records

Figure 16-1. *In a database table, all the data about a person or thing is listed in a record, and each record is divided into categories called* fields

include. Include one field for each category of information you care to know about a person or thing.

A Relational Database

Access 97 is a *relational database*, which means that data is not stored in a single, very large table. Instead, data is stored in several different tables, all of which are related to one another in such a way that you can join the data from different tables if need be, or retrieve information from several tables at once.

To understand how a relational database works, consider Figure 16-2, which shows what is called a *flat-file database.* A flat-file database, contrary to a relational database, consists of a single large table, not several different tables. The flat-file database in Figure 16-2 lists the names of contacts. Notice that much of the data stored in the database table is repetitive: the contacts in the database table work for either of two companies, AirTech or DynoAir. Each time you enter information about a person or thing—that is, each time you enter a record—in a flat-file database, you have to enter all the data. In the case of the table in Figure 16-2, you have to enter the name, address, city, state, and zip code of either the AirTech company or the DynoAir company.

With a relational database, on the other hand, you wouldn't have to enter the name, address, city, state, and ZIP code of AirTech or DynoAir each time you entered a new contact name in the database table. All you would enter is the contact's last name, first name, and the name of the company that he or she works for. A separate table, also part of the database, would list the addresses of AirTech, DynoAir, and other companies you do business with. If you wanted a complete list like the one in Figure

ACCESS

	Last	First	Company	Address	City	State	Zip	Phone
	Plescoe	Wilma	AirTech	12 Duncan	Bitz	TX	67521	555-1344
	Ritz	Roscoe	AirTech	12 Duncan	Bitz	TX	67521	555-1344
	Weaver	James	AirTech	12 Duncan	Bitz	TX	67521	555-1344
	Strayhorn	Jules	DynoAir	333 Maples	Las Pulgas	TX	60432	555-8991
	McCreedy	Lionel	DynoAir	333 Maples	Las Pulgas	TX	60432	555-8991
	Munoz	Rebecca	AirTech	12 Duncan	Bitz	TX	67521	555-1344
	Dyer	George	DynoAir	333 Maples	Las Pulgas	TX	60432	555-8991
	Ng	Andrew	DynoAir	333 Maples	Las Pulgas	TX	60432	555-8991
▶								

Figure 16-2. *An old-fashioned, flat-file database. In a relational database like Access, repetitive information like that shown in this database is eliminated*

16-2, you would ask the database for a report that lists contacts, the companies they work for, and the address and phone numbers of those companies.

In a relational database, it is possible to gather information from different tables and assemble that information in one place. In fact, you are encouraged to divide your database into tables. You save time that way, because you don't have to enter repetitive information in many different fields. Instead of entering the same address over and over again, you would enter it only once, in an Addresses table. You also cut down on data-entry errors by saving data in different tables because you don't have to enter the same data over and over.

Getting Information from Forms, Queries, and Reports

Tables are the means of storing information in a database, but storing information is only half the story. Besides storing information, a database is a means of *getting* information. Basically, the three ways to get information from a database are by means of a form, a query, or a report.

Forms

Figure 16-3 shows a form. Most *forms* display one record—and they display that record very succinctly. Forms are one of the best ways to view data in a database, although you can also enter data on a form. In the form in Figure 16-3, for example, the field names are clearly labeled. You can tell precisely what each piece of information—what each field—is.

Queries

Queries are the means of gathering information from a database and organizing it in a different way. In effect, a query is a question. For example, you could query a database

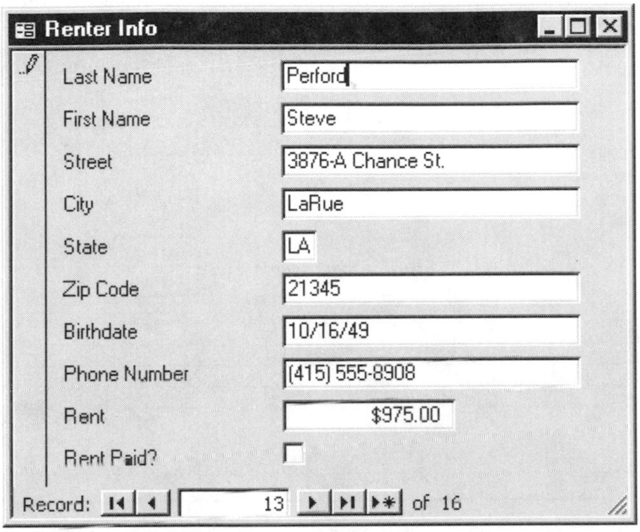

Figure 16-3. *On a form, you can see data more clearly. You can also enter data on forms*

to gather the names of people who live in Connecticut and whose incomes are between $30,000 and $40,000 a year. Or, if your database is an inventory of the items in a store, you could query to find out how many light bulbs in the $1 to $3 price range are in stock. The simple query shown in Figure 16-4 asks a renters database who didn't pay the rent this month. The results of the query produced two names, as shown in the figure.

Reports

Reports like the one shown in Figure 16-5 neatly organize and summarize information in a database. Reports are meant to be printed. Data from a report can come from a database table or a query. Access offers many preformatted layouts, so you don't have to be a layout artist to create a fancy report.

Designing Your Database

Before you touch the keys of the computer, you need to sit down with a scratch pad and pencil and choose a design and structure for your database. In the first place, you need to decide which fields to include in the database. How many distinct pieces of information does your database require? If you operate a video rental shop and you

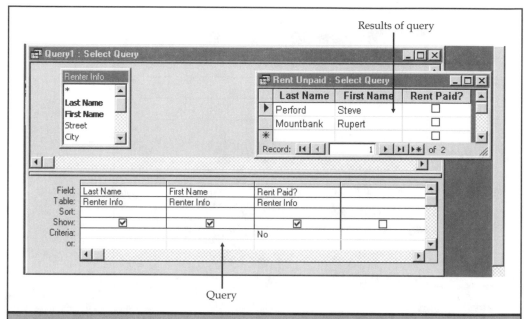

Results of query

Query

Figure 16-4. *A query is a question you ask of a database. This query asks, "Who failed to pay the rent this month?"*

List of Renters

Last Name	First Name	Street	City	State	Zip Code
Hornsby	Roger	11 Cortland St.	Pierspont	PA	21345
Birthdate	Phone Number	Rent			
12/24/65	(415) 555-9807				$1,000.00

Last Name	First Name	Street	City	State	Zip Code
Martinez	William	12 Castro St.	Pierspont	PA	21345
Birthdate	Phone Number	Rent			
17/31/58	(415) 555-3689				$660.00

Last Name	First Name	Street	City	State	Zip Code
Danforth	Peter	122 W. Third Street	Pierspont	PA	21345
Birthdate	Phone Number	Rent			
08/16/61	(212) 555-0687				$550.00

Last Name	First Name	Street	City	State	Zip Code
Creegan	Megan	12234 Monterey Blvd.	Pierspont	PA	21345
Birthdate	Phone Number	Rent			
12/24/51	(212) 555-9876				$850.00

Last Name	First Name	Street	City	State	Zip Code
Derwood	Jane	1712 Lemay St.	New Orleans	LA	21345
Birthdate	Phone Number	Rent			
08/30/29	(415) 555-8976				$450.00

Monday, February 24, 1997

Page 1 of 3

Figure 16-5. *Reports present another way to see the data in a database*

are putting together a database of all the videos in stock, your database obviously needs a title field. How about a director field, a lead actor field, and lead actress field? What if someone asks if the shop carries Biker flicks? Perhaps you should have a genre field as well. Having a Yes/No field that indicates whether each video has been checked out would be an excellent idea. In the database, include fields for each type of information you conceivably might need some day.

When it comes to choosing which fields to include in the database, it is better to err on the side of too much than too little. On the other hand, don't include frivolous information or information that can be derived through a calculation. Entering data in a database is tedious work to begin with, and if you have to enter data in more fields than are really necessary, the work becomes all the more tedious.

After you have decided which fields to include, it is time to divide the fields into database tables. As "A Relational Database" earlier in this chapter explained, creating more than one table for different types of information makes it easier to enter data, because you don't have to enter repetitive information time and time again. Put repetitive information in its own table. For example, if you were creating a database of employees in a large corporation, you could create a Worksite table with the address and telephone number of each worksite. Meanwhile, in the Employee table that lists each employee, you could include a Worksite field. The relationship between two such tables is shown in the following illustration. Table relationships like the one shown here are an important aspect of Access databases. In Chapter 17, you will learn how to forge relationships like the one shown in the illustration.

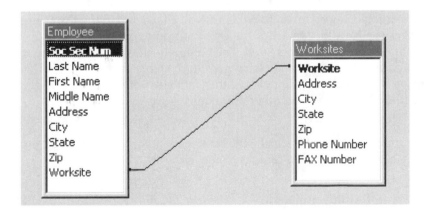

The last thing to consider when you draw up plans for your database is the *primary key,* also known as the unique field. In most database tables, one field or one combination of fields should contain data that is different from record to record, and that field is the primary key. In the database table shown here, for example, Item Number is the primary key, because no two items in the Item Number field can have the same number. In database tables in which information about people is kept, a

Social Security number field is often used as the primary key, because no two Social Security numbers can be the same.

Item Number	Description	Price	Qty per Box	Boxes per Case
12349	Buggy Bumper	$14.23	4	4
76532	Hanging Dice	$5.95	25	2
75983	Eat Fords Decal	$4.19	70	4
78734	Shag Seat Cover	$119.99	2	8
		$0.00	0	0

Part Inventory : Table

When you create a database table, Access asks for the primary key. Primary key fields make it easier for Access to organize records and identify records in databases.

A Quick Geography Lesson

Access 97 is a little different from the other Office 97 programs in several respects. One important difference is that, in Access, you create, open, and design tables, queries, forms, reports, macros, and modules starting from the Database window. The Database window, shown in Figure 16-6, is the first thing you see when you open a database file. It is the Access Grand Central Station. Although tables, queries, reports, and all the other parts of the database are stored in one file, you open them by way of the Database window.

To create a table, query, form, or whatnot, you click a tab in the Database window and then click the New button. Click the Open button to open a table, query, form, or whatnot that you have already created. The Design button is for switching to Design view so you can tell Access exactly what goes in the table, form, report, or whatnot. Moreover, by right-clicking on an item in the Database window, you can open it, print it, rename it, or delete it, among other things, as Figure 16-6 shows.

TIP: *Press F11 or click the Database Window button to get back to the Database window when you are working in a table, query, form, or report.*

Access treats the different parts of a database like files. If you open a database table, for example, and decide to work on a query, you have to save the table before you can close it. In fact, if you try to close a table or any other part of a database without saving the changes you made to it, a message box appears and asks if you want to save the changes you made. Instead of closing a part of a database when you

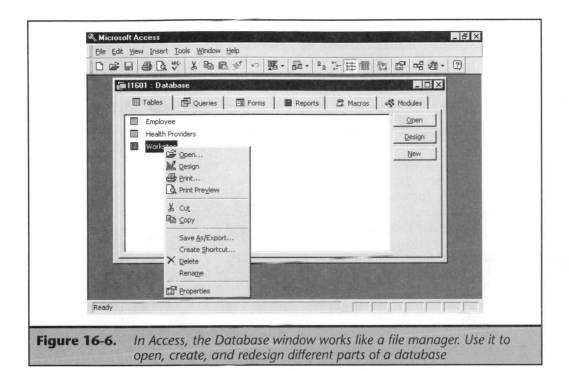

Figure 16-6. *In Access, the Database window works like a file manager. Use it to open, create, and redesign different parts of a database*

want to work on another part, you can click the Minimize button. For this illustration, I opened the three tables shown in Figure 16-6 and then minimized them:

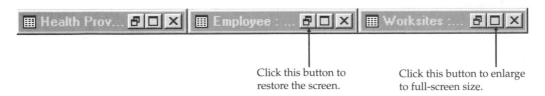

Click this button to restore the screen.

Click this button to enlarge to full-screen size.

By clicking the Restore or Maximize button on the title bar of one of these tables, or by choosing its name from the Windows menu, you can restore it to the screen.

Creating a Database

Access offers two ways to create a database—with the Database Wizard or from scratch. Both techniques are described in the pages that follow.

ACCESS

WARNING: Access is different from the other Office 97 programs in that you have to save and name the database file you create from the moment you create it. Before you create your new database, prepare a folder for storing it and be prepared to enter a meaningful name for the database file.

Creating a Database with the Database Wizard

Access offers 22 databases that you can create either from templates or by means of the Database Wizard. The 22 preformatted, ready-made databases are fine for doing common database tasks such as tracking expenses or keeping tabs on the members of an organization. After you create a database with the Wizard or a template, you get a handful of queries, forms, and reports, all ready to go. And if the queries, forms, and reports aren't quite right, you can always refine them by using the techniques described throughout Part IV.

NOTE: When you create a database with the Wizard, Access creates what it calls the Switchboard, another way apart from the Database window to open database tables, forms, queries, and whatall. Some Access users prefer the Switchboard to the Database window. See "The Switchboard for Working with a Database" later in this chapter for more information.

Access offers the following ready-made databases:

Address Book
Asset Tracking
Book Collection
Contract Management
Donations
Event Management
Expenses
Household Inventory
Inventory Control
Ledger
Membership
Music Collection
Order Entry
Picture Library
Recipes
Resource Scheduling
Service Call Management
Students and Classes
Time and Billing
Video Collection
Wine List
Workout

Follow these steps to create a ready-made database with the help of the Database Wizard:

1. If you just started Access, click the Database Wizard option button in the Microsoft Access dialog box and then click OK. If the program is running already, choose the File menu New Database command and click the Databases tab in the New dialog box.

2. In the New dialog box, click the type of database you want to create and then click OK. You see the File New Database dialog box.

3. Find and double-click on the folder that the database file is to be stored in, enter a name for the file in the File name box, and click the Create button.

4. A dialog box tells you what the database is good for storing. Click the Next button.

5. As shown in Figure 16-7, the next dialog box wants to know which fields to include in the database table or tables. Fields you may or may not want are shown in italics in the right side of the dialog box. Click a table name in the left side of the dialog box and then click the check box next to an italicized field name if you want an optional field.

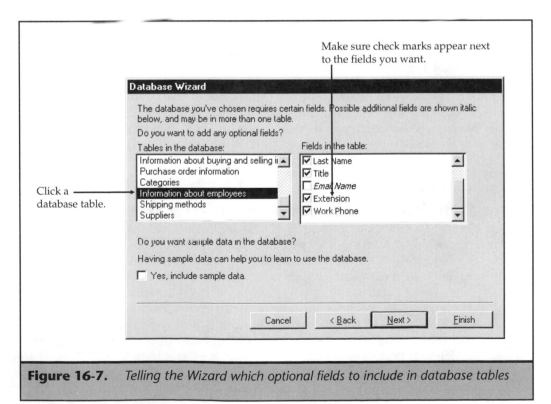

Figure 16-7. *Telling the Wizard which optional fields to include in database tables*

NOTE: If you want to include sample data in the database, click the Yes, include sample data check box. Sample data is especially useful if you are new to working with databases.

6. Click the Next button after you have told Access which fields to include in the database table or tables. The next screen asks what screen displays should look like in your database.

7. Try clicking on a few display names. When you do so, the sample display changes. When you have found a display that suits you, click the Next button.

8. The next dialog box wants you to choose a style for the reports you will generate and print from your new database. Click a few style names until you find the one that tickles your fancy, and then click the Next button.

9. In the next dialog box, enter a title for your database in the text box if you don't like the title that Access suggests. Titles appear on reports. Click Next when you have finished.

NOTE: To include a picture, perhaps a corporate logo, on reports, click the Yes, I'd like to include a picture check box and then click the Picture button. In the Insert Picture dialog box, find and click on the clip art file whose picture you want to appear on reports, and then click OK. The picture appears in the upper-left corner of reports.

10. The last dialog box simply asks if you want to start working with the database immediately. Click Finish in this dialog box.

Depending on how large a database you created, it can take a while for Access to create the sundry parts of your database. Twiddle your thumbs awhile. When the database has been constructed, you see a Switchboard like the one shown in Figure 16-8. A Switchboard is an alternative means of working with a database.

The Switchboard for Working with a Database

If you created your database file with the Database Wizard, you have an alternative means for working with your database—the Switchboard. Figure 16-8 shows the Switchboard. As well as starting from the Database window, you can start from the Switchboard and click a button when you want to view or enter data in part of your database.

When you open the database, you see the Switchboard. To close the Switchboard, click the Exit button. Usually, the Exit button is the last button. To open the Database window, click its Restore or Maximize button. You will find the Database along the bottom of the screen, as shown in Figure 16-8.

Click here to close the Switchboard.

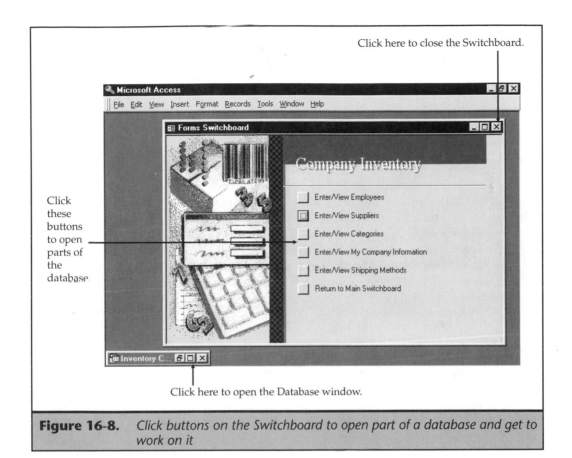

Click these buttons to open parts of the database

Click here to open the Database window.

Figure 16-8.   *Click buttons on the Switchboard to open part of a database and get to work on it*

Creating a Database from Scratch

Creating a database from scratch is easy in the short term. However, instead of relying on Access to create the tables, forms, and queries as you can do when you create a database with the Database Wizard, you have to create those things yourself. Follow these steps to create a database from scratch:

1. If you just opened Access, click the Blank Database option button in the Microsoft Access dialog box and then click OK. If you have already opened Access, either press CTRL+N or click the New Database button. You see the General tab of the New dialog box.

2. Click the Blank Database icon and then click OK. You see the File New Database dialog box.

3. Find the folder in which you want to save the file and double-click it, and then enter a name for the database in the File name text box. Click Create when you have finished.

You see the Database window with its six tabs: Tables, Queries, Forms, Reports, Macros, and Modules. This is the starting point for creating the different parts of the database.

Creating and Refining Database Tables

The first step in creating a database is to create the tables. Tables are where the raw data is stored. After you have entered data in the database tables, you can start pestering the database for information about the people or things that your database is supposed to keep track of.

The following pages explain how to design a table by adding the fields. You also learn how to select data types for the fields and establish field properties to make entering the data easier. These pages also explain how to choose a primary key for a table and how to index a table. Finally, because appearances count, you also learn how to change a table's appearance.

Creating a Database Table

Access offers three ways to create a database table. You can start in Design view and enter the field names yourself, create a table with Access's Table Wizard, or import the data from a table you already created. The Table Wizard can be very helpful when it comes to creating a table, but even if you create a table with the Wizard you have to refine it to make it work for your data.

No matter which method you choose for designing a table, you start from the Database window (click the Database Window button or press F11 if you don't see it). In the Database window, click the Tables tab and then click the New button. You see the New Table dialog box:

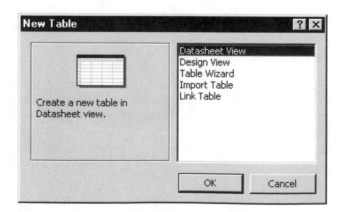

This dialog box is where you decide how to create your table:

- *Design View*   Choose Design View and click OK to design the table yourself. "Designing and Refining a Database Table" in Chapter 17 tells what to do next if you go this route.

- *Table Wizard*   Choose Table Wizard and click OK to get Access's help in designing and creating the table. "Creating a Table with the Table Wizard," later in this chapter, explains what to do next.

- *Import Table*   Choose Import Table and click OK to import a table from another Access database; from an Excel spreadsheet; or from a dBASE, Microsoft FoxPro, or another ODBC database; or from a text file. See "Importing Data from Another Table or Program," later in this chapter, to find out what to do next.

Creating a Table with the Table Wizard

After you click New on the Tables tab in the Database window, choose Table Wizard, and then click OK in the New Table dialog box. In order to create a table with the Table Wizard, follow these steps:

1. In the first Table Wizard dialog box, which is shown in Figure 16-9, choose the table in the Sample Tables box that best describes the database table that you want to create.

2. In the Sample Fields box, click on a field that you want for your table and then click the topmost button, the one that points to the right. When you do so, the field name is moved into the Fields in my new table box.

3. Repeat step 2 as many times as necessary to move fields from the Sample Fields box to the box on the right. If you make a mistake and accidentally move a field into the box on the right, select it and then click the arrow that points to the left.

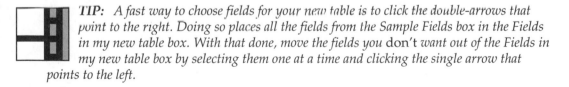 **TIP:** *A fast way to choose fields for your new table is to click the double-arrows that point to the right. Doing so places all the fields from the Sample Fields box in the Fields in my new table box. With that done, move the fields you* don't *want out of the Fields in my new table box by selecting them one at a time and clicking the single arrow that points to the left.*

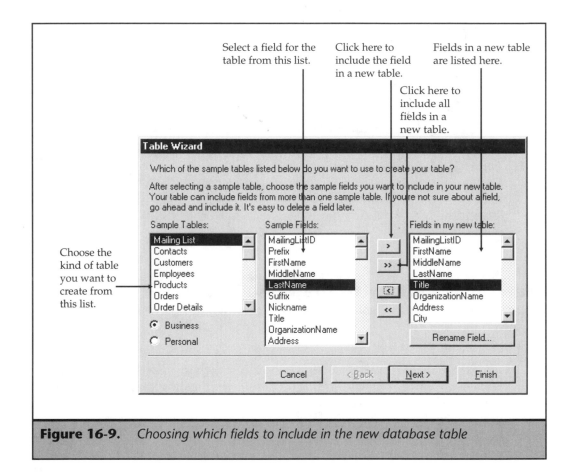

Select a field for the
table from this list.

Click here to
include the field
in a new table.

Fields in a new table
are listed here.

Click here to
include all
fields in a
new table.

Choose the
kind of table
you want to
create from
this list.

Figure 16-9. *Choosing which fields to include in the new database table*

TIP: *To rename a field, select it in the Fields in my new table box and then click the Rename Field button. You see the Rename field dialog box. Enter a new name and click OK. By the way, contrary to what you might think by reading about field names in the Table Wizard, field names can include blank spaces and be more than one word long. If you plan to export information to another database system, however, it's best to omit blank spaces in field names.*

4. Click the Next button. The next dialog box asks for a table name and whether you want the Wizard to choose a primary key for you:

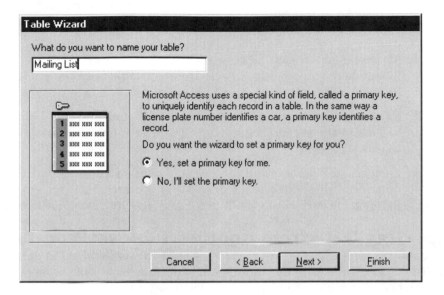

5. Enter a name for your table if Access's name doesn't suit you.

6. Click the Yes or No option button to answer the question concerning whether you want to choose a primary key yourself or let Access choose one ("Designing Your Database," earlier in this chapter, explains what a primary key is). If you click No, a dialog box appears and asks which field is the primary key and what kind of data is stored in that field. It isn't really necessary to choose a primary key now, so you can bypass the question and choose one later if you want. See "Choosing the Primary Key" in Chapter 17 for more information.

7. Click the Next button.

8. If your database already includes a table, the next dialog box asks how the table you are creating relates to the table or tables already in the database. If you are lucky, the Database Wizard may be able to create a relationship for you. Whether or not the Wizard can do that, however, I recommend bypassing this dialog box. In the next chapter, "Forging the Relationships Between Tables" explains how to chart the relationships between tables in a database. It isn't really necessary to do it from this unwieldy dialog box.

ACCESS

9. Click the Next button. You see the last Database Wizard dialog box, which simply asks what you want to do now that you have created a database table:

■ *Modify the table design*   Choose this option and click Finish to go to Design view, where you can refine the design of the table (see "Designing and Refining a Database Table" in Chapter 17).

■ *Enter data directly into the table*   Choose this option and click Finish to switch to Datasheet view and begin entering data (see "Entering Data in a Table" in the next chapter).

■ *Enter data into the table using a form that the wizard creates for me*   Choose this option and click Finish to tell Access to create a form in which to enter data for the table (see "Forms for Entering and Viewing Data" in Chapter 17).

Importing Data from Another Table or Program

If the data you want to use for your new table already exists in another database or spreadsheet, you can import the information into a new table. Follow these steps to import data from elsewhere into an Access database table:

1. Make sure that the source file and program are open.

2. Click the Table tab in the database window, if necessary, and then click the New button.

3. Choose Import Table and click OK in the New Table dialog box. You see the Import dialog box.

4. Find and click on the database file with the data you want to import. If you are importing data from an Excel file or other database program besides Access, open the Files of type drop-down list and choose the type of file whose data you need. Click the Import button when you have finished.

What happens next depends on where the data comes from. If you are importing data from another Access file, you see a dialog box similar to the following. It wants to know which table to get the data from. You can click the Options button to tell Access precisely how to import the data. You can, for example, import only the structure of a table, not the data itself.

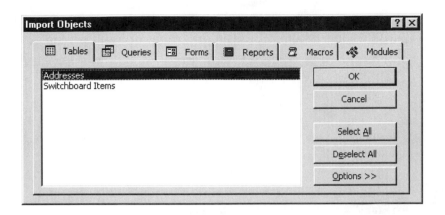

If you import data from an Excel file, Access asks which worksheet to get it from and helps you pinpoint which parts of the worksheet to import. Keep answering the questions and clicking Next in the Wizard dialog boxes until the data is imported.

ACCESS

The Complete Reference

Office
97

Chapter 17

Building Your Database Tables

This chapter explains how to design a database table, establish relationships between the different tables so you can work with more than one at the same time; change the appearance of a table; and, last but not least, enter the data itself. It also explains how to create and design forms for entering and viewing data.

In the course of this chapter, you will learn ways to make sure that data is entered accurately. You can do that by making rules—Access calls them "properties"—for each field in a table. For example, you can tell Access to allow only two letters to be entered in a State field (two being the number of letters in standard state abbreviations such as CT, RI, NY, and so on). Or you can tell Access only to permit numbers, not letters, to be entered.

This chapter also offers techniques for viewing tables. Eventually, you will be the judge of which view is best for viewing and entering the data in tables; this chapter explains how to change views and makes suggestions about which view is best in different situations. At the end of this chapter, you learn how to print a database table and export data to other Access files and database programs.

Opening a Database Table

To open a database table, start at the Database window. This window appears automatically if you created your database without the help of the Database Wizard. If you used the Wizard to create your database, you see the Switchboard onscreen when you open a new database file instead of the Database window. To see the Database window, which is shown in the following illustration, press F11 or click the Database window button.

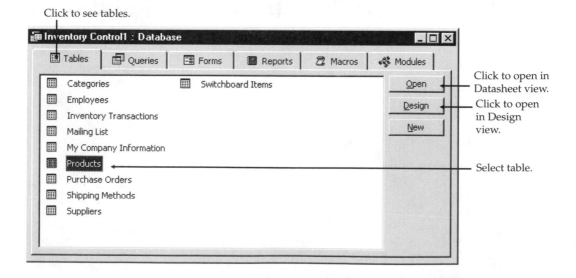

Click to see tables.

Click to open in Datasheet view.

Click to open in Design view.

Select table.

After the Database window is onscreen, click the Tables tab, if necessary, to see the tables in the database, click the table you want to open, and then click either the Open or the Design button:

- *Open*   Opens the table in Datasheet view so you can view records, enter new records, or delete records.
- *Design*   Opens the table in Design view so you can change the structure of a table, add new fields, delete fields, or change field settings.

TIP: *You can also open a database table by right-clicking on its name on the Tables tab. From the shortcut menu, choose Design to open the table in Design view; choose Open to open the table in Datasheet view.*

Read on to find out more about the two views and why you would choose one or the other.

Ways of Viewing Tables

Access offers two ways to view database tables—in Datasheet view or Design view. Figure 17-1 shows a table in Datasheet view, and Figure 17-2 shows the same table in

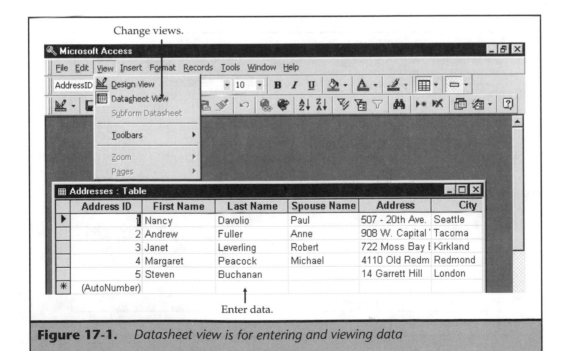

Figure 17-1.   *Datasheet view is for entering and viewing data*

Design view. Use Datasheet view to enter data in a table. Design view is for designing the database table—that is, for telling Access which fields go in the table, what kind of data is allowed in each field, and how the data is formatted.

To change views of a table, choose either the View menu Datasheet command or the View menu Design command. The next section in this book, "Designing and Refining a Database Table," explains how to add fields to a table and set properties for the fields. "Entering Data in a Table," toward the end of this chapter, explains how to enter data in Datasheet view.

LEARN BY EXAMPLE
Open the Figure 17-1 (Views) file on the companion CD if you care to experiment with views.

Designing and Refining a Database Table

Designing a table is a big job, especially when it comes to choosing what kind of data goes in each field. The following pages explain how to create a new field, choose a data type for the field, and establish a field's properties (the settings that determine how data is displayed and stored). These pages also explain how to edit fields, move and copy them, and establish the primary key for a table.

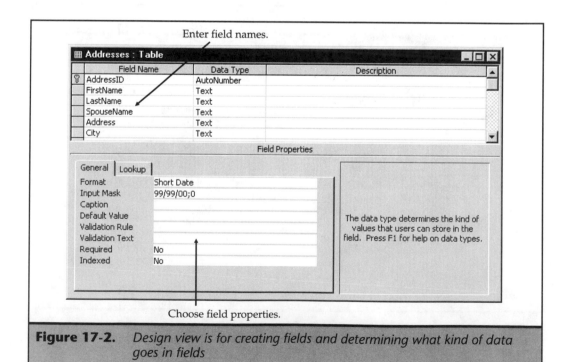

Figure 17-2. *Design view is for creating fields and determining what kind of data goes in fields*

TIP: Access offers a thing called the Table Analyzer Wizard that looks at tables and tells you whether they should be broken into two or more tables. If you find yourself entering the same data time and time again in a table, your table might need breaking up. To use the Table Analyzer Wizard, choose the Tool menu Analyze command, and then click Table.

Creating a Field

To create a field in a database table, follow these steps:

1. Switch to Design view, if you are not already there, by choosing the View menu Design command.

2. Tell Access where the new field is to go:

   ■ If you are creating the first field in the table, the cursor is in the first row and you are ready to go.

   ■ To insert a field between fields that are already there, select the field below which the new field is to go and either click the Insert Rows button or right-click and choose Insert Rows from the shortcut menu. To select a field, click the small square to its left. In this database table, I want to insert a field between FirstName and LastName, so I have selected the LastName field:

Field Name	Data Type	Description
🔑 AddressID	AutoNumber	
FirstName	Text	
▶ LastName	Text	
SpouseName	Text	

Click to select field. ──

NOTE: The order in which fields are entered in Design view determines where the fields appear in Datasheet view. The topmost field in the Design view window is the leftmost field in the Datasheet view window; the last field in the Design view window is the rightmost field in the Datasheet view window.

3. Enter a name for the field in the Field Name box. Names can be 64 characters long, but they ought to be considerably shorter so they fit onscreen in Datasheet view and don't take up too much space on forms.

WARNING: Including spaces in field names in Access database tables is perfectly OK, but some database programs do not permit spaces in field names. If you intend to export databases from Access to other database programs, don't include blank spaces in field names.

4. Click in the Data Type box to the right of the field name. The word "Text" appears in the Data Type box. However, if numbers, dollar amounts, or other types of data besides text are to be stored in the field, click the down arrow in the Data Type box and choose a different data type (the next sidebar explains what the data types are):

```
Text
Memo
Number
Date/Time
Currency
AutoNumber
Yes/No
OLE Object
Hyperlink
Lookup Wizard...
```

5. Enter a few words in the Description box, if necessary, to describe the data that is to be stored in the field. The words you enter appear on the status bar when you are working with a field in Datasheet view.

6. If you want, choose field properties from the bottom half of the dialog box to tell Access how to handle the data you will enter in the field. (See "Establishing Field Properties for Easier Data Entry," later in this chapter.)

You can also get Access's help to create a new field. To do so, make sure the insertion point is in the Field Name box below where you want the new field to be located. Right-click in the Field Properties pane in the lower portion of the window, and then click Build on the shortcut menu. You see the Field Builder dialog box shown in Figure 17-3. Click the Business or Personal option button to tell Access what type of fields you need, and then, in the Sample Tables box, click the table that most resembles the one you are working on. New field names appear in the Sample Fields box. Click a field name and then click OK.

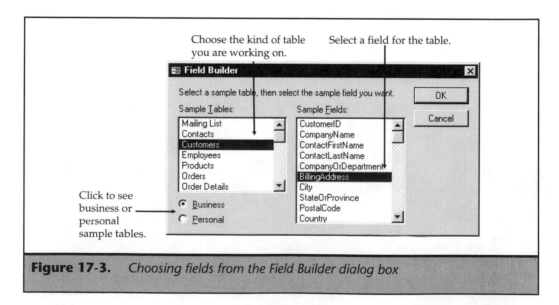

Figure 17-3. Choosing fields from the Field Builder dialog box

The Data Types

When you create a field, Access asks you to choose a data type. Following are explanations of the ten data types:

Data Type	What It Is For
Text	For storing text (names, for example), combinations of text and numbers (street addresses), and numbers that aren't meant to be calculated (Social Security numbers and telephone numbers). A text field cannot be longer than 255 characters.
Memo	For storing long notes. Choose this data type when you want to include long descriptions in a database table.
Number	For storing numbers that are to be used in calculations.
Date/Time	For storing dates and times. (To choose how the date or time is formatted, click the Format box in the Field Properties part of the Design View dialog box and choose a format from the drop-down menu.)
Currency	For storing monetary figures that are to be used in calculations.
AutoNumber	For entering numbers in sequence each time you add a new record to the table. For example, the first record is 1; the second, 2; and so on. Each number can only be used once in the field. By choosing the AutoNumber data type, you make sure that the data in the field is unique and is not repeated. Use the AutoNumber data type for the primary key field if no other field in the table stores unique, one-of-a-kind numbers such as Social Security numbers or item numbers. To make the AutoNumber field assign random numbers instead of sequential numbers, click in the New Values box on the lower half of the Design view dialog box and choose Random from the drop-down menu instead of Increment.
Yes/No	For storing either-or data, such as Yes/No, True/False, Checked Out?, Beautiful/Ugly. When you choose this data type, a box appears in the field. Checking the box means Yes, True, checked out, Beautiful, and so on; an empty check box means No, False, not checked out, ugly; and so on.

OLE Object	For storing text, spreadsheets, pictures, sounds, and other data created in Word, Excel, or other programs. The Memo data entry type is fine for entering a paragraph or two; but if you want a page or more to appear in a database table, you are better off choosing the OLE Object data type.
Hyperlink	For storing hyperlinks. Hyperlinks are described in Chapter 26 of this book.
Lookup Wizard	For retrieving values either from another database table or from a list of values in a combo box. When you choose this data type, the Lookup Wizard comes onscreen so you can designate which table to get the data from or enter the values that will appear in the combo box. See "Creating a Data-Entry Drop-Down List," later in this chapter, for more information.

Moving, Copying, Deleting, and Renaming Fields

After you have gone to the trouble of creating all the fields for the database table, you might discover to your dismay that fields are in the wrong order, that some fields don't belong in the table, or that some fields need new names. The following pages explain how to move, delete, and rename fields. You will also find instructions for copying fields.

Moving and Copying Fields

Move a field when you want it to appear in a different place in the table. To move a field, follow these steps:

1. Select the field by clicking on the box to its left. The field is highlighted.
2. Drag the field up or down across the small squares to the left of the fields. As you drag, a gray line appears between fields to show where the field will land when you release the mouse button.
3. Release the mouse button.

TIP: You can also move fields in Datasheet view. To do so, click the field name at the top of the database table and drag to the left or right. A black line appears between columns to show where the field will go. When the black line is in the right place, release the mouse button. However, moving fields in Datasheet view only changes the table's layout; it doesn't change its underlying structure. When you export the table, for example, its fields will be in their Design view order.

Copy a field when all its settings—its data type and field properties—can be used over again in another field. After you have copied the field, be sure to rename it. Identical fields cannot appear in the same table. To copy a field, follow these steps:

1. Select the field to be copied by clicking the box to its left in Design view.

2. Press CTRL+C or right-click and choose Copy from the shortcut menu.

3. Click on the field that you want the copy to appear above. In this illustration, for example, the copy will appear between the SendCard and Birthdate fields:

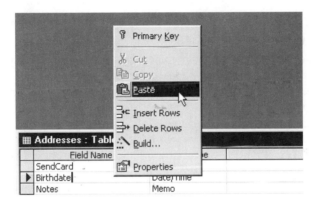

4. Either press CTRL+V or right-click and choose Paste on the shortcut menu.

5. Change the field name for the field you copied.

Renaming a Field

To rename a field, all you have to do is start in Design view, click in the box where the field's name is, delete the name that is there, and enter a new name. It doesn't matter if the field whose name you change is linked to a field in another table, because changing the name of a field doesn't affect the relationships between tables.

WARNING: *If you change the name of the field that you created with the Table Wizard or the Field Builder, the name change won't appear when you switch to Datasheet view. To make the name change appear in Datasheet view, either make the name change in Datasheet view by right-clicking on the column name, choosing Rename Column, and entering a new name, or else change the field's Caption property in Design view. See "Establishing Field Properties for Easier Data Entry," later in this chapter.*

Deleting a Field

Think twice before you delete a field. After you delete it, all the data is lost from every record in the database table. You can't recover it. Follow these steps to delete a field:

1. In Design view, select the field you want to delete by clicking the little box to its left. The field is highlighted.

2. Either click the Delete Rows button or right-click and choose Delete Rows.

3. When Access asks if you really want to go through with it, click Yes.

 WARNING: *Before you can delete a field that is related to a field in another table, you have to end the relationship. See "Forging the Relationships Between Tables" later in this chapter.*

Establishing Field Properties for Easier Data Entry

As shown in Figure 17-4, the lower half of the Design View window offers boxes for choosing properties for fields. Properties make data entry easier. They also help make entries more accurate, make searches go faster, and make sorting faster. You can do yourself and the people who enter data in your database tables a big favor by carefully choosing property settings.

Each so-called property is designed to make data entry go more smoothly. The Field Size property, for example, determines how many characters can be entered in a field. For a State field, you could enter **2** in the Field Size property box and thereby make sure that no one enters three letters for a state abbreviation instead of the

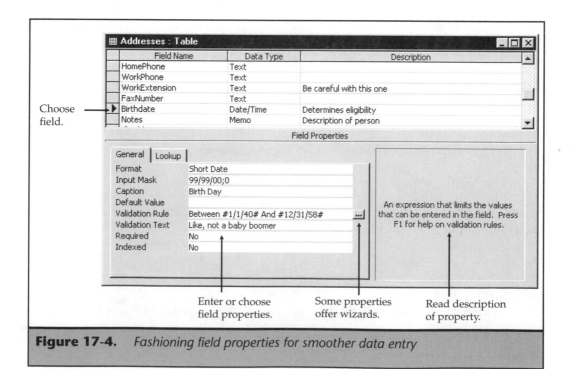

Figure 17-4. *Fashioning field properties for smoother data entry*

requisite two. Or, if the majority of the people whose records you want to enter live in California, you can make CA the default property for the State field. That way, CA appears in the State field automatically and you save yourself the trouble of entering those letters over and over again.

LEARN BY EXAMPLE
To try your hand with field properties, open the Figure 17-4 (Properties) *file on the companion CD.*

Which field properties appear in Design view depends on which data type you chose for the field you created. The following pages explain all the different field properties, when to use them, and how to use them.

WARNING: *Before you choose properties for a field, make sure that the cursor is in the correct field in the top half of the window in Design view. Properties settings apply to whatever field the cursor is in.*

TIP: *For detailed information about a property, click in its property box and then press* F1.

Allow Zero Length

The Allow Zero Length property allows zero-length strings to appear in the field. A *zero-length string* is an empty string (two quotation marks with no text between them). It indicates that there is no value for a field. The default setting is No.

Enter a zero-length string to indicate that the field is not applicable. For example, if you did not know a person's e-mail address, you could leave the field blank; but if you knew that the person did not have an e-mail address, you could enter a zero-length string to record that information in the database table.

Caption

Enter a word or two to describe the field in the Caption box if you don't care for the field name. The word or words you enter will appear in Datasheet view, on reports, and on forms in place of the field name. In Figure 17-4, for example, "Birth Day" has been entered in the Caption box, so "Birth Day" and not "Birthdate" will appear on reports, on forms, and in Datasheet view.

Decimal Places

The Decimal Places property determines how many spaces can appear to the right of the decimal point. This property only affects how numbers and currency figures are displayed, not their real value. Choose a number from the drop-down list or choose Auto. The Auto option displays the number of decimal places that the Format property allows (see "Format," below).

Default Value

The Default Value property enters a value in each new record so you don't have to enter it yourself. Enter a default value—it can be a word, abbreviation, or number—when you know that the majority of the records you will enter require a certain value. You can always delete the default value and enter a different value. If the majority of the people whose records you enter live in Daly City, you can make Daly City the default value; and if a person lives in Colma instead of Daly City, all you have to do is delete Daly City and enter **Colma** in its place.

 TIP: When you see an ellipses (three dots) next to a field property text box, it means that a wizard is available to help you set the field property value. Figure 17-4 shows the three dots next to the Validation Rule text box. Wizards are also available for the Input Mask and Default Value boxes.

Field Size

The Field Size property determines how many numbers or characters at maximum can be entered in the field. Use the Field Size property to make data entry more accurate. If the field stores phone numbers, for example, and you know that no phone number can be longer than 14 characters, enter 14 in the Field Size box.

Format

The Format property is for determining the format in which dates, times, numbers, currency figures, and Yes/No data types are displayed. Table 17-1 illustrates the different formats.

You can also format text in or tell Access what should be entered in Memo and Text fields. To do so, enter one of the following four characters in the Format box:

Character	What It Does
@	Tells Access that a text character or a blank space is required in the field
&	Tells Access that a text character is not required in the field
<	Requires all characters in the field to be lowercase
>	Requires all characters in the field to be uppercase

Indexed

Indexes make searching and sorting operations go faster. In large databases, however, they also make table updates take longer and require more disk space for storing the data. With the Indexed property, you can tell Access that you want to index a field in a table. No is the default choice. The indexing choices are

■ *Yes (Duplicates OK)* Indexes the field and allows duplicate values to appear in the field.

■ *No (No Duplicates)* Indexes the field and prevents duplicate values from appearing in the field.

Format	Example
Date/Time	
General Date	7/31/98 5:29.24 PM
Long Date	Monday, July 31, 1998
Medium Date	31-Jul-98
Short Date	7/31/98
Long Time	5:29:24 PM
Medium Time	5:29 PM
Short Time	17:29
Number *and* Currency	
General Number	4455.78
Currency	$4,455.78
Fixed	4455.78
Standard	4,455.778
Percent	78.00%
Scientific	46E+03
Yes/No	
True/False	True
Yes/No	Yes
On/Off	On

Table 17-1. *Formats for Dates, Numbers, Currency Figures, and Yes/No Field Types*

NOTE: Later in this chapter, "Indexing a Table Field" explains indexing in detail.

Input Mask

The Input Mask property lays down blank spaces and punctuation in the field so that numbers and letters can be entered accurately. The following illustration shows an input mask for entering a telephone number. As soon as you move the cursor into a field that has an data input mask, punctuation marks and blank spaces appear so you know how many numbers or letters to type.

Work Phone
(504) 555-9922
(504) 555-9933
(504) 555-9944
(504) 555-9955
(171) 555-5858
( ) -   ⟵———— Input mask

Input masks can be very sophisticated. Suffice it to say, you can create an input mask by entering the punctuation marks, a 9 where optional numbers appear, and a 0 where numbers are required. For example, to create the input mask shown in the previous illustration, enter the following in the Input Mask text box: **(999) 000-0000**. The punctuation marks—the parentheses and hyphen—will always appear in the field. The three-digit area code is optional, so 9s are used for its placeholders. The seven-digit telephone number is required, so 0s are used for its placeholders.

TIP: To create sophisticated input masks, click the three dots beside the Input Mask text box to open the Input Mask Wizard and get help there. The Input Mask Wizard is not loaded as part of a typical installation in Office 97. You likely have to reinstall the program to use the Input Mask Wizard. See Appendix A.

New Values

For use with the AutoNumber data type, the New Values property determines whether the numbers are generated sequentially or at random. To make the AutoNumber field assign random numbers instead of sequential numbers, choose Random; otherwise, keep the default Increment setting.

Required

The Required property tells Access whether an entry has to be made in the field. The default value is No; but if you choose Yes for this property but fail to enter a value in the field in question, you see this message box:

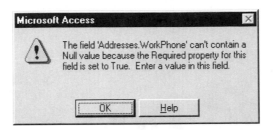

Validation Rule

The Validation Rule lets you set down rules that have to be followed in order for data to be entered in the field. For example, you could require date entries to fall within a certain time period. Or you could require numbers or currency figures to be above or below a certain number. To create a validation rule, you enter an expression in the Validation Rule text box. In Figure 17-4, for example, the expression Between #1/1/40# And #12/31/58# tells Access not to allow date entries in the field unless they fall between January 1, 1940 and December 31, 1958.

WARNING: *To use dates in an expression, the dates must be enclosed by number signs.*

The best way to create an expression, especially if you are not up on your math, is to click the three dots beside the Validation Rule text box. You see the Expression Builder shown in Figure 17-5. By clicking buttons, by choosing functions, constants, or operators, and by entering text in the text box, you can construct expressions. Click OK when you have finished constructing your expression. Following are some sample expressions from Access's Help files:

Examples of field validation rules

ValidationRule setting	ValidationText setting
<>0	Please enter a nonzero value.
0 Or >100	Value must be either 0 or over 100.
Like "K???"	Value must be four characters beginning with the letter K.
<#1/1/96#	Enter a date before 1996.
>=#1/1/97# And <#1/1/98#	Date must be in 1997.

NOTE: *By choosing a data type, you are already establishing a validation rule. Letters, for example, cannot be entered in fields to which the Number or Currency data types have been assigned.*

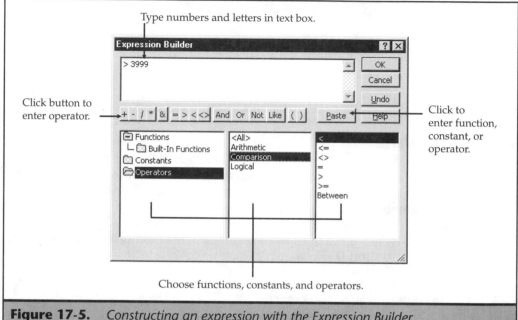

Type numbers and letters in text box.

Click button to enter operator.

Click to enter function, constant, or operator.

Choose functions, constants, and operators.

Figure 17-5. *Constructing an expression with the Expression Builder*

Validation Text

If you established a validation rule for a field and someone enters data that breaks the rule, Access displays a standard error message. You can, however, write an error message of your own by entering it in the Validation Text text box. This error message, for example, warns data-entry employees not to get droopy-eyed while they work:

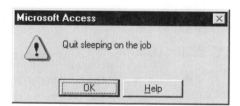

Creating a Data-Entry Drop-Down List

Instead of entering data in a field, you can choose data from a drop-down list. Choosing data from a list not only makes entering data go faster, it makes entries more accurate. With a list, you can be sure that you or others are entering data correctly in the database table. Access offers two ways to create a drop-down list for entering data.

You can type the items that appear on the list yourself, or you can get the items for the list from a column in a database table.

Both techniques are described in the following pages. Type the list yourself if the items on the list are not likely to change. By getting the items from a database table, you can access a completely up-to-date list of items. As the number and variety of items in the database table changes, so will the number and variety of items on your drop-down list, because items on the list will come from a database table.

LEARN BY EXAMPLE
Open the Figure 17-7 (Lookup) file to see examples of drop-down lists in database tables.

Creating the List Yourself

The following illustration shows a drop-down list with county names. Instead of entering these county names, users can simply choose a name from the list. That saves time and makes sure that the county name is entered correctly.

Last Name	First Name	County
Williamson	Gil	

Los Angeles
Riverside
San Bernardino
San Diego

Follow these steps to create a drop-down list of your own:

1. In Design view, click in the field in which you want to create a drop-down list.

2. In the Data Type column, click to open the drop-down list and choose Lookup Wizard. You see the first Lookup Wizard dialog box.

3. Click the I will type the values that I want option button and then click Next. As shown in Figure 17-6, the second Lookup Wizard dialog box appears. This is where you type the values that will appear on the list.

4. Under Col1, type each item that is to appear on the drop-down list. When you have finished, click Next.

NOTE: *You can create a multicolumn drop-down list by entering the number of columns you want in the Number of columns box and entering choices under each column.*

5. In the next Lookup Wizard dialog box, enter a name for the field in your database table, if necessary. Then click the Finish button.

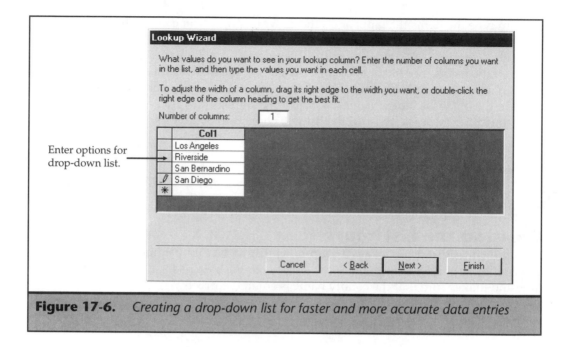

Enter options for drop-down list.

Figure 17-6. *Creating a drop-down list for faster and more accurate data entries*

If you click the Lookup tab on the bottom of the Design View window, you will see everything you care to know about the drop-down list:

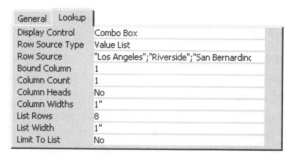

Getting Items on the List from a Database Table

Follow these steps to get items on your drop-down list from another table or from a query in the database:

1. In Design view, click in the field in which you want to create a drop-down list.

2. In the Data Type column, click to open the drop-down list and choose Lookup Wizard. The first Lookup Wizard dialog box appears.

3. The I want the lookup column to look up the values in a table or query option button is already selected, so click the Next button. The next Lookup Wizard

dialog box asks for the name of the table or query where the column whose values you want for your list is located.

4. Click the Tables, Queries, or Both option button; if necessary, click a table; then click the Next button. As shown in Figure 17-7, the next dialog box asks for the name of the column whose values you want for the list.

5. Click a column name on the left side of the dialog box, and then click the arrow that points to the right. The column name moves to the right side of the dialog box. Repeat this step if you want to add more than one column to the combo box; otherwise, click the Next button.

6. If necessary, adjust the width of the column or columns in the next dialog box either by dragging the right side of the column heading or by double-clicking on the right side of the column heading. Then click Next.

7. In the next Lookup Wizard dialog box, enter a name for the field in your database table, if necessary. Then click the Finish button.

8. In the message box that appears, click Yes. Access has to create a relationship between your table and the other table or query so that you can draw upon values in the other table or query.

9. Switch to Datasheet view, click in the new field you created, and see if the drop-down list appears.

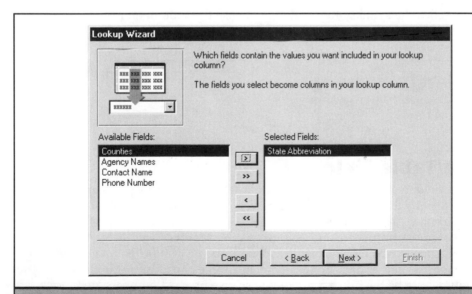

Figure 17-7. *Click the field whose values you want for the drop-down list and then click the arrow that points to the right*

Choosing the Primary Key

So important is choosing a primary key, Access reminds you to choose one if you try to leave Design view without having done so. A *primary key* is the means by which Access identifies each record in the table. Therefore, the field that you choose for the primary key must be one whose entries are different from record to record. Invoice numbers, social security numbers, account numbers, and check numbers are often chosen for the primary key, because these numbers always differ from record to record. A last name field, however, would be a poor choice for the primary key, because common names like Martinez and Smith are likely to repeat themselves in a database table.

If you can't find a field in your database table that can serve as the primary key, you can either choose a combination of fields or choose the AutoNumber data type for a field and make that field the primary key. Fields assigned the AutoNumber data type are required to be different from record to record. If you choose a combination of fields for the primary key, make sure you choose a combination that will not ever repeat itself. For example, in a database table with employee names and pay dates, you could make the combination of names and pay dates the primary key, the idea being that no employee would be paid twice.

Follow these steps to choose the primary key for the database table:

1. In Design view, select the field or fields for the primary key. To select a field, click the small box to its left. To select more than one field, hold down the CTRL key as you click the small boxes.

2. Either click the Primary Key button or choose the Edit menu Primary Key command. A small key appears in the box beside the field or fields you chose:

	Field Name	Data Type	Description
Primary ⟶ ⚷	Social Security Number	Text	
key field.	Last Name	Text	
	First Name	Text	

Indexing a Table Field

By indexing a field in a table, you can make data searches go faster. You can also sort table records faster and generate reports faster. An indexed field is a bit like having a second primary key—it tells Access that the field is an important one and that you intend to use it for sorting, searching, and generating reports.

When you choose which fields to index, choose the pivotal fields in the table from which you expect to gather data. For example, in a table of products, the Product Number field would be the primary key field because product numbers are unique and can't be repeated, but you would likely generate reports based on product names, in which case you would index the Product Name field.

WARNING: *It takes Access longer to update tables, especially large ones, in which fields have been indexed.*

By choosing the View menu Indexes command, you can open the Indexes dialog box and see which fields in a table have been indexed, as well as which field is the primary key field. Figure 17-8 shows the Indexes dialog box.

LEARN BY EXAMPLE
To experiment with indexes, open the Figure 17-7 (Indexes) *file on the companion CD.*

Indexing One Field

Follow these steps to index a table field:

1. In Design view, click the field that you want to index.

2. Click the General tab, if necessary, at the bottom of the Design View window.

3. Click the down arrow in the Indexed box at the bottom of the General tab and choose an indexing option:

   ■ *Yes (Duplicates OK)* Indexes the field and allows duplicate values to appear in the field.

   ■ *No (No Duplicates)* Indexes the field and prevents duplicate values from appearing in the field.

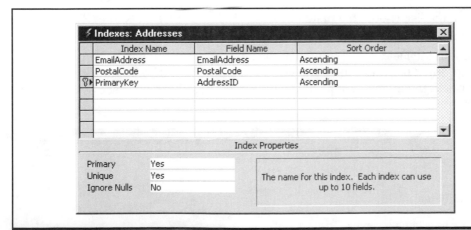

Figure 17-8. *The Indexes dialog box shows which fields in the table have been indexed. Use this dialog box as well to create an index based on two or more fields*

ACCESS

TIP: By default, indexed fields are sorted in ascending order. To index a field in descending order, choose the View menu Indexes command to open the Indexes dialog box (see Figure 17-8), click in the Sort Order column beside the field whose index order you want to change, and choose Descending from the drop-down list.

Indexes Based on More than One Field

Sometimes it is necessary to index two or even three fields at the same time. For example, if you index the Last Name field and two or more people in the database table have the same last name, it is necessary as well to index the First Name field. That way, if there are two Johnsons, two Martinezes, two Wongs, or the names of two other people with a common last name in the table, Access can look to the First Name field to "break the tie" and sort Billy Bob Johnson before Lilly Mae Johnson, for example.

Follow these steps to create an index based on two fields instead of one:

1. In Design view, click anywhere in the database table.

2. Choose the View menu Indexes command or click the Indexes button on the Standard toolbar. You see the Indexes dialog box (see Figure 17-8). In this dialog box, you will create a name for the two- or three-field index and tell Access which fields to include in the index.

3. On a blank line in the Index Name column, enter a name for the new index you want create.

4. Click in the Field Name column beside the name you just entered. An arrow appears in the column.

5. Click the arrow to open a drop-down list of all the fields in the database table.

6. From the list, choose the first field for the index. For a Last Name/First Name index, for example, choose Last Name.

7. Click in the Field Name column in the next row in the dialog box, open the drop-down list, and choose the second field for the index. When you have finished, the Indexes dialog box looks something like the one shown in this illustration:

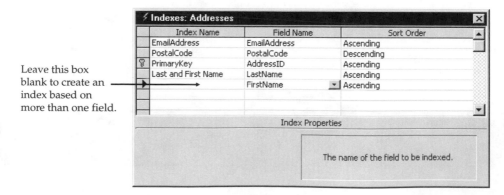

Leave this box blank to create an index based on more than one field.

Forging the Relationships Between Tables

As "A Relational Database" in Chapter 16 explained, you don't have to store all the data in a single table. In fact, you *shouldn't* store all the data in a single table, because that makes entering the data harder and it uses up valuable disk space. Instead, you can store the data in several tables, pass information back and forth between tables, query several tables at the same time, create forms that draw data from different tables, and generate reports from different tables. The hitch is this: Access cannot work with several tables or create queries, forms, or reports from several different tables unless you have established relationships between the tables.

A relationship matches data from fields in different tables, usually from fields that have the same name. Figure 17-9 shows the relationships among seven tables in a database. In the figure, a line has been drawn from table to table when two tables have a relationship. Notice that relationships are forged so that data from one table can be used in another table. Moreover, relationships are usually forged by using the primary key fields from tables. The Inventory Transactions table shown roughly in the

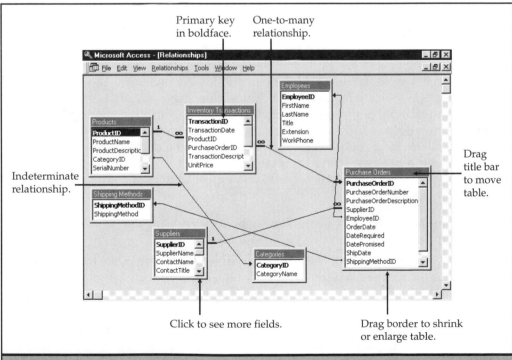

Figure 17-9. *To see the relationships between tables in a database, click the Relationships button in the Database window or choose the Tools menu Relationships command*

middle of Figure 17-9, for example, gets product ID numbers from the ProductID field—a primary key—in the Products table to its left.

This part of the chapter explains how to forge relationships like the ones shown in Figure 17-9 between tables, find out if relationships have already been created between tables, and sever relationships between tables. You also learn about the different relationships that can be forged and what referential integrity is.

LEARN BY EXAMPLE

On the companion CD is a sample database file called Figure 17-9 (Relationships) *that you can use to experiment with forging relationships between tables.*

Seeing the Relationships Between Tables

When you create a database with the Database Wizard, Access forges relationships between the tables in the database automatically. And when you create a database table with the Table Wizard, Access asks if you want to forge a relationship with the table or tables that you already created. Therefore, if you are fond of wizards and used one to create the database or database tables, relationships may already exist between the tables in your database.

Viewing Tables in the Relationships Window

Whether relationships already exist or not, it is easy to find out where relationships have been forged between tables. To find out, choose the Tools menu Relationships command or click the Relationships button in the Database window. You see the Relationships window (see Figure 17-9) if relationships have already been forged. If they haven't been forged, you see the Show Table dialog box (see Figure 17-10).

In the Relationships window, each table is represented by a box and lines are drawn to show the relationships between tables. Field names in boldface are primary key fields. If yours is a database with a lot of tables, you might have to do some dragging and clicking in the Relationship window to untangle the tables and see precisely where the relationships are.

- *Moving tables* To move a table box in the window, drag its title bar to a new place.

- *Changing table size* To make a table box larger or smaller, move the pointer over its border, and when you see a two-headed arrow, click and drag the border.

- *Seeing the field names* A scroll bar appears in the table box if all the fields can't be displayed at once. Click the arrows in the scroll bar (or enlarge the table box) to read the field names.

TIP: *To see only the relationships between one table and the tables to which it is related, click the table and then click the Show Direct Relationships button on the Relationship toolbar. Click the Show All Relationships button when you want to see the relationships among all the tables in the database.*

TIP: *To remove a single table from the Relationships window, right-click it and choose Hide Table from the shortcut menu. Click the Show All Relationships button to get it back again.*

Relationships Between Tables

In the Relationships window, tables that have a one-to-many relationship show the number 1 on the "one" side and an infinity symbol (∞) on the "many" side. If you designed your database carefully and accurately, the majority of the relationships in the table should be of the one-to-many variety. Access creates a one-to-many relationship when one of the fields being related is either a primary key field or an indexed field to which you have assigned the No (No Duplicates) setting (see "Indexing a Table Field," earlier in this chapter, for more information).

By far, the majority of relationships are one-to-many. The one-to-many relationship shown in the following illustration, for example, forges a relationship between an Employee table and a Health Plan table. Health plan numbers must be unique and not appear more than once in the Plan Number field of the Health Plan table (the "one" side), but health plan numbers can appear more than once in the Plan Number field of the Employee table (the "many" side), because more than one employee can belong to the same health plan.

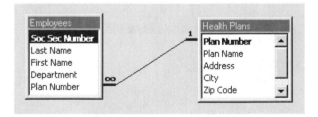

NOTE: *Besides one-to-many relationships, you can forge one-to-one, indeterminate, and many-to-many relationships. One-to-one relationships show a 1 on each side of the relationship line. A simple line is drawn between tables whose relationship is indeterminate. Many-to-many relationships are rare. They require a third, intermediary table. Look up "Relationship" in the Access Help program for more information.*

Mapping Relationships Between Tables

To forge relationships between tables, you start by displaying the tables between which you want to create relationships in the Relationships window. Then you draw lines between fields on the tables.

Displaying Tables in the Relationships Window

Follow these steps to display the tables that you want to form relationships between in the Relationships window:

1. If necessary, close all the tables in the database.

2. Click the Relationships button in the Database window or choose Tools menu Relationships command. The Relationships window appears, as does the Show Table dialog box shown in Figure 17-10. (If the Show Table dialog box does not appear automatically, click the Show Table button.)

 TIP: *If you have opened the Relationships window before to create relationships between tables, the Relationships window opens with the table boxes already on display. To place a new table or query in the Relationships window, click the Show Table button on the Relationship toolbar. You will see the Show Table dialog box.*

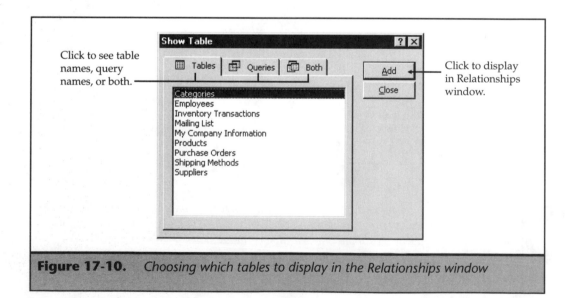

Figure 17-10. *Choosing which tables to display in the Relationships window*

3. Click the Queries tab or Both tab, if necessary, to see the names of queries or of both tables and queries.

4. Click the table or query you want to place in the Relationships window.

5. Click the Add button.

6. Repeat steps 3 through 5 until all the tables or queries between which you want to forge relationships are in the Relationships window.

7. Click the Close button.

TIP: *Right-click a table and choose Hide Table from the shortcut menu to remove a table from the Relationships window. Click the Show All Relationships button to get the table back again.*

Drawing the Lines Between Tables

After the tables (or tables and queries) are in the Relationships window, you can forge relationships betwixt them. Follow these steps to so:

1. Drag a field from one table box and drop it in the field in another table box. When you drag the field into the second table box, the pointer changes into a rectangle. By the way, it doesn't matter which table box you start from. In other words, you can drag the field from table to table in either direction.

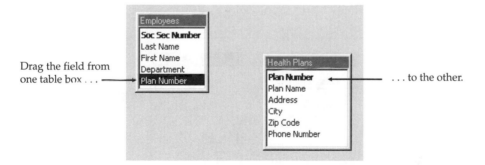

Drag the field from one table box . . .

. . . to the other.

WARNING: *You can't create a relationship using fields that aren't of the same data type. For example, you can't create a relationship between a number field and text field.*

2. Release the mouse button. The Relationships dialog box appears, as in Figure 17-11. The name of the field you dragged and the field you dropped it on appear in the dialog box. At the bottom of the dialog box, you can see what kind of relationship you are creating.

ACCESS

3. Click the Enforce Referential Integrity check box if you want the rules of referential integrity to apply to the relationship. See the sidebar "What Is Referential Integrity?" to find out what those rules are. The sidebar also explains what the Cascade Update Related Fields and Cascade Delete Related Records check boxes are for.

NOTE: If you opt against applying the rules of referential integrity, the line that is drawn between the tables will show an indeterminate relationship without 1s or the infinity symbol.

4. Click the Create button. You go straight to the Relationships window, where a line has been drawn to mark the relationship.

TIP: Click the Join Type button to open the Join Properties dialog box and tell Access how to display records by default when you create a query with the two tables in the relationship. Queries are discussed in the next chapter.

When you have finished forging relationships between tables and you close the Relationships window, Access asks if you want to save your changes to the layout in the window. The relationships themselves have already been saved—you saved them when you clicked the Create button in the Relationships dialog box. Access only wants to know whether to save the positions of the table boxes onscreen so that the table boxes appear in the same places next time you open the Relationships window. Click Yes or No.

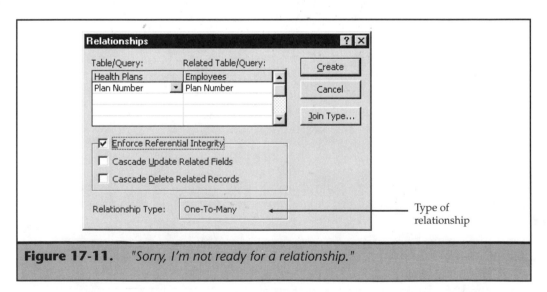

Figure 17-11.   *"Sorry, I'm not ready for a relationship."*

What Is Referential Integrity?

Referential integrity, a particularly hideous database term, refers to the rules by which Access makes sure that relationships between tables are valid and that you don't delete or change field values in one table that are necessary for another table. By clicking the Enforce Referential Integrity check box in the Relationship dialog box, you make sure that one side of the relationship works in tandem with the other side in the following ways:

- A value in a field on the "many" side of the relationship is valid only if it matches a value on the "one" side. For example, suppose there is a relationship between two tables, one called Health Plans and one called Employees, and the relationship is forged on a field in each table called Plan Number. In this case, you couldn't enter a health plan number in the Employees table (the "many" side) unless it was listed already in the Plan Number field of the Health Plans table (the "one" side). You could, however, leave the Plan Number field blank in the Employees table under the rules of referential integrity. If you tried to enter a health plan number in the Employees table that didn't match any values in the Health Plans table, you would see this dialog box:

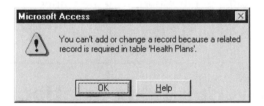

- A value on the "one" side of the relationship cannot be deleted or changed if it is matched by a value that has been entered on the "many" side. To use the example of the Health Plans and Employees table again, suppose that the two tables are joined on the Plan Number field. The Health Plans table holds the master list of plan numbers, some of which have already been entered in the Employees table. If you try to change or delete a plan number in the Health Plans table, Access will not permit it under the rules of referential integrity, because values on the "one" side can't be deleted or changed if they match values that have been entered on the "many" side of the table. If you try to delete or change a value on the "one" side that has been entered on the "many" side, you see this dialog box:

ACCESS

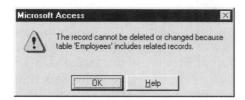

The Relationships dialog box offers two check boxes for keeping referential integrity but also allowing records on the "one" side to be deleted or changed:

- *Cascade Update Related Fields* Click this check box and Access allows you to change values on the "one" side of the relationship even if the values have already been entered on the "many" side. When you change a value on the "one" side, matching values in related records on the "many" side are likewise changed.

- *Cascade Delete Related Records* Click this check box and Access lets you delete values on the "one" side of the relationship. When a value is deleted on the "one" side, matching values in related records on the "many" side are also deleted.

How the word "cascade" got mixed up with these option names I will never know. Perhaps the propeller-head who invented the options invented them while honeymooning in Niagara Falls.

Changing and Severing Table Relationships

Follow these steps to change a relationship between two tables or end the relationship altogether:

1. In the Relationships window (click the Relationships button or choose the Tools menu Relationships command to get there), right-click on the line that marks the relationship between two tables. You see the following shortcut menu:

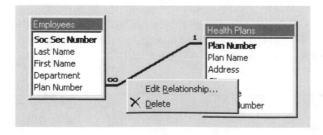

NOTE: *Sometimes when you click the line between tables, you see a shortcut menu with options for displaying tables in the Relationships window. Keep right-clicking. Eventually, you see the shortcut menu for editing and deleting relationships.*

2. Either edit the relationship or delete it:

- *Edit the relationship* Click the Edit Relationship option to open the Relationships dialog box (see Figure 17-11). From there, you can choose options to change the relationship.

- *Delete the relationship* Click the Delete option to sever the relationship between the two tables.

Changing a Table's Appearance

Thus far in this chapter, you have learned how to design database tables and forge relationships between them. To actually see the data in a table, however, you switch to Datasheet view. To do so, either choose the View menu Datasheet command or, if you are starting from the Tables tab of the Database window, double-click a table name or click it and then click the Open button.

One way to enter data is to do it in Datasheet view, so taking the time to make the table more legible is definitely worthwhile if you have a lot of data to enter. The following pages explain how to make columns wider and rows taller, change the arrangement of columns, and change the look of a datasheet.

LEARN BY EXAMPLE
To experiment with the commands for changing a datasheet's appearance, open the Figure 17-12 (Datasheet) *file on the companion CD.*

Changing the Look of a Datasheet

To change the way that a datasheet looks onscreen, you can do any number of things. You can change the font of the text or change what Access calls the "cell effects"—the gridline, gridline color, and background color. Figure 17-12 shows four data sheets whose fonts, font sizes, background colors, gridlines, and gridline colors have been formatted in different ways.

Change the font of the text in a datasheet by choosing the Format menu Font command. In the Font dialog box, choose a font, font size, and font style for the text. You can also change the color of text in the Font dialog box.

Change the look of the datasheet by choosing the Format menu Cells command. You see the Cells Effects dialog box shown in Figure 17-13. By experimenting with the Gridlines Shown, Cell Effect, Gridline Color, and Background Color check boxes;

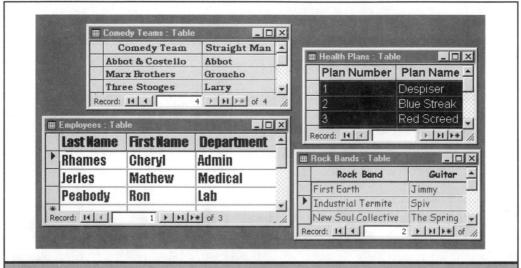

Figure 17-12. *By changing fonts and experimenting with "cell effects," you can radically change the way a datasheet looks*

drop-down lists; and option buttons, you can design a datasheet to suit your taste. Keep your eye on the Sample box as you experiment. The Sample box shows precisely what your design looks like. Click OK when you have put together the perfect datasheet design.

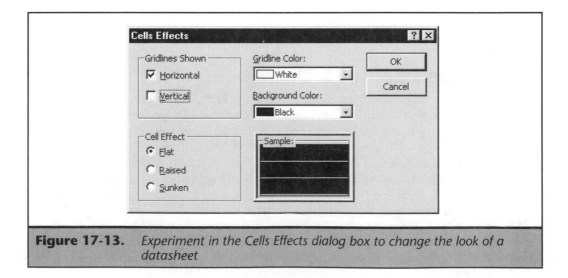

Figure 17-13. *Experiment in the Cells Effects dialog box to change the look of a datasheet*

TIP: Another way to change the appearance of a datasheet is to click the Fill/Back Color, Font/Fore Color, Gridlines, and Special Effects buttons on the Formatting toolbar. Clicking these buttons and choosing options from the drop-down menus is a quick way to experiment with a datasheet's appearance.

Changing the Width of Columns and the Height of Rows

The techniques for changing the width of columns and the height of rows are the same in Access as they are in Excel:

- *Column width* To change the width of a column, move the pointer into the right side of the heading of the column you want to widen or make narrower. The *column heading* is the gray field name at the top of the column. When the pointer changes into a double-headed arrow, click and drag the boundary between column headings to make the column wider or narrower.

TIP: The fastest way to adjust the width of a column is to double-click on the right side of its column heading (the field name at the top of the column). Double-clicking there tells Access to make the column wide enough for its widest entry.

- *Row height* When you change the height of one row, you also change the height of all the rows in the table. To change the height of the rows, move the cursor onto the boundary between two of the small boxes on the left side of the datasheet. When the cursor changes into a double-headed arrow, click and drag up or down to make the columns taller or shorter.

Changing the Order of Columns

Change the order of columns in a datasheet by dragging the column headings to new places. To do that, click on a column heading. When you do so, the entire column is selected. Next, drag the column to the left or right. As you drag, a black line appears between columns to show where the column will land after you move it. When the black line is in the right place, release the mouse button.

NOTE: Changing the order of columns in Datasheet view only changes the layout of the fields. To change the actual order of fields, do so in Design view.

Entering Data in a Table

After you have gone to all the trouble of creating database tables and forging relationships between tables, it is time to hunker down and enter the data. The following pages explain tried-and-true techniques for entering data quickly and accurately. They also explain how to edit the data in a database table, in case you don't enter it correctly the first time.

Access offers two ways to enter data in a table: on the datasheet and on a form. Creating a form for entering data in a database table is explained in "Forms for Entering and Viewing Data," later in this chapter. To open the datasheet and start entering data in a table, either choose the View menu Datasheet command or, if you are starting from the Tables tab of the Database window, double-click a table name or click it and then click the Open button.

LEARN BY EXAMPLE
To test drive the techniques described in the following pages for entering data in a datasheet, open the Figure 17-14 (Enter Data) *file on the companion CD.*

Entering Data in a Datasheet

The pages that follow explain how to enter data in a datasheet, as well as how to enter data in memo fields, and how to hide and freeze columns so you never lose sight of where you are entering data in a datasheet.

TIP: Don't worry about whether you are entering data in the first record or last record in a datasheet. It doesn't matter where you enter the data. Access gives you lots of opportunities to sort or rearrange records on the datasheet, as the next chapter explains.

To enter data in a datasheet, go to the last record. To get there, either click the New Record button or scroll to the bottom of the datasheet and click in the first field of the last, empty record. After you type the first character in the new record, a picture of a pencil appears to the left of the record so you know where you are entering data. Meanwhile, Access inserts a new blank row at the bottom of the table and marks the new row with an asterisk:

	Reesin	Roger	(415) 555-2431
	Keeger	Bill	(415) 555-3551
✎			
✳			

Enter data in the first field and press the TAB key or press ENTER when you have finished. The cursor moves to the next field so you can enter data there. When you have entered data in all the fields in the record, press ENTER or TAB again. The cursor moves to the next row so you can enter another record.

NOTE: At the bottom of the datasheet, Access tells you how many records are in the database table and which record the cursor is in.

Formatted Fields, Input Masks, and Drop-Down Lists

That's all there is to it. The only unusual things to notice about entering data on a datasheet is that you don't have to worry about formatting when you enter data in a field that has been formatted in a certain way. You encounter punctuation marks when the cursor is in a field with an input mask, and you see an arrow when the cursor is in a field to which you have attached a drop-down list, also known as a lookup table. The following illustrations show a field that has been formatted for entering currency figures, a field with an input mask, and a field with a drop-down list:

Do the following when you encounter formatted fields, input masks, and drop-down lists:

- *Formatted fields* Enter the value and let Access format the field for you. For example, if you type **432.1** in the Cost field shown in the previous illustration and press TAB or ENTER, Access formats the entry as follows: $4,321.10. You don't have to worry about entering the dollar sign, comma, or trailing zero because the field has been formatted with the Currency data type.

- *Input masks* Enter the numbers or letters without any concern for punctuation marks. Access bypasses punctuation marks and moves the cursor directly to the next place where a number or letter needs to be entered.

- *Drop-down lists* Click the down arrow and choose an item from the list.

Entering Data in Memo Fields

As you know if you read "Creating a Field" earlier in this chapter, Access gives you the opportunity to create Memo fields for storing long notes in a database table. However, entering a long note on the datasheet is well-nigh impossible. To enter a note in a Memo field, move the cursor into the field and press SHIFT+F2. You see the Zoom dialog box shown in Figure 17-14. Enter your note and click OK or press ENTER. Only the first few words of a note appear on the datasheet, but you can read a note on a datasheet by moving the cursor into the Memo field and pressing SHIFT+F2.

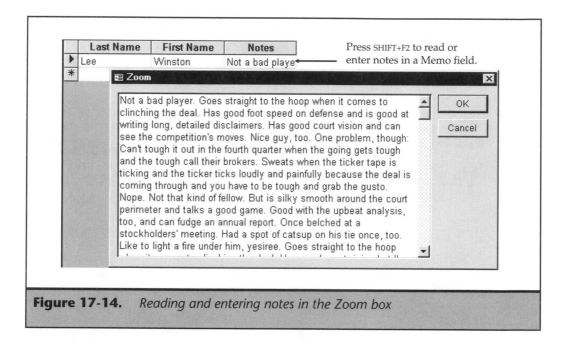

Figure 17-14. *Reading and entering notes in the Zoom box*

Freezing and Hiding Columns so You Can See What You Are Doing

As you enter data on the outskirts of a datasheet, it is sometimes hard to tell what data to enter. When the cursor is in the eighth or ninth column, for example, you lose sight of the fields in the first and second column that usually identify the name of the person or thing whose data you are entering. You can, however, "freeze" the first and second column—or any column for that matter—so that columns stay onscreen no matter how far you stray to the outskirts of the datasheet. And you can also hide columns so that fewer appear on the datasheet.

FREEZING COLUMNS IN ONE PLACE

Follow these steps to "freeze" a column or columns so that they can always be seen:

1. Select the column or columns that are to stay onscreen. To select a single column, click its column heading. To select several columns, click the first, then hold down the SHIFT key as you click the last one. Columns are highlighted onscreen after they have been selected.

2. Choose the Format menu Freeze Columns command.

Now when you move around in the datasheet, the columns you "froze" stay onscreen. To "unfreeze" a column or columns, choose the Format menu Unfreeze All Columns command.

HIDING COLUMNS ON THE DATASHEET

Follow these steps to hide a column or columns:

1. Select the column or columns that you want to hide. To select a column, click its column heading. Select several columns by clicking the first, then holding down the SHIFT key as you click the last one.

2. Choose the Format menu Hide Columns command.

The columns disappear. You can hide as many different columns as you want. When the hide-and-seek game is over and you need to see the columns again, choose the Format menu Unhide Columns command, click beside the names of the columns you want to unhide in the Unhide Columns dialog box, and click the Close button:

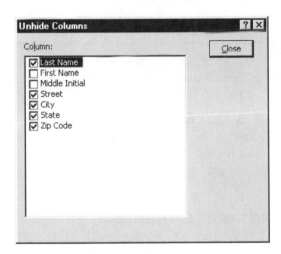

Editing Data in a Datasheet

To edit data in a datasheet, click inside the field whose data needs editing and delete or enter new characters. If you want to replace the data in a field, select the data and start typing. The old data is instantly erased and is replaced with the numbers or characters you type.

So much for basic editing techniques. The following pages explain how to move around in a datasheet, delete records, and delete columns.

WARNING: You can't edit data in the following kinds of fields: AutoNumber fields, locked fields, fields in queries that establish relationships between fields, and calculated fields.

Press	To Move
↑	To the previous record
↓	To the following record
TAB or ENTER	To the next field in the record
SHIFT+TAB	To the previous field in the record
CTRL+HOME	To the first field in the record
CTRL+END	To the last field in the record
PGUP	Up one screen
PGDN	Down one screen

Table 17-2.   *Moving Around in a Datasheet*

Moving Around a Datasheet

Table 17-2 explains keyboard techniques for getting around in a datasheet. Besides pressing keys, you can click the buttons or work the scrollbar on the bottom of the datasheet to move the cursor. Figure 17-15 explains what the buttons on the bottom of the datasheet do.

Deleting Records and Columns

Deleting a record on a datasheet isn't a big deal, but deleting a column is. When you delete a column, you delete an entire field in the database. In other words, you delete part of each record you have entered so far. Think twice before doing that. In fact, I recommend switching to Design view to delete a field, because Design view affords a better look at the structure of the table and how the fields fit together (see "Moving, Copying, Deleting, and Renaming Fields," earlier in this chapter, to learn how to delete a field in Design view).

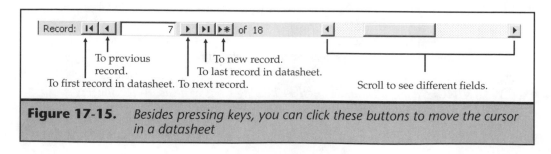

Figure 17-15.   *Besides pressing keys, you can click these buttons to move the cursor in a datasheet*

WARNING: *When you delete a column or record, you can't get the data back. It is gone forever. Access doesn't let you click the Undo button, for example, to get it back.*

 WARNING: *Deleting a field may adversely affect the forms and reports that get their data from the table.*

DELETING A RECORD

To delete a record, follow these steps:

1. Select the record you want to delete by clicking the small box to its left. To select several records, click the box to the left of the first one, and then SHIFT+click the box to the left of the last one.

2. Click the Delete Record button.

3. Click Yes when Access asks if you really want to delete the record.

 WARNING: *If the record you want to delete is related to records in another table, deleting the record deletes the records in the other table as well. Access displays a dialog box to warn you about it if you try to delete a record that has relatives elsewhere. Click No in the dialog box to keep from deleting the records, then choose the Tools menu Relationships command to open the Relationships window and investigate the relationship. Refer to "Seeing the Relationships Between Tables," earlier in this chapter, for more information.*

DELETING A COLUMN

If you disregarded my advice about deleting columns and want to delete columns in Datasheet view, follow these steps:

1. Select the column or columns you want to delete. To do so, either click the column heading or SHIFT+click column headings to select more than one.

2. Choose the Edit menu Delete Column.

3. Click Yes in the dialog box that asks if you really want to go through with it.

 WARNING: *Before you can delete a field that is related to a field in another table, you have to end the relationship. See "Forging the Relationships Between Tables," earlier in this chapter.*

Forms for Entering and Viewing Data

Besides viewing and entering data in Datasheet view, *forms* are the chief means of viewing and entering data in a database table. Access forms are very much like the forms you fill out to apply for a job or a driver's license. Each field is labeled and asks

ACCESS

for or offers information of some kind. The form shown in Figure 17-16, for example, solicits and displays information about the members of an organization. There are fields for each member's name, address, phone number, and dues amount. When you enter data in a form like this, it is entered in its underlying database table. When you view data or query data by means of a form, the data comes from a database table.

If you look closely, however, you will see that this form does more than enter data in a database table. Along the bottom of the form are buttons called Committees, Payments, Preview Invoice, and so on. By clicking one of these buttons, you can open another form and view data from the Committees, Payments, or Invoice database tables.

Forms can be far more sophisticated than datasheets. For one thing, you can usually see all the fields in a record on a form. And you can also clearly see where data is supposed to be entered because each place on the form is clearly labeled. Moreover, you can create more than one form for a database table—or you can link a form to several database tables and assemble information from several different places at once.

The following pages explain how to create a form, print a form, enter data in a form, copy data from one form to another, and delete a record from a form.

LEARN BY EXAMPLE
To experiment with the techniques in this chapter for creating forms, open the Figure 17-16 (Forms) *file on the companion CD.*

EXAMPLES

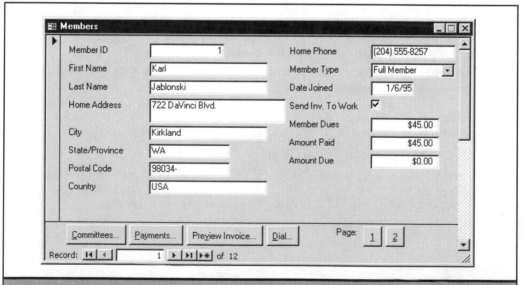

Figure 17-16. *Forms present another way to enter and view data in a database table*

Creating a Form

Access offers no less than three ways to create a form: in Design view, with an AutoForm option, and with the Form Wizard. The least sophisticated but by far the easiest method of creating a form is to use an AutoForm option. With an autoform, you get one text box, check box, or drop-down menu for each field in your database table. To create forms that draw upon data from more than one table or query, create your form with the Form Wizard or in Design view. By the way, if you used the Database Wizard to create your database, chances are that Access already created a form or two for your database.

To begin creating a form, start from the Forms tab of the Database window. Forms that you or Access already created appear on the Forms tab. To create a new form, click the New button on the Forms tab. You see the New Form dialog box shown in the following illustration:

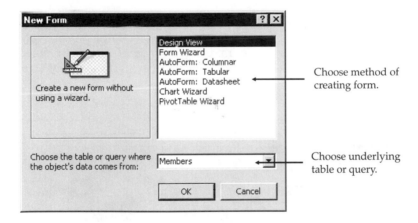

If you intend to create an autoform, choose a table or query from the drop-down list at the bottom of the dialog box. Access will create a form for each field in the database table. You need not choose a table or query to create a form in Design view with the Form Wizard, Chart Wizard, or Pivot Table Wizard option in the dialog box.

Choose one of the following means of creating a new form:

■ *Design View* For creating the form yourself, one control—that is, one text box, one check box, or one command button—at a time. For more information, look up "Design view, forms" in the Index tab of the Help dialog box.

■ *Form Wizard* For letting the Form Wizard do the work. The Form Wizard asks questions about which fields to include in the form and creates the form when you are finished answering questions. See "Creating a Form with the Form Wizard," later in this chapter.

- *AutoForm: Columnar* For creating a two-column form in which the text boxes and other controls are left-aligned, one below the other. The form in Figure 17-16 is a columnar form, as is the topmost form in Figure 17-17. To learn about this and the other autoform options, see "Creating a Form with Access's AutoForms," later in this chapter.

- *AutoForm: Tabular* For creating a form in which the text boxes and other controls appear in a table format, as shown in Figure 17-17.

- *AutoForm: Datasheet* For creating a form that looks exactly like a datasheet, as shown in Figure 17-17.

- *Chart Wizard* For creating a form with the Chart Wizard that shows data from a chart.

- *Pivot Table Wizard* For creating a form that gathers information from an Excel pivot table.

TIP: Data input masks, formats, drop-down lists, and data type settings made in Design view to a table appear on the form as well when you create a form for entering and viewing the data in a database table. You can create special formats for entering data in a form, but it is far easier to do that in Design view in a table than it is in Design view in a form.

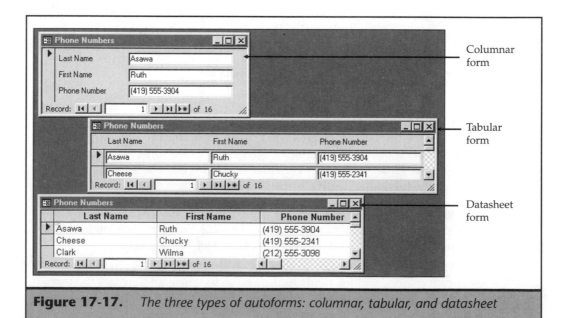

Figure 17-17.   *The three types of autoforms: columnar, tabular, and datasheet*

Creating a Form with Access's AutoForms

After you have clicked the New button on the Forms tab of the Database window, chosen which table or query to be the basis of the form in the New Form dialog box, and chosen an AutoForm option, Access creates the form nearly instantaneously. Figure 17-17 shows the three types of autoforms you can create. On your new form is one text box, check box, or drop-down menu for each field in the table. That's all there is to it. See "Entering, Viewing, and Editing Data on Forms," later in this chapter, to learn how to enter data in forms.

TIP: Access offers a very fast way to create a columnar autoform. On the Tables or Queries tab of the Database window, click the table or query for which you want to create a form. Then, either choose the Insert menu AutoForm command or click the arrow beside the New Object button on the Database toolbar and choose AutoForm.

Creating a Form with the Form Wizard

The Form Wizard is the way to go if you want to create a sophisticated form that draws on data from more than one table without having to enter into the dreaded realm of Design view. Besides drawing upon data from more than one table or query, forms created with the Wizard can include command buttons and other amenities. And they look good, too, because you get to choose one of Access's pretty designs for your form.

WARNING: To create a form with fields from more than one table, the tables must be related to one another. See "Forging the Relationships Between Tables," earlier in this chapter.

To create a form with the Form Wizard, follow these steps:

1. Start from the Forms tab of the Datasheet window and click the New button. You see the New Table dialog box.

2. Click Form Wizard and then click OK. You see the first Wizard dialog box shown in Figure 17-18. This dialog box wants to know which fields to include on the form.

3. In the Tables/Queries drop-down list, choose the first table or query from which to get fields for the form.

4. Click a field in the Available Fields box, and then click the triangle that points to the right to enter the field in the Selected Fields box. You can click the double triangle to enter all the fields in the Available Fields box in the Selected Fields box.

5. Repeat steps 3 and 4 until all the fields you want for the form are assembled in the Selected Fields box.

6. Click the Next button. As shown in Figure 17-19, you see a dialog box that asks how you want to view your data. What this dialog box really wants to know is which of the tables or queries whose fields you choose for the form should take precedence over the others. Fields from the table or query you click in the box on the left side of the dialog box appear in the top half of the form.

NOTE: If you are including fields from only one table or query on the form, the Wizard bypasses the dialog box shown in Figure 17-19. Instead, you see a dialog box for choosing a columnar, tabular, datasheet, or justified form. Figure 17-7 demonstrates what three of the forms are. The Justified option creates columnar, right-aligned fields on the form.

7. In the box in the upper-left corner of the dialog box, click on the name of the table or query whose fields are to appear on the top of the form.

8. Choose the Form with subform(s) or Linked forms option button:

   ■ *Form with subform(s)* Places fields from secondary tables or queries at the bottom of the form.

   ■ *Linked forms* Creates a button on the form that you can click to access fields from the secondary tables or queries.

9. Click the Next button. The next dialog box asks you to choose a layout for the form.

10. Click option buttons until you see a preview form in the dialog box that suits you, and then click the Next button. The next dialog box asks you to name forms and subforms that comprise your new form.

11. Enter form and subform names and click the Finish button. Your new form appears onscreen.

Entering, Viewing, and Editing Data on Forms

After you have created a form, you can start entering data in it. The following pages explain how to enter data, move from record to record in a database table while forms are onscreen, delete a record, copy data from one record to another record, and print a form.

To open a form, go to the Forms tab of the Database window and either double-click the form you want to open or click the form and then click the Open button.

NOTE: "Finding Data in a Database Table" at the start of the next chapter explains how to find a record in a table.

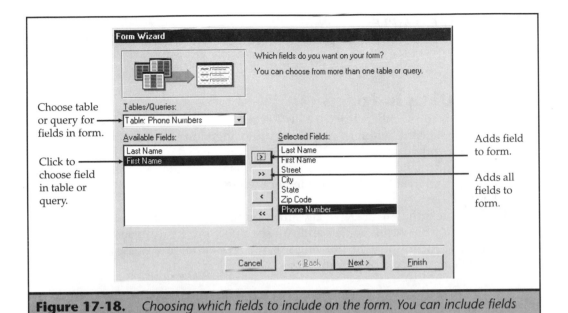

Figure 17-18. *Choosing which fields to include on the form. You can include fields from more than one table or query*

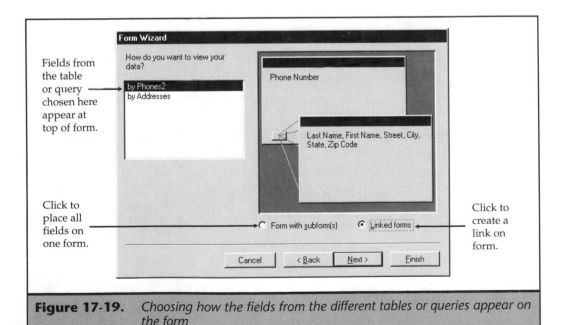

Figure 17-19. *Choosing how the fields from the different tables or queries appear on the form*

ACCESS

LEARN BY EXAMPLE
To practice entering data on forms, open the Figure 17-A (Forms) *file on the companion CD.*

Entering Data in Forms

To enter data in a form, either click the New Record button on the Form View toolbar or click the New Record button next to the record navigation buttons at the bottom of the form. When you do so, an empty form appears onscreen. Enter data in the fields. To move to the next field after you finish entering data, press the TAB or ENTER key. You can also move from field to field by clicking or by pressing the UP ARROW or DOWN ARROW key.

When you press the TAB or ENTER key after you have entered data in the last field, the data on the form is saved on disk and you see a new, empty form onscreen. (If you are working on a form/subform, pressing TAB or ENTER either moves the cursor to the subform or to a new record on the subform.)

Viewing Records on Forms

Use the toolbar along the bottom of the Form window to move from record to record and view the data in forms:

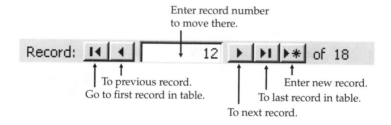

You can also use the following keyboard techniques to move from record to record:

Key	Moves To
HOME	First field in record
END	Last field in record
PGUP	To previous record
PGDN	To next record

And these keyboard techniques can come in handy when you are entering data in a multitable form with subforms:

Key	What It Do
CTRL+TAB	Leaves a subform and moves to the next field in the main form
CTRL+SHIFT+HOME	Moves to the first field in the main form
CTRL+SHIFT+TAB	Leaves a subform and moves to the previous field in the main form

Deleting Records

To delete a record on a form, display it onscreen and click the Delete Record button on the Form View toolbar. Click Yes when Access asks if you really and truly want to delete the record. But remember, you can't get the data back after you delete a record. Deleted records are gone for good.

Copying Data from One Record to Another

Oftentimes the data in one record is similar to the data in another. To save a little time, you can copy one record and then change whatever needs changing to enter a new record. Follow these steps to copy data from one record to another:

1. Display the record that you want to copy.
2. Click in the vertical bar on the left side of the form. Clicking the vertical bar selects the data in the record.

Click here to select record data. →

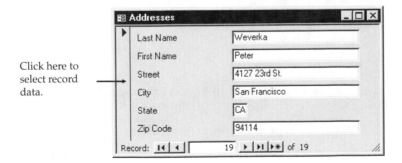

3. Choose the Edit menu Copy command.
4. Click the New Record button.
5. Click the vertical bar on the left side of the blank form.

6. Choose the Edit menu Paste command. Except for primary key data and data in a field that has been indexed and is supposed to be unique, the data is copied to the new record.

7. Change the data in the form as necessary.

Printing a Form

Follow these steps to print a record in a form:

1. To print a single record, display it onscreen. To print several records or all of the records on the forms, it doesn't matter where you start.

2. Press CTRL+P or choose the File menu Print command. You see the Print dialog box.

3. Tell Access what you want to print:

   ■ Click the Selected Record(s) option button to print the form that is displayed onscreen.

   ■ Click the All button to print forms for all the records in the table.

   ■ Enter record numbers in the Pages From and To boxes to print several forms in sequence.

4. Click the OK button.

Printing a Database Table

Follow these steps to print all or some of the records in a database table:

1. Open the database table by double-clicking it on the Tables tab of the Database window.

2. Choose File menu Print command.

3. Tell Access what you want to print:

   ■ Click the Selected Record(s) option button to print only a few records in the datasheet that appears onscreen.

   ■ Click the All button to print all the records in the table.

   ■ Enter record numbers in the Pages From and To boxes to print several records in sequence.

4. Click the OK button.

 TIP: *Click the Print Preview button to see beforehand what the records will look like after they are printed.*

Exporting Data to Other Programs and Databases

After you have carefully and thoughtfully entered data in an Access database table, you might decide that your data is needed elsewhere. The following pages explain how to copy data to another database program and how to copy data from one Access database to another Access database. You will also find instructions for copying a table's design but not its data from one Access database to another.

Copying Data to Another Program

Access has a special command, File menu Save As/Export command, for copying a database table to a new file so that other database programs, and Excel too, can make use of the data. Follow these steps to make a copy of an Access database table so that users of other programs can have the data:

1. Starting from the Tables tab of the Database window, open the table whose data you want to copy. To do that, double-click on the table name on the Tables tab.

2. With the table onscreen, choose the File menu Save As/Export command. A dialog box asks if you want to copy the table for use within the database you are working on or for use with an outside database.

3. Make sure the To an External File or Database button is selected, and then click OK. You see the Save Table As dialog box:

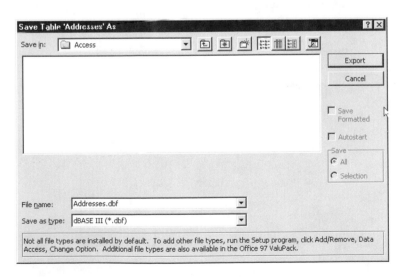

4. In the Save as type drop-down list, choose a file format that permits your friends or colleagues to use the data in the database table.

 TIP: *If the program your friends or colleagues use isn't on the drop-down list, choose the Rich Text Format option. Rich Text Format is the* lingua franca *of the computer world. With Rich Text Format, programs can pass data back and forth without losing sophisticated data formats.*

5. Enter a name for the copy in the File name box.

6. Choose a folder to store the file in.

7. Click the Export button.

Depending on the type of export you are performing, Access may start a wizard to help you copy the data. Follow the instructions in the wizard dialog boxes until the copy procedure is completed.

Copying Data to Another Access Database

Follow these steps to copy the data in a database table from one Access database to another Access database:

1. Open the Tables tab in the Database window.

2. Click the table you want to copy.

3. Choose the Edit menu Copy command. The entire database table is copied to the Clipboard.

4. Close the Access database.

5. Open the Access database into which you want to copy the table.

6. Choose Edit Paste. You see the Paste Table As dialog box:

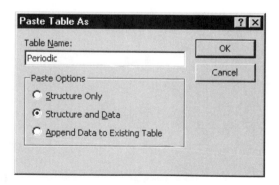

7. Make sure that the Structure and Data option button is selected. With this option, you copy the design of the database table and the data as well.

 TIP: *Choose the Structure Only option to copy the design of a table, but not its data, from one Access database to another.*

8. Enter a name for the table in the Table Name box.

9. Click OK.

The
Complete
Reference

Office
97

Chapter 18

Sorting, Filtering, and Querying
a Database

The last two chapters explained how to enter and view data in a database. In this chapter, you learn how to pester a database for information. This chapter explains how to dig into a database and find the information you have so carefully and thoughtfully stored there. You will also learn how to find specific records in a database, filter data to derive information of a certain kind, sort data to arrange it in a new way, and query a database to get information.

No doubt you have received lots of junk mail in your life. You might be interested to know that your name was chosen as the result of a query. That's right—you lived in a certain postal code, purchased products from the mailer before, or met some other condition that deemed you worthy of being sent a solicitation of some kind. In this chapter, you learn the same techniques the big companies use to cull information from a database.

In general terms, there are four ways to draw data out of a database:

- *Find it*   Use Access's Edit menu Find command to locate specific records.

- *Filter it*   Find all the records that share a field value in a database table. For example, you can find the records of all the people who live in Florida. Or you can find the records of all the inventory items that cost more than $400.

- *Sort it*   Rearrange the records in a database table in a new way to make records easier to find.

- *Query it*   Find records throughout an entire database that meet certain criteria. If you set up and enter data correctly in a database, for example, you can find all the people in three Los Angeles ZIP codes who own sports utility vehicles and have incomes over $50,000 a year.

Each method of getting data out of a database is described in the following pages.

Finding Data in a Database Table

To find a single record in a table, use the Edit menu Find command. You might use this command to find records that need changing or deleting. The following pages explain how to find data in a database table and how to replace the data if it needs replacing.

Finding Specific Records

Follow these steps to find data in a database table:

1. Open the table by double-clicking it on the Tables tab of the Database window.

2. Click in the field you want to search if you happen to know in which field the data you are looking for is located. If the data might be found in more than one field, it doesn't matter which field the cursor is in when you start the search.

WARNING: *Be sure to complete step 9 in this list of instructions if you want to search in more than one field.*

3. Press CTRL+F, click the Find button, or choose the Edit menu Find command. You see the Find in field dialog box shown in Figure 18-1.

4. Enter the text or numbers you are looking for in the Find What box.

5. In the Search drop-down list, choose Up or Down instead of All if you know where the record is and you want to search in one direction.

6. To speed up the search, choose an option from the Match drop-down list:

   ■ *Any Part of Field* The search stops on the letters or numbers you entered in the Find What box no matter where it encounters them in fields. This is the broadest way to search. For example, a search for the letters *con* finds *Conner, ex-con, con, 113 Condor Dr.,* and *University of Connecticut.*

   ■ *Whole Field* The search stops on the letters or numbers you entered only if the letters or numbers stand by themselves in a field. This is the narrowest way to search. A search for *con* finds *con* and *Con,* but not *Conner, ex-con, 113 Condor Dr.,* or *University of Connecticut* because *con* is a part and not the sum of those entries.

   ■ *Start of Field* The search stops on the letters or numbers you entered if they appear at the start of a field. A search for *con* finds *Con* and *Conner,* but not *ex-con, 113 Condor Dr.,* or *University of Connecticut.*

ACCESS

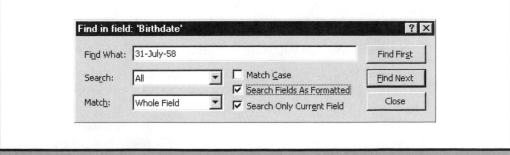

Figure 18-1. *Telling Access how to search the database table*

7. Click the Match Case check box if you know the correct combination of upper- and lowercase letters you are looking for and you entered the right combination of letters in the Find What box.

8. Click the Search Fields As Formatted check box if you are searching in a field that has been formatted a specific way. As "Establishing Field Properties for Easier Data Entry" in Chapter 17 explained, dates, times, numbers, currency figures, and Yes/No data types are formatted in specific ways. To find data in a field that has been formatted, the Search Fields As Formatted check box must be checked and the text or numbers in the Find What box must be formatted correctly as well. For example, the search in Figure 18-1 will find *31-July-58* but will bypass *July 31, 1958* in the Birthdate field. Only by entering *31-July-58* in the Find What box can I expect to find people born on that day.

9. If you want to search in more than one field, click to remove the check mark from the Search Only Current Field check box. Notice that the dialog box changes names when you clear the check mark. Now the dialog box is simply called "Find."

10. Click the Find First button. If the letters or numbers can be found, Access highlights the first place where they appear in the database table.

11. Click Find Next to find the next set of letters or numbers. You can click Find Next as many times as it takes to find the letters or numbers.

12. Click the Close button when your search is over.

Finding and Replacing Data

As well as finding data in a database table, you can find data and replace it with other data. You might do this to correct data-entry errors. For example, if you discovered to your dismay that Waukegan, the crown jewel of the state of Illinois, had been misspelled time and time again in your database table, you could search for the incorrect *Woukigan* and replace it with the correctly spelled *Waukegan*.

Follow these steps to find and replace data in a database table:

1. Open the database table that you want to rummage around in.

2. If you know in which field the data you want to replace is found, click in that field (and be sure to click the Search Only Current Field check box in the Replace dialog box).

3. Press CTRL+H or choose the Edit menu Replace command. You see the Replace dialog box shown in Figure 18-2. If you searched for or searched for and replaced text or numbers since you opened the database table, the items you searched for earlier appear in the Find What and Replace With dialog box.

4. Enter the text or numbers you are looking for in the Find What box.

5. Enter the replacement text or numbers in the Replace With box. Be sure to enter the correct combination of upper- and lowercase letters.

6. If you want to search and replace in a certain direction, open the Search drop-down menu and choose Up or Down.

7. Click the Match Case check box if you know the correct combination of upper- and lowercase letters you are looking for.

WARNING: *Under no circumstances should you uncheck the Match Whole Field check box. If you ignore my advice and uncheck the box, Access replaces parts of field entries, which can have untoward consequences. For example, a search for* **Brook** *would also find* **Brooklyn,** *and if the replacement text was* **Briock,** *the result would be a new entry,* **Briocklyn,** *which is phonetically correct but a misspelling of the New York borough.*

8. Click the Find Next button. Access finds the text or numbers you are looking for if they are in the database table.

9. Either click the Replace or Replace All button:

   ■ *Replace* Replaces the text or numbers that Access found with the replacement text. Click Find Next again to find the next instance of the text or numbers.

   ■ *Replace All* Replaces all occurrences of the text or numbers in the database with the replacement text.

WARNING: *Click the Replace All button at your own risk. By "replacing all," you don't get the chance to review each replacement as it is made. Moreover, Access doesn't offer an Undo command for reversing the replacements. They are permanent.*

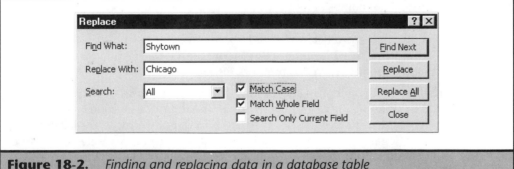

Figure 18-2. *Finding and replacing data in a database table*

ACCESS

> **TIP:** *You can also find and replace data by running an update query. See "Update: Updating Records in a Database" later in this chapter.*

Filtering to Find Data

Filtering means to find all the records in a database table that share the same or nearly the same field values. Unlike a Find operation, you can find more than one record at a time when you filter a database table. For example, you might filter a database table to find all the people who live in Florida. Or you might filter it to find all the people whose income is $40,000 or more. You can use more than one criterion to filter data. For example, you could filter a database to find the records of all the people who live in Florida, have incomes above $40,000, and own their own homes.

Access offers three ways to filter a database table. You can filter by form, filter by selection, or filter by exclusion. Either way, the general idea is to choose a field value from the database table and then filter the table to find or exclude all records that have the same value.

- *By form* Choose values from drop-down lists to tell Access which records you want to get, and then give the filtering command. Filter by form when you want to filter a database table using several different criteria. For example, you could search in a Videos database table for all movies that star either Humphrey Bogart or George Raft. What's more, you can use comparison operators in a filter by form. For example, you can search for videos that cost less than $35.

- *By selection* Starting in Datasheet view, select a value or values in a single record that you want to find throughout the database table, and then give the filtering command. For example, to find all movies with Humphrey Bogart in them in a Videos database table, select Bogart's name. The filtering operation will throw up the names of all movies in which Humphrey Bogart played. It is hard to choose different filtering criteria with the "by selection" method, however. In other words, it is hard to look for two things at once—for example, movies that star either Humphrey Bogart or George Raft. And you can't use comparison operators with this method, either.

- *By exclusion* Starting in Datasheet view, select a value or values and then filter the database. You see all the records in the database *except* those in which the value or values you selected are found. For example, by selecting Humphrey Bogart's name and then filtering by exclusion in a Videos database table, you could find all the movies in the table except those in which Humphrey Bogart starred.

Filtering by form, by selection, and by exclusion are discussed on the following pages. You also learn how to save the results of a filtering operation on a form or in a report. There is another method of filtering called Advanced Filter/Sort. However, it has more in common with query operations and is discussed later in this chapter under "Advanced Filter/Sort: Sorting on Two Fields."

LEARN BY EXAMPLE
To try your hand at filtering a database table, open the Figure 18-3 (Filter) *file on the companion CD and filter away.*

Filtering by Form

Follow these steps to filter a database by form:

1. Open the database table you want to filter by double-clicking its name on the Tables tab of the Database window.

2. Click the Filter by Form button on the Table Datasheet toolbar or choose the Filter by Form command from the Records menu Filter submenu. The Datasheet changes into a tabular form, as shown in Figure 18-3.

TIP: If you or someone else filtered the database already, criteria from the last filtering operation appear in the first row of the form. Click the Clear Grid button on the Filter/Sort toolbar to remove the criteria and start anew.

Filters vs. Queries

Filtering is a sophisticated means of finding more than one record in a database table. Query a database table if you frequently use the same criteria to gather information or you want to include information from more than one database table.

When you filter a database table, you can use standard comparison operators to find records whose values are greater than, less than, equal to, less than or equal to, greater than or equal to, or not equal to a value that you enter. For example, you could find items of a certain kind that cost $20 or more. However, you can't use expressions to find records whose values fall within a certain range. In other words, to find items that cost between $20 and $22, you can't filter a database table. To do that, you have to construct a query.

Access remembers the last filtering operation you did so you can filter in the same way a second time, but you can't store several different filtering criteria and call on each one whenever you need it. You can, however, save the results of a filtering operation in a form or report.

By the way, it is possible to filter the results of a query. To do so, open the query on the Queries tab of the Datasheet window and then give a filtering command.

You can filter for values by using comparison operators.
Click here to filter the table.
Choose criteria from the drop-down lists.

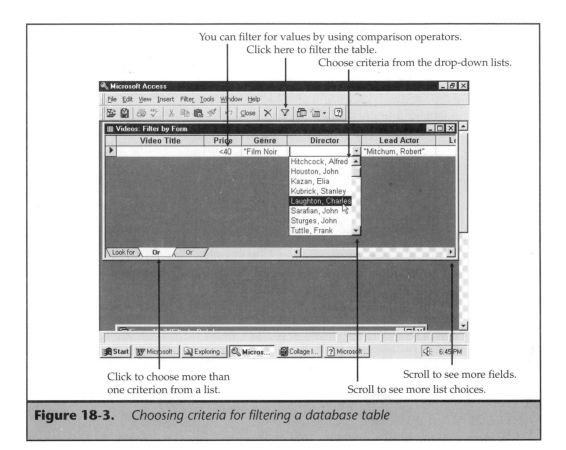

Click to choose more than
one criterion from a list.

Scroll to see more fields.
Scroll to see more list choices.

Figure 18-3. *Choosing criteria for filtering a database table*

Field names appear across the top of the form. Notice the down-arrow in the first field. By clicking that down-arrow, or by moving to another field and clicking the down-arrow there, you can open a drop-down list with all the values that were entered in each record of the database. In Figure 18-3, an inventory database table called Videos is being filtered to locate *film noirs* that cost less than $40, were directed by Charles Laughton, and star the great Robert Mitchum. On the Director drop-down list are the names of all the directors that were entered in the database table.

3. Enter the criteria for the filtering operation:

■ *Choosing criteria from lists* To search for values in the table, open as many drop-down lists as necessary and choose values. Values are listed in alphabetical order. You might have to scroll to get to the bottom of the list and find the value you are looking for.

- ■ *Or operator for making more than one selection from the same list* To choose more than one value from the same drop-down list, click the Or tab along the bottom of the window and then make another selection from the list. A new Or tab appears each time you make another selection from the same list.

- ■ *Comparison operators for choosing relative values* Enter a number and a comparison operator in a numeric field to look for monetary and numerical values in the database table. In Figure 18-3, the *<40* tells Access to look for videos that cost less than $40. Table 18-1 describes the comparison operators you can use.

TIP: *To remove a criterion from the form, select it and press the* DELETE *key. To remove a criterion you entered by means of an Or operator, click the Or tab for the criterion you entered and then choose the Edit menu Delete command.*

4. Click the Apply Filter button when you are done entering the filtering criteria. The results of the filter appear in the Form window.

My search for a *film noir* directed by Charles Laughton and starring the great Robert Mitchum turned up—what else?—*Night of the Hunter,* as the following illustration shows. If I was a clerk at a video store and someone called to ask if the store carried that movie, whatyamacallit, with Robert Mitchum that was like really, really creepy and was directed by that fat English guy, you know, Charles Laughton, I could find out very quickly if the store carried that video and what its title is by filtering the Videos database table:

Video Title	Price	Genre	Director	Lead Actor
Night of the Hunter	$35.00	Film Noir	Laughton, Charles	Mitchum, Robert

5. Click the Remove Filter button to return to the database table.

Next time you click the Filter by Form button and see the form onscreen, the filtering criteria you so laboriously constructed appears on the form in case you want to filter the database table all over again. Click the Clear Grid button on the Filter/Sort toolbar if you want to start all over and enter new criteria. To conduct the same filtering operation, simply click the Apply Filter button.

TIP: *After you have filtered records from a database table, you can filter the records that are left. In this way, by filtering and filtering, you can trim the database table down to size and find the records you are looking for.*

Operator	Name	Example (27..23)
<	Less than	<25 finds 24, 23
<=	Less than or equal to	<=25 finds 25, 24, 23
>	Greater than	>25 finds 27, 26
>=	Greater than or equal to	>=25 finds 27, 26, 25
=	Equal to	=25 finds 25
<>	Not equal to	<>25 finds 27, 26, 24, 23

Table 18-1.   *Comparison Operators for Filtering Operations*

Creating a Form or Report with the Results of a Filtering Operation

After you have finished a filtering operation, you can save the results in a form or report (Chapter 19 explains reports). To save filtering results in a form or report, follow these steps:

1. With the results of the filtering operation onscreen, click the down-arrow beside the New Object button and choose either AutoForm or AutoReport.

2. Click Yes in the message box that appears and advises you to save the database table from which you filtered data.

3. If you created a form, it appears onscreen; if you created a report, you see your report in the Print Preview screen.

4. Click the Save button if you created a form: press CTRL+S or choose the File menu Save command to save a report.

5. In the Save As dialog box, enter a name for your form or report and click OK:

6. Close the form or report to see the filtering results again.

7. Click the Remove Filter button to get back to the database table.

Forms are kept on the Forms tab of the Database window; reports are kept on the Reports tab. Go to the Forms or Reports tab and double-click a form or report to open it.

Filtering by Selection

Filtering by selection is a primitive version of filtering by form. It is harder to do, makes it hard to enter more than one search criterion, and doesn't permit the use of comparison operators. As far as I know, the only advantage of filtering by selection is that you can do it in a hurry.

Follow these steps to filter by selection:

1. Open the database table you want to filter by double-clicking its name on the Tables tab of the Database window.

2. Choose criteria for the filtering operation:

   ■ *Search for one field value* Click in a field whose data value you want to search for. In the following illustration, I clicked on Ford, John in the Director field. This filtering operation will turn up all movies in the Videos database table that were directed by John Ford:

Video Title	Price	Genre	Director	Lead Actor
Long Goodbye, The	$54.00	Film Noir	Altman, Robert	Gould, Elliot
Magnificent Seven	$54.00	Western	Sturges, John	Brynner, Yul
Maltese Falcon	$36.00	Drama	Houston, John	Bogart, Humphrey
My Darling Clementine	$35.00	Western	Ford, John	Fonda, Henry
Night at the Opera, A	$24.00	Comedy	Wood, Sam	Marx Brothers

   ■ *Search for two or more values in the same field* Select two or more values in the same field to search for values in the same field. In the following illustration, for example, I have selected Sturges, John; Huston, John; and Ford, John to find all movies in the database table that were directed by those three directors:

	Video Title	Price	Genre	Director	Lead Actor	▲
	Long Goodbye, The	$54.00	Film Noir	Altman, Robert	Gould, Elliot	
▶	Magnificent Seven	$54.00	Western	Sturges, John	Brynner, Yul	
	Maltese Falcon	$36.00	Drama	Houston, John	Bogart, Humphrey	
	My Darling Clementine	$35.00	Western	Ford, John	Fonda, Henry	
	Night at the Opera, A	$24.00	Comedy	Wood, Sam	Marx Brothers	

Selecting field values this way is kind of tricky. To do it, gently move the pointer to the left side of the first field value you want to select, and when the pointer changes into a cross, drag downward across the other values.

TIP: *Unfortunately, you can only select more than one value in the same field or more than one value in two different fields if the values are next to each other in the database table. You can, however, move records (rows) or move fields (columns) in the database table so that they are next to each other, and then select them. But why bother? Filter by form, not by selection, when you want to select criteria from more than one field or in more than one field.*

■ *Search for values in two or more different fields* Select two or more values in different fields to search for values in different fields. In the following illustration, for example, I have selected Western in the Genre field and Ford, John in the Director field to search for all westerns that were directed by John Ford. To select fields this way, gently move the pointer to the left side of the first field value you want to select, and when the pointer changes into a cross, drag to the right across the other field values.

	Video Title	Price	Genre	Director	Lead Actor	▲
	Long Goodbye, The	$54.00	Film Noir	Altman, Robert	Gould, Elliot	
	Magnificent Seven	$54.00	Western	Sturges, John	Brynner, Yul	
	Maltese Falcon	$36.00	Drama	Houston, John	Bogart, Humphrey	
▶	My Darling Clementine	$35.00	Western	Ford, John	Fonda, Henry	
	Night at the Opera, A	$24.00	Comedy	Wood, Sam	Marx Brothers	

3. Click the Filter by Selection button on the Table Datasheet toolbar. The table shrinks considerably and you see the results of the search in the Table window.

4. Click the Remove Filter button or choose the Records menu Remove Filter/Sort command to see all the records in the database table again.

Filtering by Exclusion

Filtering by exclusion is a simple operation and is done very much like a filter by selection. To filter by exclusion, open the database table, click a field whose value you want to exclude from the database table, choose the Records menu Filter command,

and click Filter by Excluding Selection. In spite of its name, you can't select more than one value to exclude with the Filter by Excluding Selection command.

In the following illustration, for example, I clicked Western in the Genre field. When I choose the Filter by Excluding Selection command, Access will show me all the movies in the database table *except* westerns.

Video Title	Price	Genre	Director	Lead Actor
Long Goodbye, The	$54.00	Film Noir	Altman, Robert	Gould, Elliot
Magnificent Seven	$54.00	Western	Sturges, John	Brynner, Yul
Maltese Falcon	$36.00	Drama	Houston, John	Bogart, Humphrey
My Darling Clementine	$35.00	Western	Ford, John	Fonda, Henry
Night at the Opera, A	$24.00	Comedy	Wood, Sam	Marx Brothers

Click the Remove Filter button to see all the records again, including the ones you excluded.

Sorting, or Arranging, Records in a Database Table

Sort means to arrange the records in a database table in an entirely new way. By sorting a database table, you can locate information faster. And before you print a database table, you should sort it so that the records appear in the order you want them to appear. To sort a table, you start by selecting the field, or column, on which the table is to be sorted, and then you click either the Sort Ascending or Sort Descending button to sort the records in the column in ascending or descending order:

- *Ascending order* Arranges text entries in alphabetical order from A to Z (California, Nebraska, Wisconsin); numbers from smallest to largest (4, 27, 146); and dates from earliest in time to latest in time (31-Jul-58, 4-Mar-97, 16-Oct-06).

- *Descending order* Arranges text entries from Z to A (Wisconsin, Nebraska, California); numbers from largest to smallest (146, 27, 4); and dates from latest in time to earliest in time (16-Oct-06, 4-Mar-97, 31-Jul-58).

 WARNING: Sorting a table only changes its appearance onscreen. The records revert to their primary key order when the table is closed. If you find yourself sorting records often, create a query that permanently sorts the records in the way you want them to appear onscreen.

The following two illustrations show the same information in the same database table. However, in the illustration on the left, the records have been sorted in ascending order in the Video Title field; in the illustration on the right, the records have been sorted in descending order on the Year field:

Video Title	Year
▶ 39 Steps, The	1935
Bicycle Thief, The	1949
Casablanca	1942
City of Women	1980
Dr. Strangelove	1964
Gone with the Wind	1939
High Noon	1952
I'm All Right, Jack	1960
Long Goodbye, The	1973
Magnificent Seven	1960

Video Title	Year
▶ City of Women	1980
Long Goodbye, The	1973
Dr. Strangelove	1964
I'm All Right, Jack	1960
Magnificent Seven	1960
High Noon	1952
Bicycle Thief, The	1949
Casablanca	1942
Gone with the Wind	1939
39 Steps, The	1935

Follow these steps to sort a database table:

1. In Datasheet view, click anywhere in the field, or column, that the table is to be sorted on.

2. Click the Sort Ascending or the Sort Descending button on the Table Datasheet toolbar.

TIP: *To sort a table on two or three fields instead of one, you have to query it. For example, to sort by last name, then by first name so that Smith, Michael comes before Smith, Steven, you have to query the table. See "Advanced Filter/Sort: Sorting on Two Fields," later in this chapter.*

Querying a Database for Information

Thankfully, the word *query* means the same thing in computerese as it means in what computer programmers call "human-readable language." "To query" means the same thing to a computer programmer as it does to a poet—it means *to ask*. When you query a database, you ask it for information of some kind.

The rest of this chapter concerns queries. It explains how queries work and what the different kinds of queries are. It describes how to construct a query using expressions and numeric-, date-, and time-based criteria. You also learn how to save a query and run it again, as well as modify a query so it digs up the information you are looking for. Finally, this chapter explains the details of constructing and running queries with Access.

LEARN BY EXAMPLE

To try your hand at querying a database, open the Figure 18-4 (Query) *file on the companion CD.*

An Introduction to Querying

Queries run the gamut from the very simple to the very complex. For example, you could construct a query that finds purchase orders submitted on a particular date for a particular item. Or you could construct a query that finds purchase orders for the same item made during a three-month period in states where sales tax is charged, and obtain the total amount of sales tax that was charged for the item during the three months.

NOTE: *These pages outline the procedures for creating a query from scratch. However, you can also create a query with the Query Wizard. How to use the Query Wizard to create different kinds of queries is discussed throughout this chapter.*

Unlike a filtering operation, which can look in one table only, a query can gather information from as many as all the tables in a database. Figure 18-4 shows two tables being queried, Products and Inventory Transactions. When you construct a query, the first thing you do is tell Access which tables to look in.

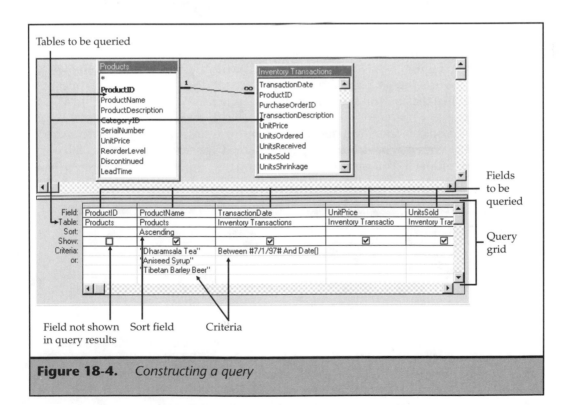

Figure 18-4. *Constructing a query*

ACCESS

After you have told Access which tables to query, the next step is to tell the program which fields to look in. In Figure 18-4, the first row of the *query grid* shows that five fields will be queried, two from the Products table (Product ID and ProductName) and three from the Inventory Transactions table (TransactionDate, UnitPrice, and UnitsSold).

As you construct a query, you can ask Access to sort the results. To do so, make a choice on the Sort row of the query grid. In Figure 18-4, the results of the query will be sorted in ascending order—that is, alphabetical order—by product name.

A query tells Access which fields to look in to gather information, but that doesn't mean that each field in which Access looks has to be on the results table. By removing the check mark from the box in the Show row, you tell Access *not* to include a field in the query results. In Figure 18-4, no check mark appears in the ProductID check box, so this field will not appear on the query results.

The bottom of the query grid is where you establish the criteria, also known as the *conditions*, for the query. This query asks for information about three products— Dharamsala Tea or Aniseed Syrup or Tibetan Barley Beer. For the period between 7/1/97 and today's date, this query wants to know when units of these products were sold, what the unit price of each transaction was, and how many units were sold as part of each transaction.

To run a query after you have finished constructing it, you press the Run button or choose the Query menu Run command. When I clicked the Run button, I got the results shown in Figure 18-5. Now I can see price fluctuations and judge which of my three exotic products is most popular with the health food set. Query results appear on a datasheet like the one you see in Datasheet view when you are working on a database table.

After you finish constructing a query, the next step is to save it and give it a name. The names of queries that have been saved and named appear on the Queries tab of the Database window so you can run them over and over again.

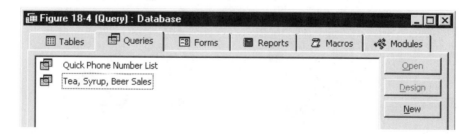

A query doesn't actually store any data. All it does is store criteria, table names, field names, and other information for searching in database tables. However, you can enter data in a query datasheet. The data you enter is stored in the tables that were accessed when the query was created. For example, if I enter a record or change a value in the query datasheet shown in Figure 18-5, the new data is stored in the

Product Name	Transaction Date	Unit Price	UnitsSold
Aniseed Syrup	11/30/97	$33.00	3
Aniseed Syrup	11/30/97	$22.00	22
Aniseed Syrup	11/27/97	$43.00	17
Aniseed Syrup	11/12/97	$10.00	44
Aniseed Syrup	11/2/97	$3.00	3
Aniseed Syrup	11/1/97	$6.00	4
Dharamsala Tea	11/30/97	$43.00	5
Dharamsala Tea	11/26/97	$33.00	4
Dharamsala Tea	11/5/97	$11.00	5
Dharamsala Tea	11/1/97	$4.00	3
Tibetan Barley Beer	11/30/97	$43.00	6
Tibetan Barley Beer	11/25/97	$44.00	25
Tibetan Barley Beer	11/11/97	$19.00	12
Tibetan Barley Beer	11/1/97	$2.00	4

Figure 18-5. *The results of the query shown in Figure 18-4*

Products and Inventory Transactions table, the two tables from which I constructed the query.

By keeping a query on hand on the Queries tab of the Database window, you can run the query time and time again. Each time you run it, you get an up-to-date picture of the records in the database tables that the query was designed to access.

TIP: As you can from database tables, you can create forms and reports from queries. To do so, click the arrow beside the New Object button when the query results are onscreen and choose either AutoForm or AutoReport on the drop-down menu.

Constructing a Select Query

No matter which way you query a database, the techniques for creating the query, choosing which tables to query, choosing which fields to query, entering the criteria, and running the query are the same. The following pages explain how to create and generate a *select query*, the standard type of query on which all the others are built.

TIP: The following pages describe how to construct a select query yourself, but you can also construct one with the Query Wizard. See "Constructing a Select Query with the Query Wizard" later in this chapter.

The Fifteen Types of Queries

Access offers no less than 15 kinds of queries. Queries in the following list that can be created with the Query Wizard have an asterisk beside their name.

Type of Query	What it Does
Append	Copies data from one or several different tables to a single table.
Advanced Filter/Sort	Sorts data on two or more fields instead of one. This type of query works on one database table only. As explained in "Sorting, or Arranging, Records in a Database Table," earlier in this chapter, you can sort a table on one field by selecting the field in Datasheet view and clicking the Sort Ascending or Sort Descending button. However, to sort on two, three, or more fields, you have to run an Advanced Filter/Sort query.
AutoLookup	Automatically enters certain field values in new records.
Calculation	Lets you add a field in the query results table for making calculations with the data that the query returns. In a database that tracked rental properties, for example, you could query to find out how much rental income each property generates, and then see how much income each property would generate if rents were increased across the board by 7 percent.
Crosstab*	Displays information in a matrix instead of a standard table. Crosstab queries make it easier to compare the information in a database.
Delete	Permanently deletes records that meet certain criteria from the database. Use this type of query, for example, to remove outdated records that were entered before a certain date.
Find Duplicates*	Finds all records with field values that are also found in other records. This query is useful for finding all the people in a database who live in the same ZIP code or have the same blood type, for example.
Find Unmatched*	Compares database tables to find records in the first table for which a match cannot be found in the second table. This query is useful for maintaining referential integrity in a database.

Make-Table	Creates a table from the results of a query. This type of query is useful for backing up records.
Parameter	Displays a dialog box that tells the data-entry person what type of information to enter.
Select*	Gathers information from one, two, or more database tables. The select query is the standard query on which all others are built. Also known as a *simple query.*
SQL	Uses an SQL (structured query language) statement to combine data from different database tables. SQL queries come in four kinds: a Data Definition query creates or alters objects in a database; a Pass Through query sends commands for retrieving data or changing records; a Subquery queries another query for certain results; and a Union query combines fields from different queries.
Summary	Finds the sum, average, lowest or highest value, number of, standard deviation, variance, or first or last value in the field in a query results table
Top-Value	Finds the highest or lowest values in a field. You can find the highest or lowest 5, 25, 100, or whatever values. Or you can choose percentages or enter your own percentage setting to find values in the highest or lowest 5, 25, or whatever percent.
Update	Finds records that meet certain criteria and updates those records *en masse.* This query is useful for updating records. For example, to increase the price of all items in a database by a certain percentage, use an update query.

Creating the Query

To tell Access that you want to create a query, start from the Query tab of the Database window and either click the New button or choose the Insert menu Query command. You see the New Query dialog box shown in the following illustration. Query Wizards are available for creating simple (also known as select) queries, crosstab queries, and queries for finding duplicate records and unmatched records. Choose a Wizard option to create one of those queries. To design your own query, make sure Design View is selected in the New Query dialog box, and then click OK.

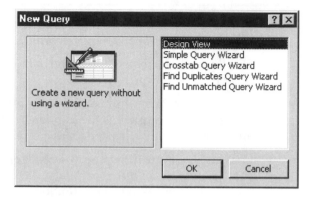

The Query Design window and Show Table dialog box appear so you can tell Access which tables to query. Read on.

Choosing Which Tables to Query

Choose which table or tables to query from the Tables tab of the Show Table dialog box shown in the following illustration. And yes, you can construct queries from queries you have already constructed by choosing those queries on the Queries tab. The Both tab lists both tables and queries in case you want to start from there.

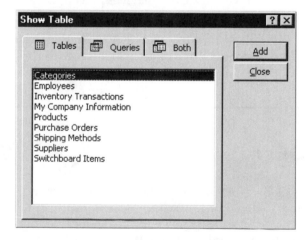

To choose each table or query that your new query will gather data from, click it in the Show Table dialog box and then click the Add button. Keep clicking tables or queries and clicking the Add button until you have "loaded" all the tables or queries you need for the new query. Click the Close button when you are done. The tables and queries you chose appear on the top of the Query Design window, as shown in Figure 18-6.

TIP: *If you loaded a table in the Query Design window but regret having done so, right-click on its field list box and choose Remove Table from the shortcut menu. To add a table you forgot to add, click the Show Table button on the Query Design toolbar to bring back the Show Table dialog box.*

The next step in constructing the query is to tell Access which fields to include. To get a fix on which fields are in each table, and to make it easier to work with the fields, drag the border that divides the top half of the Query Design window from the query grid downward. That gives you more room to work. Drag the bottom border of the table boxes downward as well so you can see all the field names. Later, when it is time to focus on the query grid, you can drag the northern border of the grid upward.

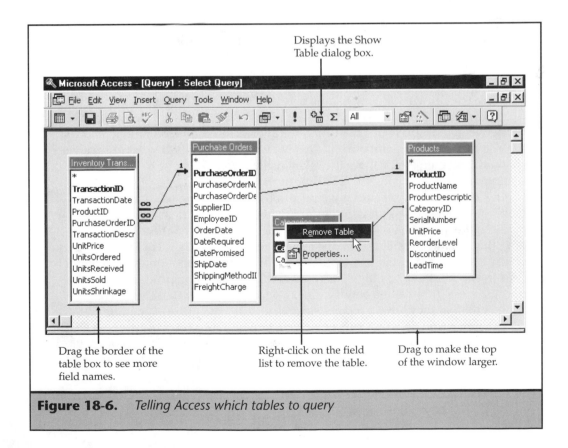

Figure 18-6. *Telling Access which tables to query*

Joining the Tables for the Query

In a query of two or more tables, Access displays records from the different tables when the values in the fields by which they are joined match. For example, in a query that brings together data from an Employee Address table and an Employee Phone Number table, Access looks for matching names in the Last Name field of each table, and when it finds a matching name, say, Jane Perez, it displays Jane's address and phone number in the query results.

However, before Access can query more than one table and find matches, fields from the different tables must be joined. In other words, relationships must have been established between the tables. You can tell if relationships have been established because, if they have, Access draws lines between field names, as Figure 18-6 shows.

Access joins tables automatically in the Query Design window under the following conditions:

- Relationships were established before you started constructing the query.

- The same field name appears in different tables, the same data type was assigned to both fields, and one of the fields is a primary key field.

The Query Design window provides a mechanism for joining tables, but you are better off establishing relationships before you arrive in the Query Design window. ("Forging the Relationships Between Tables" in Chapter 17 explains how to create relationships between tables.) If relationships have not been established yet between the tables you chose for your query, I strongly recommend choosing the File menu Close command, clicking No when asked if you want to save your changes, and then establishing the relationships. You will have to start all over with your query, but you will save time in the long run.

If you decide to disregard my advice about establishing relationships between tables in the Query Design window, or if you need to establish relationships between the queries you have decided to query, establish relationships by dragging a matching field from one table or query to another. For example, click on the Product ID field in one table box and drag-and-drop it on the Product ID field in another table box to tell Access to look for matching product IDs in the query. Access draws a line between the two tables to show that they have been joined and that they have a relationship.

Whatever you do, don't run a query on tables that haven't been joined. The query will be utterly useless, because Access will join every record in one table with every record in the other table and you might end up with thousands upon thousands of records in the query results.

Choosing Which Fields to Query

The next step is to tell Access which fields from the tables to include in the query. Do that by copying field names from the table box or boxes to the Field row in the query grid. Each field you copy to the Field row of the query grid will appear on the query results table (unless you click the Show button, but that subject is discussed a little later in this chapter).

Following are instructions for choosing which fields to query and rearranging the field names—that is, the columns—on the query grid.

Rearranging Columns on the Query Grid

The order in which field names appear in the columns on the query grid is the order in which they will appear in the query results. In Figure 18-7, for example, the PurchaseOrderID field comes first, then the PurchaseOrderNumber field, then the OrderDate field. Follow these steps to change the order of columns on the query grid:

1. Gently move the pointer to the small rectangle at the top of the column you want to move.

2. When you see an arrow that points downward, click to select the column. The column is highlighted, as shown in this illustration:

Click here to select and move the column.

The black line shows where the column will move.

3. Click again on the small rectangle at the top of the column and drag toward the left or right. As you drag, a black line appears between columns to show where the column will land when you release the mouse button.

4. When the black line is in the right place, release the mouse button.

Use the techniques outlined in Figure 18-7 and described here to copy field names onto the Field row in the query grid:

- *Choose tables and fields from menus*   Click on the Table row, open the drop-down list and choose a table name, and then click directly above in the Field row, open the drop-down menu, and choose a field name. In Figure 18-7, the OrderDate field is being chosen this way.

- *Drag a field*   Drag a field name from the table box to the Field row.

- *Double-click a field name*   Double-clicking a field name copies the field name to the Field row in the next available column. For example, if the third column is the first empty column, double-clicking a field name copies it to the third column.

- *CTRL+click field names*   By CTRL+clicking the field names in a table box, you can select several field names at once and copy them onto the Field row. Hold down the CTRL key and click each field name you want to copy. Then point to one of the selected fields and drag the field names *en masse* onto the query

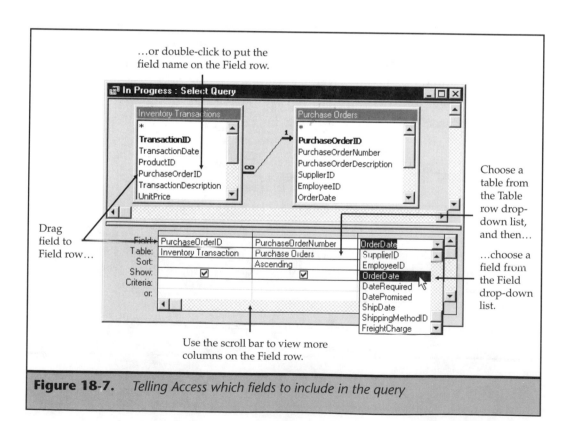

Figure 18-7.   *Telling Access which fields to include in the query*

grid. The first field name in the block lands in the first empty Field column, and the others land to its right.

You may use the scroll bars below the Design window and query grid to scroll side to side and see the tables and different field columns. Try dragging the boundary lines between columns in the query grid if you are having trouble reading field names.

TIP: *If you mistakenly copy the wrong field name to the Field row, either delete it and substitute the right name or open the drop-down list on the Field row and choose the correct field name.*

TIP: *By double-clicking the asterisk at the top of a table box or dragging it onto the Field row, you can copy all the fields in a table to the Field row at once. Use the asterisk method only to tell Access to include all the fields in a table in a query. When you copy fields with the asterisk method, only the table name and an asterisk appear on the Field row. Field names do not appear across the columns of the query grid.*

Deciding How to Sort the Query Results

Unless you tell it otherwise, Access sorts query results on the primary key field or, if there isn't a primary key field, on the leftmost field in the query grid. You can, however, decide for yourself which field is the one on which the query results are sorted, and if you want to sort on more than one field, you can do that as well by following these steps:

■ *Sorting on one field* To choose a single field on which to sort the results, click on the Sort row in the field, open the drop-down menu, and choose Ascending or Descending, as shown in the following illustration:

Field:	Last Name	First Name	Middle Initial	Address
Table:	Outlaws	Outlaws	Outlaws	Outlaws
Sort:	Ascending	Ascending	Ascending	
Show:	☑	☑	Ascending	☑
Criteria:			Descending	
or:			(not sorted)	

The leftmost field is sorted first, then next field, then next.   Choose the type of sort from the drop-down menu.

■ *Sorting on more than one field* To sort the results on more than one field, click on the Sort row in each field and choose Ascending or Descending from the drop-down list. Then, make sure that the first field to be sorted appears to the left of the other fields to be sorted on the query grid, that the second field to be sorted appears directly to the right of the first field to be sorted, and so on. In the illustration, for example, the query results will be sorted in ascending order (alphabetical order) by last name, then first name, then middle initial.

NOTE: "Sorting, or Arranging, Records in a Database Table," earlier in this chapter, explains the difference between ascending and descending sorts.

Deciding Which Fields Appear in the Query Results

It isn't necessary to include all the fields that you query in the query results. In fact, sometimes including all the fields is pointless. For example, if you design a query to find people who live in a single county or ZIP code, you need not include the County or Zip Code field in the query results, because that would be redundant. Every record the query turns up would list the same county or ZIP code.

To keep a field from appearing in query results, click to remove the check mark from the Show box. In this illustration, the Birthdate, Squire, Province, and Castle fields will be queried; and the query will list, from oldest to youngest, each squire, the province where he lives, and the castle he inhabits. However, the squires are getting quite old, and to spare them any embarrassment concerning their ages, the Birthdate field will not appear in query results, because no check mark appears in its Show box:

Field:	Birthdate	Squire	Province	Castle
Table:	Squires	Squires	Castles	Castles
Sort:	Descending			
Show:	☐	☑	☑	☑
Criteria:				
or:				

Entering the Query Criteria

Include criteria on the Criteria line of the query grid when you want to query for certain kinds of records. For example, to query for the records of people who live in San Francisco, the query grid looks like this:

Field:	Last Name	City	Annual Income	Birthdate
Table:	City Address	City Address	Vitals	Vitals
Sort:				
Show:	☑	☑	☑	☑
Criteria:		"San Francisco"		
or:				

In a similar way, by making an entry in the Criteria line of the Annual Income field, you could query for people who earn between $50,000 and $65,000 a year. By making an entry in the Criteria line of the Birthdate field, you could query for people born after 1 January 1958. Or, you might query for the records of people who meet *all three* of those criteria, in which case the query grid looks like this:

Field:	Last Name	City	Annual Income	Birthdate
Table:	City Address	City Address	Vitals	Vitals
Sort:				
Show:	☑	☑	☑	☑
Criteria:		"San Francisco"	Between 45000 And 65000	>=#1/1/58#
or:				

Besides querying for records that meet criteria in different fields, you can require records to meet more than one criterion in the same field. Consider the criteria in the following illustration. This query not only seeks the records of people who earn between $50,000 and $65,000 annually, were born after 1 January 1958, and live in San Francisco, but it seeks people in Los Angeles, San Diego, and San Jose. So this query asks the database for the records of San Franciscans, Los Angelenos, San Diegans, and San Josians who earn between $50,000 and $65,000 annually and were born after 1 January 1958:

Field:	Last Name	City	Annual Income	Birthdate
Table:	City Address	City Address	Vitals	Vitals
Sort:				
Show:	☑	☑	☑	☑
Criteria:		"San Francisco"	Between 45000 And 65000	>=#1/1/58#
or:		"Los Angeles"		
		"San Diego"		
		"San Jose"		

Notice that the Criteria line on the query grid in the previous two illustrations includes two expressions: Between 45000 And 65000, and >=#1/1/58#. By building expressions like these, and by entering criteria in different fields and in the same field, you can construct very sophisticated queries and get very specific kinds of information from a database.

The following pages explain how to query a database by using text, numeric, and date expressions, as well as wildcards. You also learn how to enter criteria on the Criteria lines of the query grid.

Guidelines for Entering Criteria on the Query Grid

Unless you enter the criteria correctly, Access can't query a database. In fact, if you enter criteria incorrectly, the program shows you a message window with a cryptic explanation of why your criteria are wrong. Following are guidelines for entering criteria on the query grid:

- *Quote marks (") and number signs (#)* As the previous two illustrations show, Access puts quotation marks around text criteria and number signs around date criteria. However, you do not need to enter those symbols yourself. The program enters them for you after you move the cursor out of the criteria box.

- *Number formats* Do not enter commas when you enter numbers on the query grid. For example, to enter the number 45,000, you need only enter **45000**. If you include a comma in numbers or currency figures, Access flashes a message that says you created the expression incorrectly.

- *Date formats* You can enter dates in all three of Access's date formats. For example, to find records dated December 31, 1978, you can enter the date in the query grid in any of the following ways: 12/31/78, 31-Dec-78, or December 31, 1978. Whichever way you type the date, Access puts number signs around it and changes it to this format on the query grid: #12/31/78#.

- *Operator names* It doesn't matter whether you enter operator names such as Not and Between in all uppercase or all lowercase letters. Access capitalizes the first letter and lowercases the other letters for you.

Text Criteria

Text criteria are the simplest and easiest types of criteria—not to mention the most commonly used type of criteria—you can use in queries. To enter text criteria, all you do is enter letters on the query grid. For example, to query a database for orders that were shipped to cities named Rome, you include the City field in the query and the name *Rome* on the Criteria line in the City field:

Field:	Order Number	Name	City	Country	
Table:	Text Based Criteria	Text Based Criteria	Text Based Criteria	Text Based Criteria	
Sort:					
Show:	☑	☑	☑	☑	
Criteria:			"Rome"		
or:					

Two operators, Not and Like, can come in handy when you are working with text criteria. The Not operator tells Access to exclude a criterion from the search. By using the Like operator along with the asterisk wildcard, you can search for groups of records. For example, entering **Like F*** in the Shipped To field of a query grid finds the records of companies whose names begin with the letter *F*. Entering *Like [A-E]** finds the records of companies whose names begin with the letter *A, B, C, D,* and *E*. Entering *Like *Ltd.* finds the records of companies whose names end with the Ltd. suffix.

In the following illustration, the query finds orders that were shipped to companies whose names begin with the letter *T* that are located in cities named Rome, but not in Rome, Italy. A query like this one would turn up Tarantino Produce in Rome, New York, USA; but not Tarantino Produccia in Rome, Italy:

Field:	Order Number	Name	City	Country	
Table:	Text Based Criteria	Text Based Criteria	Text Based Criteria	Text Based Criteria	
Sort:					
Show:	☐	☑	☑	☑	
Criteria:		Like "T*"	"Rome"	<>"Italy"	
or:					

Numeric Criteria

Use numeric criteria in Number and Currency fields to find specific kinds of records. Table 18-2 lists the operators you can use in Numeric and Currency fields. Use these operators liberally and often to query databases and get detailed information about the people or things that your database is meant to track.

Operator	Name	Example (*in Cost field*)	Query Results
=	Equal to	=49.95	Items that cost exactly $49.95
<>	Not equal to	<>	Items that do not cost $49.95
<	Less than	<49.95	Items that cost less than $49.95
<=	Less than or equal to	<=49.95	Items that cost $49.95 or less
>	Greater than	>49.95	Items that cost more than $49.95
>=	Greater than or equal to	>=49.95	Items that cost $49.95 or more
Between... And...	Between	Between 49.95 And 59.95	Items that cost between $49.95 and $59.95

Table 18-2. *Operators for Use in Numeric Fields in Queries*

ACCESS

As an example of how to use numeric operators to pinpoint specific records in a database, the following query finds donors whose annual income is between $150,000 and $200,000 and who donated $15,000 or more to charities (and God bless them every one):

Field:	Last Name	First Name	Total Charity Contribution	Income
Table:	Generous Peop	Generous Peo	Generous People	Generous People
Sort:	Ascending			
Show:	☑	☑	☑	☑
Criteria:			>=15000	Between 150000 And 200000
or:				

Date Criteria

All the numeric operators that can be used in numeric fields on a query grid can also be used in date fields (see Table 18-2). For example, entering **<3/8/97** in a field called Ship Date finds all shipments that were made before (are less than) 8 March 1997. Entering **Between 3/8/97 And 3/15/97** finds shipments that were made between 8 March and 15 March 1997.

TIP: *Access offers a function called Date() that represents today's date and can be useful in date expressions. For example, to find shipments made between today's date, whatever it happens to be, and 1 April 1997, you can enter the following expression:* **Between 4/1/97 And Date()**.

As an example of using date criteria in a query, the following query finds the records of people born in the years 1946 to 1958 to whom a CD called "Disco Wonderland Retrospective" was shipped after 2 February 1997:

Field:	Name	Birthdate	Date Shipped	CD: Disco Wonderland
Table:	Baby Boomer:	Baby Boomers	Baby Boomers	Baby Boomers
Sort:	Ascending			
Show:	☑	☑	☑	☑
Criteria:		Between #1/1/46# And #12/31/58#	>#2/2/97#	
or:				

Seeing and Saving the Results of a Query

After you have laboriously constructed your query, it is time to run it. To do so, either click the Run button or choose the Query menu Run command. The results of the query appear on a datasheet that looks exactly like a table looks in Datasheet view.

The Expression Builder for Creating Expressions

Besides creating expressions yourself, you can do it by getting the Expression Builder's help. The Expression Builder offers buttons and tools for creating expressions. To use it, right-click on the query grid where the expression will go and choose Build from the shortcut menu. You see the Expression Builder dialog box shown in Figure 18-8.

By clicking buttons; by choosing functions, constants, or operators; and by entering text in the text box, you can construct expressions. Click OK when you are done constructing your expression.

In database parlance, the datasheet is called a *dynaset.* It's called that ("What do you get when you cross a dinosaur with a dinette set?") because the results of a query represent a subset of all the data and because query results are considered "dynamic"—you can alter them and your alterations are made as well on the database tables from which the data came.

The records you enter or edits you make on a dynaset are recorded on the underlying tables from which you got the data in the first place. Many Access users find entering data on a query datasheet, or dynaset, easier, because they can work with a subset of the fields in a table. However, unless all the fields in a database table also appear on the query results table, records that are entered in the query results

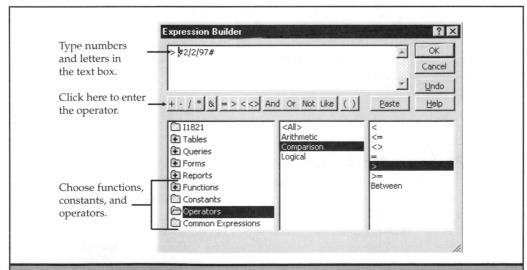

Figure 18-8.   *Instead of creating expressions on your own, you can get the Expression Builder's help*

table are incomplete. For example, if you queried a table for six of its eight fields, six fields appear on the query. If you then enter a record on the query, it is recorded on the table, but data is recorded in only six of the eight fields.

What's more, all the formats that apply to fields in the database table also apply on the results table. For example, if the database table stipulates that a field name be no longer than 20 characters, the same is true on the query results table.

 TIP: You can remove fields, insert fields, or change the order of fields on the dynaset. To do so, see "Moving, Copying, Deleting, and Renaming Fields" in Chapter 17. The same techniques for working on a table in Datasheet view also apply to working on the table that shows the results of a query.

After you have finished examining the results of a query, save it by clicking the Save button. A box appears so you can give the query a name. Enter a name and click the OK button.

Viewing, Running, and Modifying Queries You Already Created

Queries that have been constructed and saved appear on the Queries tab of the Database window. To open a query so you can view its results, run it again, or perhaps modify it, click the Queries tab, click the query you want to use again, and then click either the Design or the Open button:

- *Design button*   Opens the query in Design view so you can modify it or run it. To modify it, click the Show Table button to add new tables to the query if that's what you want to do, or else change the field names and criteria on the query grid. When you are ready to run it again, click the Run button or choose the Query menu Run command.

- *Open button*   Runs the query and displays the results.

The Different Kinds of Queries

Thus far, you have learned how to construct a select query, the standard type of query, but the remainder of this chapter describes how to create the other kinds of queries, as well as how to create a select query with the Query Wizard. The select query is the foundation on which all the others are built. If you need instructions for selecting tables for a query, or selecting fields for a query, or doing all the other standard things that have to be done to construct a query, refer to the preceding pages in this book. Meanwhile, read on to learn about the different kinds of queries you can create with Access.

Constructing a Select Query with the Query Wizard

The middle third of this chapter describes how to create a select query on your own. You can, however, create a select query with the Query Wizard by following these steps:

1. Starting from the Queries tab of the Database window, click the New button. You see the New Query dialog box.

2. Click the Simple Query Wizard option and then click OK. You see the first Wizard dialog box, shown in Figure 18-9, which asks which tables to query and which fields in those tables to query.

3. Open the Tables/Queries drop-down list and choose the first table or query that you intend to query. Its fields appear in the Available Fields box.

4. Either click the double arrows that point to the right to move all the fields from the Available Fields box to the Selected Fields box, or click on fields one at a time and then click the arrow that points to the right to move fields one by one into the Selected Fields box.

5. Repeat steps 3 and 4 until you have selected all the tables and all the fields you want to query.

6. Click the Next button to open the next Wizard dialog box. It asks if you want a detailed or summary query.

NOTE: Later in this chapter, "Summary: Getting Comprehensive Information About Data in a Field" explains how to run a summary query.

7. Click Next to create a detailed query. The next dialog box asks for a query name. The name you enter will appear on the Query tab.

8. Enter a name for your query.

9. Click one of the option buttons on the dialog box:

   ■ *Open the query to view information* Click this button and then click Finish to run the query. You see the query results on a datasheet.

   ■ *Modify the query design* Click this button and then click Finish to open the Query in Design view, where you can enter criteria on the query grid. After you have entered the criteria, click the Run button.

LEARN BY EXAMPLE
Open the Figure 18-9 (Query Wizard) *file on the companion CD if you would like to try creating a select query with the Query Wizard.*

ACCESS

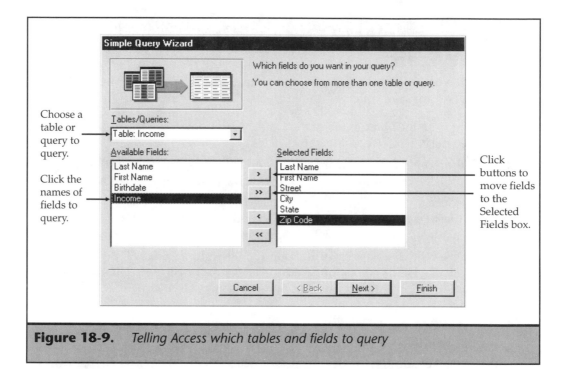

Figure 18-9. *Telling Access which tables and fields to query*

Advanced Filter/Sort: Sorting on Two Fields

To filter a single database table and sort it on two or more fields at the same time, choose the Records menu Filter command and then click Advanced/Filter Sort. As "Sorting, or Arranging, Records in a Database Table" earlier in this chapter explained, you can sort a table on one field by selecting the field in Datasheet view and then clicking the Sort Ascending or Sort Descending button. However, to sort on two, three, or more fields, you have to run an Advanced Filter/Sort query (or run a select query).

NOTE: An advanced filter/sort is not technically a query, and certain database mavens would take issue with my including it here, but it is included in this section because advanced filter/sorts are constructed exactly like queries.

To perform an advanced filter/sort, follow these steps:

1. Open the table that you want to filter and sort by double-clicking its name on the Table tab of the Database window.

2. Choose the Records menu Filter command and then click Advanced/Filter Sort. You see the Filter window:

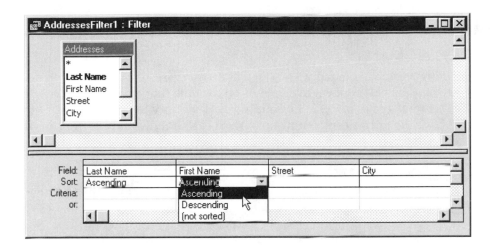

NOTE: *If instructions from a previous filter appear on the filter grid, click the Clear Grid button.*

3. Tell Access which fields to include in the filter operation by displaying them on the Field row (see "Choosing Which Fields to Query," earlier in this chapter, if you need help).

4. On the Sort box of each field on which you intend to sort the table, open the drop-down menu and choose Ascending or Descending:

   ■ *Ascending order* Arranges text entries in alphabetical order from A to Z (Cleveland, New York, West Hollywood); numbers from smallest to largest (5, 26, 144); and dates from earliest in time to latest in time (31-Jul-57, 4-Mar-96, 16-Oct-05).

   ■ *Descending order* Arranges text entries from Z to A (West Hollywood, New York, Cleveland); numbers from largest to smallest (144, 26, 5); and dates from latest in time to earliest in time (16-Oct-05, 4-Mar-96, 31-Jul-57).

5. If necessary, move the foremost field on which the table will be sorted to make sure that it is on the left of the other fields to be sorted on the query grid. When Access sees that more than one field needs to be sorted, it sorts the leftmost field first. To learn how to move a field in the query grid, see "Rearranging Columns on the Query Grid," earlier in this chapter.

6. Click the Apply Filter button.

TIP: *You can enter criteria on the query grid as part of an advanced filter/sort operation. See "Entering the Query Criteria," earlier in this chapter.*

Calculation: Performing Calculations on Query Returns

By performing a calculation query, you can make a query results table work like a spreadsheet and have it perform calculations on the data that the query returns. In a database that tracks sales prices, for example, you can query to find many different items and have the query results show how much each item would cost if prices were increased by 3 percent.

EXAMPLES

LEARN BY EXAMPLE

To try your hand at calculating the results of a query, open the Figure 18-10 (Calculation Query) *file on the companion CD.*

Follow these steps to create a calculation query:

1. Create a new query, choose which tables to query, and choose which fields to query.

2. Click the Table row of a blank column.

3. From the drop-down list, choose the table with the field that you want to use in the calculation. For example, if the field you want to use is called Price and it is in the Items table, choose the Items table from the drop-down list.

4. Click directly above the Table row, in the Field row.

5. Click to open the drop-down list and choose the name of the field you want to use in the calculation. Figure 18-10 shows the Price field being chosen.

6. Click directly to the right of the field name you just entered and type an operand and number. In Figure 18-10, I entered ***1.03** to calculate a 3 percent rise in prices.

7. Press the ENTER key. When you do so, Access inserts the letters *Expr1* (for Expression 1) and encloses the field name in brackets, as shown in Figure 18-10.

8. Run the query by clicking the Run button.

The following illustration shows the results of the query shown in Figure 18-10. For this query, I did two calculations on the items in the Price field, one to see how prices would rise if I increased them by 3 percent, or 1.03 (Expr1); and one to see how much prices would rise if I increased them by 7 percent, or 1.07 (Expr2):

Item	Price	Expr1	Expr2
Cat	$49.00	50.47	52.43
Dinosaur	$4,500.00	4635	4815
Dog	$48.00	49.44	51.36
Parrot	$123.00	126.69	131.61
Weasal Rat	$50.00	51.5	53.5
*	$0.00		

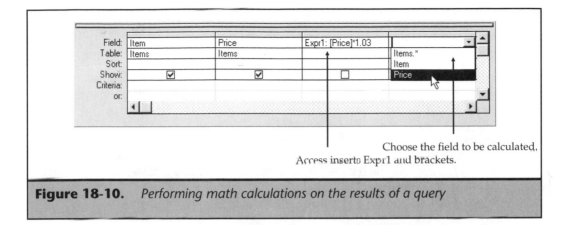

Choose the field to be calculated, Access inserts Expr1 and brackets.

Figure 18-10. *Performing math calculations on the results of a query*

Crosstab: Displaying Query Results in a Matrix

A crosstab query makes it easier to compare, or cross-tabulate, information. To see the advantages of a crosstab query, study the following two illustrations. The first shows a table with horses' names, races in which the horses ran, and the prize money they won. However, horses' names and sweepstakes' names repeat themselves in the first two columns, so it is hard to make a realistic comparison of the horses to see which won more money.

Horse	Sweepstakes	Prize Money	Race ID
LaSerella	The Brown Derby	$4,400.00	1
Lady Fair	Kentucky Home	$65,000.00	2
Swan's Delay	The Freakness	$115,000.00	3
Lady Fair	The Brown Derby	$23,000.00	5
Swan's Delay	Kentucky Home	$32,000.00	6
Sky's Limit	The Brown Derby	$13,000.00	7
LaSerella	Kentucky Home	$23,000.00	8
Lady Fair	The Freakness	$78,000.00	9

The following illustration shows the results of a crosstab query on the table. Horses' names have been grouped in the left-hand column and you can clearly see how much money each horse won, if any, in each sweepstakes race. Moreover, the crosstab query has added a "total of" column so you can see each horse's total winnings:

Horse	Total Of Prize Money	Kentucky Home	The Brown Derby	The Freakness
Lady Fair	$166,000.00	$65,000.00	$23,000.00	$78,000.00
LaSerella	$27,400.00	$23,000.00	$4,400.00	
Sky's Limit	$13,000.00		$13,000.00	
Swan's Delay	$147,000.00	$32,000.00		$115,000.00

LEARN BY EXAMPLE
Open the Figure 18-11 (Crosstab Query) *file on the companion CD to try your hand at creating a crosstab query.*

When you construct a crosstab query with the Query Wizard, the Wizard asks three questions about how to translate the data on the table into the data on the query results:

1. *For row labels in the left-hand column of the query results* From which column in the database table should the query get row labels? In the query results shown in the preceding illustration, row labels came from the Horse column of the database table. For each name in the Horse column of the table, Access created a row on the query results.

2. *For column headings in the query results* From which column in the database table should the query get column headings? In the previous illustration, column headings came from the Sweepstakes column. For each sweepstakes name in the Sweepstakes column, Access created a column in the query results.

3. *For the numeric data in the query results* From which column heading in the table should the query get the numeric data that fills most of the table? In the illustration, numeric data came from the Prize Money column.

The Query Wizard asks a fourth question, too. It asks if you want to total, average, count the number of, or do a number of other mathematical things to the data in the table. For the sample illustration, I had the Query Wizard total the prize money won by each horse.

WARNING: To run a crosstab query, the table you are querying must include at least one field that stores numbers—that is, one numeric, date, or currency field. Moreover, if the data is to come from two or more tables, query the tables with a simple, select query. After you have assembled the data from the different tables in a select query, run a crosstab query on the select query.

By far the easiest way to create a crosstab query is to do so with the Query Wizard. Follow these steps to create a crosstab query:

1. Starting from the Query tab of the Database window, click the New button.

2. In the New Query dialog box, choose Crosstab Query Wizard and click OK. You see the first Wizard dialog box, which asks which table or query you want to query.

3. Choose a table or query. If necessary, click the Queries or Both option button to see the query that you want to query.

4. Click the Next button. The next dialog box asks, "Which field's values do you want as row headings?" The wizard is asking you question number 1 in the list

of questions above. The wizard wants to know where to get the names or numbers that will go in the left-hand column of the query results and identify each row of data.

5. Click one field name in the Available Fields box and then click the arrow that points to the right to move that field into the Selected Fields box.

 TIP: Watch the Sample box in the Query Wizard dialog box. It gives a fair idea of what the query results table will look like when you are done creating it.

6. Click the Next button. The next dialog box asks, "Which field's values do you want as column headings?" This is question 2 in the list above. The wizard is asking where in the table or query being queried to get the column names for the query results table.

7. Click the field whose values you want to appear in the column headings across the top of the query results table you are about to create.

8. Click the Next button. The next dialog box asks question 3 (and 4) above. As shown in Figure 18-11, it wants to know which numeric value to place in the query results table and whether or not to summarize the data in each row.

9. Click the name of the numeric field in the table you are querying that holds the values you want to compare in your crosstab query.

10. If you want to add a column to the query results table that summarizes each row, make sure a check mark appears in the Yes, include row sums check box, and then choose the means by which the data will be summarized by clicking an option in the Functions box. For example, SUM totals the rows and adds a "total of" column. AVG averages the numbers in the rows. Count counts how many entries are in each row.

11. Click the Next button.

12. Enter a name for the crosstab query. The name you enter will appear on the Queries tab in the Database window.

13. Click the Finish button. The results of the query appear onscreen.

Summary: Getting Comprehensive Information About Data in a Field

The previous part of this chapter explained how to summarize a row of data in a crosstab query. You can create a query that summarizes all the data in a field as well, as long as the row, or field, in the database table or query that you are querying stores numeric data. Only numeric data can be "summarized." A summary query can find the

Click the field where the data values
for rows and columns come from.

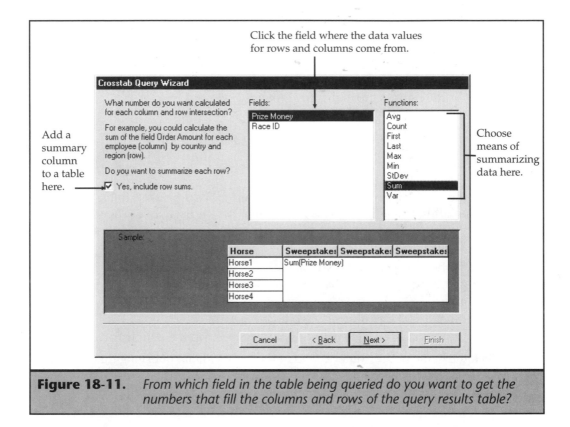

Add a
summary
column
to a table
here.

Choose
means of
summarizing
data here.

Crosstab Query Wizard

What number do you want calculated
for each column and row intersection?

For example, you could calculate the
sum of the field Order Amount for each
employee (column) by country and
region (row).

Do you want to summarize each row?

☑ Yes, include row sums.

Fields:

Prize Money
Race ID

Functions:

Avg
Count
First
Last
Max
Min
StDev
Sum
Var

Sample:

Horse	Sweepstakes	Sweepstakes	Sweepstakes
Horse1	Sum(Prize Money)		
Horse2			
Horse3			
Horse4			

Cancel   < Back   Next >   Finish

Figure 18-11. *From which field in the table being queried do you want to get the numbers that fill the columns and rows of the query results table?*

sum, average, lowest or highest value, number of, standard deviation, variance, or
first or last value in a field in a query results table.

Figure 18-12 shows a database table along with three summary queries that were
made on the data in the table. The first summary query, called Average Sales by
Region, shows the average sales in the West, North, South, and East region. The
second query shows total sales by region and the third shows the maximum amount
sold by the best-performing salesperson in each region. Notice how a summary query
displays results in only one row and that the query added the letters AvgOf, SumOf,
and MaxOf to the column headings.

Access offers a menu with functions for summarizing the data in a field. Table 18-3
explains the different functions and why you would use them.

EXAMPLES

LEARN BY EXAMPLE
*Open the Figure 18-12 (Summarize Query) file on the companion CD if you want to
experiment with summary queries.*

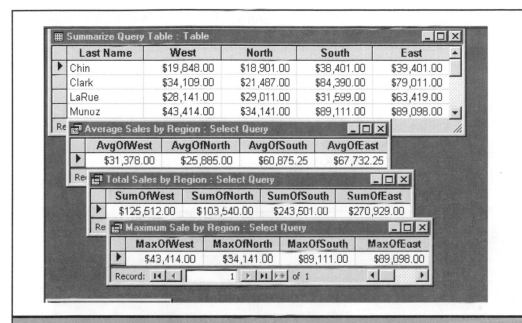

Figure 18-12. *A database table (top) and three summary queries made on the data in the table: Average Sales by Region, Total Sales by Region, and Maximum Sales by Region*

Function	What It Does
Sum	Totals the values in the field
Avg	Finds the average value in the field
Min	Finds the lowest value in the field
Max	Finds the highest value in the field
Count	Counts the number of values in the field
StDev	Finds the standard deviation of the values in the field
Var	Finds the variance of the values in the field
First	Finds the first value in the field
Last	Finds the last value in the field

Table 18-3. *Functions for Use with Summary Queries*

Follow these steps to create a query that summarizes data in a query results table:

1. Create a new query, choose which tables to query, and choose which fields to query.

2. Choose the View menu Totals command or click the Totals button on the Query Design toolbar. A Total row and the words "Group By" appear on the query grid.

3. Click on the Total row of the field you want to summarize.

4. Open the drop-down menu on the Total row and choose the function from the drop-down menu that describes how you want to summarize the row (see Table 18-3):

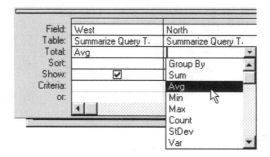

5. Repeat steps 3 and 4 for each field you want to summarize.

6. Click the Run button or choose the Query menu Run command.

TIP: *You can also run a summary query with the Query Wizard. In the wizard's second dialog box, click the Summary radio button and the Summary Options button. In the next dialog box, click the Sum, Avg, Min, or Max check box for each field you want to summarize.*

Top Value: Finding High and Low Values in Fields

The previous part of this chapter explained how to find the highest and lowest value in a field by performing a summary query. However, if you want to find the high and low values, there is a quicker way. You can find the highest or lowest 5, 25, 100, or whatever values, or find the values in the highest or lowest percentile of a database table, by following these steps:

1. Create a new query, choose which tables to query, and choose which fields to query.

2. On the query grid in the field in which you want to find the highest or lowest values, click the Sort row.

3. Click Ascending or Descending on the drop-down menu:

- *Ascending*   Click to find low values in the field.

- *Descending*   Click to find high values in the field.

4. Click to open the Top Values menu on the Query Design toolbar:

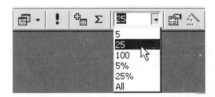

5. If you chose Ascending, either enter a number or percentage or choose a number or percentage to find low values in the field; if you chose Descending, either enter a number or percentage or choose a number or percentage to find high values. To enter a number, click in the Top Values box, type the number, and press the ENTER key. To enter a percentage, enter a number followed by the percent sign, and then press the ENTER key.

6. Click the Run button to run the query.

Update: Updating Records in a Database

An update query finds records that meet certain criteria and updates those records *en masse.* Update queries are especially useful for updating telephone numbers, addresses, and other types of information that typically are stored in several different database tables.

EXAMPLES

LEARN BY EXAMPLE
On the companion CD is a file for practicing update queries called Figure 18-13 (Update Query).

To see how an update query works, suppose you keep a database in which one table lists college courses and the other lists information about professors. Each course is assigned one professor, but Professor Jacobson leaves and is replaced by Professor Hernandez. Rather than go into the college courses table, find courses taught by Jacobson, and change Jacobson to Hernandez in the Professor field, you could run an update query that finds Jacobson and changes her name to Hernandez. In a very large database, being able to make updates automatically is invaluable.

ACCESS

Finding Duplicate Fields and Unmatched Records

The New Query dialog box—the one you see when you click the New button on the Query tab—offers Query Wizards for finding duplicate fields in a table and records in one table for which matches can't be found in another:

- *Find Duplicates* The Find Duplicates Query Wizard lists all the records in a table that share field values with other records. For example, the records of people who live in the same ZIP code are listed, as are the records of people who live in the same city or have the same blood type. Besides running the Find Duplicates Query Wizard to locate like-minded records, you can also use it before you choose the primary key field or index a field to find out whether duplicate values exist in a field. As you surely must know, duplicate values cannot appear in a primary key field.

- *Find Unmatched Records* The Find Unmatched Query Wizard compares two tables to find out whether matches exist between the records in one table and the records in another. Records for which matches can't be found are listed. For example, in a comparison of an Inventory table and a Product Description table, the Find Unmatched Query Wizard could find items in the Inventory table that haven't been assigned a product number that is listed in the Product Description table. Finding records for which matches don't exist is useful for maintaining referential integrity in a database (see the box "What Is Referential Integrity?" in Chapter 17 if the concept is foreign to you).

The Find Duplicates and Find Unmatched Query Wizards work like all the Wizards—they hold your hand throughout and help you find the records you are looking for. The only thing you need to know about the two wizards is that they are not installed as part of a "typical" Office 97 installation. For instructions about installing them, see Appendix A.

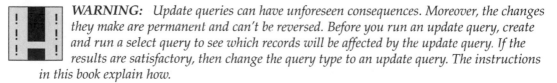 *WARNING: Update queries can have unforeseen consequences. Moreover, the changes they make are permanent and can't be reversed. Before you run an update query, create and run a select query to see which records will be affected by the update query. If the results are satisfactory, then change the query type to an update query. The instructions in this book explain how.*

Follow these steps to run an update query:

1. Create a new query and make sure to add the table with the data you want to change and the table from which the new data will come.

2. Choose the fields that you want to appear in the query results table.

3. Click on the Criteria row of the field that you want to update and enter the value that is to be updated. In Figure 18-13, Professor Jacobson is going to be "updated" and replaced by Professor Hernandez.

4. Click the View button to switch to Datasheet view. Access shows you the table that will be updated when you finish the update query.

WARNING: *Make absolutely certain that the table you see after you switch to Datasheet view is indeed the one that you want to update and that the selection criteria was entered correctly.*

5. Click the View button again to return to Design view.

6. Click the arrow that points down beside the Query button and choose Update Query from the drop-down menu. A new row called Update To appears on the query grid.

7. On the Update To row, enter the new, updated value. In Figure 18-13, the value is a name, Hernandez.

8. Click the Run button or choose the Query menu Run command. A dialog box asks if you want to go through with it. Changes made by an update query are permanent and can't be reversed.

9. Click the Yes button.

NOTE: *An update query does not produce a dynaset. To see the result of an update query, close the query without saving it, and then open the source table to see the result of the update.*

Append: Copying Data to a New Table

An append query copies records from one table and pastes them in another table. For an append query to work, field types in both tables must be the same. In other words, when you create an append query, the first thing you do is formulate the query that will retrieve the records you want to copy to a table. Then you tell Access which table to copy the records to. Then you start the show, retrieve the copies into the table, and hope for the best.

LEARN BY EXAMPLE
To try your hand at running an append query, open the Figure 18-B (Append Query) *file on the companion CD.*

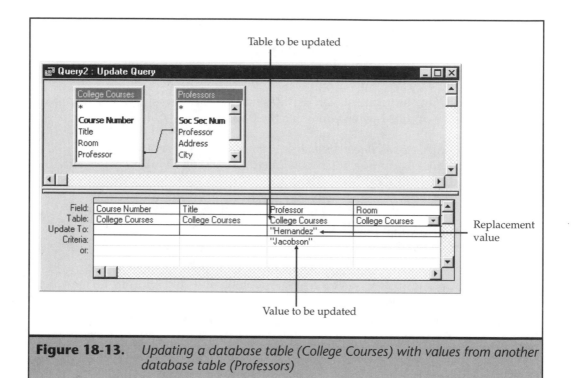

Figure 18-13. *Updating a database table (College Courses) with values from another database table (Professors)*

Follow these steps to create and run an append query:

1. Create a query that retrieves the records you want to copy into a table. Choose which tables to query and choose which fields to query.

2. Run the query to see which records will be copied.

3. Click the View button to return to Design view.

4. Click the arrow that points down beside the Query Type button on the Query Design toolbar and choose Append Query. You see the Append dialog box:

5. From the Table Name drop-down list, choose the name of the table that the records from your query will be copied to.

6. Click the OK button. Access adds a new line to the query grid: Append To.

7. If the field names in the destination table do not match the field names in the source table, click on the Append To line of the first field, open the drop-down list, and choose a field name from the table whose records you are copying. In this illustration, values from the Price field in one table are being copied to the Cost field in another table:

Field:	Product Number	Product Name	Cost		
Table:	Products	Products	Products		
Sort:					
Append To:		Item	Price		
Criteria:			Items.*		
or:			Number		
			Item		
			Price		

WARNING: In order to copy values from a field in one table to another, the fields must have been assigned the same data type. For example, only data in currency fields can be copied to a currency field in another table. In the illustration shown here, you couldn't copy values from the Item field into the Cost field, because Item has been assigned the Text data type and Cost has been assigned the Currency data type.

8. Repeat step 7 for each field whose name does not have a matching field name in the destination table.

WARNING: You cannot copy records with fields to which the AutoNumber data type has been assigned from one table to another. When you copy records to a table that includes a field with autonumbers, the copied records are assigned new autonumbers.

9. Choose the Query menu Run command or click the Run button.

10. Click Yes in the dialog box that asks if you really want to go through with it.

Make-Table: Creating a Table from Query Results

Use a make-table query when you want to back up or archive records. A make-table query copies records from database tables and stores the records in a new table. Follow these steps to create and run a make-table query:

1. Create a new query, choose which tables to query, and choose which fields to query.

ACCESS

2. On the query grid, carefully enter criteria for choosing the records for the new table. For example, to create a backup table of sales transactions made in 1995, you might enter **Between 1/1/95 And 12/31/95** in the Transaction Date field of your query. See "Entering the Query Criteria," earlier in this chapter.

3. Run the query to see which records will be included in the new query.

4. Click the View button to return to Design view.

5. Click the arrow that points down beside the Query Type button on the Query Design toolbar and choose Make-Table Query. You see the Make Table dialog box:

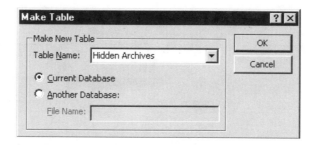

6. Enter a name for your new table in the Table Name box and click OK.

7. Click the Run button or choose the Query menu Run command. A dialog box appears and tells you how many records (rows) are in your new table.

8. Click the Yes button.

You can find your new table on the Tables tab of the Database window. Take note, however, that the new table does not have a primary key field. If you intend to mate your table with or create a relationship between the new table and other tables in the database, open it in Design view and designate a primary key.

Delete: Querying to Delete Records from Tables

Before you read about delete queries, take heed: delete queries permanently delete records from a database. Before you run a delete query, run a make-table query that assembles all the records you intend to delete. That way, if you regret deleting the records, you can get them from the table you made.

That said, delete queries are excellent for removing the deadwood from a database. Use this type of query to remove outdated records that were entered before a certain date or to remove the names of industrial spies who have been caught and are no longer of use to the company you work for.

Follow these steps to create and run a delete query:

1. Create a new query, and, on the query grid, carefully enter criteria for choosing which records to delete. To delete records that were entered before a certain date, for example, you could enter an expression in the Date of Sale field. See "Entering the Query Criteria," earlier in this chapter.

2. Click the arrow that points down beside the Query Type button on the Query Design toolbar and choose Delete Query. As shown in this illustration, a new row called Delete appears in the query grid and the word "Where" appears on each line in the Delete row:

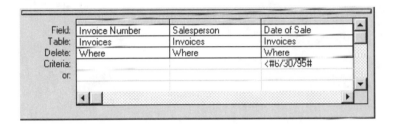

3. Click the Run button or choose the Query menu Run command. A dialog box appears and tells you how many records will be deleted if you click Yes. You backed up the records you are about to delete with a make-table query, right?

4. Click Yes if you answered "yes" to the question posed at the end of step 4. If you answered "no," click the No button.

Chapter 19

Generating Reports and Mailing Labels

No doubt one of the reasons people go to such lengths to create databases is so they can present the data in printed form for others to admire. Chapter 19 explains how to create and print reports. Of course, you can also admire data on the computer screen, but reports are especially designed to be printed. As the following pages explain, Access offers several different kinds of reports, and you can get quite fancy if you want to.

This chapter also explains how to print mailing labels from the names and addresses in a database table or query. You are hereby encouraged to use Access-generated labels for mass mailings and bulk mailings. Moreover, if you intend to do a bulk mailing, you can sort the addresses by ZIP code as you print them and save yourself the trouble of sorting them yourself before you take them to the post office. The post office, you must know if you do bulk mailings, requires letters to be sorted by ZIP code.

Generating a Report

Access offers three ways to generate a report: with an AutoReport, with the Report Wizard, or from scratch. AutoReports and the Report Wizard are covered in the following pages. This book does not cover creating reports on your own because doing so is far too much trouble and you can't hope to match the snazzy designs that you can get very simply with AutoReports or the Report Wizard. Every design innovation you can make on your own can be made easily and quickly with the Report Wizard.

Time-Saving Tips for Creating Reports

It is much easier to create a report from a query than it is to create a report from a table or from several tables. Access's Report Wizard offers a bunch of options for determining which fields from which tables to put in a report, but you can dispense with all those options simply by creating a query that brings together all the data you want the report to display. With a query, you decide from the get-go what goes in the report and you don't have to fool with field options.

You can also save time by sorting the query results on the field that is to be the prominent field in the report. For example, if the report is supposed to display information about people, sort the query on the last name field. If the report is supposed to present data about automobile parts, sort the report on the part name or part number field. By sorting the query results beforehand, you can bypass the options in the Report Wizard for sorting the report because the data will have already been sorted. "Deciding How to Sort the Query Results" in Chapter 18 explains how to sort a query.

Yet another shortcut for creating reports is to give the query the name that you want the report to have. In the case of AutoReports, Access simply names the report after the table or query from which the data came. By carefully naming the query, you make sure that the AutoReport has a descriptive name.

Choosing How to Create Your Report

No matter which method you choose to create a report, you start the same way:

1. From the Database window, click the Reports tab.

2. Click the New button on the Reports tab. You see the New Report dialog box shown in Figure 19-1.

3. Choose the query (or table if you disregard my advice about creating reports) from which to get the data for the report from the drop-down list at the bottom of the dialog box.

4. Choose a means of creating a report:

   ■ *Report Wizard* Opens the Wizard, after which you are asked a bunch of questions about what the report should look like. See "Creating a Report with the Report Wizard," later in this chapter.

   ■ *AutoReport: Columnar* Creates a report in which the data is displayed in a single column. With this kind of report, data is shown a record at a time. See "Creating an AutoReport," later in this chapter.

   ■ *AutoReport: Tabular* Creates a report in which data is shown in a table. You can see several records at once in a tabular report. See "Creating an AutoReport," later in this chapter.

5. Click OK.

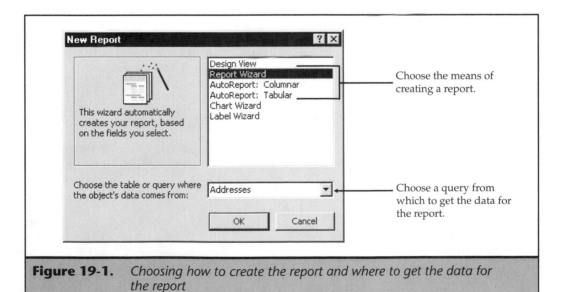

Figure 19-1. *Choosing how to create the report and where to get the data for the report*

Columnar, Tabular, or Justified Reports?

When you create an AutoReport, Access gives you the choice of creating a columnar or tabular report. And when you create a report with the Report Wizard, the program gives you the choice of creating a columnar, tabular, or justified report. What is the difference between the three?

The following illustration shows a *columnar report*. Columnar reports present data much like it is presented in a form. Labels appear on the left and the data itself is presented in a single column:

First Name	Dan
Street	122 W. Third Street
City	Duhere
State	IL
Zip Code	33337
Last Name	Williams
First Name	Reginald
Street	34457 Wilcox Blvd.
City	Los Angeles
State	CA
Zip Code	90047

Tabular reports present the data in a table format so that you can see several records at once, as the following illustration demonstrates. Create a tabular report when you want the report to show a list of the data in the database table or query:

Last Name	First Name	Street	City	Stat	Zip Code
Danforth	Dan	122 W. Third Street	Duhere	IL	33337
Williams	Reginald	34457 Wilcox Blvd.	Los Angeles	CA	90047
Roger	McRee	2719 44th St.	San Francisco	CA	94114
Dubain	Duffy	2718 Douglas St.	Waukeegan	IL	33337
Clarkson	William	229 E. Rainy St.	Checker	OR	96789
Manfred	Lois	338 Miner Rd.	Danforth	KS	41327

A *justified report* is a sort of hybrid between a columnar and a tabular report. In a justified report, fields and values appear in rows, and values appear directly below field names:

Last Name	First Name		Street
Danforth	Dan		122 W. Third Street
City	**State**	**Zip Code**	
Duhere	IL	33337	
Last Name	**First Name**		**Street**
Williams	Reginald		34457 Wilcox Blvd
City	**State**	**Zip Code**	
Los Angeles	CA	90047	

Creating an AutoReport

After you click the New button on the Reports tab of the Database window and then choose AutoReport: Columnar or AutoReport: Tabular in the New Report dialog box, there isn't anything more to do to create an AutoReport. Twiddle your thumbs until the AutoReport appears onscreen.

When you first see them, AutoReports appear on the Print Preview screen, as shown in Figure 19-2. (See "Using Print Preview" in Chapter 2 if you don't know your way around the Print Preview screen.) If you like the looks of your AutoReport and want to keep it, choose the File menu Save command, enter a name for your report in the Save As dialog box, and click OK. The names of reports that have been saved appear on the Reports tab of the database window.

An AutoReport gets its title from the query from whence it came. For example, the AutoReport shown in Figure 19-2 came from a query called "Phone Numbers," so the words "Phone Numbers" appear at the start of the report. Along the bottom of each page of an AutoReport is a footer with the day of the week, date, page number, and total number of pages in the report, as shown here:

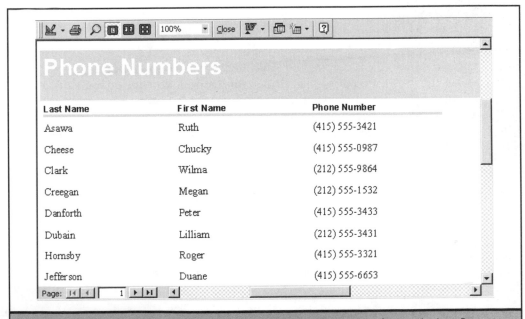

Figure 19-2. *The title of the AutoReport appears at the top of page 1. AutoReport titles come from the names of queries*

TIP: You can create a columnar AutoReport from a database table or the results of a query by clicking the arrow that points down beside the New Object button and choosing AutoReport while the table or query results are onscreen.

Creating a Report with the Report Wizard

The Report Wizard, like its cousin the Table Wizard and Design Wizard, asks you a bunch of questions about what you want your report to look like and then spits out a report. Follow these steps to create a report with the Report Wizard:

1. From the Reports tab of the Database window, click the New button. You see the New Report dialog box (see Figure 19-1).

2. From the drop-down list at the bottom of the dialog box, choose the query that will provide raw data for the report. (See "Time-Saving Tips for Creating Reports" at the start of this chapter if you don't understand why choosing a query instead of a table is so important, or why it is necessary to sort the query as well. For information about sorting a query, see "Deciding How to Sort the Query Results" in Chapter 18.)

3. Click the Report Wizard option and click OK in the New Report dialog box. You see the first Wizard dialog box, which wants to know which fields from the query to include in the report.

4. Click the double arrows that point to the right to move all the fields from the Available Fields box to the Selected Fields box. You can select individual fields by clicking the single arrow, but if you took my advice and you are creating your report from a query, you don't have to do that.

5. Click the Next button. As shown in Figure 19-3, the next dialog box wants to know if data in the report should have what Access calls "grouping levels." Grouping levels aren't necessary for a report, and if you decide not to include them, simply click the Next button. For Figure 19-3, I chose two grouping levels (Zip Code and State) for a report. The following illustration shows what a report with these two grouping levels looks like after it has been printed:

Zip Code	State	Last Name	First Name	Street	City
02134					
	NY				
		Wong	Mariam	178 E. Lansing	Checkers
21347					
	Fl				
		Perford	Steve	3876-A Chance	Niler
24127					
	NJ				
		Hornsby	Harried	11 Cortland St.	East Rutherfo

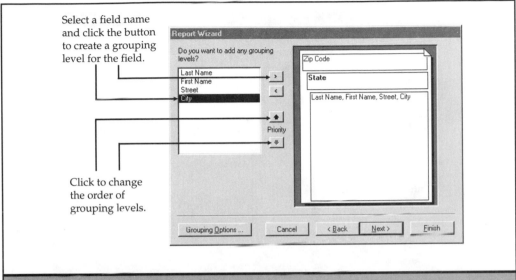

Figure 19-3. *Choosing "grouping levels"—better known as headings and subheadings—for the report*

6. For each field you want as a "grouping level," if you indeed want grouping levels, click its name in the box on the right and then click the button with the arrow that points to the right. The field name moves into the box on the right. You can include as many grouping levels as you wish. Click the Priority button to change the hierarchy of grouping levels.

7. Click the Next button. The next dialog box wants to know how to sort the records in the report. You, however, took my advice and sorted the records in the query before you started creating your report, so you can ignore this dialog box.

8. Click the Next button. The next dialog box asks if you want a columnar, tabular, or justified report, and whether to print the report in landscape mode. If you opted for grouping levels, you get several other choices as well.

 TIP: *Click the Landscape option button if the query on which you base your report includes a lot of fields and you are creating a tabular or justified report. With a landscape report, you can fit more fields across the page.*

9. Click a button to tell Access what kind of report you want. "Columnar, Tabular, or Justified Reports?" earlier in this chapter explains the three main kinds of reports.

10. Click the Next button. The next dialog box asks what you want the report to look like:

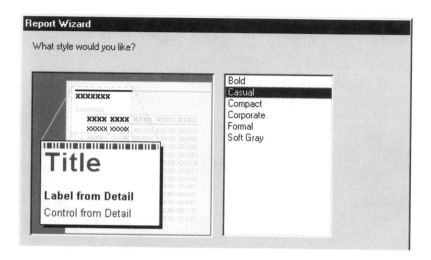

11. Click style options until you've found the one that tickles your fancy, and then click the Next button.

12. In the last Wizard dialog box, enter a name for your report and then click the Finish button. The name you enter will appear at the top of the first page in the report and appear as well on the Reports tab of the Database window. Your new report appears on the Print Preview screen (see Figure 19-2).

The title you entered in step 12 appears at the start of the report. Along the bottom of each page is a footer with the day of the week, date, page number, and total number of pages in the report.

Opening a Report You Already Created

To open a report, go to the Reports tab of the Database window and double-click the report's name. Reports remain up-to-date as the data in the database changes. For example, if you enter a new record or change part of an existing one and open a report that "reports on" the data you entered or altered, the report shows the changes you made.

Printing a Report

To print a report in its entirety, go to the Reports tab of the Database window, right-click on the report, and choose Print from the shortcut menu. If you want to print part of the report instead of all of it, double-click the report's name to open it, and then choose the File menu Print command. In the Print dialog box, click the Pages From option button, enter the number of the first page to print in the From box and the last page to print in the To box, and then OK.

Saving a Report as a Word Document

You can save a report as a Word document. Once the database is in Word, you can change the fonts, headers and footers, and other formats. Follow these steps to save a report in Word:

1. In Access, open the report by double-clicking its name on the Reports tab of the Database window. The report opens on the Print Preview screen.

2. Click the arrow that points down beside the OfficeLinks button on the Print Preview toolbar and choose Publish It with MS Word from the drop-down menu. A dialog box tells you that the report is being "output" to MS Word. Soon the report opens in Word as a rich text format (RTF) file.

3. In Word, choose the File menu Save As command to save the file under a name and in a folder of your choice.

Generating Mailing Labels

One of the nicest features of Access is being able to produce mailing labels quickly. All you have to do is query the database to produce the names and addresses for which you want to make labels. With that done, you take a very serious look at the labels on which you want to print the addresses. Make sure you know the dimensions of the labels you intend to print on, because Access needs to know that in order to print labels. The program works very well with Avery brand labels; with other labels, you have to try your luck. Once you have assembled the names and addresses and examined the labels, you can let the Label Wizard do the rest of the work.

TIP: *If you are printing the labels for a bulk mailing, sort the query results on the Zip Code field before you create the labels. That way, you can save a little time sorting the mail.*

Follow these steps to generate mailing labels with Access:

1. From the Database window, click the Reports tab.

2. Click the New button on the Reports tab. You see the New Report dialog box:

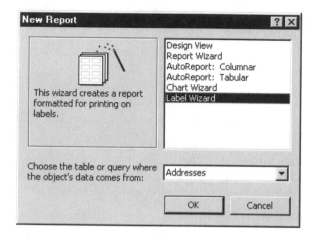

3. Choose the query from which the names and addresses will come from the drop-down list at the bottom of the dialog box.

4. Click the Label Wizard option and then click OK. You see the first Wizard dialog box. It wants to know what size labels you will print on, as well as other information about printing:

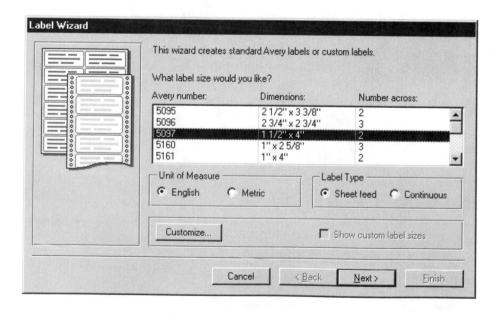

5. In the scroll list, find and click on the kind of labels you will print on. The Dimensions column shows label sizes (click the Metric option button if you are more at home with the metric system or you purchased your labels from a French drugstore) and the Number across column shows how many labels appear across the page. If you are using Avery brand labels, all you have to do is look at the number on the package the labels came from and click that number in the dialog box.

NOTE: If labels are fed continuously, not one sheet at a time, to your printer click the Continuous option button.

6. Click the Next button. The next dialog box asks about font name, font size, and other settings having to do with the appearance of text on the labels.

7. Choose new font and text color settings to your heart's desire, but make sure that the text doesn't grow so large it can't fit on the labels.

8. Click the Next button. As shown in Figure 19-4, the next dialog box asks you to construct a prototype label from the fields in the Available fields box.

9. Click the field name that is to appear first in the label, and then click the button with the arrow on it to move the field name into the Prototype label box.

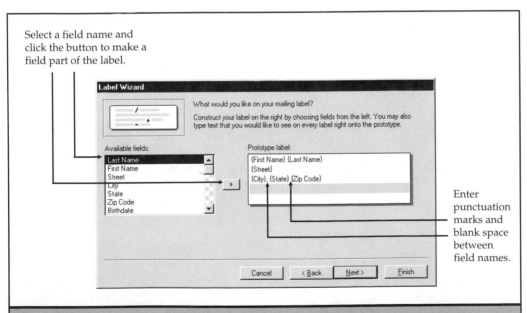

Figure 19-4. *When you tell Access which fields to print on the labels, make sure to put blank spaces and perhaps punctuation marks between fields*

ACCESS

10. Enter a space, line return, or a punctuation mark, as shown in Figure 19-4. To do so, press the SPACEBAR, ENTER, or comma, dash, or other punctuation key on the keyboard.

11. Repeat steps 9 and 10 for each field that is to appear on the label. Be sure to enter blank spaces, line returns, and perhaps punctuation marks between fields.

12. Click the Next button. The next dialog box wants to know how to sort the fields, but you took my advice and sorted them before you met the Label Wizard, right?

13. Click the Next button.

14. Enter a name for the labels. The name you enter will appear on the Reports tab of the Database window.

15. Click the Finish button. The labels appear on the Print Preview screen.

16. To print the labels now, insert the labels in your printer, choose the File menu Print command, and click OK in the Print dialog box.

To print the labels in the future, all you have to do is put labels in your printer, open the Reports tab of the Database window, right-click on the labels report, and choose Print from the shortcut menu.

Part V

Microsoft PowerPoint

Chapter 20

Creating a PowerPoint
Presentation

This chapter is the first in Part V, which explains how to use Microsoft PowerPoint, Office 97's presentation program. To borrow a term from the classroom, PowerPoint is *an audiovisual* program. Use it to present ideas, sales pitches, budgets, plans—you name it—to groups of people.

In PowerPoint, you create what the program calls *slides,* but don't be confused by that term. A slide is simply an image. Yes, you may take the slides you create with PowerPoint to the local graphics shop and turn them into slides or overhead transparencies, but that isn't absolutely necessary because PowerPoint slides can be shown on computer screens.

This chapter starts by explaining how to create what PowerPoint calls a presentation. A *presentation* is a series of slides whose goal is to dazzle or persuade an audience. As you will see shortly, PowerPoint offers many predesigned presentations. You don't have to be an artist to create a professional-looking presentation with this program. If you are not the adventurous kind or if you are in a hurry, you can create a "paint by numbers" presentation in a matter of minutes.

Besides creating a presentation, this chapter explores different ways of viewing your work, how to enter the text on the slides, and how to format the text on the slides.

Creating a Presentation

PowerPoint offers no less than three ways to create a presentation: from a template, with the AutoContent Wizard, or from scratch. All three techniques are described on the following pages.

When you use a template or design a presentation with the AutoContent Wizard, you end up with a generic presentation complete with headings, text, and a full-fledged design. All you have to do is replace the generic headings and text with headings and text of your own. And you might have to remove or add a slide or two, of course.

Figure 20-1 shows the dialog box you see when you start PowerPoint. From here, you can create a presentation or open a presentation you have already created. Read on for the dirty details.

What Is the Best Way to Create a Presentation?

All the techniques for creating a presentation have advantages and disadvantages. With the AutoContent Wizard, you get PowerPoint's help in deciding which design is the best for you—but you don't see the design until the presentation has been created. With a template, on the other hand, you get to see the design from the get-go—but PowerPoint offers no advice about which design is best. Both AutoContent and template presentations come with generic text and titles that you can use as a starting point for your own text and titles.

Whatever you do, don't worry about creating a perfect presentation the first time around. PowerPoint gives you ample opportunities to change a presentation's design, as well as add and remove slides.

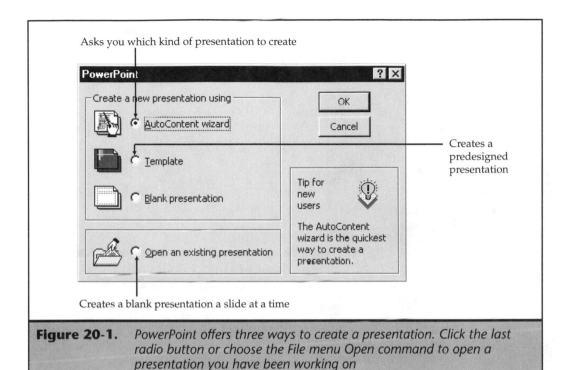

Asks you which kind of presentation to create

Creates a predesigned presentation

Creates a blank presentation a slide at a time

Figure 20-1. *PowerPoint offers three ways to create a presentation. Click the last radio button or choose the File menu Open command to open a presentation you have been working on*

Creating a Template with the AutoContent Wizard

As the "Tips for new users" in the lower-right corner of the PowerPoint dialog box in Figure 20-1 says, the AutoContent Wizard is the quickest way to create a presentation. For new users, and for users in a hurry, it truly is the quickest way. The AutoContent Wizard asks a series of questions about the purpose of your presentation, what you want to communicate, and by what means you will present it. On the basis of the answers you give, it chooses a design for the slides and provides generic headings and text.

Follow these steps to create a PowerPoint presentation with the AutoContent Wizard:

1. From the PowerPoint dialog box (see Figure 20-1), click the AutoContent Wizard option button, if necessary, and then click OK.
   You see the following illustration. In the course of choosing a presentation with the AutoContent Wizard, you will be asked questions about the presentation type, output options, presentation style, and presentation options.

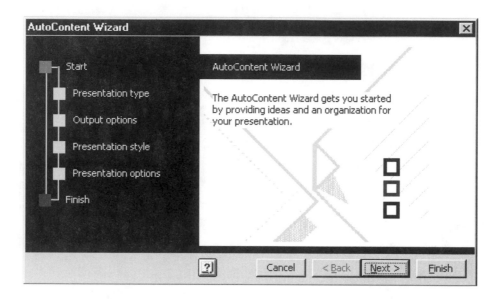

TIP: If the PowerPoint dialog box isn't onscreen, you can still create a presentation with the AutoContent Wizard by choosing the File menu New command, clicking the Presentations tab in the New Presentation dialog box, and double-clicking the AutoContent Wizard icon.

2. Click the Next button.

   The next dialog box asks what kind of presentation you want to give. The presentations are organized by category. To begin with, all presentations are shown in the box on the right, but to pare down the list, click the category name button that best describes the type of presentation you want to create. A short list of presentations appears in the box on the right.

3. Click a category name button and, in the box on the right, click the type of presentation you want to create.

4. Click the Next button.

The next dialog box asks if you are indeed trying to create a presentation or if the presentation is meant to be shown on the Internet or at a kiosk. A kiosk presentation is one that repeats itself over and over again. Perhaps you've seen them at shopping malls.

NOTE: Chapter 27 explains how to create a web page with PowerPoint. "Showing a Timed Kiosk Presentation" in Chapter 22 explains how to show a kiosk presentation in PowerPoint.

5. Click the Presentation, informal meeting, handout option button, if necessary. Otherwise, just click Next.

The next dialog box asks by what medium you will show the presentation and whether you will print handouts of the slides you create ("Printing Handouts of Slides for the Audience to Take Home" in Chapter 22 covers that topic).

6. Click the option button next to the medium by which you will show the slides, tell PowerPoint whether you will print handouts, and then click the Next button.

The next dialog box asks for a title for the presentation, your name, and "additional information." Figure 20-2 shows the first slide in a presentation created with the AutoContent Wizard. In the figure, you can see where the text that is entered in this dialog box goes on the title slide. The generic presentation style was chosen for this slide. If you choose a different style, the title, name, and additional information are formatted differently.

7. Enter a title, your name or a company name, and additional information, if you so desire. You can leave the text boxes blank if you want.

8. Click Next and then click Finish.

9. Choose the File menu Save command or click the Save button to save the new presentation.

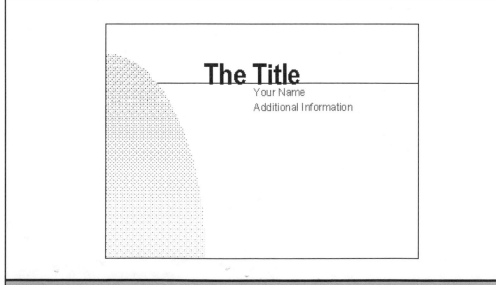

Figure 20-2.   *What you enter in the AutoContent Wizard dialog box goes on the first slide in the presentation*

POWERPOINT

As Figure 20-3 shows, the new presentation appears in Outline view. "Ways of Viewing and Working on Slides," the next part of this chapter, explains Outline view in detail. For now, all you need to know is that Outline view is the best view for entering text and that the generic headings and text in the new presentation offer suggestions for writing headings and text of your own.

Creating a Presentation with a Template

A template does what the AutoContent Wizard does, only it does it in a shorter time. When you create a presentation with a template, you end up with a predesigned bunch of slides and generic text like that in Figure 2-3. The difference is, the presentation is created very quickly. PowerPoint doesn't query you to find out what kind of presentation you want to create. All you do is review presentations on the Presentations tab of the New Presentations dialog box, click the presentation you want, and click OK.

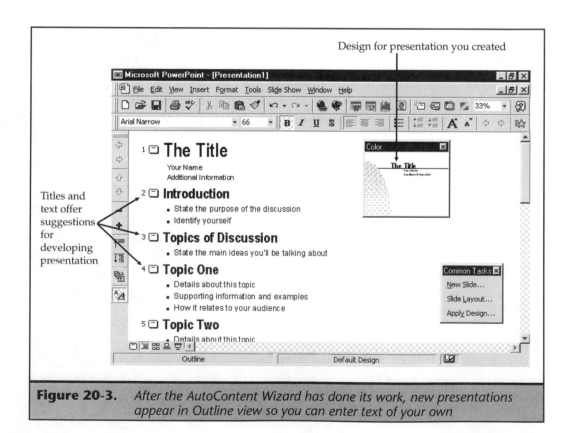

Figure 20-3. *After the AutoContent Wizard has done its work, new presentations appear in Outline view so you can enter text of your own*

HEADSTART

On the companion CD that comes with this book are about two dozen templates for creating PowerPoint presentations. Besides the templates that come with Office 97, you can use these templates, as well. See Appendix C for information.

To create a PowerPoint presentation from a template, follow these steps:

1. In the PowerPoint dialog box that you see when you start the program, click the Template option button and then click OK. You see the New Presentation dialog box.

TIP: You can create a presentation from a template without starting from the PowerPoint dialog box. To do so, choose the File menu New command.

2. Click the Presentations tab. It is shown in Figure 20-4.

3. Read the names of the icons to find the one that best describes the kind of presentation you want to create, then click the icon and look in the Preview box. Click as many icons as you like until you find one that does the job.

4. Click OK when you've found a suitable presentation. The title slide of the presentation appears onscreen.

5. Choose the View menu Outline command or click the Outline View button in the lower-left corner of the screen. Your presentation looks something like Figure 20-3.

6. Save and name your presentation.

See "Ways of Viewing and Working on Slides," the next part of this chapter, to learn how to enter your own text in Outline view in place of the generic headings and text that appears in the presentation. Notice that the generic text offers suggestions for developing a presentation.

Creating a Presentation from Scratch

Yet another way to create a presentation is to create it from the ground up. With this technique, you add one slide at a time to the presentation.

To create a slide presentation without any help from a template or the AutoContent Wizard, click the New button if the PowerPoint dialog box (see Figure 20-1) is not onscreen; if it is onscreen, click the Blank presentation option button and then click OK. You see the New Slide dialog box with its 12 so-called AutoLayouts. Later in this chapter, "Inserting a New Slide in a Presentation" tells how to add a slide from this dialog box to a presentation. Add the slides one at a time. Be sure to save and name the presentation when you have finished creating it.

POWERPOINT

... and see if it's the template you want.

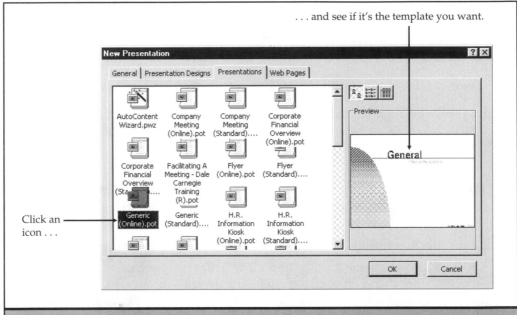

Click an icon . . .

Figure 20-4. *Click a template icon and glance in the Preview box to see if its design meets your approval*

Ways of Viewing and Working on Slides

One of the hardest things to do when you create a presentation is get a fix on how it is taking shape. When you concentrate on the slides' appearance, it is easy to lose sight of a spelling or grammar error. And when you concentrate on the text, it is easy to lose sight of the slides' appearance. For that reason, PowerPoint offers a number of different ways to view the slides in a presentation. You can view them one at a time, view several at once, view one in excruciating detail, or focus on the text in the presentation.

Figure 20-5 shows the four views of a presentation: Slide view, Outline view, Slide Sorter view, and Slide Show view. To change views, either click a button in the lower-left corner of the screen or choose an option from the View menu (press ESC to leave Slide Show view). Table 20-1 compares and contrasts the different ways of viewing slides.

LEARN BY EXAMPLE

To explore the different ways of viewing PowerPoint presentations, open the Figure 20-5 (Views) *file on the companion CD that comes with this book.*

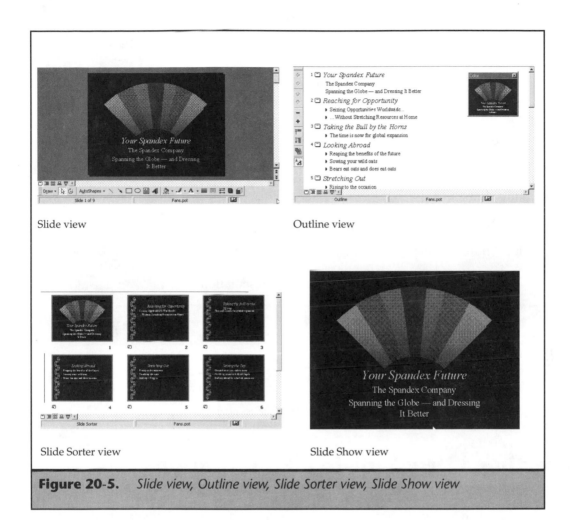

Figure 20-5. *Slide view, Outline view, Slide Sorter view, Slide Show view*

Inserting, Deleting, Rearranging, and Copying Slides

At some point or other, as your presentation takes shape and you sculpt it into a masterpiece, you have to add and remove slides. When you add a slide, you have the choice of adding one of PowerPoint's 12 preformatted slides, called AutoLayouts. You can save a lot of work by choosing a preformatted slide. PowerPoint offers preformatted charts and organization charts, preformatted bulleted lists, boxes for importing clip art, and preformatted tables.

View	Description
Slide	Shows a single slide. All PowerPoint's menus and buttons are available in this view. Good for laying out text and importing clip art images.
Outline	Shows the text in the presentation. From this view, you can focus on the presentation's content. Good for entering and editing text.
Slide Sorter	Shows several slides at once (to see more or less than six slides, use the Zoom drop-down list box). Good for moving and deleting slides.
Slide Show	Shows a single slide that fills the entire screen. This is what the slide looks like in a presentation. Good for dress-rehearsing a presentation.

Table 20-1. *Ways of Viewing a Presentation*

LEARN BY EXAMPLE

To test your ability at inserting and deleting slides, open the Figure 20-A (Add and Remove) *file on the companion CD.*

Inserting a New Slide in a Presentation

Follow these steps to insert a slide in a presentation:

1. Switch to Slide Sorter view by clicking the Slide Sorter View button in the lower-left corner of the screen or by choosing the View menu Slide Sorter command.

2. Click where the new slide is to go in the presentation. If you've noticed, slides are numbered in Slide Sorter view. Click to the right of slide 4, for example, to place a new slide between slides 4 and 5. To get to the slides at the end of a presentation, click the down arrow on the scroll bar.

3. Click the New Slide button, press CTRL+M, or choose the Insert menu New Slide command. You see the New Slide dialog box shown in Figure 20-6.

4. Click the kind of slide you want to insert. The box in the lower-right corner of the dialog box describes the slide that has been selected. The slide in the lower-right corner is a blank slide.

5. Click OK.

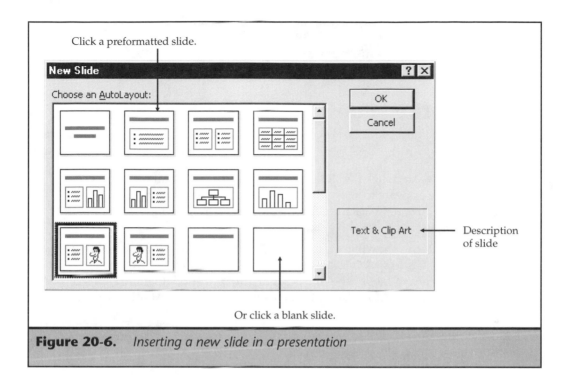

Figure 20-6. *Inserting a new slide in a presentation*

Deleting a Slide from a Presentation

To delete a slide, either do it from Outline or Slide Sorter view:

■ *Slide Sorter view* Click the slide. A black box appears around the slide to show it has been selected. Press the DELETE key.

 TIP: *To select more than one slide in Slide Sorter view, hold down the SHIFT key and start clicking on the slides you want to select.*

■ *Outline view* Click on a slide icon, the small square to the left of the slide. When you do so, all the text in the slide is highlighted, as the following illustration shows. Next, press the DELETE key. (If clip art images or notes pages are attached to the slide, PowerPoint informs you by way of a message box that you are about to delete them as well. Click OK.)

Rearranging the Slides

To move a slide to a new place in a presentation, you can start from either Slide Sorter view or Outline view:

- *Slide Sorter view*   Click the slide you want to move and start dragging. A vertical line appears to show where the slide will land when you release the mouse button. Release the mouse button when the slide is where you want it to be.

- *Outline view*   As shown in Figure 20-7, click the Collapse All button on the Outline toolbar to see only the title for each slide. Next, click on the icon of the slide you want to move. The title is highlighted to show that the slide has been selected. Click the Move Up or Move Down button on the Outline toolbar.

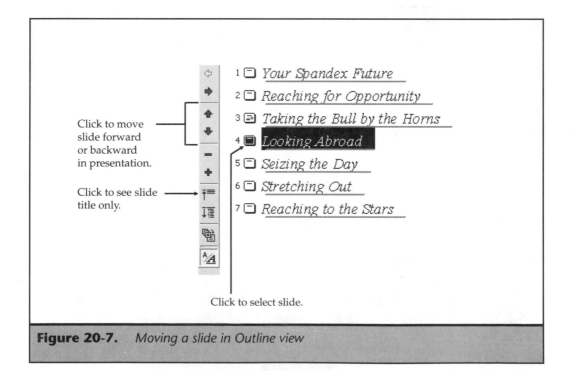

Figure 20-7.   *Moving a slide in Outline view*

Copying a Slide

Follow these steps to copy a slide:

1. Switch to Slide Sorter view.
2. Right-click on the slide you want to copy and choose Copy from the shortcut menu.

3. Click between slides in the presentation where the copy of the slide is to go.
4. Right-click and choose Paste from the shortcut menu.

Entering and Formatting the Text

Besides the standard Font and Font Size commands that can be found in all the Office 97 programs, PowerPoint offers a couple of amenities of its own for formatting text. This part of the chapter explains how to enter, edit, and format text. It explains how to align text on slides and control the amount of space between lines. And you also find instructions for moving from slide to slide in the different views and importing text from a Word document.

Writing the Words on the Slides

This part of the chapter explains how to enter the words that appear onscreen during a presentation. With PowerPoint, you can fool your colleagues and business associates into thinking that you are a layout artist. The program offers many easy-to-use tools for doing that. When it comes to writing the words, however, you are on your own.

PowerPoint can't tell you what to say, but at least it makes entering words—after you've decided what the words are—pretty easy.

The following pages offer advice for entering the text. They also explain how to keep speaker's notes for each slide so that you remember what to say at presentations as each slide appears onscreen. And you will also find a neat trick for using the headings in a Word document for the titles and text in a PowerPoint presentation.

 TIP: Words on the slides in a presentation are like headings in a document—they announce the topic, they don't explain it in detail. You, as the speaker, fill in the details. Slides with a lot of text on them annoy the audience. Text on slides should be short, sweet, and to the point.

LEARN BY EXAMPLE
EXAMPLES   *To practice entering the text for a presentation, open the Figure 20-8 (Enter Text) file on the companion CD.*

Which Is the Best Way to Enter the Text?

The best way to enter text depends on how you created your presentation. If you used a template or the AutoContent Wizard, PowerPoint has provided "placeholder text" and all you have to do is switch to Outline view and replace PowerPoint's text with your own. Outline view is by far the easiest and most practical way to enter text. Outline view was invented to help users focus on the content of a presentation—that is, on the words. In Outline view, you can read the headings and text on several different slides. And the Outline toolbar offers several buttons to help with entering text.

Another way to enter the text is to get it from a Word document. PowerPoint offers a special command for importing the headings from a Word document and using them for the slide titles and text in a PowerPoint presentation.

Entering the Text in Outline View

To enter text in Outline view, switch to Outline view by choosing the View menu Outline command or clicking the Outline View button in the lower-left corner of the screen. If you used a template or the AutoContent Wizard to create your presentation, replace the text that is already there with text of your own. If you are working with a blank slide, simply type the text you want to appear on the slide. To help you stay focused, the Outline toolbar on the left side of the screen offers a number of handy buttons. The buttons are explained in Table 20-2 and labeled in Figure 20-8.

Entering Text—and Text Boxes—in Slide View

When you insert a new slide in a presentation and choose an AutoLayout for the new slide (see "Inserting a New Slide in a Presentation," earlier in this chapter), PowerPoint

Button	What It Does
Promote	Moves a subheading or bulleted point in a slide up one level. For example, if you click on a subheading below the first heading on a slide and then click the Promote button, the subheading becomes a first heading and therefore becomes the first heading in a brand-new slide.
Demote	Moves a title, subheading, or bulleted point down one level in the hierarchy.
Collapse	Shows only the first heading in a slide. Click on a first heading and then click this button if you only want to see the first heading.
Expand	Shows all the subheadings under the first heading in a slide.
Collapse All	Shows only the first heading of each slide in the entire presentation.
Expand All	Shows all the text in all the slides in the presentation.
Show Formatting	Shows/hides the font formatting when working in Outline view In Slide Sorter view, toggles between showing all text and graphics and showing only the slide titles.

Table 20-2. *Outline Toolbar Buttons*

provides text boxes for entering the text. As this illustration shows, all you have to do is switch to Slide view, click in a text box, and start typing to enter a title or text for the new slide:

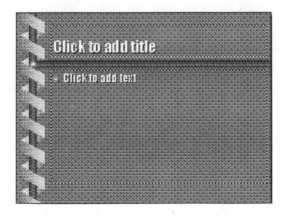

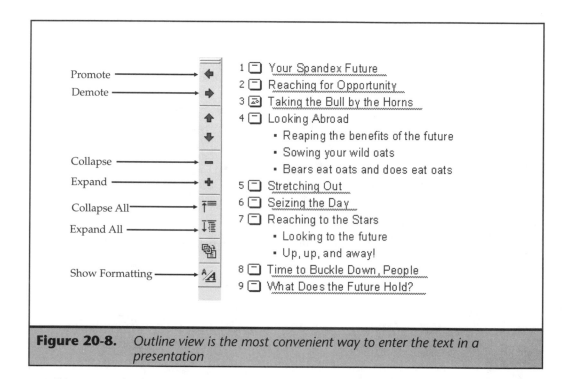

Figure 20-8. *Outline view is the most convenient way to enter the text in a presentation*

For blank slides, however, you have to create a text box yourself before you can enter the text if you want to work in Slide view. Follow these steps to create a text box and enter text inside it:

1. Switch to Slide view.

TIP: *It's better to work in Outline view on a blank slide. That way, you don't have to go through the trouble of creating a text box.*

2. Choose the Insert menu Text Box command. The pointer changes into an arrow that points down.

3. Click in what is to be one corner of the text box, and then drag across the slide. A box appears to show roughly how big the text box will be when you release the mouse button.

4. Release the mouse button when the text box is the right size.

5. Enter the text. As Figure 20-9 shows, the text box gets larger to accommodate the text you enter. When you press ENTER to begin a new line, the font size shrinks by roughly one half. PowerPoint shrinks the font size at the second line because it believes the second line is a subheading.

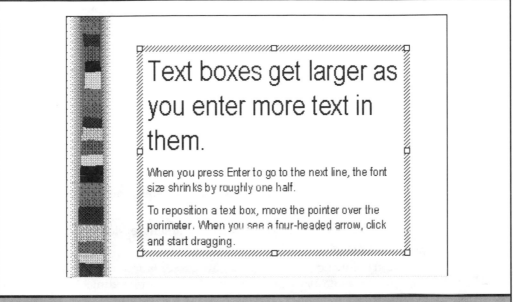

Figure 20-9. *You can insert a text box anywhere on a slide. To insert a text box, choose the Insert menu Text Box command*

TIP: To reposition a text box, move the pointer over the perimeter. When the pointer changes into a four-headed arrow, click and drag the text box to a new location.

Importing the Text from a Word Document

Personally, I think the easiest way to enter the text for a slide presentation is to simply get it from a Word 97 document. PowerPoint offers a special command for doing just that: the Insert menu Slides from Outline command. If you think about it, headings in a Word document are very much like text in a presentation—headings hit the high points and announce the topic that is under review.

WARNING: There appears to be a bug in the program, and some users report having trouble importing text from a Word document to PowerPoint. You can get around the problem, however, by converting the Word document to Rich Text Format (RFT) before importing the words into PowerPoint.

To insert headings from a Word document, you must have assigned styles to the headings (styles are explained in Chapter 8). As Figure 20-10 shows, headings assigned the Heading 1 style become slide titles in a presentation; all headings beyond Heading 2 headings are put in bulleted lists, with each kind of heading—Heading 3, 4, and so on—indented farther form the left margin. PowerPoint ignores text that wasn't assigned a heading style and does not bring it into the presentation along with the headings. In Figure 20-10, the Word document is shown in Outline view. You can see what happened to the headings when they were turned into a PowerPoint slide by looking on the right side of the figure. PowerPoint creates one slide for each Heading 1 in the Word document.

Follow these steps to use the headings from a Word document in a PowerPoint presentation:

1. Either create a new Word document and write the headings or open the Word document whose headings you want for a PowerPoint presentation.

2. Choose the View menu Outline command to see the headings only.

3. If necessary, write or edit the headings. Be sure to assign a heading style to each one.

4. Save the document. If necessary, convert the document to Rich Text Format and then close it.

5. Switch to PowerPoint and either create a new presentation or place the cursor at the point in a presentation where you want to import headings from the Word document.

6. Choose the Insert menu Slides from Outline command. You see the Insert Outline dialog box.

7. Find and click on the Word document whose headings you want to import.

8. Click the Insert button.

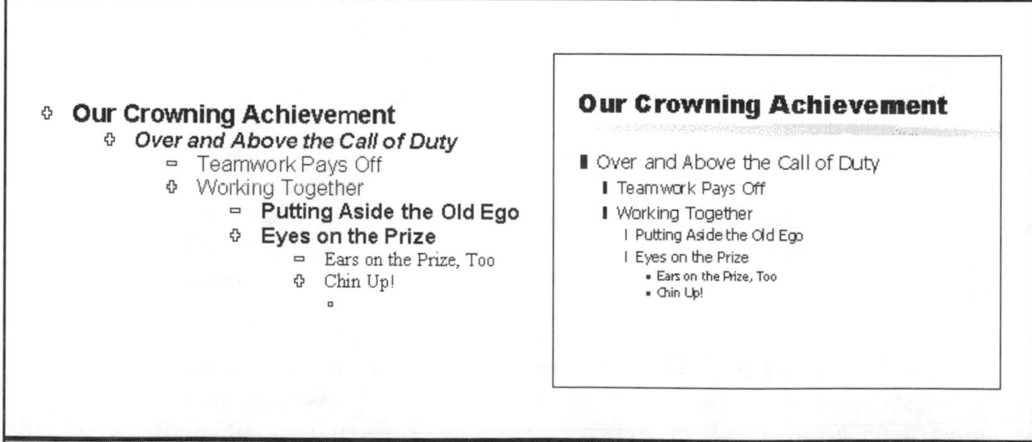

Figure 20-10. *Headings in a Word document (left) can be used as the text in a PowerPoint slide (right)*

Writing the Words You Will Speak at the Presentation

Nobody wants to commit a gaff during a presentation, so PowerPoint gives you the opportunity to write note pages. *Note pages* are notes on the slides, or the text of a presentation, or whatever will help you most when it comes time to deliver your little masterpiece. Viewers of the presentation don't see the note pages.

As Figure 20-11 shows, the note page for each slide is saved with an image of the slide itself. You can print note pages and read from them or refer to them during presentations. Be sure to be clear and grammatical if you intend to print and distribute your note pages. Don't embarrass yourself by subjecting others to a poorly written collection of sorry notes.

Follow these steps to record notes about a slide:

1. Select the slide in whatever view you happen to be in.

2. Choose the View menu Notes Page command or click the Notes Page View button in the lower-left corner of the screen. You see the slide and, below it, a blank page.

3. Click the Zoom drop-down list and choose 66% or 75% to see what you type more clearly.

4. Click in the text box at the bottom of the page and type your notes. You can call on all the text-formatting commands as you do so.

Figure 20-11.   *Viewers can't see notes pages—but you can. Use them to help give the presentation*

POWERPOINT

TIP: *Use the scroll bar to get from slide to slide in Note Pages view.*

Formatting the Text on Slides

Most of the common Office tools described in Part I of this book also work for formatting text on a slide. The techniques for choosing a font are the same in Word as PowerPoint, for example. Both programs have a Bullets button. The Align buttons work the same as the Align buttons in Excel.

More so than the other programs in Office 97, however, PowerPoint presentations are meant to be seen and not read. Therefore, the programs offer buttons that you can click to change font sizes and line spacing by increments and "eyeball" the text to make sure it looks right. As shown in Figure 20-12, select the text whose font size or line spacing you want to change and then click these buttons:

- Increase Paragraph Spacing or Decrease Paragraph Spacing to increase or decrease the amount of space that appears between lines.

- Increase Font Size or Decrease Font Size to enlarge or shrink the size of letters.

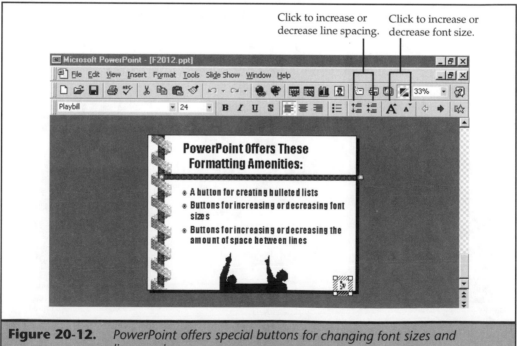

Figure 20-12. *PowerPoint offers special buttons for changing font sizes and line spacing*

The Complete Reference

Office 97

Chapter 21

Customizing Your Presentation

This chapter picks up where the last chapter left off and explains how to put the finishing touches on a slide presentation. It explains how to change the layout of a slide, choose a background for the slides in a presentation, or choose one of PowerPoint's designs. It describes how to control the transition between slides or "build" slides onscreen one line at a time. In this chapter, you learn how to make the slides in a presentation consistent with one another by using the so-called slide master, PowerPoint's equivalent of styles in a Word document. You also learn how to include graphs, charts, and tables on slides, and how to create a "multimedia" presentation with animation, sound, and video clips.

Deciding on the Look of Slides

This part of the chapter explains the basics of choosing what slides look like. PowerPoint makes it pretty easy to experiment with slides' appearance, and you are hereby invited to toy with all the techniques described in the following pages until you find a look that will catch the eye of your audience.

Following are instructions for choosing a new layout for slides, choosing one of PowerPoint's designs, and creating a design of your own. To make sure that all slides in a presentation are consistent with one another—that slide titles and bulleted text are the same font and same font size—PowerPoint has a thing called a *master slide*. Master slide settings apply to all the slides in a presentation. The following pages explain how master slides work, and how to include footers on slides.

EXAMPLES

LEARN BY EXAMPLE
Open Figure 21-A (Look of Slides) *file on the companion CD to try out the techniques described in the following pages.*

Choosing a Different Layout for a Slide

"Inserting a New Slide in a Presentation" in Chapter 20 explained how to create a new slide with one of PowerPoint's preformatted layouts. You can save yourself a lot of work by choosing a preformatted slide. Suppose, however, that you choose the wrong format. Does PowerPoint in its benevolence let you apply a new format to a slide you already created? Indeed it does. Follow these steps to apply a new format to an old slide:

1. In Slide view, display the slide that is to be given a new layout.

2. Click the Slide Layout button or choose the Format menu Slide Layout command. You see the Slide Layout dialog box shown in Figure 21-1. The layout in the blue box is the one that has been selected for the slide.

3. Click a new layout in the Slide Layout dialog box.

4. Click the Apply button.

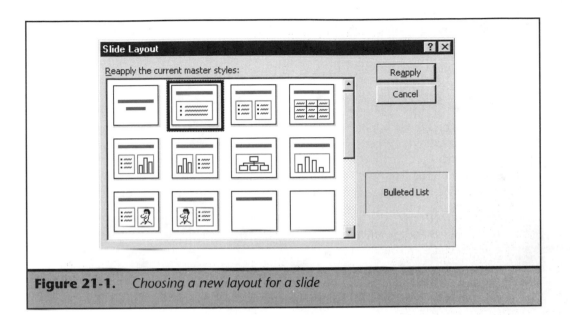

Figure 21-1. *Choosing a new layout for a slide*

You likely have to do a bit of reformatting after a slide is given a new layout. To do that, use the tools on the Formatting toolbar.

TIP: *If you bend a slide out of shape by formatting it and regret having done so, you can get the original format back. To do so, click the Slide Layout button, click the Reapply button in the Slide Layout dialog box, and click OK.*

Applying a New Design to a Presentation

As you know if you created your presentation with a template or the AutoContent Wizard, PowerPoint offers many designs for slide presentations. You can choose one of PowerPoint's designs and apply it to a finished presentation in about a second flat. And PowerPoint gives you the opportunity to look over the designs before you choose one.

HEADSTART
You can also use a PowerPoint template from the CD that comes with this book to change the design of a presentation. See Appendix C.

Follow these steps to choose one of PowerPoint's designs for all the slides in a presentation:

1. Click the Apply Design button or choose the Format menu Apply Design command. You see the Apply Design dialog box shown in Figure 21-2.

POWERPOINT

2. Click a design name in the box on the left and then glance at the preview box. Keep clicking design names until you find a suitable design.

3. Click the Apply button.

Choosing a Background Color for Slides

When it comes to choosing a background color for one slide or all the slides in a presentation, you have the option of putting a single color in the background or putting different colors behind titles, bulleted lists, and the rest of the slide apart from the titles and bulleted lists. The following pages describe how to apply a single background color or a motley collection of colors to the various parts of slides.

TIP: *A light background looks best on overhead transparencies. Use a dark background for 35mm slides and onscreen presentations.*

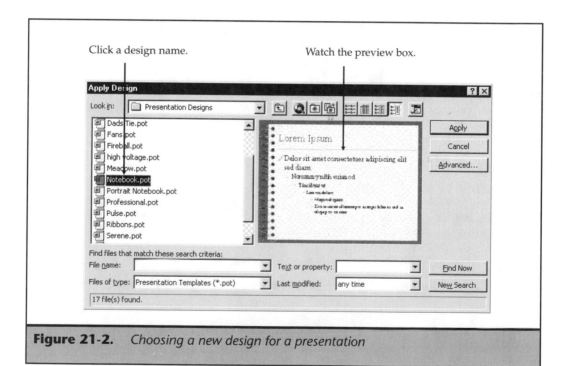

Figure 21-2. *Choosing a new design for a presentation*

Applying a Single Background Color to Slides

To apply a single background color to *all* the slides in a presentation, it doesn't matter where you start. But if you want to apply a single background color to one or a handful of slides, you have to select them first. To select a slide or slides, switch to Slide Sorter view and either click on a single slide or hold down the SHIFT key and click on the handful of slides you want to select.

 WARNING: *On a predesigned slide like the one shown in Figure 21-3, the background color need not be the predominant one. In predesigned slides, the background color is the one that is on the bottom layer. Unless you are working with single-color slides, it is sometimes hard to tell which color is actually the "background."*

Follow these steps to apply a background color to all the slides or to slides you selected:

1. Choose the Format menu Background command. You see the Background dialog box shown in Figure 21-3.

2. Click the arrow to open the drop-down list and then choose a color:

   ■ *Predefined color* Click a square on the drop-down menu to choose a predefined color.

   ■ *More Colors* Click this button and you see the Color dialog box. On the Standard tab, click a color in the rainbow assortment of colors. On the Custom tab, either click a color in the rainbow assortment or enter hue, saturation, and brightness percentages, or red, green, and blue percentages to create a color. The New box in the lower-right corner of each tab shows precisely what color you are creating.

   ■ *Fill Effects* You see the Fill Effects dialog box with its four tabs—Gradient, Texture, Pattern, and Picture—from which you can devise a color or pattern, or import a picture for the background.

3. Click the Apply to all button to give all the slides in the presentation the same color, or click the Apply button to apply the background color to the slides you selected.

Applying Your Own Background Color to Various Parts of Slides

PowerPoint offers preformatted color schemes for putting background colors on the different parts of a slide or slides. When you choose a new background color scheme,

POWERPOINT

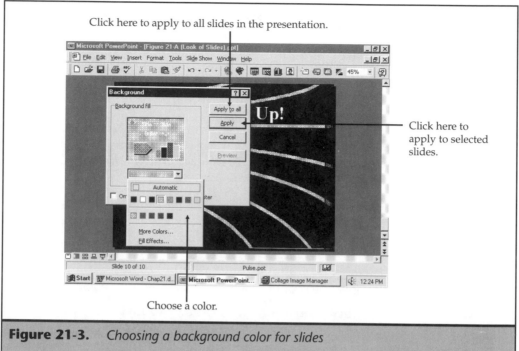

Click here to apply to all slides in the presentation.

Click here to apply to selected slides.

Choose a color.

Figure 21-3. *Choosing a background color for slides*

you can either go with one of PowerPoint's preformatted color schemes or devise a scheme of your own.

CHOOSING ONE OF POWERPOINT'S PREFORMATTED COLOR SCHEMES

Follow these steps to apply one of PowerPoint's background schemes to the different parts of a slide:

1. To change the color on all the slides in the presentation, you are all set; but to change the color on one or a handful of slides, select slides in Slide Sorter view by holding down the SHIFT key and clicking on them.

2. Choose the Format menu Slide Color Scheme command. You see the Color Scheme dialog box shown in Figure 21-4.

3. Click a Color scheme box.

4. Click the Apply to All button to change the color scheme of all the slides in the presentation or click the Apply button to change the color scheme of the slides you selected in step 1.

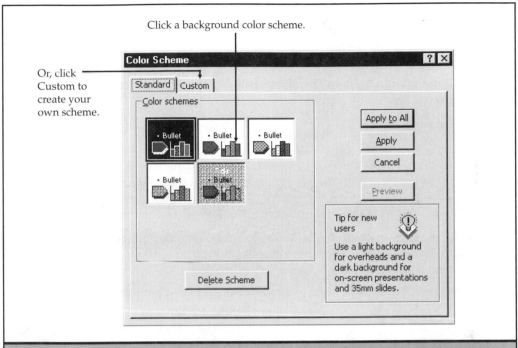

Click a background color scheme.

Or, click Custom to create your own scheme.

Figure 21-4. *Choosing a predefined color scheme. Click the Custom tab to create a color scheme of your own*

CREATING A COLOR SCHEME OF YOUR OWN

Follow these steps to apply your own colors to different parts of a slide:

1. Select slides in Slide Sorter view by holding down the SHIFT key and clicking on them if you want to change the background colors on several slides. Otherwise, to change the color scheme of all the slides in the presentation, you don't have to select any slides.

2. Choose the Format menu Slide Color Scheme command. The Standard tab of the Color Scheme dialog box appears (see Figure 21-4).

3. Click the Color scheme box that most resembles the background color scheme you want to create.

TIP: *After you create a new background color scheme, you can make it appear on the Standard tab by clicking the Add As Standard Scheme button on the Custom tab.*

4. Click the Custom tab. It is shown in Figure 21-5.

5. Under Scheme colors, click the option for the part of the slide or slides whose color you want to change.

6. Click the Change Color button. You see the Background Color dialog box with its Standard and Custom tabs. From here, you have two ways to designate a new color for the color scheme:

   ■ *Standard tab* Click a color in the rainbow assortment of colors. Click OK when you are done.

   ■ *Custom tab* Click a color in the rainbow assortment or enter hue, saturation, and brightness percentages or red, green, and blue percentages to create a color. The New box in the lower-right corner of each tab shows precisely what color you are creating. Click OK when you have chosen a color.

7. Click the Preview button. The slide or slides onscreen change to show what the color you added to the scheme looks like (you may have to drag the Color Scheme box out of the way to see the slide below it).

8. Repeat steps 5 through 7 to create more colors for your homegrown color scheme.

9. Click the Apply to All button to change the color scheme of all the slides in the presentation or the Apply button to change the color scheme of the slides you selected in step 1.

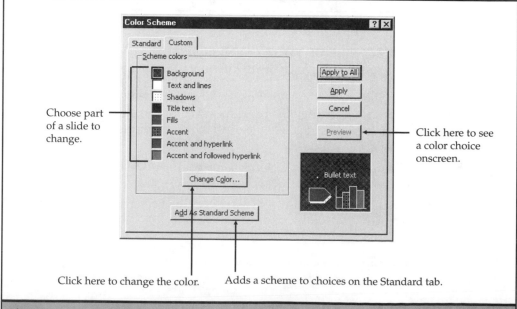

Figure 21-5. *Creating a background color scheme of your own for slides*

Master Slides for a Consistent, Professional Look

The surest way to create a professional-looking presentation is to make sure that the slides are consistent with one another. All the slide titles should be the same font and font size, as should the text in bulleted lists. If the same graphic appears on every slide, it should be the same size and appear in the same location from slide to slide. Footers on slides need to appear in the same places.

To be absolutely certain that all the slides are consistent with one another, you can do the formatting in what PowerPoint calls a *master slide.* Each presentation has two master slides, one for the title slide or slides, called the *title master,* and one for all other slides, called the *slide master.* The title master and slide master are representative slides. Format changes made on the title master are made on all title slides in the presentation; format changes made on the slide master are made to all slides in the presentation except title slides.

 NOTE: Usually, the first slide in a presentation is the title slide, but you can insert a title slide wherever you wish. In the Slide Layout dialog box (see Figure 21-1), which is used for inserting new slides in a presentation, the title slide is the one in the upper-left corner.

The following pages explain how to format text on the slide master so that text is the same font and font size from slide to slide. You also learn how to put the same text box or graphic image on each slide in a presentation and how to format text on the title master.

 LEARN BY EXAMPLE
To experiment with the slide master and title master, open the Figure 21-6 (Slide Master) *file on the companion CD.*

The Slide Master for Consistent Text Formatting

Figure 21-6 shows the slide master slide. After you change the formats on this slide, your new formats set the standard for all the slides in the presentation except title slides. Follow these steps to apply the same formats across the length and breadth of a presentation:

1. Choose the View menu Master command, and then click Slide Master. You see the slide master shown in Figure 21-6.

2. Click in the Title Area for AutoLayouts box and choose a different font and font size from the Font and Font Size menus. Click the Boldface button or format the text in other ways. For example, you can choose font color or align the text in different ways.

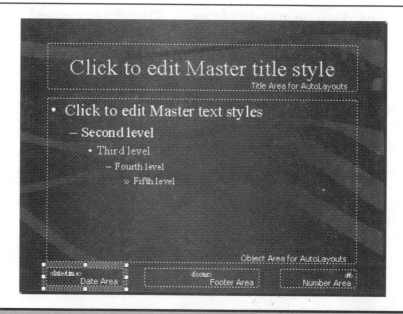

Figure 21-6. *Text formats in the slide master set the standard for formats throughout the presentation*

NOTE: *Don't bother changing the text on the slide master. All that matters is changing the text's appearance. Text on the slide master is only there for identification purposes.*

3. Click in the Object Area for AutoLayouts box and, one by one, change the font and font size of master text styles, second level text, third level text, and so on. Simply click in the text whose formats you want to change and then choose new settings from the Font and Font Size menus.

4. Click in the Date Area, Footer Area, and Number Area boxes at the bottom of the slide master and change fonts and font sizes there as well, if you want. These three boxes constitute the footer.

NOTE: *Later in this chapter, "Including Footers on Slides" explains how to put footers on all the slides in a presentation.*

5. Click the Close button in the Master toolbar.

Formatting the Title Master for Consistent Title Slides

The title master works exactly like the slide master, only the text formats made on the title master apply to title slides only. Most presentations have but one title slide. If yours has two or three, perhaps because you will cover two or three topics in the course of the presentation, you ought to go to the trouble of formatting text on the title slide to make sure your title slides are consistent with one another.

To format text on the title slide, choose the View menu Master command, click Title Master, click in the area that you want to change on the title master slide, reformat the text, and then click the Close button on the Master toolbar.

Putting the Same Image or Text on Each Slide

Figure 21-7 shows two slides with the same graphic and text on each one. Company logos, mottoes, and the like are candidates for inclusion on each slide in a presentation. To put the same graphic or text box on each slide, choose the View menu Master command, and click Slide Master to see the slide master for your presentation. A graphic or text box placed on the slide master appears on all slides:

- ■ *Graphic* See "Inserting Clip Art into a Document File" in Chapter 3 if you need help placing a clip art image.

- ■ *Text box* See "Writing the Words on the Slides" in Chapter 20 if you need help inserting a text box.

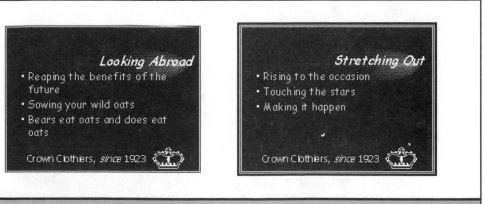

Figure 21-7. *Include graphics and text boxes on all slides in a presentation by inserting them into the slide master*

Including Footers on Slides

In the case of slides, a *footer* is a bit of text that appears along the bottom. If you tell it to do so, PowerPoint puts the date and time in the footer, text of your choice such as a company name or slogan, and a slide number on all or some of the slides in a presentation. The footer in the following illustration lists the date, the title of the presentation, and the slide number.

To include a footer on slides, follow these steps:

1. To tell PowerPoint which slides need footers, either hold down the SHIFT key and click slides in Slide Sorter view, or else don't bother selecting slides if you want all the slides or all the slides except the title slide to have footers.

2. Choose the View menu Header and Footer command. You see the Header and Footer dialog box shown in Figure 21-8.

3. If necessary, click the Date and time check box to include the date or the date and the time in the footer.

4. Click one of the option buttons to tell PowerPoint how to display the date and time:

   ■ *Update automatically* Click this option button and then click the down arrow and choose a date or a date and time format from the drop-down list. With this option, the date or the date and time will always be current. A viewer watching the presentation on April 1, 1998 at 11:30 will be reminded throughout the presentation what day and time it is—the footer in each slide will say so.

   ■ *Fixed* Click this option button and enter a date in the text box. The date you enter will appear in the footers, no ifs, ands, or buts.

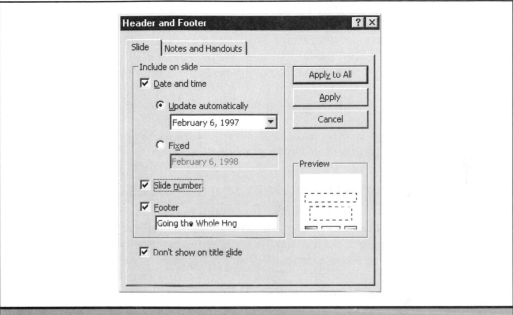

Figure 21-8. *Including a footer on the slides in a presentation*

5. Click the Slide number check box to include the slide number in the lower-right corner of the slides.

6. Click the Footer check box and enter a title, company name, aphorism, or whatever you deem important in the text box. The text you enter appears in the middle of the footer.

7. To prevent the footer information from appearing on the title slide, click to enter a check mark in the Don't show on title slide check box.

8. Click the Apply to All button to put the footer on all the slides in the presentation or the Apply button to put footers only on the slides you selected in step 1.

Giving an "Animated" Slide Presentation

People love to see images move—how else do you account for the success of television? The makers of PowerPoint, well aware that moving images catch the eye, have included a number of features for making text and graphics move on a slide. The following pages explain how to make slides not simply appear onscreen, but appear from one side or appear in an interesting way. They also explain how to make items in bulleted lists appear one at a time and parts of a slide—the title, for example—appear from one side, drop in, or do any number of interesting but possibly distracting things.

WARNING: The techniques on the following pages for "animating" parts of a slide are dangerous. Use animation techniques well and sparingly. A slide presentation with too many animations distracts the audience and keeps it from focusing on the real purpose of a presentation—to communicate ideas and plans.

Controlling Transitions Between Slides

At the movies you must have noticed how sometimes the camera goes from a soft focus to a sharp focus. Blurred images turn slowly into images you can see and understand. In PowerPoint, you can make images arrive onscreen in a similar fashion. Instead of just appearing, slides can float in from the right side of the screen, for example, or "explode" onto the screen. *Transition* is the term PowerPoint uses to describe the way that slides arrive onscreen. The program offers 42 transitions in all.

EXAMPLES

LEARN BY EXAMPLE

To see examples of slide transitions, open the Figure 21-9 (Transitions) *file on the companion CD.*

When you assign transitions to slides, you can assign the same transition to all the slides at once or assign different transitions to different slides. Don't worry about the strange names that PowerPoint gives transitions. As you choose one, you get a chance to preview it and see precisely what it does. Follow these steps to choose a transition for slides:

1. In Slide Sorter view, select the slide or slides to which you want to assign a transition. To select more than one slide, hold down the SHIFT key as you click each one. If you want to assign the same transition to all the slides in the presentation, it doesn't matter how you start.

2. Either choose the Slide Show menu Slide Transition command or right-click and choose Slide Transition from the shortcut menu. You see the Slide Transition dialog box shown in Figure 21-9.

3. Click the Effect drop-down list and choose a transition. As soon as you do so, the little doggy in the window disappears and a key appears in its place. Look closely at how the key appears in the dialog box—that is how the slide will appear onscreen if you keep the transition you chose in the Effect drop-down list. To choose a different transition, select it from the drop-down list and watch the dog and key show. Keep going until you find a transition that tickles your fancy.

Watch the transition occur. Choose a transition.

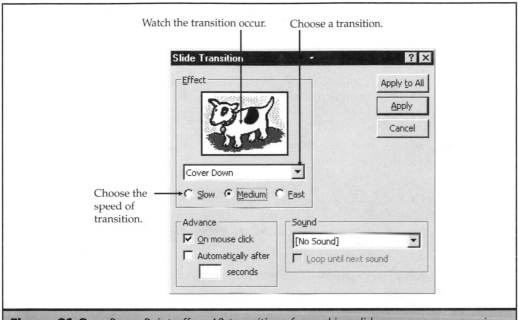

Choose the speed of transition.

Figure 21-9. *PowerPoint offers 42 transitions for making slides appear onscreen in unusual ways*

TIP: You can also select a transition from the Slide Transition Effects drop-down list on the Slide Sorter toolbar.

4. Click the Slow, Medium, or Fast option button to tell PowerPoint how fast or slow to make the transition occur. Again, the dog jumps and the key lands so you can see what the slow, medium, and fast speeds are.

5. Click the Apply to All button to assign the transition to all the slides in the presentation, or click the Apply button to assign the transition to the slides you selected in step 1.

TIP: To remove a transition, open the Slide Transition dialog box and choose No Transition on the Effects drop-down list.

NOTE: At the end of this chapter, "Including Sounds as Part of a Slide Transition" explains how to make sounds as well as sights a feature of slide transitions.

POWERPOINT

Making Bulleted Lists on Slides Appear One Bullet at a Time

Another way to keep the audience enthralled is to make bulleted lists appear on the slides one bulleted item at a time. PowerPoint gives you a bunch of different choices as to how the bullets arrive onscreen. They can drop from the sky, flash, or simply appear. Unfortunately, however, the program doesn't offer a preview screen so you can see what your choices on the Preset Animation menu mean. To make the bulleted items appear, you click the mouse during the slide presentation. Each time you click, another bulleted item appears.

LEARN BY EXAMPLE
Open the Figure 21-B (Preset Animation) *file on the companion CD to see and experiment with shooting bullets in PowerPoint presentations. Be sure to click to make the bullets appear in the slide show.*

Follow these steps to emphasize bulleted points in slide presentations by making the bulleted items appear one by one:

1. In Slide Sorter view, select each slide with a bulleted list in your presentation if you want to make all the bulleted points appear one at a time. To select the slides, click them as you hold the SHIFT key down. Otherwise, click a single slide with a bulleted list.

2. Right-click and choose Preset Text Animation from the shortcut menu.

3. Choose an animation technique from the submenu.

TIP: *You can also apply text animation effects from the Text Preset Animation drop-down list on the Slide Sorter toolbar.*

Animating Different Parts of a Slide

The previous handful of pages explained how to make a whole slide or the bulleted items on a slide drop onto the screen, fly in from the left, or do any number of acrobatic tricks. You can make different parts of a slide—the heading, the entire bulleted list (not just each bullet), a graphic, or a text box—perform acrobatic tricks as well. What's more, if more than one part of a slide is to perform acrobatically, you can tell which part performs first and which part performs last.

WARNING: *Unless you're going for laughs, do not animate more than two—or at the very most, three—parts of a slide. Animation can be very, very distracting.*

Follow these steps to animate different parts of a slide:

1. Find the inanimate slide that you want to animate, select it, and switch to Slide view.

2. Click a text box or graphic on the slide, then right-click and choose Custom Animation. You see the Custom Animation dialog box shown in Figure 21-10.

3. Under Entry animation and sound, click to open the first drop-down list, and choose an animation effect.

4. If you want and if your system is capable of producing sounds, click the second drop-down list and choose a sound to announce the arrival of the part of the slide onscreen.

5. Click to open the After animation drop-down list and tell PowerPoint what the object you are animating is supposed to do after it lands onscreen:

   - *Don't Dim* Lets the object stay onscreen.

   - *Hide After Animation* Makes the object disappear after it arrives onscreen.

   - *Hide on Next Mouse Click* Makes the object disappear when you next click the mouse to bring something else onscreen.

6. If the part of the slide you are dealing with concerns text, choose from the following options:

   - *Introduce text* Tell PowerPoint to make the text appear all at once, a word at a time, or a letter at a time.

   - *Grouped by* For text boxes in which more than one level of text appears, makes the text in the level you choose from the drop-down list appear first.

   - *In reverse order* Makes lists appear backward. In a numbered list, for example, step 5 appears first and step 1 appears last.

7. Click the Preview button to get a look at what your many choices do. The sample slide "animates" and does what the slide will do when you actually show it. You can click the Stop button (it appears where the Preview button used to be) if the performance takes too long and you want to halt it.

8. Repeat steps 2 through 7 for any other objects on the slide that you want to animate.

9. To control the order in which animated objects will appear on the slide, click the part of the slide you want to control in the Animation order box. In the preview box, a box appears around the part of the slide you selected.

10. Click the up or down arrow to the right of the Animation order box to tell PowerPoint when the thing you selected in step 7 is to appear. The thing at the top of the list appears first.

11. Click OK.

Click buttons to change the order in which parts of a slide appear.

This box shows which part of the slide you selected.

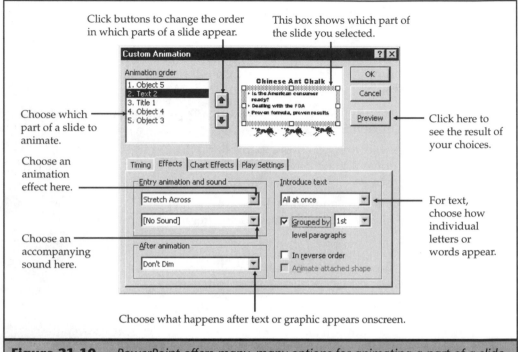

Choose which part of a slide to animate.

Choose an animation effect here.

Choose an accompanying sound here.

Click here to see the result of your choices.

For text, choose how individual letters or words appear.

Choose what happens after text or graphic appears onscreen.

Figure 21-10. *PowerPoint offers many, many options for animating a part of a slide. Don't overdo it, however*

TIP: *In Slide view, you can "animate" a slide by choosing the Slide Show menu Animation Preview command.*

EXAMPLES

LEARN BY EXAMPLE
To try your hand at animating the different parts of a slide, open the Figure 21-10 *(Animation) file on the companion disk.*

The Fast but Dicey Way to Animate Slides

Instead of fishing around in the Slide Transition or Custom Animation dialog boxes (see Figures 21-9 and 21-10), you can animate slides very quickly in Slide Sorter view. To do so, follow these steps:

1. In Slide Sorter view, select a slide or slides.

2. As shown in Figure 21-11, click to open the Slide Transition Effects drop-down list and choose a transition for the slide or slides.

3. Click to open the Text Preset Animation drop-down list and choose an animation option for the main text on the slide (the text directly below the title).

In Slide Sorter view, icons appear below slides to which animation effects have been assigned. You can see the icons in Figure 21-11.

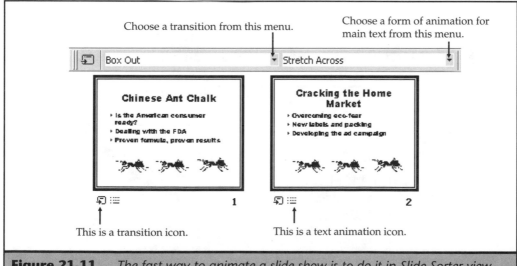

Figure 21-11. *The fast way to animate a slide show is to do it in Slide Sorter view*

POWERPOINT

Including Graphs, Charts, Tables, and Columns in Slides

The following pages explain how to include specialty items on slides—graphs, charts, tables, and two-column text. As shown in Figure 21-12, PowerPoint gives you an opportunity to insert preformatted slides—some of which are preformatted for charts, tables, and clip art—when you insert a new slide in a presentation. By all means choose a preformatted slide. Those slides make it very easy to import graphs, charts, and clip art images, as the following pages demonstrate.

An Organization Chart Slide

To include an organization chart on a slide, start by inserting an organization chart slide from the New Slide dialog box (see Figure 21-12). Then, on the slide, enter a title for the chart and double-click the box that says "Double click to add a chart." The Organization Chart window appears, as shown in Figure 21-13.

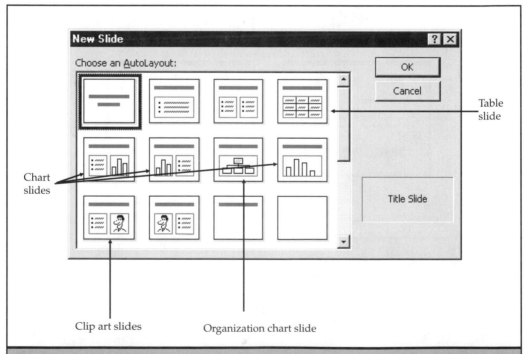

Figure 21-12. *The preformatted slides are a big help when it comes to including charts, tables, and clip art on slides*

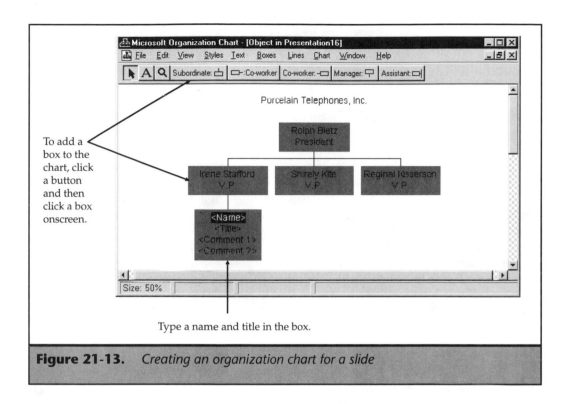

To add a box to the chart, click a button and then click a box onscreen.

Type a name and title in the box.

Figure 21-13.   *Creating an organization chart for a slide*

Enter a title for the chart at the top of the screen, and then click in each box, delete the placeholder text, and type the names and titles of the people over whom you crack the whip or under whom you bend when the whip is cracked. The boxes get larger and smaller to accommodate the names and titles. To add a new box to the chart, click one of the five buttons along the top of the screen—Subordinate, Co-worker, and so on—and then click the box on the screen to which you need to attach the subordinate, co-worker, and so on.

When you are done, choose the File menu Update presentation command, then click the Microsoft PowerPoint button on the taskbar to see what the chart looks like on the slide. If need be, click the Microsoft Organization Chart button on the taskbar to return to the Organization Chart window and continue to fiddle with the chart. Close the Organization Chart application when your chart is tip-top. To open the Organization Chart application after you have closed it, double-click the organization chart on the PowerPoint slide.

A Table Slide

To include a table on a slide, insert a Table slide from the New Slide dialog box (see Figure 21-12). Then enter a title for the table and double-click where the slide says to "Double click to add table." You see the Insert Word Table dialog box:

POWERPOINT

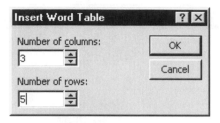

Tell PowerPoint how many rows and columns you want, and then click OK. You see a table with the gridlines showing. Enter the numbers, labels, and whatnot for the table. You can use the Font and Font Size menus to change the look of text. In fact, if you look closely, you will see that the PowerPoint toolbars and menus have flown the coop and the Word toolbars and menus appear in their places. See "Working with Tables in Word" in Chapter 9 to find out all the secrets of creating tables with the Word toolbars and menus.

When you have finished creating the table, click outside of the table to restore PowerPoint's toolbars and menus. If you need to go back to your table and dicker with it after you have finished creating it, double-click the table. You see the Word menus and toolbars again.

 TIP: *Another way to enter a table on a slide is to import it from Word, Excel, or Access. Make sure the table will fit on the slide, copy it to the Clipboard, and then paste it in the slide.*

A Graph

PowerPoint offers no less than three preformatted slides for graphs. To include a graph on a slide, choose one of the three preformatted slides in the New Slide dialog box (see Figure 21-12) and click OK. Then, enter a title for the slide and double-click in the slide where it says to "Double click to add chart." Soon the Microsoft Graph application appears onscreen and you see a datasheet and prototype graph like the ones in the following illustration. Chapter 13 explains how to fashion a chart with this application. If you are not up for making the trip to Chapter 13, simply replace the data in the datasheet with data of your own.

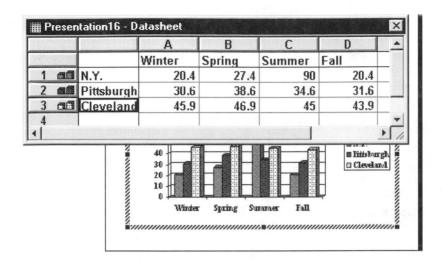

When you are done creating your graph, click on the slide. The datasheet disappears and you see the graph in all its glory. To see the datasheet again and re-enter numbers or labels for the graph, double-click the graph.

Two Columns

Here's a little trick for creating two columns on a slide: choose the Two-Column Text slide in the New Slide dialog box (see Figure 21-12). PowerPoint gives you two bulleted lists, but you can make those lists into ordinary columns by selecting them and clicking the Bullets button. After that, you get normal, all-American columns. By the way, the columns are not newspaper-style columns—text does not spill over from one column to the next.

Getting Fancy with Sound and Video

Provided your system is set up to handle it, you can include video clips and sound recordings in a PowerPoint presentation. When a video clip or sound is attached to a slide, it appears as an icon. You can either double-click the icon to play the video clip or sound, or arrange for PowerPoint to play it automatically when the slide appears onscreen.

POWERPOINT

WARNING: Sound and video take up a lot of disk space. Moreover, if you intend to include sound and video sequences in your slide presentation, be sure to test the presentation on the computer on which the presentation will be run. That way, you can see if the sound and video play at acceptable speeds. It is embarrassing to have to wait two minutes for a video sequence to start running during a presentation.

Inserting a Video Clip

When you insert a video clip, you can use either one of your own or one from the Microsoft Clip Gallery. To insert a clip of your own, choose the Insert menu Movies and Sounds command, click Move from File, find the video-clip file in the Insert Movie dialog box, and click OK. Follow these steps to insert a video clip from the Microsoft Clip Gallery in a slide presentation:

1. Choose the Insert menu Movies and Sounds command, and then click Movie from Gallery to open the Clip Gallery.

2. Click the Videos tab. It is shown in Figure 21-14.

3. Find a clip that piques your interest and click on it.

4. Click the Play button to see what it does.

5. Click the Insert button when you've found a video clip that you like.

Figure 21-14. *Inserting a video clip on a slide. You can get video clips from the Microsoft Clip Gallery*

The following illustration shows what the clip looks like when it lands on the slide. You can drag the clip to a new location on a side. Double-click a video clip to play it during a presentation. To play it when the slide appears onscreen, right-click the video clip, choose Custom Animation from the shortcut menu, and turn a few pages back to "Animating Different Parts of a Slide" and Figure 21-10 for all the details.

LEARN BY EXAMPLE
Open the Figure 21-14 (Video Clip) *file on the companion CD if you want to see firsthand how video clips on slides work.*

Including Sounds in Slides

PowerPoint offers three ways to attach sounds to a slide: by importing a sound file from Microsoft's Clip Gallery, by importing a sound file of your own, or by including sound as part of a slide transition. To import your own sound file, choose the Insert menu Movies and Sound command, click Sound from File, find the sound file in the Insert Sound dialog box, and click OK. The other two techniques for inserting a sound file are described on the following pages.

Inserting a Sound from the Clip Gallery

Follow these steps to insert a sound from Microsoft's Clip Gallery:

1. Choose the Insert menu Movies and Sound command, and click Sound from Gallery. You see the Clip Gallery dialog box.

2. Click the Sounds tab.

3. Click the sound of your choice, click the Play button, and listen carefully.

4. Click Insert when you've found the sound you want.

A very small icon—it looks like a speaker—appears on the slide. By double-clicking the icon during a presentation, you can play the sound:

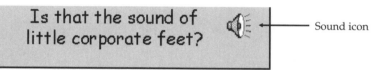

Is that the sound of little corporate feet?

Sound icon

TIP: *Drag sound icons to the lower-right corner of slides. That way, you always know where they are. You can enlarge a sound icon by dragging one of its corners.*

Including Sounds as Part of a Slide Transition

Another way to include sound in a slide show is to include a sound as part of a slide transition. "Controlling Transitions Between Slides," earlier in this chapter, gave the lowdown on slide transitions. Follow these steps to make sounds a part of slide transitions:

1. In Slide Sorter view, select the slide or slides to which you want to assign a sound transition. To select more than one slide, hold down the SHIFT key as you click each one. If you want to assign the same sound to all the slides in the presentation, it doesn't matter how you start.

2. Choose the Slide Show menu Slide Transition command. You see the Slide Transition dialog box shown in Figure 21-15.

3. On the Sound drop-down menu, choose a sound to accompany the transition.

4. Click the Loop until next sound check box if you want the sound to play continuously while the slide is onscreen.

5. Click the Apply to All button to assign the sound to all the slides in the presentation, or click the Apply button to assign the sound to the slides you selected in step 1.

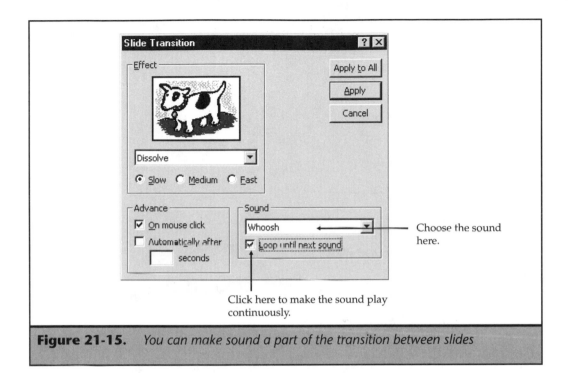

Choose the sound here.

Click here to make the sound play continuously.

Figure 21-15. *You can make sound a part of the transition between slides*

TIP: *To remove a sound, open the Slide Transition dialog box and choose No Sound on the Sound drop-down menu.*

The
Complete
Reference

Office
97

Chapter 22

Showing a Presentation

The previous two chapters explained how to prepare a slide presentation. In this short chapter, you learn to go give a show, make it lively, and print a presentation so that the audience can take it home, ponder it, and marvel at how satisfying and enriching it was.

This chapter explains how to run a presentation and designate some slides as "hidden" so that you have the option of showing them or not showing them during the show. It explains how to start a presentation and move from slide to slide. You don't have to show the slides in order if you decide not to. You will learn two or three tricks for adding a little drama to the show. You also will learn how to draw onscreen during a show and how to black out the screen. If you have ever wanted to create a kiosk presentation that repeats itself until the cows come home, or learn how to take notes during a presentation (and include the notes as part of the handout that the audience receives after the show), read on.

This chapter also reviews how to print transparencies, print slides on paper, print speakers notes, and print handouts for the audience. It also tells how to print slide transparencies.

Dress-Rehearsing a Presentation

Before you give a presentation, be sure to dress-rehearse it two or three times. And as you dress-rehearse, try timing the presentation to see how long it takes. That way, you will know how long to book the conference room and whether your presentation is too long or too short. In case your presentation falls short of its allotted time, you can create two or three hidden slides and show them only in the event that the presentation takes less time than you expected.

TIP: You might dress-rehearse the presentation on the computer that you will use for the genuine presentation.

The following pages explain how to time a presentation and how to create and show hidden slides.

LEARN BY EXAMPLE
To practice timing a presentation, open the Figure 22-A (Timing) *file on the companion CD.*

Timing a Presentation

These instructions explain how to dress-rehearse a slide show and find out how long each slide stayed onscreen and how long the entire show lasted. When you are done timing the presentation, PowerPoint will ask if you want to be able to see how long you lingered with each slide and whether you want each slide to advance automatically after a certain amount of time. If you answer yes, the number of seconds each slide was presented will appear below each slide in Slide Sorter view and slides will advance after the number of seconds has passed. Follow these steps to find out how long it takes to give your presentation:

1. Switch to Slide Sorter view.

2. Either click the Rehearse Timings button on the Slide Sorter toolbar or choose the Slide Show menu Rehearse Timings command. The first slide fills the entire screen. In the lower-right corner of the slide, the Rehearsal dialog box tells how long the first slide in the presentation has been onscreen and how long the slide show has taken so far:

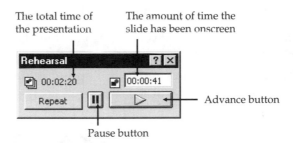

The total time of the presentation

The amount of time the slide has been onscreen

Advance button

Pause button

3. Pretend that you are giving the presentation and discuss the first slide. Say everything that you intend to say about this slide. The clock on the right side of the Rehearsal dialog box records how long the slide has been onscreen. If you think your slide will engender a discussion, take that into account, too, and leave the slide onscreen longer.

NOTE: Later in this chapter, "Printing the Speaker's Notes Along with Slide Images" explains how to print the speaker's notes, if you jotted down any. You might print the speaker's notes and read them as you time your presentation.

4. Click the Advance button to go to the next slide and pretend that you are showing it to an audience, too. The clock on the right side of the Rehearsal dialog box is reset to 00:00:00, but the clock on the left, which records the entire presentation, not each slide's stay onscreen, continues to tick.

TIP: Click the Pause button to stop the clocks from running if your dress-rehearsal is interrupted by a phone call, a hungry cat, or some other distraction. To start all over and "show" a slide from the beginning, click the Repeat button.

5. When you click the Advance button after showing the last slide, you see a message box like the one in the next illustration. It tells how long the presentation took to show *in toto,* and asks if you want to record "the new slide timings" and use them to view the slide show:

POWERPOINT

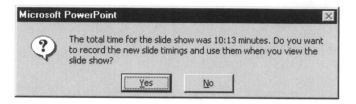

By "use them," PowerPoint is referring to the fact that you can make slides advance automatically during a show after a certain number of seconds. If you click the Yes button in this dialog box, slides will appear onscreen during the show for the same amount of time you allowed them to stay onscreen during the rehearsal. Instead of pressing N or PGDN or clicking to advance the slides, you can make slides advance automatically after a certain number of seconds.

6. Click the Yes or No button. If you click Yes, another dialog box asks if you want the amount of time each slide stayed onscreen to be listed in Slide Sorter view.

7. Click Yes or No. If you click Yes, listings appear below each slide in Slide Sorter view to show how long it will stay onscreen:

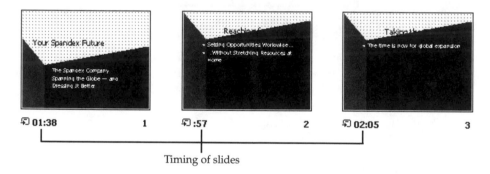

Timing of slides

NOTE: *Advancing slides automatically after a certain amount of time is useful in kiosk presentations. "Showing a Timed Kiosk Presentation," later in this chapter, gives all the details of creating a presentation that loops and loops and repeats itself until you or someone else tells it to stop.*

Designating Some Slides as "Hidden"

A hidden slide is like an insurance policy in case a presentation falls short of the time you allotted for it. Rather than stare at the audience and ad-lib for ten minutes, you can create two, three, four, or another number of hidden slides. If you come to the end of a show a few minutes early, simply show a hidden slide and discuss it. The following pages explain how to "hide" a slide and how to show a hidden slide during a presentation.

LEARN BY EXAMPLE
Open the Figure 22-1 (Hide Slide) *file on the companion CD to practice hiding slides and showing them during presentations.*

Telling PowerPoint to Hide a Slide

Follow these steps to "hide" a slide:

1. Create a few slides you can call on in case of an emergency.

TIP: *A quick way to create a gratuitous hidden slide is to select all the slides in the presentation except the first one in Slide Sorter or Outline view and then click the Summary Slide button. PowerPoint creates a summary slide with all the titles of the slides you selected in a bulleted list. Move the new summary slide to the end of the presentation.*

2. Switch to Slide Sorter view.

3. Select the slide or slides that you want to hide. To select more than one, hold down the SHIFT key and click on slides.

4. Click the Hide Slide button or choose the Slide Show menu Hide Slide command. A slash appears across the slide number to show that the slide has been hidden:

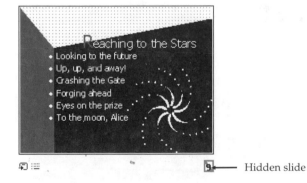

Hidden slide

To "unhide" a slide, select it in Slide Sorter view and click the Hide Slide button.

TIP: *Put hidden slides at the end of the presentation. That way, you always know where they are.*

Showing a Hidden Slide in a Presentation

Unless you happened to have created the presentation and know where the hidden slides are, you can show an entire presentation without encountering them.

POWERPOINT

PowerPoint bypasses hidden slides unless you tell it specifically to display them. Follow these steps to show a hidden slide during a presentation:

1. Right-click anywhere on a slide.

2. As shown in Figure 22-1, click the Go command on the shortcut menu.

3. Chose By Title on the submenu. You see a list of all the slides in the presentation. Parentheses appear around the numbers of the slides that have been hidden. In Figure 22-1, slides 7, 8, and 9 are hidden slides.

4. Click the hidden slide that you want to display.

TIP: *If you know that the next slide in a presentation is a hidden slide and you want to show the hidden slide, press* H. *The computer beeps if the next slide is not a hidden one.*

Giving a Presentation

You will be pleasantly surprised to find out how easy it is to give a presentation. After you have gone to all the trouble of creating it, giving it is by contrast a piece of cake. The following pages explain how to give a presentation from first slide to last and how

Figure 22-1.   *Displaying a hidden slide. On the By Title submenu, parentheses appear around the numbers of slides that have been hidden*

to jump around in a presentation and show the slides out of sequence. These pages also explain how to draw on slides and black out the screen. You also learn how to create a kiosk presentation in which slides appear onscreen after specific time intervals.

To start showing a presentation, choose the View menu Slide Show command or choose the Slide Show menu View Show command.

Moving from Slide to Slide

When you show slides, you can do so by going from the first to the last, or you can jump from place to place. Following are instructions for doing both.

LEARN BY EXAMPLE
To try your hand at giving a presentation, open the Figure 22-2 (Present) *file on the companion CD.*

Viewing the Slides in Order

To give a slide show from first slide to last slide, choose the View menu Slide Show command or choose the Slide Show menu View Show command. You see the first slide onscreen. PowerPoint offers no less than five ways to see the next and subsequent slides:

- Click with the mouse.
- Press N (for next).
- Press the PGDN key.
- Right-click and choose Next from the shortcut menu.
- Click the button in the lower-left corner of the screen and choose Next from the shortcut menu.

When the presentation is over, the screen returns to whichever view it was in when you started the presentation. Press ESC to end a presentation before it reaches the end.

WARNING: *"Giving an 'Animated' Slide Presentation" in Chapter 21 explained how to make parts of a slide appear one at a time. If you told PowerPoint to make parts of a slide appear that way, clicking, pressing N, pressing the PGDN key, and all the other means of going from slide to slide instead make the different parts of a slide appear. Only after the entire slide arrives onscreen does clicking, pressing N, and so on advance the presentation to the next slide.*

Viewing Slides Anywhere in a Slide Show

Suppose an attentive busybody asks a question in the middle of a slide presentation, and to answer it you have to go back to a slide that you showed already or go forward to a slide near the end of the presentation. PowerPoint offers a bunch of different ways to skip around to different slides.

To go backward slide by slide in a presentation, do the following:

- Press P (for previous).
- Press the PGUP key.
- Right-click and choose Previous from the shortcut menu.
- Click the button in the lower-left corner of the screen and choose Previous from the shortcut menu.

To go backward or forward anywhere you wish in a presentation, follow these steps:

1. Either click on the button in the lower-left corner of the window or right-click anywhere on the screen.
2. As shown in Figure 22-2, choose Go from the shortcut menu.
3. Choose By Title from the submenu.
4. Click the title of the slide you want to see onscreen.

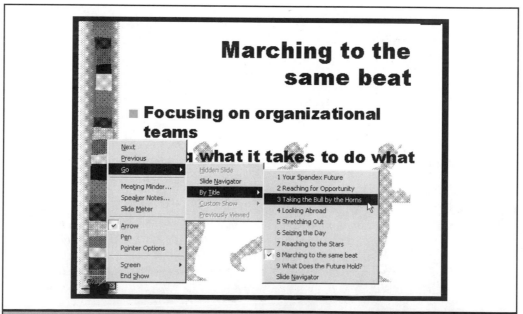

Figure 22-2. *You can go to any slide in a slide show by choosing the Go menu By Title command*

Techniques for Making a Show Livelier

To add a bit of spice to a show, you might try drawing on the screen or blacking out the screen. In Figure 22-3, the presenter has underlined the word "future" on the slide and drawn Xs in the boxes on the right. Presumably, the presenter did this as part of the talk to show how keen the company is to seize future opportunities and how able the company is to do that thanks to the creativity, vision, and pep of its employees. In the course of a presentation, you might black out the screen when the members of the audience start discussing a topic among themselves and no longer need to focus on a slide.

The following pages explain how to use the pen, change the color of the pen, and black out the screen.

Using the Pen for Emphasis

How to choose a color for the pen is explained shortly. Meanwhile, read on to learn how to draw with the pen.

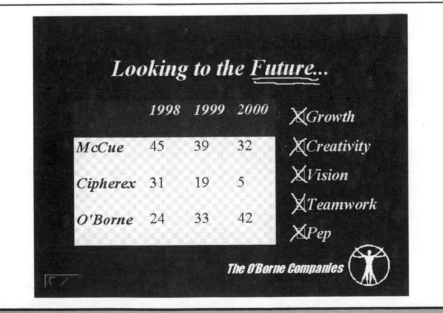

Figure 22-3. *Draw on the screen to highlight important parts of a presentation*

DRAWING WITH THE PEN

To draw with the pen during a presentation, follow these steps:

1. Right-click and choose Pen from the shortcut menu. The pointer changes into a pen.

2. Drag the pointer to draw lines and shapes onscreen.

3. Press ESC when you have finished using the pen.

 TIP: *Hold down the* SHIFT *key as you drag the mouse if you want to draw a straight line.*

Pen marks are not permanent. They are much easier to erase than graffiti. As soon as you move to the next slide, the pen marks are wiped clean. Return to the slide again and you see that all the pen marks are gone. However, if you must remove pen marks right away, right-click, choose Screen, and then choose Erase Pen.

 WARNING: *Be careful not to press* ESC *twice when you have finished using the pen. Pressing once removes the pen; pressing once again ends the slide presentation.*

CHOOSING A COLOR FOR THE PEN

To choose a color for the pen, follow these steps:

1. Right-click and choose Pointer Options from the shortcut menu.

2. Choose Pen Color on the submenu.

3. Choose a new color.

To get the default ink color back, right-click, choose Pointer Options, choose Pen Color, and choose Reset. (The default pen color changes—it always matches the color of the slide text.)

Blacking Out the Screen

An audience usually stares at the slide onscreen, but if you want it to focus on you, the speaker, you can always black out the screen. To do so, follow these steps:

1. Right-click and choose Screen from the shortcut menu.

2. Choose Black Screen.

To see the presentation again, simply click onscreen.

Showing a Timed Kiosk Presentation

Perhaps you've seen a kiosk-style presentation at a shopping mall or other place where particular people congregate. A kiosk presentation is one that plays over and over. After the last slide appears, the first appears, and the saga begins all over again.

To create a kiosk presentation with PowerPoint, you tell the program how many seconds to leave each slide onscreen, set the works in motion, and let it run until you or someone else presses ESC. "Timing a Presentation," earlier in this chapter, explained how to measure how long each slide stays onscreen during a rehearsal. One way to tell PowerPoint how long to leave each slide onscreen during a kiosk presentation is to time the presentation and tell PowerPoint to record the settings. This way, PowerPoint leaves each slide onscreen the same amount of time it stayed onscreen during the rehearsal.

See "Timing a Presentation," earlier in this chapter, if you want to use the rehearsal method to determine how long to leave each slide onscreen. The other way to handle a kiosk presentation is to simply tell PowerPoint how long to leave each slide onscreen. Follow these steps to do so:

1. In Slide Sorter view, click on a single slide if you want it to stay onscreen a certain amount of time. Otherwise, to tell PowerPoint to leave all the slides onscreen the same amount of time, it doesn't matter how you start.

2. Choose the Slide Show menu Slide Transition command. You see the Slide Transition dialog box shown in Figure 22-4.

3. Clear the check mark from the On mouse click check box.

4. Click the Automatically after check box.

5. In the seconds box, enter how many seconds the slide or slides should stay onscreen before the following slides or slides appear automatically.

6. Click the Apply to All button to make all the slides in the presentation appear onscreen for the same amount of time, or click the Apply button to make only the slides you selected in step 1 appear onscreen for the same amount of time.

7. Choose the Slide Show menu Set Up Show command.

8. Click the Loop continuously until 'Esc' check box.

9. Click OK.

Printing a Presentation

Giving a presentation on a computer screen, by way of a slide projector, or in overhead transparencies is not the only way to present your masterpiece. You can also print it.

POWERPOINT

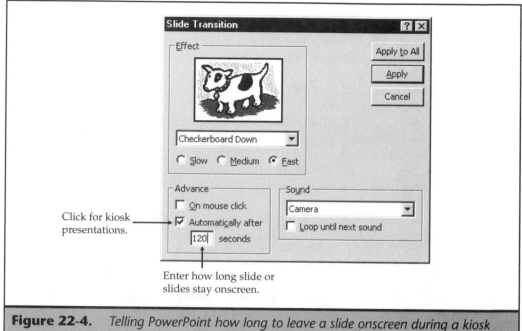

Click for kiosk presentations.

Enter how long slide or slides stay onscreen.

Figure 22-4. *Telling PowerPoint how long to leave a slide onscreen during a kiosk presentation*

In fact, printing it in the form of a handout is a good idea, because it gives the audience a chance to look over the slide presentation after it is over.

PowerPoint offers two ways to print a presentation. You can print the slides, or you can print the slides along with the speaker's notes. The following pages explain how to print hard copies of the slides and print the speaker's notes. They also explain how to print slide transparencies.

EXAMPLES

LEARN BY EXAMPLE
Open the Figure 22-5 (Printing) file on the companion CD to get some practice printing slides and speaker's notes.

Printing the Speaker's Notes Along with Slide Images

Most people aren't very good at extemporizing, so they need speaker's notes to read from during a presentation. "Writing the Words on the Slides," in Chapter 20, describes how to enter speaker's notes. When you print the speaker's notes, you get one page

Taking the Minutes of the Meeting

During a presentation, you can add to the speaker's notes that pertain to a slide, take minutes, or jot down what PowerPoint calls "action items"—a better word is "work assignments"—and display all the action items you jotted down on a slide that appears at the end of the presentation.

- *Adding to speaker's notes*   To add to or create new speaker's notes while a presentation is in progress, right-click on a slide and choose Speaker Notes. As shown in the following illustration, a window appears with the notes you already jotted down, if you jotted down any. The audience cannot see this window. Type a few words of wisdom and then click the Close button.

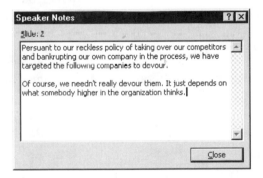

- *Taking the minutes*   To take the minutes of a meeting in order to collect them in a Word document when the meeting is over, right-click on a slide and choose Meeting Minder. You see the Meeting Minder dialog box shown in the following illustration. Enter the minutes and click OK.

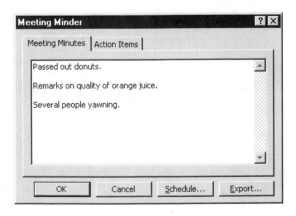

When the presentation is over, you can assemble all the minutes you took throughout the slide presentation into a single Word document. To do so, save the PowerPoint presentation and choose the View menu Slide Show command. Then right-click on a slide; choose Meeting Minder; click the Meeting Minutes tab, if necessary; and click the Export button. A dialog box asks if you want to send the meeting minutes and action items to Microsoft Word. Click the check box, if necessary, and then click the Export Now button. If Word isn't running already, it starts running. You see a new document with your minutes in it. Name and save the document.

■ *Jotting down "action items" for the last slide* To record work assignments—or "action items," as Microsoft so cavalierly calls them—as you present each slide, right-click on a slide, choose Meeting Minder from the shortcut menu, and click the Action Items tab. Then enter a description of the task in the Description box, the person who the task is assigned to, and the date it is supposed to be done, as shown in the following illustration. Enter as many assignments as you want at one time. All action items entered on the Action Items tab appear in an action-packed slide that PowerPoint creates and puts at the end of the presentation.

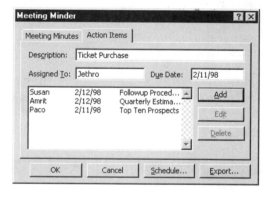

for each slide in the presentation. At the top of the page is an image of the slide; at the bottom are your notes. Follow these steps to print the speaker's notes:

1. From any view, choose the File menu Print command. You see the Print dialog box shown in Figure 22-5.

2. In the Print what drop-down list, choose Notes Pages.

3. Click OK.

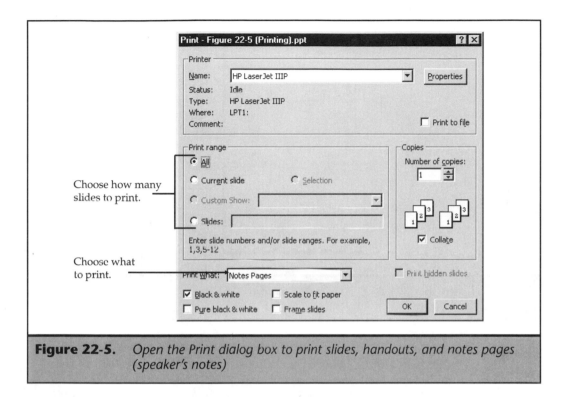

Choose how many slides to print.

Choose what to print.

Figure 22-5. *Open the Print dialog box to print slides, handouts, and notes pages (speaker's notes)*

PowerPoint prints a copy of the slide at the top of the page and your notes at the bottom.

NOTE: *Chapter 2 explains all the details of printing in an Office 97 program.*

Making the Notes Pages Presentable

If you intend to hand out the speaker's notes along with slide images to the audience, you ought to make the notes presentable. In other words, you ought to format the text, and perhaps include a header or footer on the pages. All that can be done from a thing that PowerPoint calls the "notes master."

Follow these steps to lay out the notes pages so that they look good to the audience who will receive them:

1. Choose the View menu Master command, and then click Notes Master. You see the notes master shown in Figure 22-6.

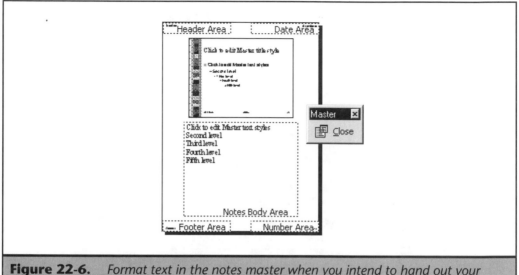

Figure 22-6. *Format text in the notes master when you intend to hand out your speaker's notes to the audience*

2. Click in the Notes Body Area box and choose a different font and font size from the Font and Font Size menus for each level of text you've included in your notes. Titles are first-level text, text goes on the second level, and bulleted lists go on the third level. Click the Boldface button or format the text in other ways. For example, you can align the text in different ways. Don't bother changing the text on the notes master. All that matters is changing the text's appearance. Text on the notes master is only there for identification purposes.

3. In the Date Area and Number Area, click in the text and change the text formatting.

4. Click in the Header Area and Footer Area and change the text formatting there as well. To enter text for a header or footer, click the Zoom drop-down list and choose 75% to see what you are doing, then scroll to the header and footer respectively, select the text between the angle brackets (<>), delete the text, and enter text of your own. The text you enter between the brackets will appear in the header and footer on all the pages you print.

5. Click the Close button on the Master toolbar.

Printing Handouts of Slides for the Audience to Take Home

Besides printing speaker's notes and slides, you can print only the slides. PowerPoint calls a sheet with slides on it a "handout." You can print two, three, or six slides per page. Follow these steps to print the slides in a presentation so the audience can take the slides away when the presentation is over:

1. Choose the File menu Print command. You see the Print dialog box shown in Figure 22-7.

2. In the Print what drop-down list, choose a Handout option to tell PowerPoint how many slides to print on each page.

3. Click the check boxes at the bottom of the dialog box to tell PowerPoint how the slides should look.

   ■ *Black & white* Converts colors to gray shades.

   ■ *Pure black & white* Does not allow gray shades, but displays images in black and white only.

   ■ *Scale to fit paper* Makes slides larger or smaller so they fit across the page.

   ■ *Frame slides* Draws a thin line around the border of slides.

4. Click OK.

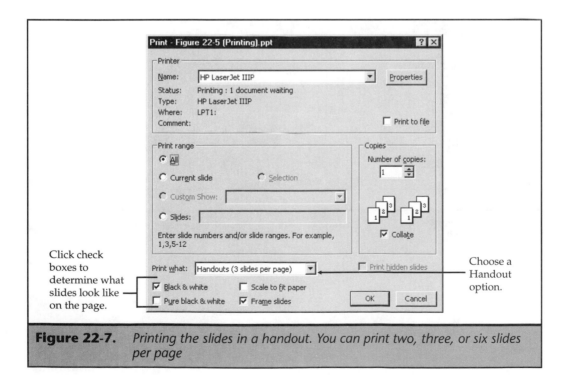

Click check boxes to determine what slides look like on the page.

Choose a Handout option.

Figure 22-7. *Printing the slides in a handout. You can print two, three, or six slides per page*

POWERPOINT

TIP: *To print the slides in color, remove the check mark from the Black & white check box.*

Printing Transparencies

To print transparencies, start by loading your printer tray with transparencies. You might have to consult the dreary manual that came with your printer to find out if it can handle transparencies and which kind of transparencies to use. Follow these steps to tell PowerPoint that you want to print transparencies:

1. Choose the File menu Page Setup command. You see the dialog box shown in Figure 22-8.
2. In the Slides sized for drop-down list, choose Overhead.
3. If necessary, change the Width, Height, and Slides settings.
4. Click OK.

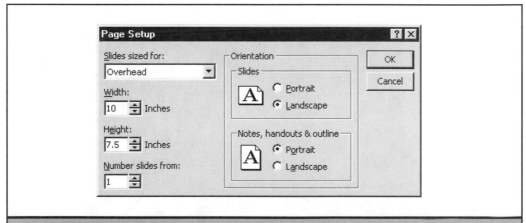

Figure 22-8. *Choose Overhead in the Slides sized for drop-down menu to print slide transparencies*

Part VI

Microsoft Outlook

The Complete
Reference

Office
97

Chapter 23

Using Outlook for E-Mail

This chapter, the first in Part VI, explains how to use Outlook to communicate with coworkers, friends, and colleagues by way of a network or the Internet. Besides helping you send and receive e-mail, the program is also what software marketers call a "personal information manager." That means you can use it to keep address lists, schedule meetings, and organize work schedules. Chapter 24 explains the personal information manager side of Outlook.

In this chapter, you familiarize yourself with the Outlook screen and learn how to get from place to place. Then you learn how to send, forward, and receive e-mail messages. Unfortunately, e-mail having become a way for people in crowded offices to document their every decision, action, and thought, many Outlook users receive hundreds of e-mail messages a week. This chapter explains how to organize those messages in folders so you can keep track of them. It also explains how to delete messages, flag urgent messages, request replies for messages, and send files along with e-mail messages.

A Quick Geography Lesson

The primary difference between Outlook and the other Office 97 programs is that in Outlook you start from a different screen, depending on what you want to do. For example, to open incoming e-mail messages, you go to the Inbox screen. To find a colleague or friend's address, you go to the Contacts screen.

Figure 23-1 shows the Inbox screen, the one that appears when you start Outlook. On the left side of this screen is something called the *Outlook bar*. Notice the icons and the three buttons—the Outlook button, the Mail button, or the Other button—in the Outlook bar:

- ■ *Button* Click a button and you see a new set of icons in the Outlook bar.
- ■ *Icon* Click an icon and you see a new screen. To get to some icons, you have to click the down arrow at the bottom of the Outlook bar.

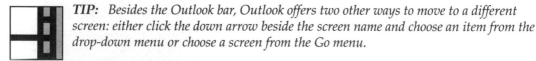

TIP: *Besides the Outlook bar, Outlook offers two other ways to move to a different screen: either click the down arrow beside the screen name and choose an item from the drop-down menu or choose a screen from the Go menu.*

Table 23-1 explains where clicking an icon on the Outlook bar takes you. In the table, icon names appear under button names. That is because, when you click one of the three buttons, a new set of icons appears in the Outlook bar.

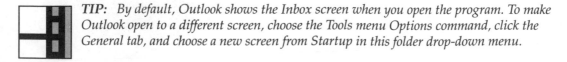

TIP: *By default, Outlook shows the Inbox screen when you open the program. To make Outlook open to a different screen, choose the Tools menu Options command, click the General tab, and choose a new screen from Startup in this folder drop-down menu.*

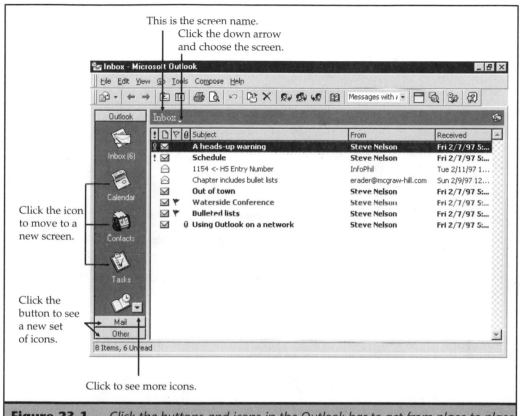

This is the screen name.
Click the down arrow
and choose the screen.

Click the icon
to move to a
new screen.

Click the
button to see
a new set
of icons.

Click to see more icons.

Figure 23-1. *Click the buttons and icons in the Outlook bar to get from place to place in Outlook*

Composing E-Mail Messages

This part of the chapter explains how to send e-mail messages with Outlook. It tells how to compose a message, give Outlook the recipient's e-mail address, and shoot your message into cyberspace—or across a network, if your computer happens to be connected to one of those. Before you attempt to send or receive e-mail with Outlook, you need to know which services the program works with, so that is covered in the following pages, as well. You also learn how to flag messages in different ways and send a file along with your message.

OUTLOOK

Icon	Opens This Screen
Outlook Button	
Inbox	The Inbox screen for composing, opening, replying to, and forwarding e-mail messages
Calendar	The Calendar screen for scheduling appointments and meetings
Contacts	The Contacts screen for recording names and addresses
Tasks	The Tasks screen for planning projects and tasks
Journal	The Journal screen for recording work activity
Notes	The Notes screen for jotting down notes, reminders, and epiphanies
Deleted Items	The Deleted Items screen with all e-mail messages that you deleted
Mail Button	
Inbox	The Inbox screen for composing, opening, replying to, and forwarding e-mail messages (this icon also appears when you click the Outlook button)
Sent Items	The Sent Items screen with copies of all e-mail messages you sent
Outbox	The Outbox screen with e-mail messages that have not been sent yet
Deleted Items	The Deleted Items screen with e-mail messages that you deleted
Other Button	
My Computer	The My Computer screen for finding and opening documents on your computer
My Documents	The My Documents screen with items you are storing in the My Documents folder
Favorites	The Favorites screen with shortcut icons for opening folders and files

Table 23-1.   *Buttons and Icons in the Outlook Bar*

E-Mail Programs That Outlook Works With

Outlook is designed to work with the following e-mail services:

- Internet Mail
- Lotus cc:Mail
- Microsoft Exchange Server
- Microsoft Mail
- The Microsoft Network (MSN)

To use Outlook with an online service such as CompuServe or America Online that isn't yet part of the Mighty Microsoft Monopoly, you or the network administrator who handles your system must install a connector. For more information about connectors, how they work, and where to find them, consult the network administrator or the technical support staff of the online service that you subscribe to.

Composing a Message

This part of the chapter gives bare-bones instructions for composing and sending an e-mail message. Later on, you will find out how to flag messages, attach files to messages, and send copies of messages. The techniques that follow are techniques you will use each time you send an e-mail message with Outlook.

WARNING: PowerPoint gets e-mail addresses from the Contacts List; the Address Book; or, if your computer is connected to a network, the Global Address List. As part of composing a message, you tell PowerPoint where to send it by choosing a name and address from the Contacts List, Address Book, or Global Address List. Before you send the message, therefore, you must have entered it already in the Contacts List, Address Book, or Global Address List. See "Keeping a List of Contacts" in Chapter 24 to learn how to enter someone's name and addresses (e-mail and otherwise) on the Contacts List or Address Book.

Follow these steps to send an e-mail missive with Outlook:

1. Go to the Inbox screen (see Figure 23-1) and either click the New Mail Message button, the leftmost button on the Standard toolbar, or press CTRL+N. You see a Message window like the one in Figure 23-2.

2. Click the To button to tell Outlook who will receive the message. You see the Select Names dialog box in Figure 23-3.

3. In the Show Names from the drop-down list, click the name of the list where the e-mail address is stored. In Figure 23-3, the Contacts List has been chosen.

4. In the list of names on the left, click the name of the person you want to send a message to. To send the message to more than one person, hold down the CTRL key and click each name.

5. Click the To button. The name or names appear to the right of the To button in the Message Recipients box.

6. Click OK. You return to the Message window (see Figure 23-2).

7. In the Subject line, enter a subject for the message. Be sure to enter descriptive words on the Subject line. If the person to whom you send this message receives lots of e-mail, she or he needs to know how important this message is and whether to answer it today or a fortnight from now. By entering a descriptive subject, you help the recipient prioritize your message.

 TIP: Notice, on the taskbar, a button called by whatever name you entered in step 7. Outlook treats messages as computer files. Because, in effect, you have opened a new file, a button for your new file appears on the taskbar. You can click another button, do work elsewhere, and return to finish composing your message later by clicking its button on the taskbar.

8. In the box on the bottom half of the window, type your message.

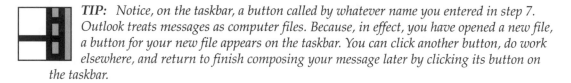 *TIP: To get more room to type your message, click the Message Header button. Doing so removes the To, Cc, and Subject boxes. Click the button again to see the boxes again.*

9. Click the Send button. Outlook closes the Message window and you see the Inbox screen again.

If your computer is connected to a network, the message is sent right away. If this message is to travel over the Internet, however, the message lands on the Outbox screen. It stays there until you choose the Tools menu Check for New Mail command. As Outlook collects mail, it also sends e-mail messages. See "Sending Messages," later in this chapter, for the details.

 TIP: If you are in the middle of composing a message and decide you don't want to compose or send it after all, choose the File menu Close command and click the No button when Outlook asks if you want to save the changes to your message.

Sending Copies and Blind Copies of Messages

At the same time as you send a message, you can send copies and blind copies of the message as well. What is the difference between a copy and a blind copy? When a copy of a message is sent, the person who receives the message is told that a copy has been sent and is given the name of the person it was sent to. When a blind copy of a

Click to send a message.

Click to tell Outlook who to send messages to.

Enter the subject of the message.

Type the message.

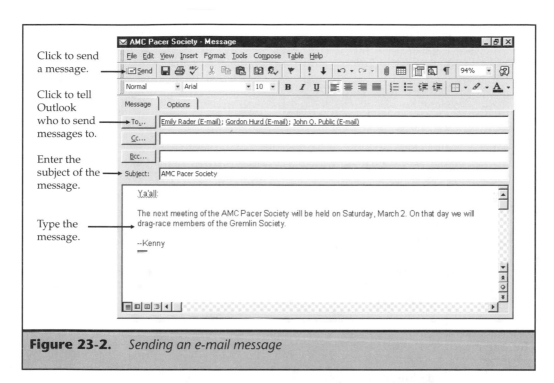

Figure 23-2. *Sending an e-mail message*

Choose where addresses are stored.

Click here to enter names in the To box.

Click or CTRL+click recipients' names.

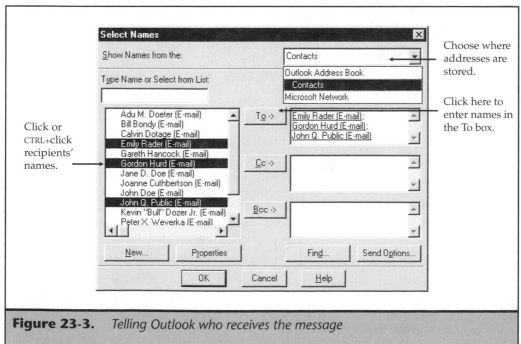

Figure 23-3. *Telling Outlook who receives the message*

Is Word Your E-Mail Editor?

The first time you start Outlook, a message box appears and asks if you want Word to be your e-mail editor. I hope you clicked Yes. By clicking Yes, you get to use all of Microsoft Word's buttons and menus to format the messages you send. If you clicked No, don't despair. You can still make Word your e-mail editor by following these steps:

1. Choose the Tools menu Options command. You see the Options dialog box.

2. Click the E-Mail tab.

3. Click the Use Microsoft Word as an e-mail editor check box.

4. Click OK.

Making Word your e-mail editor offers many advantages. You can do almost everything in the Message window that you can do in a Word document—create a table, insert a graphic, and comment on the text.

message is sent, the person who receives the message is *not* told that it has been sent to a third party as well.

Send copies and blind copies of messages at the same time that you send messages. To do so, follow these steps:

1. From the Inbox screen (see Figure 23-1), either click the New Mail Message button or press CTRL+N.

2. When the Message window opens (see Figure 23-2), click the To button. You see the Select Names dialog box.

3. In the Show Names from the drop-down list, click the name of the list where the e-mail address is stored.

4. As "Composing a Message," earlier in this chapter, explained how to do, tell Outlook who is to receive the message.

5. To choose the recipients of copies of the message, select their names in the box on the left and click the Cc button. (*Cc* stands for *carbon copy*. Using carbon dating techniques, archaeologists have determined that this term comes from the days of the typewriter, when copies were typed on carbon paper.)

TIP: *Hold down the* CTRL *key and click names to select more than one name.*

6. To choose the recipients of blind copies of the message, select their names and click the Bcc: button. (*Bcc* stands for *blind carbon copy*.)

Sends copies

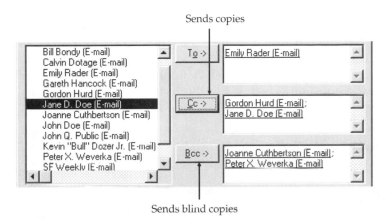

Sends blind copies

7. Click OK to close the Select Names dialog box.
8. Click the Send button in the Message window.

Calling Recipients' Attention to Urgent Messages

Outlook offers two ways to tell others that the messages you sent are urgent and need immediate attention. The first is to click the Importance: High button (the exclamation point) on the Standard toolbar in the Message window. (You may need to maximize the Message window in order to see the Importance: High button.) Provided the person who receives the message receives it with Outlook, he or she sees a red exclamation point beside the message in the Inbox screen:

! ✉   **Everything is overdue!**   **Peter Weverka**

And when the recipient opens the message, he or she sees the following words near the top of the Message window:

ⓘ This message was sent with High importance.

NOTE: *You can flag a message as well as prioritize it, and both the priority level and the flag will appear in the recipient's message window.*

Creating a Distinctive AutoSignature

An AutoSignature is a name, a name and address, or perhaps a pithy saying with which a user of Outlook always ends his or her messages. I knew somebody who always ended his e-mail messages with an AutoSignature calling for the goddess Vishnu the Destroyer to ascend to earth and simultaneously destroy and rejuvenate, but that's another story.

To create an AutoSignature and tell Outlook to append it automatically to the end of all your e-mail messages, follow these steps:

1. Compose an e-mail message.

2. At the end of the message, create what you want your AutoSignature to be. You might format it in an unusual way.

3. Select the text of the AutoSignature.

4. Choose the Tools menu AutoSignature command. You see the AutoSignature dialog box:

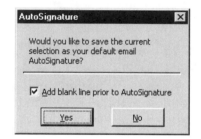

5. Click the Yes button.

6. Click OK when Outlook tells you that the AutoSignature has been saved.

Next time you create a new e-mail message or reply to a message that someone has sent you, you will see your AutoSignature as soon as the Message window opens. You can delete it if you decide not to use it in a particular message. To keep the AutoSignature from appearing at all, choose the Tools menu AutoSignature command. You see a dialog box that asks if you want to delete the

AutoSignature. Click Yes, and then click OK when Outlook tells you that the thing has been deleted.

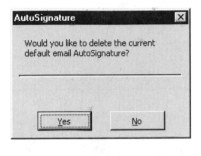

You can also draw a recipient's attention to an urgent, pressing, and vital message by flagging it. Provided the recipient reads the message in Outlook, the subject line of a message that has been flagged appears in red in the Inbox screen, and a red flag appears as well:

✉ ⚑   **What did you call me?**   **Peter Weverka**

Outlook offers many different ways to flag a message. Instructions to the recipient concerning what to do about the message appear near the top of the Message window. This flagged message simply asks the recipient for a reply:

When you flag a message, you can request the recipient to respond by a certain date. If the recipient fails to do so, an Overdue dialog box like the one in the following illustration appears in the middle of the screen. The recipient can click the Dismiss button to make the dialog box disappear, click Open to open the message, or click Postpone and choose how long to procrastinate by choosing an option from the Click Postpone drop-down list:

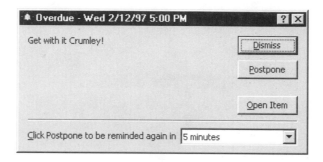

Following are instructions for flagging the messages in different ways.

TIP: *Here's a surefire way to flag a message and get the recipient's attention: After you finish typing the message, choose the Format menu Background command and then choose Red or Pink from the drop-down menu. A fiery red or a hot-pink message will put the fear of God in them—provided, of course, that the recipient uses Outlook to read e-mail messages.*

High- and Low-Priority Messages

Prioritizing a message is easy. In the Message window, as you compose the message, either click the Importance: High or Importance: Low button on the Standard toolbar. The buttons appear next to one another on the toolbar. The High button is a red exclamation point; the low button is a red arrow that points down.

Flagging a Message

To flag a message, follow these steps:

1. In the Message window, click the Flag Message button on the Standard toolbar. The Flag Message dialog box appears:

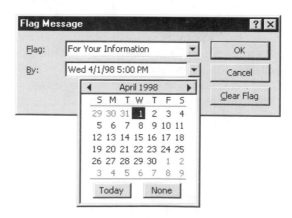

2. From the Flag drop-down menu, choose how you want to label your message. Among the choices are Review, No Response Necessary, and Call.

3. If you want the recipient to reply by a certain date, click the By drop-down arrow and select a date from the calendar. Click the arrows at the top of the Calendar to go backward or forward in time.

4. Click OK.

A notice appears in the Message window. The choices in the Flag Message dialog box shown in step 1 yield the following message, which the recipient of the message will also see.

> ⓘ For Your Information by Wednesday, April 01, 1998 5:00 PM.

TIP: *To remove a flag from a message, click the Flag button and then click Clear Flag in the Flag Message dialog box.*

Private, Personal, and Confidential Messages

Another way to flag a message is to post the word "Private," "Personal," or "Confidential" near the top of the message window. Of course, you could always tell the recipient in the message that the words you are sending are confidential, private, or personal, but stamping one of the three words on a message may make it seem more official.

To stamp the word "Private," "Personal," or "Confidential" on a message, follow these steps:

1. In the Message window where you compose the message, click the Options tab.

2. Click the down arrow on the Sensitivity drop-down menu and choose an option:

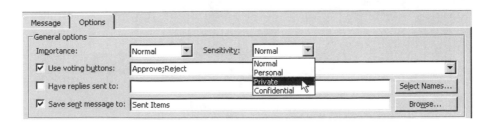

3. Click the Message tab to get back to writing your message.

When the recipient receives the message, he or she will see, near the top of the Message window, a yellow sign with an exclamation point, the words "Please treat this as," and the word "Private," "Personal," or "Confidential." Not only is this message confidential, it has been given a high-importance rating:

> ⚠ Please treat this as Confidential.
> This message was sent with High importance.

Sending Files Along with Messages

Outlook makes it pretty easy to send a file along with a message. As shown in Figure 23-4, all you have to do is click the Insert File button (the paperclip) on the Standard toolbar. You see the Insert File dialog box. Find and click the file you want to send

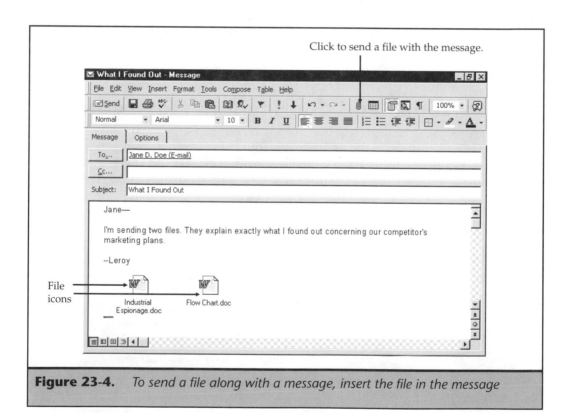

Figure 23-4. *To send a file along with a message, insert the file in the message*

along with your message, and then click OK. As the figure shows, a file icon appears in the Message window. You can send as many files as you want this way. When you send the e-mail message, the file is sent right along with it.

WARNING: *You can't send a file if you move it to a different folder after you insert it in a message. If you move the file, Outlook won't know where to find it when sending times comes.*

NOTE: *Later in this chapter, "Opening and Storing a File That Someone Sent You" explains how to open and store a file that has been sent to you.*

Sending Messages

Having explained everything there is to know about messages except how to send them, this part of the chapter explains how to send the messages you so thoughtfully composed, arranged to send copies and blind copies of, "autosigned," flagged, stamped as confidential, and attached files to. The following pages explain how to send files over a network and the Internet. They also explain how to tell Outlook when to deliver messages, how to find out when a message arrived, and how to change or delete a message before you send it.

Sending Messages Over a Network or the Internet

When you click the Send button in the Message window, your e-mail message is sent right away if your computer is connected to a network. However, if the message is to travel over the Internet and you haven't signed on to a network yet, or you have signed on to a network but you want to send the message over the Internet, you have to tell Outlook to send the message.

Follow these steps to send a message you have composed if it was not sent automatically:

1. From the Inbox screen, choose the Tools menu Check for New Mail command. When Outlook checks for new mail, it collects mail that has been sent to you as well. You see the Delivering Messages dialog box, followed shortly by a dialog box for connecting to the service from which you collect mail. The following illustration shows the dialog box for connecting to the Microsoft Network.

OUTLOOK

Using Outlook on a Network

You can use Outlook to send e-mail as well as files to other local area network users as long as your computer is connected to a local area network that includes an Exchange server. Moreover, the Exchange server administrator must have set up an Exchange account for you. If you have an Exchange account and if the other users on the network make use of the Calendar in Outlook, you may even be able to use Outlook to schedule group meetings. Exchange server, by the way, runs on a Windows NT server and is part of the Microsoft BackOffice. However, how the Exchange server works shouldn't be of any concern to you—worrying about the Exchange server is the network administrator's business. If you have questions about Exchange server, talk to your network administrator.

Except for a few minor differences, Outlook works the same on a network as it does on an online service. If you are using Outlook on a network, take note of the following differences:

- On a network, you usually don't do anything special to send or retrieve messages. When you click the Send button in the Message window, Outlook immediately and automatically sends the message to the Exchange server. Meanwhile, the Exchange server also automatically delivers e-mail messages that others sent you.

- Your Address Book includes another set of people, called the Global Address List. The Global Address List names and identifies the local area network users to whom you can send e-mail. (To see the Global Address List, choose the Tools menu Address Book command and select Global Address List from the Show Names From list box.)

- Provided that others on the network are using Outlook and the Exchange administrator has set up the network correctly, network users can schedule meetings with others on the network. For this to work, the Exchange administrator must have set up Exchange so that one Outlook user can view another's Outlook Calendar. Moreover—and this is important—other Outlook users must be using the Calendar as their scheduling tool.

- Network users may also see and be able to use the Send To command on the File menu in Word, Excel, and PowerPoint. (For more information about the Send To commands, see Chapter 5.)

You can use Outlook as an e-mail client both with the Microsoft Network online service and on a local area network that includes an Exchange server. It's also possible to use Outlook as an e-mail client with other online services such as CompuServe if you or the network administrator installs what's called a connector. For more information about all this, consult your network administrator or the online service's technical support staff.

NOTE: *If your system is capable of getting mail from more than one source, choose the Tools menu Check for New Mail On command. You see the Check for New Mail On dialog box. Click next to the service from which you want to get mail and then click OK.*

2. Click the Connect button and complete whatever rigmarole you have to complete to be connected. You see the Delivering Message dialog box again. When the mail has been sent and delivered, you are returned to the Inbox, where you see your new mail. See "Receiving Messages," later in this chapter, if you need advice about reading messages.

TIP: *If you are getting mail from more than one source, you can make the source you use most often the default choice and the one that Outlook gets mail from when you choose the Tools menu Check for New Mail command. From the Inbox, choose the Tools menu Options command, click the E-mail tab in the Options dialog box, click next to a mail source in the Check for new mail on box, and click OK.*

Choosing When Messages Are Delivered

If your computer is connected to a network and you have signed on, messages are sent as soon as you click the Send button in the Message window. If the message goes over the Internet or you haven't signed on to a network yet, messages are sent as soon as you choose the Tools menu Check for New Mail command. Suppose, however, that you want to wait a few days before sending a message. You can tell Outlook when to send a message by following these steps:

1. Compose the message in the Message window.
2. Click the Options tab. It is shown in Figure 23-5.

3. Under Delivery options, click the Do not deliver before down arrow and click the date on the calendar before which the message is not to be delivered. Outlook will not deliver the message before 5:00 P.M. on the date you choose. To choose a date, click on it. To go from month to month, click the arrow on either side of the month name.

4. Click the Expires after down arrow and choose an expiration date, if you want. If you do not connect to a network or the Internet between the delivery date and the expiration date, the message is not sent.

5. Click the Send button.

Getting Notification When Messages Are Delivered and Read

Also on the Options tab in the Message window (see Figure 23-5) are check boxes for being informed when messages are delivered and when they are read. You cannot track messages that are sent over the Internet. Only messages sent on networks and intranets can be tracked this way.

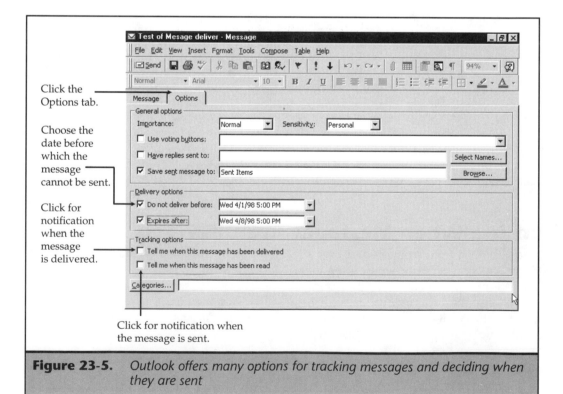

Figure 23-5. *Outlook offers many options for tracking messages and deciding when they are sent*

Follow these steps to receive notification when a message is read or delivered:

1. Compose the message in the Message window.
2. Click the Options tab.
3. Click the Tell me when this message has been delivered check box. If you can't see this option, maximize the message window.
4. Click the Tell me when this message has been read check box.
5. Click the Send button.

 TIP: *If you want, you can be informed when* all *of your messages are delivered and read without having to visit the Options tab. Starting from the Inbox, choose the Tools menu Options command; click the Sending tab in the Options dialog box; and, under Tracking Options, click the Tell me when all messages have been delivered and Tell me when all messages have been read check boxes.*

Changing and Recalling Messages

Suppose you compose a message to somebody, click the Send button in the Message window, and regret sending the message. Can you recall the message? Can you head it off at the pass before it is sent? It depends on whether you are connected to a network. Network users can recall messages. As for people using Outlook over the Internet, the only way to recall a message is to go to the Outbox screen, hope the message has not been sent yet, and either change or delete the message there.

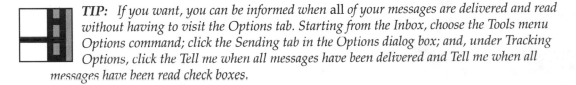 **WARNING:** *Messages sent by way of the Internet cannot be recalled after they are sent.*

Changing or Deleting Messages That Haven't Been Sent

If the message hasn't been sent yet, you can find and open it or else delete it in the Outbox screen. Follow these steps to do so:

1. Click the Mail button in the Outlook bar.
2. Click the Outbox icon. You see the Outbox screen shown in Figure 23-6.
3. Click the message you want to delete or change.
4. Either delete or change the message:

   - *Deleting* Click the Delete button to delete the message.
   - *Changing* Double-click the message. The Message window opens. Change the text of the message, the address, the delivery settings, or whatever else needs changing. Then click the Send button.

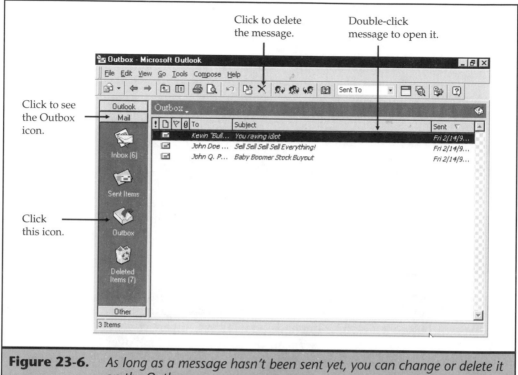

Figure 23-6. *As long as a message hasn't been sent yet, you can change or delete it on the Outbox screen*

Recalling a Message That Has Been Sent

Follow these steps to recall an embarrassing or inaccurate message that you sent over a network or intranet:

1. Click the Mail button in the Outlook bar.

2. Click the Sent Items icon. You see the Sent Items screen with copies of all the messages you sent.

3. Open the message you want to recall.

4. Choose the Tools menu Recall This Message command.

5. Click the Delete unread copies of this message from Inboxes check box.

Where Outlook Stores Copies of Sent Messages

Copies of the messages you send are kept on the Sent Items screen. Click the Mail button and then the Sent Items icon in the Outlook bar to open the Sent Items screen. With that done, double-click a message to open and read it.

    After a while, the number of sent items gets large and takes up valuable disk space. To remove items from the folder, hold down the CTRL key as you select the items you want to remove, and then click the Delete button.

WARNING: *It isn't always possible to recall messages that have been sent. Ask your network administrator for more information.*

Receiving Messages

The command for receiving e-mail messages is the same as the command for sending them: the Tools menu Check for New Mail command. The following pages explain the ins and outs of retrieving mail. They also explain how to preview messages after they arrive, read messages, delete messages, and arrange messages on the Inbox screen. You will also find instructions here for replying to and forwarding messages.

Collecting and Reading Your E-Mail

Collecting e-mail messages is as easy as choosing the Tools menu Check for New Mail command and, in the case of the Internet, clicking all the right buttons to get connected. What those buttons are depends on the Internet provider you use.

    If you use more than one Internet provider, or if your computer is connected to both a network and the Internet, you have to tell Outlook where to go to collect the mail. To do that, choose the Tools menu Check for New Mail On command. The Check for New Mail On dialog box appears. Click next to the service from which you want to get mail and then click OK.

    Mail arrives in the Inbox, as shown in the following illustration. A closed envelope appears next to messages that haven't been read yet. Messages that have been read show an open envelope. The lower-left corner of the Inbox screen tells how many messages are in the Inbox and how many remain unread. In the illustration, you see exclamation points, flags, and paperclip icons next to some of the messages. The first part of this chapter explains what those icons mean.

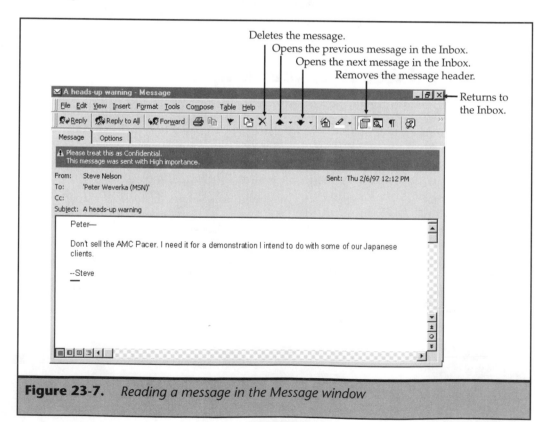

TIP: *After you open a message for the first time and return to the Inbox screen, the message is shown in Roman type instead of boldface and an open envelope icon appears beside it. If for some reason you want to indicate that you haven't read the message, perhaps to remind yourself to return to it again, select the message and choose the Edit menu Mark As Unread command.*

To read a message on the Inbox screen, double-click it. You see a message like the one in Figure 23-7.

Figure 23-7. *Reading a message in the Message window*

TIP: *Clicking the Message Header button makes it easier to read long messages. When you click this button the To, Cc, and Subject are removed from the top of the Message window.*

After you have read the message, either choose the File menu Close command or click the Close button in the Message window to return to the Inbox screen.

Speed Techniques for Reading and Handling Messages

Some poor souls receive hundreds and hundreds of e-mail messages a week. Rather than slog through all those messages one at a time, you can take advantage of the buttons in the Inbox screen and Message window to dispatch messages quickly. Following are techniques for reading e-mail as fast as possible.

Previewing the Messages

In the Inbox screen, click the AutoPreview button to read the first two lines of all unread messages. As the last two messages in the following illustration show, you can read an entire message by previewing it if the message is short enough:

✉	**Out of town**	**Steve Nelson**	**Fri 2/7/97 5:...**
	Just a quick reminder. This is my last day in the office until February 24th. I won't be picking up my messages or e-mail while I'm on vacation.		
	Note, however, that Kaarin Dolliver, my editorial assistant, will be available to deal with any		
! ✉	**Schedule**	**Steve Nelson**	**Fri 2/7/97 5:...**
	Just for your information, the technical editor has only sent me chapters 1, 2, 3, 5, 11, 13, and 15. I'm still wanting for 12, 14, and 25 through 31... <end>		
✉ ⚑	**Waterside Conference**	**Steve Nelson**	**Fri 2/7/97 5:...**
	Should I be getting a box of cigars? It seems like a good idea to me. <end>		

Deleting Messages

When you delete a message with the Delete button in a Message window, Outlook immediately opens the previous message in the Inbox screen. You don't go back to the Inbox screen to choose another message to open.

Jumping to Different Messages

After you have opened a message, you needn't return to the Inbox screen to open another one. To go to the previous or next message in the Inbox screen, click the Previous Item or Next Item button. The next or previous message, whether you've already read it or not, is opened and the message you were looking at is closed.

Moreover, if you click the drop-down menu attached to either of these buttons, you see a list of items you can go to, as the following illustration shows. For example, click Item from Sender to open the previous or next item in the Inbox from the person who sent you the message you are looking at. Click Flagged Message to see the next or previous flagged message you were sent.

OUTLOOK

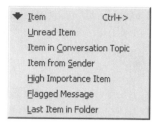

▼ Item	Ctrl+>
Unread Item	
Item in Conversation Topic	
Item from Sender	
High Importance Item	
Flagged Message	
Last Item in Folder	

Deleting a Message

Outlook gives you lots of opportunities for deleting messages. Wherever you see the Delete button, all you have to do to delete a message is select it and click the Delete button. The Delete button, a crayon-drawn *X*, is located on the Standard toolbar in every Outlook screen.

When you delete a message, it doesn't disappear for good. Deleted messages land in the Deleted Items screen. This screen works like the Windows Recycle Bin. If you regret deleting a message, you can click the Mail button in the Outlook bar and then click the Deleted Items icon to open the Deleted Items screen. From there, you can resuscitate the message by copying it to a different folder.

However, letting deleted messages languish in the Deleted Items screen takes up disk space. Periodically open the Deleted Items screen, hold down the CTRL key and click on the messages that need deleting, and then click the Delete button.

> **TIP:** *To delete all the messages in the Deleted Items screen, choose the Tools menu Empty Deleted Items command.*

Opening and Storing a File That Someone Sent You

As shown in the following illustration, files appear as icons in the message window when someone sends you a file. To open a file, click on it, and when a frame appears around the file icon, double-click.

I'm sending two files. They explain exactly what I found out concerning our competitor's marketing plans.

--Leroy

Industrial
Espionage.doc   Flow Chart.doc

To save a file in the folder of your choice, choose the File menu Save Attachments command. You see the Save All Attachments dialog box. To begin with, all the files that were sent along with the e-mail message are selected. What you do next depends on whether or not you want to save all the files to the same folder:

- *Files to same folder* Click OK. You see the Save All Attachments dialog box. Find and click on the folder to which you want to save the files, and then click the Save button.

- *Files to different folders* Click some of the files to "unselect them," and then click OK. In the Save All Attachments dialog box, find and click on the folder in which the files are to be saved, and then click the Save button. Back in the Save All Attachments dialog box, start all over again to save the other files.

Replying to and Forwarding Messages

Outlook makes it pretty easy to reply to and forward messages. To reply to a message, all you have to do is click one of the two buttons on the left side of the Message window—Reply or Reply to All—and enter the text of a reply. To forward a message, all you have to do is click the Forward message and give Outlook the name and addresses of the parties to whom the message will be forwarded. The following pages explain how to reply to and forward messages.

Replying to a Message

When you reply to a message, you don't have to know the e-mail address of the person to whom you are replying. Outlook keeps that information for you. All you have to do is click the Reply or Reply to All button and enter the text of your reply. Follow these steps to reply to a message:

1. Click the Reply or Reply to All button:

   - *Reply* Click this button to reply to the person who sent you the message.

   - *Reply to All* Click this button to reply to the person who sent you the message, as well as all the people to whom copies of the message were sent. As shown in Figure 23-8, the names of people who received copies appear next to the Cc: button in the RE: Message window.

   After you click a button, you see the RE: Message window, as shown in Figure 23-8. What Outlook calls the "memo header"—the name of the person the message is from, when the message was sent, who it was sent to, the names of people who received copies (if any), and the subject of the message—appears in the text box along with the text of the message.

2. Click below the message and write your reply. The words you type appear in red and a vertical line appears in the left margin beside the words. If the

OUTLOOK

person who receives the reply also has Outlook, the red text will not be red, but blue. If you want, you can delete the memo header and all or as much of the original message as you like. You needn't include all of it in the reply.

TIP: *Click the Message Header button to remove the Cc: and Subject: lines from the screen and get more room to write your reply.*

3. Click the Send button.

TIP: *In your reply, you can call on all the techniques described in "Composing E-Mail Messages," earlier in this chapter, to flag the message, attach a file, or send your reply to others besides those people listed on the To: and Cc: lines of the memo header.*

Forwarding a Message

To forward a message, all you have to do is click the Forward button in the Message window. A "memo header" with the author's name, the names of the people to whom

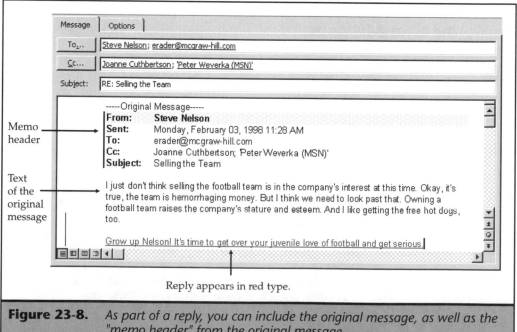

Memo header

Text of the original message

Reply appears in red type.

Figure 23-8. *As part of a reply, you can include the original message, as well as the "memo header" from the original message*

Finding Out Someone's E-Mail Address

When you reply to a message, you don't need to know the e-mail address of the person you are replying to. But suppose you want to know it? Suppose you want to make note of it and keep the e-mail address on your Contacts List so you can send e-mail to this person weeks or months from now?

You can get another's e-mail address by looking in the From column of the Inbox screen. If necessary, drag the column boundary to the left to make the From column wider so that you can read the entire e-mail address.

If an address doesn't appear in the From column, follow these steps to obtain an e-mail address:

1. Open a message from the person whose address you need.

2. Choose the File menu Properties command.

3. Click the Internet tab. The address appears on this tab.

the message and copies of the message were sent, and the subject of the message, appears at the top of the FW: Message window, as shown in this illustration:

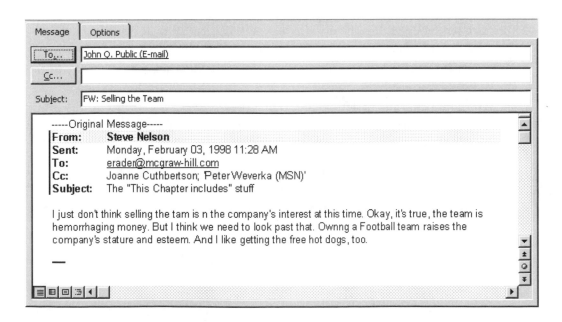

OUTLOOK

Click the To button and tell Outlook who the message is to be forwarded to in the Select Names dialog box. See "Composing a Message," near the start of this chapter, if you aren't sure how the Select Names dialog box works.

Storing and Organizing Messages

If you are one of those important personages who gets lots and lots of e-mail, you can do yourself a big favor by storing e-mail messages in different folders. For example, you might create a folder for each project, plan, scheme, or undertaking in which you are involved. Then, as e-mail messages come flooding in, you can store each one in the appropriate folder and find and read it when the right time comes. Following are instructions for creating folders for storing messages and for storing messages in the folders you have created.

Creating a Folder for Messages

Follow these steps to create a folder for storing messages:

1. From the Inbox screen, click the Move to Folder button.

2. Choose Move to Folder from the drop-down menu. You see the Move Items dialog box.

3. Click the plus sign beside the Personal Folders icon.

4. Click the Inbox folder. The new folder you will create will be a subfolder of the Inbox folder.

5. Click the New button. You see the Create New Folder dialog box shown in Figure 23-9.

6. Type a name for the folder in the Name box.

7. Enter a description of the messages you will put in the folder at the bottom of the dialog box.

 TIP: If you intend to store a lot of messages in the new folder, leave the check mark in the Create a shortcut to the folder in the Outlook Bar check box. That way, all you have to do is click the shortcut in the Outlook bar to open the new folder you are creating.

8. Click OK. Back in the Move Items dialog box, the folder you created appears as a subfolder of the Inbox folder.

9. Click OK.

 TIP: To delete or rename a folder you created, click the Folder List button and then find and click on the folder in question. Next, choose the File menu Folder command. On the submenu, choose either Delete or Rename.

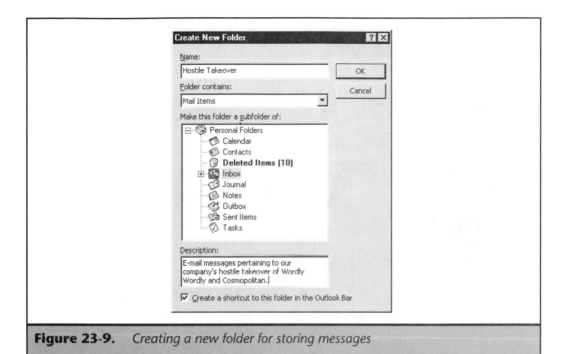

Figure 23-9.   *Creating a new folder for storing messages*

Storing and Opening Messages in Folders

To store a message in a folder you created, follow these steps:

1. Starting in the Inbox screen, click the Folder List button. As shown in Figure 23-10, a list of folders appears to the left of the e-mail messages.

TIP: *You can drag the boundary between the folders and e-mail message to the right to read the folder names.*

2. Click the plus sign beside the Inbox folder to see its subfolders.

3. Click the message that you want to move to a folder. To select several messages, hold down the CTRL key as you click each one.

4. Drag the message to the folder.

5. Click the Folder List button to remove the folders from the screen.

TIP: *After you have dragged one message to a folder, you can move another message to the same folder by clicking the message, clicking the Move to Folder button, and, on the drop-down menu, clicking the name of the folder you want to move the message to.*

OUTLOOK

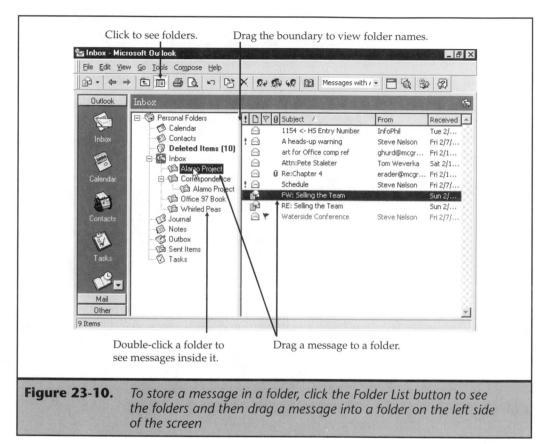

Click to see folders.   Drag the boundary to view folder names.

Double-click a folder to   Drag a message to a folder.
see messages inside it.

Figure 23-10.   *To store a message in a folder, click the Folder List button to see the folders and then drag a message into a folder on the left side of the screen*

To read and perhaps reply to a message you stored in a folder, follow these steps:

1. Click the Folder List button to see the folders.
2. Click the plus icon next to the Inbox folder to see its folders.
3. Double-click on the folder whose messages you want to see.

The Complete Reference

Office
97

Chapter 24

Using Outlook as a Personal
Information Manager

This chapter explains the personal information manager side of Outlook. If you peered into the last chapter, you know that Outlook can be used to send and receive e-mail. This chapter explains how to use the program to bring order to the chaos of your life.

On the personal information manager side of Outlook are five screens:

Screen	What It Is For
Calendar	Scheduling appointments, meetings, and events, and seeing on the Calendar screen where you are supposed to be on a daily, weekly, or monthly basis.
Contacts	Keeping detailed information about the addresses, phone numbers, and e-mail addresses of your friends, colleagues, and clients.
Tasks	Juggling work assignments. Tasks appear on both the Tasks screen and Calendar screen.
Journal	Keeping track of the files you work on, how long you work on each one, and who you send e-mail to and receive e-mail from.
Notes	A place for jotting down reminder notes.

The following pages explain how to organize yourself with these screens.

NOTE: "A Quick Geography Lesson," at the start of Chapter 23, explains how to open the different screens in Outlook.

Keeping a List of Contacts

As you know if you read the last chapter, Outlook gets e-mail addresses from the Contacts screen. Besides e-mail addresses, you can keep street addresses, Web page addresses, phone numbers of all types and varieties (pager numbers, fax numbers), and even miscellaneous information such as birthdays, on the Contacts List.

Read on to learn how to enter a new contact on the list, find a contact on the list, and tell Outlook to dial a contact's phone number or send him or her an e-mail message.

Entering Contacts on the List

To enter a contact on the Contacts List (click the Contacts icon in the Outlook bar to get there), start by clicking the New Contact button. You see the Contacts dialog box shown in Figure 4-1. On this screen are four tabs: General, Details, Journal, and All Fields. Only the General tab needs filling out, but you can fill in the other three, too, if

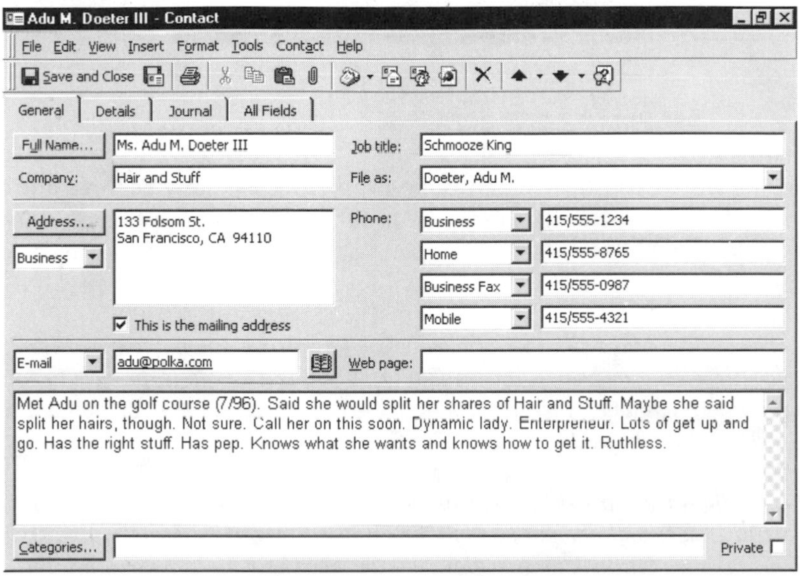

Figure 24-1. Enter data about colleagues, friends, and clients in the Contacts dialog box

you want to keep dossiers on your friends, colleagues, and clients. When you are done filling out the Contacts dialog box, click the Save and Close button. Following are the details about filling in these tabs.

TIP: If the contact whose data you want to enter works for the same company as a contact whose data you have entered already, you can get a head start entering the data. In the Contacts List, click the name of the contact whose data you have already entered in the Contacts List. Then, instead of clicking the New Contact button to enter contact information, choose the Contacts menu New Contact from Same Company command.

General Tab

The General tab is for entering names, addresses, e-mail addresses, Web page addresses, phone numbers, and all-purpose descriptions of the person in question. How to enter information on this tab is fairly self-explanatory. Click the Full Name button and Address button to enter the name and address one part at a time. By default, the name you enter appears in the Contacts List last name first, followed by first name, followed by middle initial, but you can make it appear any number of ways by making a choice from the File as drop-down menu:

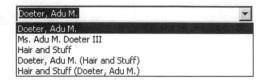

By choosing from drop-down menus, you can enter as many as three addresses and three e-mail addresses, and as many as 18 different types of phone numbers, ranging from Business to Mobile to Teletype. Notice the text box for entering a web page address, too.

 TIP: *The bottom of the Contacts dialog box is for jotting down a few words about the colleague, client, or friend. If your Contacts List is a long one, be sure to enter descriptions so that when the time comes to weed names from the list, you will be able to tell who is who and whether each name needs weeding.*

 NOTE: *"Phoning and E-Mailing Contacts," later in this chapter, explains how you can get Outlook to dial phone numbers. Don't worry about punctuation marks in phone numbers, because Outlook ignores punctuation marks when it dials numbers. Moreover, you don't have to enter a 1 to use the AutoDialer because the AutoDialer dials it for you when you dial numbers outside your area code.*

Details Tab

The Details tab is for—what else?—entering excruciating details about the contact. On the tab are text boxes for entering anniversary dates, birthdays, department names, and other such arcana.

Journal Tab

Don't worry about the Journal tab for now. As "The Journal for Recording Day-to-Day Events," later in this chapter, explains, you can tell Outlook to record when you send e-mail messages to this contact. The dates that e-mail was sent will appear on the Journal tab.

All Fields Tab

The All Fields tab is simply a shortcut for viewing data about the client. At the top of the tab is the Select from drop-down menu. By making a choice from this menu, you can see quickly what it is you want to know about the contact.

Finding a Contact in the Contacts List

Contact lists can get very long, so Outlook offers a number of different ways to find a contact. Figure 24-2 outlines the several different ways. Following are all the details:

- *Click a letter button* Click a letter button and Outlook takes you down the list to entries that are filed under the letter you clicked.

- *Use the scroll bar* Either click arrows on the scroll bar at the bottom of the screen or drag the scroll box to move through the list.

- *Change the view* Make a choice from the Current View drop-down list to display more or fewer contacts onscreen.

- *Click the Find Items button* If you can't remember a name but know it is associated with a certain company or address, click the Find Items button and, in the Find dialog box, enter the company name or street name you do know in the Search for the word(s) dialog box and click the Find Now button. If Outlook can find the name, it lists it in the dialog box.

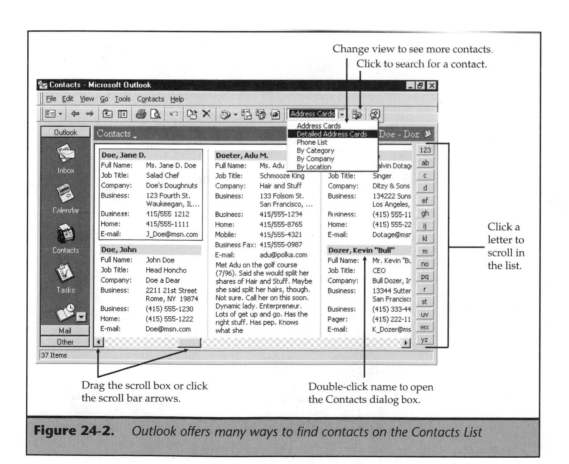

Figure 24-2. *Outlook offers many ways to find contacts on the Contacts List*

After you find a contact, double-click its name at the bottom of the Find Contacts dialog box to open the Contact dialog box and see all the details. You can dial a contact's number from the Contacts dialog box. You can also send e-mail messages. Read on.

Phoning and E-Mailing Contacts

As long as your computer is connected to a modem, Outlook can dial telephone numbers on the Contacts List for you. And you can also e-mail a contact from the Contact dialog box.

To e-mail a contact, follow these steps:

1. Open the Contacts dialog box for a contact.

2. Click the New Message to Contact button, as shown in Figure 24-3. You see the Message window, where you can compose the message (see "Composing E-Mail Messages" in Chapter 23 if you need help). Outlook alerts you if the recipient has more than one e-mail address. It puts all the recipient's known e-mail addresses in the To: box and expects you to remove the one you don't want to use.

Also in the Contacts dialog box is a button for opening a contact's Web page—the Explore Web Page button.

Follow these steps to tell Outlook to dial a telephone number for you:

1. Open the Contacts dialog box for the person you want to call.

2. Click the AutoDialer button (the one with the telephone on it). As shown in Figure 24-3, you see the New Call dialog box.

3. If the person you want to call has more than one telephone number, click the down arrow to open the Number drop-down list and choose the correct number.

4. Click the Start Call button and lift the receiver. The Call Status dialog box appears.

5. Click the Talk button in the Call Status dialog box.

6. When you have finished talking to the contact, hang up the phone and click the End Call button.

7. Click the Close button.

You don't have to bother about dialing a 1 or 9 when you use the AutoDialer. Outlook is supposed to take care of that on its own. If it is not dialing correctly, however, click the Dialing Properties button in the New Call dialog box (see Figure 24-3) and tell Outlook what is the proper way to dial a call from the phone you are using.

The Calendar for Scheduling Appointments, Meetings, and Events

Outlook offers the Calendar screen for making sure you don't miss activities you have scheduled for yourself. After you schedule an activity, it appears on the Calendar screen, where you can see daily appointments (in Day view), appointments for an entire week (in Week view), or appointments for an entire month (in Month view).

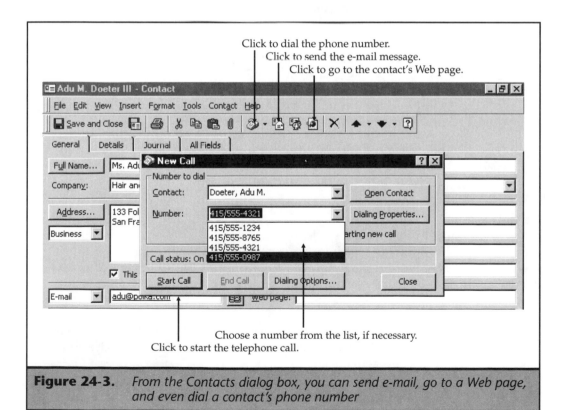

Figure 24-3. *From the Contacts dialog box, you can send e-mail, go to a Web page, and even dial a contact's phone number*

Figure 24-4 shows the Calendar screen in Day view. The Calendar was devised to tell you at a glance where you are expected to be and what you are expected to do each day, week, and month. Use the Calendar to schedule your time better.

As Figure 24-4 shows, Outlook makes a somewhat arbitrary distinction between appointments, meetings, and events when it comes to scheduling. Following is an explanation of appointments, meetings, and events.

Appointments

An *appointment* is an activity that occupies a specific time period. For example, the job interview that takes place between 2:00 and 2:30 in Figure 24-4 is an appointment. The manicure appointment that takes place between 5:00 and 5:15 is a *recurring* appointment—it happens every Wednesday. The alarm bell icons you see in Figure 24-4 mean that Outlook will make the computer chime a few minutes before the appointment or meeting takes place.

Meetings

A *meeting*, like an appointment, occupies a specific time period, but it involves other people besides yourself. If you are using Outlook at home, the difference between an appointment and a meeting doesn't matter at all; but if your computer is connected to a network and the network uses Microsoft Exchange Server, you can send invitations to others on the network at the same time as you schedule a meeting.

In Figure 24-4, a meeting takes place between 11:00 and 11:30, and a recurring meeting takes place between 3:00 and 4:00. Notice the two small heads in the 11:00 and 3:00 time slots—those heads tell you that a meeting has been scheduled. The revolving arrows mark recurring meetings or recurring appointments.

TIP: *If you are not working on a network or not working on a network that uses the Microsoft Exchange Server, don't bother scheduling meetings. Schedule appointments and events instead.*

Events

An *event* is an activity that occupies at least 24 hours of time. The classic example of an event is a birthday. Schedule a birthday so as not to forget a loved one's or boss's special day. An all-day trade show, for example, would also be scheduled as an event. Events appear at the top of the window on the Calendar screen. In Figure 24-4, the user has designated April Fool's Day as an event (probably a lot of prankstering goes on in the office that day).

The following pages explain how to schedule one-time and recurring appointments, meetings, and events, as well as how to view your schedule in different ways and delete, edit, and reschedule activities.

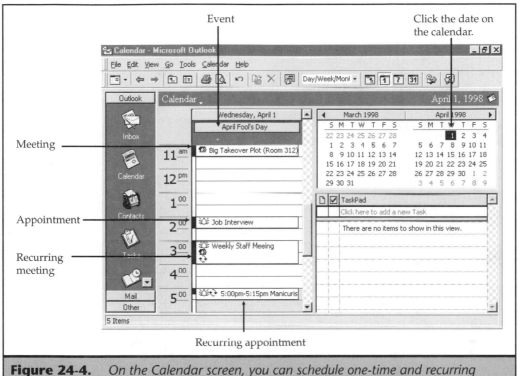

Figure 24-4. *On the Calendar screen, you can schedule one-time and recurring events, meetings, and appointments*

NOTE: *"A Quick Geography Lesson," at the start of Chapter 23, explains how to open the Calendar screen and other Outlook screens.*

Scheduling One-Time Appointments, Meetings, and Events

To schedule a one-time appointment, meeting, or event, follow these steps:

1. Switch to Day view, if necessary, by clicking the Day button or choosing the View menu Day command.

2. In the calendars on the right side of the Calendar screen, click the day when the activity is to take place. If the month in which the activity is to take place

is not in view, click the arrow to the left or right of the month names to see different months.

3. Click on the hour in the day when the activity is to start.

4. Choose an option from the Calendar menu: New Event, New Appointment, or New Meeting Request. You see a dialog box similar to the Appointment dialog box shown in Figure 24-5. The three dialog boxes are exactly alike, except the Meeting dialog box offers the To: button for inviting others on your network to a meeting.

5. Using Table 24-1 as your guide, fill in the dialog box.

6. Click the Save and Close button.

Part of Screen	What It Is For
Subject	Why the appointment, meeting, or event is being scheduled. What you type in this box appears on the Calendar screen.
Location	Where the activity takes place. As you enter locations, Outlook remembers them. Click the arrow to open the drop-down list and choose from locations you entered previously.
Start time	When the activity begins. If you clicked the right hour before you opened the dialog box, the right hour should appear here. If it doesn't, click the down arrow to open the drop-down list and make a new choice.
End time	When the activity ends. If necessary, make a new choice from the drop-down menu.
All day event	Click this check box if the activity is to last all day. When you schedule an event, this check box is already checked.
Reminder	Click this check box if you want Outlook to play a two-note chime to remind you of the upcoming event. Click the down arrow and choose how many minutes or hours in advance the chime is to sound.
Show time as*	If your computer is on a network that uses the Microsoft Exchange Server, choose how the activity is to appear to others on the network who can view your calendar schedule.

Table 24-1.   *Filling in the Appointment, Meeting, and Event Dialog Boxes*

Part of Screen	What It Is For
Text box	Jot down a note about what you would like the appointment, meeting, or event to accomplish. Or perhaps jot down directions how to get there.
Categories	You can display activities on the Calendar screen by category. If you want to categorize this activity, choose a category from the drop-down list. (You might have to maximize the window to see this button.)
Private*	Click this check box to keep others on the network from seeing this activity on your calendar. (You might have to maximize the window to see this check box.)

* These options are for people whose computers are connected to a network that uses the Microsoft Exchange Server.

Table 24-1. *Filling in the Appointment, Meeting, and Event Dialog Boxes (continued)*

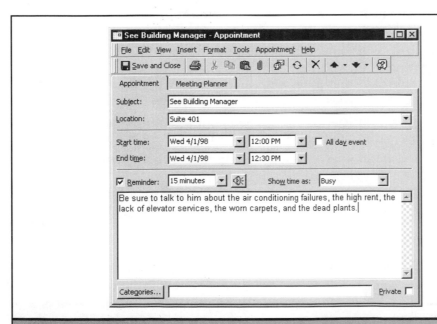

Figure 24-5. *Scheduling a one-time appointment, meeting, or event. Table 24-1 explains how to fill in this dialog box*

OUTLOOK

Scheduling Recurring Appointments, Meetings, and Events

Follow these steps to schedule a recurring appointment, meeting, or event:

1. If necessary, click the Day button or choose the View menu Day command to switch to Day view.

2. On one of the calendars in the upper-left corner of the Calendar screen, click on the first or nearest day on which the recurring activity is to take place. For example, if the activity takes place on the first of the month, click the first of the month. If it takes place on Wednesdays, click a Wednesday.

3. Click the hour in the day at which the recurring activity takes place.

 TIP: *To turn a one-time activity into a recurring activity, open it in the Calendar window and, when you see the Appointment, Meeting, or Event dialog box, click the Recurrence button. To open an activity in the Calendar window, move the pointer across it, and when the pointer changes into a four-headed arrow, double-click.*

4. Choose an option from the Calendar menu: New Recurring Event, New Recurring Appointment, or New Recurring Meeting. You see the Appointment Recurrence dialog box shown in Figure 24-6.

5. Under Appointment time, make choices from the drop-down lists to tell Outlook how long the activity lasts.

6. Under Recurrence pattern, click the Daily, Weekly, Monthly, or Yearly option button. Depending on which button you click, you see a different array of choices to the right of the option buttons. If necessary, use the drop-down lists to more adequately tell Outlook when the meeting takes place.

7. Under Range or recurrence, click an option from the drop-down menus or click radio buttons to tell Outlook how far into the future these meetings will "recur."

8. Click OK. You see an Appointment, Meeting, or Event dialog box similar to the one in Figure 24-5.

9. Turn back a few pages and follow steps 5 and 6 under "Scheduling One-Time Appointments, Meetings, and Events."

Getting a Look at Your Schedule

After you have scheduled a bunch of activities, how can you find out what you are supposed to do and where you are supposed to be? Outlook offers several different

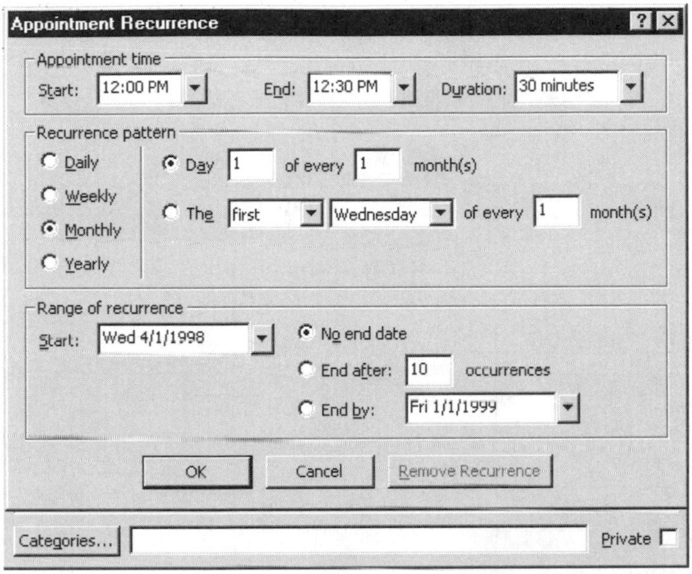

Figure 24-6. *Scheduling an appointment, meeting, or event that takes place each day, week, month, or year*

ways to look at your schedule. They are outlined in Figure 24-7. The following list explains them in detail:

- *Changing views* To see daily appointments, weekly appointments, or monthly appointments, either click the Day, Week, or Month button on the toolbar or choose the View menu Day, Week, or Month command. Figure 24-7 shows the Calendar screen in Week view. (Figure 24-4 shows it in Day view.)

- *Seeing specific types of activities* By making a selection from the Current View drop-down list, you can see only appointments, events, annual events, recurring appointments, or certain categories of events.

- *Seeing a single activity* To open the Appointment, Meeting, or Event dialog box and get all the details about an appointment, move the pointer across the activity and double-click.

TIP: *To get more room to see calendar dates on the Calendar screen, drag the border between the calendar dates and TaskPad, as shown in Figure 24-7.*

OUTLOOK

Choose daily, weekly, or monthly view.

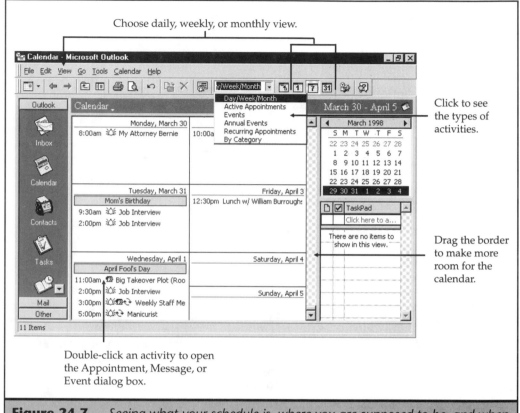

Click to see the types of activities.

Drag the border to make more room for the calendar.

Double-click an activity to open the Appointment, Message, or Event dialog box.

Figure 24-7. *Seeing what your schedule is, where you are supposed to be, and when you are supposed to be there*

TIP: *Wherever you are on the Calendar screen, you can always click the Go To Today button to view today's activities.*

Deleting, Rescheduling, and Editing Calendar Activities

Activities often need to be postponed, delayed, shelved, or rescheduled, so Outlook gives you the opportunity to delete, move, and edit calendar activities on the Calendar screen. Following are directions for doing so.

Deleting an Activity

If an appointment, meeting, or event gets canceled, you can delete it from the Calendar screen by clicking on it and then clicking the Delete button. If the activity is a recurring activity, you see the following dialog box:

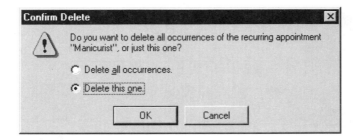

Click the Delete all occurrences radio button and click OK if you are deleting a recurring appointment, meeting, or event. Otherwise, simply click OK.

Rescheduling an Activity

To reschedule an activity, drag it to a new location. To do that, move the pointer over the left edge of the activity you want to reschedule. When you see a four-headed arrow, click and drag the activity either to a new time or new day. You can reschedule an activity several months in advance by displaying the calendar month to which the activity will be rescheduled in the upper-right corner of the Calendar screen and then dragging the activity to a day on the calendar.

Editing an Activity

To edit a calendar activity, click to select it on the Calendar screen, and then double-click the item. You see the Activity, Meeting, or Event dialog box, where you can choose new options or enter new text.

The Tasks Screen for Managing Your Time Better

It's not easy to juggle several different tasks at once; but to help you become a better juggler, Outlook offers the Tasks screen. As Figure 24-8 shows, the Tasks screen tells

OUTLOOK

	!	0	Subject	Status	Due Date	% Complete	Categories
				Not St...	None	0%	
☑	!		Curry Favor with Higherups	In Pro...	None	0%	
☑	!		Write speech for CEO	In Pro...	Thu 2/27/97	25%	
☑	!		Placate Spouse	Waitin...	None	25%	Personal
☑			~~Compose Sonnet for Convention Ke...~~	~~Compl...~~	~~Fri 2/21/97~~	~~100%~~	
☑	!		Write Takeover Bid	In Pro...	Tue 2/18/97	50%	
☑	↓		Clean Out Desk	Deferred	Mon 2/17/97	0%	Personal

6 Items

Figure 24-8. *The Tasks screen shows how far along each task is, when it is due, and whether it is overdue. This figure shows the Tasks screen in Detailed List view*

you which tasks need doing, how urgent each one is, when tasks need to be completed, and whether a task is overdue. By making entries in and studying the Tasks screen, you can manage your time better and perhaps get everything done.

The due date of each task appears on the Tasks screen. Overdue tasks appear in red. Tasks that have been completed are crossed off. Outlook offers many ways to view the Tasks screen. As shown in Figure 24-8, Detailed List view shows each task's status; how close you have come to completing each task; whether the task has been given a high priority or not; and which category, if any, each task falls in. Because tasks often have to be juggled along with meetings and appointments, tasks also appear on the Calendar screen on what Microsoft calls the "TaskPad" (never confuse the TaskPad with what hippies used to call the "crash pad"). Compare Figure 24-8 to the following illustration, which shows tasks on the TaskPad:

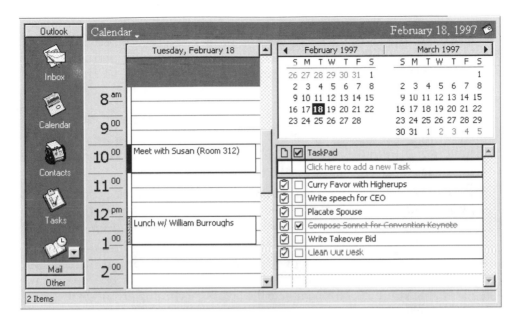

The following pages explain how to enter tasks on the Tasks screen, view tasks In different ways, update tasks, delete tasks, and assign a task to someone else by way of the Tasks screen.

Entering Tasks on the Tasks Screen

Outlook offers a fast way and a slow way to enter a task on the Tasks screen. The fast way is to click near the top of the screen where it says "Click here to add a new Task." After you click, enter a few words to describe the task. To assign a due date, click the down arrow under Due Date, choose a date from the calendar, and press the ENTER key, like so:

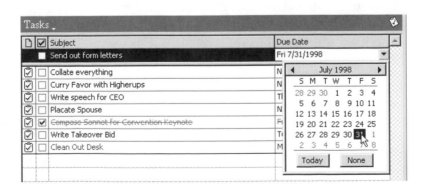

Doing it the fast way is fine if you intend only to view tasks in Simple List view. However, to prioritize tasks, track how close or far they are from completion, be reminded when they are due to be finished, keep notes about them, and even track things such as mileage and how many hours you worked on a task, you have to take the slow route by following these steps:

1. Click the New Tasks button or press CTRL+N. You see the Task dialog box shown in Figure 24-9.

2. In the Subject text box, enter a description of the task. What you enter appears on the Tasks screen and the TaskPad of the Calendar screen.

3. Under Due date, click the Due option button if the task is to be completed by a certain day. Click the drop-down arrow and choose the day from the mini-calendar. If you started the task already, open the Start drop-down list and tell Outlook when you started this task.

4. Under Status, click the drop-down arrow and choose a status demarcation that best describes the task; prioritize the task with the Priority drop-down list; and tell Outlook how complete the task is by clicking arrows in the % Complete box.

5. To be reminded when the task falls due, click the Reminder check box and then choose when you want to be reminded by making a choice in the drop-down menu. Reminders come in the form of a two-note chime that Outlook plays over the speaker in your computer.

6. Enter a few words in the text box to describe the task.

7. You can categorize tasks in different ways and view tasks in specific categories on the Tasks screen. To do so, click the Categories button and choose a category or two.

8. Click the Private check box if you are working on a network with the Microsoft Exchange Server and you don't want others to see this task on your Tasks list.

9. Click the Status tab and fill it out if you want to get very specific about the task and what it demands of you.

10. Click the Save and Close button.

TIP: *If someone assigns you a task by way of an e-mail message, you can save yourself a bit of trouble by dragging the e-mail message to the Tasks screen. To do so, click the e-mail message in the Inbox and gently drag it to the Task icon. The Task dialog box opens and you see the text of the message in the text box. Fill out the other parts of the Tasks dialog box and click the Save and Close button.*

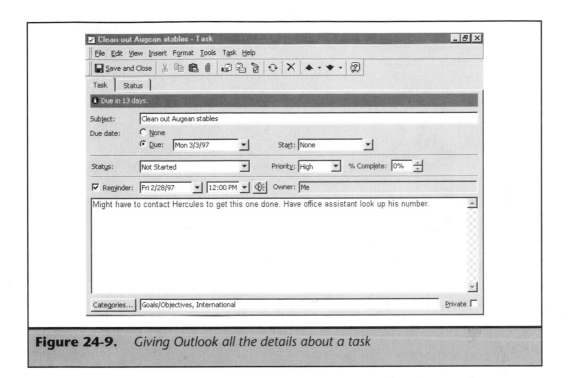

Figure 24-9. *Giving Outlook all the details about a task*

Seeing the Tasks That Need to Be Done

After you have entered the numerous tasks that you are expected to do, how can you get a fix on all the tasks and tell which one to tackle first? To do that, click the Current View down on the toolbar and choose one of the ten views:

A new set of tasks appears on the screen, depending on which view you chose. All views except Simple List tell you the task's status, how near it is to completion, and which category it was filed under, if any.

Choose Task Timeline view and click the Week or Month button on the toolbar to see a timeline that shows when tasks are due and when you are supposed to be working on them. Timelines appear for tasks for which you have designated a start date and due date. For tasks to which only a due date is assigned, a box with a check mark appears on the due date. As the following illustration shows, you can move the pointer on top of a timeline or due date to see which task it represents:

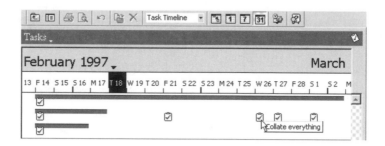

Updating and Deleting Tasks on the Tasks Screen

Following are instructions for keeping the Tasks screen up to date and deleting tasks in the Task screen.

Updating the Tasks Screen

To tell Outlook that a task has been completed, that a due date needs changing, that a task needs to be prioritized in a different way, or do whatever it takes to update a task, double-click it on the Tasks screen. The Task dialog box opens (see Figure 24-9). From there, you can choose options to your heart's content.

A faster but not as thorough way to update a task is to simply delete characters and enter new ones on the Tasks screen. Some views offer drop-down menus in the Status and View Date columns for changing the status of a task or the day it is due:

☑	↓	Clean Out Desk	Deferred ▼	n 2/17/97	0%	Personal
			Not Started			
			In Progress			
			Completed			
			Waiting on someone else			
			Deferred			

TIP: In Simple List view, simply click the empty box next to a task to show that it has been completed.

Deleting a Task

After you have completed a task, you can take great pleasure in removing it from the Tasks screen. To do that, simply click a task to select it and then click the Delete button.

Assigning a Task to Someone Else

As long as your computer is connected to a network that uses the Microsoft Exchange Server, you can hand off a task to someone else by way of the Tasks screen. Follow these steps to do so:

1. Choose File menu New command, and then click Task Request. You see a Task dialog box similar to the one in Figure 24-9, but this Task dialog box also has a To button.

2. Fill in the Task dialog box (see "Entering Tasks on the Tasks Screen," earlier in this chapter, if you need help).

3. Click the To button and tell Outlook to whom you want to assign the task.

4. Click the Send button.

In due time you receive a notice in your Inbox from the other person about whether or not he or she cares to do the task you assigned.

The Journal for Recording Day-to-Day Events

The Journal is an electronic log of the files you work on and the e-mail messages you receive and send to others. The program is set up to record the sending of e-mail messages and work done to Access, Excel, PowerPoint, and Word files. For Figure 24-10, I asked the Journal to show me the e-mail messages that I sent or received and the Word files that I worked on during the morning of February 19, 1997. By double-clicking the e-mail message, I can learn the details of whom the message was sent to and how much time I spent composing the message. And I can open the message as well. By double-clicking a Word file, I can find out how long I worked on the file and even open the Word file directly from the Journal screen.

The following pages explain how to record entries on the Journal screen, how to view the entries in different ways, how to open files, and how to delete entries.

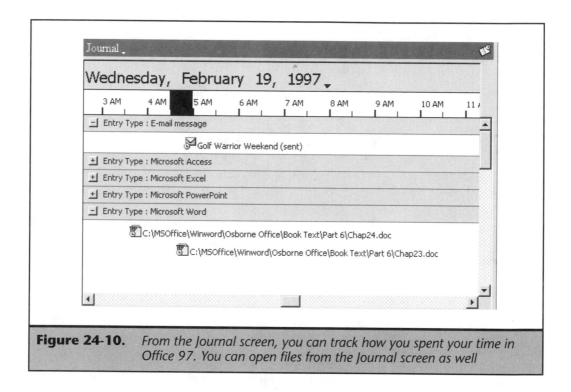

Figure 24-10. *From the Journal screen, you can track how you spent your time in Office 97. You can open files from the Journal screen as well*

Recording Entries in the Journal

Outlook can record certain kinds of events automatically on the Journal screen. E-mail transmissions, meeting requests, and work done to files that were created with one of the programs in the Office 97 suite can be recorded automatically if you so choose. UFO sightings, United States World Cup championships, and other extraordinary events have to be recorded manually. Following are instructions for making automatic and manual entries on the Journal screen.

Automatic Journal Entries

To begin with, Outlook is set up to record work done in Access, Excel, PowerPoint, and Word automatically. But you can decide for yourself what is recorded on the Journal screen by following these steps:

1. Choose the Tools menu Options command to open the Options dialog box.

2. Click the Journal tab. It is shown in Figure 24-11.The top half of the tab is for telling Outlook what type of e-mail activities to record and with whom to record them. The bottom half of the tab is for telling Outlook to record activities in Microsoft Office computer programs.

3. Under Automatically record these items, click next to the activities you want to record in the Journal.

4. Under For these contacts, click beside the names of the people who are important enough to be included in Journal entries.

5. Under Also record files from, click to remove the check mark beside the names of the Office programs you do *not* care to track with the Outlook. To begin with, the Journal tracks activity in all the Office programs.

> **TIP:** *Normally when you double-click an entry on the Journal screen, you see a dialog box that says how long you worked on the file or message and offers other details as well. However, if you want to double-click to open messages and files instead, click the Opens the item referred to by the journal entry option button on the Journal tab. This option button is for people who want to make the Journal the starting point for doing their work. You can also open messages and files by right-clicking on the Journal screen.*

6. Click OK.

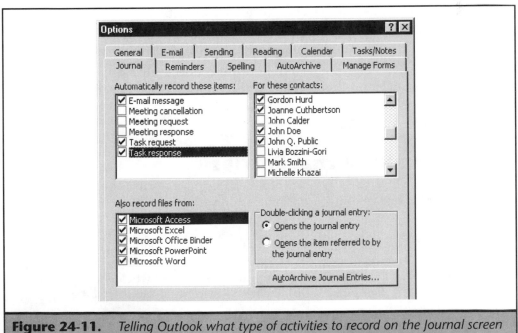

Figure 24-11.   *Telling Outlook what type of activities to record on the Journal screen*

OUTLOOK

Manual Journal Entries

To record an event such as a phone call that the Journal screen can't record automatically, or to record an event that the Journal screen hasn't been set up to record automatically, follow these steps:

1. Click the New Journal button or press CTRL+N. You see the Journal Entry dialog box shown in Figure 24-12.

2. In the Subject box, enter a short description of the activity. What you enter will appear on the Journal screen.

3. Open the Entry type drop-down menu and choose the option that best describes the activity.

4. If the activity involves someone who is listed on your Contacts List, click the button to the right of the Contacts dialog box. You see the Select Names dialog box. Click a contact name, click the Add button, and click OK. Back in the Journal Entry dialog box, you can enter a company name in the Company box if one isn't entered automatically.

5. Under Start time, change the start date and time, if necessary, and if this is an activity whose duration you can record, you can click the Start Timer button to move the clock and find out how long the activity lasts.

6. Enter a few words in the text box to describe the activity.

7. If you want to, click the Categories button and choose categories that describe this activity. You can display journal entries on the Journal screen by category.

8. Click the Private button if your computer is connected to a network that uses the Microsoft Exchange Server and you don't want others nosing around on your Journal screen.

9. Click the Save and Close button.

Looking at Your Journal Entries

Figure 24-13 outlines the ways to view entries on the Journal screen. Following are instructions for looking at your journal entries and perhaps opening a file from the Journal screen:

■ *Choosing which type of entries to display*   Click the plus sign next to an entry type to display its entries onscreen. In Figure 24-13, the plus sign beside Entry Type: Microsoft Word has been clicked and the screen shows which Word files were worked on. To hide entries, click the minus sign beside an entry type.

■ *Choosing how entries are displayed*   Open the Current View menu on the toolbar to change the way entries are displayed. To see phone call entries, choose Phone Calls, the bottom-most option on the drop-down menu.

■ *Choosing a time period* Click the Day, Week, or Month button on the toolbar to tell Outlook to display a day's worth, a week's worth, or a month's worth of entries. Use the scroll bar on the bottom of the screen to move backward or forward in time. (This option is only available when the Current View is set to By Type, By Contact, or By Category.)

■ *Viewing the details of an entry* Right-click an entry, and then choose Open Journal Entry to open the Journal Entry dialog box (see Figure 24-12) and learn more about the entry. The Journal Entry dialog box tells, among other things, when and how long you worked on the file or message.

> **WARNING:** *The time listing in the Journal Entry dialog box isn't necessarily accurate. The Journal only measures how many hours and minutes you actually worked on the file, not how many hours and minutes the file was open. For example, if you open two Word files simultaneously and work with each for an hour, the Journal only records 1 hour total for both files, not 2 hours total. The clock ticks only when the file is open and active.*

■ *Opening a message or file* To open a message or file, select an entry, right-click, and choose Open Item Referred To on the shortcut menu.

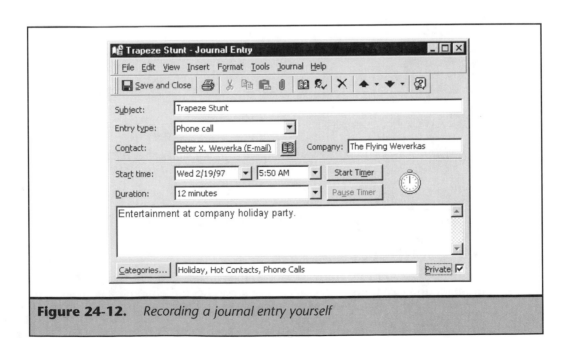

Figure 24-12. *Recording a journal entry yourself*

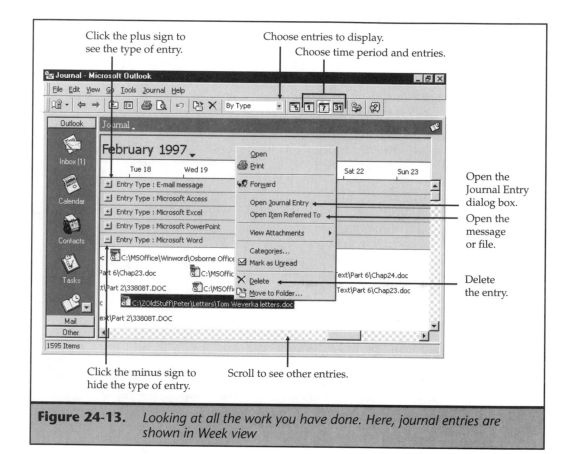

Click the plus sign to see the type of entry.

Choose entries to display.

Choose time period and entries.

Open the Journal Entry dialog box.

Open the message or file.

Delete the entry.

Click the minus sign to hide the type of entry.

Scroll to see other entries.

Figure 24-13.   *Looking at all the work you have done. Here, journal entries are shown in Week view*

TIP: *To delete an entry on the Journal screen, select it and either click the DELETE button or right-click and choose Delete from the shortcut menu.*

The Notes Screen for Jotting Down Reminders

The Notes screen is the computer equivalent of a refrigerator door. As Figure 24-14 shows, you can jot down reminder notes to yourself and keep them on the Notes screen. The notes look like the yellow "sticky" notes that are always falling off refrigerator doors and landing in the trash.

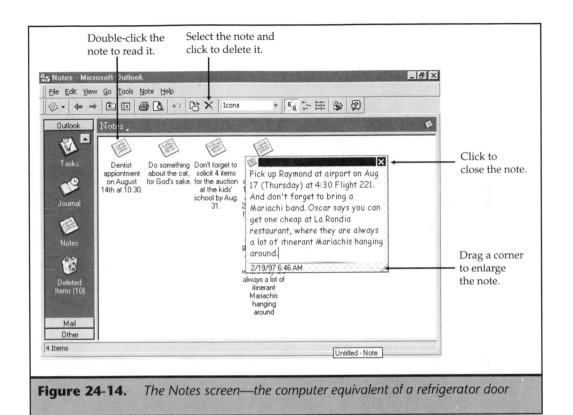

Figure 24-14. *The Notes screen—the computer equivalent of a refrigerator door*

To write a note to yourself, start by clicking the Note icon on the Outlook bar, and then click the New Note button. A Note box appears onscreen. Type the note. When you are done, click the Close button (the *X*) in the upper-right corner of the note. The note gets pasted onscreen beside the other notes you have written.

If you can't read a note onscreen, double-click it. The Note box appears. Drag the lower-right corner of the Note box if you can't read the note in its entirety.

To delete a note, click it and then click the Delete button.

OUTLOOK

Part VII

Web Publishing with Office

The Complete Reference

Office 97

Chapter 25

Office and Internet

As you undoubtedly know, the Internet—and especially the World Wide Web—are red-hot in the personal computer industry. Among both manufacturers and software developers (who want to sell users new products) and homes and businesses (who want to use the Internet for getting and sharing better and more information), the Internet has become the driving force in the world of computers. Microsoft (along with every other software development company) knows all this and, predictably, has built into the newest release of Microsoft Office 97 a plethora of tools and features for working with the Internet. This chapter essentially starts the discussion of how Office relates to the Internet by providing a primer on what the Internet and World Wide Web are and by explaining how you connect Office document files to the Internet.

NOTE: The four chapters that follow this one emphasize using Office programs for web publishing.

A Primer on the Internet and the World Wide Web

The Internet seems to confuse a lot of people, but it actually isn't all that hard to understand or even to use. New users should benefit, however, by getting an overview of what the Internet is and how it works, which is exactly what this section does.

What the Internet Is

In a nutshell, the Internet is a network of computers that people use for moving information from one computer to another computer. Sometimes this network shares information simply by moving a file from one computer to another computer (very much like when you move a file from one disk to another disk on your desktop computer or on a local area network). Other times the Internet shares information in a more structured and unique way.

NOTE: To be extremely precise, the Internet is actually a network of networks, but this point is irrelevant for most Internet users and casual web publishers.

Reviewing Popular Internet Protocols and Services

Perhaps the most common way that the Internet shares information is by passing e-mail messages from one computer to another. But there are several other methods that the Internet provides for people who want to share information. Table 25-1 lists

Protocol	Description
file	The file protocol moves files to and from a local drive. (A local drive is one connected either to your desktop or laptop computer or to another computer on your local area network).
ftp	The ftp, or file transfer protocol, moves files to and from ftp servers.
gopher	The gopher service creates a set of cascading menus for finding resources (usually files) stored on the Internet.
http	The http, or hypertext transfer protocol, moves HTML documents—also known as web pages—from web servers to web clients like your desktop or laptop computer. The http protocol, by the way, is what the World Wide Web uses to share information.
mail	The mail service lets people (or more precisely, mail servers) pass e-mail messages back and forth.
nntp	The nntp, or network news transfer protocol, moves newsgroup articles—basically e-mail messages—to and from nntp servers.
telnet	The telnet protocol lets you essentially turn your computer into a dumb terminal (a monitor and keyboard) and then log on to a server and connect to another computer. It is often used to access online library catalogs.

Table 25-1.   *Internet Information-Sharing Methods*

and describes some of the more common information-sharing methods—basically protocols—that web browsers like Internet Explorer or Netscape recognize in a URL.

 NOTE: Some entries in Table 25-1 are called "protocols," and some are called "services." For purposes of the discussion here, however, this distinction is irrelevant. You can simply think of all of these items as methods for sharing information.

A Brief Overview of Client-Server Computing
One interesting and important feature of the Internet is that it uses a client-server computing architecture. What this means is that whenever two computers share information, one computer acts as client while the other computer acts as a server. In a client-server relationship, the client computer essentially requests the server computer

to perform certain operations. The server computer then responds to the request—either granting the request or denying it.

As you might guess, the fact that there are essentially two computers involved in any exchange of information means that the client computer needs to be running client software (to make the request) and the server computer needs to be running server software (to respond to the request).

Office 97 comes with some Internet client software. For example, in the Office program, you receive a recent version of Microsoft's Internet Explorer web browser. It works as client software for all of the Internet's information-sharing methods: ftp, http, gopher, file, and so on. Outlook, as you might guess, works as client software for sharing information using the mail service. And Windows itself comes with several other client software programs, including ftp (this is another ftp client) and telnet. But recognize that you may need to acquire appropriate client software before using other, more specialized information-sharing methods.

NOTE: Both Windows 95 and Windows NT 4.0 (as well as their successors) also come with other more esoteric Internet clients, including PING (a client utility for testing Internet connections) and TRACERT (a client utility for identifying the route an Internet connection between two computers takes). For more information about these other clients, refer to Windows online help, the Windows documentation, or a thorough book on using Windows and the Internet.

One other point related to the Internet's client-server computing model bears mentioning: While the Internet is amazingly robust considering all it's doing, with so many hardware and software elements involved, it doesn't always work perfectly. If you consider the basic components already mentioned—a client computer, client software, a server computer, and then server software—you easily and correctly deduce that if one component of this connection isn't working correctly, you can't share any information.

NOTE: The preceding paragraph mentions only the most prominent hardware and software elements involved in any information exchange involving the Internet. It turns out, however, that there are actually many other, less apparent components to the connection, such as the telephone lines and cables that connect the client and server.

What a Packet-Switched Network Is

There's one final piece of background information that you'll probably find illuminating—at least in the long run. It turns out that the Internet uses a packet-switched network. That doesn't mean much to you if you're not a networking engineer, but the relevancy of this technology is easy to understand.

First, however, it's helpful if you understand about the other general type of network that's available, a circuit-switched network. With a circuit-switched network, when two people or computers (or anything else) communicate, the communication connection is dedicated to and used solely by the two people or computers communicating.

The most common example of a circuit-switched network is the telephone system. When you call a friend or associate and successfully complete the connection (because the other person picks up the phone), that connection (your phone, his phone, one of the telephone companies switches, some telephone cable and so forth) is used solely by the two of you. Similarly, if you use your computer to connect to a local bulletin board system, again the connection is used solely by your computer and the bulletin board system's computer.

A packet-switched network, however, works very differently. Whenever a client or a server communicate, the information is broken down into little chunks called *packets*. These packets are then identified, addressed, and numbered: packet 1 of 10, packet 2 of 10, packet 3 of 10, and so on. Then, these packets are pumped out onto the Internet (where they get all mixed up with the packets that every other client and server are exchanging) and sent off to the appropriate client or server. Once the packets reach their destination, the receiving computer reassembles the packets.

The most common, everyday example of a packet-switched network is the postal service. If you live in Seattle and mail some friend in San Francisco a couple of letters, the two letters get mixed with everyone else's mail as soon as you drop them into the letter box. And they stay "mixed up" as the two letters move from Seattle to San Francisco. Ultimately, however, the postal carrier, in effect, reassembles the information you've sent (the two letters) and drops them into your friend's mail box.

There's more to learn about packet-switched networking than the preceding paragraphs describe, of course. But even with this basic information, one important characteristic of the Internet becomes very clear: You share the Internet's carrying capacity—its bandwidth—with everyone else who's also using it to move information. And that means the whole system slows down when people's usage increases because they're sending more information.

 NOTE: Technically speaking, bandwidth refers to the amount of data that a computer can push through a particular connection in a set time interval. You typically measure modem bandwidth, for example, in kilobits per second. And people typically measure the bandwidth of the high-speed cables that make up the backbone of the Internet in megabits per second.

What the World Wide Web Is

As mentioned earlier, one of the more popular ways that the Internet lets people share information is through the World Wide Web. The Web, as it's often called, is popular for two basic reasons. One reason is that the http protocol lets web browsers transfer interesting information (as described in the next paragraph). The other reason for the popularity of the Web is that it's extremely easy to use once you install the web client software (and get it working correctly).

The bit about the http protocol letting web browsers transfer interesting information is perhaps the Web's most powerful feature. http lets people move multimedia documents—called web pages—from a server computer to a client computer. In other words, with the http protocol, it's possible to move a web page document that has text (one medium), pictures (another medium), sound (still another medium), and video (yet another medium). The web, then, lets people create and view multimedia documents. Figure 25-1 shows one example of a web page: that of the President of the United States.

As mentioned, a second reason for http's and the web's popularity exists. The web is easy to use. Really easy. In general, to move from one web page to another web page you click a hypertext link, called a hyperlink in the parlance of the Internet. A *hyperlink* is simply a bit of text or a picture that points to another web page. In other words, you move from web page to web page simply by clicking the mouse. For example, if you display the web page shown in Figure 25-1 and click the hyperlink identified in that figure, your web browser displays the web page shown in Figure 25-2.

NOTE: *The Windows online Help program also makes use of clickable hypertext links, as you probably know.*

Figure 25-1. *The home page of the president of the United States*

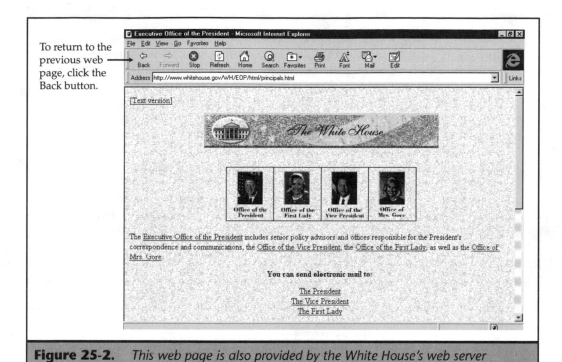

To return to the previous web page, click the Back button.

Figure 25-2.   *This web page is also provided by the White House's web server*

NOTE: The server computer that supplies a collection of web pages (or web site) is called a web server.

In summary, the Internet's http protocol represents an extremely powerful way to transfer information. Because the Web consists of multimedia documents, you can create web pages using HTML that present almost any type of information (see Chapter 26 for information about HTML and web publishing). And because one only needs to know how to use a mouse to move between these web pages, browsing the web is only slightly more complicated than paging through a book.

Understanding URLs

While it is possible to use the World Wide Web simply by clicking hyperlinks, you'll find it extremely beneficial to understand what URLs, or uniform resource locators, are and how they work.

A URL identifies a specific Internet resource: a web page, a file on an ftp server, a Telnet connection, an e-mail address, and so on. In other words, the URL is the computer equivalent of a person's address. Given a person's complete address—the

A Few Words About Intranets

Because the http protocol and HTML are so powerful, they aren't only used on computers and networks connected to the Internet. More and more organizations are also setting up internal-to-the-organization web sites, often called *intranets,* that let employees easily access information. For example, some companies publish their human resources literature on an internal web, thus making it easier to keep this information accessible and up-to-date.

One noteworthy point concerning an intranet is that people are much less likely to experience bandwidth bottlenecks over a local area network. The Ethernet networking protocol used in a local area network, for example, transmits data at 10 megabits per second, roughly six times the speed of the fast 1.5 megabits-per-second T1-line connection that some companies use to connect their networks to the Internet. And it transmits data at more than 300 times the speed of the typical user's 28.8 kilobits-per-second modem.

street and, if necessary, apartment numbers, the city, and the state—you should be able to locate the person's home or business.

Because URLs are so important, they appear by default in the Address box at the top of most web browser clients. Predictably, every web page has a unique URL. Figure 25-3, for example, shows a web page at the Microsoft Corporation web site.

While URLs look like ciphers the first few times you see them, they're actually fairly easy to interpret and read. In general, URLs consist of three parts: the protocol or service name, the server name, and the path name of the file (this might be an HTML document, for example).

 NOTE: Web page designs and content change regularly. So don't expect the real-life web pages shown in this chapter to look the same if you visit them as part of following along with your reading. Undoubtedly, they will have changed between the time this chapter was written and the time you read the chapter.

The first part of the URL is the protocol or service name. (It's a bit imprecise, but from this point forward in the chapter we will simply call this the protocol name.) In Figure 25-3, for example, the protocol name is the http:// portion of the URL. (If you remember the table shown earlier in the chapter, you'll remember that the hypertext transfer protocol, which makes the World Wide Web possible, is called http.)

If an Internet resource uses another information-sharing method, however, the protocol or service name is different. Figure 25-4 shows the URL for a resource that uses the ftp protocol, for example.

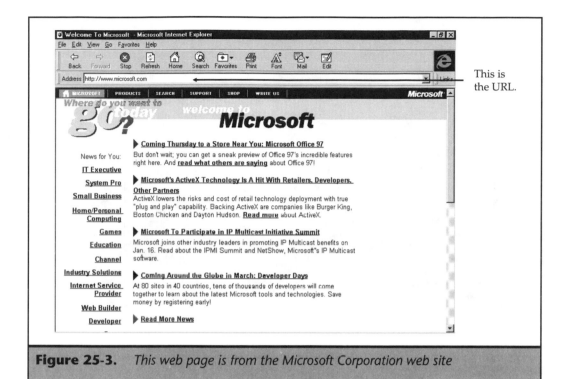

This is the URL.

Figure 25-3.   *This web page is from the Microsoft Corporation web site*

The next part of a URL is generally the server name. This names the server computer (actually the server network) that's running the server software and on which is stored the Internet resources you want to retrieve. While it's not an ironclad convention, people often name servers by combining the common abbreviation used to identify the World Wide Web, www, and the network domain name. In the case of the Microsoft Corporation web site URL shown in Figure 25-3, for example, the server name is www.microsoft.com. Similarly, in the case of the Microsoft Corporation ftp site URL shown in Figure 25-4, the server name is ftp.microsoft.com.

The last part of a URL supplies the complete path name of the Internet resource you want to retrieve. The path name starts with the / character, then names the folder (or perhaps the folder and subfolder), and then (usually) names the file.

NOTE: *URLs don't always name a file. If you visit the home page of a large corporation's web site, for example, the URL will show only the server address—that is, until you link to a folder or subfolder within the web site.*

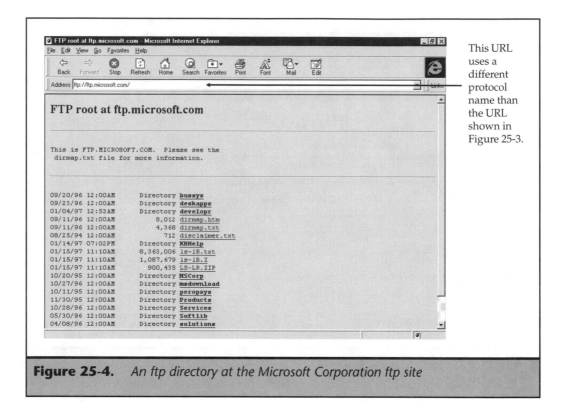

This URL uses a different protocol name than the URL shown in Figure 25-3.

Figure 25-4. *An ftp directory at the Microsoft Corporation ftp site*

Working with Hyperlinks

With knowledge of what the Internet is, how the World Wide Web works, and what URLs do, you'll find it easy to work with Office's new hyperlinks feature. Office's hyperlinks feature lets you place URLs into almost any Office document file: Word documents, Excel workbooks, PowerPoint presentations, Access databases, and even Outlook message items. Once you've placed a hyperlink into a document file, you can retrieve the Internet resource identified by the hyperlink's URL simply by clicking it.

NOTE: *If you don't have a permanent connection to the Internet, you may need first to connect to the Internet. When this is the case, Windows asks you if you want to make the connection and, assuming that you indicate you do, makes the dial-up networking connection.*

Creating a Hyperlink

The general rules for creating hyperlinks are quite straightforward:

- You must provide the actual URL, which makes sense since that's the way you describe what Internet resource you want to retrieve.

- You can optionally provide clickable text or a clickable picture that can be used to represent the hyperlink.

In general, you accomplish both tasks by using the Insert menu Hyperlink command or the Standard toolbar Insert Hyperlink button. Specifically, you follow these steps:

1. If you want to use existing document file text or an existing picture, select it.

2. Choose the Insert menu Hyperlink command or click the Insert Hyperlink button, which appears on the Standard toolbar. The Office program displays the Insert Hyperlink dialog box (see Figure 25-5).

3. Enter the URL of the Internet resource that you want to reference with the hyperlink. If you want to reference a local file, you can click the Browse button to the right of the Link to File or URL text box. When you do, the Office program displays the Link to File dialog box (see Figure 25-6), which you can use to identify the file you want to reference.

4. Optionally, use the Named location in file text box to identify a Word bookmark, Excel worksheet, or Access object if you're creating a hyperlink that references a local file instead of an Internet resource. If you don't know the name of the Word bookmark, Excel worksheet range, or Access object that you want to reference, click the Browse button to the right of the Named location in file text box. When you do, the Office program displays a dialog box you can use to identify the bookmark, worksheet range, slide, or database object. Figure 25-7 shows the Bookmark dialog box, which you would use to specify a Word bookmark.

NOTE: You only need to provide an e-mail address when you create an e-mail hyperlink. You don't need to provide the protocol.

5. If you want the URL to be relative, check the Use relative path for hyperlink box. If you use this option, you don't need to supply the path name for finding some Internet resource or local file. The Office program just assumes that the active web directory or file folder is the one with the resource or file you want.

You can activate this list box to see URLs you've recently retrieved with your web browser client.

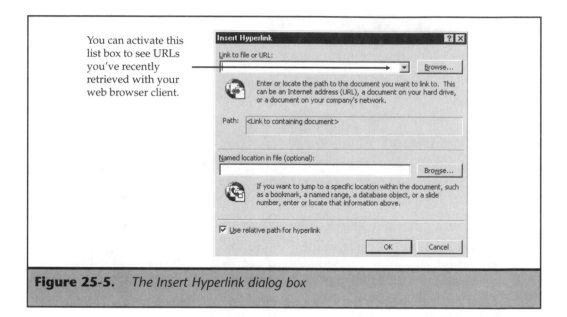

Figure 25-5. *The Insert Hyperlink dialog box*

Use the Look in box to identify the folder that holds the file.

Once you see the file listed in this box, double-click it.

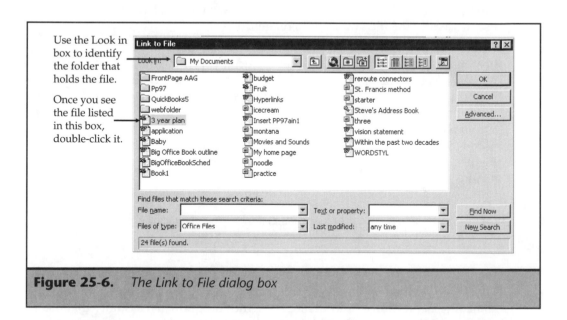

Figure 25-6. *The Link to File dialog box*

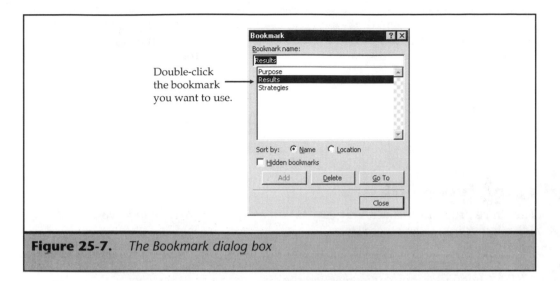

Double-click
the bookmark
you want to use.

Figure 25-7. *The Bookmark dialog box*

Once you create a hyperlink, you can begin using it. To make it easier to identify the hyperlink, Office programs do several things. If the hyperlink relies on clickable text, the Office program colors the hyperlink text blue and also underlines it:

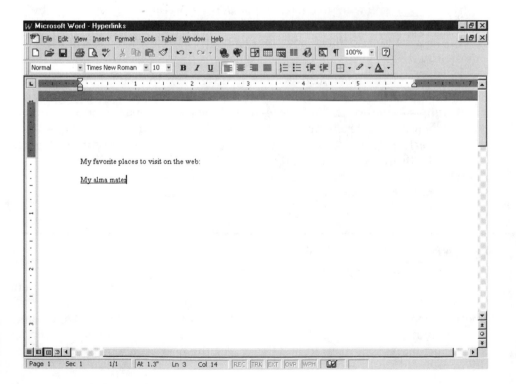

If you point to the hyperlink—and it doesn't matter whether the hyperlink uses clickable text or a clickable picture—the Office program changes the mouse pointer into a pointing hand and displays a pop-up box showing the URL:

Editing Hyperlinks

The Office programs make it very easy to edit or update the hyperlinks you create. To edit a hyperlink, follow these steps:

1. Right-click the hyperlink so that the Office program displays a shortcut menu.

2. Choose the shortcut menu Hyperlink command and then choose the Hyperlink submenu Edit Hyperlink command. The Office program displays the Edit Hyperlink dialog box (see Figure 25-8).

3. Edit the URL shown in the Link to file or URL text box. As when you create a hyperlink, if you want to reference a local file, you can click the Browse button to the right of the Link to file or URL text box. When you do, the Office program displays the Link to File dialog box (see Figure 25-6), which you can use to identify the file you want to reference.

4. If necessary, edit the Named location in file text box to identify the correct Word bookmark, Excel worksheet range, or Access database object if you're creating a hyperlink that references a local file instead of an Internet resource. As when you create a hyperlink, if you don't know the name of the Word bookmark, Excel worksheet range, or Access object that you want to reference, click the Browse button to the right of the Named location in file text box. When you do, the Office program displays a dialog box, which you can use to identify the bookmark, worksheet range, slide, or database object.

Automatic Hyperlinks

While you can create hyperlinks with any of the Office programs, Word and Outlook will automatically create hyperlinks if you enter a URL into the document file or something that looks like a URL. You can't turn off Outlook's automatic hyperlinks feature, but you can turn off Word's. If you don't want Word to create these automatic hyperlinks, choose the Tools menu AutoCorrect command, click its AutoFormat As You Type tab, and then check the Internet and network paths with hyperlinks box.

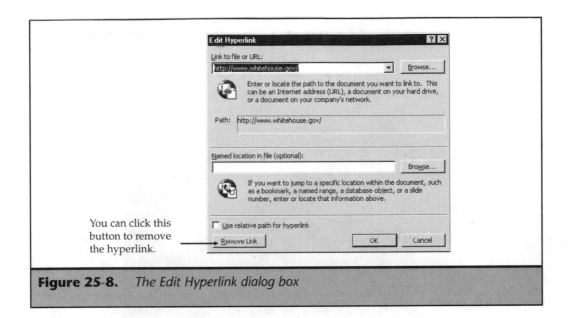

You can click this
button to remove
the hyperlink.

Figure 25-8. *The Edit Hyperlink dialog box*

Using Office's Web Toolbar

When you view an Internet resource in an Office program window—such as by
adding a hyperlink to an Office document and by then clicking the hyperlink—the
Office program adds a new toolbar to the program window, as shown in Figure 25-9.

You can use the toolbar to move to web pages and local files you've recently
accessed using a hyperlink. Most of the toolbar buttons and boxes that the Web toolbar
displays are easy to use, but a few are more complicated, so the next paragraphs
quickly describe all of the toolbar's buttons and boxes.

NOTE: *Chapter 30 describes web browsing and web browser mechanics in much
greater detail than the paragraphs that follow. For this reason, if you're still new to the
World Wide Web, you may want to refer there for more information.*

Back and Forward

The Back and Forward buttons move you to the previous web page or the next web
page. The Back button, of course, moves you back to the web page you were
previously viewing:

This is
the Web
toolbar.

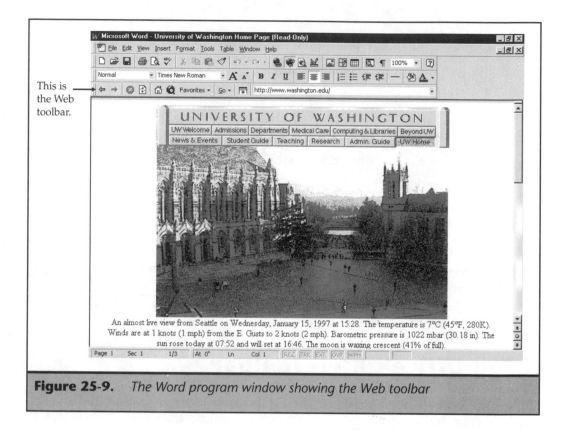

Figure 25-9. *The Word program window showing the Web toolbar*

The Forward button moves you forward to next web page you were viewing:

You may be interested in knowing that your web browser caches, or stores copies of, recently viewed web pages. For this reason, clicking the Back and Forward buttons to view a web page you've already retrieved from a web server lets you very quickly see a page you want revisit.

NOTE: *You can customize a web browser's caching of recently visited web pages in a variety of ways. For more information about how to do this, refer to Chapter 30.*

Stop Current Jump

The Stop Current Jump button tells your web browser to stop retrieving a web page from a web server:

If a web page is taking a long time to grab (more than about a minute), you can use this tool to abort the retrieval operation. (If you tell a web browser to grab another new web page before it has successfully retrieved an already requested web page, the web browser also aborts the first retrieval operation.)

Refresh Current Page

The Refresh Current Page button tells your web browser to grab a new copy of a web page from the web server:

You use this tool when web page information changes frequently and you want to make sure you have the most-recent version of the web page, or when your web browser has retrieved a web page from your local cache.

Start Page

The Start Page button moves you to your start, or home, page:

As you may know, the start page is just the default web page a web browser loads. Typically, the software developer who makes the web browser sets your start page to his or her corporate web site. You can and should consider changing your start page to another web site or page, however, if you don't use the information provided by this start page setting.

NOTE: The Go button, described in one of the paragraphs that follow, provides a command you can use to set your start page to the open web page.

Search the Web

The Search the Web button displays the default search service form:

As with a start page, the software developer who makes the web browser sets your default search service form, but you can and should consider changing your default search service form so that it represents the service you know best. The Go button, described in one of the paragraphs that follow, also provides a command you can use to specify which search service you want to use as your default.

 NOTE: For more information about how you use an Internet search service, refer to Chapter 30.

Favorites

The Favorites button displays a menu of commands that you can use to add web pages and other Internet resources to a list of your favorite Internet places. You also can use the command menu to jump to one of these favorite places:

If you choose the Favorites menu Add to Favorites command, for example, the Office program displays the Add To Favorites dialog box:

You use the Save in drop-down list box to specify where you want to save the name of the favorite web page (typically, you save the name of the web page in your Favorites folder). Be sure that the Save as type box shows the type as Internet Shortcuts.

NOTE: When you add a web page to your Favorites folder, what you're actually doing is creating an Internet shortcut that points to the web page's URL and then storing this Internet shortcut in the Favorites folder.

To later open a web page for which you've created an Internet shortcut, choose the Favorites menu Open Favorites command. Then, when the Office program displays the Favorites dialog box, double-click the Internet shortcut for the web page you want to open:

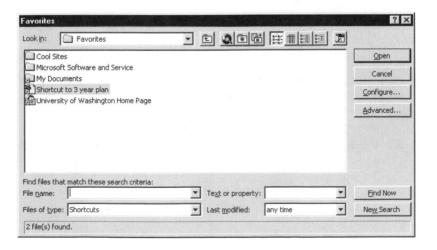

NOTE: *You can also open a web page for which you've added an Internet shortcut to the Favorites folder simply by choosing the web page from the Favorites menu.*

Go

The Go button displays a menu of commands you can use to move to a different web page:

Most of the Go menu commands simply let you move to a web page. If you choose the Go menu Open command, for example, the Office program displays the Open Internet Address dialog box, where you can enter the address of the file you want to open. If you choose the Go menu Back or Forward command, the Office program tells your web browser to move back to the previous page or forward to the next web page.

TIP: *The Back and Forward commands, in other words, are equivalent to the Back and Forward buttons that appear on the toolbar itself.*

The Go menu Set Start Page and Set Search Page commands work a bit differently, however. If you choose the Go menu Set Start Page command, for example you change your start page to whatever web page you are currently viewing. Similarly, if you choose the Go menu Set Search Page command, you can change your default search service to whatever web page you are currently viewing. (For this to make sense, of course, the web page you're currently viewing needs to show a search service form.)

Address

The Address combo box shows the current page's URL:

```
http://www.washington.edu/                    ▼
```

You can also use the Address combo box for entering a new URL or for selecting a recently used URL. (To select a recently used URL, activate the Address drop-down list and select one of its entries.)

The
Complete
Reference

Office
97

Chapter 26

Web Publishing with Word

P erhaps the major new capability of Word 8 (the version of Word that comes with the Office 97 suite) is that it lets you create HTML documents—the building blocks used for creating web sites. This means that for very simple web authoring and HTML editing tasks, most people never need to learn or work with specialized web authoring programs like Microsoft FrontPage or Adobe PageMill.

 NOTE: Appendix B describes what FrontPage is, how you use it, and what it does that you can't do (or can't easily do) with the simpler web authoring capabilities of a program like Word.

Creating a Blank Web Page with Word

To create an empty web page, or HTML document, you run a special Web Page Wizard. If you've worked with the File menu New command or employed any of Word's other document creation wizards, you'll find the steps necessary to create a blank web page very easy.

One item to note is that before you add some types of information to a web page—such as a graphic image—you need to first save the web page. For this reason, this section also describes how you save and then later open web pages.

A Quick Primer on HTML

The acronym HTML stands for hypertext markup language. In essence, HTML is simply a set of instructions to a web browser. These instructions describe how the web browser should display text contained in the HTML document; typically provide that text; and identify graphic images, sounds, and video clips that should be displayed when someone (or more precisely someone's web browser) requests the web page.

While not that long ago, web authors worked with HTML to create web pages, that's no longer true. HTML is still the language used to create web pages. But as a web author, you don't need to even see it and you certainly don't need to learn the actual commands or HTML syntax. Using a program like Word, you can simply provide the content—the actual text, pictures, and other information—that you want to show in your web page and then tell the program like Word how it should format this content. Word then writes the actual HTML code for you. (To see the HTML instructions that Word creates for a web page, choose the View menu HTML Source command.)

Running the Web Page Wizard

The Web Page Wizard works like Word's other document creation wizards. To run the Web Page Wizard, follow these steps:

1. Choose the File menu New command.

2. When Word displays the New dialog box (see Figure 26-1), click its Web Pages tab.

NOTE: *The More Cool Stuff template opens a Word document that describes other web authoring tools available for use with Word and Office. This document includes a hyperlink to Microsoft's web server, which is where you can find these tools.*

3. Double-click the Web Page Wizard. When you do, Word starts the wizard.

4. When the wizard's first dialog box asks you what kind of web page you'd like, select one of the entries from the dialog box's only list box. Then click Next.

5. When the wizard's second dialog box asks you what visual look you'd like for your web page, again select one of the entries from the dialog box's only list box. Then click Finish. The wizard finishes, opening a new, blank web page, such as that shown in Figure 26-2.

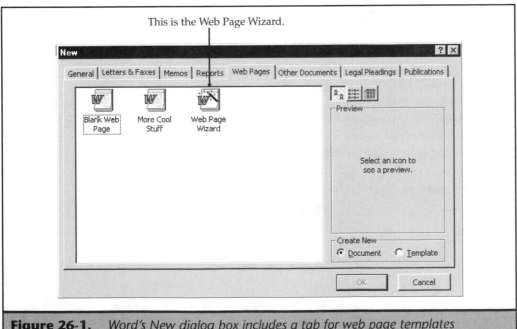

Figure 26-1. *Word's New dialog box includes a tab for web page templates and wizards*

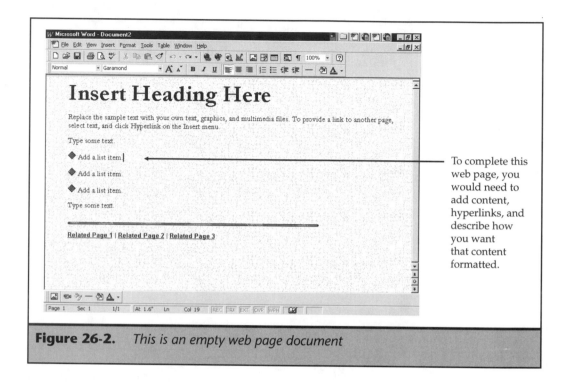

To complete this web page, you would need to add content, hyperlinks, and describe how you want that content formatted.

Figure 26-2. *This is an empty web page document*

LEARN BY EXAMPLE

If you want to follow along with the discussion here, note that the companion CD includes several sample web pages created using the Web Page Wizard. You can open Figures 26-B through 26-J to see what you can do with the different web page types and styles. You can also open Figure 26-K and click the hyperlink at the bottom of this sample home page to see what the same page looks like in each of the different styles.

Saving Your New Web Page

Once you've created a blank web page, you should save it, because while you can add text to a web page you haven't yet saved, you can't add other types of content, such as graphic images. To save a web page for the first time, choose the File menu Save As command. When Word displays the Save As dialog box, shown in Figure 26-3, follow these steps:

1. Use the Save in drop-down list box to select the folder in which you want to save the web page. You should set up a separate folder used exclusively for the web pages that make up a web site—and then use the folder to store all of your web page documents and the components of those web page documents.

NOTE: *If you have questions about how any of the command buttons on the Save As dialog box work – such as the Create New Folder button, refer to Chapter 2.*

2. Enter the filename you want to use for the new web page into the File name box.

3. Verify the Save as type box shows file type as HTML Document. (It should.) Then click Save.

Naming Your Web Page

While Windows 95, Windows NT, and their successors let you name your web pages and graphic images anything you want, you should generally use standard MS-DOS file naming conventions if it's possible that someone using a computer running MS-DOS will view or save the web page or graphic image you're creating. This means that your file name should use eight characters or less. You can use any letters or numbers in your web page file name, but there are other characters you can't use (such as spaces, slashes, question marks, and asterisks). To see a list of the other sorts of characters you can't use, refer to a good book on using MS-DOS.

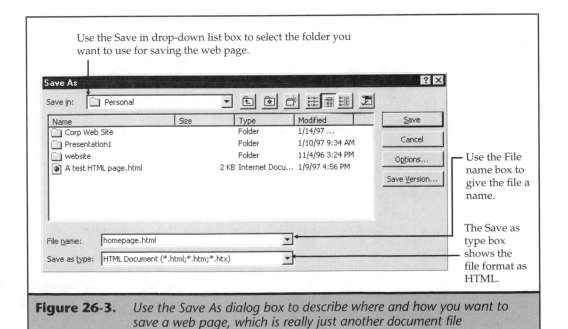

Figure 26-3. *Use the Save As dialog box to describe where and how you want to save a web page, which is really just another document file*

Resaving a Web Page

Once you save a web page, its new name appears on the document window's title bar. When you want to save it again, you simply click the Save button or choose the File menu Save command. Word saves the web page in the same location and with the same name. (Note that this means Word replaces your old version of the web page with the new version of your web page.)

 NOTE: Word's File menu also shows the Save as Word Document command. You can use this new command, Save as Word Document, to create a regular Word document file that shows the same information as your web page document.

Saving a Web Page with a New Name

You can save multiple copies of a web page simply by giving the copies new names or by placing the copies in a different folder. (Typically, you'll want to give the copied web page a new name so that you don't get the document files mixed up.) To save a web page with a different name or in a different location, choose the File menu Save As command. Then use the Save As dialog box to specify either a new file name or a new folder location. (This business of specifying either a new file name or a new folder location works the same way as it does the time you originally specify a file name or folder location.) As when you originally saved the web page, be sure that the Save as type shows the file format as HTML document.

 NOTE: Chapter 2 describes special save options available for regular Word documents such as automatic backup copies and password protection. These same options work for web pages. If you have questions about using any of these options, refer to Chapter 2.

Opening Web Pages for Editing

You open web pages (for purposes of editing them) by clicking Word's Open button or by choosing the Word File menu Open command. You can't open a web page you want to edit with the Start button's Documents menu or using the Windows Explorer. If you open an HTML document in either of these ways, Windows uses the Internet Explorer to open the web page for viewing and not for editing.

To open an existing document with Word's Open button or the File menu Open command, click the button or choose the command to display the Open dialog box shown in Figure 26-4, and then follow these steps:

1. Select the HTML Document entry from the Files of type drop-down list box.

2. Use the Look in drop-down list box to select the folder that stores the web page you want to open.

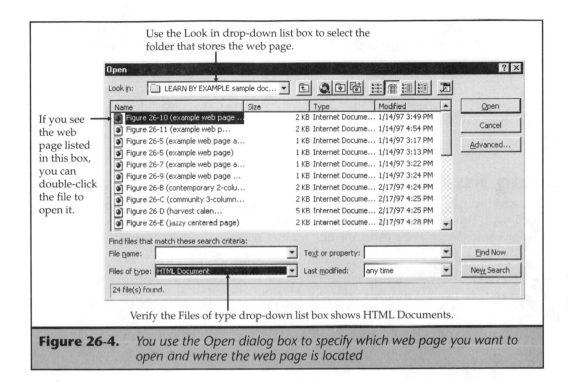

Use the Look in drop-down list box to select the folder that stores the web page.

If you see the web page listed in this box, you can double-click the file to open it.

Verify the Files of type drop-down list box shows HTML Documents.

Figure 26-4. *You use the Open dialog box to specify which web page you want to open and where the web page is located*

NOTE: *If the file you're looking for isn't in the default folder, activate the Look in drop-down list box to display a list of your drives. Click the drive that contains the document file you want, and then double-click folders until you locate your file. Alternatively, you can start looking through the folder hierarchy by clicking the Up One Level button next to the Look in drop-down list box.*

3. When you see the HTML document listed, double-click it, or, alternatively, enter the web page's URL into the File name box. Note that if you know the name and path of a document file, you can also enter this information into the File name drop-down list box.

NOTE: *You can also typically use the File menu to re-open the four document files—including web pages—that you used most recently. They are listed at the bottom of the File menu. Just click a file to open it.*

Adding Content to Your Web Page

After you create a blank web page, you're ready to begin adding content to the web page: text, pictures, video, and even sound. In most cases, you do this in the same

manner that you do for a regular Word document. If you're well-versed in the
mechanics of using Word, you should have no trouble adding content to you
web pages.

NOTE: *You create hyperlinks for HTML documents in the same way you create
hyperlinks for regular Word documents.*

Adding Text

You add text to a web page in the same way that you add text to a regular Word
document. You can type the text into a web page. You can copy text from some other
document file, such as by using the Edit menu Copy, Cut, and Paste commands.

NOTE: *Chapter 1 describes (briefly) how you enter text into a document file. Chapter 3
describes how you copy and move text.*

Figure 26-5 shows an example web page with a bit of text. To make the text more
interesting to look at, the web page text includes formatting.

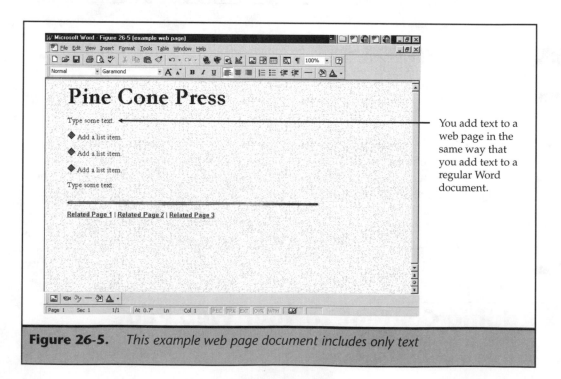

Figure 26-5. *This example web page document includes only text*

LEARN BY EXAMPLE
You can open the example web page shown in Figure 26-5, Figure 26-5 (example web page), from the companion CD if you want to follow along with the discussion here. Note that this sample document is an HTML document so it uses the file extension, HTM.

You can also insert the textual portion of an existing document file into a web page document. To do this, you take the following steps:

1. Choose the Insert menu File command. When you do, Word displays the Insert File dialog box shown in Figure 26-6.

2. Use the Look in drop-down list box to select the folder that stores the document file you want to insert.

3. Optionally, use the Range text box to specify that only a portion of the selected file should be inserted. You can enter either a Word document bookmark or an Excel worksheet range into the Range box.

4. Activate the Files of type drop-down list box and select the file format of the document file you want to insert. If the document file is a Word document, for example, select the Word document entry from the list box.

5. When you see the document file listed in the Insert File dialog box, double-click it. Word inserts the document file's text into the web page at the insertion point. Figure 26-7 shows the web page from Figure 26-5 after a bit of text has been inserted into the web page.

LEARN BY EXAMPLE
If you want to follow along with the discussion here, note that the companion CD includes a small Word document that includes the newly inserted text shown in Figure 26-7, Figure 26-A (text for insertion). The companion CD also includes the completed web page document shown in Figure 26-7, Figure 26-7 (web page after text insertion).

Adding Pictures

You can add pictures to web page document, too. And, not surprisingly, this process also works the same with a web page document as it does with a regular Word document.

One of the ways, for example, that you can add pictures to a web page document is by using the Clip Gallery. Chapter 3 describes how you use this tool, so refer there if you have questions about how to do this.

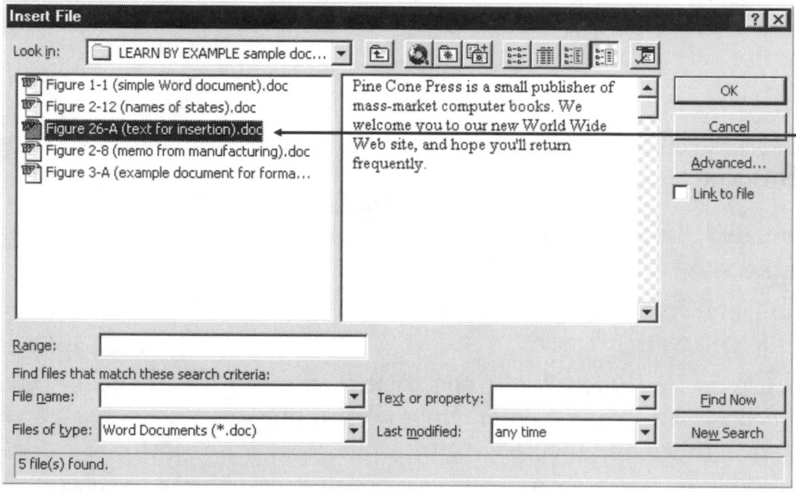

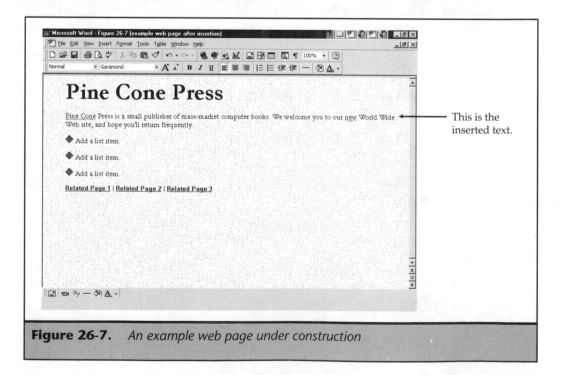

Once you see the document file listed here, double-click it to insert it.

Figure 26-6. *You can use the Insert File dialog box to identify and then insert a document file into a web page*

This is the inserted text.

Figure 26-7. *An example web page under construction*

You can also add pictures to a web page by inserting the graphic image file. To do this, you take the following steps:

1. Choose the Insert menu Picture command and then choose the Picture submenu From File command. When you do, Word displays the Insert Picture dialog box, shown in Figure 26-8.

2. Use the Look in drop-down list box to select the folder that stores the graphic image you want to insert.

3. Activate the Files of type drop-down list box and select the All Pictures file format.

4. When you see the graphic image file listed in the Insert Picture dialog box, double-click it. Word inserts the graphic image into the web page at the insertion point. Figure 26-9 shows the web page from Figure 26-7 after inserting clip art and graphic images.

After you add a graphic image to a web page, you can easily move and copy the graphic image by using the mouse. For example, if you want to move the graphic image to some other location—perhaps you accidentally inserted the image at the wrong location—you can simply drag it to the correct location.

TIP: *You can see what your web page looks like in a web browser window by choosing the File menu Web Page Preview command.*

If you want to copy the graphic image so you can also use it in some other location, you can hold down the CTRL key and the drag the image. (When you hold down the CTRL key, Word makes a copy of the image and it's this copy you're dragging to a new location—not the original graphic image.)

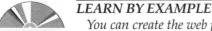

LEARN BY EXAMPLE
You can create the web page shown in Figure 26-9 by opening the sample web page shown in Figure 26-7, Figure 26-7 (web page after text insertion), *and by then adding the clip art and graphic images shown. The companion CD also includes the completed web page document shown in Figure 26-9,* Figure 26-9 (example web page with images).

NOTE: *As you add graphic images to your web pages, bear in mind that most web browsers support only two graphic image file formats: GIF and JPEG (also known as JPG). Word will convert most graphic images that are not of these graphic image file formats, but you will almost certainly want to limit yourself to using these two formats to prevent any distortion or loss of graphic image quality in a file type conversion.*

Once you see the graphic image listed here, double-click it to insert it.

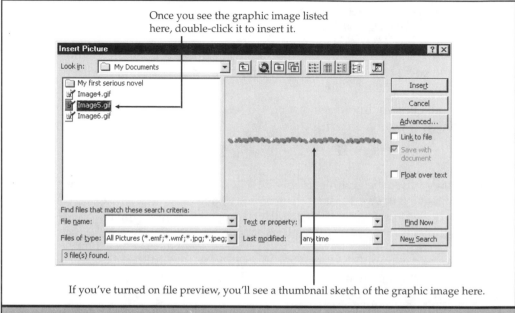

If you've turned on file preview, you'll see a thumbnail sketch of the graphic image here.

Figure 26-8. *You can use the Insert Picture dialog box to identify and then insert a graphic image into a web page*

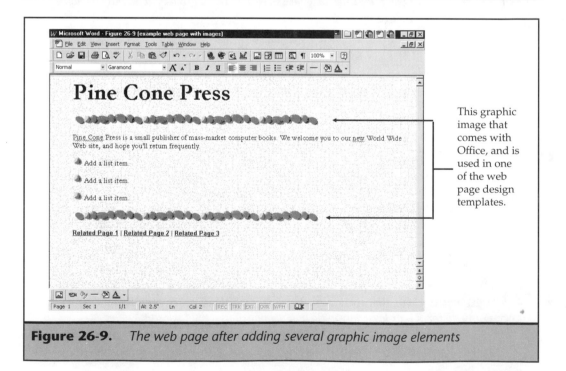

This graphic image that comes with Office, and is used in one of the web page design templates.

Figure 26-9. *The web page after adding several graphic image elements*

Adding Sound

You can add two types of sounds to a web page, which a web browser will play if the computer running the web browser client is multimedia capable and has the right software, configured correctly:

- Background sounds, which play whenever someone opens the web page or refreshes the web page
- Sound objects, which play whenever they're opened (such as when someone double-clicks them)

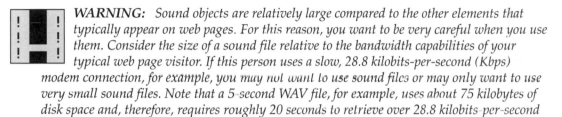 *WARNING: Sound objects are relatively large compared to the other elements that typically appear on web pages. For this reason, you want to be very careful when you use them. Consider the size of a sound file relative to the bandwidth capabilities of your typical web page visitor. If this person uses a slow, 28.8 kilobits-per-second (Kbps) modem connection, for example, you may not want to use sound files or may only want to use very small sound files. Note that a 5-second WAV file, for example, uses about 75 kilobytes of disk space and, therefore, requires roughly 20 seconds to retrieve over 28.8 kilobits-per-second modem connection.*

Adding a Background Sound

To add a background sound to a web page, follow these steps:

1. Choose the Insert menu Background Sounds command and then choose the Background Sound submenu Properties command. When you do, Word displays the Background Sound dialog box.

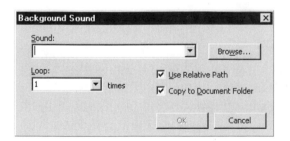

2. Click the Browse button to display the Browse dialog box. Word displays the File Open dialog box.

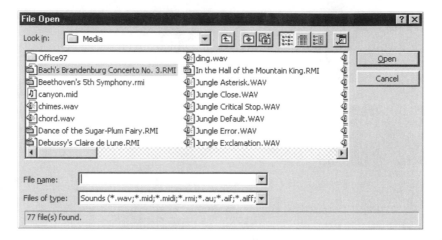

3. Use the Look in drop-down list box to select the folder that stores the sound you want to insert.

4. Activate the Files of type drop-down list box and select the Sounds file format.

5. When you see the sound file listed in the File Open dialog box, double-click it. Word redisplays the Background Sound dialog box.

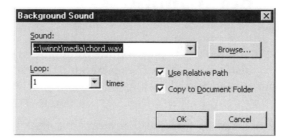

6. Use the Loop drop-down box to specify how many times you want the background sound to play. (If you want the background sound to play over and over, select Infinite from the Loop drop-down list box.)

7. Check the Use Relative Path box if you will store the sound file in the same folder as the web page. (This is usually a good idea.)

8. Check the Copy to Document Folder box if you want Word to copy the sound file from its current location to the same folder in which the web page document is stored. (Again, this is usually a good idea.) Then click OK.

Word will play the background sound as it's added to the page so that you know what your web page sounds like as it's opened. You can also play and stop playing a background sound by using the two other commands appearing on the Background

Sound submenu: Play and Stop. The Play command, of course, plays the web page's background sound. The Stop command stops the playing of a web page 's background sound.

NOTE: *The Clipart folder on the Microsoft Office CD includes several dozen example sound files, which you can use to experiment with background sounds.*

You can also add sound objects to a web page. A sound object isn't played automatically, however. A sound object is played when someone viewing the web page double-clicks the sound object. (The President of the United States web site at http://www.whitehouse.gov, for example, has a sound object that plays Socks the cat's meow.)

To add a sound object to the web page, you can use the Clip Gallery—and this is probably the easiest way to place a sound object into a web page. The only prerequisite is that the sound object needs to be listed in the Clip Gallery.

NOTE: *Chapter 3 describes how you work with the Clip Gallery.*

You can also use the Insert menu Object command to add a sound object to a web page. You will need to do this when a sound object hasn't been listed in the Clip Gallery. To use the Insert menu Object command, follow these steps:

1. Choose the Insert menu Object command. Word displays the Object dialog box.

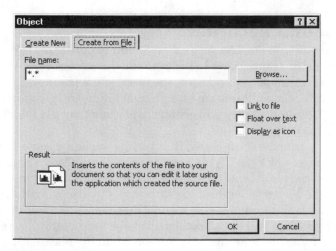

2. Click the Create from File tab.

3. Enter the complete path name for the sound object file you want to link into the File name text box. Or, if you don't know the complete path name, click the Browse command button and then use the Browse dialog box to locate and identify the sound object file. The Browse dialog box works like the Open dialog box, which Office programs display when you choose their File menu Open command.

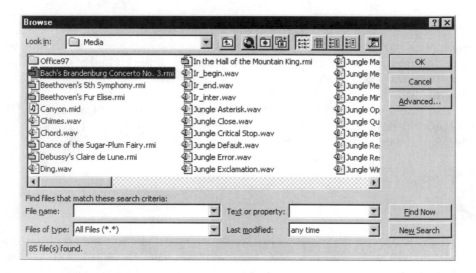

4. Click OK to insert the sound file.

Using Sound Recorder

Windows comes with an accessory called Sound Recorder that lets you play, record, and modify sound files. In order to use this accessory, your computer must have a properly installed sound card, speakers, and a microphone. Unless all three of these multimedia additions are of high quality (meaning probably fairly expensive) the sound quality you achieve will more than likely not meet your satisfaction.

To record a sound to be inserted into your web page, choose the Insert menu Object command. Click the Create New tab and choose Wave Sound from the list box, and then click OK. Windows opens Sound Recorder. Before you begin recording, you'll want to set the audio properties by choosing the Audio Properties command from the Edit menu. Click the Record button to begin recording, and when you have finished, click the Stop button. To return to your web page, choose Exit & Return to document from the File menu.

Adding Video

As mentioned in the opening paragraph of the chapter, you can add video clips to a web page, too. A video clip object is played when someone viewing the web page double-clicks or points to the video clip object. The viewer must also, of course, have all of the necessary software in order to be able to do this.

> **WARNING:** *Video clips are much larger than any of the other elements you place on a web page. As with sound files, then, you'll want to consider the relationship between the physical size of any video clips you add to a web page and the typical web visitor's Internet or intranet connection. Video clips can easily be upward of 500 kilobits in size, or about twice the size of common short sound clips. If the people visiting the web site use very slow connections, you may want to avoid the use of video images altogether or use only very short (and therefore very small) video images.*

The easiest way to add a video clip object to a web page is by using the Clip Gallery. (Chapter 3 describes how you do this.) You can also use the Insert menu Video command. (And, in fact, you'll need to do this if the video clip you want to add to a web page isn't in the Clip Gallery.)

To use the Insert menu Video command, follow these steps:

1. Choose the Insert menu Video command. Word displays the Video Clip dialog box.

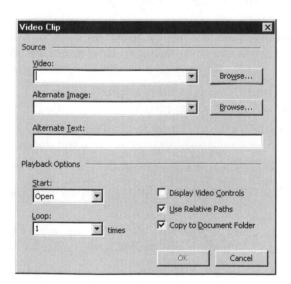

2. Click the Video text box's Browse button to display the Browse dialog box. Word displays the File Open dialog box.

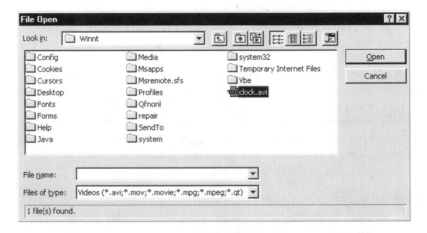

3. Use the Look in drop-down list box to select the folder that stores the video clip you want to insert.

4. When you see the video clip file listed in the File Open dialog box, double-click it. Word redisplays the Video Clip dialog box.

5. Click the Alternative Image text box's Browse button to display another File Open dialog box.

6. Use the Look in drop-down list box to select the folder that stores the alternative image you want someone to see if their web browser doesn't play video clips.

7. When you see the alternate image file listed in the File Open dialog box, double-click it. Word redisplays the Video Clip dialog box.

8. Use the Alternate Text text box to enter the alternative text you want someone to see if their web browser doesn't play video clips and doesn't show graphic images.

9. Use the Start drop-down list box to specify when the video clip should play:

   ■ Choose Open if you want the video clip to play when someone opens the web page.

   ■ Choose Mouse-over if you want the video clip to play when someone moves the mouse pointer over the video clip placeholder.

   ■ Choose Both if you want the video clip to play both when someone opens the web page and when someone moves the mouse pointer over the video clip placeholder.

10. Use the Loop drop-down list to specify how many times the video clip should play. You can choose a specific number of plays or select Infinite from the box.

11. Check the Display Video Controls box if you want the web browser to show play, stop, and pause buttons so the web page viewer can control how the video clip plays.

12. Check the Use Relative Paths box if you will store the video clip file in the same folder as the web page. (This is usually a good idea.)

13. Check the Copy to Document Folder box if you want Word to copy the video clip file from its current location to the same folder in which the web page document is stored. (Again, this is usually a good idea.) Then click OK.

NOTE: *The Mmedia subfolder of the Clipart folder on the Microsoft Office CD also includes several example video clips, which you can use to experiment with placing video clips on web pages.*

Formatting Your Web Page

You can perform all of the same document formatting for a web page that you can for a regular Word document. Because how you perform this formatting is described earlier in the book in Chapter 3, that information isn't repeated here. It is useful, however, for you to be aware of several special formatting options you have available for web pages.

Inserting Horizontal Lines

You can add interesting horizontal lines and borders to visually break up your web pages by using the Insert menu Horizontal Line command. When you choose this command, Word displays the Horizontal Line dialog box. To use one of the horizontal lines shown in the Horizontal Line dialog box, simply double-click it.

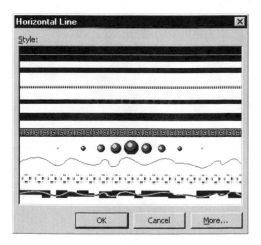

Adjusting the Web Page Background

When you create a web page using the Web Page Wizard, Word selects a background pattern fill effect and color for your web page. You aren't forced to use these selections, however. (Note that the selections are based on your answers to the Web Page Wizard's questions.) You can change both the pattern effect and its color. Keep the legibility factor in mind, however, as you change the background of your web page. You probably don't want to use a background that is so busy that it makes your viewers dizzy as they read the text on your page. You also don't want to use a dark background color if you want dark font color, and so on.

To change the background pattern color, you take the following steps:

1. Choose the Format menu Background command. Word displays a box of colored squares.

2. To use one of the colors shown in the background colors box, click it.

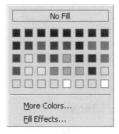

3. If you don't want to use any of the colors shown in the background colors box, click the More Colors button. Word displays the Colors dialog box with the Standard tab showing.

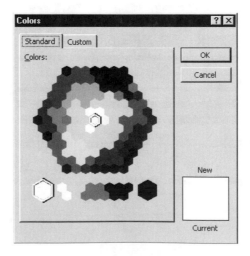

4. If you want to use the Standard tab of the Colors dialog box, click one of the honeycombs shown in the colors grid.

5. If you don't want to use the Standard tab of the Colors dialog box and instead want to mix your own color, click the Custom tab. Word displays the Custom tab of the Colors dialog box.

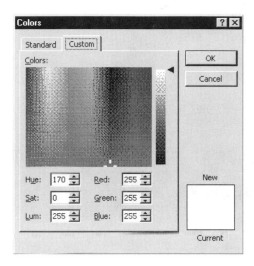

6. To use the Custom tab of the Colors dialog box, you can click a pixel in the colored rainbow-like picture that makes up most of the dialog box. Alternatively, you can precisely describe the color by using either the Hue, Sat (saturation), and Lum (luminance) boxes or the Red, Green, and Blue boxes. You can also use the luminosity slider bar to adjust the luminance of the selected color.

NOTE: You can describe, or mix, any color using the Hue, Sat, and Lum boxes or by using the Red, Green, and Blue boxes. Note, however, that the colors you pick for a web page may look different when viewed by a web site visitor.

To change the background pattern effect, you take the following steps:

1. Choose the Format menu Background command. Word displays the Background box of colored squares.

2. Click the Fill Effects button. Word displays the Fill Effects dialog box.

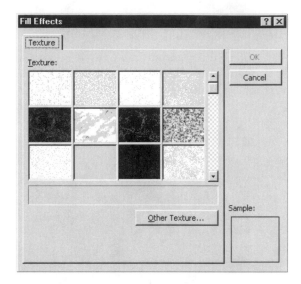

3. If you see a background fill effect in the texture list box that you want to use, double-click it. You can scroll down the texture list box to see additional background fill effects.

4. If you don't see a background fill effect in the texture list box that you want to use, click the Other Texture command button. Word displays the Select Texture dialog box.

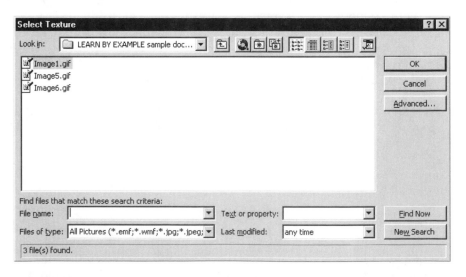

5. Use the Look in drop-down list box to select the folder that stores the graphic image you want to use in a pattern to create a background fill effect.

6. Activate the Files of type drop-down list box and select the All Pictures file format.

7. When you see the graphic image file listed in the Select Texture dialog box, double-click it. Word redisplays the Fill Effects dialog box, and now the Texture list box shows a new texture—a pattern that repeats the graphic image you selected. To use this fill effect as the web page background, double-click it.

Formatting Graphic Images

If you want to specify how a web page's text wraps (or doesn't wrap) around a graphic image you've placed on the page, you can right-click the image and choose the shortcut menu Format Picture command. When Word displays the Picture dialog box, click the Position tab and then use the Text wrapping buttons—None, Left, and Right—to describe how text should wrap around the selected graphic image. You can use the Distance from text boxes—Vertical and Horizontal—to specify how much space goes between the edge of the graphic image and the text.

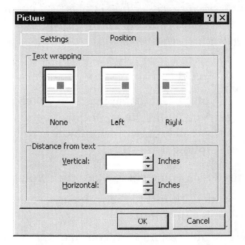

NOTE: Notice that on the Position tab, the Text wrapping button faces show (approximately) what the different text wrapping options look like.

If you click the Picture dialog box's Settings tab, you can check the Use absolute path box to indicate that the web browser should just assume that the graphic image is located in the same folder as the web page. You can also use the Text text box to provide placeholder text, which a web visitor sees in place of the graphic image if he or she is waiting for the graphic image to load or is viewing only the textual portion of a web page.

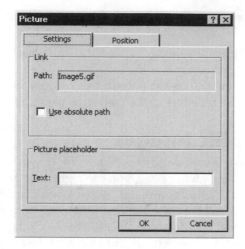

NOTE: *You don't use the Format Picture command to specify or make changes to a video clip's settings. To specify a video clip's settings, you use the Insert menu Video command. To make changes to a video clip's settings, you right-click the video clip and choose the shortcut menu Properties command.*

Adding Scrolling Text

You can tell Word that some of the text that appears on a web page should scroll, or move, across the web page. As with the other special effects you can create in Word, however, keep in mind that not all browsers can handle scrolling text. To add this scrolling text to a web page, follow these steps:

1. Click the line onto which you want to place the scrolling text.

2. If you've already added the text to the web page, select the text and then click the Standard toolbar's Cut button.

3. Choose the Insert menu Scrolling Text command. Word displays the Scrolling Text dialog box.

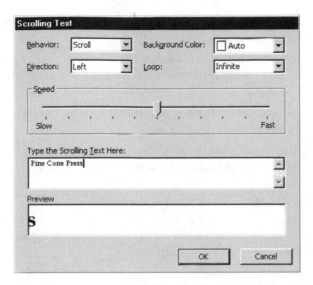

4. Type the text that you want to scroll into the Type the Scrolling Text Here box. Or, if you cut the text from the web page, click this text box and then press CTRL+V. (You press these two keys simultaneously to paste the clipboard contents into the text box.)

5. Use the Behavior drop-down list's entries to specify how you want the scrolling text to scroll:

   ■ Choose Scroll if you want the text to scroll across the screen and ultimately disappear.

   ■ Choose Slide if you want the text to scroll across the screen and then stop when it hits the side of the web page.

   ■ Choose Alternate if you want the text to scroll back and forth across the screen—visually bouncing between the sides of the web page.

6. Use the Direction drop-down list's entries—Left and Right—to specify whether the scrolling text should move from left to right or from right to left.

7. Use the Background Color drop-down list—which is simply a box of colored buttons and descriptions—to indicate what color the scrolling text's box should be.

8. Use the Loop drop-down list box to indicate how many times the text should scroll.

9. Finally, use the Speed slider button to adjust the speed of scrolling text. Figure 26-10 shows a web page that uses a scrolling text element.

LEARN BY EXAMPLE
You can open the web page shown in Figure 26-10, Figure 26-10 (example web page with scrolling text), *from the companion CD if you're following along with the discussion here in front of your computer.*

TIP: *To delete scrolling text, click the box that shows the scrolling text and then press DELETE.*

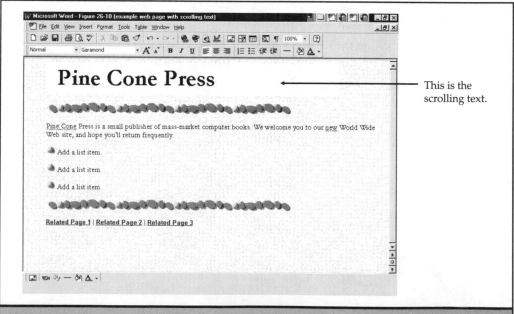

Figure 26-10. *This web page uses a scrolling text element for its title*

Creating a Form

Word includes some rudimentary tools for creating web page forms. You can't create fully functional forms with Word because to do that requires additional system files, including server software for handling the form. Nevertheless, you can, in effect, rough out a web page form by adding form buttons, boxes, and lists.

To create a web page form, you simply add form elements: check boxes, text boxes, submit and reset command buttons, option buttons, drop-down list boxes, list boxes, scrolling text boxes (also known as text areas), password boxes, and hidden fields. Forms are useful if you want to get information back from your viewers. You might create a form for viewers to send comments, or for them to submit orders for products you sell, or for them to send in their contact information. You add the elements of a form by following the same set of basic steps:

1. Choose the Insert menu Forms command so that Word displays the Forms submenu.

2. Choose the Forms submenu command that adds the form element you want to place onto the web page.

3. Resize the form element, as needed, by dragging its selection handles.

4. As needed, add text describing the form element.

Table 26-1 identifies and describes each of the commands on the Forms submenu. Figure 26-11, which follows the table, shows an example web page form under construction. Callouts identify several key elements of the form's structure. Notice, too, that web page text identifies and describes the web page form elements.

TIP: *After you finish creating a web page form, you can choose the File menu Web Page Preview command to see what your form looks like.*

Command	Description
Check Box	Adds a check box at the insertion point location. Check boxes are good for yes-or-no or multiple-choice questions.
Option Button	Adds a single option button at the insertion point location. (Word considers all of the option buttons you add to be part of the same option button set.) Option buttons are good for yes-or-no or multiple-choice questions.
Dropdown Box	Adds a one-line drop-down list box at the insertion point location. Drop-down boxes are good for choosing an item from a list.
List Box	Adds a multi-list box at the insertion point location. List boxes are good for choosing an item from a longer, often more complicated list.
Text Box	Adds a text box at the insertion point location. Text boxes are good for requesting names or addresses and other short answers.
Text Area	Adds scrolling text at the insertion point location. Text areas are good for long comment requests.
Submit	Adds a command button labeled "Submit" at the insertion point location. A submit button is obligatory in a form.
Image Submit	Chooses the Insert Picture command for you (so you can insert a picture at the insertion point location) and then turns whatever graphic image you insert into a Submit command button.
Reset	Adds a command button labeled "Reset," which returns all form elements to their original state.
Hidden	Adds a hidden field to the form at the insertion point location.
Password	Adds a password box to the form at the insertion point location. (A password box is just a text box that doesn't show you what you enter, displaying asterisk characters instead.) This is good if you are requesting personal information that people would generally want kept secure.

Table 26-1.   *Forms Menu Commands*

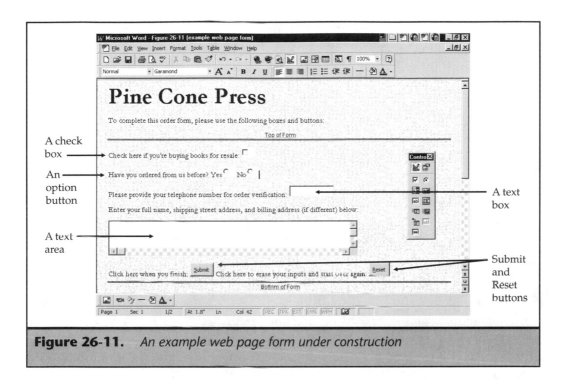

Figure 26-11. *An example web page form under construction*

EXAMPLES

LEARN BY EXAMPLE
If you want to follow along with the discussion here, you can open the example web page form shown in Figure 26-11, Figure 26-11 (example web page form) *from the companion CD.*

Working with Web Page Properties

When you create a web page, Word lets you work with two additional HTML document properties: base URLs and language encoding settings. To make these changes, you choose the File menu Properties command when the web page document is open. When you do, Word displays the Document Properties dialog box.

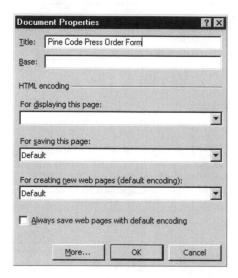

A base URL, in effect, amounts to a default web server name. Because you supply this default web server name as a web page property, you don't have to supply it every time you create a new hyperlink, thereby saving you significant amounts of time. For example, perhaps all or most of the web pages referenced by hyperlinks on a particular web page reside on this web server:

http://www.company.com/

You can enter this bit of information once in the Document Properties dialog box. Any time you provide a hyperlink in the web page that doesn't supply a web server address, the web browser will assume that it can, in effect, fill in the missing portion of the URL by looking at the base URL. For example, if you create a hyperlink that references the web page,

reports/intro.htm

a web browser can build the complete URL by combining the base URL and the relative URL supplied by the hyperlink:

http://www.company.com/reports/intro.htm

Language encoding deals with the fact that web site visitors may use a different language and, therefore, a different set of characters for viewing web page documents. By selecting languages from the Document Properties three drop-down list boxes, you can control which language's character set is used to display the web page, save the web page, and to create new web pages.

Testing Your Web Page

After you've created a web page, you need to save it in Word. Then you'll want to test it by viewing it in a web browser. Office comes with a recent version of the Internet Explorer web browser. But note that different web browsers display the same web page differently. For this reason, if the people viewing your web page will do so using other web browsers—such as a version of Netscape Navigator—you'll also want to test your web page by viewing it with these other web browsers.

All of the popular Windows-based web browsers let you open a web page stored on a local drive using their File menu Open command. This command, for the most part, works like the equivalent command in Word. You choose the command and then use the dialog box that the web browser displays to identify the web page. (In Internet Explorer and Netscape Navigator, you do need to click a standard Browse button in order to display a dialog box that lets you search your local drive's folders.)

One final comment concerns text-only browsers. Some people use text-only web browsers, for example. And other people, to increase the speed with which a web browser retrieves web pages, view only the textual portion of a web page. Be sure, therefore, to also test how your web pages look when viewed with a text-only browser or when only the textual portion of the web page is retrieved.

The Complete Reference

Office 97

Chapter 27

Web Publishing with PowerPoint

L ike Word, which is described in the preceding chapter, PowerPoint also lets you create HTML documents—the building blocks used to create web sites. If you're a proficient PowerPoint user—and you aren't familiar with a more powerful web authoring program such as Microsoft FrontPage—you can productively use PowerPoint to create simple web pages or to create rough drafts of more sophisticated web pages.

It's worthwhile to note here, too, that while some users might choose to use Word rather than PowerPoint for their web authoring activities (because they're more familiar with Word), that probably doesn't make sense. PowerPoint provides tools to easily create an entire set of web pages—such as those you might use for a personal web site. Word, in comparison, really emphasizes the creation of single, stand-alone web pages. For this reason, many web authors may want to first create a set of rough draft web pages using PowerPoint and then later edit individual web page documents using Word.

NOTE: Appendix B briefly describes what FrontPage is, how you use it, and what it does that you can't do (or can't easily do) with the simpler web authoring capabilities of a program like PowerPoint.

Creating Web Page Content

If you don't have an existing presentation from which you would like to create a set of web pages, you create web page content by running PowerPoint's AutoContent Wizard. (If you do have an existing presentation that you would like to save as an HTML document, skip ahead to the section called "Creating Your Web Pages.") The AutoContent Wizard provides several web page outlines that you can use as the basis of your web pages, including corporate home pages and personal home pages. You can choose any of these styles, but regardless of the style you choose, you must indicate that you will show your PowerPoint presentation using the Internet/Kiosk option when the AutoContent Wizard displays the dialog box shown in Figure 27-1.

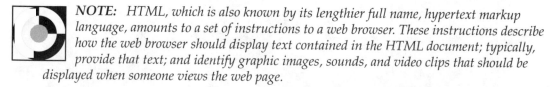

NOTE: HTML, which is also known by its lengthier full name, hypertext markup language, amounts to a set of instructions to a web browser. These instructions describe how the web browser should display text contained in the HTML document; typically, provide that text; and identify graphic images, sounds, and video clips that should be displayed when someone views the web page.

Perhaps predictably, the choice to show a presentation using the Internet affects some of the questions asked by the AutoContent Wizard. For example, after you do indicate that you want to show the presentation using the Internet (see Figure 27-1), the AutoContent Wizard requests information that would only be used on a web page (see Figure 27-2.) Furthermore, when you indicate you want to show the presentation using the Internet, the AutoContent Wizard also selects a PowerPoint design template

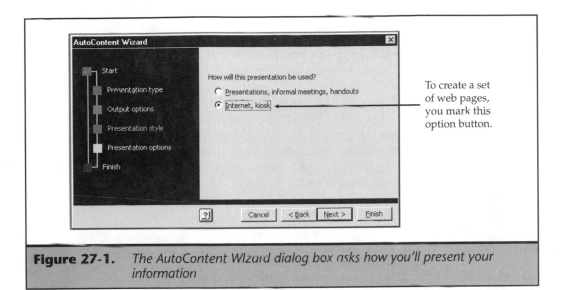

To create a set of web pages, you mark this option button.

Figure 27-1. *The AutoContent Wizard dialog box asks how you'll present your information*

that works well for web pages. Other than these minor differences, however, running the AutoContent Wizard to produce a set of web pages works just like running the AutoContent Wizard to produce any other PowerPoint presentation: you simply answer questions by clicking buttons and checking boxes, and you provide a bit of information by filling in a handful of text boxes.

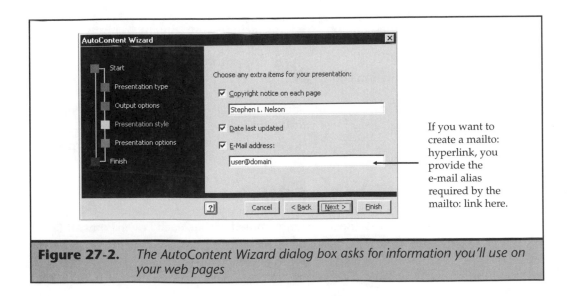

If you want to create a mailto: hyperlink, you provide the e-mail alias required by the mailto: link here.

Figure 27-2. *The AutoContent Wizard dialog box asks for information you'll use on your web pages*

About Mailto: Hyperlinks

You can create hyperlinks that point not to an Internet resource such as a web site or an FTP server, but instead provide another person's Internet e-mail address. When you click one of these hyperlinks, the web browser starts your e-mail client, creates a new message item, and then addresses the new message to the person whose e-mail address is provided as part of the hyperlink.

To create a URL for a mailto: hyperlink, you specify the protocol name as mailto: and then follow the protocol name with the e-mail address. For example, to create a URL for a mailto: hyperlink that lets you send e-mail to the President of the United States, you combine mailto: with president@whitehouse.gov as shown here:

    mailto:president@whitehouse.gov

After you run the AutoContent Wizard, you finish the PowerPoint presentation in the usual way. For example, you edit the presentation's outline, add graphic images, and perhaps insert sound and video clip objects. All of these tasks work the same way as described in this book's earlier chapters on PowerPoint. Figure 27-3 shows an outline of a presentation created as the basis for a set of web pages.

LEARN BY EXAMPLE
You can open the example presentation shown in Figure 27-3, Figure 27-3 (example Power Point presentation), *from the companion CD if you want to follow along with the discussion here.*

When you finish the presentation—and this includes any content and hyperlinks—you need to save it. Again, you do this in the usual way. Simply choose the File menu Save As command and then use the Save As dialog box to describe what name you want to use for the presentation and where it should be stored.

NOTE: For more information about adding content to a Power Point presentation, refer to Chapters 20, 21, and 22. For more information about creating a hyperlink, refer to Chapter 25.

Creating Your Web Pages

Once you create and then save the presentation, you use the presentation as the basis for creating a set of HTML documents. As noted earlier, each PowerPoint slide becomes an HTML document. To do this, choose the File menu Save As HTML command. PowerPoint then starts the Save As HTML Wizard:

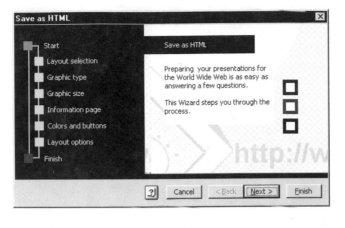

To use the Save As HTML Wizard, you take the following steps:

1. Click the Next button, provided in the first wizard dialog box, to continue to the wizard's second dialog box. The wizard's second dialog box asks you to choose a layout for your web pages.

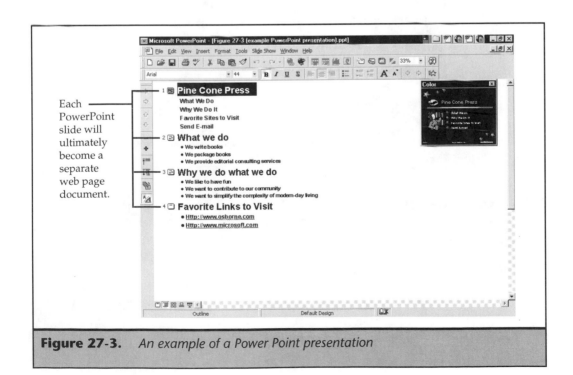

Figure 27-3. *An example of a Power Point presentation*

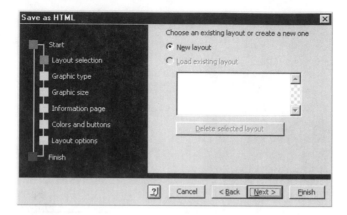

2. You can click either the New layout option button (you'll do this if this is the very first time you're using the Save As HTML Wizard) or you can click one of the existing layouts shown in the list box.

3. Click Next to continue to the wizard's third dialog box.

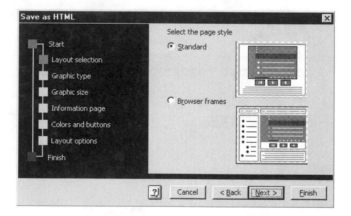

4. Indicate whether your web pages will use browser frames by clicking either the Standard or the Browser frames option button in the wizard's third dialog box. Browser frames break the web browser window into subwindows, or panes, which can then be used to show different web pages. Browser frames, therefore, can be rather useful. You might choose to show a web site's table of contents in one frame and then another web page—the one actively being viewed—in the other frame. Note, however, that some web browsers don't support the use of frames.

5. Click Next to continue to the wizard's fourth dialog box.

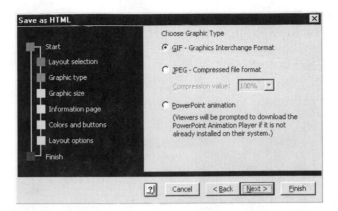

6. Indicate which file format you want to use for your graphic images. You'll typically choose either the GIF or the JPEG option button. Both graphic image file formats work with almost all web browsers. Note that if you choose the JPEG file format, you can indicate an image compression percentage. Choosing any compression value less than 100% will make your images smaller (and therefore quicker to retrieve) but also reduce their quality. You probably don't want to use the PowerPoint Animation format unless you are sure that your viewers' browsers support browser extensions.

7. Click Next to continue to the wizard's fifth dialog box.

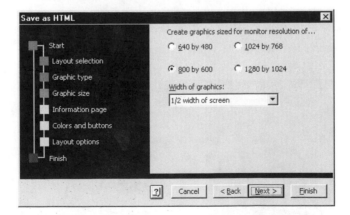

8. Indicate which monitor resolution you want to assume web site visitors will use to view your web pages by marking the option buttons shown on the fifth dialog box. (The typical screen resolution is usually either 640 by 480 or 800 by 600.) Use the Width of graphics drop-down list box to select a

defaultsize for the graphic images you'll place (and the AutoContent Wizard will place) on the web pages. If you're in doubt about either of these settings, it's best to go with the smaller values, so that you can be sure that your graphics won't be too large for your viewers' screens and won't take too long to load.

9. Click Next to continue to the wizard's sixth dialog box.

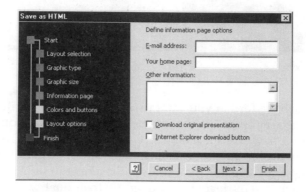

10. Use the sixth dialog box to provide general information about your web site, such as your home, or introduction, page and an e-mail address for any mailto: hyperlinks. This dialog box also includes boxes that, if checked, add hyperlinks to your introduction page so that web site visitors can download the latest version of the Internet Explorer web browser from Microsoft's web site and the complete PowerPoint presentation used to create the web site.

11. Click Next to continue to the wizard's seventh dialog box.

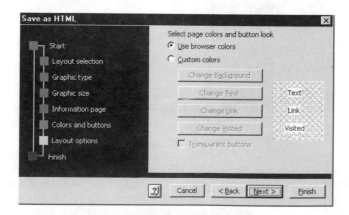

12. Optionally, use the wizard's seventh dialog box to select custom colors for the web pages. To do this, you click the Custom colors option button and then

use the Change Background, Change Text, Change Link, and Change Visited command buttons to specify which colors you want used for various elements of the web page. When you click any of these command buttons, the Save As HTML Wizard displays a pop-up dialog box from which you select a color by clicking. You can use any colors you want, but make sure that the text colors you choose are legible on the background color. Also, you probably want to have unique text, link, and visited-link colors.

13. Click Next to continue to the wizard's eighth dialog box.

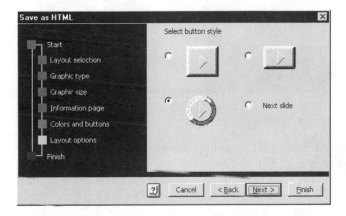

14. Select a visual look for the web page's command buttons.

15. Click Next to continue to the wizard's ninth dialog box.

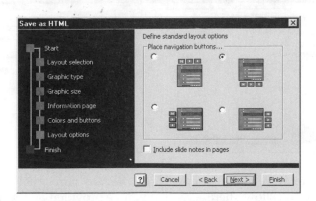

16. Use the Place navigation buttons option buttons to select a location for the command buttons that web site visitors will use to move between your web site's pages. Notice that next to the option buttons, the Save As HTML Wizard shows pictures of how the web pages will look with the navigation buttons in

the different locations. If the Place navigation buttons option buttons aren't available to you, don't worry, because they are only available for certain layouts.

17. Click Next to continue to the wizard's tenth dialog box.

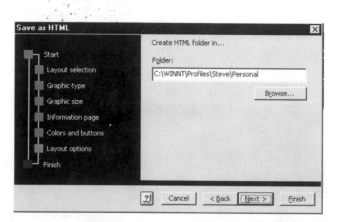

18. Provide a name and location for the new folder that PowerPoint should use to store the web pages you're creating. You can enter a complete path name in the Folder text box. Or, alternatively, you can click the Browse command button to display the Folder for HTML files dialog box, which you can use to identify where you want your web page documents stored. To use the Folder for HTML files dialog box, select a folder from the Look in drop-down list box.

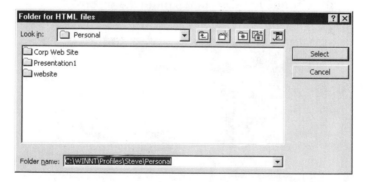

19. Click Next to move to the Save As HTML Wizard's final dialog box. This dialog box, which isn't shown here, says that you've provided all the information the wizard needs to create the set of web pages.

20. Click Finish. The Save As HTML Wizard displays a dialog box that asks if you'd like to name the HTML conversion settings (your answers to the Save As HTML Wizard's questions). Enter a name and then click Save.

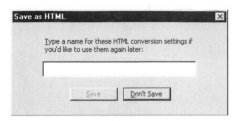

NOTE: *If in step 20 you name a set of conversion settings, you can later reuse these conversion settings by choosing them from the list box in step 2.*

After you complete step 20, the Save As HTML Wizard creates HTML documents for each of your presentation slides, placing the new HTML documents in a new subfolder inside the folder you selected in step 18. The wizard isn't creative about the way it names the new HTML documents. The HTML document created from the first PowerPoint slide is named sld001.htm. The HTML document created from the second PowerPoint slide is named sld002.htm. The subsequent HTML documents are named following the same pattern: sld003, sld004, and so on.

To name the subfolder used to store the HTML documents and their building blocks, the wizard uses the name of the original PowerPoint presentation. For example, if the name of the original PowerPoint presentation used to create the HTML document is webpages, then the wizard creates a new subfolder named webpages and stores the web pages and the web page components in this subfolder.

TIP: *To test the web pages you create using PowerPoint, open them with your web browser.*

Changing Your Web Pages

You can edit your web page documents in a variety of ways. If you want to make changes to your web pages using PowerPoint, you need to first make any changes in the original PowerPoint presentation and then resave the document. Then, after you've done this, you rerun the Save As HTML Wizard to create a new set of HTML documents. (In effect, when you do this, you're simply creating a new set of HTML documents—not editing the existing documents.)

You can also use another HTML editor to make changes to an original web page document. For example, you can use Word to edit a document. To do this, start Word, choose the File menu Open command to open the HTML document, make your changes, and then resave the web page document.

NOTE: *To open HTML documents saved in Word, you'll need to select the All Files entry from the Files of type drop-down list box.*

One advantage of editing an HTML document created by PowerPoint with another HTML editing tool is that you may get to more easily add other sorts of objects to the web page or use additional formatting. For example, with Word, you can create horizontal lines, easily edit and add large quantities of text, and use background sounds. Word also lets you create simple web page forms.

NOTE: *For more information about using Word to edit HTML documents, refer to Chapter 26.*

The Complete Reference

Chapter 28

Web Publishing with Excel

E xcel's Internet Assistant Wizard lets you take an Excel worksheet range, convert it into a web page, or HTML document, and then place it into a web page. The wizard also lets you add Excel charts to new web pages. While Excel doesn't, therefore, provide HTML editing tools, it can be very useful for Office users who want to use information from Excel workbooks in their web pages.

NOTE: *Appendix B briefly describes what FrontPage is, how you use it, and what it does that you can't do (or can't easily do) with the simpler web authoring capabilities of a program such as Excel.*

Creating Web Page Content

You don't do anything special to create Excel worksheet ranges or charts that you want to use for web pages. You build them in the usual way. To create a worksheet range you'll later use in a chapter, for example, you place labels, values, and formulas into worksheet cells, and then you add any formatting necessary to make the information more interesting or legible. To create a chart, you first collect the to-be-charted data and then you use the Chart Wizard to create the chart. Figure 28-1, for example, shows a simple Excel workbook with a small table and a simple column chart such as you might use in an HTML document.

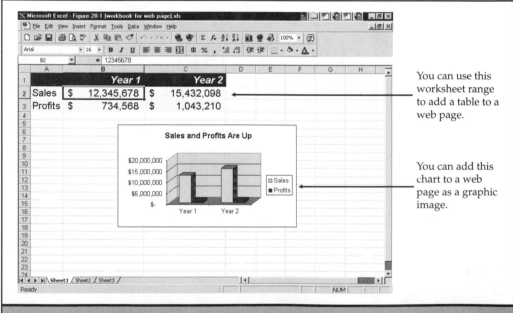

Figure 28-1. *A simple Excel workbook with information such as you might use in a web page*

NOTE: For more information about creating Excel workbooks, refer to Chapters 11, 12, and 13.

LEARN BY EXAMPLE
You can open the sample Excel workbook shown in Figure 28-1, Figure 28-1 (workbook for web page), from the companion CD if you want to follow along with the discussion here. The next section describes how to use an Excel workbook like the one shown in Figure 28-1 to add a table and a chart to a web page.

Creating Your Web Pages

Once you have an Excel workbook with the information that you want to add to a web page, you use Excel's Internet Assistant Wizard either to create a new HTML document with the Excel information or to edit an existing document by adding the information.

To add Excel worksheet ranges and Excel charts to a new web document, you take the following steps:

1. Choose the File menu Save As HTML command. Excel then starts the Internet Assistant Wizard. The wizard attempts to identify which worksheet ranges and charts you want placed on the new web page, listing these items in the Ranges and charts to convert list box.

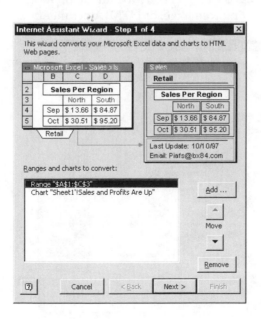

WEB PUBLISHING WITH OFFICE

2. If you want to remove a worksheet range or chart from the list of items that Excel will use to create the web page, click the item and then the Remove button.

3. If you want to add a worksheet range or chart to the list of items that the Internet Assistant Wizard will use to create the web page, click the Add button so that the Internet Assistant Wizard displays a dialog box you can use to identify another worksheet range. To identify the new worksheet range, select it in the workbook.

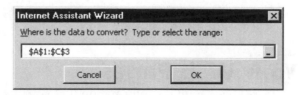

4. To rearrange the order in which the Internet Assistant Wizard adds the worksheet ranges and charts to the web page, use the Move buttons.

   ■ To move an item down the page, select it and then click the Move button that shows a downward-pointing arrow head.

   ■ To move an item up the page, select it and then click the Move button that shows an upward-pointing arrow head.

5. Click Next. The Internet Assistant Wizard next asks whether you want to create a new web page, or HTML document, or add the items you've selected to an existing web page, or HTML document.

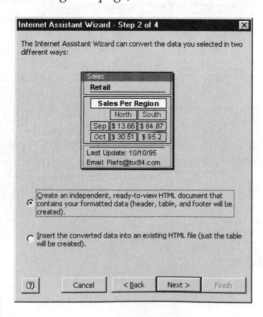

6. Click the option button that indicates you want to create an independent HTML document, and then click Next.

7. When the Internet Assistant Wizard displays its third Internet Assistant Wizard dialog box, use it to name and briefly describe the new HTML document:

- Enter a title for the web page into the Title text box. The title will appear in the Title bar of the window.

- Provide a header for the web page by entering text into the Header text box. The header will appear on the first line in the window.

- If you want, you can also provide additional web page text by entering this into the Description below header text box.

- Add a horizontal line before and after the Excel items you place on the web page by checking the two boxes related to inserting horizontal lines.

- Optionally, provide additional information for the page by filling in the Last Update on, By, and Email boxes that appear at the bottom of the dialog box. If you would like visitors to send their comments about your web page, you will want to include your e-mail address here.

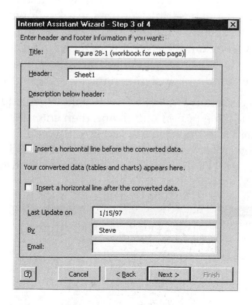

8. Click Next. The Internet Assistant Wizard displays its fourth and final dialog box.

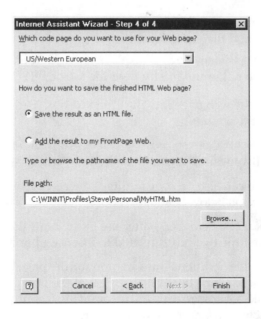

9. Indicate which code page, or character set, you want to use for your web page by selecting your alphabet description from the drop-down list box. If you created your Excel workbook characters from English or any western European language, for example, you choose the US/Western European option. If you created your Excel workbook using some other character set—Japanese, for example—select this character set from the drop-down list.

10. To tell the Internet Assistant Wizard to create a new web page, click the Save the result as an HTML file option button and then enter the complete path for the HTML document into the File path text box. If you don't know the path name, click the Browse button and then use the Save Your HTML document as dialog box to name the HTML document and specify its storage location.

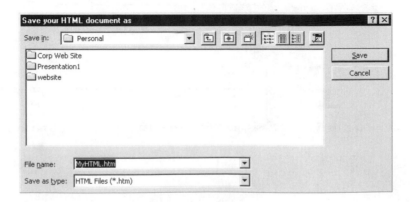

NOTE: *You can also tell the Internet Assistant Wizard to add the web page to a FrontPage web, if you've installed FrontPage on your computer. If you choose this option, the wizard prompts you for the name of the FrontPage web to which you want to add the new HTML document. For more information about FrontPage, refer to Appendix B.*

11. Click Finish. The Internet Assistant creates the new web page using the specified name and location.

Figure 28-2 shows an example web page created by adding a table (based on an Excel worksheet range) and a chart, displayed with the Internet Explorer web browser.

LEARN BY EXAMPLE
The companion CD includes a copy of the web page document shown in Figure 28-2, Figure 28-2 (web page with Excel items).

To add an Excel worksheet range to an existing web document—you can't add a chart to an existing document—you take the following steps:

1. Using an HTML editor such as Microsoft Word, open the HTML document to which you want to add the Excel worksheet range. (The worksheet range gets

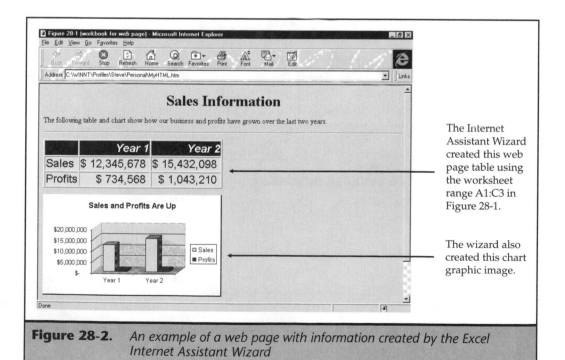

Figure 28-2.   *An example of a web page with information created by the Excel Internet Assistant Wizard*

added as a table.) Then, enter the following HTML instruction at the exact location where you want the new table placed:

= <!-##Table##->

2. Save and then close the HTML document. You can also close your HTML editing program.

NOTE: If you use Word for editing the existing HTML document, know that you can display the actual HTML instructions for the open web page by choosing the View menu HTML Source command.

3. Start Excel and then open the Excel workbook with the worksheet range you want to use as a web page table.

4. Choose the File menu Save As HTML command. Excel then starts the Internet Assistant Wizard. The wizard attempts to identify which worksheet ranges and charts you want placed on the new web page, listing these items in the Ranges and charts to convert list box.

NOTE: You can't add charts to an existing web page—you can only add Excel worksheet ranges.

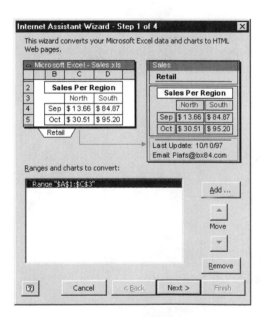

5. If you want to remove a worksheet range from the list of items that the wizard will use to create the web page, click the item and then the Remove button.

6. If you want to add a worksheet range to the list of items that the wizard will use to create the web page, click the Add button so that the Internet Assistant Wizard displays a dialog box you can use to identify another worksheet range. To identify the new worksheet range, select it in the workbook.

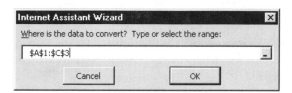

7. To rearrange the order in which the Internet Assistant Wizard adds the worksheet ranges to the web page, use the Move buttons.

   ■ To move an item down the page, select it and then click the Move button that shows a downward-pointing arrow head.

   ■ To move an item up the page, select it and then click the Move button that shows an upward-pointing arrow head.

8. Click Next. The Internet Assistant Wizard asks whether you want to create a new web page, or HTML document, or add the items you've selected to an existing web page, or HTML document.

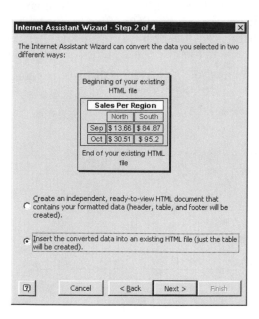

9. Click the option button that indicates you want to add the Excel item to an existing web page, and then click Next. The Internet Assistant displays the third dialog box.

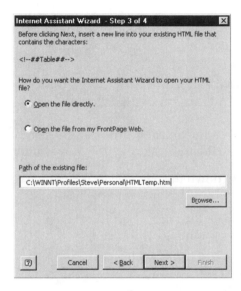

10. Click the Open the file directly option button and then enter the complete path for the HTML document into the Path of the existing file text box. (If you don't know the path name, click the Browse button and then use the Select Your HTML file dialog box to identify the .htm document and its location.)

11. Click Next. The Internet Assistant Wizard displays its fourth and final dialog box.

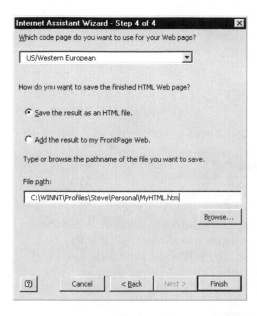

12. Indicate which code page, or character set, you want to use for your web page by selecting your alphabet description from the drop-down list box. If you created your Excel workbook characters from English or any western European language, for example, you choose the US/Western European option. If you created your Excel workbook using some other character set—Japanese, for example—select this character set from the drop-down list.

13. To tell the Internet Assistant Wizard to create a new web page, click the Save the result as an HTML file and then enter the complete path for the HTML document into the File path text box. If you don't know the path name, click the Browse button and then use the Save your HTML document as dialog box to name the HTML document and specify its storage location.

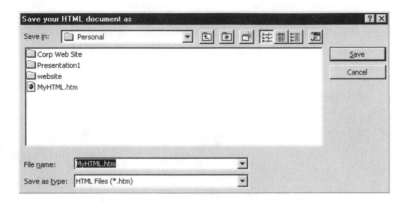

NOTE: *You can also tell the Internet Assistant Wizard to add the web page to a FrontPage web, if you've installed FrontPage on your computer. If you choose this option, the Internet Assistant Wizard prompts you for the name of the FrontPage web to which you want to add the new HTML document. For more information about FrontPage, refer to Appendix B.*

14. Click Finish. The Internet Assistant creates the new web page using the specified name and location.

Changing Your Web Pages

You can't actually use Excel for HTML editing. So, you won't use it for making changes to a web page you create or a web page you modify. You can, however, use another HTML editor to make changes to an original web page document. For example, you can use Word to edit a web page you've created with Excel and its Internet Assistant Wizard. To do this, start Word, choose the File menu Open command to open the HTML document, make your changes, and then resave the web page document.

NOTE: *To open HTML documents, you'll need to select the HTML Document entry from the Files of type drop-down list box.*

If you do use another HTML editing tool such as Word, you may get to more easily add other sorts of objects to the web page or use additional formatting. For example, with Word, you can create horizontal lines, easily edit and add large quantities of text, and use background sounds. Word also lets you create simple web page forms.

NOTE: *For more information about using Word to edit HTML documents, refer to Chapter 26.*

Creating Forms with Excel

Excel comes with an add-in tool called the Web Form Wizard. You can use this tool to construct the basic building blocks a web site administrator uses to set up and then use web page forms. To install this add-in, you choose the Tools menu Add-Ins command and check the Web Form Wizard box on the Add-Ins dialog box. (The Add-Ins dialog displays a long list of check boxes so you have to scroll down the list to see the Web Form Wizard check box.)

Once you install the Web Form Wizard add-in, you need to create a form. You can use the Forms toolbar to add option buttons, drop-down list boxes, and the like. To display the Forms toolbar, choose the View menu Toolbars command and the Toolbars submenu Forms command. You can enter the options you want displayed in your lists off to the side of the range of cells you are using as your form. You can then link the range to the list by right-clicking the form field and choosing the shortcut menu Format Control command. Click the Control tab and enter the input range in the Input range box, as shown here.

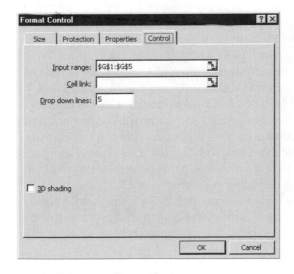

To make check boxes or option buttons marked or unmarked by default, right-click the check box or option button and choose the shortcut menu Format Control command. In the Format Control dialog box, click the Control tab, and then mark either the Checked or Unchecked option button.

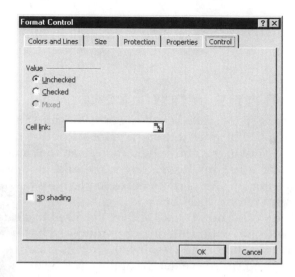

Once you have your form completed, you will want to protect your worksheet so that visitors to your web form can only enter data into specific cells. To do this, select the cells into which you want your visitors to enter information. Then choose the Format menu Cells command. Click the Protection tab and clear the Locked check box. When you have finished unlocking these cells, you lock all others so that they cannot be changed. You do this by choosing the Tools menu Protection command and the Protection submenu Protect Sheet command.

Once your form is complete and protected, you run the Web Form Wizard by choosing the Tools menu Wizard command and then the Wizard submenu Web Form command. The Web Form Wizard will take you through a series of steps that ask you to specify which form fields and cells you want visitors to fill out with data. The Web Form Wizard asks you to describe and name the confirmation message file you want your visitors to receive once they fill out and submit your form. The Web Form Wizard will also create a database for receiving the data your visitors submit. In order for the Web Form Wizard to work properly, you should see your Web administrator for help in configuring the data-gathering system.

Note that if you want to create web page forms, while you can use Excel and its Web Form Wizard, you'll find the process much easier if you simply move up to using a real, full-featured web publishing program such as Microsoft FrontPage.

Chapter 29

Web Publishing with Access

A ccess includes a Publish to the Web Wizard that lets you publish database objects as web pages. Interestingly, you can publish either static, unchanging "pictures" of database objects or dynamic, continually updated "pictures" of database objects. In both cases, however, you'll find it surprisingly easy to publish database information.

Creating a Web Database

Before you can publish database information using Access's Publish to the Web Wizard, you'll need to create and then fill the database. This chapter doesn't describe how you create and fill a database. Chapters 16–19 describe how you do this; you may want to refer there if you have questions.

> *NOTE: If you are going to use a database's information for web publishing, you'll probably want to consider this fact when you design the database, its forms, and its reports.*

Using the Publish to the Web Wizard

After you've created or located the database with the objects you want to publish, you use the Publish to the Web Wizard to identify the objects you want to include on web pages and to describe how you want the web pages to look.

> *NOTE: The Publish to the Web Wizard creates a separate web page for each datasheet, each form, and for each page of a report.*

To use the Publish to the Web wizard, you take the following steps:

1. Open the database with objects you want to publish to web pages.
2. Choose the File menu Save As HTML command. Access starts the Publish to Web Wizard, and it displays its first dialog box.

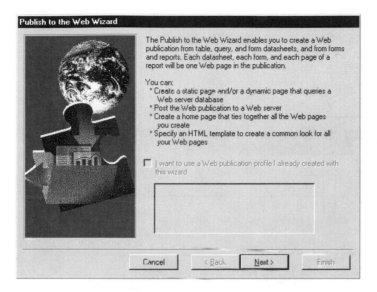

The following describes the "Publish to the Web Wizard" dialog box shown:

> **Publish to the Web Wizard**
>
> The Publish to the Web Wizard enables you to create a Web publication from table, query, and form datasheets, and from forms and reports. Each datasheet, each form, and each page of a report will be one Web page in the publication.
>
> You can:
> * Create a static page and/or a dynamic page that queries a Web server database
> * Post the Web publication to a Web server
> * Create a home page that ties together all the Web pages you create
> * Specify an HTML template to create a common look for all your Web pages
>
> ☐ I want to use a Web publication profile I already created with this wizard
>
> Cancel   < Back   Next >   Finish

3. Click the Next button so that the wizard displays the dialog box shown in Figure 29-1.

4. Select the database objects you want to publish. To do this, click a tab to show the tab's category of database objects. Then, check the boxes that represent the specific database objects.

5. Click the Next button so that the wizard displays the dialog box shown next. Then enter into the text box the complete path name for the default HTML template you want to use as the basis for designing your web page. The HTML template will provide such things as background and text colors and layout. If you don't know the complete path name of the HTML template, click the Browse button. Then select the HTML template from the Select an HTML Template dialog box, which the wizard displays.

TIP: *You aren't required to specify an HTML document template.*

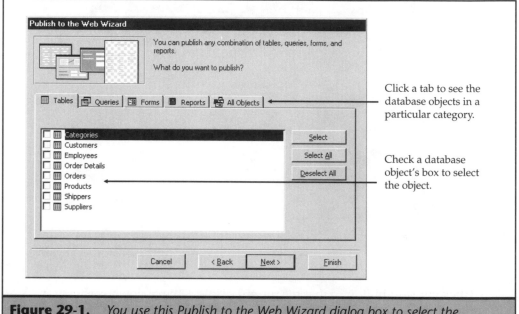

Figure 29-1. *You use this Publish to the Web Wizard dialog box to select the database objects you want to publish*

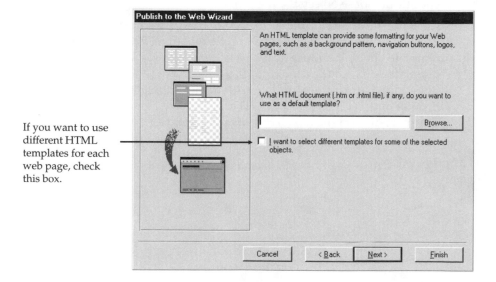

6. Click the Next button so that the wizard displays the dialog box shown in Figure 29-2.

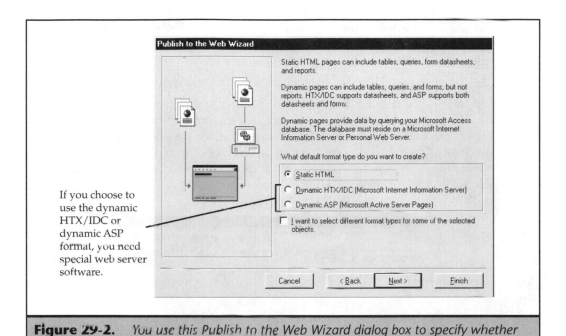

If you choose to use the dynamic HTX/IDC or dynamic ASP format, you need special web server software.

Figure 29-2. *You use this Publish to the Web Wizard dialog box to specify whether you want to use dynamically updated web pages or static web pages*

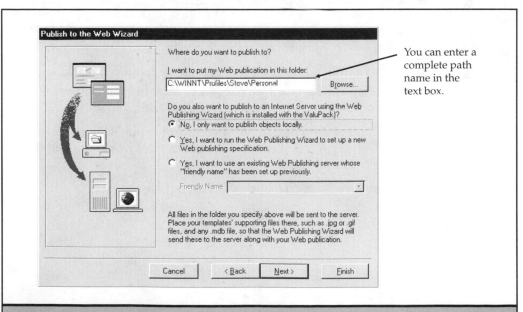

You can enter a complete path name in the text box.

Figure 29-3. *You use this Publish to the Web Wizard dialog box to identify the folder you want to use to store the pages the Publish to Web Wizard will create*

7. If you want to work with traditional, static web pages, mark the Static HTML option button. If you want to work with dynamic web pages, mark one of the other option buttons.

8. Click Next so that the wizard displays the dialog box shown in Figure 29-3.

9. Provide a name and location for the new folder that Access should use to store the web pages you're creating. You can click the Browse command button to display the Choose a directory for the objects you have selected dialog box, which you can use to identify where you want your web page documents stored. To use the Choose a directory for the objects you have selected dialog box, select a folder from the Look in drop-down list box.

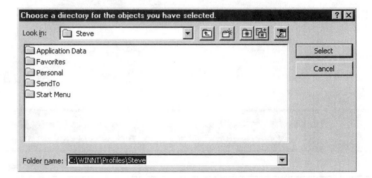

10. Use the option buttons provided by the dialog box shown in Figure 29-3 to indicate where you want to publish the new pages:

   ■ Choose the first option button—the one that refers to publishing objects locally—if you'll place the new web pages on a local machine either for use in a simple intranet or as a temporary storage location.

   ■ Choose the second or third option box if you want to publish your new web pages to a web server. (For information about how this works, consult the web server's site administrator.)

11. Click Next so that the wizard displays the dialog box shown here:

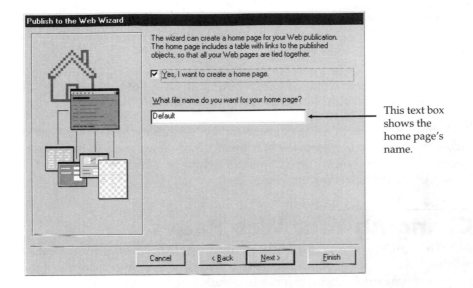

This text box shows the home page's name.

12. Check the box shown on the preceding illustration if you want to create a home page that acts as a table of contents listing all of your published database objects. You typically want to use this option whenever you're publishing multiple database objects. If you do check the box, use the text box to name the home page.

13. Click Next so that the wizard displays the dialog box shown here:

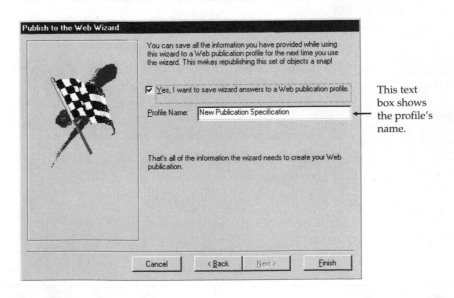

This text box shows the profile's name.

14. Check the box shown in the preceding illustration if you want to save the database web publishing information you just created in the wizard. If you do check the box, use the text box to name the profile.

15. Click Finish. The Publish to the Web Wizard creates HTML documents using the database objects you selected. You can try it out by opening the HTML document in your web browser.

Figure 29-4 shows a home page created by the Publish to the Web Wizard. (The Figure uses information from the Northwind Traders sample database that comes with Access.) Figure 29-5 shows the Customers web page, which appears if you click the Customers hyperlink shown in Figure 29-4.

Changing Your Web Pages

As with Excel, you can't actually use Access for HTML editing. For this reason, you won't use Access for making changes to a web page that you create using the Publish to the Web Wizard—except by rerunning the wizard.

NOTE: By using an HTML editor—such as Word—you can add other objects to the web page or use additional formatting.

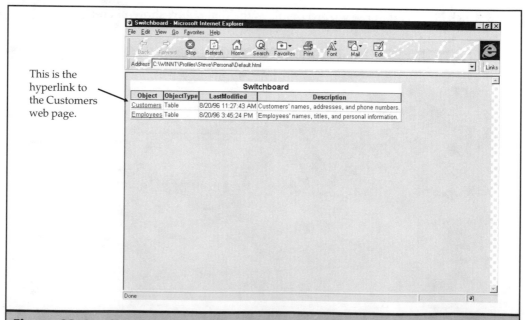

This is the hyperlink to the Customers web page.

Figure 29-4. *You create this web page by indicating you want a home page that lists the published database objects*

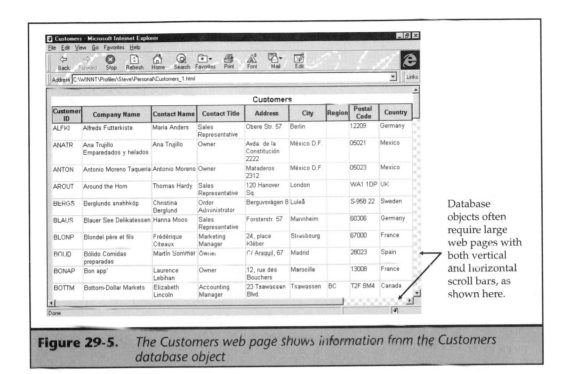

Figure 29-5. *The Customers web page shows information from the Customers database object*

You can use another HTML editor to make changes to web page documents you create with Access, however. For example, you can use Word to edit a web page you've created with Access and its Publish to the Web Wizard. To do this, start Word, choose the File menu Open command to open the HTML document, make your changes, and then resave the web page document. (To open HTML documents, you'll need to select the HTML Document entry from the Files of type drop-down list box.) For more information about using Word to edit HTML documents, refer to Chapter 26.

Chapter 30

Internet Explorer and Office

Office comes with the Internet Explorer, Microsoft's web browser software. For this reason, this chapter provides a fast-paced description of how you use this tool to view and access Internet resources. (If you're an experienced Internet Explorer user—or you've used another graphical web browser—you won't need this primer information.) Following that discussion, the chapter describes in some detail how you use Internet search services such as Yahoo! and AltaVista to find information.

Using Internet Explorer

Internet Explorer isn't difficult to use. In fact, the ease with which it's possible to browse web servers and web pages largely explains the popularity of the Internet, and in particular the World Wide Web. Nevertheless, using Internet Explorer (or any other web browser) can be confusing if you're new to the logic and operation of web browsers.

NOTE: For the purposes of this chapter, you'll find it extremely valuable to possess the information contained in the first section in Chapter 25.

Starting Internet Explorer

You start the Internet Explorer the same way you start other programs. You can, for example, click the Start button and choose Internet Explorer from the Programs menu.

You can open a document file that Windows knows needs to be opened with a web browser. (For example, you can open an HTML, or web page document.) And you can double-click the Internet shortcut icon, which may appear on your Windows desktop.

If you connect to the Internet using Windows' dialup networking feature, however, you can't begin to view web documents that aren't on your own computer or local area network until you first connect to an Internet service provider's network. Once you make this connection, however, your computer actually becomes part of the Internet for the duration of the connection.

NOTE: Windows 95, Windows NT, and their successor versions let you make two types of dialup networking connections: PPP (which stands for Point-to-Point Protocol) and SLIP (which stands for Serial Line Internet Protocol). If you have a choice—and your Internet service provider is the person who gives or doesn't give this choice—make your connection using PPP. PPP results in a faster connection, and it's generally easier to set up.

You can make your dialup networking connection in two basic ways. It's quite likely that you can simply start Internet Explorer. As a general rule, if you either

directly or indirectly request to view some web page and the Internet Explorer senses
that you aren't connected to the Internet, the Internet Explorer prompts you to make
the dialup networking connection. For example, if you're using Microsoft Network as
your Internet service provider, Windows displays the Microsoft Network Sign In
dialog box, and you provide your user name and password.

After you provide the sign-on information, Windows connects your computer to
the Microsoft Network and the Internet.

A second way to connect to the Internet (so you can begin viewing web pages)
also exists. You can tell Windows to make the dialup networking connection first.
For example, you can start the Dial-up Networking program by clicking the Start
button and choosing the Programs menu Accessories command and the Accessories
submenu Dial-Up Networking command.

The first time you make a dialup networking connection, by the way, you need to
describe in precise technical detail how the connection is made. To do this, you need to
get detailed instructions from your Internet service provider. Note that one of the
advantages of using a large Internet service provider such as the Microsoft Network is
that you don't have to get mired in the technical details of making a dialup
networking connection. You simply install Microsoft Network by running the
Microsoft Network Setup Wizard, and it does most of the rest of the work of
configuring the dialup networking connection. Note also that not all Internet service
providers, regardless of size, support dialup networking.

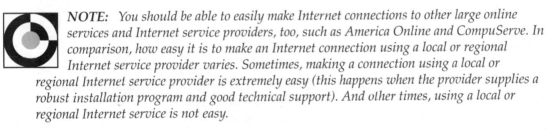

*NOTE: You should be able to easily make Internet connections to other large online
services and Internet service providers, too, such as America Online and CompuServe. In
comparison, how easy it is to make an Internet connection using a local or regional
Internet service provider varies. Sometimes, making a connection using a local or
regional Internet service provider is extremely easy (this happens when the provider supplies a
robust installation program and good technical support). And other times, using a local or
regional Internet service is not easy.*

After you successfully make the dialup networking connection and start Internet
Explorer, you see your start page, as shown in Figure 30-1. Some people also call the
first page you see a home page. Note that it may take several seconds for your
computer and web browser to retrieve the start page from the web server on which it
resides. But after Internet Explorer loads your start page, you can begin moving to
other web pages in a variety of ways.

Viewing Web Pages

You can move from one web page to another web page in a variety of ways: by
clicking hyperlinks, by entering URLs directly into the Address box, by using the Back
and Forward buttons, and by selecting web pages from either your history list or
favorite places folder.

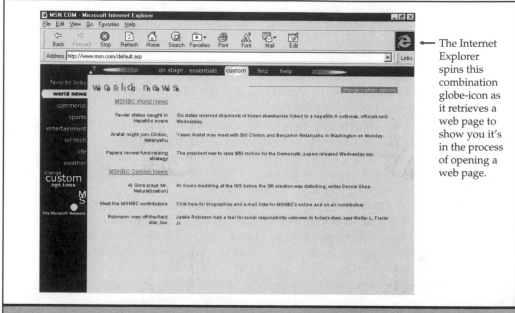

The Internet Explorer spins this combination globe-icon as it retrieves a web page to show you it's in the process of opening a web page.

Figure 30-1.   *The Internet Explorer showing a custom MSN start page*

Clicking Hyperlinks

As described in Chapter 25, the easiest way to move from one web page to another web page is by clicking a hyperlink. You can typically identify hyperlinks three ways. First, the web page itself usually identifies any hyperlinks, either by providing description text such as "click here" or by formatting the text or graphic image in a certain way. Typically, for example, textual hyperlinks show in color and with underlining to stand out on the web page:

News for You:

IT Executive

System Pro

Small Business

Home/Personal Computing

Games

Your web browser also identifies hyperlinks, however, and it does so in two ways, as shown in Figure 30-2. If you mouse over a hyperlink, the web browser changes the mouse point to a pointing finger. Sometimes, the web browser also displays a pop-up box that names the hyperlink.

Using the Back, Next, Stop, and Refresh Buttons

As you move from web page to web page, you may notice that Internet Explorer activates the Back and Forward buttons, which show on its toolbar. You can click the Back button to redisplay the web page you were just viewing. If you've just clicked the Back button, you can click the Forward button to go back to the web page you were viewing before you clicked the Back button.

TIP: *If you want to change the font point size of the text shown in the Internet Explorer program window, click the Font toolbar button. Repeatedly clicking this button cycles through a variety of larger and smaller font point sizes.*

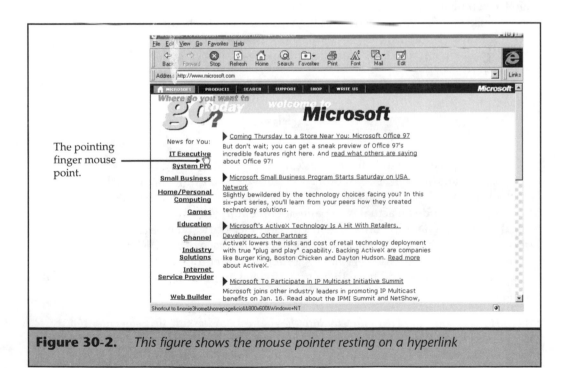

Figure 30-2.   *This figure shows the mouse pointer resting on a hyperlink*

Because Internet Explorer caches, or stores, web pages you've recently viewed on your desktop or laptop computer, you'll find that Internet Explorer redisplays web pages very quickly.

 NOTE: Later in the chapter, the section entitled, "Fine-Tune the Cache" describes how you can adjust and fine-tune the web page cache.

If you want to retrieve a new copy of a web page—perhaps because the web page is frequently updated or because you want to make sure that you're grabbing the web page from its web server and not from a local cache, you click the Refresh button.

If a web page takes a long time to retrieve, you can click the Stop button to tell Internet Explorer that it should give up on retrieving a web page you've requested. (Anything more than about a minute is a long time if you're using a dialup networking connection.)

Entering a URL into the Address Box

While clicking hyperlinks and toolbar buttons is the easiest way to move from web page to web page, you (thankfully) aren't limited to following a trail of hyperlinks. You can also enter a URL directly into the Address box. To do this, click the Address box and then type the URL. If you want to view the web pages at the web site http://www.whitehouse.gov/, for example, you simply type this URL into the Address box.

You don't need to include the http:// prefix if you're visiting a web server. Internet Explorer (as well as most other web browsers) assume that the URL you've entered is for a web site if you don't specify the Internet protocol. You also typically don't need to include an actual web page document in your URL; web servers will typically supply a default home page if you don't identify some other page by name. This means that it's usually quickest to just enter the piece of the URL that falls between the http:// and the very next /. Entering this chunk of the URL takes you to the default home page, and from there you can click hyperlinks to get to the different web page documents.

 TIP: As you enter URLs directly into the Address box, be sure that you enter the periods as periods (and not as commas) and that you enter the slashes as slashes (and not as backslashes).

The Address Box, as you'll notice from Figure 30-2, is actually a combo box. If you activate its drop-down list, Internet Explorer displays a list of URLs for web pages and servers you've recently visited. To revisit any of the web pages or servers you see listed, select it from the list.

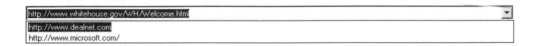

NOTE: *The Internet Explorer actually maintains a history list of web pages and web sites you've visited. It's this list you see when you activate the Address drop-down list box.*

Using a Favorite Places Folder

If you find or discover a web page that you want to revisit, you can tell Internet Explorer to record the web site's URL in your Favorite Places folder. To add the web page you're currently viewing to the Favorite Places folder, choose the Favorites menu Add To Favorites command. Then, when Internet Explorer displays the Add to Favorites dialog box, click the Create in button so that Internet Explorer expands the dialog box to show the Favorites folder's subfolders, select the folder you want to store the web page's URL in, and then click OK.

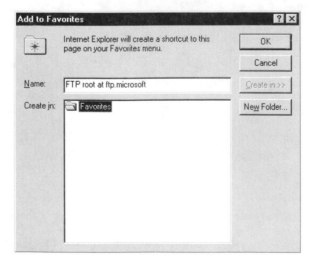

NOTE: *If you want to create a new subfolder, select the folder into which you want to place the subfolder, click the New Folder button, and then enter a name for the new folder using the dialog box that Internet Explorer provides.*

To view a web page you've recorded in the Favorites folder, you activate the Favorites menu and then click the web page (if it's listed on the Favorites menu). To visit a web page you've recorded in a subfolder in the Favorites folder, activate the Favorites menu, click the subfolder you used to store the web page, and then click the web page. (The Favorites menu, in other words, lists the web pages you've recorded in the Favorites folder and any subfolders you've created in the Favorites folder.)

Saving Web Page Information

You can save the information shown in the Internet Explorer window in a couple of predictable ways. You can, for example, print the web page. And you can save the HTML document (or some portion of the HTML document) to your desktop's or laptop's local drive.

Printing HTML Documents

You can always print an HTML document displayed in the Internet Explorer window. To do so, click the Print command button to display the Print dialog box. Then use its buttons and boxes to describe how you want the web page printed.

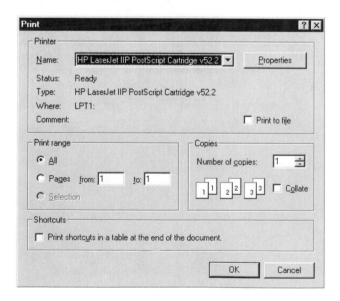

NOTE: *For more information about how you print document files—including HTML documents—refer to Chapter 2.*

Saving HTML Documents

You can save the text that a web page shows by choosing the File menu Save As File command. When Internet Explorer displays the Save As dialog box, shown in Figure 30-3, use the Save in drop-down list box to indicate the folder where the file should be stored. Then use the File name box to name the HTML document. Note that while you can specify the file format as either HTML or plain text, if you do create an HTML document, the HTML document won't show any of its graphical images. You need to separately save any graphic images you want to keep, as described in the paragraph that follows this one.

Saving Graphic Images

You can save a graphic image shown on a web page by right-clicking the image and then choosing the shortcut menu Save Picture as command. When you do this, the Internet Explorer displays the same Save As dialog box that you use to save an HTML or plain text file. You use its Save in drop-down list box to indicate the folder where the graphic image should be stored. Optionally, you can use the File name box to provide a new name for the graphic image and the Save as type drop-down list box to specify a different file format than the image's native format (gif or bmp).

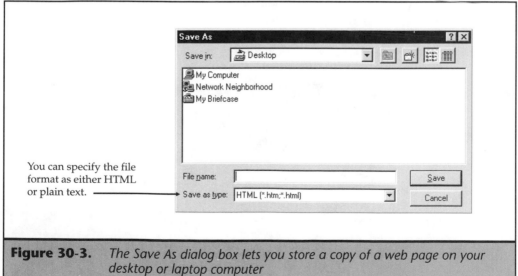

You can specify the file format as either HTML or plain text.

Figure 30-3. *The Save As dialog box lets you store a copy of a web page on your desktop or laptop computer*

Retrieving Files Via Web Pages

Many web pages include hyperlinks that point not to other web pages, but instead point to a file. When you click the hyperlink, your web browser downloads the file. If you do click a hyperlink that points to a downloadable file, Internet Explorer displays the dialog box that follows:

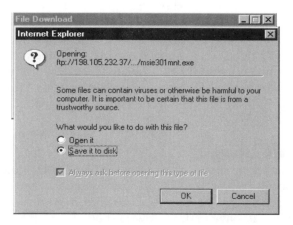

To confirm that you do indeed want to either save or open the file, click the appropriate option button and then OK. You probably want to think twice about downloading files unless you are fairly certain the source is reputable because it is very easy to get viruses from the Internet, and even if you are running an antivirus program, you aren't protected from each and every virus. After you click OK, Internet Explorer next displays the Save As dialog box (as shown in Figure 30-3), which you can use to specify where the file should be saved and what it should be named. When you provide this information and click OK, Internet Explorer begins downloading the file, displaying the dialog box that follows to apprise you of its progress. To stop downloading a file, of course, you just click Cancel.

Accessing Other Internet Resources

Internet Explorer lets you access Internet resources in addition to those provided by web sites. You can retrieve files from FTP sites, use Gopher menus, Telnet, and even browse and post newsgroup articles.

Using FTP Sites

You can view and retrieve files from FTP sites by entering the FTP site's URL into the Address box. Figure 30-4, for example, shows the Microsoft Corporation FTP site root directory. To move to a subdirectory, you click the directory name. To retrieve a file, you right-click the file, choose the Save Target As command from the shortcut menu, and then complete the Save As dialog box that Internet Explorer displays.

NOTE: The FTP protocol is specifically tailored for moving files between Internet computers.

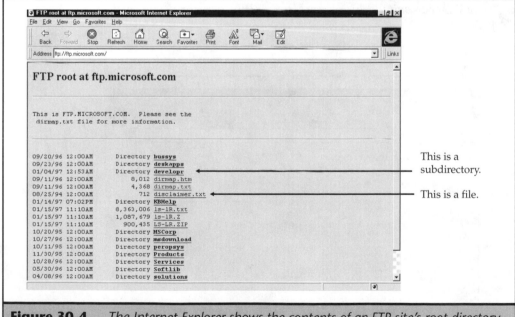

This is a subdirectory.

This is a file.

Figure 30-4.   *The Internet Explorer shows the contents of an FTP site's root directory*

Using Gopher Sites

Gopher servers create menus of Internet resources. To use a Gopher server, you first enter the Gopher server's URL into the Address box. Then, you begin choosing menu commands. At first, the menu commands you choose will just display submenus of commands, as shown in Figure 30-5. But ultimately, as you burrow down through the levels of menus, you'll find files you can open or retrieve.

Using Telnet Sites

Some hyperlinks you click lead to Telnet sites. When you connect to a Telnet site, your computer in effect becomes a dumb terminal connected to the Telnet site's computer. If you initiate a Telnet session, Internet Explorer starts the Telnet client that comes with Windows 95, Windows NT, and their successors, as shown in Figure 30-6.

When you finish working with a Telnet site, follow whatever instructions you were given for logging off of the Telnet site and then choose the Connect menu Disconnect command.

 NOTE: *For more information about working with the Windows Telnet client, refer to the Windows online help or a good book on Windows and the Internet.*

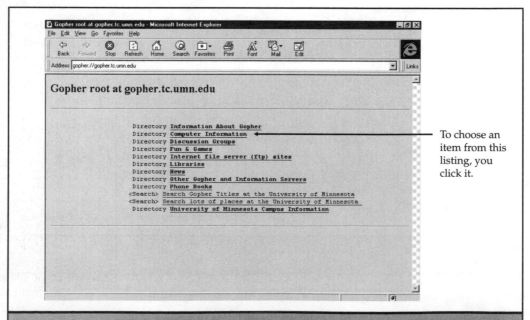

Figure 30-5. *The Internet Explorer shows the contents of a Gopher site's root directory*

Once you start a Telnet session, you follow the Telnet site's onscreen instructions for working with the system.

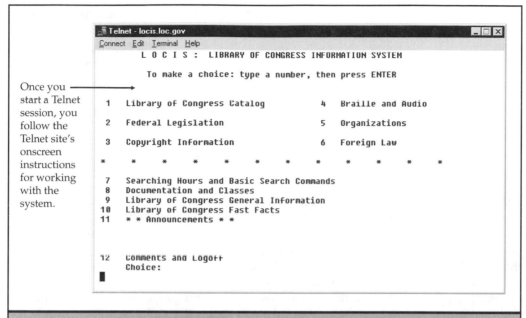

Figure 30-6. *When you click a Telnet hyperlink, the Internet Explorer starts the Windows Telnet client*

Using Internet Mail

You can send and receive Internet Mail from within the Internet Explorer program. To do this, click the Mail button and choose the New Message command from the menu that Internet Explorer displays. Internet Explorer then starts Outlook so you can create and send a message item.

NOTE: For more information about sending e-mail or about Outlook, refer to Chapter 23.

Troubleshooting Common Problems

While the Internet, and especially the World Wide Web, are easy to use, you may encounter several problems as you start out. For the most part, however, these problems are relatively easy to address.

Slow Transmission Times

Perhaps the most common problem that people encounter is slow transmission. Richly illustrated HTML documents—the kind that are most fun to view—take time to download from a web site. And this is especially true when you're connecting to the web site over a slow, 28.8Kbps dialup networking connection. HTML documents that include sound, video, and other exotic objects take even longer. Fortunately, there are several things you can do to at least mitigate the problem of slow transmission times.

CHOOSE A SMART START PAGE   As mentioned as the beginning of the chapter, Internet Explorer loads a start page every time it starts. While that's usually fine, it doesn't make sense to spend any time waiting for Internet Explorer to load a start page you don't read. You can change the start page that Internet Explorer loads by choosing the View menu Options command, clicking the Navigation tab, and then entering the URL of the start page you do want to load into the Address box.

SKIP THE PICTURES, SOUNDS, AND VIDEO   One other technique you can easily use to speed up transmission time is to *not* load the pictures, sounds, and video for each web page you open. To make this adjustment, you choose the View menu Options command and click the General tab, shown in Figure 30-8. Then you uncheck the Show Pictures, Play Sounds, and Play Videos boxes.

If you want to see a graphic image that should appear on a web page, you click the graphic image's placeholder. To see all of a web page's images, choose the View menu Options command, click the General tab, and check the Show Pictures, Play Sounds, and Play Videos boxes; then click the Refresh button.

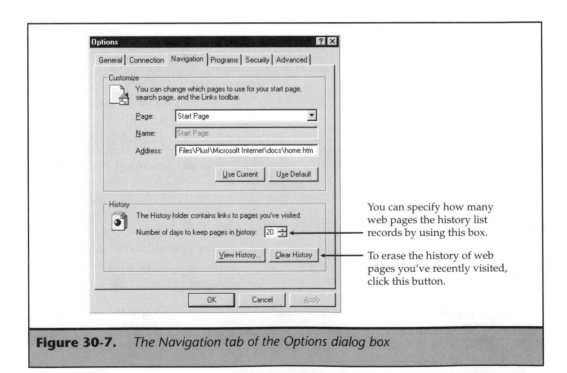

Figure 30-7.   *The Navigation tab of the Options dialog box*

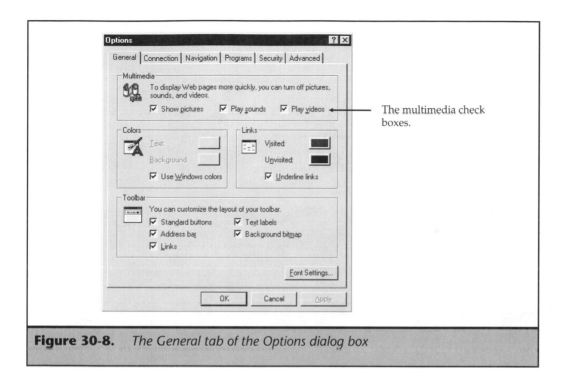

The multimedia check boxes.

Figure 30-8.   *The General tab of the Options dialog box*

FINE-TUNE THE CACHE   As mentioned earlier in the chapter, Internet Explorer stores, or caches, copies of web pages, graphic images, sounds, and videos you've recently opened. With this cache, Internet Explorer can retrieve a web page you've just looked at by grabbing the web page from your local drive (which takes only a split second) rather than by grabbing the web page from a remote web server (which may take several seconds or even several minutes).

You can adjust and possibly improve the way the Internet Explorer cache works by choosing the View menu Options command, clicking the Advanced tab, and then clicking the Settings button so that Internet Explorer displays the Settings dialog box, shown in Figure 30-9.

When Internet Explorer displays the Settings dialog box, you can use the option buttons to specify when Internet Explorer should check if it needs to retrieve a new copy of the web page from the remote server. Internet Explorer doesn't grab a new copy of a web page unless it sees the web page has changed since the last time you opened and cached the web page. If Internet Explorer doesn't grab a new copy of the web page, it retrieves the web page from your document cache and not from the remote web server.

The Settings dialog box's slider button controls how much disk space is allocated to your document cache. You can adjust this button to increase or decrease the size of the document cache and, therefore, the number of HTML documents and graphic images stored in the cache.

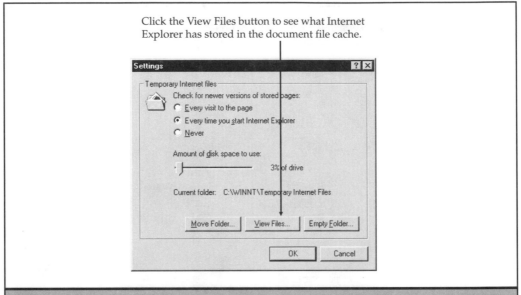

Click the View Files button to see what Internet Explorer has stored in the document file cache.

Figure 30-9. *The Settings dialog box lets you fine-tune Internet Explorer's cache*

Poor Graphic Image Quality

If your web page images don't look sharp and crisp, the problem may not be with the web browser, the HTML document, or the graphic image. You may need to adjust your computer's display settings. To do this, minimize any program windows so that the Windows desktop shows. Then follow these steps:

1. Right-click the Windows desktop so that the shortcut menu shows.

2. Choose the Properties command from the shortcut menu.

3. When Windows displays the Display Properties dialog box, click the Settings tab, as shown in Figure 30-10.

4. Activate the Color Palette drop-down list box and choose the entry that describes the largest number of colors.

5. Optionally, use the Desktop Area slider button to increase the screen resolution.

6. To verify that your new settings work, click the Test button.

7. If step 6 indicates that your new display settings do work, click the Display Properties dialog box's OK button when Windows finishes the test and redisplays the dialog box. Or, Windows might tell you that you need to restart your computer for the new settings to take effect. If this is the case, make sure you have everything saved and then restart your computer.

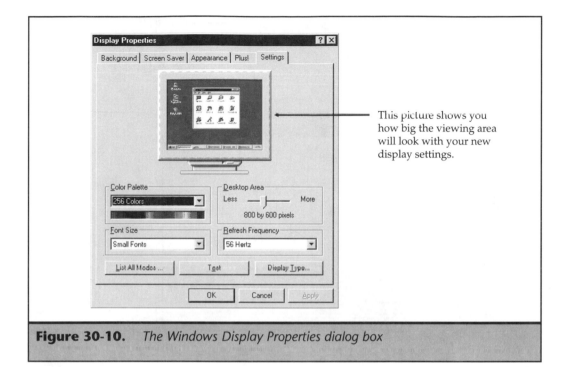

This picture shows you how big the viewing area will look with your new display settings.

Figure 30-10. *The Windows Display Properties dialog box*

Web Site Connection Problems

If you can't connect to a web site, your problem typically falls into one of three categories: a problem with the connection itself, a problem with the remote web server, or a bad URL. Typically, you can easily identify all problems. And once you identify the problem, you can begin working on a solution.

BAD CONNECTIONS   The first thing you should check when you can't connect to a particular web site is the connection itself. As you may recall from the Chapter 25 discussion, "What the Internet Is," an Internet connection requires that the client computer, the client software, the server computer, and the server software work together. It's occasionally the case, predictably, that one or more parts of the process aren't working. How you verify a connection depends on the connection itself.

If you've connected to the Internet using some other Internet service provider and Window's Dial-up Networking utility, for example, you can display the Dial-up Networking window:

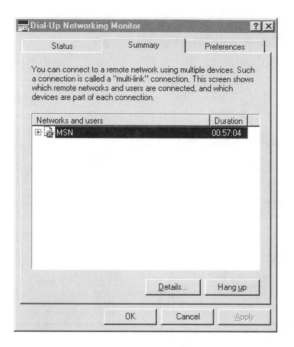

 TIP: *To display the Dial-up Networking window, click the Dial-up Network shortcut on the taskbar. You should see two buttons in the window. The top one will say Disconnect if you are currently connected. If you see the Connect button instead, it means you lost your connection. Click this button to reconnect.*

BAD URLS If you can't connect to a web site and you're sure your connection is working, you may have entered the URL incorrectly. URLs aren't exactly easy to enter. You need to make sure that you type everything just right and that you punctuate and capitalize the URL correctly. You need to be careful, for example, that you use periods and not commas and slashes rather than backslashes. If you check for these sorts of obvious errors, you have two other tacks you can attempt:

- You can simplify the URL so that you land at the web site's root directory. Then, once there you can (hopefully) use hyperlinks to move to the web page you want to view. For example, if you can't open the web page at http://www.company.com/folder/subfolder/page1.htm, you can enter the URL as http://www.company.com and then hope that the web server's default home page contains hyperlinks that point to the HTML document named page1.htm.

- You can find another web page that shows a hyperlink to the page you want and then use this hyperlink to move to the page. For example, you may be able to use a search service to find the URL. (The final section of this chapter, "Using a Search Service," explains how these handy tools work.)

BAD WEB SERVERS   If you know a connection is working and you know the URL is correct, the remote web server just may not be working. It may be too busy to respond to your request, for example. (This often happens with very popular web servers that are operated by very small web publishers.) The web server may be temporarily shut down for regular maintenance. Or, the web server may simply have permanently disappeared. In any of these cases, your only real recourse is to just attempt a connection later.

Viruses

Before closing this brief discussion of troubleshooting Internet-related and web-related problems, it's worth mentioning one final point: If you're indiscriminate about the web sites you visit and about the files you download, you should probably acquire and regularly use virus protection software. You can't catch a virus simply by opening web pages. You can, however, catch a virus by saving files to your desktop or laptop computer's local drive. If you're interested in more information about virus protection, consider visiting the web site at http://www.thunderbyte.com/.

Using a Search Service

As a practical matter, one of the biggest challenges in using the World Wide Web as a tool is that it's often very difficult to find information. This isn't surprising, really. Two problems confront web site visitors: the staggering volume of the information available and the oftentimes poor quality of the information. Tens of thousands of web sites exist, supplying millions of pages of information. And if you sift through even a few dozen pages, you'll encounter voluminous quantities of advertising, sloppily prepared and hastily presented information, and much suspect data.

At this point in the life of the web, you don't have many options available for dealing with the poor information problem (other than just limiting yourself to high-quality web sites you discover or learn about). You can, however, use search services to deal with the quantity of information problem.

Understanding How Search Services Work

Search services attempt to organize and bring structures to the Internet's—and in particular to the web's—vast resources. In general, these tools work in one of two ways: as directory-style services or as index-style services.

NOTE: *There are many search services and few fall neatly and completely into just one of the aforementioned categories. Many work partly as a directory and partly as an index.*

Directory-Style Services

A directory-style search service organizes its information about the web's content in a directory that works very much like a book's table of contents. In a book, you can use a good table of contents to first find a chapter with the information you need and then to locate within that chapter a section with the information you need. A directory-style search service works in the same basic way by organizing directory information in categories, subcategories, sub-subcategories, and so on. You locate the category with the information you need, and then the subcategory, and then the sub-subcategory.

One common characteristic of a directory-style search service is that web publishers themselves are responsible for getting their web sites and web pages entered into the directory. For example, if you want your web site to be listed in the Yahoo! search service's directory, you must contact Yahoo! and ask to have your web site added.

Index-Style Services

An index-style directory organizes its information in a huge index, not altogether unlike the index in a reference book. To use a reference book's index, for example, you attempt to look up a term or phrase in the index. If you locate the term or phrase in the index, you'll find a list of page numbers, which you can turn to. To use an index-style search service, you supply a term or phrase to the search service. The search service then looks up the term or phrase in its index and supplies a list of web pages you can move to by clicking hyperlinks.

In general, index-style search services build and then regularly update their indexes by using programs called web spiders. A web spider searches through every web page it can find, creating an index of the web page's information. To move from web page to web page, the spider follows each of the hyperlinks it finds.

Index-style search services aren't perfect, however. It typically takes a while for a web spider to find and index a page—particularly one that's not referenced by numerous other hyperlinks. What's more, some web spiders don't reindex web pages as they change—which means that the search service's index becomes more and more out of date over time.

NOTE: *The very powerful AltaVista search service reportedly takes about a week to create its index.*

Using a Directory-Style Service Like Yahoo!

To use a directory-style search service, you take the following steps:

NOTE: Perhaps the most popular directory-style search service is Yahoo! at http://www.yahoo.com/. For this reason, the instructions that follow use the Yahoo! search service. Other directory-style search services work in the same basic way, however.

1. Open the search service's start page by entering its URL into the Internet Explorer's Address box. Internet Explorer displays a start page like the one shown in Figure 30-11.

2. Use the search service's start page to find the category that best describes the information you're looking for and then, when you find it, click the category's hyperlink. For example, if you want to learn more information about a particular university, you click the Universities hyperlink, which appears under the Education hyperlink. When you do this, the search service displays a new page listing the information subcategories within the selected category (see Figure 30-12).

3. Find the subcategory that best describes the information you're looking for and then, when you find it, click the category's hyperlink. For example, if you want to learn more information about a particular university in Argentina, you click the Argentina hyperlink. When you do this, the search service displays a new page listing the information within the select subcategory—in this case, a list of universities in Argentina (see Figure 30-13).

4. Use the open web page to find the information you're looking for and then, when you find it, click the information's hyperlink. For example, if you want to learn more information about the first university listed in Figure 30-13, you click its hyperlink.

NOTE: You may need to repeat step 3 described in the preceding sequence more than one time if the directory-style search service organizes a particular set of information with more than just categories and subcategories.

Using an Index-Style Service Like AltaVista

To use an index-style search service, you take the following steps:

NOTE: One of the most powerful index-style search services is AltaVista at http://www.altavista.digital.com/. For this reason, the instructions that follow use the AltaVista search service. Other index-style search services work in same basic way, however.

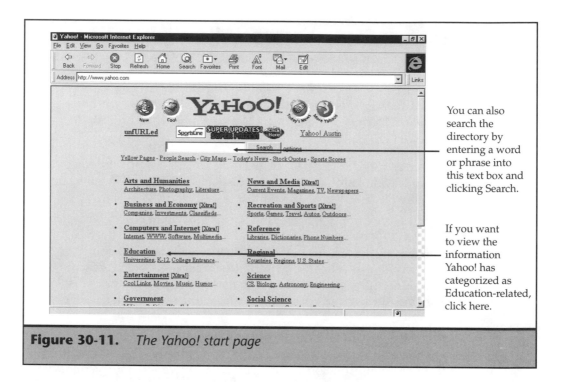

You can also search the directory by entering a word or phrase into this text box and clicking Search.

If you want to view the information Yahoo! has categorized as Education-related, click here.

Figure 30-11. *The Yahoo! start page*

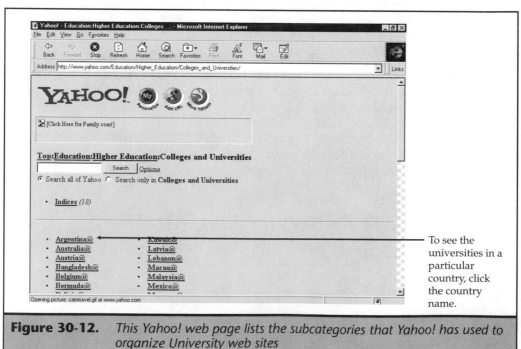

To see the universities in a particular country, click the country name.

Figure 30-12. *This Yahoo! web page lists the subcategories that Yahoo! has used to organize University web sites*

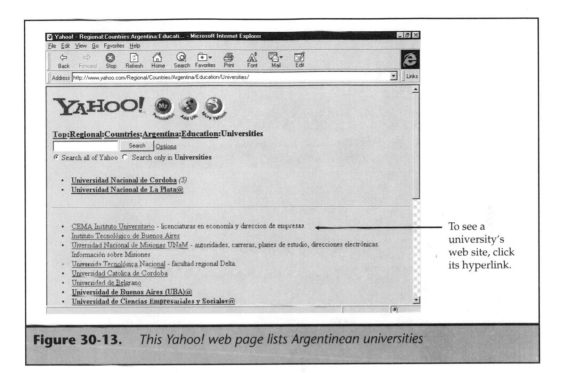

To see a university's web site, click its hyperlink.

Figure 30-13.   *This Yahoo! web page lists Argentinean universities*

1. Open the search service's start page by entering its URL into the Internet Explorer's Address box. Internet Explorer displays a start page like the one shown in Figure 30-14.

2. Enter a word or phrase that best describes the information you're looking for into the text box provided. For example, if you want to learn more information about St. Augustine, enter **Augustine** into the text box.

NOTE: Different index-style search services work differently, but, in general, if you enter more than one word, enclose the words in quotations if you want the search service to treat the words as a phrase. For example, if you wanted to search for web pages that used the phrase St. Augustine, *you would enclose this entry in quotation marks.*

3. Click the Submit button. When you do this, the search service displays the first portion of a list (usually a lengthy list) of web pages that use the word or phrase you specified (see Figure 30-15).

4. Use the listing of web pages to find the information you're looking for and then, when you find it, click the information's hyperlink. For example, if you want to learn more information about St. Augustine Sailing, you click the first hyperlink shown in Figure 30-15.

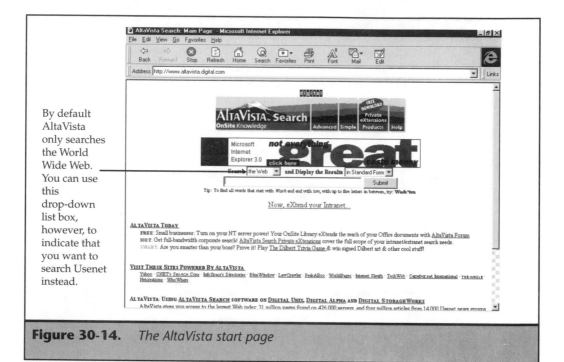

By default AltaVista only searches the World Wide Web. You can use this drop-down list box, however, to indicate that you want to search Usenet instead.

Figure 30-14. *The AltaVista start page*

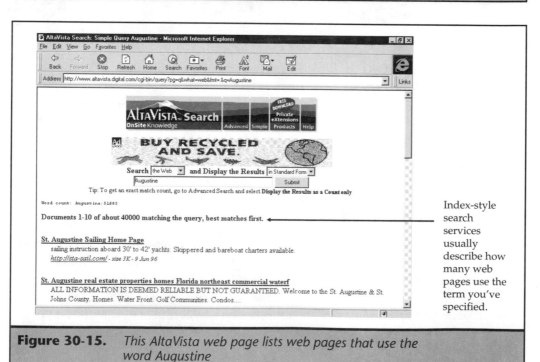

Index-style search services usually describe how many web pages use the term you've specified.

Figure 30-15. *This AltaVista web page lists web pages that use the word Augustine*

NOTE: *When using the AltaVista search service, if you don't see listed the information you want, you can scroll to the bottom of the web page and then click the page number hyperlinks to see additional listings of hyperlinks.*

What to Do When a Search Service Doesn't Work

Search services, as you'll find as soon as you begin using them, aren't perfect. Certainly, they make it much easier to find information on the Internet, but they won't always help you find the information you need or want. For this reason, don't rely solely on search services. If you stumble upon some interesting web site while browsing, for example, add it to your Favorites folder. If you hear about or see the URL for an interesting web site, write it down someplace so you can later try it. Record the URLs to interesting web sites.

What's more, do consider learning to use more than one search service. Resources that don't appear in one search service often do appear in another.

Finally, you really should learn to use a couple of search services well if you plan to spend much time browsing the World Wide Web. A few minutes of time spent learning about Yahoo! or AltaVista in depth, for example, will deliver tremendous time savings over the course of year.

Part VIII

Appendixes

The Complete Reference

Office 97

Appendix A

Installing Microsoft Office 97

This appendix describes how to install and reinstall Office 97. It explains the questions you need to ask yourself before you install the program, what to do before you start installing it, how to install Office 97 for the first time, and how to reinstall the program to load more or fewer Office 97 features onto your system. To install Office 97, you need

- Either the Office 97 CD-ROM or the handful of disks for installing the program

- Windows 95, Windows NT, or a higher version of Windows on your computer

- At least 8MB of memory (says Microsoft); actually, to run Office 97 and not be frustrated by delays and slowdowns, you need at least 16MB of memory, especially if you intend to install and run the two memory-hungry programs in the Office 97 suite, PowerPoint and Access

- At least 119MB of empty disk space for what Microsoft calls a "typical" installation, or as much as 166MB if you want to install all parts of the Office 97 program

TIP: To find out how much empty disk space—also known as free space—is on your computer, open the My Computer utility by double-clicking it on the Windows desktop. When the My Computer window appears, right-click on the icon that represents the part of the computer on which you will load Office 97 (most likely the C drive, Disk1_vol1 [C:]). On the shortcut menu, choose Properties. The General tab of the Properties dialog box appears and tells you how much free, or empty, space is on your computer.

Before You Install Office 97

Microsoft recommends closing all the programs before installing Office 97. Microsoft also says you should back up important files—not program files, but personal files: letters to your mom, novels, legal documents, and the like. During the course of writing this book and others about the Office 97 programs, I have installed and reinstalled the program many times and never lost a file. However, for the record, I want you to know what Microsoft recommends.

When you install Office 97, the program asks if you want a Typical installation, a Custom installation, or a Run from CD-ROM installation:

- *Typical* Installs the most widely used features of all the Office programs— Word, Excel, PowerPoint, Outlook, and Access—as well as popular features that are common to all the programs, such as the spell checker and clip art utility.

- *Custom* Lets you pick and choose which programs to install, as well as which features of each program to install and which common features to install.

TIP: *Microsoft says that the Custom installation is for "expert users." Not so. The Custom installation is for anyone who wants to decide for himself or herself what to put on the computer. As the following pages will show, a Custom installation is not as difficult as Microsoft makes it out to be. If you're running short on disk space, or if you don't care to use one or two or three of the Office 97 programs, by all means opt for a Custom installation.*

■ *Run from CD-ROM* Lets you run Office 97 from the CD-ROM. With this choice, you only need 24MB of free disk space. However, running Office 97 from a CD is very time-consuming and is not recommended. A CD-ROM drive runs much, much slower than your computer's hard disk.

The important thing to remember about installing Office 97 is that it doesn't matter if you get it right the first time. If you forgot to install a certain feature or a certain program, or if you regret installing a certain feature or a certain program, all you have to do is reinstall Office 97. You can reinstall the program as many times as you wish.

Retaining an Office 95 Program

If Office 95 is loaded on your computer and you install Office 97, the setup program searches for old 1995 editions of the Office programs, deletes them, and replaces them with the brand-new 1997 editions. No problem there. However, what if you want to keep a 1995 edition of an Office program? For example, suppose you want to keep Word 95 and Word 97 on your computer?

The only way to keep an Office 95 program on your computer and still load Office 97 programs is to do the following:

1. Uninstall Office 95. (To do that, put the Office 95 CD in the CD-ROM drive, click the Start button, choose the Settings menu Control Panel command, and click Add/Remove Programs. In the Add/Remove Properties dialog box, click Office 95, click the Add/Remove button, and then follow the directions for removing Office 95.)

2. Reinstall Office 95, but this time when you install the program, install it to a different directory than the default directory that Microsoft recommends.

When you install Office 97, the Office 97 programs will fall in a different directory than the old Office 95 program or programs that you retained and you will be able to use both Office 95 and Office 97 programs.

Installing Office 97 for the First Time

Follow these steps to install Office 97 for the first time:

1. Close the programs that are open on your computer, if any are open.

2. Do the following, depending on how you intend to install the program:

   ■ *From the CD*   Put the Office 97 CD in the CD-ROM drive. If the installation program does not start automatically, the folder for the CD-ROM drive contents appears. Double-click setup.exe to start the installation.

   ■ *From floppy disks*   If you are installing the program from floppy disks, put Setup Disk 1 in drive A, click the Start button, and choose Run. Then type **a:\setup** in the Run dialog box and click OK.

3. Speed-read the copyright warning and click the Continue button. You see the Name and Organization Information dialog box.

4. Enter your name and, if you are so inclined, the company you work for, and then click OK. The next screen asks you to confirm the name and company name you entered. Click OK.

WARNING: What you enter in the Name and Organization dialog box is more important than you may think. The name and company name you enter appear all over Office 97. For example, by choosing the Tools menu AutoText command and then clicking Signature in Microsoft Word, you can make the name you enter in the dialog box appear automatically. Make sure what you enter in the dialog box is accurate.

5. If you are installing from a CD, the next dialog box prompts you to type your CD key. You can find the CD key on the back of the case that the CD was shipped in. Do not lose this number. You will be asked for it if you ever need to completely reinstall the program.

6. The following dialog box lists a product ID number for your copy of Office 97. Jot down the number in case you need to identify yourself to Microsoft's Customer Support staff in the event of an emergency, and then click OK.

7. The first Setup dialog box appears and recommends installing Office 97 in the C:\Program Files\Microsoft Office folder. Click OK in this dialog box.

WARNING: The first Setup dialog box offers you the opportunity to install Office 97 in a folder of your choice by clicking the Change Folder button. Do not avail yourself of this opportunity. Office 97 works best when you install it in the default folder. If Office 95 programs are already in the C:\Program Files\Microsoft Office folder and you want to keep an Office 95 program or two, see "Retaining an Office 95 Program" earlier in this chapter.

In the next few minutes, the Office 97 setup program examines your hard disk to see what is there and which files need to be loaded. After that, you see a

Setup dialog box that asks what kind of installation you want: Typical, Custom, or Run from CD-ROM.

8. Choose the kind of installation you want by clicking a button. "Before You Install Office 97," at the start of this appendix, explains what the three installations are. If you choose a Custom installation, see "Custom Installations: Choosing What Parts of Office 97 to Install," following, for instructions about how to pick and choose different parts of the program to load.

 NOTE: If you are installing the program from a CD, you see screens that tell you which parts of the program are being installed. If you are installing from floppy disks, you are prompted to insert them by number, one at a time.

9. Click OK when you see the dialog box that tells you that the setup process is complete.

Custom Installations: Choosing What Parts of Office 97 to Install

When you choose a Custom installation or reinstallation, you get the chance to tell Office 97 which programs to install, what parts of each programs to install, and which common Office tools to install.

Figure A-1 shows the first dialog box that you see when you opt for a Custom installation or reinstallation. In this dialog box and the others that you see when you tell Office 97 what to install, a white check box with a check mark in it means to install all parts of the item; a gray box with a check mark in it means to install some parts of the item; and an empty white box means to install no parts of the item.

If I were to click Continue in the dialog box shown in Figure A-1, the setup program would install all of Microsoft Binder, parts of Excel, Word, PowerPoint, Access, and Outlook, and no Web Page Authoring features whatsoever.

To change how many parts of an item are installed, click the item in this dialog box and then click the Change Option button. When you do so, you see a dialog box like the one in Figure A-2. To get to this dialog box, I clicked Microsoft Word and then the Change Option button. The Microsoft Word dialog box in Figure A-2 lists all the major components of Microsoft Word. The boxes in this dialog box mean the same as the ones in the previous dialog box—that none, some, or all of the different components will be installed.

From this dialog box, I can either click the Select All dialog box to install all the Word features, or I can select an item and choose which of its parts to install:

■ Click the Select All button to install all the features of a program.

■ Click an option in the dialog box and click the Change Option button to install some of the features. When you select an option by clicking it, the dialog box describes the parts of the option. In Figure A-2, for example, I selected Proofing Tools. The Description box tells me that the proofing tools are the "Thesaurus, Hyphenation, and Grammar utilities."

For Figure A-3, I clicked Proofing Tools in the Microsoft Word dialog box (see Figure A-2). Now, in the Proofing Tools dialog box, I have the opportunity to choose which proofing tools I want to install by clicking the boxes next to Grammar, Hyphenation, Thesaurus. To install all of the proofing tools, I can click the Select All button and then click OK.

After you click OK in a dialog box, you climb the ladder and go back to the previous dialog box, where you can pick and choose more items and options.

Starting with the dialog box shown in Figure A-1 (it's called Custom or Maintenance, depending on whether you are installing or reinstalling Office 97), you can drill down through dialog boxes and tell Office 97 precisely which parts of the program to install. Be sure to read the descriptions to find out what the items you install are good for. Click Continue in the Custom or Maintenance dialog box when you have told Office 97 what to install.

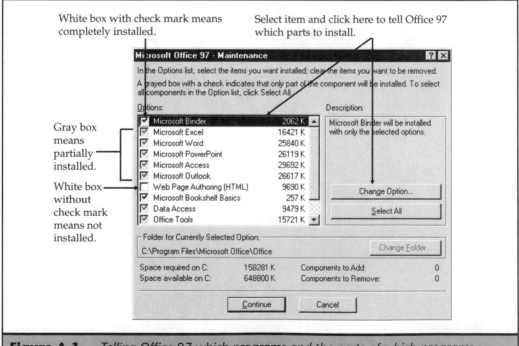

Figure A-1.   *Telling Office 97 which programs and the parts of which programs to install*

Select item and click here to install some or no features.

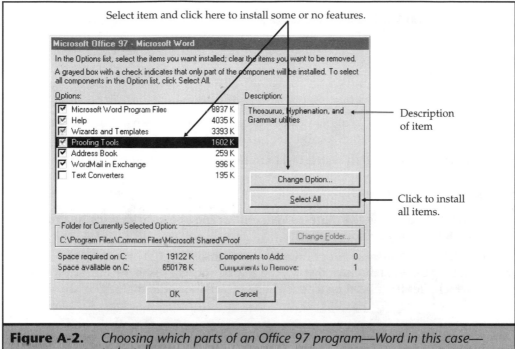

Figure A-2. *Choosing which parts of an Office 97 program—Word in this case—to install*

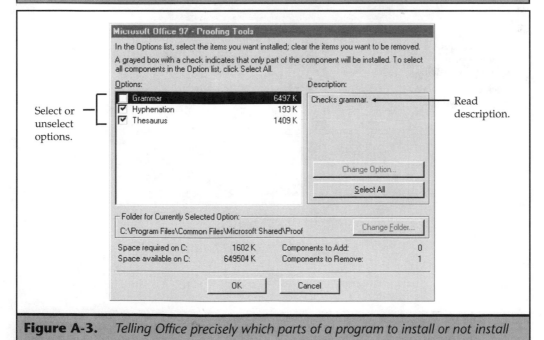

Figure A-3. *Telling Office precisely which parts of a program to install or not install*

Reinstalling Office 97

Reinstall Office 97 if you think that program files have been corrupted and the program isn't working right or if you want to install a part of the program that you didn't install the first time around. Follow these steps to reinstall Office 97:

1. Close the programs that are open on your computer, if any are open.

2. Put the Office 97 CD in the CD-ROM drive. If you are reinstalling the program from floppy disks, put Setup Disk 1 in drive A.

3. Click the Start button on the taskbar, choose Settings, then choose Control Panel. The Control Panel opens.

4. Double-click Add/Remove Programs.

5. In the Add/Remove Programs Properties dialog box, click Office 97 and then click the Add/Remove button.

6. Click OK if the setup program asks you to insert the CD or a disk (you did that in Step 2). For a moment or two, the setup program scans the hard disk to see which files have been installed. Then you see the Setup dialog box shown here.

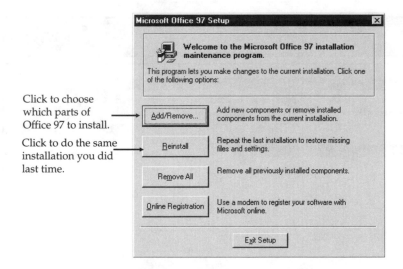

Click to choose which parts of Office 97 to install.

Click to do the same installation you did last time.

7. Click either the Add/Remove button or the Reinstall button:

■ *Add/Remove* Lets you pick and choose which parts of Office 97 to install. See "Custom Installations: Choosing What Parts of Office 97 to Install," earlier in this chapter, to see what to do if you click this button.

■ *Reinstall* Installs the same program files that were installed the last time you installed or reinstalled Office 97. If you click this button, the reinstallation begins immediately. Click OK when you see the dialog box that tells you that the setup process is complete.

Appendix B

Introducing FrontPage

Office doesn't, at least as of this writing, include Microsoft FrontPage. Nevertheless, Office users interested in web publishing will benefit by knowing exactly what FrontPage is, how it works, and what web publishing capabilities it provides that you don't get with programs like Word or PowerPoint. For these reasons, this appendix discusses these topics.

What FrontPage Is

FrontPage is actually a collection of web publishing software programs. When you acquire FrontPage you get

- FrontPage Explorer, which you can use to design web sites and set up web site folders and ready-to-edit HTML documents

- FrontPage Editor, which you can use to create HTML documents—including forms

- Microsoft Image Composer, which you can use to create and edit graphic images

- Personal Web Server, which you can use to test FrontPage web sites and even to publish small intranet web sites

While some of this functionality exists in Word, Excel, PowerPoint, and Access, none of the regular Office programs do as much as FrontPage does and none of them do it as well. In point of fact, much of the web authoring functionality you see in the individual Office programs reportedly comes from FrontPage.

How FrontPage Works

Using FrontPage is really a three-step process: designing a web site, creating the HTML documents, and then publishing the web site to a web server.

Designing a Web Site

Unlike the document-centric approach used with Office's programs, you begin any FrontPage web publishing project by designing and describing your web site. To do this, you typically use one of the FrontPage Explorer's Web Wizards, as shown in Figure B-1. FrontPage Explorer provides Web Wizards for constructing all sorts of different web sites—including interactive web sites. As you would expect, to use one of these wizards, you start it and then answer the questions it poses.

One of the big benefits of using FrontPage Explorer to design a web site is that FrontPage Explorer arranges and organizes all of the web site's components—HTML documents, graphic images, and so on—and then creates a map that shows how these web site components relate to one another, as shown in Figure B-2.

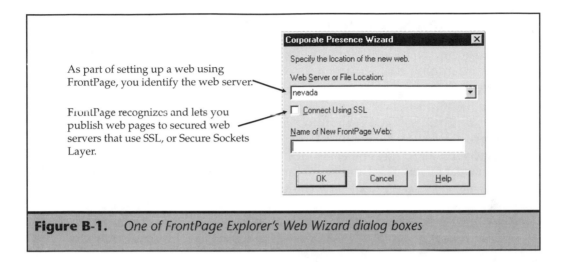

As part of setting up a web using FrontPage, you identify the web server.

FrontPage recognizes and lets you publish web pages to secured web servers that use SSL, or Secure Sockets Layer.

Figure B-1. *One of FrontPage Explorer's Web Wizard dialog boxes*

NOTE: *FrontPage comes with a rich set of web-specific clip art that you can use for your web pages.*

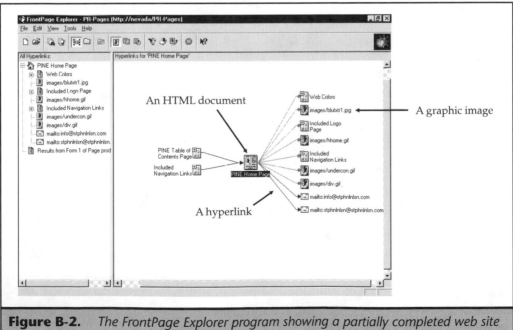

An HTML document

A graphic image

A hyperlink

Figure B-2. *The FrontPage Explorer program showing a partially completed web site*

Creating and Editing Web Content

After you design a web site and create an overall structure for it, you edit its foundational web pages and add new web pages and graphic images. To work with the HTML documents themselves, you use FrontPage Editor (see Figure B-3), a powerful, easy-to-use HTML editor. FrontPage Editor supplies all of the HTML editing tools built into Word—as well as many more.

To work with images and clip art, you use Microsoft Image Composer, a powerful illustration program (see Figure B-4). Using Image Composer, for example, you can manipulate and edit images and art so they work well for your web pages.

As you create your HTML documents and graphic images, not surprisingly, FrontPage makes it easy to test your web site's operation. FrontPage includes a small but full-featured web server, called Personal Web Server, that you can use to experiment with all elements of your web site, including web page forms and WebBots.

NOTE: WebBots are special instructions—beyond those that HTML can provide—to a web server.

As with Word, to add textual content, you can type it into the document, copy it into the document, or insert a file containing the text.

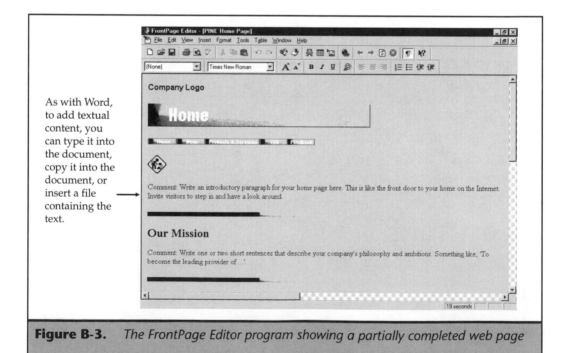

Figure B-3. *The FrontPage Editor program showing a partially completed web page*

APPENDIXES

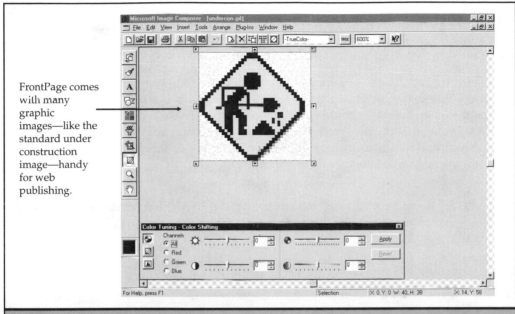

FrontPage comes with many graphic images—like the standard under construction image—handy for web publishing.

Figure B-4.   *The Image Composer program showing an image being edited for a page*

Publishing and Administering a Web Site

FrontPage also helps with the final tasks related to web publishing—the work of actually moving a web site (and all of its components) to a web server and the work of administering a web site on an ongoing basis. FrontPage Explorer, for example, includes a wizard that you can use to move a FrontPage web site to a web server. What's more, FrontPage Explorer includes web administration utilities that make it possible and relatively painless to administer a web site. FrontPage Explorer, for example, provides tools that web site administrators can use to control access to a web site's components and to describe who can make changes to a web site.

Why FrontPage Is Special

From the perspective of the Microsoft Office user, FrontPage is special for three very understandable reasons: its look and feel, its extra HTML editing functionality, and its web site design and administration functionality. All three items deserve brief further discussion.

Regarding FrontPage's look and feel, you should know that FrontPage's appearance and operation closely resemble those of the Microsoft Office programs. Therefore, if you've learned how to use Word with some modicum of proficiency, you already know much of what you need to know to operate the programs that make up the FrontPage suite of programs: FrontPage Explorer, FrontPage Editor, and Image Composer.

NOTE: Microsoft originally purchased the company that developed FrontPage, Vermeer, because of FrontPage's similarity to its Office programs.

Regarding FrontPage's superior HTML editing capabilities, you'll probably find it useful to know that the WebBots that FrontPage Editor lets you add to your HTML documents mean that you can do more in the web pages you create with FrontPage than you ever can with, say, Word or PowerPoint. You can use WebBots, for example, to place time and date stamps in your web pages, to schedule when images appear, and even to create web site-specific search services.

NOTE: In order for the WebBots you place into an HTML document to work, you must publish the web site to a web server that uses the FrontPage Server Extensions.

Finally, as alluded to earlier in this chapter, FrontPage Explorer provides a wizard that you can use to move a FrontPage web (including all of its HTML document, graphic images, and other components) to a web server.

Using FrontPage

The earlier paragraphs of this appendix describe what FrontPage is and why you might choose to use it. This section of the chapter will now describe in step-by-step form the key tasks you would use FrontPage for as a part of constructing an actual Internet or intranet web site:

- Running the Create Wizard to set up a web site
- Importing textual information from other documents
- Using Microsoft Image Composer to add and edit art for your web pages
- Adding web pages to your web site and linking the pages together
- Creating and working with forms and WebBots.

Run the Create Wizard

Using the Create Wizard is the quickest way to create a professional-looking FrontPage web. It can save you hours upon hours of time designing the framework of your web and linking all of the separate pages together. The Create Wizard is very easy to use—within a matter of minutes, you can have an entire web site ready for you to enter content into. To run the Create Wizard, simply follow these steps:

1. Start FrontPage. You can do this by clicking the Start button and choosing the Programs menu Microsoft FrontPage command.

2. In the Getting Started with Microsoft FrontPage dialog box, mark the Create a New FrontPage Web from a Wizard or Template option button and click OK.

3. Select one of the templates or wizards from the Template or Wizard list box shown in Figure B-5 and click OK.

4. Choose a web server or file location onto which you want to store your site from the Web Server or File Location drop-down list box, as shown in Figure B-6. You can include the port number as is shown (8080) if your web server is not mounted on the standard port. You can also type the path name of a folder on your hard disk onto which you want to temporarily store your web if you don't have authoring access on your web server.

5. Check the Connect using SSL box if you want to connect to the web server using the Secure Socket Level protocol, which is just a special, secure protocol. If you don't know, ask your web administrator.

6. Enter a name for the new web. In Figure B-6, I named the example web KD_Books.

TIP: *FrontPage doesn't let you use spaces, but which other characters you can and cannot use depends on your server.*

7. If the Name and Password Required Dialog Box appears on your screen, it means that you are not yet authorized as an administrator to create a new

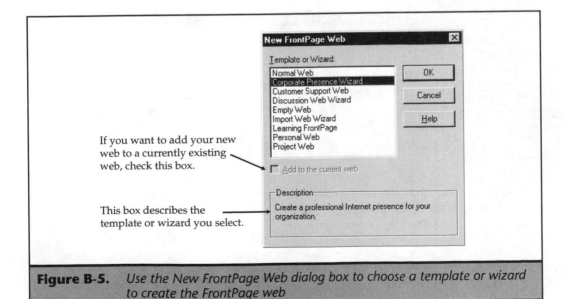

If you want to add your new web to a currently existing web, check this box.

This box describes the template or wizard you select.

Figure B-5. *Use the New FrontPage Web dialog box to choose a template or wizard to create the FrontPage web*

Corporate Presence Wizard ✕

Specify the location of the new web.

Web Server or File Location:

montana:8080 ▼

☐ Connect Using SSL

Name of New FrontPage Web:

KD_Books

[OK] [Cancel] [Help]

Figure B-6. *Use this dialog box to tell FrontPage what you want to name your web and where you want to store it*

FrontPage web in the root FrontPage web. Enter your administrator name and password as shown here or contact your web administrator for help. Click OK and FrontPage launches the wizard or template you chose in step 3. If you chose Corporate Presence Wizard or Discussion Web Wizard in step 3, follow along with the rest of these steps. If you chose Import Web Wizard, skip ahead to the section called "Import Files into FrontPage." If you chose any of the other templates or wizards, you're already ready to begin entering content into your web pages.

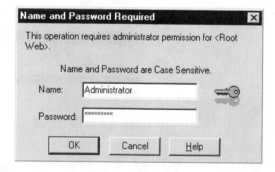

Name and Password Required ✕

This operation requires administrator permission for <Root Web>.

Name and Password are Case Sensitive.

Name: Administrator

Password: ✕✕✕✕✕✕✕✕

[OK] [Cancel] [Help]

NOTE: *Your name and password are case-sensitive. If you enter them incorrectly, FrontPage will redisplay the same dialog box so that you can try again. Make sure that you don't have your CAPS LOCK on.*

8. Click Next to begin the Web Wizard or template. The following illustration shows the first dialog box of the Corporate Presence Web Wizard.

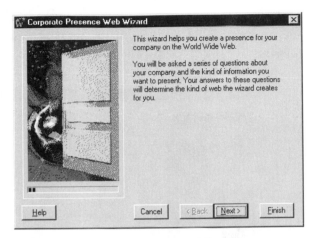

9. Choose which pages you want to include in your new web site and click Next. Note that you can add and delete pages from your web site later if you change your mind.

10. For each page you chose to include in the previous step, the wizard asks you what you want to include on that page, as shown next for the home page. Depending on how many pages you have, the wizard takes you through quite a few dialog boxes. Just choose what you want included on each page and continue to click Next. Remember that you can add or remove things manually from your pages once they are created.

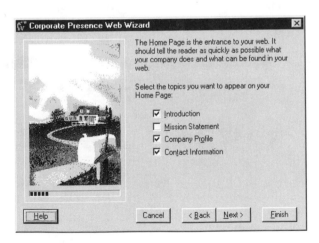

TIP: *If you are including a Feedback form, and are planning on using Microsoft Access or Excel for manipulating the data you receive from your visitors, mark Yes, use tab-delimited format in the dialog box that defines your Feedback file.*

11. Once you have gone through all of your pages and described what you want on each one, the wizard asks you for some general information that will apply to all of your pages, as shown here. Click Next when you are done.

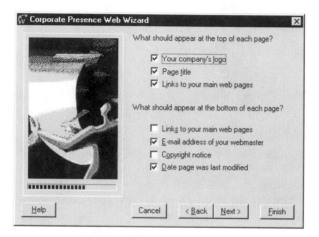

12. The wizard asks you to pick a style for your web site. Mark one of the option buttons and click Next.

13. The wizard asks you to pick the background and text colors for your web site pages as shown here. If you choose to change the colors FrontPage suggests, make sure that you consider the legibility of your pages as you make your choices, and also make sure that each of your text and link colors is unique and distinguishable from the others.

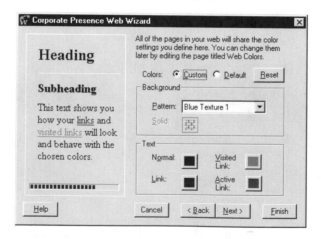

14. If you are running the Discussion Web Wizard instead of the Corporate Presence Wizard as in this example, you will see one more dialog box asking if you want to frame your web, then click Finish and you're done.

    NOTE: *Frames are not supported in all browsers. Unless you are certain of the browser software visitors to your web site will be using, you may not want to frame your web.*

15. The wizard displays a series of dialog boxes for you to fill out the company information you want included on your web, as illustrated here. Click Finish when you're done, and FrontPage creates your new web site.

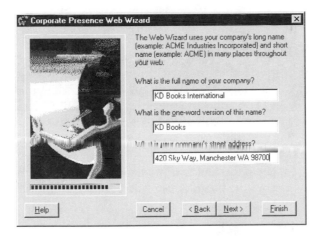

16. Once you have created a web site, FrontPage displays the To Do list. You can edit the contents of your web by selecting a task from the list and then clicking Do Task.

Import Files into FrontPage

The Import Web Wizard makes it very simple for you to import Office document files and other files into FrontPage. The easiest way of doing this is by running the Import Wizard. Before you can begin using the Import Web Wizard, you must have all of the files you want to import stored in the same folder on your computer. You can then start the wizard in one of two ways:

- When you first open FrontPage, you can mark the Create a New FrontPage Web With the Import Wizard button.

- If you already have FrontPage open, you can click the New button and choose Import Web Wizard from the Template or Wizard list box.

To run the wizard once you start it, follow these steps:

1. In the Import Web Wizard dialog box, name your new web and specify the web server or file location on your computer in which you want your new web stored.

2. Click OK to launch the Import Web Wizard.

3. In the first Import Web Wizard dialog box, enter the complete path name of the folder in which you've stored all of the files you want to import, as shown in Figure B-7. If you don't know the path name, click the Browse button to find and select it.

4. Click Next to continue.

5. In the Edit File List dialog box shown in Figure B-8, select any files you want excluded from your web and click the Exclude button, then click Next.

6. Click Finish and the Import Web Wizard imports the files you selected into a new web.

Add Art to Your Web

To create and edit graphic images, which FrontPage calls *sprites*, you use Microsoft Image Composer. You can also open the program by choosing the Tools menu Show Image Editor command or by clicking the Show Image Editor toobar button in the FrontPage Explorer window. Figure B-9 shows an empty Image Composer window.

Open a Sprite

To open a graphic image in the Image Composer, click the Open button. When the Image Composer displays the Open dialog box, locate the graphic image you want to

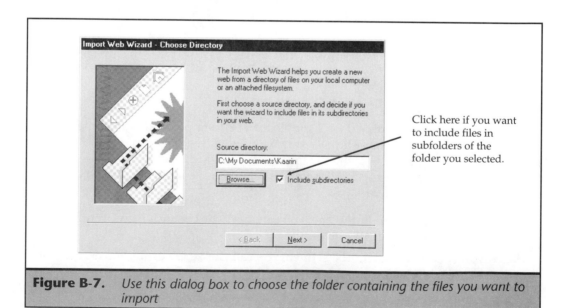

Figure B-7.   *Use this dialog box to choose the folder containing the files you want to import*

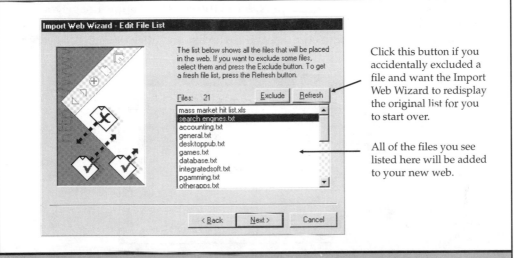

Figure B-8.   *Use this dialog box to specify which files you want to import*

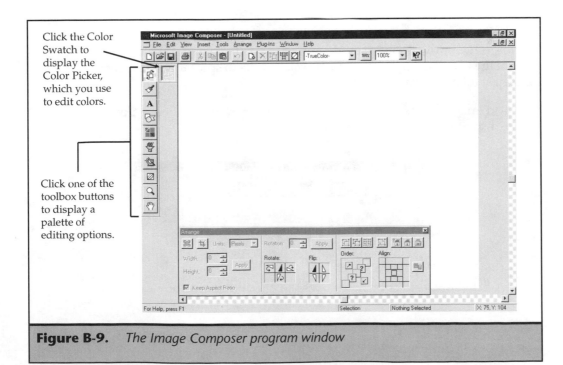

Figure B-9.   *The Image Composer program window*

edit. In the Files of type drop-down list box, select the type of graphic image you're looking for, or if you don't know, select the All Supported Formats entry. Once you have located the file you want to edit, select it in the list and click Open.

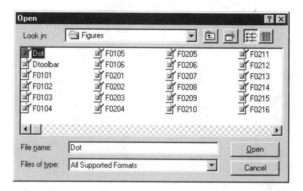

NOTE: *The Image Composer can read several types of image files; but if you haven't yet created or scanned your image, and you are planning to use Image Composer to edit it and add it to your web, you will want to save it as one of the file types listed in the Files of type box.*

Create a Text Sprite

Creating a text sprite is really simple, and once you have one created, you can use some of the Image Composer's many special effects to spice it up. To create a text sprite, just follow these steps:

1. In Image Composer, click the Text toolbox button. The Image Composer displays the Text palette shown here:

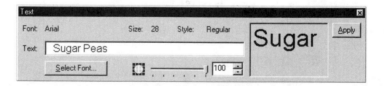

2. In the text box, type your text.

3. Click the Select Font button to display the Font dialog box shown here:

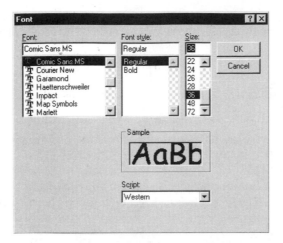

4. Choose a font from the Font list box, a font style from the Font style list box, and a font size from the Size list box.

5. Click OK.

6. Click Apply and the Image Composer creates the text sprite.

NOTE: To change the color of your text sprite, see the section later in this appendix, "Change the Color of a Sprite."

Create a Graphic Sprite

You can use Image Composer to create complex graphic sprites from scratch or add graphic designs to existing graphic images. The Image Composer has so many tools you can use in your artistic pursuits that it is impossible to describe each one individually here. There are, however, two basic things you can add to sprites: shapes and hand-drawn designs. To add shapes to your sprite, click the Shapes toolbox button to display the Shapes-Geometry palette shown here:

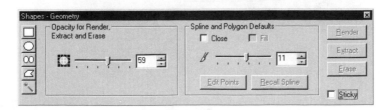

Click one of the basic shape buttons along the left side of the Shapes-Geometry palette, draw the shape by dragging the mouse across the screen, and then click Render to add the shape.

TIP: The smaller the opacity value in the Shapes-Geometry palette, the more see-through a shape will be. If a shape has 100-percent opacity, you won't be able to see through it at all.

To add painted hand-drawn designs and effects to your graphic sprite, click the Paint toolbox button to display the Paint palette shown in Figure B-10.

NOTE: You must have a sprite already open in order to use the paint tools. If you want a fresh canvas on which to paint, draw a rectangle (or any other shape) using the Shapes-Geometry palette.

Click one of the tools at the left and then define the size of the tool using the list box in the middle of the palette. You can define the color of the paint by clicking the Color Swatch and choosing a new color in the Color Picker dialog box.

Save a Sprite

To save a sprite, click the Save button on Image Composer's toolbar. Image Composer displays the Save As dialog box shown here:

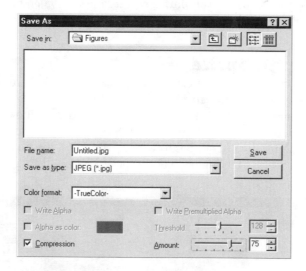

In the Save in drop-down list box, locate the folder in which you want to save the graphic image. Use the File name text box to name the file, select a file format in the Save as type drop-down list box, and then click Save.

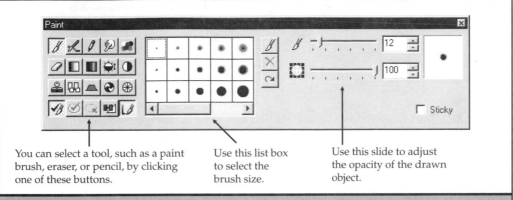

You can select a tool, such as a paint brush, eraser, or pencil, by clicking one of these buttons.

Use this list box to select the brush size.

Use this slide to adjust the opacity of the drawn object.

Figure B-10. *The Paint palette provides several options for adding graphic art effects*

A Note About Graphic Image File Formats

Most web pages use either JPEG or GIF images for two basic reasons: First, all web browsers include the ability to view JPEG and GIF images. Second, both of these formats can be compressed and so are smaller in size and take less time for viewers to load. If you've spent much time surfing the Web, you know how irritating it can be to wait for large images to load. To spare your web site visitors this time cost and annoyance, you'll probably want to both limit the number of graphics you include on each page and save the images as either JPEG or GIF files, as well.

To save your image as a JPEG file, choose the JPEG entry from the Save as type drop-down list box. Check the Compression box and use the Amount slider to adjust the file compression. The more you move the slider to the right, the more image quality you lose, but the smaller your image file becomes (and therefore takes less time to load).

To save your image as a GIF file (commonly used by CompuServe), select the CompuServe GIF entry from the Save as type drop-down list box. If you have specified a color as transparent, the Transparent color box will be checked, and the color swatch beside the box will show the replacement color (which should probably be the same as your web page's background color).

Crop a Sprite

To crop a sprite, follow these steps:

1. Select the sprite you want to crop by clicking it.

2. Click the Arrange toolbox button to display the Arrange Palette shown here:

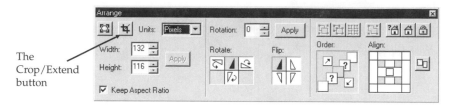

The Crop/Extend button

3. Click the Crop/Extend button. When you do this, Image Composer adds blue cropping handles to the corners and sides of your sprite.

TIP: *Before you crop, always make sure you see the blue cropping handles. If the handles are black, it means you haven't clicked the Crop/Extend button and Image Composer will resize the sprite instead of cropping it as you drag the handles. After each crop you make, you need to click the Crop/Extend button before you can continue cropping.*

4. Drag the cropping handles inward to crop the image down to just a piece of the sprite. The following illustration shows a sprite of Dot, one of the Office Assistants, that I have cropped:

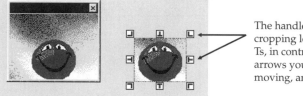

The handles you use for cropping look like blue Ls and Ts, in contrast to the black arrows you use for selecting, moving, and resizing.

5. Click the Save button to save the cropped image.

Resize a Sprite

To resize a sprite, follow these steps:

1. Select the sprite you want to resize by clicking it.

2. Drag the selection handles inward or outward to decrease or increase the sprite's size, as shown in the following illustration. Keep image quality in mind, however, as you resize sprites. Sure, you can make a small and wide sprite long and tall, to fit in an area shaped so, but the sprite will be terribly distorted if you do so. You also shouldn't plan on taking a very small sprite and increasing its size by several factors unless you want a very grainy image.

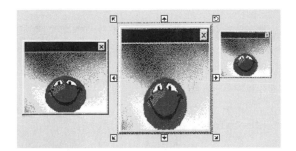

TIP: *To keep the same ratio of width to height (this is called the sprite's aspect ratio), hold down the SHIFT key as you drag a corner handle.*

3. Click the Save toolbar button to save the resized sprite.

Rotate and Flip a Sprite

To rotate a sprite, follow these steps:

1. Click the sprite to select it. Image Composer adds selection handles to the sprite. Notice how the handle in the upper-right corner looks like a circular arrow, as shown here. This is called the rotation handle. When you move the mouse pointer over this handle, it also becomes a circular arrow.

2. Click the rotation handle and turn the sprite clockwise or counterclockwise by dragging with the mouse.

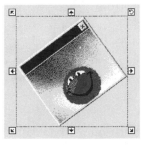

TIP: *You can also click the Arrange toolbox button and use the Rotation box in the Arrange palette to specify a specific angle of rotation.*

To flip a sprite, follow these steps:

1. Select the sprite by clicking it.

2. Click the Arrange toolbox button.

3. In the Arrange palette, click one of the Flip buttons: flip horizontally, flip vertically, or flip both to flip the sprite as shown here:

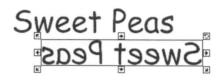

Duplicate and Group Sprites

Rather than spending a lot of time trying to re-create identical sprites, you can just duplicate a sprite. Duplicating a sprite is even easier than copying it and pasting it using the toolbar, a familiar Office technique. To duplicate a sprite, all you have to do is select the sprite you want to duplicate and click the Edit menu Duplicate command. Image Composer stacks another copy of the image on top of the original. You can continue to duplicate the same sprite if you need more copies, as shown here:

 TIP: *To move a sprite, just select it and drag it using the mouse.*

If you have several sprites that you want to edit together as one image, you need to first group them. In the next illustration, I have a number of individual-shaped sprites that I want to group into one design so that I can move them as one image as I need to. To group sprites, follow these steps:

1. Select the first sprite you want to include in the group by clicking it.

2. Select all other members of the group by holding down the CTRL key while you click each one.

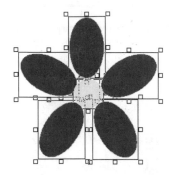

APPENDIXES

TIP: *To select all of the sprites on a page, choose the Edit menu Select All command.*

3. Click the Arrange toolbox button.

4. On the Arrange palette, click the Group button.

TIP: *To ungroup sprites you have previously grouped, select the group by clicking it, click the Arrange button, and then click the Ungroup button on the Arrange palette.*

Change the Color of a Sprite

To change the color of a graphic or text sprite, select the sprite you want to recolor and click the Patterns and Fills toolbox button. In the Patterns and Fills palette, choose Current Color Fill from the list box. Click the Current Color Swatch to display the Color Picker shown in Figure B-11.

Once you have chosen a new color in the Color Picker, click OK and then click Apply in the Patterns and Fills palette to apply the new color to the selected sprite.

Other Special Effects with Sprites

Microsoft Image Composer allows you to perform a lot of neat editing tricks to your graphic images beyond the basic image editing functions already described. This appendix is too short to discuss all of the special effects you can do with Image Composer, but it will briefly illustrate Image Composer's capabilities. Once you've mastered the basic image editing techniques listed above, take the time to experiment with Image Composer's graphic editing capabilities for yourself—just make sure that you first create a copy of the graphic image you intend to insert in your web so that you aren't experimenting with the original (just in case you change your mind after saving changes).

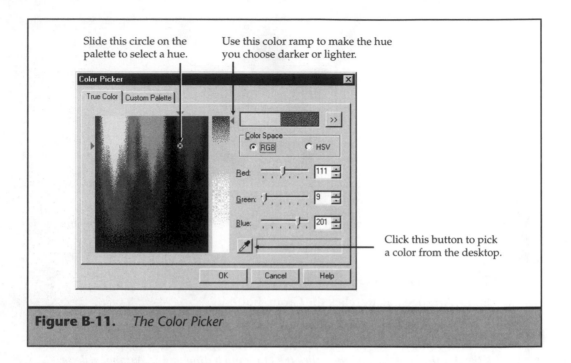

Slide this circle on the palette to select a hue.

Use this color ramp to make the hue you choose darker or lighter.

Click this button to pick a color from the desktop.

Figure B-11.   *The Color Picker*

For a brief overview of some of Image Composer's special effects, select an image you want to experiment with. Click either the Warps and Filters or the Art Effects toolbox button. Use the drop-down list box and the list box in the palette Image Composer displays to define a special effect and then click Apply to apply it to the selected sprite. There are too many effects to list and show all of them here, but the following illustration shows what a few of the effects can do to two sprites, a text sprite and a simple graphic sprite:

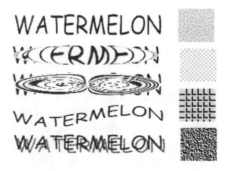

TIP: *If you don't like an effect you add to a sprite, click the Undo toolbar button.*

Add a Web Page

Once you have created a web site, it's simple to add another web page to it. First, you need to open FrontPage Editor. You can do this in one of two ways:

- By choosing the Tools menu Show FrontPage Editor command
- By double-clicking an existing web page to open it in FrontPage Editor

Once you have opened the FrontPage Editor program, just follow these steps to create a new web page:

1. Choose the File menu New command. FrontPage Editor displays the New Page dialog box shown here:

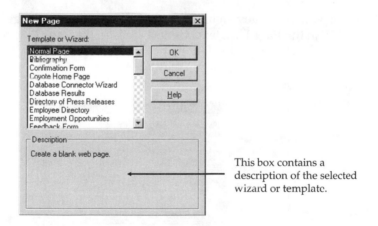

This box contains a description of the selected wizard or template.

NOTE: *If you click the New tool on FrontPage Editor's Standard toolbar, FrontPage will create an Untitled Normal (blank) page.*

2. Select a template or wizard for your new page in the Template or Wizard list box and click OK.

3. For most of the options listed in the Template or Wizard list box, this is all you have to do. FrontPage creates the new page and you're ready to edit it and add content to it, and then save it when you're through. If, however, you chose a wizard in the previous step, the wizard begins. In the case of the Personal

Home Page Wizard, it asks you what you want included on your new page, as shown here. Just check the boxes for the sections you want and click Next.

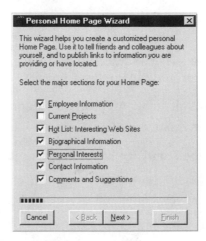

4. The wizard requests a file name and title for the new page. Enter a relative URL in the Page URL text box and a title in the Page Title text box. (A relative URL just means that you don't need to include the path name.) The page title is what viewers will see when they open the page.

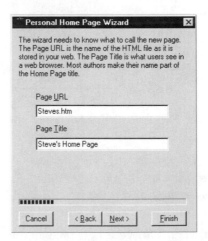

5. The wizard takes you through a series of dialog boxes so that you can further define the sections you chose to include in step 3. Then it asks how you want the sections organized, as shown here:

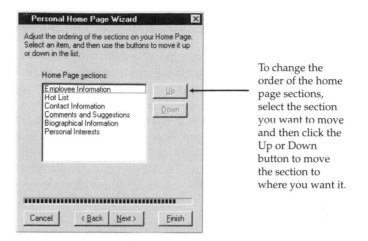

To change the order of the home page sections, select the section you want to move and then click the Up or Down button to move the section to where you want it.

6. Click Finish when you reach the end of the wizard and FrontPage creates your new page and display it in FrontPage Editor. Figure B-12 shows the personal home page added to the web site.

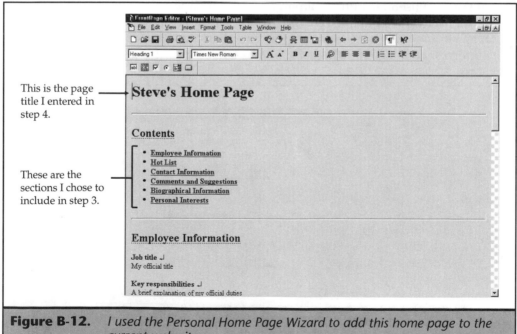

This is the page title I entered in step 4.

These are the sections I chose to include in step 3.

Figure B-12.   *I used the Personal Home Page Wizard to add this home page to the current web site*

Linking Pages

Once you have created a new page, you need to link it to the other pages in your web site. To do this, first open a page in the web site that you want to link to the new page. Then, select the text or graphic you want to become a hyperlink to the new web page. (If you don't already have a chunk of text or a graphic image on the page that you want to use as the hyperlink, you need to create that first.) Choose the Insert menu Hyperlink command. Click the Current FrontPage Web tab to display the dialog box shown in Figure B-13. Enter the name (the relative URL) of the new page in the Page text box (or click the Browse button if you don't remember the new page's name). In the Bookmark text box, you can enter the name of a bookmark field in the new page that you want the hyperlink to link to. If the current page has frames, you can enter the name of the frame that you want the hyperlink to display the new page in. Click OK when you have finished.

> **TIP:**   *You use the other tabs on the Create Hyperlink dialog box to create hyperlinks to web pages that are currently open (but aren't necessarily in the current web), to World Wide Web sites, or to a new page to be created.*

Create a Form

One of the most useful features of FrontPage, as compared to the Office suite of programs, is its ability to allow you, the user, to create detailed forms with ease. FrontPage includes several form templates, as well as a wizard for creating your own custom forms (I don't go into this here, but it is fairly simple to run. All you have to do

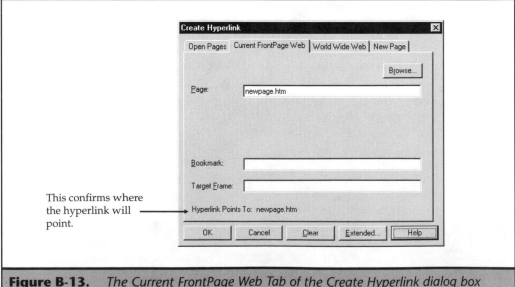

This confirms where the hyperlink will point.

Figure B-13.   *The Current FrontPage Web Tab of the Create Hyperlink dialog box*

is choose Forms Wizard in the New Page dialog box when you create a new page.) To create a form page based on one of FrontPage's existing templates, just follow these steps:

1. Open FrontPage Editor and choose the File menu New command.

2. Select a Form from the Template or Wizard dialog box and click OK:

   ■ Confirmation Forms let you confirm the receipt of forms from viewers.

   ■ Feedback Forms allow viewers to provide you with feedback about your organization, products, services, or web site.

   ■ Survey Forms allow you to conduct a survey of your viewers.

3. Save the form and then edit it and add text to fit your needs.

Working with Forms and WebBots

Once you create a form, you will need to modify it to collect the information you need from your viewers. You will more than likely have to add fields to your forms or delete fields that you don't need. To do this, you use the Forms toolbar and the Insert WebBot button on the Standard toolbar. The Forms toolbar should be displayed by default whenever you open a form in FrontPage Editor. If you don't see the Forms toolbar, however, you can display it by choosing the View menu Forms Toolbar command.

ADD TO AND MODIFY FIELD GROUPS ON FORM TEMPLATES

FrontPage's form templates come with groups of fields so that the individual fields will recognize each other. For example, in the Feedback Form shown in Figure B-14, the radio buttons (also known as option buttons) together comprise a group called MessageType. This group is configured so that viewers can mark only one of the radio buttons.

If you create a form based on one of FrontPage's templates, chances are that you will want to modify the predefined groups by adding an option, deleting an option, or changing what is selected by default. To add a field to a group of radio buttons or check boxes, right-click a member in the group and choose the shortcut menu Form Field Properties command. Note what is listed in the Group Name text box and close the dialog box. Add the form field that you want by placing the insertion point where you want the new field to go, then clicking the Forms toolbar button for the field you want to insert. Right-click the field and choose the shortcut menu Form Field Properties command. FrontPage Editor displays the dialog box shown in Figure B-15. In the Group Name text box, make sure that the name is the same as the one you just saw for the existing group member. In the Value text box, type a unique value (what you want the field to be called). Mark the initial state as either Selected or Not, and click OK, then type a name for the new field either beside or above the new field, as needed.

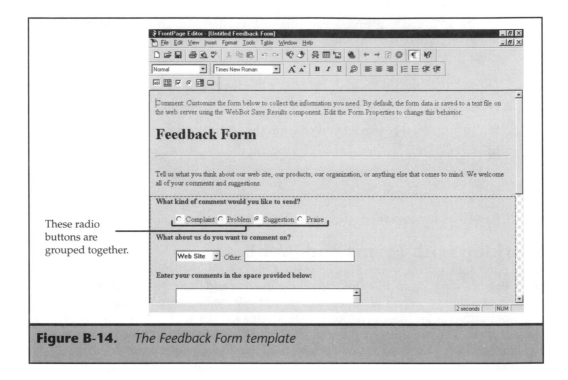

These radio buttons are grouped together.

Figure B-14. *The Feedback Form template*

ADD NEW FIELDS AND FIELD GROUPS TO FORMS

You add form elements—text boxes, scrolling text boxes or areas, check boxes, radio buttons, drop-down menus or list boxes, and push buttons (also known as command buttons)—by following the same set of basic steps:

1. Open the form you want to edit in FrontPage Editor.
2. Position the insertion point where you want the new form element.
3. Click the Forms toolbar button that corresponds to the field you want to insert.

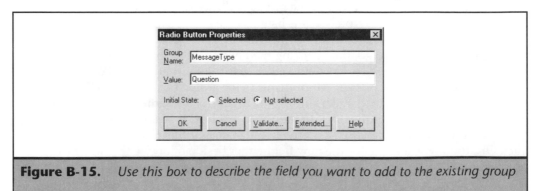

Figure B-15. *Use this box to describe the field you want to add to the existing group*

4. Right-click the new form element and choose the shortcut menu Form Field Properties command. FrontPage displays a dialog box similar to the one shown in Figure B-16.

5. Enter the name of the new form element and any other appropriate information in the Form Field Properties dialog box and click OK.

6. Resize the form element, as needed, by selecting it and dragging its sizing handles.

7. As needed, add text describing the form element.

To add a choice to the list, click the Add button. In the Add Choice dialog box shown here, enter the name of the choice in the Choice text box. In the Initial State box, mark whether or not you want the choice selected as a default choice.

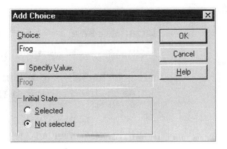

 TIP: *To change the initial state of a choice, select the choice from the list and click the Modify button. In the Initial State box, mark either Selected or Not Selected and click OK.*

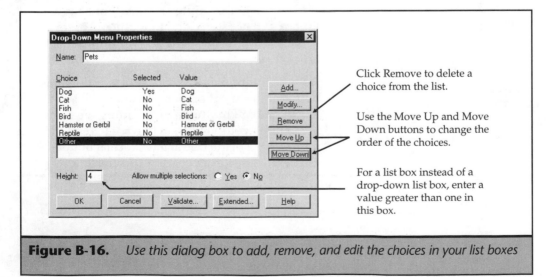

Figure B-16. *Use this dialog box to add, remove, and edit the choices in your list boxes*

Table B-1 identifies and describes each of the Forms toolbar's buttons. Figure B-17 shows an example web page form under construction. Notice, too, that web page text identifies and describes the web page form elements.

Button	Name	Description
	One-Line Text Box	Adds a text box at the insertion point location. These are used for short, often one-word, answers.
	Scrolling Text Box	Adds a text area box at the insertion point location. These are used for longer, sentence-style answers.
	Check Box	Adds a check box at the insertion point location. These are used for yes or no type responses.
	Radio Button	Adds a single radio button (option button) at the insertion point location. (FrontPage considers all of the option buttons you add to be part of the same option button set.) These are often used for a set of mutually exclusive answers, for example Visa or MasterCard.
	Drop-Down Menu	Adds a one-line drop-down list box or a multiline list box at the insertion point location. These are good for choosing a single answer from a longer list of choices.
	Push Button	Adds a Submit, Reset, or Customized command button at the insertion point location. All forms require Submit buttons; Reset buttons are useful if you think your viewers will want to reset the form to get a blank one again. Normal buttons can be used to run a program you create.

Table B-1.   *The Forms Toolbar Buttons*

About Form Handlers

Form handlers are the programs on your server that handle the information viewers provide when they submit a form. When you create a form using one of the templates FrontPage provides, FrontPage automatically uses the corresponding form handler. If you create a form using the Form Wizard, or if you create a form from scratch, you need to specify a form handler by selecting one of the following:

- **WebBot Discussion component.** This form handler collects the information users submit with a form and formats the information into an HTML page so that it can be added to the discussion web and to the table of contents and index.

- **WebBot Registration component.** This form handler adds a viewer to the database of a service you offer on your web site.

- **WebBot Save Results component.** This form handler collects the information users submit with a form and formats it and stores it in a file. This is the form handler you would use to collect survey information from viewers.

- **Custom ISAPI, NSAPI, or CGI Script.** These are custom scripts or programs that you create and then tell FrontPage to run when the viewer requests them. ISAPI is a high-performance script similar to CGI. NSAPI is a web server application for Netscape.

- **Internet Database Connector.** This is a script that allows visitors to access databases.

ADD WEBBOT COMPONENTS

You can use WebBot components to make your sites interactive without having to program CGI scripts. For example, with the click of a button, you can add a fully functional search engine to your web site. Table B-2 lists FrontPage's WebBots and what they are used for.

To insert a WebBot component, click the Insert WebBot Component button on the Standard toolbar in FrontPage Editor (it's the button that looks like a little robot). In the Insert WebBot Component dialog box shown here, choose the WebBot you want to insert from the list:

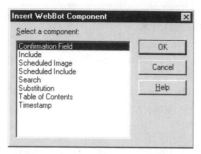

Once you have chosen the WebBot component you want to insert and have clicked OK, FrontPage will display another dialog box asking you to define the specifics of your WebBot, as shown here for the Confirmation WebBot. For the Scheduled Include or Scheduled Image WebBots, however, this means defining what file or image you want inserted and the timeframe during which you want it inserted. In the case of the Time Stamp WebBot, this means describing time and date style, and so forth.

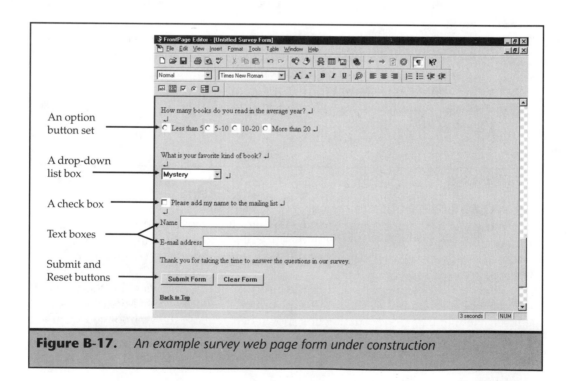

Figure B-17. *An example survey web page form under construction*

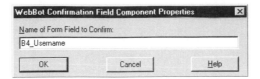

WebBot Component	What It Does
Confirmation Field	Inserts the contents of a form field. You would typically use this in a confirmation form to confirm that the information a user provided was correct.
Include	Inserts the contents of another web page. You would typically use this to create a single page that summarized several sites or so that you could update your entire site by only updating one page.
Scheduled Image	Inserts the image you specify during the time frame you specify.
+Scheduled Include	Like the Include WebBot, it inserts the contents of another web page, but only during the time frame you specify.
Search	Inserts a search engine feature that allows viewers to search your web for a word or phrase and then returns a list of hyperlinks to the pages or discussion groups that include the requested search string.
Substitution	Inserts a web page configuration variable such as the page author's name, the URL, the name of the person who last modified the page, and so forth.
Table of Contents	Creates an outline of your web site with hyperlinks to each page.
Time Stamp	Inserts the time and date the page was last updated.

Table B-2.   *FrontPage's WebBots*

Appendix C

Making Use of the Companion CD

On the CD that comes with this book are over 50 prefabricated templates that you can use to create Word files, Excel spreadsheets, and PowerPoint presentations. Also on the CD are nearly 200 sample files that you can use to experiment with the Word, Excel, PowerPoint, and Access commands described in this book. And you will also find 10 shareware programs.

This appendix explains how to make use of the templates and files that are on the CD. It tells you how to load templates onto your computer from the CD and explains what the different templates are. It also tells you how to make use of the sample documents and how to load the shareware on your computer.

NOTE: "Creating New Document Files" in Chapter 2 explains how to create a file with a template.

Copying Templates to Your Computer

On the CD, Word templates, Excel templates, and PowerPoint templates are each in their own folder. Follow these steps to copy the templates on the CD to your computer:

1. Place the CD in the CD drive.

2. Click the Start button on the taskbar and choose the Programs menu Windows Explorer command to open the Windows Explorer.

3. In the left window pane in the Windows Explorer, click the plus sign next to the drive D icon (or whichever drive your CD is on). You see the folders on the CD.

4. In the right window pane, click on the Headstart Templates folder and then double-click on the folder whose templates you want to use. The templates appear in the right window pane.

5. Find the C:\Program Files\Microsoft Office\Templates folder in the left window pane. To get there, click the plus sign next to the Program Files folder, then click the plus sign next to the Microsoft Office folder, and then click the plus sign next to the Templates folder. You see the Templates folder and all of its subfolders.

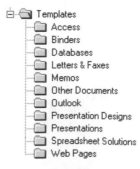

6. On the right window pane, which should still display the contents of the folder you selected in step 4, select the templates to be copied.

7. Drag the templates in the right window pane to the proper destination folder on the left window pane. I suggest putting templates in the following folders:

- *Word* Put Word templates in the Templates folder, not in any of the subfolders. That way, you can see the templates on the General tab of the New dialog box when you choose the File menu New command to create a new document.

- *Excel* Put Excel templates in the Spreadsheet Solutions folder. That way, you can find them on the Spreadsheet Solutions tab of the New dialog box when you choose the File menu New command to create a new worksheet.

- *PowerPoint* Put PowerPoint templates in the Presentation Designs folder. That way, you can find them on the Presentation Designs tab of the New Presentation dialog box when you choose the File menu New command or click the Template option button in the PowerPoint dialog box to create a presentation.

8. Click the Close button to close the Windows Explorer.

How to Use the Sample Documents

Throughout this book are "Learn by Example" notes that mention sample documents on the CD. On the CD are about 175 sample files. To try out a Word, Excel, PowerPoint, or Access sample file, you don't have to copy it to your computer. You can simply open a sample file on the CD, experiment with it, and close it. If you try to save a sample file, your computer will tell you that it is "read-only" and therefore can't be changed. You can commandeer a sample file and use it on your own, but to do so you have to copy it from the CD to your computer first. You can do whatever you please with sample files that have been copied from the CD to the computer's hard disk.

Sample files are organized into folders, with one folder for each part of the book. Follow these steps to open a sample file:

1. Make sure that the CD is in the CD drive.

2. Click the Start button on the taskbar and choose the Programs menu Windows Explorer command to open the Windows Explorer.

3. In the Windows Explorer's left window pane, click the plus sign next to the drive D icon (or whichever drive your CD is on). You see the folders on the CD.

4. In the right window pane, double-click on the folder with the sample file you want.

5. Double-click the sample file you want to use to open it.

Headstart Templates on the CD

The companion CD that comes with *Microsoft Office 97: The Complete Reference* offers more than 50 Office templates. Following are descriptions of the different templates and explanations concerning how to use them. First, the Excel templates, since they are the most complicated.

The Excel Templates

On the companion CD are 19 Excel workbook templates. The Excel templates fall, roughly speaking, into these five categories:

- Business planning templates
- Capital budgeting templates
- Loan amortization templates
- Future value compounding templates
- Personal financial planning templates

Templates in the five categories work in a different manner, so the paragraphs that follow briefly describe what the templates in each category do.

Business Planning Templates

On the companion CD are three business planning templates: 12moplan.xls, 5yrplan.xls, and pvcanal.xls. The first two templates, 12moplan.xls and 5yrplan.xls, collect a large set of inputs and then make the calculations necessary to create a *pro forma* financial statement (an income statement, a balance sheet, and a cash flow statement). What's more, both templates also calculate many standard financial ratios. Figure C-1 shows the Forecasting Inputs worksheet of the Excel template that lets you build a 5-year business plan.

The 12moplan.xls and the 5yrplan.xls templates work in almost the exact same way. The only difference is that the 12moplan.xls template forecasts profits, cash flows, and financial conditions on a *monthly basis* for a year, whereas the 5yrplan.xls template forecasts profits, cash flows, and financial conditions on an *annual basis* for five years. (The 12moplan.xls template does summarize its monthly amounts by also showing annual profits and cash flows, as well as the year-end financial condition.)

Figure C-2 shows the Balance Sheet worksheet for the 5yrplan.xls template. The Balance Sheet worksheet (as well as the other worksheet pages that show calculation results) do not provide cell comments to describe their values. If you use the 5yrplan.xls or the 12moplan.xls template, the authors assume that you understand enough about financial and managerial accounting to work comfortably with simple financial statements.

Point to an input cell to display a cell comment that describes what you should enter there.

	A	B	C	D	E	F	G
		Year	Year	Year	Year	Year	Year
1		0	1	2	3	4	5
2	Forecasting Inputs						
3	**Balance Sheet Forecasting Inputs:**						
4	Begining Cash	50,000					
5	Yield on Cash & Equivalents			%	5.00%	5.00%	5.00%
6	Accounts Receivable	80,000					
7	Number of Periods of Sales in A/R			7	0.17	0.17	0.17
8	Inventory	10,000					
9	Inventory Purchased/Produced		50,000	50,000	50,000	50,000	50,000
10	Other Current Assets	7,000					
11	Changes in Other Current Assets		1,000	1,000	1,000	1,000	1,000
12	Plant, Property, & Equipment	50,000					
13	Changes in P.P.& E		17,500	17,500	17,500	17,500	17,500
14	Accumulated Depreciation	25,000					
15	Changes in Accum. Depreciation		17,500	17,500	17,500	17,500	17,500
16	Other Noncurrent Assets	2,500					
17	Changes in Other Noncurrent Assets		100	100	100	100	100
18	Accounts Payable	8,000					
19	Number of Periods Cost of Sales in A/P		0.17	0.17	0.17	0.17	0.17
20	Accrued Expenses	10,000					
21	Number of Periods Op'g Expenses in A/E		0.04	0.04	0.04	0.04	0.04
22	Other Current Liabilities	2,500					
23	Changes in Other Current Liabilities		100	(100)	100	(100)	100
24	Long-Term Liabilities	10,000					
25	Changes in Long-Term Liabilities		(1,000)	(1,000)	(1,000)	(1,000)	(1,000)

Cell B4 commented by sln

Figure C-1. *The Forecasting Inputs worksheet of the 5yrplan.xls Excel template*

WARNING: *Both the 12moplan.xls and the 5yrplan.xls templates are very large—more than 2 megabytes in size. Because the templates are so large, you need to use them on a computer that has plenty of memory (probably at least 16 megabytes). Either that, or make sure that you don't open other large document files at the same time.*

The third business planning template, pvcanal.xls, makes profit-volume cost calculations, including the break-even point calculations. Like the other two business planning templates, pvcanal.xls uses separate worksheet pages to organize information. The first worksheet page, for example, lets you collect and store the inputs for a profit-volume cost analysis, as shown in Figure C-3.

Other worksheet pages show the results of the profit-volume analysis. For example, one worksheet page describes a business's break-even point (the sales volume at which a firm makes no money but also loses no money). Another worksheet page shows how profits and costs vary as sales revenue changes. Still another

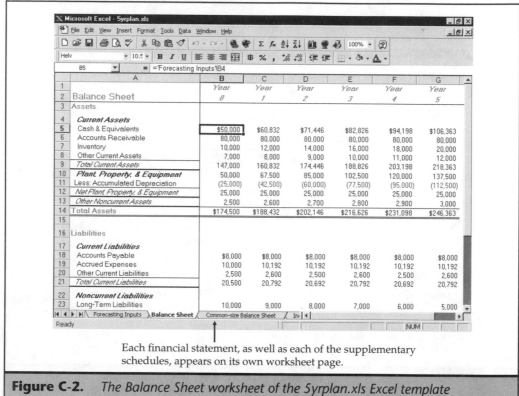

Each financial statement, as well as each of the supplementary schedules, appears on its own worksheet page.

Figure C-2. *The Balance Sheet worksheet of the 5yrplan.xls Excel template*

page—this one a chart sheet page—plots profit-volume cost data in an area chart. Figure C-4 shows the Break-even Analysis worksheet page.

NOTE: Compared to the 12moplan.xls and 5yrplan.xls templates, the pvcanal.xls template is less complicated to use, primarily because it requires fewer input values and creates simpler reports. For this reason, many users who aren't financial experts can use this tool.

Capital Budgeting Templates

The companion CD supplies two capital budgeting templates: 60mocash.xls and 10yrcash.xls. These two templates are essentially the same. Each is set up for forecasting the pre-tax and after-tax cash flows and rates of return from a capital investment (such as a new manufacturing plant or a real estate development). The difference between the two is that each uses a different forecasting horizon.

APPENDIXES

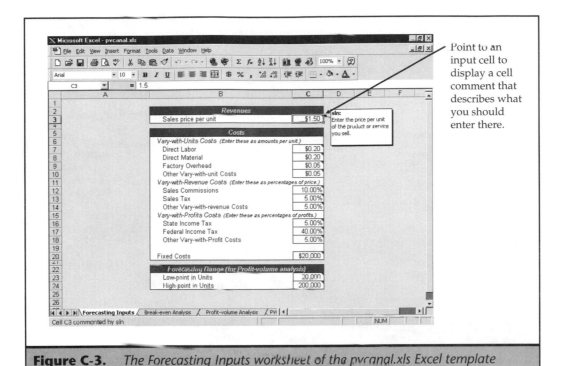

Point to an input cell to display a cell comment that describes what you should enter there.

Figure C-3. *The Forecasting Inputs worksheet of the pvcanal.xls Excel template*

Both capital budgeting templates collect a large set of inputs and then make the calculations necessary for creating *pro forma* financial statements that summarize the following:

- Operating profits (or losses)
- Capital gains (or losses) that stem from the ultimate sale or liquidation of the capital investment
- The income tax effects of the operating profits (or losses) and capital gains (or losses)
- The pre-tax and after-tax cash flows stemming from an investment

The templates then use the cash-flow information to calculate several standard, capital-budgeting benchmarks, including pre-tax and after-tax net present values, pre-tax and after-tax internal rates of return, and pre-tax and after-tax payback periods. Figure C-5 shows the Forecasting Inputs worksheet of the Excel template that lets you build a 10-year capital-budgeting plan.

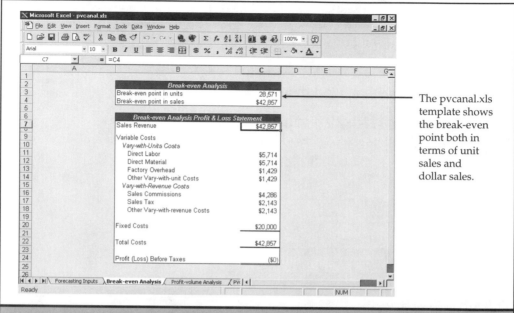

The pvcanal.xls template shows the break-even point both in terms of unit sales and dollar sales.

Figure C-4. *The Break-even Analysis worksheet of the pvcanal.xls Excel template*

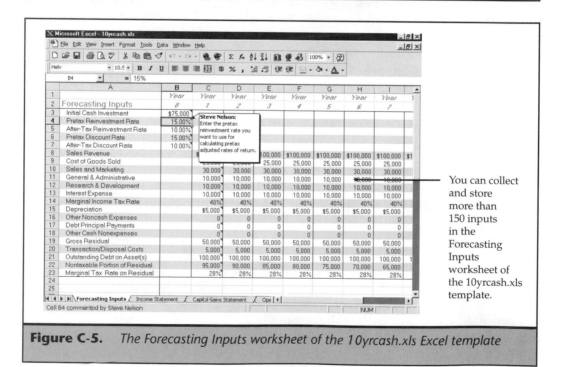

You can collect and store more than 150 inputs in the Forecasting Inputs worksheet of the 10yrcash.xls template.

Figure C-5. *The Forecasting Inputs worksheet of the 10yrcash.xls Excel template*

Figure C-6 shows the operating cash flows worksheet for the 10yrcash.xls template. The operating cash flow worksheet—along with the other worksheet pages that show calculation results—do not provide cell comments to describe their values. I assume that if you're using either the 10yrcash.xls or the 60mocash.xls template, you understand enough about standard capital budgeting techniques to work comfortably with simple financial analysis tools like the templates.

Loan Amortization Templates

The companion CD offers six Excel workbooks that let you create loan amortization templates:

- 15yr-adj.xls lets you create a loan amortization schedule for a 15-year, adjustable-interest rate mortgage or loan

- 15yrloan.xls lets you create a loan amortization schedule for a 15-year, fixed interest rate mortgage or loan

- 30yr-adj.xls lets you create a loan amortization schedule for a 30-year, adjustable-interest rate mortgage or loan

- 30yrloan.xls lets you create a loan amortization schedule for a 30-year, fixed-interest rate mortgage or loan

- 60moadj.xls lets you create a loan amortization schedule for a 60-month, adjustable-interest rate mortgage or loan

- 60moloan.xls lets you create a loan amortization schedule for a 60-year, fixed-interest rate mortgage or loan

You work with each of these templates in the same basic way. Specifically, you describe the loan's interest rate, term, and initial balance. Then you document the payment due dates. Figure C-7 shows the first portion of the 30yr-adj.xls workbook.

NOTE: All of the loan amortization templates assume monthly loan payments.

TIP: The easiest way to enter the payment due values is by entering the first two payment due dates into cells B6 and B7, selecting the range B6:B7, and then dragging the AutoFill handle into the remaining rows of the loan amortization schedule.

If you understand (even roughly) how loan payments work, you should be able to use any of the loan amortization templates to estimate the breakdown of loan payments into principal and interest and the outstanding loan balance after each payment. You don't need an undergraduate or graduate degree in finance to use these templates.

Like the other large Excel workbook templates, each financial statement and supplementary schedule appears on its own worksheet page.

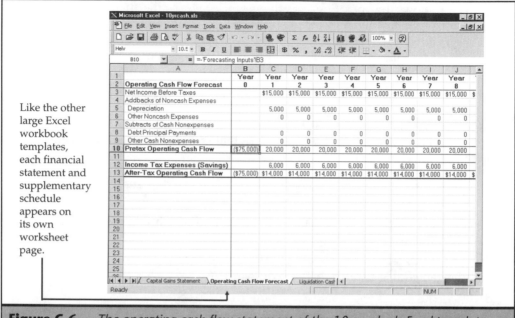

Figure C-6. *The operating cash flow statement of the 10yrcash.xls Excel template*

Enter the loan amount here.

Enter the loan term (the number of monthly payments) here.

Enter the payment due date values in column B, starting with cell B6.

Enter the payment period's interest rate into column C, starting with cell C6.

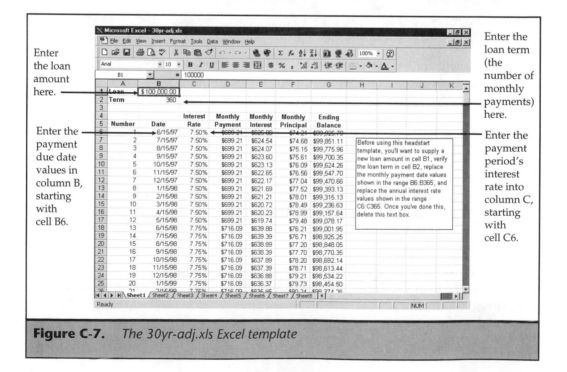

Figure C-7. *The 30yr-adj.xls Excel template*

Future Value Compounding Templates

The companion CD provides two future value compounding templates for estimating how a lump-sum investment and stream of payments (also called an *annuity*) grows over time due to compound interest:

- fv-adj-i.xls lets you use an adjustable-compound interest rate.
- fv-fix-i.xls lets you use a fixed-compound interest rate.

As the text box in Figure C-8 indicates, to use either future value compounding schedule, you supply an initial deposit amount and a regular payment amount. You then indicate whether your payments will occur as an ordinary annuity (i.e., at the end of the month rather than at the beginning of the month) by entering a *Y* for yes or an *N* for no, and then you replace the monthly payment date values shown in the range B7:B186.

> **TIP:** *You can copy the last row of the compound interest schedule to extend the forecasting horizon. You can also delete rows from the compound interest schedule if you want to shorten the forecasting horizon.*

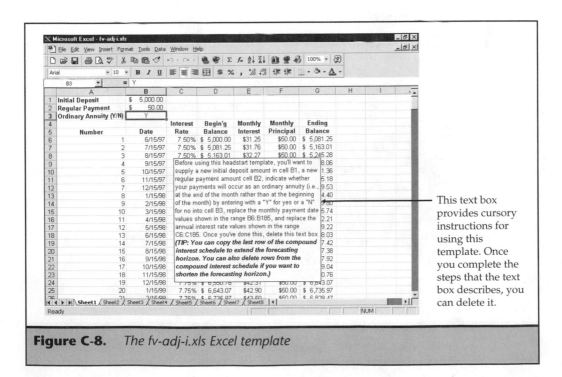

Figure C-8.   *The fv-adj-i.xls Excel template*

Personal Financial Planning Templates

The companion CD also offers half a dozen personal financial planning templates: cc_mgr.xls, college.xls, homebuy.xls, lifeinsr.xls, retire.xls, and savings.xls. Everyone who reads this book can make use of these Excel templates, so the following paragraphs describe each of these tools in detail.

CREDIT CARD ANALYZER (CC_MGR.XLS)

The Credit Card Analyzer template shown in Figure C-9 lets you estimate how quickly you can repay credit card debts. To use this template, follow these steps:

1. Enter your current credit card balance in cell D5.

2. Enter the annual credit card interest rate in cell D6.

3. Enter the minimum payment in cell D7.

4. Enter the largest monthly payment you can afford in cell D10.

5. Enter the number of months over which you want to completely repay the credit card debt in cell D11.

The Credit Card Manager template supplies cell comments that describe both the input values and the calculation results. To view a cell comment, point to the cell with the value or formula you have a question about.

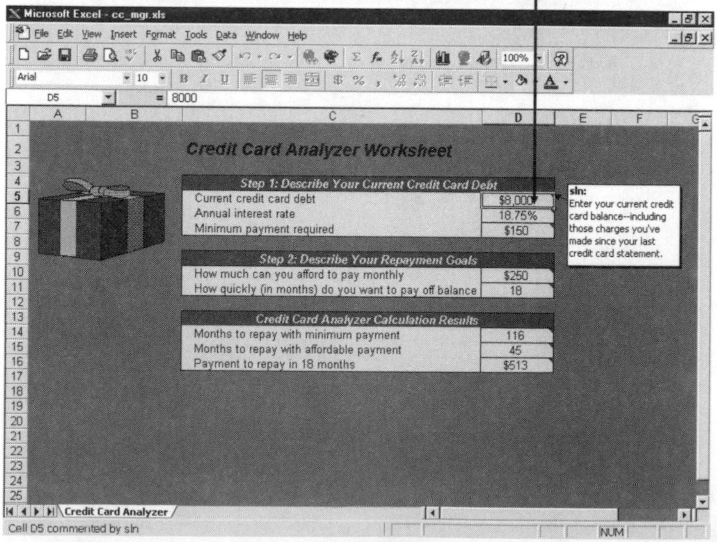

Figure C-9. *The cc_mgr.xls Excel template*

Using these inputs, the Credit Card Analyzer template calculates the number of months it will take you to repay the credit card debt if you make a minimum payment, the number of months it will take you to repay the debt if you make the largest monthly payment you can afford, and the size of the payment necessary to repay in the specified number of months shown in cell D11.

If the Credit Card Analyzer template returns an error value for the calculation result shown in cell D14, the minimum payment amount may not ever pay off the credit card balance. If the Credit Card Analyzer template returns an error value for the calculation result shown in cell D15, the largest payment you can afford may not ever pay off the credit card balance.

WARNING: *View the calculation results provided by the Credit Card Analyzer template as rough estimates. Your credit card company may calculate its interest charges differently than the template does.*

COLLEGE SAVINGS WORKSHEET (COLLEGE.XLS)

The College Savings Worksheet template shown in Figure C-10 is for estimating how much money you need to save for a child's future college expenses. To use this template, follow these steps:

1. Enter the student's current age in cell D5.

2. Enter the student's age when he or she starts college in cell D6.

3. Enter the annual estimated cost of college in current-day dollars in cell D7.

4. Enter the number of years a student will attend college in cell D8.

5. Enter the annual return on investment that you think your college savings will return in cell D11.

6. Enter the annual inflation rate you expect for the cost of attending college in cell D12.

7. Enter the amount you've already saved for the student's future college costs in cell D13.

8. Enter the amount you expect the student to contribute annually to his or her college education (these contributions can include money from scholarships, summer jobs, or part-time employment during the school year) in cell D14.

NOTE: *The College Savings Worksheet assumes that either your investment profits won't be subject to income taxes or that you will pay any income taxes on these profits out of your pocket and not out of the investment profits.*

Using these inputs, the College Savings Worksheet template calculates the annual college costs you need to fund through savings, the amount you need to have saved

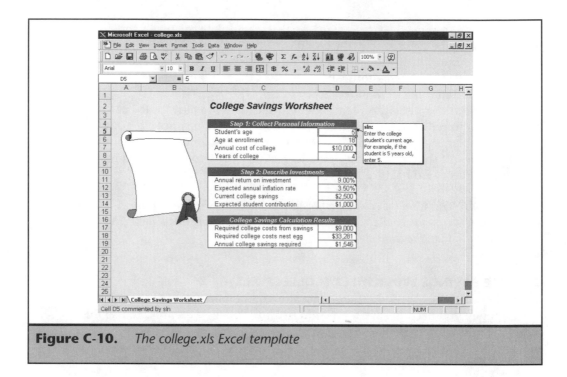

Figure C-10. *The college.xls Excel template*

by the time the student enters college to completely pay for college, and the annual college savings required between now and the time the student enters college.

By the way, the College Savings Worksheet makes one rather conservative assumption: It assumes that you will have saved the funds necessary for college by the time the student starts college. You can, however, continue to contribute to a child's college expenses out of your current income even after the student begins college.

WARNING: In using the College Savings Worksheet, be sure to experiment with a variety of input values—particularly with a range of return on investment and annual inflation rate inputs. If you underestimate the inflation rate or the annual costs of attending college or you overestimate the return on investment or the student's contribution, you won't save enough to fully fund the student's college education.

HOME AFFORDABILITY ANALYZER WORKSHEET (HOMEBUY.XLS)

The Home Affordability Analyzer Worksheet template shown in Figure C-11 is for estimating how expensive a home you can purchase based on your current financial situation. To use this template, follow these steps:

1. Enter the cash you've accumulated for a down payment and your closing costs in cell D5.

2. Enter your gross monthly income (your income before income taxes) in cell D6.

3. Enter the total debt payments you pay monthly in cell D7.

4. Enter the annual mortgage interest rate you'll pay in cell D10.

5. Enter the term of the mortgage—the number of monthly loan payments you'll make—in cell D11.

6. Enter the closing costs you expect to pay as a percentage of the home purchase price in cell D12.

7. Enter the additional monthly housing costs you expect to pay (in addition to the mortgage payment) in cell D13. This amount, for example, includes items such as property taxes and private mortgage insurance.

8. Enter the down payment percentage the lender wants you to supply in cell D16.

9. Enter the maximum debt service percentage the lender wants you to bear in cell D17.

10. Enter the maximum housing expense percentage the lender wants you to pay in cell D18.

Using these inputs, the Home Affordability Analyzer Worksheet calculates the largest monthly mortgage payment you can afford (according to the lender's

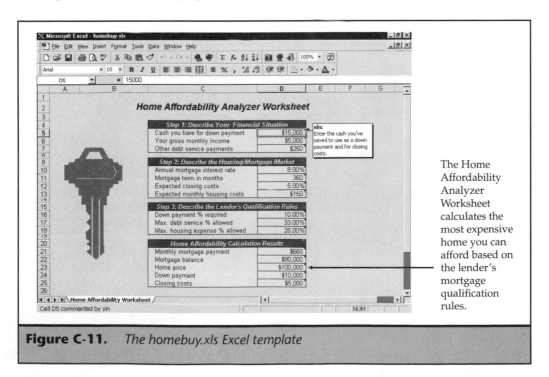

The Home Affordability Analyzer Worksheet calculates the most expensive home you can afford based on the lender's mortgage qualification rules.

Figure C-11. *The homebuy.xls Excel template*

mortgage qualification rules), the largest mortgage you can afford, the most expensive home you can afford, the down payment you'll make, and the closing costs you'll pay.

WARNING: You should not place too much reliance on the homebuy.xls template's results until you enter an up-to-date mortgage interest rate and confirm the lender's mortgage qualification rules, including the down payment percentage, the maximum debt service percentage, and the maximum housing expenses percentage.

LIFE INSURANCE PLANNER WORKSHEET (LIFEINSR.XLS)

The Life Insurance Planner Worksheet template shown in Figure C-12 is for estimating how much life insurance you need to replace your income (should you die) so that your dependents can still manage financially. To use this template, follow these steps:

1. Enter the number of earning years you want to replace in cell D5. (This might be the number of years until your youngest child graduates from college, for example.)

2. Enter the annual income you want your life insurance proceeds to replace in cell D6.

3. Enter the annual return on investment you expect your life insurance proceeds to earn in cell D10.

4. Enter the annual inflation rate you expect over the years you're replacing earnings in cell D11.

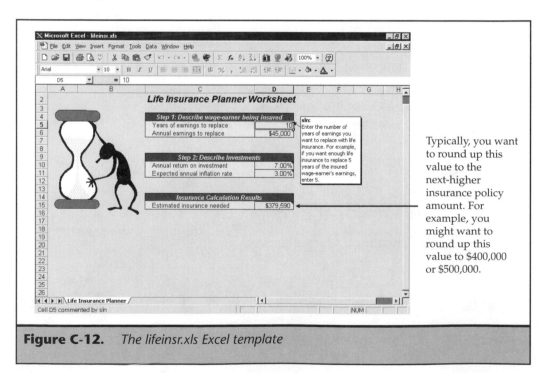

Figure C-12.   *The lifeinsr.xls Excel template*

Using these inputs, the Life Insurance Planner Worksheet estimates the size of the life insurance policy you should purchase to replace your income. The insurance proceeds, when invested, will produce a stream of payments that will initially equal the amount you entered into cell D6 and then over the years grow at the inflation rate.

RETIREMENT PLANNER WORKSHEET (RETIRE.XLS)

The Retirement Planner Worksheet template shown in Figure C-13 is for estimating how much money you need to save in order to retire with a specific level of retirement income. To use this template, follow these steps:

1. Enter your current age in cell D5.

2. Enter the age at which you want to retire in cell D6.

3. Enter the desired retirement income in cell D7.

4. Indicate the number of years you'll be retired by entering a value in cell D8. (By adding your retirement age to the number of years you expect to enjoy retirement, you are implicitly estimating how long you expect to live.)

5. Enter the annual return on investment you expect your retirement savings to earn in cell D11.

6. Enter the annual inflation rate you expect over both the years you work and the years you will be retired in cell D12.

7. Enter the amount you've already saved for retirement in cell D13.

8. Enter the annual pension or social security benefit you expect in cell D14.

Using these inputs, the Retirement Planner Worksheet estimates the amount of income you want your retirement savings to produce, the retirement nest egg you need in order to produce this income, and the amount you need to save annually between now and the time you retire to accumulate this retirement nest egg.

NOTE: If the annual retirement savings required value in cell D19 shows a negative value, it means you've already saved enough to retire—assuming, of course, that your return on investment and inflation estimates are correct.

SAVINGS PLANNER WORKSHEET (SAVINGS.XLS)

The Savings Planner Worksheet template shown in Figure C-14 is for estimating how much money you need to save in order to accumulate a specific amount. You might use this template, for example, to estimate how much you need to save to fund a major purchase (such as a home or a recreational vehicle) or a large investment

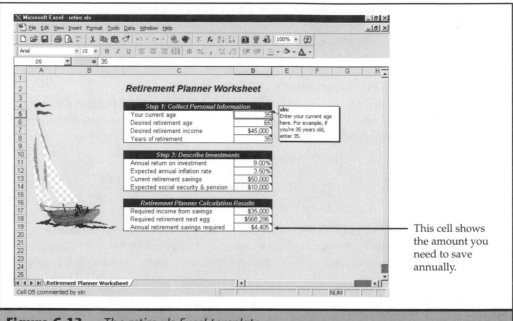

Figure C-13. *The retire.xls Excel template*

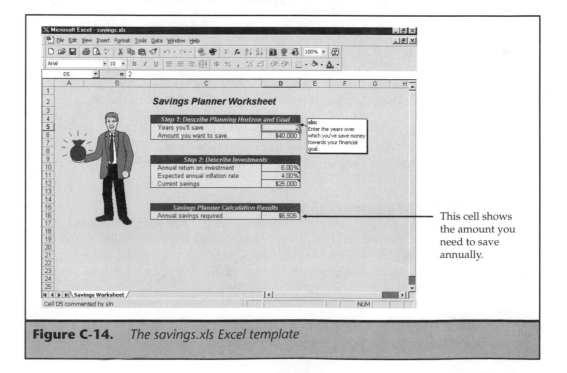

Figure C-14. *The savings.xls Excel template*

(such as a business or piece of investment real estate). To use this template, follow these steps:

1. Enter the number of years you'll save in cell D5.

2. Enter the amount you want to accumulate in cell D6.

3. Enter the annual return on investment you expect your savings to earn in cell D10.

4. Enter the annual inflation rate you expect over the years you save in cell D11.

5. Enter the amount you've already saved in cell D13.

Using these inputs, the Savings Planner Worksheet estimates the amount you need to save annually to accumulate the amount you entered in cell D6.

NOTE: The savings.xls template assumes either that you won't pay income taxes on the interest your savings earn or that you'll pay any income taxes out-of-pocket and not out of the investment's earnings.

The PowerPoint Templates

The design templates that come with PowerPoint are superb, but they have one major drawback: everybody who owns the software has them. In other words, because so many people have the same designs, the design templates that come with PowerPoint are downright conventional.

To remedy that, this book comes with 33 PowerPoint templates. Figure C-15 shows the Cello template. To use the 33 templates for your presentations, copy them to the C:\Microsoft Office\Templates\Presentation Designs folder.

TIP: To see what the templates look like, open the New Presentation dialog box in PowerPoint, click the Presentation Designs tab, click different templates, and look at the Preview screen in the dialog box. To open the New Presentation dialog box, either choose the File menu New command or, in the PowerPoint dialog box that appears when you start the program, click the Template button.

The Word Templates

On the companion CD are also 13 Word templates. To make use of these templates in your Word documents, copy them to the C:\Program Files\Microsoft Office\ Templates folder. Choose the File menu New command to create a file with one of the templates. You will find the templates on the General tab of the New dialog box if you copy them to the C:\Microsoft Office\Templates folder.

All but one of the templates provide unusual backgrounds for the page. However, the grandpa.dot template, shown in Figure C-16, offers a streamlined version of Word. Instead of the numerous commands and buttons, only essential commands and

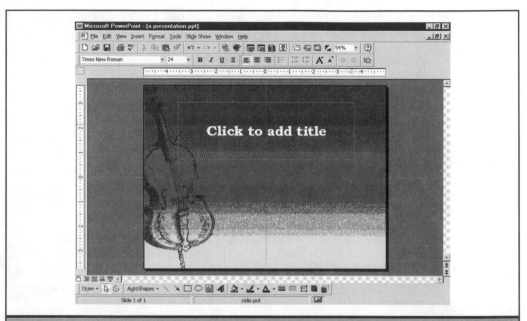

Figure C-15. *On the companion CD that comes with this book are 33 PowerPoint templates you can use for your presentations. This is the Cello template*

Figure C-16. *The grandpa.dot template for creating simple documents*

buttons are available when you create a file with this template. Use Grandpa.dot to write letters, notes, and other simple documents.

Shareware on the CD

Also on the CD are ten shareware programs. Following are descriptions of the programs and instructions for installing them on your computer.

Active Worlds Browser Version 1.1

Use Active Worlds Browser to travel through virtual reality worlds. When you use the program for the first time, it prompts you to register and obtain an immigration number. After you receive the number by e-mail, you can log on to one of several worlds and communicate with others who have one, as well. In some worlds, you can build structures, and others can see what you build. To install Active Worlds Browser, double-click Awb147 in the Active Worlds Browser folder on the companion CD. By Worlds, Inc.

Cash Express for Windows Version 3.0h

Use Cash Express for Windows to organize your personal finances. The program monitors your accounts and investments and keeps track of bills that need paying. With Cash Express, you can keep all of your financial information in one place, which makes it easier to monitor your spending habits and create simple budgets. To install Cash Express, double-click the Setup application in the Cash Express folder on the companion CD. To keep using Cash Express after the free 90-day trial period, you must register at a cost of $20. By Silicon Programming.

Hyper MPEG Player Version 0.1

Use Hyper MPEG Player to play MPEG videos. The program's controls work like VCR controls and allow you to fast-forward and rewind videos. Hyper MPEG player also lets you save a single frame in a video as a bitmap image. To begin using Hyper MPEG Player, double-click the hympeg application in the Hyper MPEG Player folder on the companion CD. By Hong Seungwook and Cho Man Jun.

Macro Mania Version 3.5

Use Macro Mania to automate keyboard tasks. Macro Mania can perform repetitive tasks such as copying and moving data between different programs for you. To install Macro Mania, double-click the Setup application in the Macro Mania folder on the companion CD. If you want to keep Macro Mania after the free trial period, you must register the program for $29.95. By Jeff Camino.

NotePad+ Version 1.1

NotePad+ is more powerful than NotePad, the Windows 95 application. It can open large files and open more than one at the same time. NotePad+ includes formatting features that are not available on the standard Windows NotePad, such as formatting fonts and font color. It also supports drag-and-drop editing. To begin using NotePad+, double-click NotePad in the NotePad+ folder on the companion CD. By Rogier Meurs.

Quick View Plus Version 4.0

Use Quick View Plus to quickly view more than 200 different file formats. This program works like the standard QuickView feature that comes with Windows 95. With Quick View plus, you can right-click a file and view it without opening the application in which the file was created. The program even lets you preview files in zipped archives. To install Quick View Plus, double-click the Setup application in the Quick View Plus folder on the companion CD. If you want to keep Quick View Plus after the free trial period, you must register the program for $49. By Inso Corp.

Second Copy 97 Version 5.11

Use Second Copy to monitor file changes and automatically make and save backup copies of files. Second Copy can back up files to a floppy disk, a network drive, or to a different disk or folder on your computer. To install Second Copy, double-click setup97 in the Second Copy 97 folder on the companion CD. If you want to keep Second Copy after the free 30-day trial period, you must register the program for $25. By Centered Systems.

TechFacts 95 Version 1.3

Use TechFacts 95 to take stock of your computer's settings. With TechFacts, you can monitor Windows, network, CMOS, DOS, and multimedia settings, and also track changes that occur as you install hardware and software. To install TechFacts, double-click Tekfct95 in the TechFacts 95 folder on the companion CD. If you want to keep TechFacts after the free trial period, you must register the program for $19.99. By Dean Software Design.

ThunderBYTE Anti-Virus for Windows 95 Version 0x0707

Use ThunderBYTE Anti-Virus to check for known and unknown viruses on your computer. ThunderBYTE's setup module checks and validates the files that are currently on your computer, and then the scan module looks for changes against the summary that the setup module generated. To install ThunderBYTE Anti-Virus, double-click the Setup application in the ThunderBYTE folder on the companion CD.

If you want to keep the program after the free 30-day trial period, you must register it for $99.95. By TCT ThunderBYTE Corp.

WinZip for Windows 95/NT Version 6.2

Use WinZip to view and extract zipped archives. WinZip's new toolbar is user friendly and makes unzipping ZIP, TAR, and GZIP archives a snap. Its Wizard feature also makes installing zipped programs easier. To install WinZip, double-click winzip95 in the WinZip folder on the companion CD. If you want to keep WinZip after the free trial period, you must register the program for $29. By Nico Mak Computing, Inc.

Index

G

WARNING: BEFORE OPENING THE DISC PACKAGE, CAREFULLY READ THE TERMS AND CONDITIONS OF THE FOLLOWING COPYRIGHT STATEMENT AND LIMITED CD-ROM WARRANTY.

Copyright Statement

This software is protected by both United States copyright law and international copyright treaty provision. Except as noted in the contents of the CD-ROM, you must treat this software just like a book. However, you may copy it into a computer to be used and you may make archival copies of the software for the sole purpose of backing up the software and protecting your investment from loss. By saying, "just like a book," The McGraw-Hill Companies, Inc. ("Osborne/McGraw-Hill") means, for example, that this software may be used by any number of people and may be freely moved from one computer location to another, so long as there is no possibility of its being used at one location or on one computer while it is being used at another. Just as a book cannot be read by two different people in two different places at the same time, neither can the software be used by two different people in two different places at the same time.

Limited Warranty

Osborne/McGraw-Hill warrants the physical compact disc enclosed herein to be free of defects in materials and workmanship for a period of sixty days from the purchase date. If the CD included in your book has defects in materials or workmanship, please call McGraw-Hill at 1-800-217-0059, 9am to 5pm, Monday through Friday, Eastern Standard Time, and McGraw-Hill will replace the defective disc.

The entire and exclusive liability and remedy for breach of this Limited Warranty shall be limited to replacement of the defective disc, and shall not include or extend to any claim for or right to cover any other damages, including but not limited to, loss of profit, data, or use of the software, or special incidental, or consequential damages or other similar claims, even if Osborne/McGraw-Hill has been specifically advised of the possibility of such damages. In no event will Osborne/McGraw-Hill's liability for any damages to you or any other person ever exceed the lower of the suggested list price or actual price paid for the license to use the software, regardless of any form of the claim.

OSBORNE/McGRAW-HILL SPECIFICALLY DISCLAIMS ALL OTHER WARRANTIES, EXPRESS OR IMPLIED, INCLUDING BUT NOT LIMITED TO, ANY IMPLIED WARRANTY OF MERCHANTABILITY OR FITNESS FOR A PARTICULAR PURPOSE. Specifically, Osborne/McGraw-Hill make no representation or warranty that the software is fit for any particular purpose, and any implied warranty of merchantability is limited to the sixty-day duration of the Limited Warranty covering the physical disc only (and not the software), and is otherwise expressly and specifically disclaimed.

This limited warranty gives you specific legal rights; you may have others which may vary from state to state. Some states do not allow the exclusion of incidental or consequential damages, or the limitation on how long an implied warranty lasts, so some of the above may not apply to you.

This agreement constitutes the entire agreement between the parties relating to use of the Product. The terms of any purchase order shall have no effect on the terms of this Agreement. Failure of Osborne/McGraw-Hill to insist at any time on strict compliance with this Agreement shall not constitute a waiver of any rights under this Agreement. This Agreement shall be construed and governed in accordance with the laws of New York. If any provision of this Agreement is held to be contrary to law, that provision will be enforced to the maximum extent permissible, and the remaining provisions will remain in force and effect.

NO TECHNICAL SUPPORT IS PROVIDED WITH THIS CD-ROM.